HOW TO PREPARE FOR THE TOEFL* TEST

Test of English as a Foreign Language

Tenth Edition

PAMELA J. SHARPE, Ph.D.
The Ohio State University

*TOEFL is a registered trademark of Educational Testing Service. Barron's Educational Series, Inc., bears sole responsibility for this book's contents and is not connected with Educational Testing Service.

To my former students at home and abroad

All inquiries should be addressed to:
Barron's Educational Series, Inc.
250 Wireless Boulevard
Hauppauge, New York 11788
http://www.barronseduc.com

Library of Congress Catalog Card No.: 00-060857
International Standard Book No. 0-7641-1766-1 (book only)
International Standard Book No. 0-7641-7467-3 (book with compact disks)
International Standard Book No. 0-7641-7500-9 (book with CD-ROM)
International Standard Book No. 0-7641-7468-1 (cassettes only package)
International Standard Book No. 0-7641-7470-3 (compact disks only package)

Library of Congress Cataloging-in-Publication Data

Sharpe, Pamela J.
How to prepare for the TOEFL test : test of English as a foreign language / Pamela J. Sharpe. — 10th ed.
p. cm.
At head of title: Barron's.
ISBN 0-7641-1766-1 (book only) — ISBN 0-7641-7467-3 (book w/ compact disks) — ISBN 0-7641-7468-1 (cassettes package) — ISBN 0-7641-7470-3 (compact disks only package)
1. English language—Textbooks for foreign speakers. 2. Test of English as a Foreign Language—Study guides. 3. English language—Examinations—Study guides. I. Title: Barron's how to prepare for the TOEFL test. II. Title.
PE1128 .S5 2001
428'.0076—dc21 00-060857

PRINTED IN THE UNITED STATES OF AMERICA
9 8 7 6 5 4 3

CONTENTS

To the Teacher

Rationale for a TOEFL Preparation Course

Although *Barron's How to Prepare for the TOEFL* was originally written as a self-study guide for students who were preparing to take the TOEFL, in the years since its first publication, I have received letters from ESL teachers around the world who are using the book successfully for classroom study. In fact, in recent years, many special courses have been developed within the existing ESL curriculum to accommodate TOEFL preparation.

I believe that these TOEFL preparation courses respond to three trends within the profession. First, there appears to be a greater recognition on the part of many ESL teachers that student goals must be acknowledged and addressed. For the engineer, the business person, the doctor, or the preuniversity student, a satisfactory score on the TOEFL is one of the most immediate goals; for many, without the required score, they cannot continue their professional studies or obtain certification to practice their professions. They may have other language goals as well, such as learning to communicate more effectively or improving their writing, but these goals do not usually exert the same kinds of pressure that the required TOEFL score does.

Second, teachers have recognized and recorded the damaging results of test anxiety. We have all observed students who were so frightened of failure that they have performed on the TOEFL at a level far below that which their performance in class would have indicated. The standardized score just didn't correspond with the score in the gradebook. In addition, teachers have become aware that for some students, the TOEFL represents their first experience in taking a computer-assisted test. The concepts of working within time limits, marking on a screen, and guessing to improve a score are often new and confusing to students, and they forfeit valuable points because they must concentrate on unfamiliar procedures instead of on language questions.

Third, teachers have observed the corresponding changes in student proficiency that have accompanied the evolutionary changes in ESL syllabus design. Since this book was first written, we have moved away from a grammatical syllabus to a notional functional syllabus, and at this writing, there seems to be growing interest in a content-based syllabus. Viewed in terms of what has actually happened in classrooms, most of us have emphasized the teaching of functions and meaning and de-emphasized the teaching of forms. As we did so, we noticed with pride the improvement in student fluency and with dismay the corresponding loss of accuracy. Some of our best, most fluent students received disappointing scores on the test that was so important to them.

Through these observations and experiences, teachers have concluded that (1) students need to work toward their own goals, (2) students need some time to focus on accuracy as well as on fluency, and (3) students need an opportunity to practice taking a standardized test in order to alleviate anxiety and develop test strategies. With the introduction of the Computer-Based TOEFL, the opportunity to gain experience taking a computer-assisted model test has also become important to student confidence and success. In short, more and more teachers have begun to support the inclusion of a TOEFL preparation course in the ESL curriculum.

Organization of a TOEFL Preparation Course

Organizing a TOEFL preparation course requires that teachers make decisions about the way that the course should be structured and the kinds of supplementary materials and activities that should be used.

Structuring

Some teachers have suggested that each review section in this book be used for a separate class; they are team teaching a TOEFL course. Other teachers direct their students to the language laboratory for independent study in listening comprehension three times a week, checking on progress throughout the term; assign reading and vocabulary study for homework; and spend class time on structure and writing. Still other teachers develop individual study plans for each student based on previous TOEFL part scores. Students with high listening and low reading scores concentrate their efforts in reading labs, while students with low listening and high reading scores spend time in listening labs.

Materials and Activities

Listening. Studies in distributive practice have convinced teachers of listening comprehension that a little practice every day for a few months is more valuable than a lot of practice concentrated in a shorter time. In addition, many teachers like to use two kinds of listening practice—intensive and extensive. Intensive practice consists of listening to problems like those in the review of listening in this book.

By so doing, the student progresses from short conversations through longer conversations to mini-talks, gaining experience in listening to simulations of the TOEFL examination. Extensive practice consists of watching a daytime drama on television, listening to a local radio program, or auditing a class. Creative teachers everywhere have developed strategies for checking student progress such as requiring a summary of the plot or a prediction of what will happen the following day on the drama; a one-sentence explanation of the radio program, as well as the name of the speaker, sponsor of the program, and two details; a copy of student notes from the audited class.

Structure. Of course, the focus in a review of structure for the TOEFL will be on form. It is form that is tested on the TOEFL. It is assumed that students have studied grammar prior to reviewing for the TOEFL, and that they are relatively fluent. The purpose of a TOEFL review then is to improve accuracy. Because accuracy is directly related to TOEFL scores and because the scores are tied to student goals, this type of review motivates students to pay attention to detail that would not usually be of much interest to them.

Among ESL teachers, the debate rages on about whether students should ever see errors in grammar. But many teachers have recognized the fact that students *do* see errors all the time, not only in the distractors that are used on standardized tests like the TOEFL and teacher-made tests like the multiple-choice midterms in their grammar classes, but also in their own writing. They argue that students must be able to recognize errors, learn to read for them, and correct them.

The student preparing for the TOEFL will be required not only to recognize correct answers but also to eliminate incorrect answers, or distractors, as possibilities. The review of structure in this book supports recognition by alerting students to avoid certain common distractors. Many excellent teachers take this one step further by using student compositions to create personal TOEFL tests. By underlining four words or phrases in selected sentences, one phrase of which contains an incorrect structure, teachers encourage students to reread their writing. It has proven to be a helpful transitional technique for students who need to learn how to edit their own compositions.

Reading. One of the problems in a TOEFL preparation course is that of directing vocabulary study. Generally, teachers feel that encouraging students to collect words and develop their own word lists is the best solution to the problem of helping students who will be faced with the dilemma of responding to words from a possible vocabulary pool of thousands of words that may appear in context in the reading section. In this way, they will increase their vocabularies in an ordered and productive way, thereby benefiting even if none of their new words appears on the test that they take. Activities that support learning vocabulary in context are also helpful.

In order to improve reading, students need extensive practice in reading a variety of material, including newspapers and magazines as well as short excerpts from textbooks. In addition, students need to check their comprehension and time themselves carefully. Many teachers are using preparation books for the General Education Degree (GED) in special reading labs for students preparing for the TOEFL. Books such as *Barron's How to Prepare for the GED* contain passages at about the same level as those on the TOEFL and include comprehension questions after each passage. Teachers report that passages on natural science, social science, and general interest only should be assigned because literature passages often require that the student read and interpret poetry and plays, and these literary readings do not appear on the TOEFL. Again, it is well to advise students of the advantages of distributed practice. They should be made aware that it is better to read two passages every day for five days than to read ten passages in one lab period.

It is also necessary for students who are preparing for the Computer-B[illegible] TOEFL to practice reading from a computer screen. The skill of scrolling through text is different from the skill of reading a page in a book. To succeed on the TOEFL and after the TOEFL, students must develop new reading strategies for texts on screens. An English encyclopedia on CD-ROM is an inexpensive way to provide students with a huge amount of reading material from all the nonfiction content areas tested on the TOEFL. By reading on screen, students gain not only reading comprehension skills but also computer confidence.

Writing. There are many excellent ESL textbooks to help students improve their writing. Because the TOEFL limits the topics to opinion, persuasion, and argument, some teachers tend to emphasize these types of topics in composition classes.

The extensive list of writing topics published in the *Information Bulletin* for the Computer-Based TOEFL offers teachers an opportunity to use actual TOEFL topics in class. In order to help students organize their thoughts, the topics can be used as conversation starters for class discussion. In this way, students will have thought about the topics and will have formed an opinion before they are presented with the writing task on the TOEFL.

It is also a good idea to time some of the essays that students write in class so that they can become accustomed to completing their work within thirty minutes.

Although teachers need to develop grading systems that make sense for their teaching situations, the scoring guide that is used for the essay on the TOEFL is general enough to be adapted for at least some of the assignments in an ESL composition class. By using the guide, teachers can inform students of their progress as it relates to the scores that they can expect to receive on the essay they will write for the TOEFL.

Networking with ESL Teachers

One of the many rewards of writing is the opportunity that it creates to exchange ideas with so many talented colleagues. At conferences, I have met ESL teachers who use or have used one of the previous editions of this book; through my publisher, I have received letters from students and teachers from fifty-two nations. This preface and many of the revisions in this new edition were included because of comments and suggestions from those conversations and letters.

Thank you for your ideas. I hope that by sharing we can help each other and thereby help our students more. Please continue corresponding by mail or by e-mail.

Pamela Sharpe
1406 Camino Real
Yuma, Arizona 85364
Sharpe@teflprep.com

Acknowledgments

It is with affection and appreciation that I acknowledge my indebtedness to the late Dr. Jayne C. Harder, Director of the English Language Institute of the University of Florida, who initiated me into the science of linguistics and the art of teaching English as a foreign language.

I am also very grateful to my parents, Robert and Lilly Sharpe, for their enthusiastic encouragement during the preparation of the manuscript and for their assistance in typing and proofreading each of the previous editions; to the late Tom Clapp, for the maturity and confidence that I gained from our marriage; to Carole Berglie of Barron's Educational Series, Inc., for her insights and guidanc[illegible] seeing the first edition of the manuscript through to publication; and to all of the editors at Barron's for their contributions to later editions.

I was particularly fortunate to be reunited for the tenth edition with the outstanding editor for the ninth edition, Marcy Rosenbaum, and the talented production manager for the ninth edition, Debby Becak, whose suggestions and designs, both large and small, improved every chapter and contributed to make this the best edition yet. I also recognize and appreciate the significant effort by my research assistant, Kathy Telford, who proved to be an invaluable member of the team for her skillful proofreading and attention to the important details in the writing process.

With the assistance of Judy Peterson and the cooperation of Roxanne Nuhaily at the English Language Program, University of California, San Diego, the items for the Computer-Adaptive Model Test were field tested; with the collaboration of Dr. Sherri McCarthy-Tucker, the items were analyzed and calibrated; in consultation with Karen McNiel and Dr. Jean Zukowski-Faust, a review of the reading level for the revised reading comprehension passages was completed, and a number of items were substantially improved.

Finally, I would like to say a special thank you to my husband, John T. Osterman, for the unconditional love, the daily interest in and support for my writing career, and the best chapter in my life story.

Permissions

With the permission of Mr. Frank Berlin, Sexton Educational Programs, New York, explanations for several of the listening comprehension problems have been adapted from previous work by the author.

With the permission of Educational Testing Service, the test instructions contained in this publication for the various sections of TOEFL have been reprinted from the *Information Bulletin* for the *Computer-Based TOEFL.* The granting of this permission does not imply endorsement by ETS or the TOEFL program of the contents of this publication as a whole or of the practice questions that it contains. Since the types of questions in TOEFL and the instructions pertaining to them are subject to change, candidates who register to take TOEFL should read carefully the edition of the *Information Bulletin* that will be sent to them free of charge with their registration material.

With the permission of the colleges and universities featured in the Appendix of this book, photographs for the Listening section of the Computer-Based Model Tests have been reprinted.

Timetable for the TOEFL

TIMETABLE FOR THE SUPPLEMENTAL PAPER-BASED TOEFL
Total Time: 3 hours

Section 1 (40 Minutes)	Listening Comprehension	50 Questions
Section 2 (25 Minutes)	Structure and Written Expression	40 Questions
Section 3 (55 Minutes)	Reading Comprehension	50 Questions
TWE (30 Minutes)	Essay	1 Question

TIMETABLE FOR THE COMPUTER-BASED TOEFL
Total Time: 4.5 hours

Tutorial (Untimed)	Computer Skills	7 Tutorials
Section 1 (40–60 Minutes)	Listening	30–50 Questions
Section 2: Part One (15–20 Minutes)	Structure	20–25 Questions
Break (5 Minutes)		
Section 3 (70–90 Minutes)	Reading	44–55 Questions
Section 2: Part Two (30 Minutes)	Essay	1 Question

Note: Actual times will vary in accordance with the time the supervisor completes the preliminary work and begins the actual test. The time for the tutorial will vary from one person to another. Format and numbers of questions will also vary from one test to another. This timetable is a good estimate.

INTRODUCTION

Study Plan for the TOEFL

Many students do not prepare for the TOEFL. They do not even read the *Information Bulletin* that they receive from Educational Testing Service along with their registration forms. You have an advantage. Using this book, you have a study plan.

Barron's TOEFL Series

There are three books in the Barron's TOEFL series to help you prepare for the Test of English as a Foreign Language. Each book has a different purpose.

Barron's Practice Exercises for the TOEFL. A book for learners at an intermediate level who need preview and practice for the TOEFL. It includes a general preview of the TOEFL examination, a review of the most frequently tested problems, and almost one thousand exercises. Two separate cassette tapes accompany the book to give you practice in listening comprehension. You may have used *Barron's Practice Exercises for the TOEFL* before using this book.

Barron's How to Prepare for the TOEFL. A book for learners at high intermediate and advanced levels who need review and practice for the TOEFL. It includes questions and answers about the TOEFL examination, a detailed review for each section of the examination, practice exercises, and eight model tests similar to the actual TOEFL examination. Several sets of additional materials are available to supplement this book, including a separate package of cassette tapes, a separate package of audio compact disks, or the book may be accompanied by compact disks for audio only, or a CD-ROM for use with a computer. A computer-adaptive test like that of the Computer-Based TOEFL is found on the CD-ROM.

Barron's Pass Key to the TOEFL. A pocket-sized edition of *Barron's How to Prepare for the TOEFL.* It is for high intermediate and advanced learners who need review and practice for the TOEFL and want to be able to carry a smaller book with them. It includes questions and answers about the TOEFL examination, basic tips on how to prepare for the TOEFL, and four model tests from *Barron's How to Prepare for the TOEFL.* One audio compact disk accompanies the book to give you practice in listening comprehension.

More About This Book

In preparing to take the TOEFL or any other language examination, it is very important to review the language skills for each section of the examination and to have an opportunity to take model tests that are similar to the actual examination.

Reviewing will help you recall some of the language skills you have studied in previous classes and other books. Taking model tests will give you the experience of taking a TOEFL before you take the actual examination. If you plan to take the Computer-Based TOEFL, it is especially important for you to practice using the CD-ROM that may accompany this book.

Remember, the purpose of the book is to provide you with a detailed review of the language skills for each section of the TOEFL examination and to provide you with opportunities to take model tests similar to the actual TOEFL examination.

By studying this book, you should renew and sharpen your skills, increase your speed, and improve your score.

Planning to Take the TOEFL

Most learners who use Barron's *How to Prepare for the TOEFL* take the test *after* they have finished studying this book.

Study Plan I—For Intermediate Level Learners

- First, use *Barron's Practice Exercises for the TOEFL.*
- Then use this book, *Barron's How to Prepare for the TOEFL.*

Study Plan II—For High Intermediate Level or Advanced Learners

- Use this book, *Barron's How to Prepare for the TOEFL.*

A Twelve-Week Calendar

Week One

- Read Chapter 2, "Questions and Answers Concerning the TOEFL."
- Write TOEFL Services for a copy of the *Information Bulletin* or download it from the TOEFL web site.
- Register for your test date.

Week Two

- Study Chapter 3, "Review of Section 1: Listening."
- Take the Listening Section of Model Test 1.
- Refer to the Answer Key in Chapter 8 and the Explanatory Answers in Chapter 9.
- Refer to Chapter 11 "Transcript for the Listening Sections of the TOEFL Model Tests."

Week Three

- Begin Chapter 4, "Review of Section 2: Structure," the Patterns.
- Complete the Practice Exercises, and refer to the Answer Key in Chapter 8.
- Mark the Problems that you need to review again.

Week Four

- Continue Chapter 4, "Review of Section 2: Structure," the Style Problems.
- Complete the Practice Exercises, and refer to the Answer Key in Chapter 8.
- Mark the Problems that you need to review again.

Week Five

- Take the Structure Section of Model Test 1.
- Refer to the Answer Key in Chapter 8 and the Explanatory Answers in Chapter 9.
- Read Chapter 6, "Review of Writing Essays."

Week Six

- Study Chapter 5, "Review of Section 3: Reading."
- Take the Reading Section of Model Test 1.
- Refer to the Answer Key in Chapter 8 and the Explanatory Answers in Chapter 9.
- Write the Essay at the end of Model Test 1.

Week Seven

- Take all three sections of Model Test 2.
- Refer to the Answer Key in Chapter 8 and the Explanatory Answers in Chapter 9.
- Write the Essay at the end of Model Test 2.

Week Eight

- Take all three sections of Model Test 3.
- Refer to the Answer Key in Chapter 8 and the Explanatory Answers in Chapter 9.
- Write the Essay at the end of Model Test 3.

Week Nine

- Take all three sections of Model Test 4.
- Take all three sections of Model Test 5: Computer-Assisted TOEFL. (If you are not preparing for the Computer-Based TOEFL, follow directions for marking in the book.)
- Refer to the Answer Key in Chapter 8 and the Explanatory Answers in Chapter 9.
- Write the Essays at the end of Model Tests 4 and 5.

Week Ten

- Take all three sections of Model Tests 6 and 7.
- Refer to the Answer Key in Chapter 8 and the Explanatory Answers in Chapter 9.
- Write the Essays at the end of Model Tests 6 and 7.

Week Eleven

- Study all the problems that you have marked in the Review Chapters.
- Review all the errors that you have made on the Model Tests.
- Take all three sections of Model Test 8.
- Refer to the Answer Key in Chapter 8 and the Explanatory Answers in Chapter 9.
- Write the Essay at the end of Model Test 8.

Week Twelve

- Review all the problems that you have marked in the Review Chapters.
- Review all the errors that you have made on all the Model Tests.
- Take the Cumulative Model Test—Computer-Adaptive TOEFL if you have the CD-ROM.

Adjusting the Calendar

Ideally, you will have twelve weeks to prepare for the TOEFL. But, if you have a shorter time to prepare, follow the plan in the same order, adjusting the time to meet your needs.

If you have taken the TOEFL before, you already know which section or sections are difficult for you. Look at the part scores on your score report. If your lowest score is on Section 1, Listening, then you should spend more time reviewing Section 1. If your lowest score is on Section 2 or Section 3, then you should spend more time reviewing them.

Plan for Preparation

To improve your scores most, follow this plan:

- ***First,*** concentrate on listening, structure, writing, and reading, instead of on vocabulary. Your score will improve, because when you are engaged in listening and reading, you are practicing skills that you can apply during the examination regardless of the content of the material. When you are reviewing structure, you are studying a system that is smaller than that of vocabulary, and, like the skills of listening and reading, has the potential for application on the TOEFL that you take. Many of the structures that you study will probably appear on the examination. But when you review lists of vocabulary, even very good lists, you may study hundreds of words and not find any of them on the examination. This is so because the system is very large. There are thousands of possible words that may be tested.
- ***Second,*** spend time preparing every day for at least an hour instead of sitting down to review once a week for seven hours. Even though you are studying for the same amount of time, research shows that daily shorter sessions produce better results on the test.
- ***Finally,*** do not try to memorize questions from this or any other book. The questions on the test that you take will be very similar to the questions in this book, but they will not be exactly the same.

What you should try to do as you use this and your other books is learn how to apply your knowledge. Do not hurry through the practice exercises. While you are checking your answers to the model tests, *think* about the correct answer. Why is it correct? Can you explain the answer to yourself before you check the explanatory answer? Is the question similar to others that you have seen before?

Plan for Additional Preparation

Although this book should provide you with enough review material, some of you will want to do more in order to prepare for the TOEFL. Suggestions for each section follow.

- ***To prepare for Section 1,*** Listening, listen to radio and television newscasts and weather reports, television documentaries, lectures on educational television stations, and free lectures sponsored by clubs and universities. Attend movies in English. Try to make friends with speakers of American English and participate in conversations.

- ***To prepare for Section 2,*** Structure, use an advanced grammar review book. If you are attending an English course, do not stop attending.

- ***To prepare for Section 3,*** Reading, read articles in English newspapers and magazines, college catalogs and admissions materials, travel brochures, and entries that interest you from American and English encyclopedias. Try to read a variety of topics—American history, culture, social science, and natural science.

- ***To prepare for the essay,*** Writing, refer to the TOEFL *Information Bulletin* for the Computer-Based TOEFL or visit the TOEFL web site at www.toefl.org. Actual essay topics for the TOEFL are listed in the TOEFL *Bulletin* and on the web site.

A Good Start

Learn to relax. If you start to panic in the examination room, close your eyes and say "no" in your mind. Tell yourself, "I will not panic. I am prepared." Then take several slow, deep breaths, letting your shoulders drop in a relaxed manner as you exhale.

Concentrate on the questions. Do not talk. Concentrate your attention. Do not look at anything in the test room except the answers that correspond to the question you are working on.

Do not think about your situation, the test in general, your score, or your future. If you do, force yourself to return to the question.

If you do not understand a problem and you do not have a good answer, do your best. Then stop thinking about it. Be ready for the next problem.

Do not cheat. In spite of opportunity, knowledge that others are doing it, desire to help a friend, or fear that you will not make a good score, *do not cheat.*

On the TOEFL, cheating is a very serious matter. If you are discovered, your test will not be scored. Legal action may be taken by Educational Testing Service (ETS).

Suggestions for Success

Your attitude will influence your success on the TOEFL examination. You must develop patterns of positive thinking. To help in developing a positive attitude, memorize the following sentences and bring them to mind after each study session. Bring them to mind when you begin to have negative thoughts.

I know more today than I did yesterday.
I am preparing.
I will succeed.

Remember, some tension is normal and good. Accept it. Use it constructively. It will motivate you to study. But don't panic or worry. Panic will cause loss of concentration and poor performance. Avoid people who panic and worry. Don't listen to them. They will encourage negative thoughts.

You know more today than you did yesterday.
You are preparing.
You will succeed.

2 QUESTIONS AND ANSWERS CONCERNING THE TOEFL

The TOEFL is the Test of English as a Foreign Language.

Almost one million students from 180 countries register to take the TOEFL every year at test centers throughout the world. Some of them do not pass the TOEFL because they do not understand enough English. Others do not pass it because they do not understand the examination.

The following questions are commonly asked by students as they prepare for the TOEFL. To help you, they have been answered here.

TOEFL Programs

What is the purpose of the TOEFL?

Since 1963 the TOEFL has been used by scholarship selection committees of governments, universities, and agencies such as Fulbright, the Agency for International Development, AMIDEAST, Latin American Scholarship Program, and others as a standard measure of the English proficiency of their candidates. Now some professional licensing and certification agencies also use TOEFL scores to evaluate English proficiency.

The admissions committees of more than 2400 colleges and universities in the United States and Canada require foreign applicants to submit TOEFL scores along with transcripts and recommendations in order to be considered for admission. Some colleges and universities in other English-speaking countries also require the TOEFL for admissions purposes.

Many universities use TOEFL scores to fulfill the foreign language requirement for doctoral candidates whose first language is not English.

Which TOEFL testing programs are available now?

Three TOEFL testing programs are available—the Supplemental Paper-Based TOEFL, the Computer-Based TOEFL, and the Institutional TOEFL. The Supplemental Paper-Based TOEFL and the Computer-Based TOEFL programs are the official administrations. The Institutional TOEFL is not an official administration.

What is the Computer-Based TOEFL program?

The Computer-Based TOEFL (CBT) was introduced July, 1998, in the United States, Canada, Latin America, Europe, Australia, Africa, the Middle East, and a limited number of Asian nations. In October, 2000, the CBT was introduced in all other Asian countries, with the exception of the People's Republic of China, where it will be given for the first time in 2002–2003, completing the worldwide phase-in of the Computer-Based TOEFL. A list of test centers established for the purpose of administering the Computer-Based TOEFL program appears in the free TOEFL *Information Bulletin* available from TOEFL Services, or on the TOEFL web site. Be sure that you request the TOEFL *Information Bulletin* for the Computer-Based TOEFL program.

What is the Supplemental Paper-Based TOEFL program?

The Supplemental Paper-Based TOEFL program is a paper and pencil version of the TOEFL that was reintroduced on a temporary basis to replace mobile computer-based testing in a few remote areas. Visit the TOEFL web site at www.toefl.org/infobull.html for a list of the areas where the Supplemental Paper-Based TOEFL is currently being offered. If you cannot use the web site, you can check at one of the United States Information Service (USIS) offices in your country for an *Information Bulletin for Supplemental TOEFL Administrations.*

What is the Institutional TOEFL program?

More than 1,200 schools, colleges, universities, and private agencies administer the Institutional TOEFL. The Institutional TOEFL is the same length, format, and difficulty as the official Paper-Based TOEFL, but the dates and the purposes of the Institutional TOEFL are different from those of the official TOEFL.

The dates for the Institutional TOEFL usually correspond to the beginning of an academic session on a college or university calendar.

The Institutional TOEFL is used for admission, placement, eligibility, or employment only at the school or agency that offers the test.

If you plan to use your scores for a different college, university, or agency, you should take one of the official TOEFL tests, either the Supplemental Paper-Based TOEFL or the Computer-Based TOEFL.

How can I order an *Information Bulletin?*

There are four ways to order a TOEFL *Information Bulletin.*

download	www.toefl.org/infobull.html
phone	1-609-771-7100
FAX	1-609-771-7500
mail	TOEFL Services P.O. Box 6151 Princeton, NJ 08541-6151 U.S.A.

Many schools also have copies of the *Information Bulletin* in their counseling centers.

Be sure that you request the correct TOEFL *Information Bulletin* for your test. Ask for either the Computer-Based *Information Bulletin* or the *Information Bulletin for Supplemental TOEFL Administrations.*

It is correct to limit your correspondence to two sentences. For example:

REQUEST FOR THE TOEFL *INFORMATION BULLETIN*

(write your address here)
(write the date here)

TOEFL Services
P.O. 6151
Princeton, NJ 08541-6151
U.S.A.

Dear TOEFL Representative:

Please send me a copy of the TOEFL *Information Bulletin* for the (write Computer-Based TOEFL or Supplemental Paper-Based TOEFL here).

Thank you for your earliest attention.

Sincerely yours,

(write your name here)

The TOEFL *Information Bulletin* is often available overseas in U.S. embassies and advising offices of the United States Information Service, binational centers, IIE and AMIDEAST Counseling Centers, Fulbright offices, and ETS Regional Registration Centers, as well as in Sylvan Technology Centers.

May I choose to take the Computer-Based TOEFL or the Supplemental Paper-Based TOEFL?

When the Computer-Based TOEFL is phased in for the area where you will take your TOEFL, you must take the Computer-Based TOEFL. All Paper-Based TOEFL tests will be replaced.

The TOEFL web site lists the areas where the Supplemental Paper-Based TOEFL has been reintroduced on a temporary basis.

Which language skills are tested on the TOEFL?

In general, the same four language skills are tested in all TOEFL programs. Listening, structure, writing, and reading are tested in three separate sections:

Section 1 Listening
Section 2 Structure/Writing
Section 3 Reading

There are some differences in the types of questions used to test the language skills, however. Charts that outline the differences between the Computer-Based TOEFL and the Supplemental Paper-Based TOEFL are printed at the beginning of each Review Chapter in this book.

On the Computer-Based TOEFL, the essay counts 50 percent of the total score for Section 2.

Does the TOEFL have a composition section?

Computer-Based TOEFL

The Computer-Based TOEFL has a Writing section. On the Writing section and on the TWE (Test of Written English), you must write a short essay on an assigned topic.

The essay should be about 300 words long. The topic is typical of academic writing requirements at colleges and universities in North America. You have 30 minutes to finish writing. Both the Writing section and the TWE are described in greater detail in Chapter 6 of this book.

Supplemental Paper-Based TOEFL

The Paper-Based TOEFL does not have a composition section, but if you take the TOEFL in August, October, December, February, or May, you will also take the TWE.

Are all the TOEFL tests the same length?

Computer-Based TOEFL

The forms for the Computer-Based TOEFL vary in length. Some items are for research purposes and are not scored. Scored items are selected by the computer, based on the level of difficulty and the number of correct responses from previous items. Difficult items are worth more points than average or easy items.

Supplemental Paper-Based TOEFL

All of the forms for the Paper-Based TOEFL are the same length.

How does the Supplemental Paper-Based TOEFL and the Institutional TOEFL compare with the Computer-Based TOEFL?

The Supplemental Paper-Based TOEFL and the Institutional TOEFL are different from the Computer-Based TOEFL not only because it is a different experience to take a test with a pencil and paper as compared with a computer but also because the test designs are different. The Supplemental Paper-Based TOEFL and the Institutional TOEFL are linear tests. This means that all the questions appear in a row, and everyone receives the same questions. The Computer-Based TOEFL has two sections, Listening and Structure, that are computer-adaptive. This means that only one question appears on the screen, and everyone does not receive the same questions. Everyone begins with a question of average difficulty. If you answer it correctly, you are given a more difficult question. If you answer it incorrectly, you are given an easier question. You receive more points for answering difficult questions correctly than you do for answering average or easy questions correctly.

For a more detailed comparison of the Paper-Based TOEFL with the Computer-Based TOEFL, please refer to the charts at the beginning of each Review Chapter in this book.

Is the Computer-Based TOEFL fair?

The Computer-Based TOEFL is fair because the computer is constantly adjusting the selection of items based on your responses. It allows you to achieve that maximum number of points that you are capable of based on your English language proficiency. In addition, everyone receives the same test content and the same proportion of question types—multiple-choice and computer-assisted.

What if I have little experience with computers?

There is a Tutorial at the beginning of the Computer-Based TOEFL to help you become familiar with the computer before you begin your test. In the Tutorial, you will review how to use a mouse, how to scroll, and how to answer all the question types on the test.

If you would like to work through the Tutorial before the day of your Computer-Based TOEFL, you can request a CD-ROM Sampler from ETS. In the United States and Canada, call 1-800-446-3319. From other countries, call 1-619-771-7243. Or, if you have access to the web, you can use the Sampler by visiting the TOEFL web site at http://www.toefl.org. There are also a few samples of the Tutorial in the TOEFL *Information Bulletin.*

Registration

How do I register for the TOEFL?

Computer-Based TOEFL

There are three ways to register for the Computer-Based TOEFL. If you plan to pay by credit card—VISA, MasterCard, or American Express—you may register by phone. Call Candidate Services at 1-800-468-6335, or phone your Regional Registration Center. The phone numbers for the regional centers are listed in the TOEFL *Information Bulletin.* If you plan to pay by check, money order, or credit card, you may register by mail. To arrange a test in the United States, Canada, Puerto Rico, or a U.S. territory, return the voucher request form in your *Information Bulletin*, along with your registration fee to TOEFL Services in Princeton, New Jersey. There is a mailing label provided in the *Information Bulletin.* To arrange a test in all other locations where the Computer-Based TOEFL is offered, return the International Test Scheduling Form to your Regional Registration Center. There are mailing labels provided in the TOEFL *Information Bulletin.* Be sure to sign the form and include your registration fee.

You will be asked to choose two days of the week and two months of the year as well as two test centers. If there are no appointments available on the dates you have requested, you will be assigned a date close to the request you have made.

Supplemental Paper-Based TOEFL

The *Information Bulletin for Supplemental TOEFL Administrations* has a registration form in it. Using the directions in the TOEFL *Information Bulletin*, fill out the form and mail it to the TOEFL Registration Office. Be sure to sign the form and include your registration fee.

Institutional TOEFL

The school, college, university, or agency that administers the Institutional TOEFL should have registration forms available. Fees vary.

The school, college, university, or agency will return your registration form and the registration fee to TOEFL Services along with the forms and fees of all of the other applicants for the Institutional Testing.

When should I register for the TOEFL?

If you are taking the TOEFL as part of the application process for college or university admission, plan to take the test early enough for your score to be received by the admission office in time to be considered with your application. Usually, a test date at least two months before the admission application deadline allows adequate time for your scores to be considered with your admission application.

Test centers often receive more requests than they can accommodate on certain dates. Try to schedule your appointment by phone or mail at least a month before the date you prefer to take the TOEFL, especially in October, November, December, April, and May.

What are the fees for the TOEFL?

Computer-Based TOEFL

In the United States, the registration fee is $110 U.S. The fee may be paid by check, credit card, money order, bank draft, or U.S. postal money order. In Canada, the fee is $118.

In other countries, the registration fee was originally advertised as $125 U.S., but TOEFL Services is now offering the Computer-Based TOEFL worldwide at $110 U.S. Because of rates of exchange, the actual cost may vary from one country to another. For exact fees in local currency, and options for payment, refer to the TOEFL *Information Bulletin*.

Supplemental Paper-Based TOEFL

The fee for the Supplemental Paper-Based TOEFL is $75 U.S.

Which credit cards will be accepted?

Only MasterCard, VISA, and American Express may be used to pay for TOEFL registration fees and services.

May I pay by check or money order?

In order to pay for the Supplemental Paper-Based TOEFL by check or money order, include payment with your registration form.

In order to pay for the Computer-Based TOEFL by check or money order, you should complete a voucher request form and mail it to the TOEFL Office with your payment. There is a special form and envelope in the middle of the *Information Bulletin for the Computer-Based TOEFL* for this purpose, or you can find these materials on the TOEFL web site. You will receive a CBT voucher by return mail.

Which currencies will be accepted?

Payments at the current exchange rate for the U.S. dollar may be made in the following currencies:

Australian Dollar
Austrian Schilling
Belgian Franc
British Pound
Danish Krone
Euro Dollar
Finnish Markka
French Franc
German Mark
Hong Kong Dollar
Irish Pound
Italian Lira
Japanese Yen
Netherlands Guilder
New Zealand Dollar
Norwegian Krone
Portuguese Escudo
Saudi Riyal
Singapore Dollar
Spanish Peseta
Swedish Kronor
Swiss Franc

Is there a fast way to send mail to the TOEFL Office?

For the fastest delivery, use the express courier delivery address:

TOEFL Services (25-Q-310)
Distribution and Receiving Center
225 Phillips Blvd.
Ewing, NJ 08628-7435
U.S.A.

Will Educational Testing Service (ETS) confirm my registration?

Computer-Based TOEFL

If you register for the Computer-Based TOEFL, you will receive an appointment confirmation number. If you do not receive an appointment confirmation number, or if you lose your appointment confirmation number, call 1-800-GOTOEFL (1-800-468-6335) in the United States or call your Regional Registration Center outside the United States. The phone numbers for regional registration centers are listed in the TOEFL *Information Bulletin*.

Supplemental Paper-Based TOEFL

If you register for the Paper-Based TOEFL, you will receive an admission ticket. Your admission ticket is your confirmation.

You must complete the ticket and take it with you to the test center on the day of the test along with your passport.

If you have not received the admission ticket two weeks before the date of your TOEFL test, call TOEFL Services or call your local representative. The phone numbers for local representatives are listed in the TOEFL *Information Bulletin*.

May I change the date or cancel my registration?

Computer-Based TOEFL

In the United States, Canada, Puerto Rico, and U.S. territories, call Candidate Services at 1-800-468-6335. Be sure to call by noon, three business days before the date of your appointment, or you will not receive a partial reimbursement of your registration fee. If you want to choose a different date, you may be asked to pay a rescheduling fee of $40 in the U.S. or $42 in Canada.

In all other locations, call your Regional Registration Center by noon, five business days before the date of your appointment, or you will not receive a partial reimbursement of your registration fee. If you want to choose a different date, you may be asked to pay a rescheduling fee of $40.

You must provide your appointment confirmation number when you call. You will be given a cancellation number.

Supplemental Paper-Based TOEFL

Test date changes and cancellations are not permitted for the Paper-Based TOEFL; however, you may receive absentee credit. If you do not take the Paper-Based TOEFL, write "absentee credit" across your admission ticket and send it to TOEFL Services. It must arrive within sixty days of your test date for you to receive $10 cash or $10 credit toward registration for a different date.

May I give my appointment to a friend?

Appointments cannot be reassigned or exchanged among friends.

How should I prepare the night before the TOEFL?

Don't go to a party the night before you take your TOEFL examination. But don't try to review everything that you have studied in this book either. By going to a party, you will lose the opportunity to review a few problems that may add valuable points to your TOEFL score. But by trying to review everything, you will probably get confused, and you may even panic.

Select a limited amount of material to review the night before you take the TOEFL.

And remember, you are not trying to score 100 percent on the TOEFL examination. No one knows everything. If you answer 75 percent of the questions correctly, you will receive an excellent score.

May I register on the day of the TOEFL?

Registration of candidates on the day of the TOEFL is permitted for the CBT only, but most of the time there is no space for candidates not pre-registered for that day.

Test Administration

Where are the test centers?

The most recent listing of the test centers for TOEFL administrations worldwide is found in the current *Information Bulletin* or on the TOEFL web site.

What kind of room will be used for the TOEFL?

Computer-Based TOEFL

Rooms used for the Computer-Based TOEFL are small. They are like the study areas in a library or a language laboratory. There are usually only six to fifteen students at individual computer stations. Each student has a headset. It is a good idea to wear clothing that allows you to adjust to warm or cold room temperatures.

Supplemental Paper-Based TOEFL

The rooms vary greatly from one test site to another. Rooms used for the Paper-Based TOEFL tend to be large. The seats are usually school desks. It is a good idea to wear clothing that allows you to adjust to warm or cold room temperatures.

What should I take with me to the examination room?

Computer-Based TOEFL

Take your appointment confirmation number and your official identification.

You will not need a watch because the computer screen has a clock face on it. Books, dictionaries, tape recorders, cellular phones, pagers, highlighters, pens, and notes are not permitted in the examination room. Some centers will have lockers for you to store your possessions, but it is really better not to take with you anything that you cannot take into the examination room.

Supplemental Paper-Based TOEFL

Take three sharpened number two pencils with erasers on them, your admission ticket, and photo identification form. In addition to your photo identification, you must have official identification with you.

It would be helpful to take a watch, although most examination rooms will have clocks. Books, dictionaries, tape recorders, cellular phones, pagers, highlighters, pens, and notes are not permitted in the examination room.

What kind of identification is required?

Computer-Based TOEFL

In the United States, only your valid passport will be accepted. In other countries, your valid passport is still the best identification, but if you do not have a passport, you may refer to the TOEFL *Information Bulletin* for special directions.

Your photograph will be taken at the test center and reproduced on all official score reports sent to institutions. Your identification will be checked against the new photograph. In addition, all Computer-Based TOEFL sessions will be videotaped.

Be sure to use the same spelling and order of your name on your registration materials or phone registration, the Test Center log that you will sign when you enter the test area, the forms on the computer screens, and any correspondence that you may have with TOEFL Services, Candidate Services, or other local representatives.

Supplemental Paper-Based TOEFL

The test center supervisor will not admit you if you do not have official identification. In the United States, only your valid passport will be accepted. The supervisor will not allow you to enter with an expired passport or a photocopy of your passport. In other countries, your valid passport is still the best identification, but if you do not have a passport, you may refer to the TOEFL *Information Bulletin* for special directions.

Be sure that your photo identification and your passport picture look like you do on the day of the examination. If not, you may not be admitted to the examination room.

Be sure to use the same spelling and order of your name on your registration materials, admission ticket, answer sheet, and any correspondence that you may have with either TOEFL Services or your Regional Registration Center.

Will I sign a confidentiality statement?

Before you begin the Computer-Based TOEFL, you will be asked to sign a confidentiality statement. You will agree to keep confidential the content of all test questions. The purpose of this procedure is to protect the security of the test.

Where should I sit?

You will be assigned a seat. You may not select your own seat.

It is usually better not to sit with friends anyway. You may find yourself looking at friends instead of concentrating on your test materials. You may even be accused of cheating if it appears that you are communicating in some way.

What if I am late?

Report to the test center thirty minutes before the appointment time for your TOEFL. You will need a half hour to check in. If you arrive late, you may not be admitted, and your fee may not be refunded.

How long is the testing session of the TOEFL?

Computer-Based TOEFL

The time for the Computer-Based TOEFL will vary, depending on your familiarity with computers. There is a computer Tutorial at the beginning of the session for those who need some practice using the computer before taking the Computer-Based TOEFL. In general, the Computer-Based TOEFL takes four hours, including the Tutorial. When you finish, you may leave the room quietly.

Supplemental Paper-Based TOEFL

The total time for the testing session of the Paper-Based TOEFL is two hours. Since the instructions are not included as part of the timed sections, the actual time that you will spend in the examination room will be about three hours. When the TWE is given with the TOEFL, the total time will be about three and one half hours. When you finish, you must sit quietly until the supervisor dismisses the group.

How much time do I have to complete each of the sections?

It is wise to work as rapidly as possible without compromising accuracy. Check the timetable for the TOEFL on page ix.

Are breaks scheduled during the TOEFL?

Computer-Based TOEFL

There is a ten-minute break scheduled during the Computer-Based TOEFL. It usually occurs between the Structure and the Reading sections.

Supplemental Paper-Based TOEFL

There are no breaks scheduled during the Paper-Based TOEFL.

Is there a place to eat lunch at the test centers?

Some of the testing centers are conveniently located near restaurants, but many, especially the mobile centers, are not. You may want to take a snack with you to eat before or after your test.

How can I complain about a test administration?

If you feel that the test situation was not fair, you have a right to register a complaint. Within three days of the date of the test, write a letter to Test Administration Services. The phone number is 1-609-771-7100. Mention the date of your test, the city, and the country. Explain why you feel that the test was not fair.

Examination

What kinds of questions are found on the TOEFL?

Computer-Based TOEFL

The majority of the questions on the Computer-Based TOEFL are multiple-choice. There are also some other types of questions on the Computer-Based TOEFL. These questions will have special directions on the screen. You will have many examples of them in the Model Tests in this book.

Supplemental Paper-Based TOEFL

All the questions on the Paper-Based TOEFL are multiple-choice.

How do I answer the test questions?

Computer-Based TOEFL

When you are presented with a multiple-choice question, read the four possible answers on the screen, point the arrow and click beside the answer that you choose. The oval will change from white to black. When you are presented with other types of questions, follow the directions on the screen.

Supplemental Paper-Based TOEFL

Read the four possible answers in your test book, and mark the corresponding space on the answer sheet, which will be provided for you at the test center.

How do I mark the answers?

Computer-Based TOEFL

Before the examination begins, you will have an opportunity to practice marking the answers to questions on the computer screen. The Tutorial will include all the different types of questions on the Computer-Based TOEFL.

MARKING THE ANSWER SCREEN: COMPUTER-BASED TOEFL

One question is shown on the computer screen. One answer is marked on the screen.

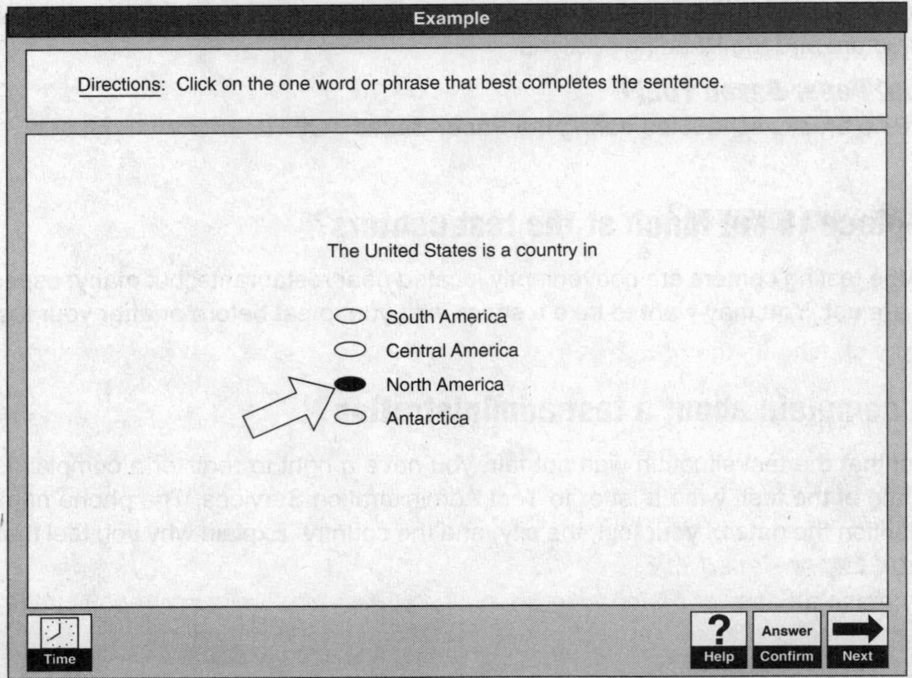

Supplemental Paper-Based TOEFL

Before the examination begins, the supervisor will explain how to mark the answer sheet. Be sure to fill in the space completely.

MARKING THE ANSWER SHEET: SUPPLEMENTAL PAPER-BASED TOEFL

One question is shown in the test book. One answer is marked on the answer sheet.

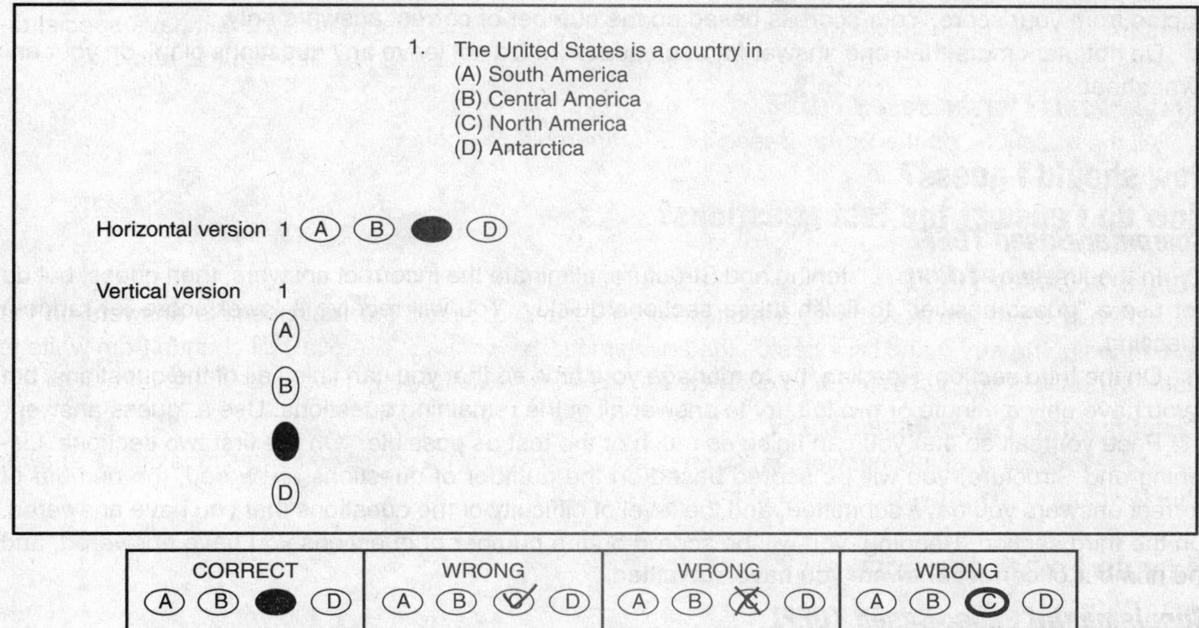

May I make notes in the test book or on the scratch paper?

Computer-Based TOEFL

There is no test book for the Computer-Based TOEFL. All of the questions and the answer options are presented on the computer screen. You may not use the scratch paper for your essay to make notes for any other section of the test.

Supplemental Paper-Based TOEFL

You are not allowed to make marks in your test book for the Supplemental Paper-Based TOEFL. You may not underline words or write notes in the margins of the test book. It is considered cheating.

May I change an answer?

Computer-Based TOEFL

On the first two sections of the Computer-Based TOEFL, Listening and Structure, you can change your answer by clicking on the new answer. You can change your answer as many times as you wish, until you click on the **Confirm Answer** button. When you click on **Confirm Answer**, you move to the next question, and you cannot go back to a previous question. On the third section of the Computer-Based TOEFL, Reading, you can change your answer as many times as you wish. You may go on to the next question and back to the previous questions. The CD-ROM that supplements this book will provide you with practice in choosing and changing answers on the computer screen.

Supplemental Paper-Based TOEFL

You may erase an answer on the answer sheet if you do so carefully and completely. Stray pencil marks may cause inaccurate scoring by the test-scoring machine.

If I am not sure of an answer, should I guess?

Computer-Based TOEFL

Try to answer every question. Your score will be based not only on the difficulty of the questions but also on the number of questions answered.

Supplemental Paper-Based TOEFL

If you are not sure of an answer, you should guess. The number of incorrect answers is not subtracted from your score. Your score is based on the number of correct answers only.

Do not mark more than one answer for each question. Do not leave any questions blank on your answer sheet.

How should I guess?

Computer-Based TOEFL

In the first two sections, Listening and Structure, eliminate the incorrect answers, then guess, but do not use a "guess answer" to finish these sections quickly. You will receive a lower score for random guessing.

On the third section, Reading, try to manage your time so that you can finish all of the questions, but if you have only a minute or two left, try to answer all of the remaining questions. Use a "guess answer."

Pace yourself so that you can finish as much of the test as possible. On the first two sections, Listening and Structure, you will be scored based on the number of questions answered, the number of correct answers you have submitted, and the level of difficulty of the questions that you have answered. On the third section, Reading, you will be scored on the number of questions you have answered, and the number of correct answers you have submitted.

Supplemental Paper-Based TOEFL

First, eliminate all of the possibilities that you know are NOT correct. Then, if you are almost sure of an answer, guess that one.

If you have no idea of the correct answer for a question, choose one letter and use it for your "guess" answer throughout the entire examination.

The "guess" answer is especially useful for finishing a section quickly. If the supervisor tells you to stop working on a section before you have finished it, answer all of the remaining questions with the "guess" answer.

What should I do if I discover that I have marked my answers incorrectly?

Computer-Based TOEFL

It is not possible to mark your screen incorrectly because the computer program will present only one question on each screen. If you change your mind after you have confirmed a response on the Listening or Structure sections, the computer will not allow you to return to a previous question on these two sections, and you will not be able to change the answer that you have confirmed.

As you see, it is very important to be sure of the answer before you click on **Confirm Answer**.

Supplemental Paper-Based TOEFL

Do not panic. Notify the supervisor immediately.

If you have marked one answer in the wrong space on the answer sheet, the rest of the answers will be out of sequence. Ask for time at the end of the examination to correct the sequence. The TOEFL test supervisor may or may not allow you to do this.

To save time finding the number on the answer sheet that corresponds to the problem you are reading, to avoid mismarking, and to save space on your desk, use your test book as a marker on your answer sheet. As you advance, slide the book down underneath the number of the question that you are marking on the answer sheet.

May I choose the order of the sections on my TOEFL?

You may not choose the order. Listening, Structure, and Reading are tested in that order. The essay is written last. When you have finished with a section, you may not work on any other section of the test.

What if I cannot hear the tape for the Listening section?

Computer-Based TOEFL

You will have your own headset for the Computer-Based TOEFL. Before the Listening section begins, you will have an opportunity to adjust the volume yourself. Be careful to adjust the volume when you are prompted to do so. If you wait until the test begins, you cannot adjust it.

Supplemental Paper-Based TOEFL

It is the responsibility of the supervisor for the Paper-Based TOEFL to make sure that everyone is able to hear the tape. If you cannot hear it well, raise your hand and ask the supervisor to adjust the volume.

May I keep my test?

TOEFL Services makes copies of TOEFL tests available for purchase. Visit the TOEFL web site for more information.

If you try to keep or copy TOEFL tests, the TOEFL Office may take legal action.

What can I do if I do not appear to take the test?

Computer-Based TOEFL

There is a $60 refund, if you cancel your test five business days before the date of your appointment.

Supplemental Paper-Based TOEFL

If you do not appear to take the test, you have a right to request a partial refund. If you enter the examination room, you cannot request a partial refund. You must make your request within sixty days of the date of the TOEFL test. Ask for "absentee credit" when you write to the TOEFL Office. The refund is $10.

Score Reports

How is my TOEFL scored?

Computer-Based TOEFL

Total Computer-Based TOEFL scores range from 0 to 300.

First, each of the three sections of the TOEFL is graded on a scale from 0 to 30. Then the scores from the three sections are added together. Finally, the sum is multiplied by 10 and divided by 3.

For example, the following scores were received on the three sections:

Listening	23
Structure and Writing	25
Reading	27
	75

75 x 10 = 750 ÷ 3 = 250 Total TOEFL Score

Supplemental Paper-Based TOEFL

Total Paper-Based TOEFL scores range from 310 to 677.

First, each of the three sections of the TOEFL is graded on a scale from 31 to 68. Then the scores from the three sections are added together. Finally, the sum is multiplied by 10 and divided by 3.

For example, the following scores were received on the three sections:

Listening Comprehension	52
Structure and Written Expression	48
Vocabulary and Reading Comprehension	50
	150

150 x 10 = 1500 ÷ 3 = 500 Total TOEFL Score

How do I interpret my score?

There are no passing or failing scores on the TOEFL. Each agency or university will evaluate the scores according to its own requirements. Even at the same university, the requirements may vary for different programs of study, levels of study (graduate or undergraduate), and degrees of responsibility (student or teaching assistant).

The following summary of admissions policies are typical of U.S. universities, assuming, of course, that the applicant's documents other than English proficiency are acceptable.

TYPICAL ADMISSIONS POLICIES OF AMERICAN UNIVERSITIES

Paper-Based TOEFL Score	*Policy*	*Computer-Based TOEFL Score*
650 or more	admission assured for graduate students	280 or more
600–649	admission assured for undergraduate students	250–279
550–599	admission probable for graduate students	213–249
500–549	admission probable for undergraduate students	173–212
450–499	individual cases reviewed	133–172
449 or less	referral to English language program probable	132 or less

Refer to the TOEFL *Information Bulletin* or web site for a detailed chart of percentile ranks for total TOEFL scores. This will help you interpret your score relative to the scores of others taking the examination.

How do the scores on the Supplemental Paper-Based TOEFL compare with those on the Computer-Based TOEFL?

A concordance table is a table that shows comparisons. A concordance table for the Paper-Based TOEFL and the Computer-Based TOEFL has been mailed to all institutions that use TOEFL scores for admissions decisions. A copy of the concordance table is printed in the TOEFL *Information Bulletin* and posted on the TOEFL web site.

A shorter version of the table follows:

Paper-Based TOEFL	*Computer-Based TOEFL*
677	300
650	280
600	250
550	213
500	173
450	133
400	97

If I score very poorly on one part of the TOEFL, is it still possible to receive a good total score?

If you feel that you have done very poorly on one part of a section, do not despair. You may receive a low score on one part of a section and still score well on the total examination if your scores on the other parts of that section and the other sections are good.

When can I see my scores?

Computer-Based TOEFL

After you complete your Computer-Based TOEFL, you can view your estimated score on the screen. You will be able to see section scores for both Listening and Reading, as well as for the multiple-choice part of the Structure section, but the essay, which is included as half of the Structure score, will not have been graded. The estimated score that you will see shows a total score range based on a very poorly written essay or on a very well written essay. For example, your score range might be 150–220.

You are entitled to five copies of your test results, including one personal copy for yourself and four official score reports.

Your official scores for all sections will be mailed to you about two to five weeks after you take your Computer-Based TOEFL, but you will have a very good idea how you performed on the test after you see the estimate.

Supplemental Paper-Based TOEFL

You are entitled to four copies of your test results, including one personal copy for yourself and three official score reports.

You will receive your copy about five weeks after you take the test.

Scores are not available by phone for the Supplemental Paper-Based TOEFL.

How can I know my scores sooner?

If your essay is typed instead of handwritten, your scores will be mailed sooner. If you would like to know your score on the same day that the report is mailed, you may use the TOEFL phone service. Using a touch-tone phone, call the TOEFL Office, and you will hear prompts to enter your appointment number, your test date, your date of birth, and a credit card number. The fee to hear your scores by phone is $10, plus any long-distance charges that apply.

To call toll-free from the United States or Canada, touch 1-888-TOEFL-44, which is 1-888-863-3544. To call with long distance charges from all other locations, touch 1-609-771-7267.

What can I do if I question my score report?

Computer-Based TOEFL

The *Information Bulletin for the Computer-Based TOEFL* includes a request form to arrange for your essay to be rescored by two graders who have not seen it previously. The fee for this service is $50.

Supplemental Paper-Based TOEFL

Occasionally, the computer will score an answer sheet incorrectly because of the way you have marked it. If you feel your score is much, much lower than you expected, you have a right to request that your answer sheet be hand scored.

Two people will score your answer sheet independently. If their results are different from that of the computer, your score will be changed. The cost of this service is $20 for the TOEFL and $45 for the TWE. You must make your request within six months of the date of the test.

To make a request, write a letter to TOEFL Services.

May I cancel my scores?

Computer-Based TOEFL

Before you view your scores, you may cancel them. If you do, they will not be sent to any institutions or to you. You will not know how you performed. If you view your scores, you may not cancel them. You will then choose four institutions to receive your score report. All of this is arranged by responding to questions on the computer screen.

Supplemental Paper-Based TOEFL

If you do not want your Paper-Based TOEFL scores to be reported, you have a right to cancel them. To cancel your test scores, you must complete the score cancellation section of your TOEFL answer sheet, or you must write, e-mail, call, or FAX TOEFL Services. If a signed request is received at TOEFL Services within seven days of the date of the test, your scores will not be reported.

How will the agencies or universities of my choice be informed of my score?

Computer-Based TOEFL

Two weeks after the testing, your official score reports will be forwarded directly to the agencies and/or universities that you designated on the information section on the computer screen on the day of the examination.

Personal copies of score reports are not accepted by institutions without confirmation by TOEFL Services. Scores more than two years old are not considered valid.

Supplemental Paper-Based TOEFL

Five weeks after the testing, your official score reports will be forwarded directly to the agencies and/or universities that you designated on an information section at the top of the TOEFL answer sheet on the day of the examination.

You may send your personal copy to an institution or agency, but the score will probably have to be confirmed by an official at TOEFL Services before you can be admitted. Scores more than two years old cannot be reported or verified.

How can I send additional reports?

Computer-Based TOEFL

There is a form in the TOEFL *Information Bulletin* that you can use to have official score reports sent to institutions that were not listed on your computer screen. In addition, the TOEFL Office provides a telephone service for additional score reports. To use the service, you will need a touch-tone phone. You will be asked for your appointment confirmation number, a credit card number, your test date, and both the institution and department codes for the schools you wish to add to your score report list. You will use the numbers on your touch-tone phone to enter the numbers for all of the dates and codes.

The fee for this service is $12 per call, and $12 for each report.

Supplemental Paper-Based TOEFL

There is a form in the TOEFL *Information Bulletin* that you can use to have official score reports sent to institutions that were not listed on your answer sheet.

You may also request official score reports by phone. To use this service, you must have your admission ticket, a credit card, and a touch-tone phone. Call 1-609-771-7267 from six in the morning to ten at night, New York time. The fee for this service is a $12 charge to your credit card per call, an $11 charge per score report, plus a charge to your telephone bill for the long distance call. Official score reports will be mailed three days after your telephone request.

May I take the TOEFL more than one time?

Computer-Based TOEFL

You may not take the Computer-Based TOEFL more than once a month. For example, if you take the Computer-Based TOEFL in July, you must wait until August to take it again.

Supplemental Paper-Based TOEFL

You may take the Paper-Based TOEFL as many times as you wish in order to score to your satisfaction.

If I have already taken the TOEFL, how will the first score or scores affect my new score?

TOEFL scores are considered to be valid for two years. If you have taken the TOEFL more than once, but your first score report is dated more than two years ago, TOEFL Services will not report your score.

If you have taken the TOEFL more than once in the past two years, TOEFL Services will report the score for the test date you request on your score request form.

Is there a direct correspondence between proficiency in English and a good score on the TOEFL?

There is not always a direct correspondence between proficiency in English and a good score on the TOEFL. Many students who are proficient in English are not proficient in how to approach the examination. That is why it is important to prepare by using this book.

What is the relationship between my score on the Model Tests in this book and my score on the TOEFL?

It is not possible to calculate an exact TOEFL score from a score that you might receive on a Model Test in this book. This is so because the actual TOEFL examination has a wider variety of problems.

The Model Tests in this book have been especially designed to help you improve your total TOEFL score by improving your knowledge of the types of problems that most often appear on the TOEFL. These problem types are repeated throughout the eight Model Tests so that you will have practice in recognizing and answering them.

By improving your ability to recognize and correctly answer those types of problems that most often appear on the TOEFL, you will improve your total TOEFL score.

Can I estimate my TOEFL score after I have prepared, using this book?

To estimate your TOEFL score, use the Score Estimates on pages 619–621 of this book.

Will I succeed on the TOEFL?

You will receive from this book what you give to this book. The information is here. Now, it is up to you to devote the time and effort. Thousands of other students have succeeded by using *Barron's How to Prepare for the TOEFL.* You can be successful, too.

Updates

Visit the TOEFL web site at **www.toefl.org** or my web site at **www.teflprep.com** for the latest information about the TOEFL.

This web site helps students and professionals prepare for the Test of English as a Foreign Language (TOEFL®). You are invited to practice with the types of questions that appear on the TOEFL, visit the TEFL Prep Center Bookstore, and ask Dr. Pamela Sharpe questions about her books. The TEFL Prep Center web site also has information about scholarships and news about the TOEFL.

Welcome ***The Practice Page*** ***The TEFL Center Bookstore*** ***TOEFL News*** ***Scholarship Opportunities*** ***Dear Dr. Sharpe***

If you are not seeing images or if the page is loading improperly, you may want to use these links to download Netscape Navigator or Internet Explorer, available at no cost.

REVIEW OF SECTION 1: LISTENING

Overview of the Listening Section

QUICK COMPARISON
PAPER-BASED TOEFL AND COMPUTER-BASED TOEFL
SECTION 1

Paper-Based TOEFL Listening Comprehension	*Computer-Based TOEFL Listening*
There are fifty questions—thirty on Part A; twenty on Parts B and C.	There are between thirty and fifty questions.
There are three types of questions—short conversations; longer conversations and class discussions; mini-talks and lectures.	There are three types of questions—short conversations; longer conversations and class discussions; mini-talks and lectures.
The three types of questions are presented in three separate parts. Part A has short conversations; Part B has long conversations and class discussions; Part C has mini-talks and lectures.	The three types of questions are presented in three sets. The first set has short conversations; the second set has longer conversations and class discussions; the third set has lectures.
Everyone taking the TOEFL answers the same questions.	The computer selects questions based on your level of language proficiency.
The test administrator plays a tape and adjusts the volume.	You have a headset to listen to the audio. You can adjust the volume before the test begins.
There are no pictures or visual cues.	Each short conversation begins with a picture to provide orientation. There are several pictures and visual cues with each longer conversation and lecture.
You hear the questions, but they are not written out for you to read.	The questions are written out on the computer screen for you to read while you hear them.
Everyone taking the TOEFL proceeds at the same pace. You cannot pause the tape.	You may control the pace by choosing when to begin the next conversation or lecture.
The section is timed. At the end of the tape, you must have completed the section.	The section is timed. A clock on the screen shows the time remaining for you to complete the section.

You may not replay any of the conversations or lectures.	You may not replay any of the conversations or lectures.
All of the questions are multiple-choice.	Most of the questions are multiple-choice, but some of the questions have special directions.
Every question has only one answer.	Some of the questions have two answers.
You answer on a paper answer sheet, filling in ovals marked (A), (B), (C), and (D).	You click on the screen in the oval that corresponds to the answer you have chosen, or you follow the directions on the screen.
You can return to previous questions, erase, and change answers on your answer sheet.	You cannot return to previous questions. You can change your answer before you click on **Confirm Answer**. After you click on **Confirm Answer**, you will see a screen that notifies you to get ready to listen to the next conversation or lecture. You cannot go back.
You may not take notes.	You may not take notes.

Directions for Section 1

Computer-Based TOEFL

The directions for the Computer-Based TOEFL are reprinted with the permission of Educational Testing Service (ETS) from the official *Information Bulletin* for the Computer-Based TOEFL.

The Listening section of the test measures the ability to understand conversations and talks in English. You will use headphones to listen to the conversations and talks. While you are listening, pictures of the speakers or other information will be presented on your computer screen. There are two parts to the Listening section, with special directions for each part.

On the day of the test, the amount of time you will have to answer all the questions will appear on the computer screen. The time you spend listening to the test material will not be counted. The listening material and questions about it will be presented only one time. You will not be allowed to take notes or have any paper at your computer. You will both see and hear the questions before the answer choices appear. You can take as much time as you need to select an answer; however, it will be to your advantage to answer the questions as quickly as possible. You may change your answer as many times as you want before you confirm it. After you have confirmed an answer, you will not be able to return to the question.

Before you begin working on the Listening section, you will have an opportunity to adjust the volume of the sound. You will not be able to change the volume after you have started the test.

QUESTION DIRECTIONS — Part A

In Part A of the Listening section, you will hear short conversations between two people. In some of the conversations, each person speaks only once. In other conversations, one or both of the people speak more than once. Each conversation is followed by one question about it.

Each question in this part has four answer choices. You should click on the best answer to each question. Answer the questions on the basis of what is stated or implied by the speakers.

Here is an example.

On the computer screen, you will see:

On the recording, you will hear:
(woman) Hey, where's your sociology book?
(man) At home. Why carry it around when we're just going to be taking a test?
(woman) Don't you remember? Professor Smith said we could use it during the test.
(man) Oh, no! Well, I've still got an hour, right? I'm so glad I ran into you!

You will then see and hear the question before the answer choices appear:

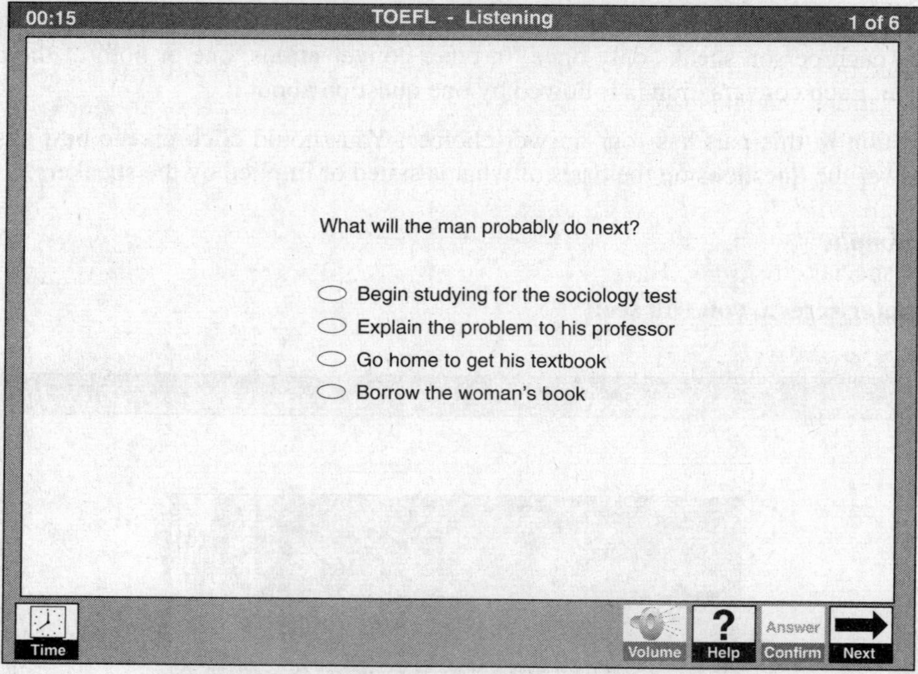

To choose an answer, you will click on an oval. The oval next to that answer will darken. **The correct answer is indicated on the next screen.**

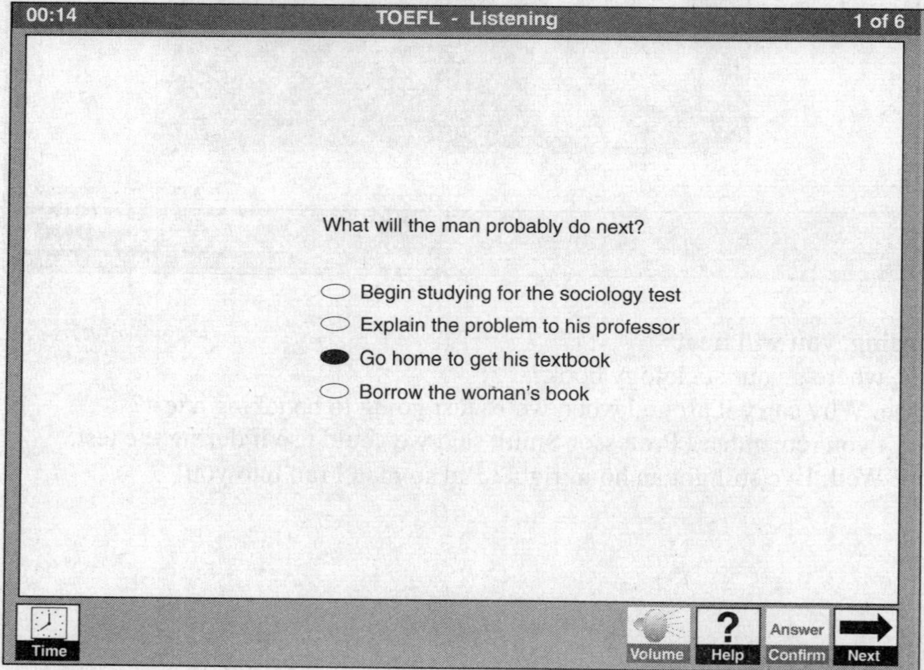

After you click on **Next** and **Confirm Answer**, the next conversation will be presented.

QUESTION DIRECTIONS — Part B

In Part B of the Listening section, you will hear several longer conversations and talks. Each conversation or talk is followed by several questions. The conversations, talks, and questions will not be repeated.

The conversations and talks are about a variety of topics. You do not need special knowledge of the topics to answer the questions correctly. Rather, you should answer each question on the basis of what is stated or implied by the speakers in the conversations or talks.

For most of the questions, you will need to click on the best of four possible answers. Some questions will have special directions. The special directions will appear in a box on the computer screen.

Here is an example of a conversation and some questions:

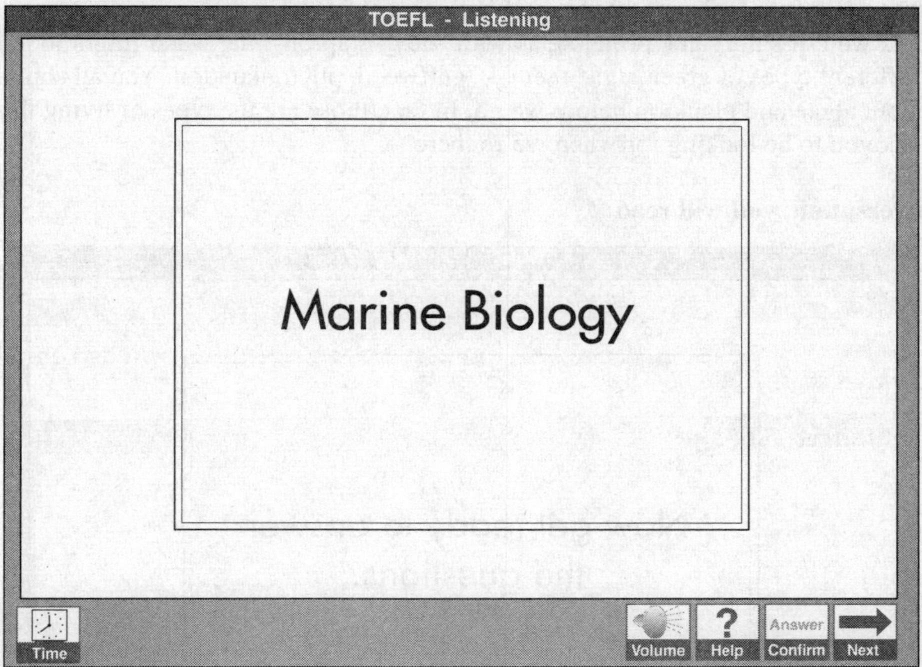

(narrator) Listen to part of a discussion in a marine biology class.

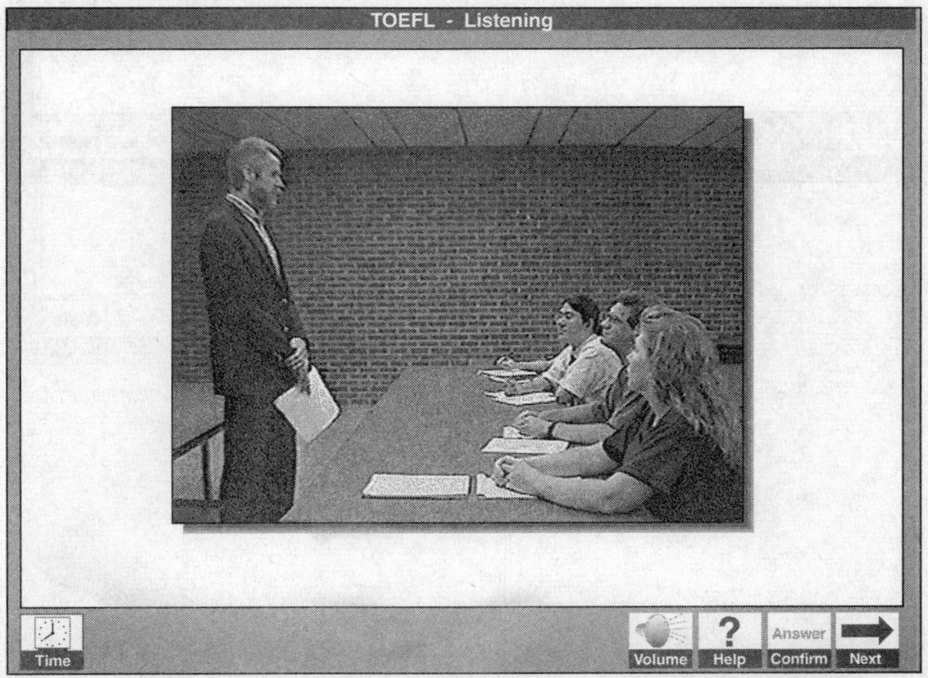

(professor) A few years ago, our local government passed a number of strict environmental laws. As a result, Sunrise Beach looks nothing like it did ten years ago. The water is cleaner, and there's been a tremendous increase in all kinds of marine life — which is why we're going there on Thursday.

(woman) I don't know if I agree that the water quality has improved. I mean, I was out there last weekend, and it looked all brown. It didn't seem too clean to me.

(professor) Actually, the color of the water doesn't always indicate whether it's polluted. The brown color you mentioned might be a result of pollution, or it can mean a kind of brown algae is growing there. It's called "devil's apron," and it actually serves as food for whales.

(man) So when does the water look blue?

(professor) Well, water that's completely unpolluted is actually colorless. But it often looks bluish-green because the sunlight can penetrate deep down and that's the color that's reflected.

(woman) But sometimes it looks really green. What's that about?

(professor) OK, well, it's the same principle as with "devil's apron": the water might look green because of different types of green algae there — gulfweed, phytoplankton. You all should finish reading about algae and plankton before we go. In fact, those are the types of living things I'm going to ask you to be looking for when we're there.

After the conversation, you will read:

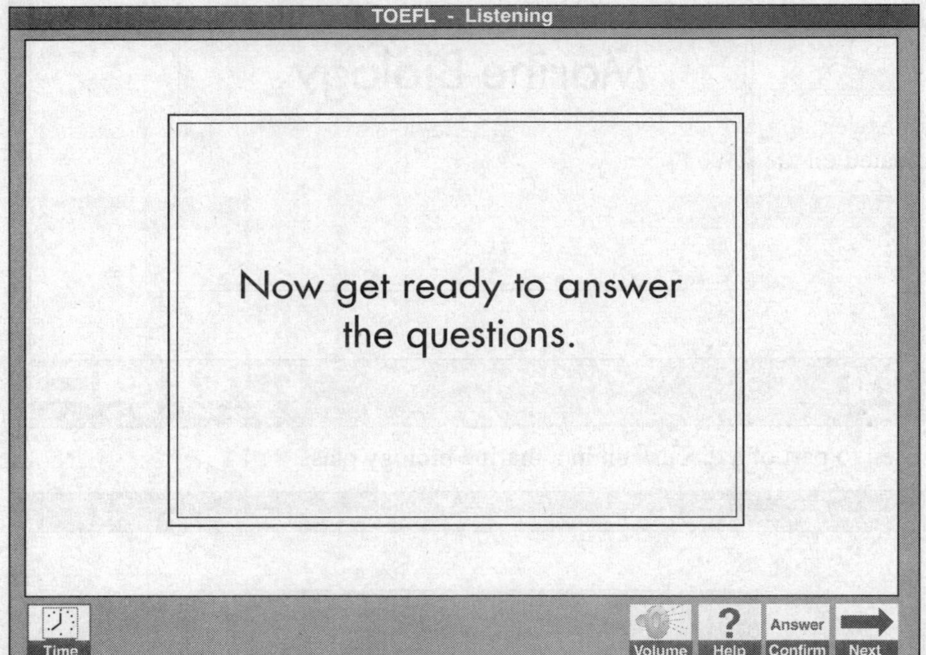

Then, the first question will be presented:

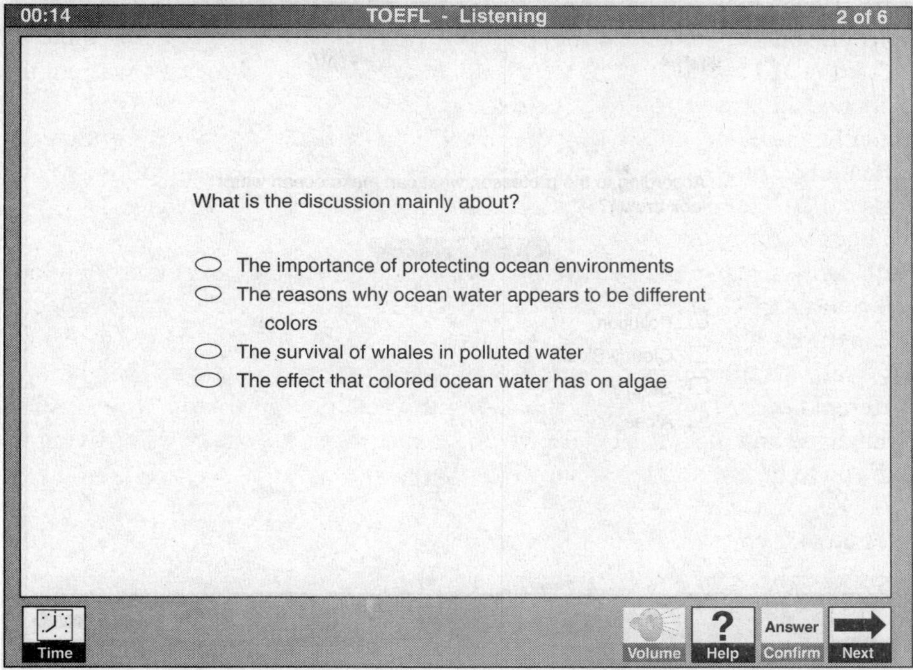

To choose an answer, you will click on an oval. The oval next to that answer will darken. The correct answer is indicated on the screen below.

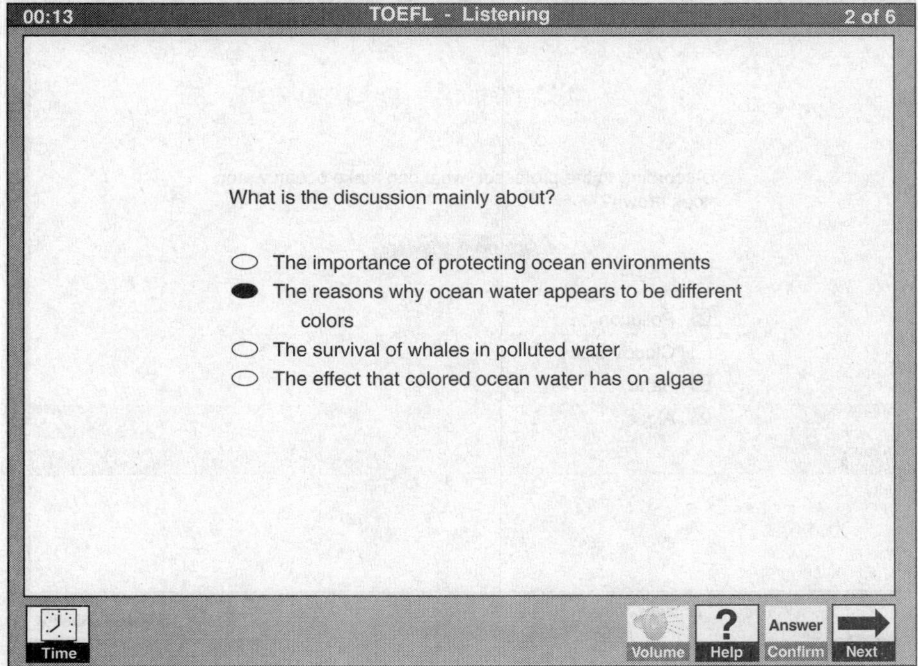

After you click on **Next** and **Confirm Answer, the next question will be presented:**

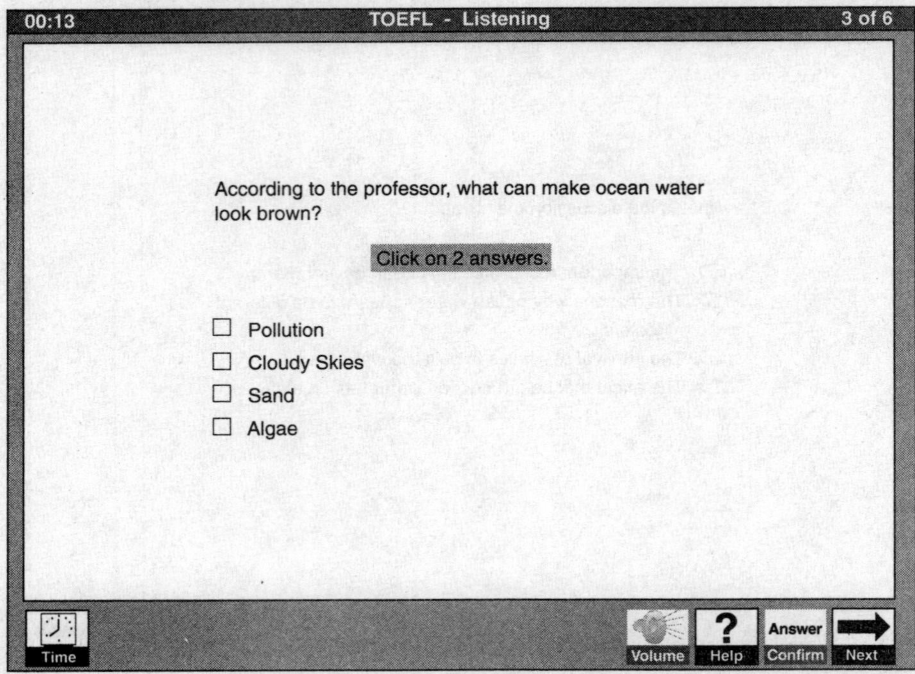

To choose your answers, you will click on the squares. An "X" will appear in each square. The correct answer is indicated on the screen below.

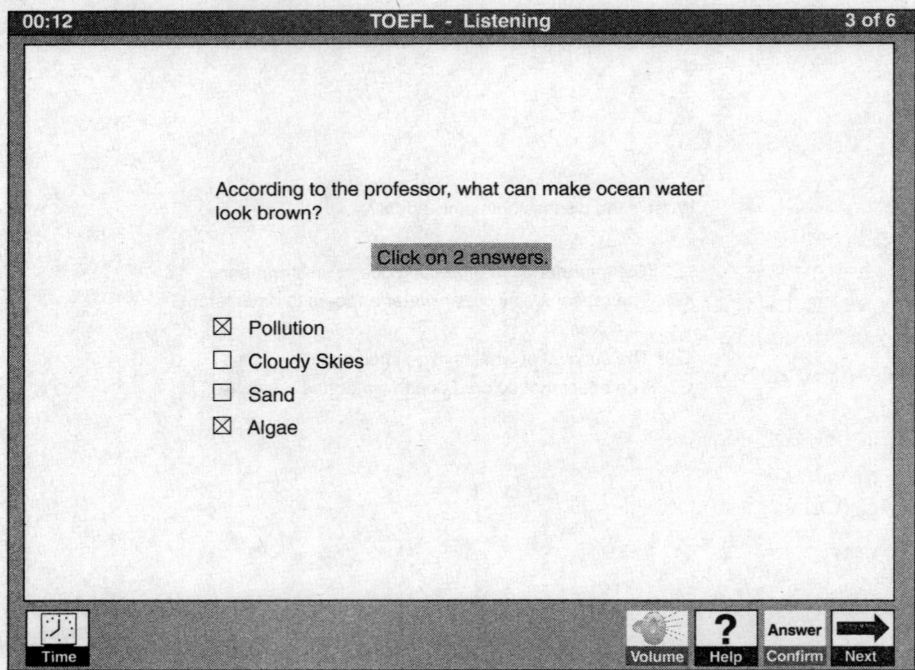

Sometimes the screen changes several times during a conversation or talk, as in the next example.

Here is an example of a talk and some questions:

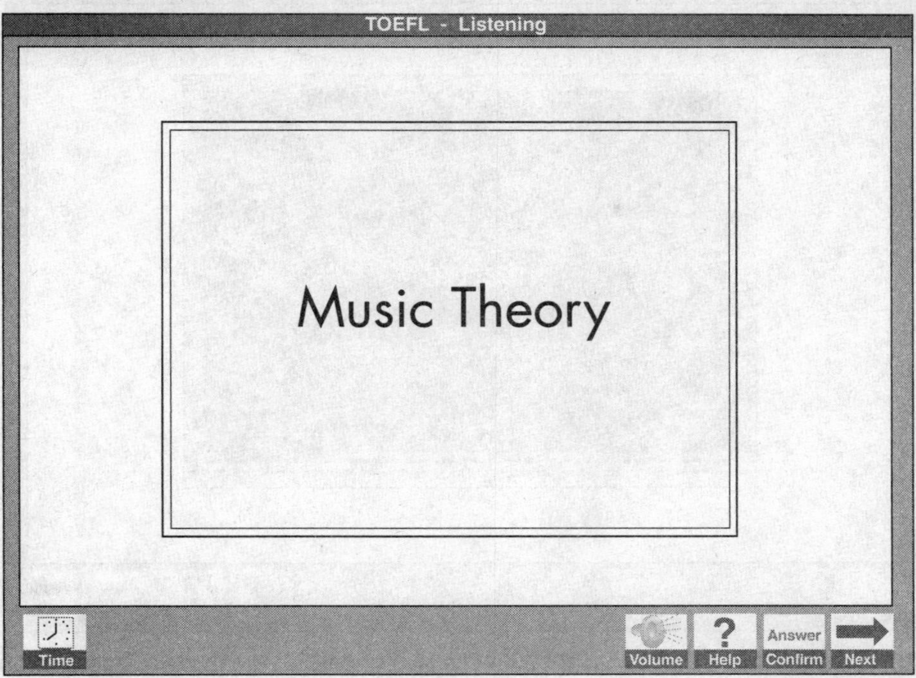

(narrator) Listen to part of a talk in a music theory class.

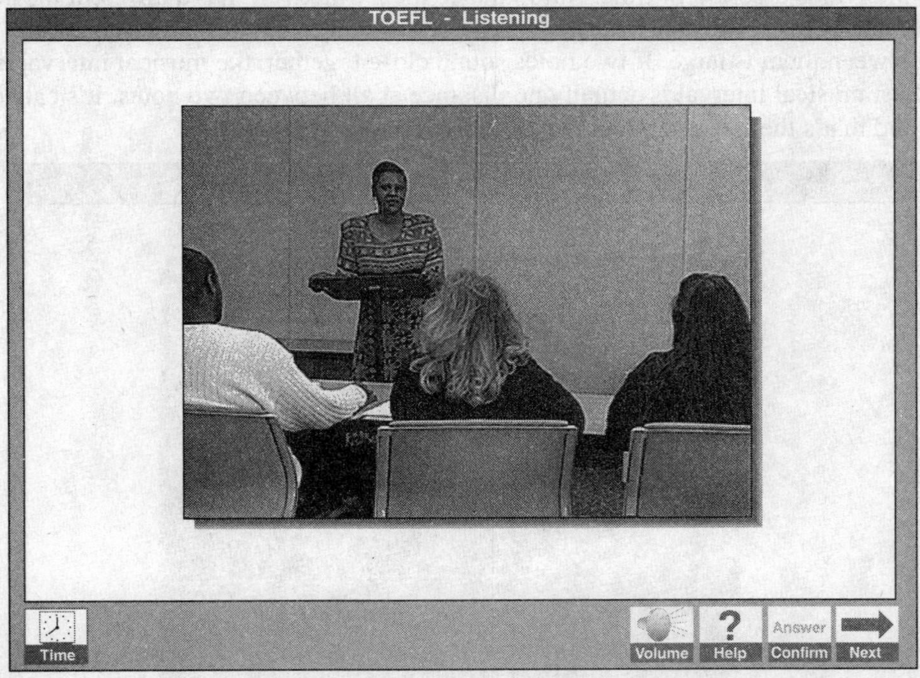

(professor) I'm sure if I asked you, you'd be able to tell me the common meaning of the word "interval."

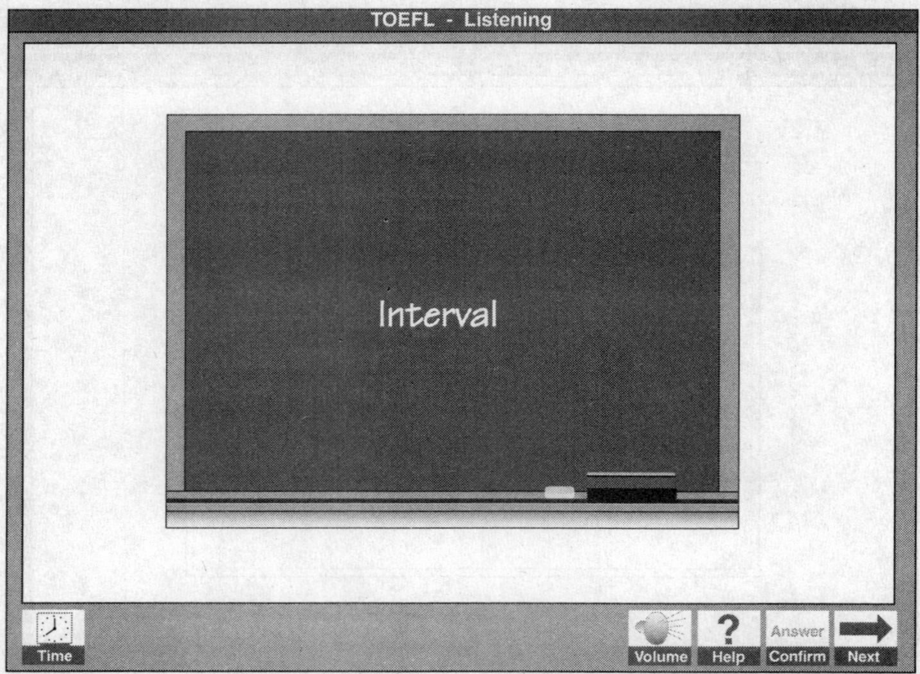

(professor) An interval is the period of time between two events. For example, buses might stop at a certain location every ten minutes — that is, at ten minute intervals. In the typical sense of the word, an interval is a period of time. But in music theory the word has a different meaning. A musical interval is the distance between two notes. So, if two notes are far apart, the musical interval between them is large. If two notes sound close together, the musical interval is small. The smallest musical interval is actually no distance at all between two notes. It's called "the unison," and that's the interval when two notes are exactly the same.

(professor) Today, I'd like to focus on a way of analyzing musical intervals by looking at the precise mathematical relationship that exists between musical notes. To do this, I've made some sounding boxes.

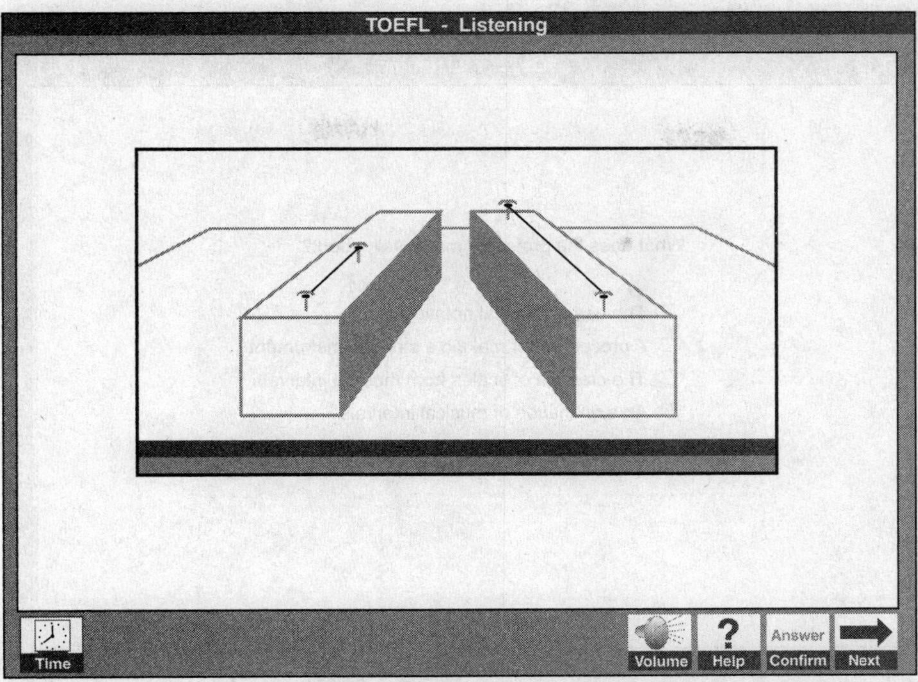

(professor) As you can see, they're just boxes made of wood with strings wrapped around two nails on the top. Now, the only difference between these two sounding boxes is the length of the string. I made the strings two different lengths to show you how this affects the sound. In fact, if you measured the length of the two strings, you'd see that the long string is exactly twice the length of the short string. So, the ratio between the short string and the long string is one to two. That's a pretty basic ratio, mathematically, and it produces one of the most basic intervals in Western music — the octave.

After the talk, you will read:

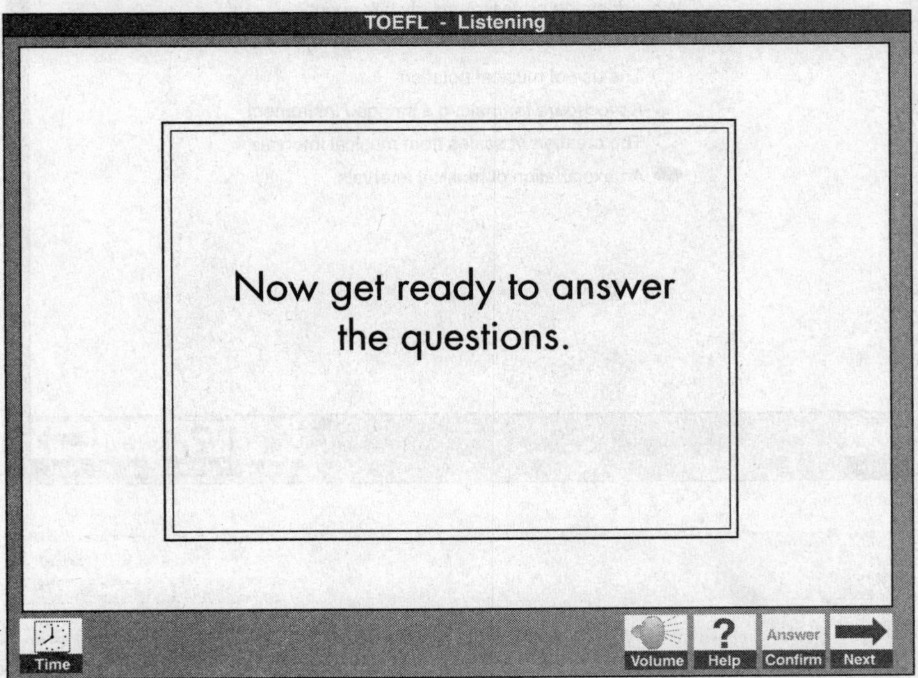

Then, the first question will be presented:

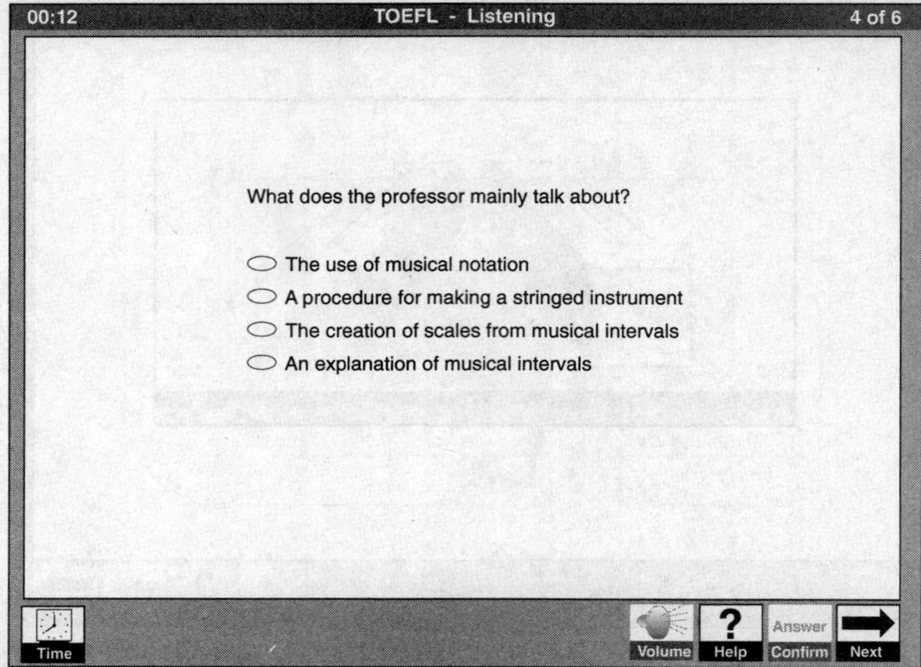

To choose an answer, you will click on an oval. The oval next to that answer will darken. The correct answer is indicated on the screen below.

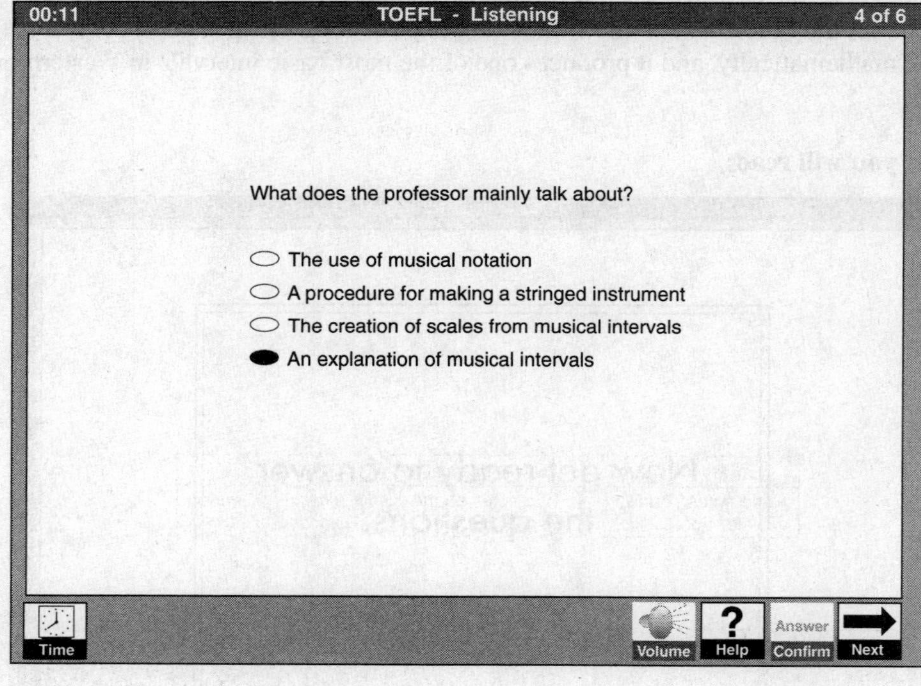

After you click on **Next** and **Confirm Answer, the next question will be presented:**

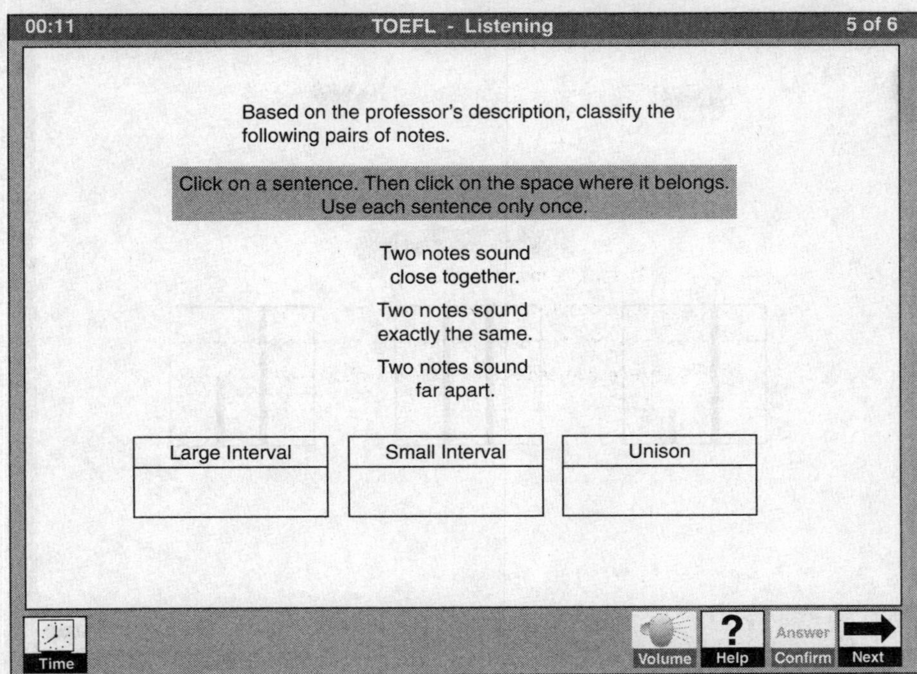

To choose your answers, you will click on a sentence and then click on the space where it belongs. As you do this, each sentence will appear in the square you have selected. The correct answer is indicated on the screen below.

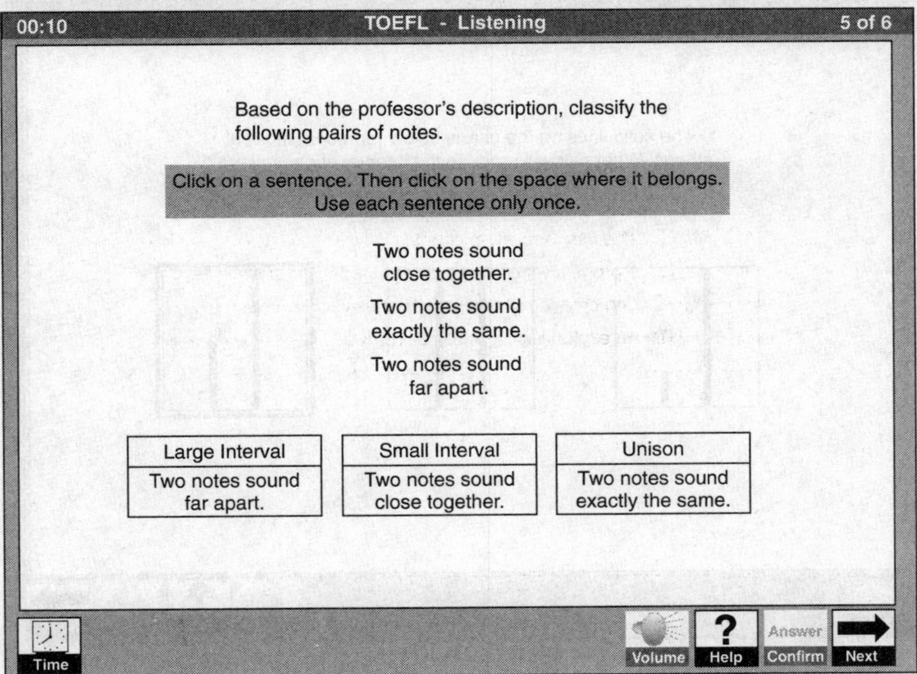

After you click on **Next** and **Confirm Answer, the next question will be presented:**

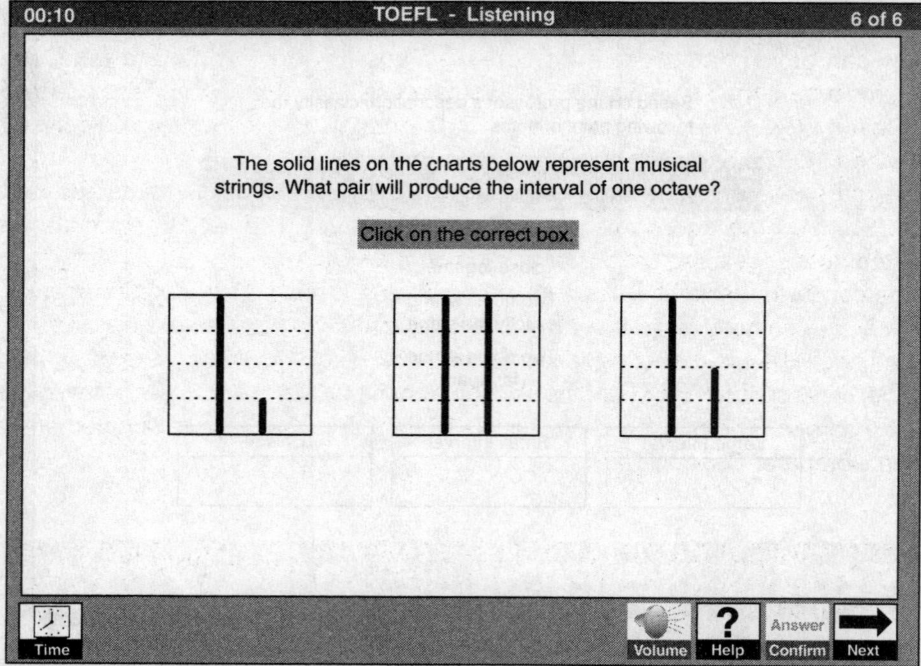

To choose your answer, you will click on the box. As you do this, the box will become highlighted. The correct answer is indicated on the screen below.

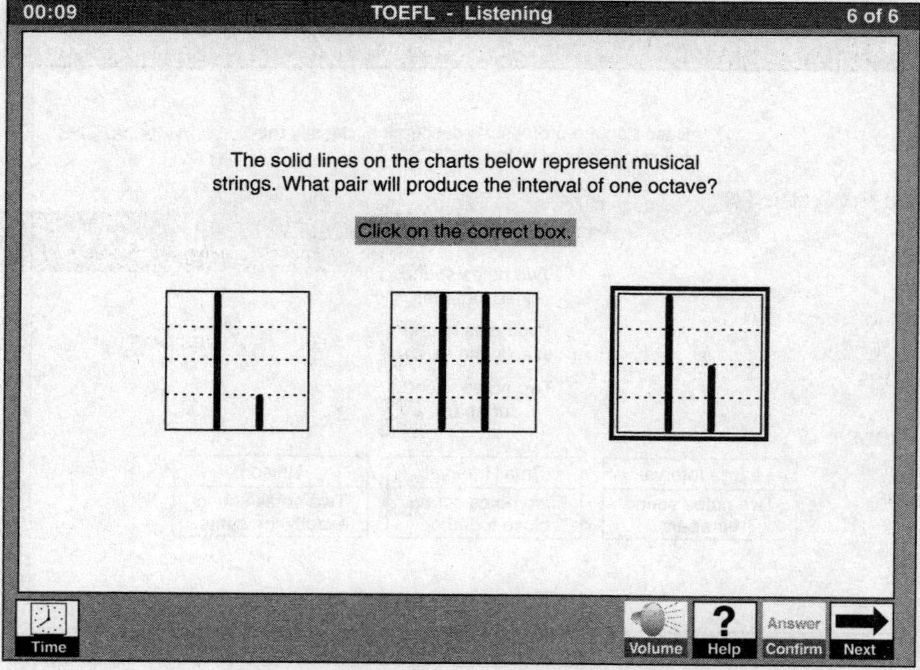

Review of Problems and Questions for the Listening Section

This Review can be used to prepare for both the Paper-Based TOEFL and the Computer-Based TOEFL. For the most part, the same types of problems are tested on both the Paper-Based TOEFL and the Computer-Based TOEFL; however, questions on Informal Conversations and Tours are found only on the Paper-Based TOEFL and are not addressed in this book.

Most of the questions on both the Paper-Based TOEFL and the Computer-Based TOEFL are multiple-choice. Some of the questions on the Computer-Based TOEFL are computer-assisted. The computer-assisted questions have special directions on the screen.

Although the computer-assisted questions in this book are numbered, and the answer choices are lettered A, B, C, D, the same questions on the CD-ROM that accompanies the book are not numbered and lettered. You need the numbers and letters in the book to refer to the Answer Key, the Explanatory Answers, and the Transcript for the Listening section. On the CD-ROM, you can refer to other chapters by clicking on the screen. The questions on the CD-ROM that is available to supplement this book are like those on the Computer-Based TOEFL.

TYPES OF PROBLEMS IN THE LISTENING SECTION

Problems like those in this Review of Listening frequently appear on Parts A, B, and C of the Listening section of the TOEFL.

Part A Short Conversations

1 Details

2 Idiomatic Expressions

3 Suggestions

4 Assumptions

5 Predictions

6 Implications

7 Problems

8 Topics

Part B Longer Conversations

9 Academic Conversations

Part C Talks and Lectures

10 Class Discussions

11 Academic Talks

12 Lectures

Types of Problems in Short Conversations

Details

Details are specific facts stated in a conversation.

In some short conversations, you will hear all of the information that you need to answer the problem correctly. You will NOT need to draw conclusions.

When you hear a conversation between two speakers, you must remember the details that were stated.

EXAMPLE

Man: Front desk. How may I help you?
Woman: I'd like to arrange a wake-up call for tomorrow morning at seven o'clock, please.

Narrator: When does the woman want to get up tomorrow?
Answer: Seven o'clock in the morning.

Idiomatic expressions

Idiomatic expressions are words and phrases that are characteristic of a particular language with meanings that are usually different from the meanings of each of the words used alone.

In some short conversations, you will hear idiomatic expressions, such as "to kill time," which means to wait.

When you hear a conversation between two speakers, you must listen for the idiomatic expressions. You will be expected to recognize them and restate the idiom or identify the feelings or attitudes of the speaker.

It will help you if you study a list of common idioms as part of your TOEFL preparation.

EXAMPLE

Man: I'm single. In fact, I've never been married.
Woman: No kidding!

Narrator: What does the woman mean?
Answer: She is surprised by the man's statement.

Suggestions

A *suggestion* is a recommendation.

In some short conversations, you will hear words and phrases that make a suggestion, such as "you should," "why don't you," or "why not."

When you hear the words and phrases that introduce a suggestion, you must be able to recognize and remember what the speaker suggested, and who made the suggestion.

EXAMPLE

Woman:	Do you know if there is a Lost and Found on campus? I left my book bag in this room earlier, and it's gone.
Man:	Too bad. Look, why don't you check with your teacher first? Maybe someone in your class turned it in.
Narrator:	What does the man suggest that the woman do?
Answer:	Ask her teacher about the book bag.

Assumptions

An *assumption* is a statement accepted as true without proof or demonstration.

In some short conversations, an assumption is proven false, and the speaker or speakers who had made the assumption express surprise.

When you hear a conversation between two speakers, you must be able to recognize remarks that register surprise, and draw conclusions about the assumptions that the speaker may have made.

EXAMPLE

Woman:	Let's just e-mail our response to Larry instead of calling.
Man:	*Larry* has an e-mail address?
Narrator:	What had the man assumed about Larry?
Answer:	He would not have an e-mail address.

Predictions

A *prediction* is a guess about the future based on evidence from the present.

In some short conversations, you will be asked to make predictions about the future activities of the speakers involved.

When you hear a conversation between two speakers, you must listen for evidence from which you may draw a logical conclusion about their future activities.

Example

Man: Could you please book me on the next flight out to Los Angeles?
Woman: I'm sorry, sir. Continental doesn't fly into Los Angeles. Why don't you try Northern or Worldwide?

Narrator: What will the man probably do?
Answer: He will probably get a ticket for a flight on Northern or Worldwide Airlines.

Implications

Implied means suggested, but not stated. In many ways, implied conversations are like prediction conversations.

In some short conversations, you will hear words and phrases or intonations that will suggest how the speakers felt, what kind of work or activity they were involved in, or where the conversation may have taken place.

When you hear a conversation between two speakers, you must listen for information that will help you draw a conclusion about the situation.

Example

Woman: Where's Anita? We were supposed to go to the library to study.
Man: Well, here is her coat, and her books are over there on the chair.

Narrator: What does the woman imply about Anita?
Answer: Anita has not left for the library yet.

Problems

A *problem* is a situation that requires discussion or solution.

In some short conversations, you will hear the speakers discuss a problem.

When you hear a discussion between two speakers, you must be able to identify what the problem is. This may be more difficult because different aspects of the problem will also be included in the conversation.

Example

Woman: It only takes two hours to get to New York, but you'll have a six-hour layover between flights.
Man: Maybe you could try routing me through Philadelphia or Boston instead.

Narrator: What is the man's problem?
Answer: His flight connections are not very convenient.

Topics

A *topic* is a main theme in a conversation or in a piece of writing.

In some short conversations, the speakers will discuss a particular topic.

When you hear a conversation, you must be able to identify the main topic from among several secondary themes that support the topic.

EXAMPLE

Man: Tell me about your trip to New York.
Woman: It was great! We saw the Statue of Liberty and the Empire State Building and all of the tourist attractions the first day, then we saw the museums the second day and spent the rest of the time shopping and seeing shows.

Narrator: What are the man and woman talking about?
Answer: The woman's trip.

Types of Problems in Longer Conversations

Academic Conversations

Academic conversations are conversations between students and professors or other academic personnel on a college or university campus.

In some longer conversations, you will hear an academic conversation between two speakers.

When you hear a conversation, you must be able to summarize the main ideas. You may also be asked to recall important details.

EXAMPLE

Marcy: Do you have a minute, Dr. Peterson?
Dr. Peterson: Sure. Come on in, Marcy. What's the problem?

Marcy: Well, I'm not sure. I got this letter, and I don't understand it very well.
Dr. Peterson: Let's see it.

Marcy: It's from the Financial Aid Office. Are they going to cancel my student aid?
Dr. Peterson: I would hope not. Hmmmn. Oh, I see. Here's what happened. You are only registered for three hours next semester.

Marcy: That's true, but I plan to register for another class during open registration. I heard about a new environmental science course, and I'm waiting for it to be assigned a sequence number.

Dr. Peterson: Well, then, you don't have a problem. You see, the terms of your grant require that you take at least six hours per semester.

Marcy: I know, but I've never gotten a letter before.
Dr. Peterson: I think it's a new procedure. Don't worry about it. Just be sure to sign up for at least three more hours before the beginning of the semester.

Marcy: Thanks, Dr. Peterson. I'm really glad you were in your office today.

Question: What is Marcy's problem?
Answer: She has received a letter from the Financial Aid Office.

Question: Why did Marcy receive a letter?
Answer: She did not register for six hours this semester.

Question: What had Marcy planned to do?
Answer: Register for three more hours during open registration.

Question: How does Marcy feel when she leaves Dr. Peterson's office?
Answer: Relieved.

Types of Problems in Talks and Lectures

Class Discussions

Class discussions are conversations that occur in classrooms.

In some talks, you will hear a class discussion between two, three, or more speakers.

When you hear a discussion, you must be able to summarize the important ideas. You will usually NOT be required to remember small details.

It will help you to audit some college classes.

EXAMPLE

Miss Richards: Good morning. My name is Miss Richards, and I'll be your instructor for Career Education 100. Before we get started, I'd appreciate it if you would introduce yourselves and tell us a little bit about why you decided to take this class. Let's start here....
Bill: I'm Bill Jensen, and I'm a sophomore this term, but I still haven't decided what to major in. I hope that this class will help me.

Miss Richards: Good, I hope so, too. Next.
Patty: I'm Patty Davis, and I'm majoring in foreign languages, but I'm not sure what kind of job I can get after I graduate.

Miss Richards: Are you a sophomore, too, Patty?
Patty: No. I'm a senior. I wish I'd taken this class sooner, but I didn't know about it until this term.

Miss Richards: Didn't your advisor tell you about it?
Patty: No. A friend of mine took it last year, and it helped her a lot.

Miss Richards: How did you find out about the course, Bill?
Bill: The same way Patty did. A friend of mine told me about it.

Question: In what class does this discussion take place?
Answer: Career Education.

Question: What are the two students talking about?
Answer: They are introducing themselves.

Question: Why is the woman taking the course?
Answer: To help her find a job after graduation.

Question: How did the students find out about the course?
Answer: From friends who had taken it.

Academic Talks

Academic talks are short talks that provide orientation to academic courses and procedures.
In some talks, you will hear academic talks on a variety of college and university topics.
When you hear a talk, you must be able to summarize the main ideas. You must also be able to answer questions about important details. You will usually not be asked to remember minor details.

EXAMPLE

Since we'll be having our midterm exam next week, I thought I'd spend a few minutes talking with you about it. I realize that none of you has ever taken a class with me before, so you really don't know what to expect on one of my exams.

First, let me remind you that I have included a very short description of the midterm on the syllabus that you received at the beginning of the semester. So you should read that. I also recommend that you organize and review your notes from all of our class sessions. I'm not saying that the book is unimportant, but the notes should help you to identify those topics that we covered in greatest detail. Then, you can go back to your book and reread the sections that deal with those topics. I also suggest that you take another look at the articles on reserve in the library. They have information in them that is not in the book, and although we didn't talk much about them in class, I do feel that they are important, so you can expect to see a few questions from the articles on the exam. Oh, yes, I almost forgot. Besides the twenty-five objective questions, there will be five essay questions, and you must choose three.

EXAMPLE

Question: What does the speaker mainly discuss?
Answer: The midterm exam.

Question: When will the students take the exam?
Answer: Next week.

Question: According to the professor, what should the students do to prepare?
Answer: Study their notes, the articles on reserve, and appropriate sections of the book.

Question: What is the format of the exam?
Answer: Twenty-five objective questions and five essay questions.

Lectures

Lectures are short talks that provide information about academic subjects. They are like short lectures that might be heard in a college classroom.

In some talks, you will hear academic information in a short lecture.

When you hear a lecture, you must be able to summarize the important ideas. You must also be able to answer questions that begin with the following words: *who, what, when, where, why?*

It will help you to listen to documentary programs on radio and television. Programs on educational broadcasting networks are especially helpful. Listen carefully. Ask yourself questions to test your ability to remember the information.

EXAMPLE

Ernest Hemingway began his writing career as an ambitious young American newspaperman in Paris after the first World War. His early books, including *The Sun Also Rises,* were published in Europe before they were released in the United States.

Hemingway always wrote from experience rather than from imagination. In *Farewell to Arms,* published in 1929, he recounted his adventures as an ambulance driver in Italy during the war. In *For Whom the Bell Tolls,* published in 1940, he retold his memories of the Spanish Civil War.

Perhaps more than any other twentieth-century American writer, he was responsible for creating a style of literature. The Hemingway style was hard, economical, and powerful. It lured the reader into using imagination in order to fill in the details.

In 1952, Hemingway published *The Old Man and the Sea,* a short, compelling tale of an old fisherman's struggle to haul in a giant marlin that he had caught in the Gulf of Mexico. Some critics interpreted it as the allegory of man's struggle against old age; others interpreted it as man against the forces of nature. This book was the climax of Hemingway's career. Two years later he was awarded the Nobel Prize for literature.

Question: What theme did Hemingway use for many of his books?
Answer: War.

Question: What was the Hemingway style?
Answer: Short and powerful.

Question: What prize did Hemingway win after he wrote *The Old Man and the Sea?*
Answer: The Nobel Prize for literature.

Question: What advice would Hemingway probably give to other writers?
Answer: Write from experience about things you have seen and people you have known.

TYPES OF QUESTIONS

Multiple-Choice Questions

Paper-Based TOEFL

1. What theme did Hemingway use for many of his books?
   (A) War
   (B) Romance
   (C) Travel
   (D) Sports

2. What was the Hemingway style?
   (A) Long descriptions
   (B) Imaginative details
   (C) Short sentences
   (D) Difficult symbolism

3. What prize did Hemingway win after he wrote *The Old Man and the Sea?*
   (A) The Nobel Prize for literature
   (B) The European Prize for best book of 1952
   (C) The Lifetime Achievement Award for literature
   (D) The American Newspapers Prize for young writers

4. What advice would Hemingway probably give to other writers?
   (A) Write for a newspaper before you begin writing novels
   (B) Create your own style of literature
   (C) Write from experience about things you have seen and people you have known
   (D) Travel in order to meet interesting people

Computer-Based TOEFL

What theme did Hemingway use for many of his books?

● War
○ Romance
○ Travel
○ Sports

What was the Hemingway style?

○ Long descriptions
○ Imaginative details
● Short sentences
○ Difficult symbolism

What prize did Hemingway win after he wrote *The Old Man and the Sea?*

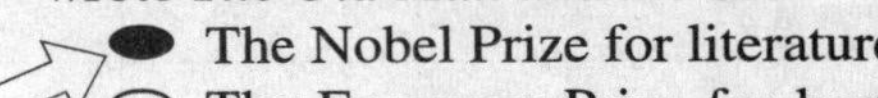

● The Nobel Prize for literature
○ The European Prize for best book of 1952
○ The Lifetime Achievement Award for literature
○ The American Newspapers Prize for young writers

What advice would Hemingway probably give to other writers?

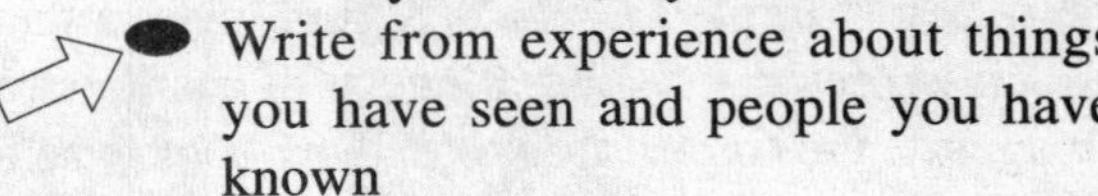

○ Write for a newspaper before you begin writing novels
○ Create your own style of literature
● Write from experience about things you have seen and people you have known
○ Travel in order to meet interesting people

Answer Sheet

1. ● Ⓑ Ⓒ Ⓓ
2. Ⓐ Ⓑ ● Ⓓ
3. ● Ⓑ Ⓒ Ⓓ
4. Ⓐ Ⓑ ● Ⓓ

Computer-Assisted Questions

Two-Answer Questions. On some of the computer-assisted questions, you will be asked to select two answers. Both answers must be correct to receive credit for the question.

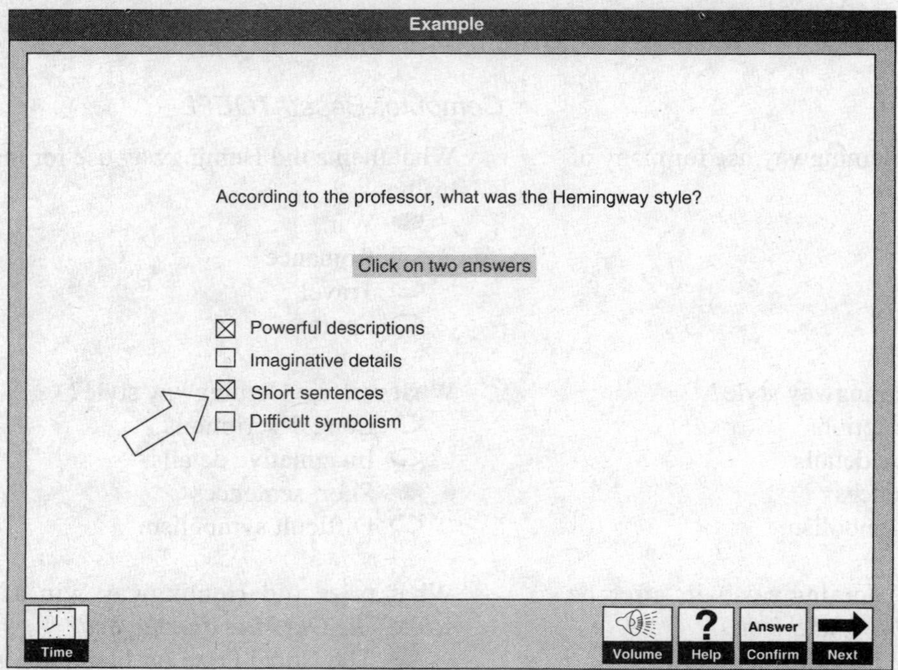

Visual Questions. On some of the computer-assisted questions, you will be asked to select a visual. The visual may be a picture, a drawing, or a diagram.

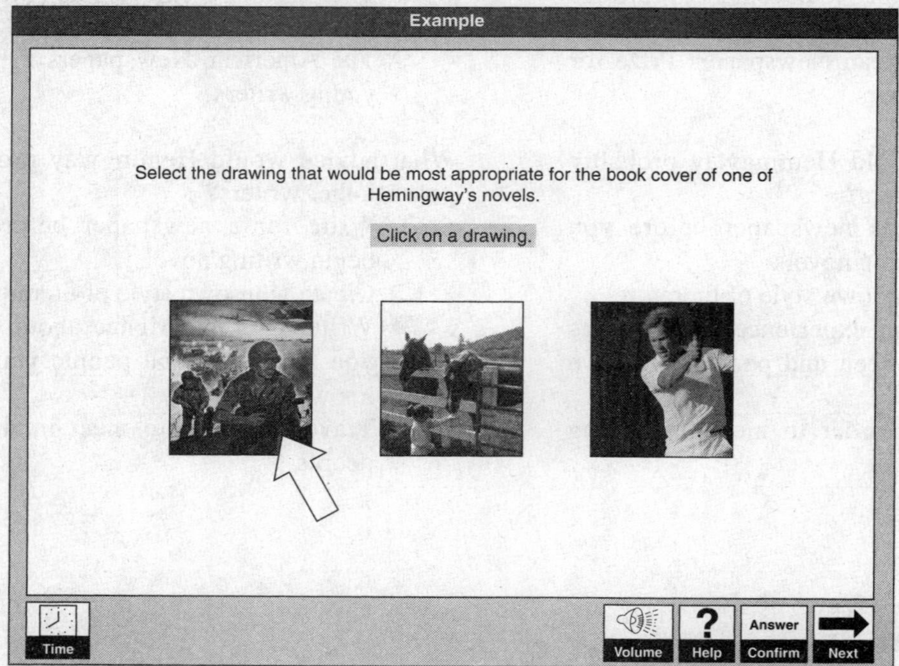

Sequencing Questions. On some of the computer-assisted questions, you will be asked to sequence events in order. The events could be historical events or the steps in a scientific process. All answers must be sequenced correctly to receive credit for the question.

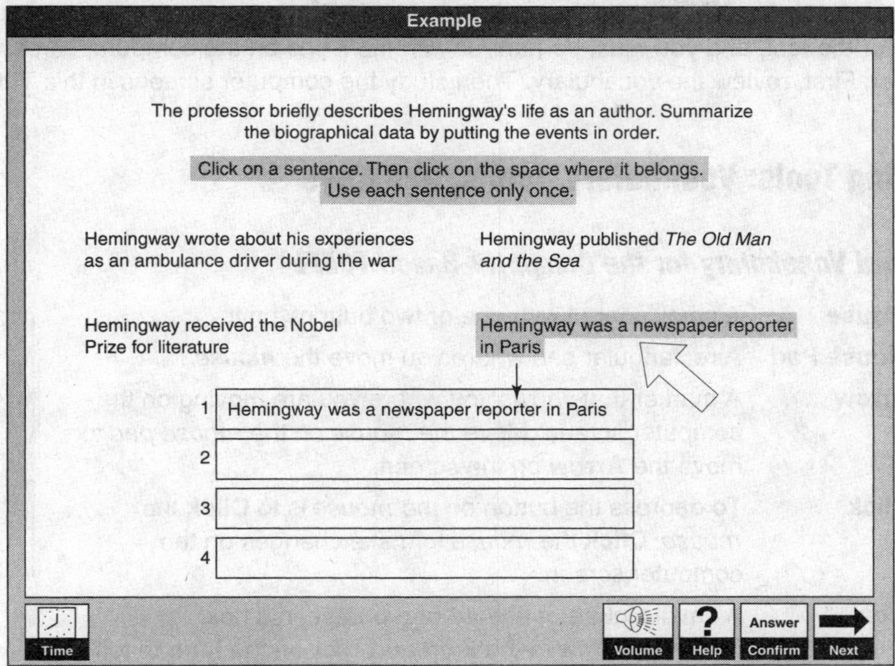

Classification Questions. On some of the computer-assisted questions, you will be asked to classify information by organizing it in categories.

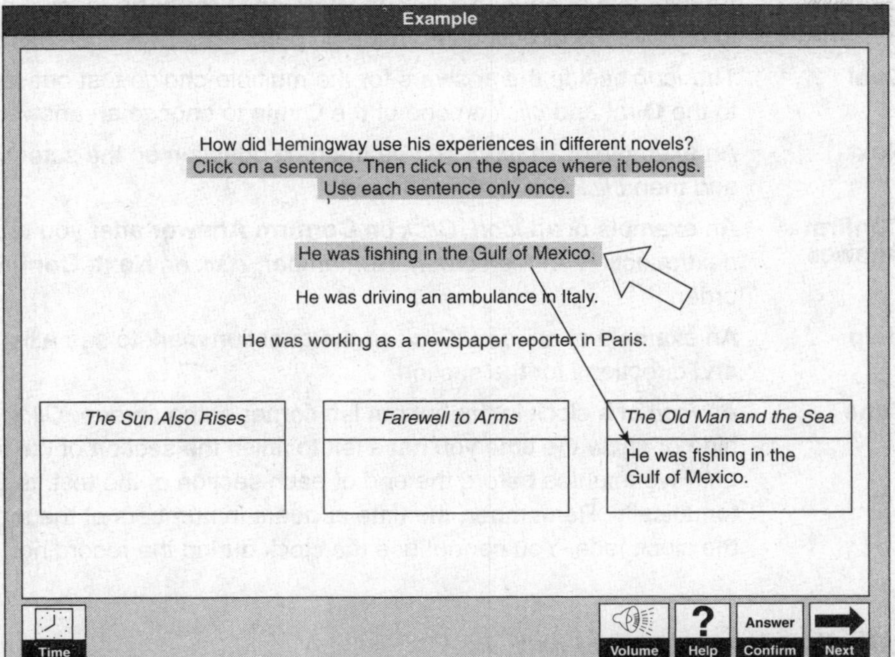

Computer Tutorial for the Listening Section

In order to succeed on the Computer-Based TOEFL, you must understand the computer vocabulary used for the test, and you must be familiar with the icons on the computer screens that you will see on the test. First, review the vocabulary. Then study the computer screens in this Tutorial.

Testing Tools: Vocabulary, Icons, and Keys

General Vocabulary for the Computer-Based TOEFL

Mouse A small control with one or two buttons on it.

Mouse Pad A rectangular pad where you move the *mouse.*

Arrow A marker that shows you where you are moving on the computer screen. Move the *mouse* on the *mouse pad* to move the **Arrow** on the screen.

Click To depress the button on the *mouse* is to **Click** the *mouse.* **Click** the *mouse* to make changes on the computer screen.

Icon A small picture or a word or a phrase in a box. Move the *arrow* to the **Icon** and *click* on the **Icon** to tell the computer what to do.

Icons for the Computer-Based TOEFL

Dismiss Directions An example of an *icon. Click* on **Dismiss Directions** to tell the computer to remove the directions from the screen.

Oval The *icon* beside the answers for the multiple-choice test questions. Move the *arrow* to the **Oval** and *click* on one of the **Ovals** to choose an answer.

Next An example of an *icon.* To see the next question on the screen, *click* on **Next** first and then *click* on **Confirm Answer**.

Confirm Answer An example of an *icon. Click* on **Confirm Answer** after you *click* on **Next** to see the next question on the screen. Remember, *click* on **Next**, **Confirm Answer** in that order.

Help An example of an *icon. Click* on the question mark to see a list of the *icons* and directions for the section.

Time An *icon* of a clock in the bottom left corner of the screen. *Click* on the clock face to hide or show the time you have left to finish the section of the test you are working on. Five minutes before the end of each section of the test, the clock will appear automatically. Remember, the time appears in numbers at the top of the screen, not on the clock face. You cannot use the clock during the recording.

Specific Vocabulary for Section 1

Volume One additional *icon* at the bottom of the screen in the Listening section. *Click* on **Volume** to go to a screen with an *up arrow* and a *down arrow. Click* on the *up arrow* to make the recording louder. *Click* on the *down arrow* to make the recording softer. Remember, you can change the volume while the speaker is giving directions, but not after the directions have concluded.

COMPUTER SCREENS FOR THE COMPUTER-BASED TOEFL

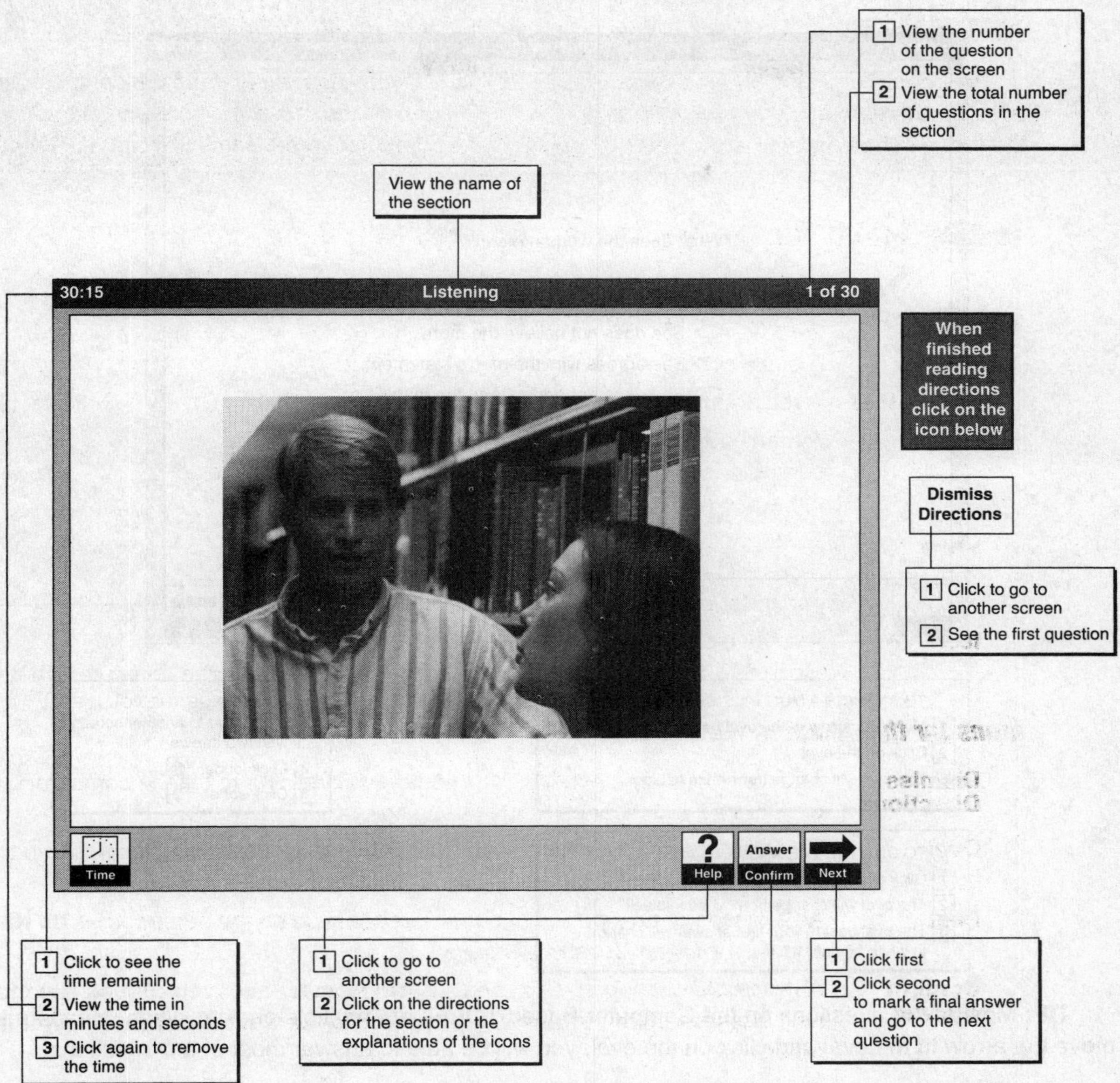

TIP: When the icons are black, you can click on them. When they are gray, they are not functioning. For example, **Confirm Answer** is gray until you click on **Next**. Then **Confirm Answer** is black. Remember the order to click on these two icons.

Computer Screens for Section 1

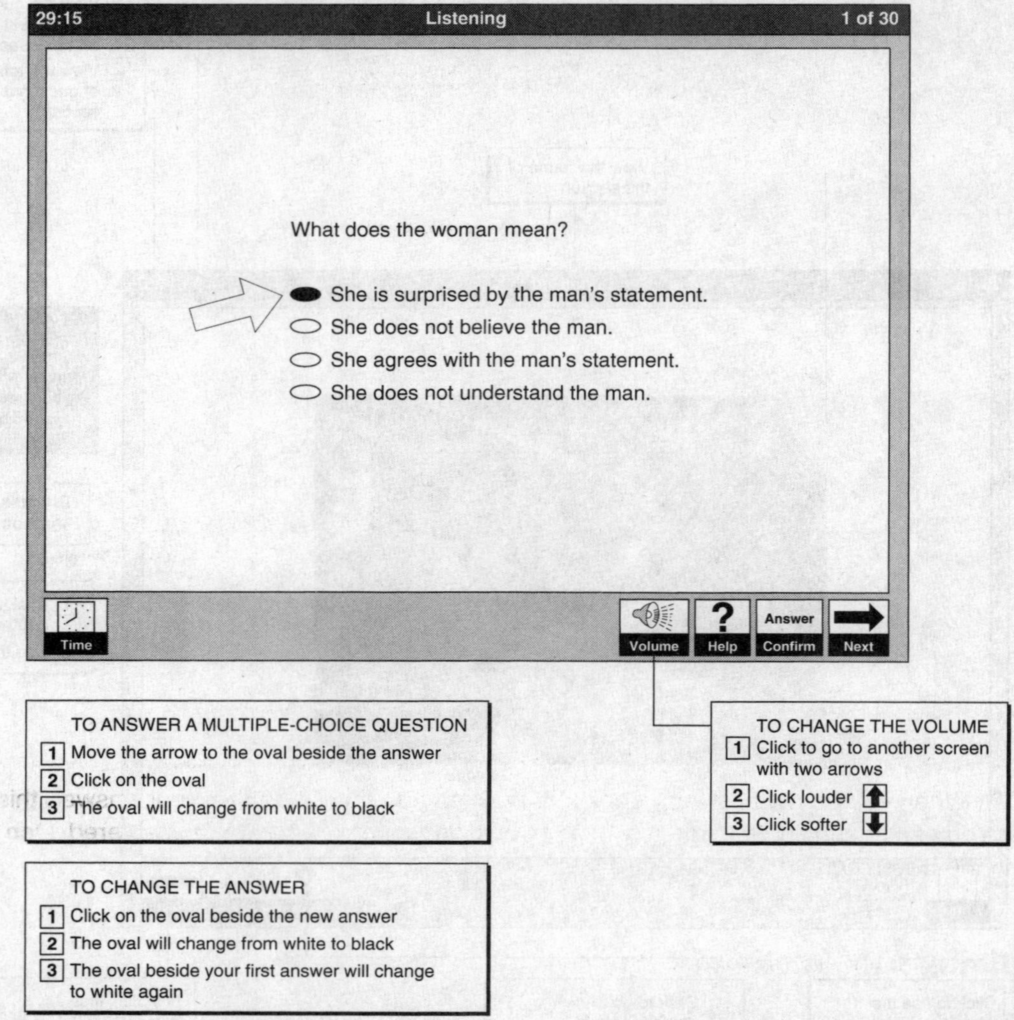

29:15
Listening
1 of 30
What does the woman mean?
She is surprised by the man's statement.
She does not believe the man.
She agrees with the man's statement.
She does not understand the man.
Time
Volume
?
Help
Answer
Confirm
Next
TO ANSWER A MULTIPLE-CHOICE QUESTION
1 Move the arrow to the oval beside the answer
2 Click on the oval
3 The oval will change from white to black
TO CHANGE THE VOLUME
1 Click to go to another screen with two arrows
2 Click louder
3 Click softer
TO CHANGE THE ANSWER
1 Click on the oval beside the new answer
2 The oval will change from white to black
3 The oval beside your first answer will change to white again

TIP: Most of the questions on the Computer-Based TOEFL are multiple-choice. When you learn to move the arrow to the oval and click on the oval, you will be able to answer most of the questions.

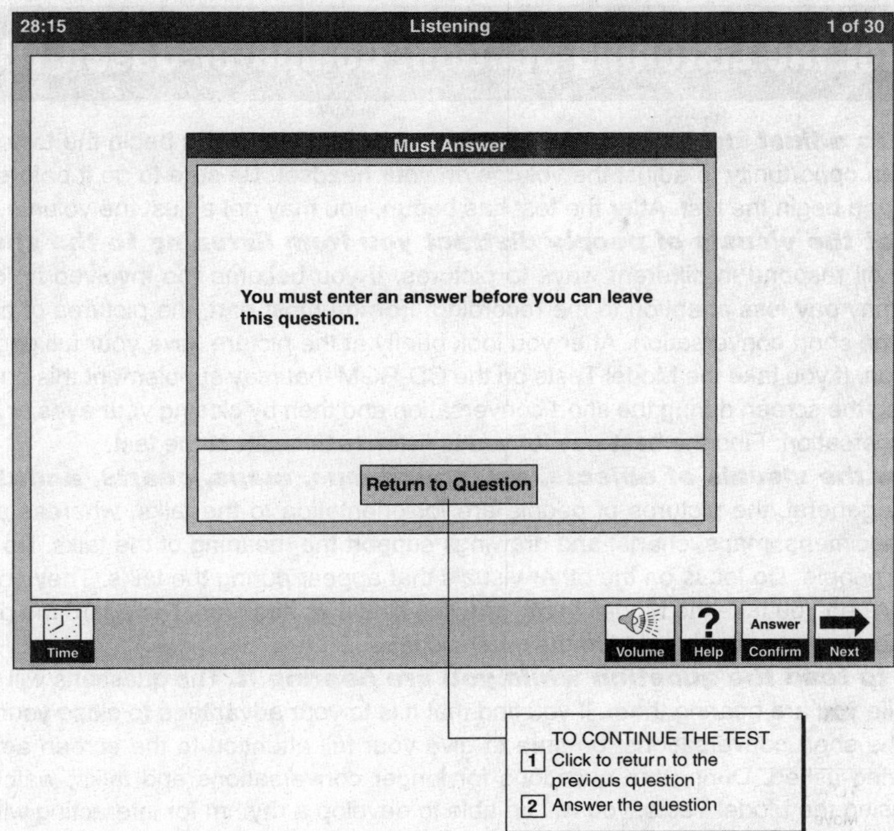

TIP: When you do not answer a question, or when you do not confirm your answer, this screen appears. You can spend a lot of time returning to questions that you have not answered. Don't skip questions in the Listening and Structure sections.

Simulations for Section 1

In order to prepare for the experience that you will have on the Computer-Based TOEFL, use the CD-ROM that supplements this book. Locate the Listening section on the Model Tests. The computer will simulate features of the Listening section on the Computer-Based TOEFL. These Model Tests are computer-assisted.

As part of your study plan, be sure to review all of the questions in all of the Model Tests. Use the Explanatory Answers on the CD-ROM or on pages 553–616. Finally, take the Cumulative Model Test on the CD-ROM. This test is computer-adaptive, which means that the computer will select questions for you at your level of language proficiency.

If you do not have a computer, you can simulate some of the features of the Computer-Based TOEFL. In Section 1 of Model Tests 1–8 in Chapter 7, the questions are written out for you to read while you listen to them. This is different from the Paper-Based TOEFL. Instead of the CD-ROM, you may be using either an audio compact disk or a cassette. Pause the tape or compact disk occasionally to give yourself more control of the time for each question. But be careful not to pause too often or you will not be able to complete all of the questions within the total time allowed for the section.

Advice for the Listening Section: Computer-Based TOEFL

Be sure to adjust the volume before you begin. Before you begin the Listening section, you will have an opportunity to adjust the volume on your headset. Be sure to do it before you dismiss the directions and begin the test. After the test has begun, you may not adjust the volume.

Do not let the visuals of people distract you from listening to the short conversations. We all respond in different ways to pictures. If you become too involved in looking at the pictures, you may pay less attention to the recording. For the most part, the pictures of people are for orientation to the short conversation. After you look briefly at the picture, give your full concentration to the conversation. If you take the Model Tests on the CD-ROM that may supplement this book, first practice by watching the screen during the short conversation and then by closing your eyes or looking away during the conversation. Find the best way for you to listen to this part of the test.

Focus on the visuals of objects, art, specimens, maps, charts, and drawings in the talks. In general, the pictures of people are for orientation to the talks, whereas the visuals of objects, art, specimens, maps, charts, and drawings support the meaning of the talks. Do not focus on the pictures of people. Do focus on the other visuals that appear during the talks. They could reappear in a question. When you take the Model Tests, practice selective attention. Disregard the pictures of the lecturer and the students, and be alert to the other visuals.

Be sure to read the question while you are hearing it. The questions will be shown on the screen while you are hearing them. If you find that it is to your advantage to close your eyes or look away during the short conversations, be sure to give your full attention to the screen again while the question is being asked. During the questions for longer conversations and talks, watch the screen carefully. By using the Model Tests, you will be able to develop a rhythm for interacting with the screen that is to your advantage.

REVIEW OF SECTION 2: STRUCTURE

Overview of the Structure Section

QUICK COMPARISON
PAPER-BASED TOEFL AND COMPUTER-BASED TOEFL
SECTION 2

Paper-Based TOEFL Structure and Written Expression	*Computer-Based TOEFL Structure*
There are two types of questions—incomplete sentences and sentences with underlined words and phrases.	There are two types of questions—incomplete sentences and sentences with underlined words and phrases.
The two types of questions are presented in separate parts. Part A has incomplete sentences, and Part B has sentences with underlined words and phrases.	The two types of questions are presented at random in one continuous section. You may see two incomplete sentences, one sentence with underlined words and phrases, another incomplete sentence, and so forth.
There are forty questions—fifteen on Part A and twenty-five on Part B.	There are between twenty and twenty-five questions.
All of the questions are multiple-choice.	All of the questions are multiple-choice.
Everyone taking the TOEFL answers the same questions.	The computer will select questions based on your level of proficiency.
Every question has only one answer.	Every question has only one answer.
You have twenty-five minutes to complete the section.	You may control the pace by choosing when to begin the next question, but the section is timed. A clock on the screen shows the time remaining for you to complete the section.
You answer on a paper answer sheet, filling in ovals marked (A), (B), (C), and (D).	You click on the screen either in the oval or on the underlined word or phrase.

You can return to previous questions, erase, and change answers on your answer sheet.	You cannot return to previous questions. You can change your answer before you click on **Confirm Answer**. After you click on **Confirm Answer**, you will see the next question. You cannot go back.
The score on Section 2 is not combined with the score on the essay in the Test of Written English (TWE).	The score on Section 2 is combined with the score on the essay in the Writing section.

Directions for Section 2

Computer-Based TOEFL

The directions for the Computer-Based TOEFL are reprinted with the permission of Educational Testing Service (ETS) from the official *Information Bulletin* for the Computer-Based TOEFL.

This section measures the ability to recognize language that is appropriate for standard written English. There are two types of questions in this section.

In the first type of question, there are incomplete sentences. Beneath each sentence, there are four words or phrases. You will choose the one word or phrase that best completes the sentence.

Here is an example.

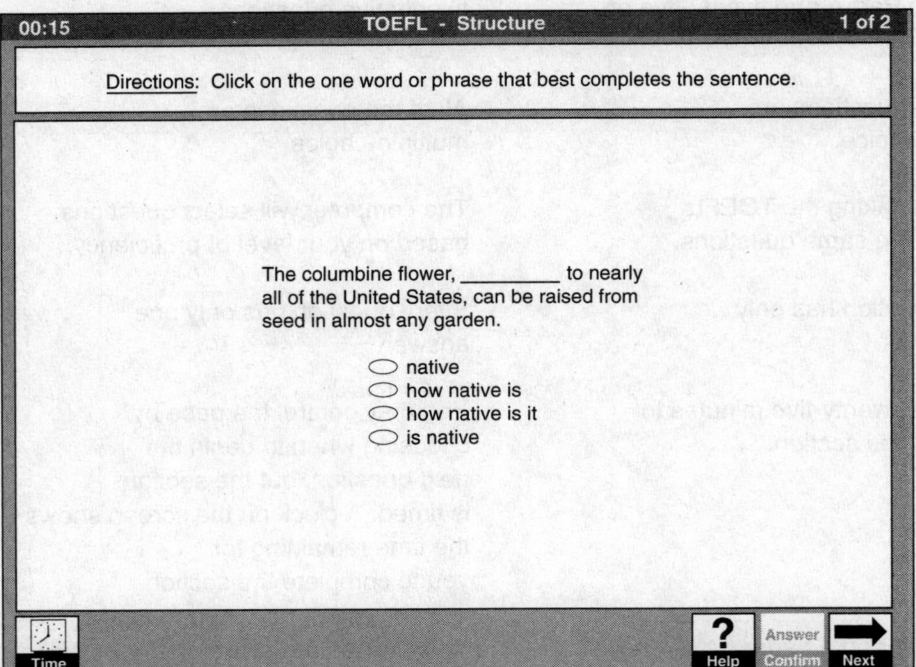

Clicking on a choice darkens the oval. The correct answer is indicated on the screen below.

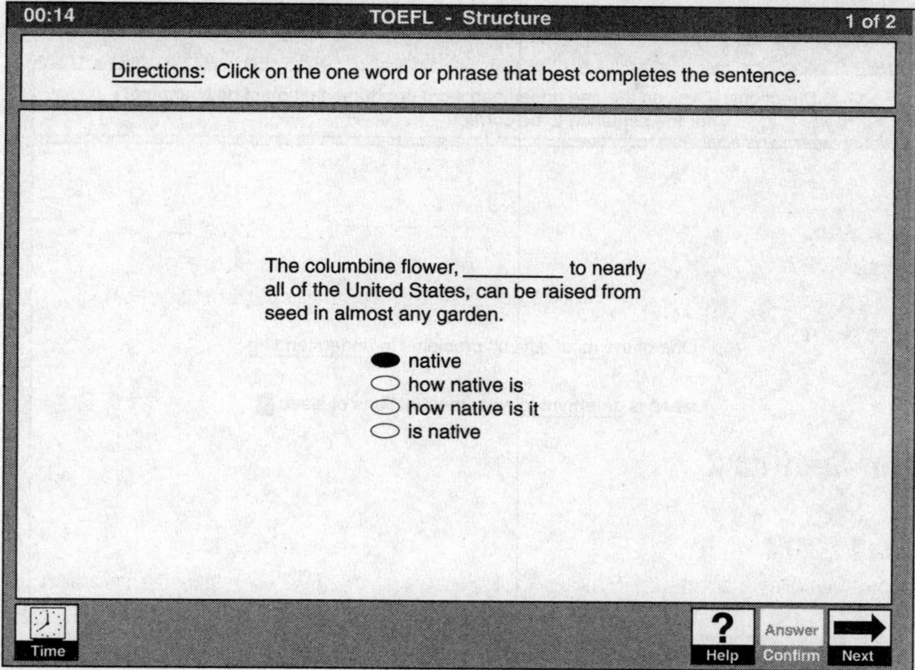

After you click on **Next** and **Confirm Answer**, the next question will be presented.

The second type of question has four underlined words or phrases. You will choose the one underlined word or phrase that must be changed for the sentence to be correct.

Here is an example:

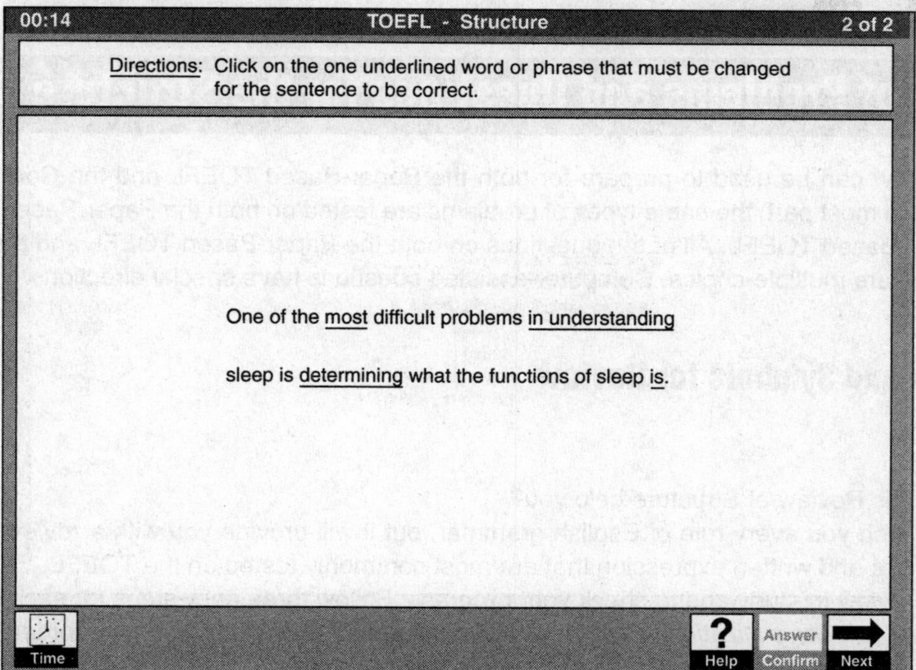

Clicking on an underlined word or phrase will darken it. The correct answer is indicated on the screen below.

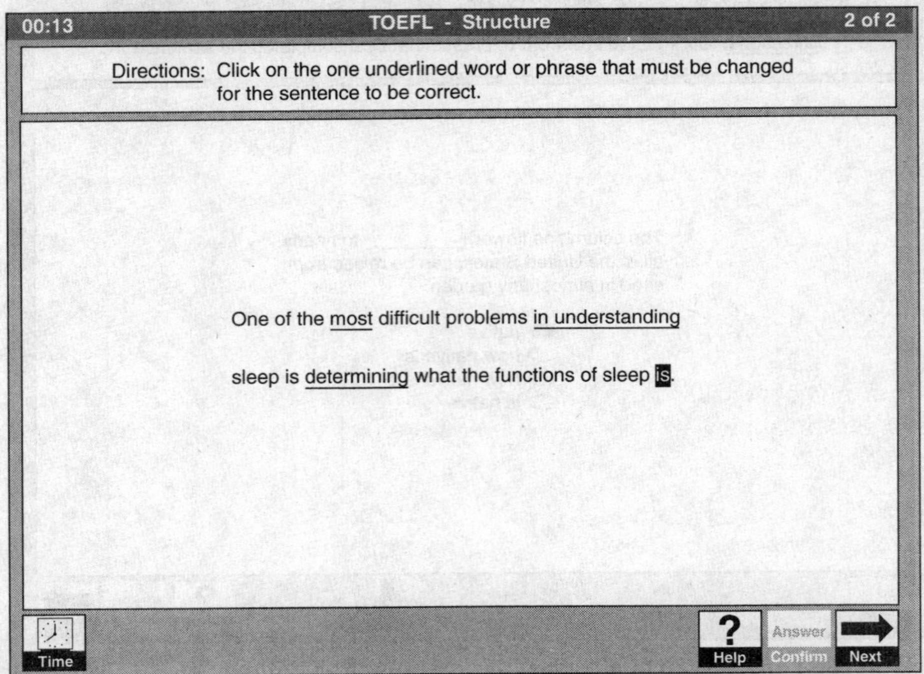

The sentence should read: One of the most difficult problems in understanding sleep is determining what the functions of sleep are. After you click on **Next** and **Confirm Answer**, the next question will be presented.

Review of Problems and Questions for the Structure Section

This Review can be used to prepare for both the Paper-Based TOEFL and the Computer-Based TOEFL. For the most part, the same types of problems are tested on both the Paper-Based TOEFL and the Computer-Based TOEFL. All of the questions on both the Paper-Based TOEFL and the Computer-Based TOEFL are multiple-choice. Computer-assisted questions have special directions.

Strategies and Symbols for Review

Strategies

How will this Review of Structure help you?

It won't teach you every rule of English grammar, but it will provide you with a review of the problems in structure and written expression that are most commonly tested on the TOEFL.

Use this review to study and to check your progress. Follow three easy steps for each problem.

1. *Review the generalization.* First, read the explanation and study the word order in the chart. Then, close your eyes, and try to see the chart in your mind.
2. *Study the examples.* Focus on the examples. First, read them silently, noting the difference between the correct and incorrect sentences. Then, read the underlined parts of the correct sentences aloud.

3. *Check your progress.* First, complete the exercise. Each exercise has two questions—one similar to Part A and the other similar to Part B on the Structure and Written Expression section of the TOEFL. Then, check your answers, using the Answer Key in Chapter 8 of this book.

If you are studying in an English program, use this review with your grammar book. After your teacher presents a grammar rule in class, find it in the table of contents of this review (see pages 68–72). Refer to the generalization, study the examples, and check your progress by completing the exercise.

When you go to your next grammar class, you will be more prepared. When you go to your TOEFL examination, you will be more confident. With preparation, you can succeed in school and on the TOEFL.

Symbols

In order for you to use the patterns and rules of style in this review, you must understand five kinds of symbols.

Abbreviations. An abbreviation is a shortened form. In the patterns, five abbreviations, or shortened forms, are used: *S* is an abbreviation for *Subject, V* for *Verb, V Ph* for *Verb Phrase, C* for *Complement,* and *M* for *Modifier.*

Small Letters. Small letters are lowercase letters. In the patterns, a verb written in small (lowercase) letters may not change form. For example, the verb *have* may not change to *has* or *had* when it is written in small letters.

Capital Letters. Capital letters are uppercase letters. In the patterns, a verb written in capital (uppercase) letters may change form. For example, the verb *HAVE* may remain as *have,* or may change to *has* or *had,* depending upon agreement with the subject and choice of tense.

Parentheses. Parentheses are curved lines used as punctuation marks. The following punctuation marks are parentheses: ( ). In the patterns, the words in parentheses give specific information about the abbreviation or word that precedes them. For example, *V (present)* means that the verb in the pattern must be a present tense verb. *N (count)* means that the noun in the pattern must be a countable noun.

Alternatives. Alternatives are different ways to express the same idea. In the patterns, alternatives are written in a column. For example, in the following pattern, there are three alternatives:

had would have could have	participle

The alternatives are *had, would have,* and *could have.* Any one of the alternatives may be used with the participle. All three alternatives are correct.

TYPES OF PROBLEMS

Patterns and rules of style like those in this Review of Structure frequently appear on Section 2 of the TOEFL.

The emphasis that is placed on various patterns and style problems changes from year to year on the TOEFL. Research indicates that those problems shown in bold print in the reference list below are most frequently tested on current examinations.

To prepare for Section 2 of the TOEFL, study the problems in this chapter. Give special attention to the problems in bold print.

PATTERNS

Problems with Verbs

Problems with Main Verbs

1 Missing Main Verb
2 Verbs that Require an Infinitive in the Complement
3 Verbs that Require an *-ing* Form in the Complement
4 Verb Phrases that Require an *-ing* Form in the Complement

Problems with Tense

5 Irregular Past Forms

Problems with Modals and Modal-Related Patterns

6 Modal + Verb Word
7 Logical Conclusions — Events in the Past
8 Logical Conclusions — Events in the Present
9 Logical Conclusions — Events that Repeat
10 Knowledge and Ability — *Know* and *Know How*
11 Past Custom — *Used to* and BE *Used to*
12 Advisability — *Had Better*
13 Preference — *Would Rather*
14 Preference for Another — *Would Rather That*
15 Negative Imperatives

Problems with Causatives

16 Causative MAKE
17 Causative GET
18 Causative HAVE
19 Causative LET
20 Causative HELP

Problems with Conditionals

21 **Factual Conditionals — Absolute, Scientific Results**
22 Factual Conditionals — Probable Results for the Future
23 Factual Conditionals — Possible Results
24 Factual Conditionals — Probable Changes in Past Results
25 Contrary-to-Fact Conditionals — Impossible Results *Were*
26 Contrary-to-Fact Conditionals — Change in Conditions *Unless*

Problems with Subjunctives

27 Importance — Subjunctive Verbs
28 Importance — Nouns Derived from Subjunctive Verbs
29 Importance — Impersonal Expressions

Problems with Infinitives

30 Purpose — Infinitives

Problems with Passives

31 **Passives — Word Order**

32 Passives — Agent

33 Passives—Infinitives

34 Necessity for Repair or Improvement — NEED

35 **Belief and Knowledge — Anticipatory *It***

Problems with HAVE + Participle

36 Duration — HAVE + Participle

37 Duration — HAVE + *Been* + Participle

38 Predictions — *Will Have* + Participle

39 Unfulfilled Desires in the Past — *Had Hoped*

Problems with Auxiliary Verbs

40 **Missing Auxiliary Verb—Active**

41 **Missing Auxiliary Verb—Passive**

Problems with Pronouns

42 Subject Pronouns

43 Subject Pronouns in Complement Position

44 Object Pronouns

45 Object Pronouns after Prepositions

46 Possessive Pronouns Before *-ing* Forms

47 Possessive Pronouns Before Parts of the Body

48 Relative Pronouns that Refer to Persons and Things

49 Relative Pronouns that Refer to Persons

50 Reflexive Pronouns

51 Reciprocal Pronouns

Problems with Nouns

52 Count Nouns

53 Noncount Nouns

54 Nouns with Count and Noncount Meanings

55 Count and Noncount Nouns with Similar Meanings

56 Noncount Nouns that are Count Nouns in Other Languages

57 Singular and Plural Expressions of Noncount Nouns

58 Classifications — *Kind* and *Type*

59 Infinitive and *-ing* Subjects

60 Qualifying Phrases with *-ing* Nouns

61 Nominal *That* Clause

Problems with Adjectives

Problems with Determiners

62 Determiners — *A* and *An*

63 Noncount Nouns with Qualifying Phrases — *The*

64 Ø Meaning *All*

65 *No* Meaning *Not Any*

66 *One of the* and *Some of the*

67 *Few* and *Little*

68 *Much* and *Many*

69 *A Little* and *Little; A Few* and *Few*

70 *Only a Few* and *Only a Little*

71 *A Large (Small) Number of* and *a Large (Small) Amount of*

72 ***Almost All of the* and *Most of the***

Problems with Other Adjectives

73 Sufficiency — *Enough* with Nouns

74 Sufficiency — *Enough* with Adjectives

75 Consecutive Order — *One, Another, the Other*

76 Consecutive Order — *Some, Other, the Other; Some, Others, the Others (the Rest)*

77 Numerical Order

78 Nouns that Function as Adjectives

79 Hyphenated Adjectives

80 Adjectives Ending in *-ed* and *-ing*

81 Cause-and-Result — *So*

82 Cause-and-Result — *Such*

83 Excess — *Too*

84 Emphasis — *Very*

85 Adjectives with Verbs of the Senses

Problems with Comparatives

86 Exact Similarity — *the Same as* and *the Same*

87 General Similarity — *Similar to* and *Similar*

88 General Similarity — *Like* and *Alike*

89 Specific Similarity — Quality Nouns

90 Specific Similarity — Quality Adjectives

91 General Difference — *Different from* and *Different*

92 General Difference — *to Differ from*

93 Comparative Estimates — Multiple Numbers

94 Comparative Estimates — *More Than* and *Less Than*

95 Comparative Estimates — *As Many As*

96 Degrees of Comparison — Comparative Adjectives

97 Degrees of Comparison — Superlative Adjectives

98 Degrees of Comparison — Irregular Adjectives

99 Degrees of Comparison — Comparative Adverbs

100 Double Comparatives

101 Illogical Comparatives — General Similarity and Difference

102 Illogical Comparatives — Degrees

Problems with Prepositions

103 Place — *Between* and *Among*

104 Place — *In, On, At*

105 Time — *In, On, At*

106 Addition — *Besides*

107 Exception — *But* and *Except*

108 Replacement — *Instead of* and *Instead*

109 Example — *Such as*

110 Condition and Unexpected Result — *Despite* and *in Spite of*

111 **Cause — *Because of* and *Because***

112 Cause — *From*

113 Purpose — *For*

114 Means — *By*

115 Time Limit — *From, To*

Problems with Conjunctions

Problems with Correlative Conjunctions

116 Correlative Conjunctions — Inclusives *both...and*

117 Correlative Conjunctions — Inclusives *both...and...as well as*

118 **Correlative Conjunctions — Inclusives *not only...but also***

119 Correlative Conjunctions — Exclusives *not...but*

Problems with Other Conjunctions

120 Affirmative Agreement — *So* and *Too*

121 Negative Agreement — *Neither* and *Either*

122 Planned Result — *So That*

123 Future Result — *When*

124 **Indirect Questions**

125 Question Words with *-ever*

Problems with Adverbs and Adverb-Related Structures

126 Adverbs of Manner

127 Adverbs of Manner — *Fast, Late,* and *Hard*

128 *Sometime* and *Sometimes*

129 **Negative Emphasis**

130 Introductory Adverbial Modifiers — *Once*

131 Introductory Adverbial Modifiers — *While*

132 *No Longer*

133 **Duration — *For* and *Since***

134 Dates

135 Pseudocomparatives

136 Generalization — *As a Whole* and *Wholly*

Problems with Sentences and Clauses

137 Sentences and Clauses

138 Clause-Marker Subjects

139 Verbs in Dependent Clauses

140 Adjective Clauses

STYLE

Problems with Point of View

1 Point of View — Verbs

2 Point of View — Reported Speech

3 Point of View — Verbs and Adverbs

4 Point of View — Activities of the Dead

Problems with Agreement

5 **Agreement — Modified Subject and Verb**

6 Agreement — Subject with Accompaniment and Verb

7 **Agreement — Subject with Appositive and Verb**

8 Agreement — Verb-Subject Order

9 Agreement — Indefinite Subject and Verb

10 Agreement — Collective Subject and Verb

11 Agreement — Noun and Pronoun

12 Agreement — Subject and Possessive Pronouns

13 Agreement — Impersonal Pronouns

14 Agreement — Subject and Appositive

Problems with Introductory Verbal Modifiers

15 Verbal Modifiers — *-ing* and *-ed* Forms

16 Verbal Modifiers — Infinitives of Purpose to Introduce Instructions

Problems with Parallel Structure

17 **Parallel Structure — In a Series**

18 **Parallel Structure — After Correlative Conjunctions**

Problems with Redundancy

19 Redundancy — Unnecessary Phrases

20 Redundancy — Repetition of Words with the Same Meaning

21 Redundancy — Repetition of Noun by Pronoun

Problems with Word Choice

22 Transitive and Intransitive Verbs — *Raise* and *Rise*

23 Transitive and Intransitive Verbs — *Lay* and *Lie*

24 Transitive and Intransitive Verbs — *Set* and *Sit*

25 Similar Verbs — *Tell* and *Say*

26 Similar Verbs — *Let* and *Leave*

27 Similar Verbs — *Borrow* and *Lend*

PATTERNS

Patterns are the parts of a sentence. In some books, *patterns* are called *structures.* In *patterns,* the words have the same order most of the time.

Some of the most important patterns are summarized in this review section. Remember, the generalizations in the charts and explanations for each pattern refer to the structure in the examples. There may be similar structures for which these generalizations are not appropriate.

Problems with Verbs

A *verb* is a word or phrase that expresses existence, action, or experience.

There are two kinds of verbs in English. They are the *main verb* and the *auxiliary verb.* In some grammar books, the *auxiliary verb* is called a *helping verb* because it is used with a *main verb.*

Every verb in English can be described by the following formula:

VERB = tense + (modal) + (have + participle) + (be + -ing) + verb word

Each of the parts of this formula will be summarized in one or more of the problems in this review. Don't spend time studying it now. Just refer to it as you progress through this review section.

PROBLEMS WITH MAIN VERBS

In English, a sentence must have a main verb. A sentence may or may not have an auxiliary verb.

Missing Main Verb

Remember that every English sentence must have a subject and a main verb.

S	V	
The sound of the dryer	bothers	my concentration

Avoid using an *-ing* form, an infinitive, an auxiliary verb, or another part of speech instead of a main verb.

EXAMPLES

INCORRECT: The prettiest girl in our class with long brown hair and brown eyes.
CORRECT: The prettiest girl in our class has long brown hair and brown eyes.

INCORRECT: In my opinion, too soon to make a decision.
CORRECT: In my opinion, it is too soon to make a decision.

INCORRECT: Do you know whether the movie that starts at seven?
CORRECT: Do you know whether the movie that starts at seven is good?

or

Do you know whether the movie starts at seven?

INCORRECT: Sam almost always a lot of fun.
CORRECT: Sam is almost always a lot of fun.

INCORRECT: The book that I lent you having a good bibliography.
CORRECT: The book that I lent you has a good bibliography.

EXERCISES

Part A: Choose the correct answer.

Arizona ____________ a very dry climate.

(A) has
(B) being
(C) having
(D) with

Part B: Choose the incorrect word or phrase and correct it.

Venomous snakes with (A) modified teeth connected to poison glands (B) in which (C) the venom is secreted (D) and stored.

Verbs that Require an Infinitive in the Complement

Remember that the following verbs require an infinitive for a verb in the complement.

agree	*decide*	*hesitate*	*need*	*refuse*
appear	*demand*	*hope*	*offer*	*seem*
arrange	*deserve*	*intend*	*plan*	*tend*
ask	*expect*	*learn*	*prepare*	*threaten*
claim	*fail*	*manage*	*pretend*	*wait*
consent	*forget*	*mean*	*promise*	*want*

S	V	C (infinitive)	M
We	had planned	to leave	day before yesterday

Avoid using an *-ing* form after the verbs listed. Avoid using a verb word after *want.*

EXAMPLES

INCORRECT: He wanted speak with Mr. Brown.
CORRECT: He wanted to speak with Mr. Brown.

INCORRECT: We demand knowing our status.
CORRECT: We demand to know our status.

INCORRECT: I intend the inform you that we cannot approve your application.
CORRECT: I intend to inform you that we cannot approve your application.

INCORRECT: They didn't plan buying a car.
CORRECT: They didn't plan to buy a car.

INCORRECT: The weather tends improving in May.
CORRECT: The weather tends to improve in May.

EXERCISES

Part A: Choose the correct answer.

One of the least effective ways of storing information is learning ________________ it.

(A) how repeat
(B) repeating
(C) to repeat
(D) repeat

Part B: Choose the incorrect word or phrase and correct it.

Representative democracy seemed evolve (A) simultaneously (B) during (C) the eighteenth and nineteenth centuries in Britain, Europe, and the United States (D).

Verbs that Require an *-ing* Form in the Complement

Remember that the following verbs require an *-ing* form for a verb in the complement:

admit	*complete*	*deny*
appreciate	*consider*	*discuss*
avoid	*delay*	*enjoy*

finish
keep
mention
miss
postpone
practice
quit
recall
recommend
regret
risk
stop
suggest
tolerate
understand

S	V	C (-ing)	M
He	enjoys	traveling	by plane

Avoid using an infinitive after the verbs listed.
Forbid may be used with either an infinitive or an *-ing* complement, but *forbid from* is not idiomatic.

EXAMPLES

INCORRECT: She is considering not to go.
CORRECT: She is considering not going.

INCORRECT: We enjoyed talk with your friend.
CORRECT: We enjoyed talking with your friend.

INCORRECT: Hank completed the writing his thesis this summer.
CORRECT: Hank completed writing his thesis this summer.

INCORRECT: I miss to watch the news when I am traveling.
CORRECT: I miss watching the news when I am traveling.

INCORRECT: She mentions stop at El Paso in her letter.
CORRECT: She mentions stopping at El Paso in her letter.

EXERCISES

Part A: Choose the correct answer.

Strauss finished __________ two of his published compositions before his tenth birthday.

(A) written
(B) write
(C) to write
(D) writing

Part B: Choose the incorrect word or phrase and correct it.

Many (A) people have stopped to smoke (B) because (C) they are afraid that it may be (D) harmful to their health.

Verb Phrases that Require an *-ing* Form in the Complement

Remember that the following verb phrases require an *-ing* form for a verb in the complement:

approve of
be better off
can't help
count on
do not mind
forget about
get through
insist on
keep on
look forward to
object to
think about
think of

S	V Ph	C (-ing)	M
She	forgot about	canceling	her appointment

Avoid using an infinitive after the verb phrases listed. Avoid using a verb word after *look forward to* and *object to*. *(Refer to page 79 for more on verb words.)*

Remember that the verb phrase *BE likely* does not require an *-ing* form but requires an infinitive in the complement.

EXAMPLES

INCORRECT: She is likely knowing.
CORRECT: She is likely to know.

INCORRECT: Let's go to the movie when you get through to study.
CORRECT: Let's go to the movie when you get through studying.

INCORRECT: We can't help to wonder why she left.
CORRECT: We can't help wondering why she left.

INCORRECT: I have been looking forward to meet you.
CORRECT: I have been looking forward to meeting you.

INCORRECT: We wouldn't mind to wait.
CORRECT: We wouldn't mind waiting.

EXERCISES

Part A: Choose the correct answer.

Many modern architects insist on _________ materials native to the region that will blend into the surrounding landscape.

(A) use
(B) to use
(C) the use
(D) using

Part B: Choose the incorrect word or phrase and correct it.

During Jackson's administration, those <u>who</u> (A) did not approve of <u>permit</u> (B) common people in the White House <u>were shocked</u> (C) by the president's insistence that they <u>be invited</u> (D) into the mansion.

Problems with Tense

Many grammar books list a large number of *tenses* in English, but the two basic tenses are present and past.

Auxiliary verbs are used with main verbs to express future and other special times.

Irregular Past Forms

Remember that past forms of the following irregular verbs are not the same as the participles:

Verb Word	***Past Form***	***Participle***
be	*was/were*	*been*
beat	*beat*	*beaten*
become	*became*	*become*
begin	*began*	*begun*
bite	*bit*	*bitten*
blow	*blew*	*blown*
break	*broke*	*broken*
choose	*chose*	*chosen*
come	*came*	*come*
do	*did*	*done*
draw	*drew*	*drawn*
drink	*drank*	*drunk*
drive	*drove*	*driven*
eat	*ate*	*eaten*
fall	*fell*	*fallen*
fly	*flew*	*flown*
forget	*forgot*	*forgotten*
forgive	*forgave*	*forgiven*
freeze	*froze*	*frozen*
get	*got*	*gotten or got*
give	*gave*	*given*
go	*went*	*gone*
grow	*grew*	*grown*
hide	*hid*	*hidden*
know	*knew*	*known*
ride	*rode*	*ridden*
run	*ran*	*run*

Verb Word	***Past Form***	***Participle***
see	*saw*	*seen*
shake	*shook*	*shaken*
show	*showed*	*shown*
shrink	*shrank*	*shrunk*
sing	*sang*	*sung*
speak	*spoke*	*spoken*
steal	*stole*	*stolen*
swear	*swore*	*sworn*
swim	*swam*	*swum*
take	*took*	*taken*
tear	*tore*	*torn*
throw	*threw*	*thrown*
wear	*wore*	*worn*
weave	*wove*	*woven*
withdraw	*withdrew*	*withdrawn*
write	*wrote*	*written*

S	V (past)	M
The concert	began	at eight o'clock

Avoid using a participle instead of a past for simple past statements.

EXAMPLES

INCORRECT: They done it very well after they had practiced.
CORRECT: They did it very well after they had practiced.

INCORRECT: Before she run the computer program, she had checked it out with her supervisor.
CORRECT: Before she ran the computer program, she had checked it out with her supervisor.

INCORRECT: We eat dinner in Albuquerque on our vacation last year.
CORRECT: We ate dinner in Albuquerque on our vacation last year.

INCORRECT: My nephew begun working for me about ten years ago.
CORRECT: My nephew began working for me about ten years ago.

INCORRECT: I know that you been forty on your last birthday.
CORRECT: I know that you were forty on your last birthday.

EXERCISES

Part A: Choose the correct answer.

Before the Angles and the Saxons __________ to England, the Iberians had lived there.
(A) coming
(B) come
(C) came
(D) did come

Part B: Choose the incorrect word or phrase and correct it.

When Columbus <u>seen</u> (A) the New World, he <u>thought</u> (B) that he <u>had reached</u> (C) the East Indies <u>by way of</u> (D) a Western route.

PROBLEMS WITH MODALS AND MODAL-RELATED PATTERNS

Modals are auxiliary verbs. They are used with main verbs to give additional meaning to main verbs. The most common modals are listed below, along with some of the additional meanings that they add to main verbs.

can	possibility, ability, permission
could	possibility, ability in the past
may	probability, permission
might	probability
must	necessity, logical conclusion
shall	future with emphasis
should	advice, obligation, prediction
will	future
would	condition

Modal + Verb Word

Remember that a *modal* is used with a *verb word*. A *verb word* is the dictionary form of the verb. In some grammar books, the *verb word* is called the bare infinitive because it appears without the word *to*. Verb words are very important in many patterns, but they are used most often with modals.

S	modal	verb word	
They	might	visit	us

Avoid using an infinitive or an *-ing* form instead of a verb word after a modal.

EXAMPLES

INCORRECT: After you show me the way, I can to go by myself.
CORRECT: After you show me the way, I <u>can</u> <u>go</u> by myself.

INCORRECT: Our friends might stopping to see us on their way to California.
CORRECT: Our friends <u>might</u> <u>stop</u> to see us on their way to California.

INCORRECT: I would, if there is time, liking to make a phone call.
CORRECT: I <u>would</u>, if there is time, <u>like</u> to make a phone call.

INCORRECT: Beth may, with effort, to pass this course.
CORRECT: Beth may, with effort, pass this course.

INCORRECT: The flight should to be on time.
CORRECT: The flight should be on time.

EXERCISES

Part A: Choose the correct answer.

By the time a baby has reached his first birthday, he should, without the help of an adult, ______ sit up or even stand up.

(A) to be able to
(B) able to
(C) to be able
(D) be able to

Part B: Choose the incorrect word or phrase and correct it.

Many birds will, in the normal course of their (A) migrations, flying (B) more than three thousand miles (C) to reach (D) their winter homes.

Logical Conclusions—Events in the Past

Remember that *must* is a modal. *Must* followed by the verb word *have* and a participle expresses a logical conclusion based on evidence. The conclusion is about an event that happened in the past.

Remember that an observation in the present may serve as the basis for a conclusion about something that happened in the past. For example, "here is a message on my desk." It may be concluded that "my friend must have called last night."

S	must have	participle	past time
My friend	must have	called	last night

Avoid using *should* or *can* instead of *must*. Avoid using a verb word instead of *have* and a participle when referring to events in the past.

EXAMPLES

INCORRECT: The streets are wet; it should have rained last night.
CORRECT: The streets are wet; it must have rained last night.

INCORRECT: This pen won't write; it can have run out of ink (in the past).
CORRECT: This pen won't write; it must have run out of ink (in the past).

INCORRECT: The ring that I was looking at is gone; someone else must buy it.
CORRECT: The ring that I was looking at is gone; someone else must have bought it.

INCORRECT: He doesn't have his keys; he must locked them in his car.
CORRECT: He doesn't have his keys; he must have locked them in his car.

INCORRECT: I don't see Martha anywhere; she must be left early.
CORRECT: I don't see Martha anywhere; she must have left early.

EXERCISES

Part A: Choose the correct answer.

The theory of Continental Drift assumes that there ___________ long-term climatic changes in many areas during the past.

(A) must have been
(B) must be
(C) must have
(D) must

Part B: Choose the incorrect word or phrase and correct it.

When the weather becomes (A) colder (B) we know that the air mass must originated (C) in the Arctic rather than (D) over the Gulf of Mexico.

Logical Conclusions—Events in the Present

Remember that *must* is a modal. *Must* followed by *be* and an *-ing* form or an adjective expresses a logical conclusion based on evidence. The conclusion is about an event that is happening now.

S	must be	-ing	present tense
My friend	must be	calling	now

S	must be	adjective	present time
He	must be	upset	now

Avoid using a verb word instead of an *-ing* form after *must be.*

EXAMPLES

INCORRECT: The line is busy; someone should be using the telephone now.
CORRECT: The line is busy; someone must be using the telephone now.

INCORRECT: Bob is absent; he must have been sick again (now).
CORRECT: Bob is absent; he must be sick again (now).

INCORRECT: He is taking a walk; he must have felt better now.
CORRECT: He is taking a walk; he must be feeling better now.

INCORRECT: She must be study at the library now because all of her books are gone.
CORRECT: She must be studying at the library now because all of her books are gone.

INCORRECT: Sarah must get a divorce (now) because her husband is living in an apartment.
CORRECT: Sarah must be getting a divorce (now) because her husband is living in an apartment.

EXERCISES

Part A: Choose the correct answer.

The general public __________ a large number of computers now, because prices are beginning to decrease.

(A) must buy
(B) must have bought
(C) must be buying
(D) must buying

Part B: Choose the incorrect word or phrase and correct it.

The American buffalo must be reproduce (A) itself (B) again because (C) it (D) has been removed from the endangered species list.

Logical Conclusions—Events that Repeat

Remember that *must* is a modal. *Must* followed by a verb word expresses a logical conclusion based on evidence. The conclusion is about an event that happens repeatedly.

S	must	verb word	repeated time
My friend	must	call	often

Avoid using an infinitive or an *-ing* form instead of a verb word after *must.*

EXAMPLES

INCORRECT: The light is always out in her room at ten o'clock; she must have go to bed early every night.
CORRECT: The light is always out in her room at ten o'clock; she must go to bed early every night.

INCORRECT: Our neighbors must having a lot of money because they are always taking expensive trips.
CORRECT: Our neighbors <u>must have</u> a lot of money because they are always taking expensive trips.

INCORRECT: He can like his job because he seems very happy.
CORRECT: He <u>must like</u> his job because he seems very happy.

INCORRECT: Her English is very good; she must spoken it often.
CORRECT: Her English is very good; she <u>must speak</u> it often.

INCORRECT: Carol always gets good grades; she should study a lot.
CORRECT: Carol always gets good grades; she <u>must study</u> a lot.

EXERCISES

Part A: Choose the correct answer.

Since more than 50 percent of all marriages in the United States end in divorce, about half of the children in America must _________ in single-parent homes.

(A) grow up
(B) to grow up
(C) growing up
(D) have grow up

Part B: Choose the incorrect word or phrase and correct it.

<u>Sheep</u> (A) <u>must have mate</u> (B) in fall <u>since</u> (C) the young <u>are born</u> (D) in early spring every year.

Knowledge and Ability—*Know* and *Know How*

Remember that *know* followed by a noun expresses knowledge.

S	KNOW	noun
I	know	the answer

Avoid using an infinitive after *know*.
Remember that *know how* followed by an infinitive expresses ability.

S	KNOW	how	infinitive	
I	know	how	to answer	the question

EXAMPLES

INCORRECT: If she knew to drive, he would lend her his car.
CORRECT: If she knew how to drive, he would lend her his car.

INCORRECT: I don't know to use the card catalog in the library.
CORRECT: I don't know how to use the card catalog in the library.

INCORRECT: Until he came to the United States to study, he didn't know to cook.
CORRECT: Until he came to the United States to study, he didn't know how to cook.

INCORRECT: Do you know to type?
CORRECT: Do you know how to type?

INCORRECT: You'll have to help her because she doesn't know to do it.
CORRECT: You'll have to help her because she doesn't know how to do it.

EXERCISES

Part A: Choose the correct answer.

In a liberal arts curriculum, it is assumed that graduates will __________ about English, languages, literature, history, and the other social sciences.

(A) know
(B) know how
(C) knowledge
(D) knowing

Part B: Choose the incorrect word or phrase and correct it.

The Impressionists like (A) Monet and Manet knew (B) to use color in order to create (C) an image of reality rather than reality itself (D).

Past Custom—*Used to* and BE *Used to*

Remember that *used to* is similar to a modal. *Used to* with a verb word means that a custom in the past has not continued.

S	used to	verb word	
He	used to	live	in the country

Avoid using a form of *be* after the subject. Avoid using the incorrect form *use to.*

Remember that *BE used to* with an *-ing* form means to be accustomed to.

S	BE	used to	*-ing* form	
He	was	used to	living	in the country

Avoid using a form of *be* after *used to.* Avoid using a verb word instead of an *-ing* form. Avoid using the incorrect form *use to.*

EXAMPLES

INCORRECT: I used to was studying at the University of Southern California before I transferred here.
CORRECT: I used to study at the University of Southern California before I transferred here.
or
I was used to studying at the University of Southern California before I transferred here.

INCORRECT: We use to go to the movies quite frequently.
CORRECT: We used to go to the movies quite frequently.
or
We were used to going to the movies quite frequently.

INCORRECT: She was used to get up early.
CORRECT: She used to get up early.
or
She was used to getting up early.

INCORRECT: He was used to drink too much.
CORRECT: He used to drink too much.
or
He was used to drinking too much.

INCORRECT: She used to speaking in public.
CORRECT: She used to speak in public.
or
She was used to speaking in public.

EXERCISES

Part A: Choose the correct answer.

Harvard __________ a school for men, but now it is coeducational, serving as many women as men.

(A) was used
(B) used to be
(C) was used to
(D) was used to be

Part B: Choose the incorrect word or phrase and correct it.

As (A) television images of the astronauts showed, even for trained professionals who (B) are used to move (C) about in a lessened gravitational field, there are (D) still problems.

Advisability—*Had Better*

Remember that *had better* is similar to a modal. Although *had* appears to be a past, *had better* expresses advice for the future.

S	had better	verb word	
You	had better	take	Chemistry 600 this semester

S	had better	not	verb word	
You	had better	not	take	Chemistry 600 this semester

Avoid using an infinitive or a past form of a verb instead of a verb word. Avoid using *don't* instead of *not.*

Examples

INCORRECT: You had better to hurry if you don't want to miss the bus.
CORRECT: You had better hurry if you don't want to miss the bus.

INCORRECT: We had better made reservations so that we will be sure of getting a good table.
CORRECT: We had better make reservations so that we will be sure of getting a good table.

INCORRECT: We had better to check the schedule.
CORRECT: We had better check the schedule.

INCORRECT: You had better don't quit your job until you find another one.
CORRECT: You had better not quit your job until you find another one.

INCORRECT: You had better don't go alone.
CORRECT: You had better not go alone.

Exercises

Part A: Choose the correct answer.

To check for acidity, one had better ______________ litmus paper.
(A) use
(B) using
(C) to use
(D) useful

Part B: Choose the incorrect word or phrase and correct it.

In <u>today's</u> (A) competitive markets, even small businesses had better <u>to advertise</u> (B) <u>on TV and radio</u> (C) in order <u>to gain</u> (D) a share of the market.

Preference—*Would Rather*

Remember that the phrase *would rather* is similar to a modal. Although *would rather* appears to be a past, it expresses preference in present and future time.

S	would rather	verb word
I	would rather	drive

S	would rather	not	verb word
I	would rather	not	drive

Avoid using an infinitive or an *-ing* form instead of a verb word.

EXAMPLES

INCORRECT: She told me that she'd rather not to serve on the committee.
CORRECT: She told me that she'<u>d rather not</u> <u>serve</u> on the committee.

INCORRECT: If you don't mind, I'd rather not going.
CORRECT: If you don't mind, I'<u>d rather not</u> <u>go</u>.

INCORRECT: He said that he'd rather went to a small college instead of to a large university.
CORRECT: He said that he'<u>d rather</u> <u>go</u> to a small college instead of to a large university.

INCORRECT: I'd rather writing this than print it because I don't print well.
CORRECT: I'<u>d rather</u> <u>write</u> this than print it because I don't print well.

INCORRECT: Greg would rather has a Pepsi than a beer.
CORRECT: Greg <u>would rather</u> <u>have</u> a Pepsi than a beer.

EXERCISES

Part A: Choose the correct answer.

Rhododendrons would rather __________ in shady places, and so would azaleas.

(A) to grow
(B) growing
(C) grown
(D) grow

Part B: Choose the incorrect word or phrase and correct it.

The Amish people, descended from the Germans and Swiss, would rather using (A) horses than (B) machines for transportation and farm work (C) because they believe that a simple life keeps them closer (D) to God.

Preference for Another—*Would Rather That*

Remember that when the preference is for another person or thing, *would rather that* introduces a clause. The other person or thing is the subject of the clause.

Although the verb is past tense, the preference is for present or future time.

S	would rather	that	S	V (past)
I	would rather	that	you	drove

Avoid using a present verb or a verb word instead of a past verb. Avoid using *should* and a verb word instead of a past verb.

S	would rather	that	S	didn't	verb word
I	would rather	that	you	didn't	drive

Avoid using *don't* or *doesn't* instead of *didn't.*

Examples

INCORRECT: I'd rather that you don't do that.
CORRECT: I'd rather that you didn't do that.

INCORRECT: Diane would rather that her husband doesn't working so hard.
CORRECT: Diane would rather that her husband didn't work so hard.

INCORRECT: The dean would rather that students make appointments instead of dropping by.
CORRECT: The dean would rather that students made appointments instead of dropping by.

INCORRECT: My roommate would rather that I don't keep the light on after ten o'clock.
CORRECT: My roommate would rather that I didn't keep the light on after ten o'clock.

INCORRECT: We'd rather that you should come tomorrow.
CORRECT: We'd rather that you came tomorrow.

EXERCISES

Part A: Choose the correct answer.

A good counselor would rather that the patient _______ his or her own decisions after being helped to arrive at a general understanding of the alternatives.

(A) makes
(B) making
(C) will make
(D) made

Part B: Choose the incorrect word or phrase and correct it.

It is said (A) that the American flag has five-pointed stars because Betsy Ross told (B) General Washington she (C) would rather that he changing (D) the six-pointed ones.

Negative Imperatives

Remember that an imperative is expressed by a verb word.

Please don't	verb word	
Please don't	tell	anyone

Avoid using an infinitive instead of a verb word.

Would you please not	verb word	
Would you please not	tell	anyone

Avoid using an infinitive instead of a verb word. Avoid using *don't* after *would you please.*

EXAMPLES

INCORRECT: Would you please don't smoke.
CORRECT: Please don't smoke.
or
Would you please not smoke.

INCORRECT: Please don't to park here.
CORRECT: Please don't park here.
or
Would you please not park here.

INCORRECT: Would you please not to be late.
CORRECT: Please don't be late.
or
Would you please not be late.

INCORRECT: Please don't to go yet.
CORRECT: Please don't go yet.
or
Would you please not go yet.

INCORRECT: Would you please don't worry.
CORRECT: Please don't worry.
or
Would you please not worry.

EXERCISES

Part A: Choose the correct answer.

Please _________ photocopies of copyrighted material without the permission of the publisher.
(A) no make
(B) don't make
(C) not make
(D) not to make

Part B: Choose the incorrect word or phrase and correct it.

Please don't parking (A) in those spaces that have signs reserving (B) them for (C) the handicapped (D).

REVIEW EXERCISE: PROBLEMS 1–15

DIRECTIONS: This Review Exercise has two parts, with special directions for each. To check your answers, refer to the key on page 527.

Part A: Choose the correct answer.

1. After her famous husband's death, Eleanor Roosevelt continued _________ for peace.
(A) working
(B) work
(C) the working
(D) to working

2. The Palo Verde tree _________ in spring.
(A) has beautiful yellow blossoms
(B) beautiful yellow blossoms
(C) having beautiful yellow blossoms
(D) with beautiful yellow blossoms

3. The great apes, a generally peaceful species, __________ in groups.
   (A) would rather living
   (B) would rather live
   (C) would rather they live
   (D) would rather lived

Part B: Choose the incorrect word or phrase and correct it.

4. Insurance rates are not the same for different people <u>because</u> (A) <u>they</u> (B) are not likely <u>have</u> (C) <u>the same risk</u> (D).

5. Many people with spinal cord <u>injuries</u> (A) can, with the <u>help</u> (B) of computer implants, <u>recovering</u> (C) some of <u>their</u> (D) mobility.

6. <u>Although</u> (A) thousands of grizzly bears <u>used to roaming</u> (B) the Western Plains of the United States, today <u>only a few thousand</u> (C) <u>exist</u> (D).

7. Although fraternal twins <u>are born</u> (A) at the same time, they do not tend <u>resembling</u> (B) <u>each other</u> (C) any more <u>than</u> (D) do other siblings.

8. Some astronomers <u>contend</u> (A) that in ancient times, the Big Horn Medicine Wheel, an arrangement of stones <u>in Wyoming</u> (B), must <u>have serve</u> (C) as <u>sighting</u> (D) points for observations of the sun.

9. Because doctors <u>are treating</u> (A) more people for skin cancer, it is widely <u>believed</u> (B) that <u>changes</u> (C) in the protective layers of the earth's atmosphere <u>must be produce</u> (D) harmful effects now.

10. Secretariat <u>run</u> (A) the Kentucky Derby in 1.59 minutes, <u>setting</u> (B) a record that <u>has remained</u> (C) unbroken <u>since 1973</u> (D).

PROBLEMS WITH CAUSATIVES

Causatives are main verbs that cause people or machines to do things or cause things to change. They are listed below in order of the most forceful to the least forceful:

make
get
have
let
help

Causative MAKE

Remember that MAKE can be used as a causative. In a causative, a person does not perform an action directly. The person causes it to happen by forcing another person to do it.

S	MAKE	someone	verb word	
His mother	made	him	take	his medicine

S	MAKE	something	verb word
I	made	the machine	work

Avoid using an infinitive or an *-ing* form instead of a verb word after a person or thing in a causative with MAKE.

EXAMPLES

INCORRECT: She made the baby to take a nap.
CORRECT: She made the baby take a nap.

INCORRECT: Professor Rogers didn't make us typed up our lab reports.
CORRECT: Professor Rogers didn't make us type up our lab reports.

INCORRECT: Are you going to make your daughter to work part time in the store this summer?
CORRECT: Are you going to make your daughter work part time in the store this summer?

INCORRECT: I can't seem to make this dishwasher running.
CORRECT: I can't seem to make this dishwasher run.

INCORRECT: Patsy makes everyone doing his share around the house.
CORRECT: Patsy makes everyone do his share around the house.

EXERCISES

Part A: Choose the correct answer.

Psychologists believe that incentives __________ to increase our productivity.
(A) make us want
(B) make us to want
(C) making us want
(D) makes us wanting

Part B: Choose the incorrect word or phrase and correct it.

<u>Too</u> much water <u>makes</u> plants <u>turning</u> brown on the edges of <u>their</u> leaves.
(A) (B) (C) (D)

Causative GET

Remember that GET can be used as a causative. In a causative, a person does not perform an action directly.

GET has less force and authority than MAKE.

S	GET	someone	infinitive	
Let's	get	Ralph	to go	with us

S	GET	something	participle	
Let's	get	our car	fixed	first

Avoid using a verb word instead of an infinitive after a person in a causative with GET. Avoid using a verb word instead of a participle after things in a causative with GET.

EXAMPLES

INCORRECT: Do you think that we can get Karen takes us to San Diego?
CORRECT: Do you think that we can <u>get</u> <u>Karen</u> <u>to take</u> us to San Diego?

INCORRECT: I want to get the house paint before winter.
CORRECT: I want to <u>get</u> <u>the house</u> <u>painted</u> before winter.

INCORRECT: Let's get some of our money exchange for dollars.
CORRECT: Let's <u>get</u> some of <u>our money</u> <u>exchanged</u> for dollars.

INCORRECT: Nora got her mother's wedding dress to alter so that it fit perfectly.
CORRECT: Nora <u>got</u> <u>her mother's wedding dress</u> <u>altered</u> so that it fit perfectly.

INCORRECT: We will have to get someone fixing the phone right away.
CORRECT: We will have to <u>get</u> <u>someone</u> <u>to fix</u> the phone right away.

EXERCISES

Part A: Choose the correct answer.

Lobbyists who represent special interest groups get _________ that benefits their groups.
(A) Congress to pass the legislation
(B) Congress passed the legislation
(C) the legislation to pass by Congress
(D) the legislation that Congress passing

Part B: Choose the incorrect word or phrase and correct it.

In order <u>to receive</u> (A) full reimbursement for jewelry that might <u>be stolen,</u> (B) the owner must get <u>all pieces</u> (C) <u>appraise.</u> (D)

Causative HAVE

Remember that HAVE can be used as a causative. In a causative, a person does not perform an action directly.

HAVE has even less force and authority than GET.

S	HAVE	someone	verb word	
My English teacher	had	us	give	oral reports

S	HAVE	something	participle	
I	want to have	this book	renewed,	please

Avoid using an infinitive or an *-ing* form instead of a verb word after a person in a causative with HAVE. Avoid using a verb word or an infinitive instead of a participle after a thing in a causative with HAVE.

Examples

INCORRECT: Tom had a tooth fill.
CORRECT: Tom <u>had</u> <u>a tooth</u> <u>filled</u>.

INCORRECT: Have you had your temperature taking yet?
CORRECT: Have you <u>had</u> <u>your temperature</u> <u>taken</u> yet?

INCORRECT: They had their lawyer to change their wills.
CORRECT: They <u>had</u> <u>their lawyer</u> <u>change</u> their wills.

INCORRECT: I like the way you had the beautician done your hair.
CORRECT: I like the way you <u>had</u> <u>the beautician</u> <u>do</u> your hair.

INCORRECT: We are going to have our car fix before we go to Toronto.
CORRECT: We are going to <u>have</u> <u>our car</u> <u>fixed</u> before we go to Toronto.

EXERCISES

Part A: Choose the correct answer.

Like humans, zoo animals must have a dentist __________ their teeth.
(A) fill
(B) filled
(C) filling
(D) to be filled

Part B: Choose the incorrect word or phrase and correct it.

Most presidential candidates have their names <u>print</u> (A) on the ballot in the New Hampshire primary election because <u>it is</u> (B) <u>customarily</u> (C) <u>the first one</u> (D) in the nation, and winning it can give them a good chance to be nominated by their parties.

Causative LET

Remember that LET can be used as a causative. In a causative, a person does not perform an action directly. With LET, a person gives permission for another person to do it.

S	LET	someone	verb word	
His mother	let	him	go	to school

S	LET	something	verb word
I	am letting	this machine	cool

Avoid using an infinitive or an *-ing* form instead of a verb word after a person or thing in a causative with LET.

EXAMPLES

INCORRECT: Professor Baker let us to write a paper instead of taking a final exam.
CORRECT: Professor Baker <u>let us write</u> a paper instead of taking a final exam.

INCORRECT: When I was learning to drive, my Dad let me using his car.
CORRECT: When I was learning to drive, my Dad <u>let me use</u> his car.

INCORRECT: Would you let us the borrow your notes?
CORRECT: Would you <u>let us borrow</u> your notes?

INCORRECT: Larry is so good-hearted, he lets people took advantage of him.
CORRECT: Larry is so good-hearted, he lets people take advantage of him.

INCORRECT: Don't let that bothers you.
CORRECT: Don't let that bother you.

EXERCISES

Part A: Choose the correct answer.

The Immigration and Naturalization Service often ________ their visas if they fill out the appropriate papers.

(A) lets students extend
(B) lets students for extend
(C) letting students to extend
(D) let students extending

Part B: Choose the incorrect word or phrase and correct it.

The National Basketball Association will not let any athlete to continue (A) playing (B) in the league unless he submits voluntarily (C) to treatment for drug addiction (D).

Causative HELP

Remember that HELP can be used as a causative. In a causative, a person does not perform an action directly. With HELP, a person assists another person to do it.

S	HELP	someone	verb word infinitive	
He	is helping	me	type	my paper
He	is helping	me	to type	my paper

Avoid using an *-ing* form instead of a verb word or an infinitive after a person in a causative with HELP.

EXAMPLES

INCORRECT: Her husband always helps her that she does the laundry.
CORRECT: Her husband always helps her do the laundry.

or

Her husband always helps her to do the laundry.

INCORRECT: Don't you help each other the study for tests?
CORRECT: Don't you help each other study for tests?
or
Don't you help each other to study for tests?

INCORRECT: My teacher helped me getting this job.
CORRECT: My teacher helped me get this job.
or
My teacher helped me to get this job.

INCORRECT: Bob said that he would help our finding the place.
CORRECT: Bob said that he would help us find the place.
or
Bob said that he would help us to find the place.

INCORRECT: This book should help you understanding the lecture.
CORRECT: This book should help you understand the lecture.
or
This book should help you to understand the lecture.

EXERCISES

Part A: Choose the correct answer.

In partnership with John D. Rockefeller, Henry Flager _________ the Standard Oil Company.
(A) helped forming
(B) helped form
(C) he helped form
(D) helping to form

Part B: Choose the incorrect word or phrase and correct it.

Doctors agree that the fluid around the spinal cord helps the nourish the brain.
(A) (B) (C) (D)

PROBLEMS WITH CONDITIONALS

Conditionals are statements with *if* or *unless.* They are opinions about the conditions (circumstances) that influence results, and opinions about the results.

There are two kinds of conditionals. In most grammar books, they are called *real* or *factual* conditionals and *unreal* or *contrary-to-fact* conditionals. *Factual conditionals* express absolute, scientific facts, probable results, or possible results. *Contrary-to-fact* conditionals express improbable or impossible results.

Factual Conditionals—Absolute, Scientific Results

Remember that *absolute conditionals* express scientific facts. *Will* and a verb word expresses the opinion that the result is absolutely certain.

CONDITION				RESULT		
If	S	V (present)	,	S	V (present)	
If	a catalyst	is used	,	the reaction	occurs	more rapidly

or

CONDITION				RESULT			
If	S	V (present)	,	S	will	verb word	
If	a catalyst	is used	,	the reaction	will	occur	more rapidly

Avoid using *will* and a verb word instead of the present verb in the clause beginning with *if.* Avoid using the auxiliary verbs *have, has, do,* and *does* with main verbs in the clause of result.

EXAMPLES

INCORRECT: If water freezes, it has become a solid.
CORRECT: If water freezes, it becomes a solid.
or
If water freezes, it will become a solid.

INCORRECT: If children be healthy, they learn to walk at about eighteen months old.
CORRECT: If children are healthy, they learn to walk at about eighteen months old.
or
If children are healthy, they will learn to walk at about eighteen months old.

INCORRECT: If orange blossoms are exposed to very cold temperatures, they withered and died.
CORRECT: If orange blossoms are exposed to very cold temperatures, they wither and die.
or
If orange blossoms are exposed to very cold temperatures, they will wither and die.

INCORRECT: If the trajectory of a satellite will be slightly off at launch, it will get worse as the flight progresses.
CORRECT: If the trajectory of a satellite is slightly off at launch, it gets worse as the flight progresses.
or
If the trajectory of a satellite is slightly off at launch, it will get worse as the flight progresses.

INCORRECT: If light strikes a rough surface, it diffused.

CORRECT: If light strikes a rough surface, it diffuses.

or

If light strikes a rough surface, it will diffuse.

EXERCISES

Part A: Choose the correct answer.

If water is heated to 212 degrees F. ________ as steam.

(A) it will boil and escape
(B) it is boiling and escaping
(C) it boil and escape
(D) it would boil and escape

Part B: Choose the incorrect word or phrase and correct it.

If a live sponge is broken into pieces, each piece would turn into a new sponge like
(A) (B) (C)
the original one.
(D)

PROBLEM 22 Factual Conditionals—Probable Results for the Future

Remember that *will* and a verb word expresses the opinion that the results are absolutely certain. In order of more to less probable, use the following modals: *will, can, may.*

If	S	V (present)		,	S	will can may	verb word	
If	we	find	her address	,	we	will	write	her

S	will can may	verb word		if	S	V (present)	
We	will	write	her	if	we	find	her address

Avoid using the present tense verb instead of a modal and a verb word in the clause of result.

EXAMPLES

INCORRECT: If you put too much water in rice when you cook it, it got sticky.
CORRECT: If you put too much water in rice when you cook it, it will get sticky.
or
It will get sticky if you put too much water in rice when you cook it.

INCORRECT: If they have a good sale, I would have stopped by on my way home.
CORRECT: If they have a good sale, I will stop by on my way home.
or
I will stop by on my way home if they have a good sale.

INCORRECT: We will wait if you wanted to go.
CORRECT: We will wait if you want to go.
or
If you want to go, we will wait.

INCORRECT: If you listen to the questions carefully, you answer them easily.
CORRECT: If you listen to the questions carefully, you will answer them easily.
or
You will answer them easily if you listen to the questions carefully.

INCORRECT: If we finished our work a little early today, we'll attend the lecture at the art museum.
CORRECT: If we finish our work a little early today, we'll attend the lecture at the art museum.
or
We'll attend the lecture at the art museum if we finish our work a little early today.

EXERCISES

Part A: Choose the correct answer.

If services are increased, taxes __________.
(A) will probably go up
(B) probably go up
(C) probably up
(D) going up probably

Part B: Choose the incorrect word or phrase and correct it.

If you don't register before the last day of regular registration, you paying a late fee.
(A) register (B) the last day (C) paying (D) a late fee

Factual Conditionals—Possible Results

Remember that although a past verb is used, the opinion is for future time. In order of most possible to least possible, use the following modals: *would, could, might.*

If	S	V (past)	,	S	would could might	verb word	
If	we	found	her address,	we	would	write	her
If	we	found	her address,	we	could	write	her
If	we	found	her address,	we	might	write	her

or

S	would could might	verb word		if	S	V (past)	
We	would	write	her	if	we	found	her address
We	could	write	her	if	we	found	her address
We	might	write	her	if	we	found	her address

Avoid using *would* and a verb word instead of a past tense verb in an "if" clause.

EXAMPLES

INCORRECT: If Jim's family meet Karen, I am sure that they would like her.

CORRECT: If Jim's family met Karen, I am sure that they would like her.

or

I am sure that they would like her if Jim's family met Karen.

INCORRECT: If you made your bed in the morning, your room looks better when you got back in the afternoon.

CORRECT: If you made your bed in the morning, your room would look better when you got back in the afternoon.

or

Your room would look better when you got back in the afternoon if you made your bed in the morning.

INCORRECT: If Judy didn't drink so much coffee, she wouldn't have been so nervous.

CORRECT: If Judy didn't drink so much coffee, she wouldn't be so nervous.

or

Judy wouldn't be so nervous if she didn't drink so much coffee.

INCORRECT: If you would go to bed earlier, you wouldn't be so sleepy in the morning.

CORRECT: If you went to bed earlier, you wouldn't be so sleepy in the morning.

or

You wouldn't be so sleepy in the morning if you went to bed earlier.

INCORRECT: If she would eat fewer sweets, she would lose weight.

CORRECT: If she ate fewer sweets, she would lose weight.

or

She would lose weight if she ate fewer sweets.

EXERCISES

Part A: Choose the correct answer.

If Americans ate fewer foods with sugar and salt, their general health ________ better.

(A) be
(B) will be
(C) is
(D) would be

Part B: Choose the incorrect word or phrase and correct it.

If drivers obeyed the speed limit, fewer accidents occur.
(A) drivers (B) speed limit (C) fewer (D) occur

Factual Conditionals—Probable Changes in Past Results

Remember that the speaker or writer is expressing an opinion about the results of the past under different conditions or circumstances. In order of the most to the least probable, use the following modals: *would, could, might.*

If	S	had	participle		,	S	would have could have might have	participle	
If	we	had	found	her address,		we	would have	written	her
If	we	had	found	her address,		we	could have	written	her
If	we	had	found	her address,		we	might have	written	her

Avoid using *would have* and a participle instead of *had* and a participle in the clause beginning with *if.* Avoid using *have* as a participle.

EXAMPLES

INCORRECT: If we had the money, we would have bought a new stereo system.
CORRECT: If we had had the money, we would have bought a new stereo system.

or

We would have bought a new stereo system if we had had the money.

INCORRECT: If the neighbors hadn't quieted down, I would have have to call the police.
CORRECT: If the neighbors hadn't quieted down, I would have had to call the police.

or

I would have had to call the police if the neighbors hadn't quieted down.

INCORRECT: If her mother let her, Anne would have stayed longer.
CORRECT: Anne would have stayed longer if her mother had let her.

or

If her mother had let her, Anne would have stayed longer.

INCORRECT: If we would have known that she had planned to arrive today, we could have met her at the bus station.
CORRECT: If we had known that she had planned to arrive today, we could have met her at the bus station.

or

We could have met her at the bus station if we had known that she had planned to arrive today.

INCORRECT: If I had more time, I would have checked my paper again.
CORRECT: If I had had more time, I would have checked my paper again.

or

I would have checked my paper again if I had had more time.

EXERCISES

Part A: Choose the correct answer.

According to some historians, if Napoleon had not invaded Russia, he ________ the rest of Europe.

(A) had conquered
(B) would conquer
(C) would have conquered
(D) conquered

Part B: Choose the incorrect word or phrase and correct it.

If dinosaurs would have (A) continued roaming (B) the earth, man (C) would have evolved quite differently (D).

Contrary-to-Fact Conditionals—Impossible Results *Were*

Remember that the verb *BE* is always *were* in contrary-to-fact conditionals.

If	S	were	
If	the party	were	on Friday, we could go

Avoid changing *were* to agree with the subject in contrary-to-fact statements.

EXAMPLES

INCORRECT: If Barbara was really my friend, she would call me once in a while.
CORRECT: If Barbara were really my friend, she would call me once in a while.
(Barbara is not my friend.)

or

She would call me once in a while if Barbara were really my friend.
(Barbara is not my friend.)

INCORRECT: If Mr. Harris is single, I could introduce him to my sister.
CORRECT: If Mr. Harris were single, I could introduce him to my sister.
(Mr. Harris is not single.)

or

I could introduce him to my sister if Mr. Harris were single.
(Mr. Harris is not single.)

INCORRECT: If the meat was a little more done, this would be an excellent meal.
CORRECT: If the meat were a little more done, this would be an excellent meal.
(The meat is not done.)

or

This would be an excellent meal if the meat were a little more done.
(The meat is not done.)

INCORRECT: If my daughter is here, I would be very happy.
CORRECT: If my daughter were here, I would be very happy.
(My daughter is not here.)

or

I would be very happy if my daughter were here.
(My daughter is not here.)

INCORRECT: This apartment be perfect if it were a little larger.
CORRECT: This apartment would be perfect if it were a little larger.
(The apartment is not larger.)

or

If it were a little larger, this apartment would be perfect.
(The apartment is not larger.)

EXERCISES

Part A: Choose the correct answer.

If humans were totally deprived of sleep, they __________ hallucinations, anxiety, coma, and eventually, death.

(A) would experience
(B) experience
(C) would have experienced
(D) had experienced

Part B: Choose the incorrect word or phrase and correct it.

If we were to consider all of the different kinds of motion in discussing the movement of an object,
(A)
it is very confusing, because even an object at rest is moving as the earth turns.
(B) (C) (D)

Contrary-to-Fact Conditionals—Change in Conditions *Unless*

Remember that there is a subject and verb that determines the change in conditions after the con-
ector *unless.*

S	V	unless	S	V	
Luisa	won't return	unless	she	gets	a scholarship

Avoid deleting *unless* from the sentence; avoid deleting either the subject or the verb from the
lause after *unless.*

EXAMPLES

NCORRECT: I can't go I don't get my work finished.
CORRECT: I can't go unless I get my work finished.

NCORRECT: They are going to get a divorce unless he stopping drugs.
CORRECT: They are going to get a divorce unless he stops taking drugs.

NCORRECT: You won't get well unless you are taking your medicine.
CORRECT: You won't get well unless you take your medicine.

NCORRECT: Dean never calls his father unless needs money.
CORRECT: Dean never calls his father unless he needs money.

NCORRECT: We can't pay the rent unless the scholarship check.
CORRECT: We can't pay the rent unless the scholarship check comes.

EXERCISES

Part A: Choose the correct answer.

Football teams don't play in the Super Bowl championship _________ either the National or the American Conference.

(A) unless they win
(B) but they win
(C) unless they will win
(D) but to have won

Part B: Choose the incorrect word or phrase and correct it.

Usually boys (A) cannot become (B) Boy Scouts unless completed (C) the fifth grade (D).

REVIEW EXERCISE: PROBLEMS 16–26

DIRECTIONS: This Review Exercise has two parts, with special directions for each. To check your answers, refer to the key on page 527.

Part A: Choose the correct answer.

1. If the Normans had not invaded England in the tenth century, the English language __________ in a very different way.
   (A) develop
   (B) developed
   (C) would develop
   (D) would have developed

2. In *The Wizard of Oz*, the wizard could not help Dorothy __________.
   (A) that she return to Kansas
   (B) return to Kansas
   (C) returning to Kansas
   (D) returned Kansas

3. If teaching __________ more, fewer teachers would leave the profession.
   (A) pays
   (B) is paying
   (C) paid
   (D) had paid

Part B: Choose the incorrect word or phrase and correct it.

4. The Food and Drug Administration, known as the FDA, makes grocers and restaurant owners
(A) known as (B) makes
pasteurized all milk before selling it.
(C) pasteurized (D) selling

5. Besides his contributions to the field of science, Franklin helped the people of Philadelphia founded
(A) his (B) helped (C) founded
an insurance company, a hospital, a public library, and a night watch, as well as a city militia.
(D) as well as

6. If baby geese are hatched in the absence of their mother, they following the first moving object they see.
(A) their (B) following (C) moving (D) see

7. The Rural Free Delivery Act was passed so that people on farms could have their mail deliver cheaper and faster.
(A) was passed (B) could (C) their (D) deliver

8. A temporary driver's permit lets the learner drives with another licensed driver in the car.
(A) drives (B) another (C) licensed (D) driver

9. Unless complications from the anesthetic, operations to remove the appendix are not
(A) (B) (C)
considered serious.
(D)

10. If the cerebellum of a pigeon was destroyed, the bird would not be able to fly.
(A) (B) (C) (D)

PROBLEMS WITH SUBJUNCTIVES

Some verbs, nouns, and expressions require a subjunctive. A subjunctive is a change in the usual form of the verb. A subjunctive is often a verb word in English.

Importance—Subjunctive Verbs

Remember that the following verbs are used before *that* and the verb word clause to express importance.

ask
demand
desire
insist
prefer
propose
recommend
request
require
suggest
urge

S	V	that	S	verb word	
Mr. Johnson	prefers	that	she	speak	with him personally

Avoid using a present or past tense verb instead of a verb word. Avoid using a modal before the verb word.

Note: The verb *insist* may be used in non-subjunctive patterns in the past tense. For example: *He insisted that I* was *wrong.*

EXAMPLES

INCORRECT: The doctor suggested that she will not smoke.
CORRECT: The doctor suggested that she not smoke.

INCORRECT: I propose that the vote is secret ballot.
CORRECT: I propose that the vote be secret ballot.

INCORRECT: The foreign student advisor recommended that she studied more English before enrolling at the university.
CORRECT: The foreign student advisor recommended that she study more English before enrolling at the university.

INCORRECT: The law requires that everyone has his car checked at least once a year.
CORRECT: The law requires that everyone have his car checked at least once a year.

INCORRECT: She insisted that they would give her a receipt.
CORRECT: She insisted that they give her a receipt.

EXERCISES

Part A: Choose the correct answer.

Less moderate members of Congress are insisting that changes in the Social Security System ________ made.

(A) will
(B) are
(C) being
(D) be

Part B: Choose the incorrect word or phrase and correct it.

Many (A) architects prefer that a dome is used (B) to roof buildings that need to conserve (C) floor space (D).

PROBLEM 28 Importance—Nouns Derived from Subjunctive Verbs

Remember that the following nouns are used in this pattern:

demand	*recommendation*
insistence	*request*
preference	*requirement*
proposal	*suggestion*

noun	that	S	verb word	
The recommendation	that	we	be	evaluated was approved

Avoid using a present or past tense verb instead of a verb word. Avoid using a modal before the verb word.

EXAMPLES

INCORRECT: He complied with the requirement that all graduate students in education should write a thesis.
CORRECT: He complied with the requirement that all graduate students in education write a thesis.

INCORRECT: The committee refused the request that the prerequisite shall be waived.
CORRECT: The committee refused the request that the prerequisite be waived.

INCORRECT: She ignored the suggestion that she gets more exercise.
CORRECT: She ignored the suggestion that she get more exercise.

INCORRECT: The terrorist's demand that the airline provides a plane will not be met by the deadline.
CORRECT: The terrorist's demand that the airline provide a plane will not be met by the deadline.

INCORRECT: He regretted not having followed his advisor's recommendation that he dropping the class.
CORRECT: He regretted not having followed his advisor's recommendation that he drop the class.

EXERCISES

Part A: Choose the correct answer.

It is the recommendation of many psychologists ________ to associate words and remember names.

(A) that a learner uses mental images
(B) a learner to use mental images
(C) mental images are used
(D) that a learner use mental images

Part B: Choose the incorrect word or phrase and correct it.

Despite (A) their insistence that he will appear (B) when there is (C) an important event, the president schedules (D) press conferences with the news media at his discretion.

Importance—Impersonal Expressions

Remember that the following adjectives are used in impersonal expressions.

essential
imperative
important
necessary

it is	adjective	infinitive	
It is	important	to verify	the data

or

it is	adjective	that	S	verb word	
It is	important	that	the data	be	verified

Avoid using a present tense verb instead of a verb word. Avoid using a modal before the verb word.

EXAMPLES

INCORRECT: It is not necessary that you must take an entrance examination to be admitted to an American university.

CORRECT: It is not necessary to take an entrance examination to be admitted to an American university.

or

It is not necessary that you take an entrance examination to be admitted to an American university.

INCORRECT: It is imperative that you are on time.

CORRECT: It is imperative to be on time.

or

It is imperative that you be on time.

INCORRECT: It is important that I will speak with Mr. Williams immediately.

CORRECT: It is important to speak with Mr. Williams immediately.

or

It is important that I speak with Mr. Williams immediately.

INCORRECT: It is imperative that your signature appears on your identification card.

CORRECT: It is imperative to sign your identification card.

or

It is imperative that your signature appear on your identification card.

INCORRECT: It is essential that all applications and transcripts are filed no later than July 1.

CORRECT: It is essential to file all applications and transcripts no later than July 1.

or

It is essential that all applications and transcripts be filed no later than July 1.

EXERCISES

Part A: Choose the correct answer.

It is necessary _________ the approaches to a bridge, the road design, and the alignment in such a way as to best accommodate the expected traffic flow over and under it.

(A) plan
(B) to plan
(C) planning
(D) the plan

Part B: Choose the incorrect word or phrase and correct it.

It is essential that vitamins <u>are</u> (A) supplied either by foods <u>or</u> (B) <u>by supplementary tablets</u> (C) for normal growth <u>to occur</u> (D).

PROBLEMS WITH INFINITIVES

An infinitive is *to* + the verb word.

Purpose—Infinitives

Remember that an infinitive can express purpose. It is a short form of *in order to.*

S	V	C	infinitive (purpose)	
Laura	jogs		to stay	fit
She	takes	vitamins	to feel	better

Avoid expressing purpose without the word *to* in the infinitive. Avoid using *for* instead of *to.*

EXAMPLES

INCORRECT: Wear several layers of clothing for keep warm.
CORRECT: Wear several layers of clothing <u>to keep</u> warm.

INCORRECT: David has studied hard the succeed.
CORRECT: David has studied hard <u>to succeed.</u>

INCORRECT: Don't move your feet when you swing for play golf well.
CORRECT: Don't move your feet when you swing <u>to play</u> golf well.

INCORRECT: Virginia always boils the water twice make tea.
CORRECT: Virginia always boils the water twice <u>to make</u> tea.

INCORRECT: Wait until June plant those bulbs.
CORRECT: Wait until June <u>to plant</u> those bulbs.

Exercises

Part A: Choose the correct answer.

In the Morrill Act, Congress granted federal lands to the states _________ agricultural and mechanical arts colleges.

(A) for establish
(B) to establish
(C) establish
(D) establishment

Part B: Choose the incorrect word or phrase and correct it.

Papyrus <u>was used</u> (A) <u>for to make</u> (B) not only paper <u>but also</u> (C) sails, baskets, <u>and</u> (D) clothing.

Problems with Passives

A passive changes the emphasis of a sentence. Usually in a passive, the event or result is more important than the person who causes it to happen.

For example, *born*, *known as*, and *left* are participles. They are commonly used with BE in passive sentences. Why? Because the person born, the person known, and the person or thing left are the important parts of the sentences.

Passives—Word Order

Remember that in a passive sentence the actor is unknown or not important. The subject is not the actor.

Passive sentences are also common in certain styles of scientific writing.

S	BE	participle	
State University	is	located	at the corner of College and Third

Avoid using a participle without a form of the verb BE.

Examples

Incorrect: My wedding ring made of yellow and white gold.
Correct: My wedding ring <u>is made</u> of yellow and white gold.
(It is the *ring*, not the person who made the ring, that is important.)

INCORRECT: If your brother invited, he would come.
CORRECT: If your brother were invited, he would come.
(It is your *brother*, not the person who invited him, that is important.)

INCORRECT: Mr. Wilson known as Willie to his friends.
CORRECT: Mr. Wilson is known as Willie to his friends.
(It is *Mr. Wilson*, not his friends, that is important.)

INCORRECT: References not used in the examination room.
CORRECT: References are not used in the examination room.
(It is *references*, not the persons using them, that are important.)

INCORRECT: Laura born in Iowa.
CORRECT: Laura was born in Iowa.
(It is *Laura*, not her mother who bore her, that is important.)

EXERCISES

Part A: Choose the correct answer.

In the stringed instruments, the tones __________ by playing a bow across a set of strings that may be made of wire or gut.
(A) they produce
(B) producing
(C) are produced
(D) that are producing

Part B: Choose the incorrect word or phrase and correct it.

Work is often measure in units called foot pounds.
(A) (B) (C) (D)

Passives—Agent

Remember that in a passive sentence, the actor is unknown or not important. The subject is not the actor.

The actor in a passive sentence is called the agent.

	by	person machine
This report was written It was printed	by by	Phil computer

Avoid using *for* or *from* instead of *by*.

EXAMPLES

INCORRECT: The decisions on cases like this are made from Dean White.
CORRECT: The decisions on cases like this are made by Dean White.

INCORRECT: Most of us are sponsored from our parents.
CORRECT: Most of us are sponsored by our parents.

INCORRECT: The car was inspected for Customs.
CORRECT: The car was inspected by Customs.

INCORRECT: The bill has already been paid Mr. Adams.
CORRECT: The bill has already been paid by Mr. Adams.

INCORRECT: State University is governed from the Board of Regents.
CORRECT: State University is governed by the Board of Regents.

EXERCISES

Part A: Choose the correct answer.

The famous architect, Frank Lloyd Wright, was greatly __________ , who wanted him to study architecture.

(A) influenced by his mother
(B) from his mother's influence
(C) his mother influenced him
(D) influencing for his mother

Part B: Choose the incorrect word or phrase and correct it.

In the ionosphere (A), gases have been partly (B) ionized for high frequency (C) radiation from the sun and other sources (D).

Passives—Infinitives

Remember that a passive infinitive can be used with a present form of the BE verb to express a future intention, and with the past form of the BE verb to express an intention that was not realized in the past.

S	BE (pres)	to be	participle	future time
The project	is	to be	completed	by 2005

S	BE (past)	to be	participle	past time
The project	was	to be	completed	by 1995

Avoid using a participle without *to* or *be* to express intention. Avoid using a verb word instead of a participle with *to be.*

EXAMPLES

INCORRECT: The play was to be cancel, but it was only postponed.
CORRECT: The play was to be canceled, but it was only postponed.

INCORRECT: The finalists are to named at the next meeting.
CORRECT: The finalists are to be named at the next meeting.

INCORRECT: The results of the exam are be announced tomorrow.
CORRECT: The results of the exam are to be announced tomorrow.

INCORRECT: We were to be notify if there was a problem.
CORRECT: We were to be notified if there was a problem.

INCORRECT: The game is to rescheduled.
CORRECT: The game is to be rescheduled.

EXERCISES

Part A: Choose the correct answer.

The TOEFL examination_______by the year 2002.

(A) completely revised
(B) is revised completely
(C) is to be revised completely
(D) completely is to revise

Part B: Choose the incorrect word or phrase and correct it.

From now on (A), new buildings in level one earthquake zones in the United States are to constructed (B) to withstand (C) a tremor without suffering (D) structural damage.

34 Necessity for Repair or Improvement—NEED

Remember that NEED may express necessity for repair or improvement.

S	NEED	*-ing* form
This paragraph	needs	revising

Avoid using an infinitive or a participle instead of an *-ing* form.

S	NEED	to be	participle
This paragraph	needs	to be	revised

Avoid using an *-ing* form instead of a participle.

EXAMPLES

INCORRECT: His car needs to fix.
CORRECT: His car needs <u>fixing</u>.
or
His car needs <u>to be fixed</u>.

INCORRECT: The rug needs cleaned before we move in.
CORRECT: The rug needs <u>cleaning</u> before we move in.
or
The rug needs <u>to be cleaned</u> before we move in.

INCORRECT: The house needs to paint, but we plan to wait until next summer to do it.
CORRECT: The house needs <u>painting</u>, but we plan to wait until next summer to do it.
or
The house needs <u>to be painted,</u> but we plan to wait until next summer to do it.

INCORRECT: Her watch needed repaired.
CORRECT: Her watch needed <u>repairing</u>.
or
Her watch needed <u>to be repaired</u>.

INCORRECT: The hem of this dress needs mended before I wear it again.
CORRECT: The hem of this dress needs <u>mending</u> before I wear it again.
or
The hem of this dress needs <u>to be mended</u> before I wear it again.

EXERCISES

Part A: Choose the correct answer.

If more than five thousand dollars in monetary instruments is transported into the United States, a report needs __________ with the Customs Office.

(A) file
(B) filing
(C) to file
(D) to be filed

Part B: Choose the incorrect word or phrase and correct it.

<u>Because</u> (A) the interstate highway system linking roads across the country <u>was built</u> (B) about forty-five years <u>ago</u> (C), most of the roads in the system now need <u>repaired</u> (D).

Belief and Knowledge—Anticipatory *It*

Remember that an anticipatory *it* clause expresses belief or knowledge. Anticipatory means before. Some *it* clauses that go before main clauses are listed below:

It is believed
It is hypothesized
It is known
It is said
It is thought
It is true
It is written

Anticipatory *it*	that	S	V	
It is believed	that	all mammals	experience	dreams

Avoid using an *-ing* form, a noun, or an infinitive instead of a subject and verb after an anticipatory *it* clause.

EXAMPLES

INCORRECT: It is hypothesized that the subjects in the control group not to score as well.
CORRECT: It is hypothesized that the subjects in the control group will not score as well.

INCORRECT: It is generally known that she leaving at the end of the year.
CORRECT: It is generally known that she is leaving at the end of the year.

INCORRECT: It is said that a buried treasure near here.
CORRECT: It is said that a buried treasure was hidden near here.

INCORRECT: It is believed that a horseshoe bringing good luck.
CORRECT: It is believed that a horseshoe brings good luck.

INCORRECT: It is thought that our ancestors building this city.
CORRECT: It is thought that our ancestors built this city.

EXERCISES

Part A: Choose the correct answer.

_________ Giant Ape Man, our biggest and probably one of our first human ancestors, was just about the size of a male gorilla.

(A) It is believed that
(B) That it is
(C) That is believed
(D) That believing

Part B: Choose the incorrect word or phrase and correct it.

That it is believed that most of the earthquakes in the world occur near the youngest mountain ranges—the Himalayas, the Andes, and the Sierra Nevadas.
(A) That it is believed (B) most of the earthquakes (C) near (D) the youngest

PROBLEMS WITH HAVE + PARTICIPLE

Have, *has*, or *had* + participle express duration of time.

Duration—HAVE + Participle

Remember HAVE + participle means that the activity is extended over a period of time. HAVE + participle is especially common with adverbs of duration such as *since* and *for*.

S	HAVE	participle	(duration)
The English language	has	changed	since Shakespeare's time

Avoid using the participle instead of HAVE + participle. Avoid using a verb word or a past form instead of a participle.

EXAMPLES

INCORRECT: We have live in Seattle for five years.
CORRECT: We have lived in Seattle for five years.

INCORRECT: Have you wrote your mother a letter?
CORRECT: Have you written your mother a letter?

INCORRECT: Ray given us a lot of help since we arrived.
CORRECT: Ray has given us a lot of help since we arrived.

INCORRECT: I have took this medication since 1985.
CORRECT: I have taken this medication since 1985.

INCORRECT: We been friends since we were children.
CORRECT: We have been friends since we were children.

EXERCISES

Part A: Choose the correct answer.

People who have very little technical background have __________ to understand computer language.

(A) learn
(B) learning
(C) learned
(D) learns

Part B: Choose the incorrect word or phrase and correct it.

Arlington National Cemetery, a memorial area that <u>includes</u> (A) the mast of the battleship *Maine*, the Tomb of the Unknown Soldier, and the eternal flame at the grave of John F. Kennedy, <u>is</u> (B) the site where the families of <u>more than</u> (C) 160,000 American veterans <u>have bury</u> (D) their loved ones.

Duration—HAVE + *Been* + Participle

Remember that HAVE + *been* + participle means that a recently completed activity was extended over a period of time.

Remember that it is a passive. The actor is not known or not important.

	HAVE	been	participle	
She	has	been	accepted	to State University

Avoid using HAVE + participle instead of HAVE + *been* + participle in a passive pattern. Avoid using *been* + participle.

EXAMPLES

INCORRECT: The party has planned for two weeks.
CORRECT: The party <u>has</u> <u>been</u> <u>planned</u> for two weeks.
(It is the party, not the people who planned it, that is important.)

INCORRECT: Your typewriter been fixed, and you can pick it up any time.
CORRECT: Your typewriter <u>has</u> <u>been</u> <u>fixed</u>, and you can pick it up any time.
(It is your typewriter, not the person who fixed it, that is important.)

INCORRECT: Wayne has elected to the student government.
CORRECT: Wayne <u>has</u> <u>been</u> <u>elected</u> to the student government.
(It is Wayne, not the people who elected him, who is important.)

INCORRECT: We been taught how to cook.
CORRECT: We <u>have</u> <u>been</u> <u>taught</u> how to cook.
(It is we, not the people who taught us, who are important.)

INCORRECT: The class been changed to room 10.
CORRECT: The class <u>has</u> <u>been</u> <u>changed</u> to room 10.
(It is the class, not the person who changed it, that is important.)

EXERCISES

Part A: Choose the correct answer.

Many books __________, but one of the best is *How to Win Friends and Influence People* by Dale Carnegie.

(A) have written about success
(B) written about success
(C) have been written about success
(D) about successful

Part B: Choose the incorrect word or phrase and correct it.

Gettysburg has been <u>preserve</u> (A) as a national historic monument <u>because</u> (B) it was the site of a major Civil War battle in which <u>many lives</u> (C) <u>were lost</u> (D).

Predictions—*Will Have* + Participle

Remember that *will have* followed by a participle and a future adverb expresses a prediction for a future activity or event.

adverb (future)	S	will	have	participle	
By the year 2010,	researchers	will	have	discovered	a cure for cancer

Avoid using *will* instead of *will have.*

EXAMPLES

INCORRECT: You will finished your homework by the time the movie starts.
CORRECT: You <u>will</u> <u>have</u> <u>finished</u> your homework <u>by the time the movie starts</u>.

INCORRECT: Jan will left by five o'clock.
CORRECT: Jan <u>will</u> <u>have</u> <u>left</u> <u>by five o'clock</u>.

INCORRECT: Before school is out, I have returned all of my library books.
CORRECT: <u>Before school is out</u>, I <u>will</u> <u>have</u> <u>returned</u> all of my library books.

INCORRECT: We have gotten an answer to our letter by the time we have to make a decision.
CORRECT: We <u>will</u> <u>have</u> <u>gotten</u> an answer to our letter <u>by the time we have to make a decision</u>.

INCORRECT: Before we can tell them about the discount, they will bought the tickets.
CORRECT: <u>Before we can tell them</u> about the discount, they <u>will</u> <u>have</u> <u>bought</u> the tickets.

EXERCISES

Part A: Choose the correct answer.

By the middle of the twenty-first century, the computer ________ a necessity in every home.

(A) became
(B) becoming
(C) has become
(D) will have become

Part B: Choose the incorrect word or phrase and correct it.

<u>It is believed</u> (A) that <u>by 2010</u> (B) immunotherapy <u>have succeeded</u> (C) in <u>curing</u> (D) a number of serious illnesses.

Unfulfilled Desires in the Past—*Had Hoped*

Remember that *had hoped* expresses a hope in the past that did not happen.

S	had hoped	that	S	would	verb word	
We	had hoped	that	she	would	change	her mind

Avoid using a verb word instead of *would* and a verb word.

Avoid using the incorrect pattern:

S	had hoped	object pronoun	*-ing* form	
We	had hoped	her	changing	her mind

EXAMPLES

INCORRECT: He had hoped that he graduate this semester, but he couldn't finish his thesis in time.
CORRECT: He had hoped <u>that he would graduate</u> this semester, but he couldn't finish his thesis in time.

INCORRECT: We had hoped him staying longer.
CORRECT: We had hoped <u>that he would stay</u> longer.

INCORRECT: They had hoped that she not find out about it.
CORRECT: They had hoped <u>that she would not find out</u> about it.

INCORRECT: I had hoped she coming to the party.
CORRECT: I had hoped <u>that she would come</u> to the party.

INCORRECT: His father had hoped that he go into business with him.
CORRECT: His father had hoped <u>that he would go</u> into business with him.

EXERCISES

Part A: Choose the correct answer.

Although research scientists had hoped that the new drug interferon ________ to be a cure for cancer, its applications now appear to be more limited.

(A) prove
(B) had proven
(C) would prove
(D) will prove

Part B: Choose the incorrect word or phrase and correct it.

President Wilson had hoped that World War I <u>be</u> (A) the last great war, but only two decades <u>later</u>, (B) <u>the Second World War</u> (C) <u>was erupting</u> (D).

PROBLEMS WITH AUXILIARY VERBS

Auxiliary verbs are additional verbs that may be used with main verbs to add meaning. For example, all of the forms of BE, HAVE, DO, and all modals are auxiliary verbs.

Missing Auxiliary Verb—Active

Remember that some main verbs require auxiliary verbs.

	BE	*-ing*	
Mom	is	watering	her plants

	HAVE	participle	
Mom	has	watered	her plants

	MODAL	verb word	
Mom	should	water	her plants

Avoid using *-ing* forms without BE, participles without HAVE, and verb words without modals when *-ing*, a participle, or a verb word function as a main verb.

EXAMPLES

INCORRECT: The party is a surprise, but all of her friends coming.
CORRECT: The party is a surprise, but all of her friends are coming.

INCORRECT: She read it to you later tonight.
CORRECT: She will read it to you later tonight.

INCORRECT: The sun shining when we left this morning.
CORRECT: The sun was shining when we left this morning.

INCORRECT: We gone there before.
CORRECT: We have gone there before.

INCORRECT: I can't talk with you right now because the doorbell ringing.
CORRECT: I can't talk with you right now because the doorbell is ringing.

EXERCISES

Part A: Choose the correct answer.

The giraffe survives in part because it ________ the vegetation in the high branches of trees where other animals have not grazed.

(A) to reach
(B) can reach
(C) reaching
(D) reach

Part B: Choose the incorrect word or phrase and correct it.

According to some scientists, the earth losing its outer atmosphere because of pollutants.
(A) (B) (C) (D)

Missing Auxiliary Verb—Passive

Remember that the passive requires an auxiliary BE verb.

S		BE	participle
The plants		are	watered
The plants	have	been	watered
The plants	should	be	watered

Avoid using a passive without a form of BE.

EXAMPLES

INCORRECT: The phone answered automatically.
CORRECT: The phone is answered automatically.

INCORRECT: They have informed already.
CORRECT: They have been informed already.

INCORRECT: These books should returned today.
CORRECT: These books should be returned today.

INCORRECT: The plane delayed by bad weather.
CORRECT: The plane was delayed by bad weather.

INCORRECT: My paper has not typed.
CORRECT: My paper has not been typed.

EXERCISES

Part A: Choose the correct answer.

Hydrogen peroxide_______as a bleaching agent because it effectively whitens a variety of fibers and surfaces.

(A) used
(B) is used
(C) is using
(D) that it uses

Part B: Choose the incorrect word or phrase and correct it.

If a rash occurs (A) within twenty-four hours after taking (B) a new medication (C), the treatment should discontinued (D).

REVIEW EXERCISE: PROBLEMS 27–41

DIRECTIONS: This Review Exercise has two parts, with special directions for each. To check your answers, refer to the key on page 527.

Part A: Choose the correct answer.

1. There are still many examples of Cro-Magnon murals _________ in the caves of France and Spain.
(A) they are left
(B) leaving them
(C) left
(D) leave

2. _________ that Lee Harvey Oswald may not have acted alone in the assassination of John Kennedy.
(A) Thinking
(B) To think
(C) It is thought
(D) The thought

3. Phosphates ________ to most farm land in America.
   (A) need added
   (B) need to add
   (C) need to adding
   (D) need to be added

Part B: Choose the incorrect word or phrase and correct it.

4. The states require that every citizen registers before voting in an election.
   (A) every (B) registers (C) voting (D) an

5. The money needed to start and continue operating a business known as capital.
   (A) The money (B) to start (C) operating (D) known as

6. The purpose of hibernation is maintain animals in winter climates where food supplies are reduced.
   (A) is (B) maintain (C) food supplies (D) are reduced

7. It is believed that, by the year 2020, many space stations will been constructed between the earth and the moon.
   (A) It is believed (B) by the year 2020 (C) will been (D) between

8. It is essential the practice a foreign language in order to retain a high level of proficiency.
   (A) the practice (B) a foreign language (C) to retain (D) a high level

9. Fewer babies born with birth defects because of advances in prenatal care during this decade.
   (A) Fewer (B) born (C) because of (D) during this decade

10. Although the sculptor had hoped that he be able to finish the large stone faces at Mount Rushmore, the work was left for his son to complete.
    (A) he be able (B) to finish (C) was left (D) to complete

CUMULATIVE REVIEW EXERCISE FOR VERBS

DIRECTIONS: Some of the sentences in this exercise are correct. Some are incorrect. First, find the correct sentences, and mark them with a check (√). Then find the incorrect sentences, and correct them. Check your answers using the key on pages 529–530.

1. In the entire history of the solar system, thirty billion planets may has been lost or destroyed.

2. A victim of the influenza virus usually with headache, fever, chills, and body ache.

3. Rubber is a good insulator of electricity, and so does glass.

4. Light rays can make the desert appears to be a lake.

5. It is essential that nitrogen is present in the soil for plants to grow.

6. A great many athletes have managed to overcome serious physical handicaps.

7. If the eucalyptus tree was to become extinct, the koala bear would also die.

8. Various species must begin their development in similar ways, since the embryos of a fish and a cat appear to be very similar during the early stages of life.

9. Some teachers argue that students who used to using a calculator may forget how to do mental calculations.

10. Last year Americans spended six times as much money for pet food as they did for baby food.

11. Secretaries are usually eligible for higher salaries when they know how shorthand.

12. A new automobile needs to tuned up after the first five thousand miles.

13. Financial planners usually recommend that an individual save two to six months' income for emergencies.

14. If a baby is held up so that the sole of the foot touches a flat surface, well-coordinated walking movements will be triggered.

15. Generally, the use of one building material in preference to another indicates that it found in large quantities in the construction area and does an adequate job of protecting the inhabitants from the weather.

Problems with Pronouns

You probably remember learning that "pronouns take the place of nouns." What this means is that pronouns often are used instead of nouns to avoid repetition of nouns.

A pronoun usually has a reference noun that has been mentioned before in conversation or in writing. The pronoun is used instead of repeating the reference noun. In some grammar books, the reference noun is called the "antecedent of the pronoun" because it has been mentioned before. "Ante" means "before." For example, in the following sentence, the word *them* is a pronoun that refers to the noun *secretaries.*

Many *secretaries* are using computers to help *them* work faster and more efficiently.

There are several different kinds of pronouns in English. Some of them are *personal* pronouns, which can be either subject or object pronouns; *possessive* pronouns; *relative* pronouns; *reflexive* pronouns; and *reciprocal* pronouns.

Subject Pronouns

Remember that personal pronouns used as the subject of a sentence or clause should be subject case pronouns.

	pronoun (subject)	V	
If the weather is good,	Ellen and I	will go	to the beach

Remember that the following pronouns are subject pronouns:

I	*we*
you	*you*
he/she	*they*
it	

Avoid using an object pronoun as a subject.

Examples

INCORRECT: When he comes back from vacation, Bob and me plan to look for another apartment.
CORRECT: When he comes back from vacation, Bob and I plan to look for another apartment.

INCORRECT: Betty studied business, and after she graduated, her and her best friend opened a book store.
CORRECT: Betty studied business, and after she graduated, she and her best friend opened a book store.

INCORRECT: After Sandy talked them into buying bikes, she and them never drove to school.
CORRECT: After Sandy talked them into buying bikes, she and they never drove to school.

INCORRECT: Frank and us are going to join the same fraternity.
CORRECT: Frank and we are going to join the same fraternity.

INCORRECT: When they have enough money, Pat and her will probably go back to school.
CORRECT: When they have enough money, Pat and she will probably go back to school.

Exercises

Part A: Choose the correct answer.

When Franklin Roosevelt became very ill, his wife began to take a more active role in politics, and many people believed that __________ and the president shared his responsibilities.

(A) she
(B) her
(C) herself
(D) hers

Part B: Choose the incorrect word or phrase and correct it.

We know that in 1000 A.D. (A) Leif Eriksson landed on the North American coast, and that him (B) and his Norwegian companions were (C) the first white men to see (D) the New World.

Subject Pronouns in Complement Position

Remember that in complement position after the verb BE, a subject pronoun must be used.

it	BE	pronoun (subject)	
It	is	he	whom the committee has named

Avoid using an object pronoun instead of a subject pronoun after the verb *BE*.

EXAMPLES

INCORRECT: It was her whom everyone wanted to win.
CORRECT: It was she whom everyone wanted to win.

INCORRECT: Is it them at the door again?
CORRECT: Is it they at the door again?

INCORRECT: This is him speaking.
CORRECT: This is he speaking.

INCORRECT: Didn't you know that it was us who played the joke?
CORRECT: Didn't you know that it was we who played the joke?

INCORRECT: I have to admit that it was me who wanted to go.
CORRECT: I have to admit that it was I who wanted to go.

EXERCISES

Part A: Choose the correct answer.

According to the Christian Bible, when the disciples saw Jesus after he had risen from the dead, they said, ______

(A) "It is him."
(B) "It is he."
(C) "It is his."
(D) "It is himself."

Part B: Choose the incorrect word or phrase and correct it.

It was her, Elizabeth I, not her father, King Henry, who led England into the Age of Empire.
(A) her (B) her father (C) who (D) led

Object Pronouns

Remember that personal pronouns used as the complement of a sentence or clause should be object case pronouns.

S	V	pronoun (object)	
They	asked	us, Jane and me,	whether we were satisfied

Remember that the following pronouns are object pronouns:

me	*us*
you	*you*
her	*them*
him	
it	

Avoid using a subject pronoun as an object.

Let	pronoun (object)	V	
Let	us (you and me)	try	to reach an agreement

Avoid using a subject pronoun after *let*.

Examples

INCORRECT: He always helps my wife and I with our tax returns.
CORRECT: He always helps my wife and me with our tax returns.

INCORRECT: Do you really believe that she has blamed us for the accident, especially you and I?
CORRECT: Do you really believe that she has blamed us for the accident, especially you and me?

INCORRECT: Let you and I promise not to quarrel about such unimportant matters anymore.
CORRECT: (You) Let you and me promise not to quarrel about such unimportant matters anymore.

INCORRECT: The bus leaves Ted and she at the corner.
CORRECT: The bus leaves Ted and her at the corner.

INCORRECT: The results of the test surprised they because everyone scored much better than expected.
CORRECT: The results of the test surprised them because everyone scored much better than expected.

Exercises

Part A: Choose the correct answer.

Moby Dick is a mythical account of evil and revenge as shown by Captain Ahab's pursuit of the whale that had wounded _________ earlier in life.

(A) he
(B) his
(C) him
(D) to him

Part B: Choose the incorrect word or phrase and correct it.

According to legend, because the Native American princess Pocahontas said that she loved he, Captain John Smith was set free.
(A) According to; (B) because; (C) he; (D) was

Object Pronouns after Prepositions

Remember that personal pronouns used as the object of a preposition should be object case pronouns.

	preposition	pronoun (object)
I would be glad to take a message	for	her

Remember that the following prepositions are commonly used with object pronouns:

among *of*
between *to*
for *with*
from

Avoid using a subject pronoun instead of an object pronoun after a proposition.

EXAMPLES

INCORRECT: The experiment proved to my lab partner and I that prejudices about the results of an investigation are often unfounded.
CORRECT: The experiment proved to my lab partner and me that prejudices about the results of an investigation are often unfounded.

INCORRECT: Of those who graduated with Betty and he, Ellen is the only one who has found a good job.
CORRECT: Of those who graduated with Betty and him, Ellen is the only one who has found a good job.

INCORRECT: Among we men, it was he who always acted as the interpreter.
CORRECT: Among us men, it was he who always acted as the interpreter.

INCORRECT: The cake is from Jan, and the flowers are from Larry and we.
CORRECT: The cake is from Jan, and the flowers are from Larry and us.

INCORRECT: Just between you and I, this isn't a very good price.
CORRECT: Just between you and me, this isn't a very good price.

Exercises

Part A: Choose the correct answer.

Since the Earth's crust is much thicker under the continents, equipment would have to be capable of drilling through 100,000 feet of rock to investigate the mantle ________ .

(A) beneath them
(B) beneath their
(C) beneath its
(D) beneath they

Part B: Choose the incorrect word or phrase and correct it.

According to Amazon legends, men <u>were forced</u> (A) <u>to do</u> (B) all of the household tasks for the women warriors <u>who</u> (C) governed and protected the cities <u>for they</u> (D).

PROBLEM 46 Possessive Pronouns Before *-ing* Forms

Remember that possessive pronouns are used before *-ing* nouns.

The following are possessive pronouns:

my	*our*
your	*your*
her	*their*
his	
its	

S	V Ph V	pronoun (possessive)	*-ing* form (noun)	
We	can count on	her	helping	us
He	regretted	their	misunderstanding	him

Avoid using subject or object pronouns between the verb and the *-ing* form.

Examples

INCORRECT: We don't understand why you object to him coming with us.
CORRECT: We don't understand why you object to <u>his coming</u> with us.

INCORRECT: I would appreciate you letting me know as soon as possible.
CORRECT: I would appreciate <u>your letting</u> me know as soon as possible.

INCORRECT: The doctor insisted on she taking a leave of absence.
CORRECT: The doctor insisted on <u>her taking</u> a leave of absence.

INCORRECT: He is surprised by you having to pay for the accident.
CORRECT: He is surprised by <u>your having</u> to pay for the accident.

INCORRECT: My father approves of me studying in the United States.
CORRECT: My father approves of <u>my studying</u> in the United States.

EXERCISES

Part A: Choose the correct answer.

One property of radioisotopes is that __________ decaying occurs in half-lives over a long period of time.

(A) they
(B) them
(C) they're
(D) their

Part B: Choose the incorrect word or phrase and correct it.

Although Barney Clark lived only a few months (A) with the artificial heart, doctors were able to learn (B) a great deal from him (C) having used (D) it.

Possessive Pronouns Before Parts of the Body

Remember that possessive pronouns are used before nouns that identify a part of the body.

		pronoun (possessive)	noun (part of body)
He	hurt	his	arm

Avoid using *the* instead of a possessive pronoun.

EXAMPLES

INCORRECT: How did you twist the ankle?
CORRECT: How did you twist <u>your ankle</u>?

INCORRECT: Kevin jammed the finger while he was fixing his car.
CORRECT: Kevin jammed <u>his finger</u> while he was fixing his car.

INCORRECT: Does Alice color the hair?
CORRECT: Does Alice color <u>her hair</u>?

INCORRECT: The arms are so long that he can't find shirts to fit him.
CORRECT: <u>His arms</u> are so long that he can't find shirts to fit him.

INCORRECT: She broke the wrist in the accident.
CORRECT: She broke <u>her wrist</u> in the accident.

EXERCISES

Part A: Choose the correct answer.

Sports medicine experts agree that ice should be applied immediately when an athlete suffers an injury to __________ leg.

(A) its
(B) an
(C) the
(D) his

Part B: Choose the incorrect word or phrase and correct it.

According to the theory of natural selection, the man who was able to use <u>the hands and feet</u> (A) most <u>freely</u> (B) <u>to walk and grasp</u> (C) was the one <u>who</u> (D) survived and evolved.

Relative Pronouns that Refer to Persons and Things

Remember that *who* is used to refer to persons, and *which* is used to refer to things.

	someone	who	
She is	the secretary	who	works in the international office

Avoid using *which* instead of *who* in reference to a person.

	something	which	
This is	the new typewriter	which	you ordered

Avoid using *who* instead of *which* in reference to a thing.

EXAMPLES

INCORRECT: The people which cheated on the examination had to leave the room.
CORRECT: <u>The people</u> <u>who</u> cheated on the examination had to leave the room.

INCORRECT: There is someone on line two which would like to speak with you.
CORRECT: There is <u>someone</u> on line two <u>who</u> would like to speak with you.

INCORRECT: Who is the man which asked the question?
CORRECT: Who is <u>the man</u> <u>who</u> asked the question?

INCORRECT: The person which was recommended for the position did not fulfill the minimum requirements.
CORRECT: The person who was recommended for the position did not fulfill the minimum requirements.

INCORRECT: The student which receives the highest score will be awarded a scholarship.
CORRECT: The student who receives the highest score will be awarded a scholarship.

EXERCISES

Part A: Choose the correct answer.

Charlie Chaplin was a comedian _________ was best known for his work in silent movies.
(A) who
(B) which
(C) whose
(D) what

Part B: Choose the incorrect word or phrase and correct it.

Absolute zero, the temperature at whom (A) all substances (B) have zero thermal energy and thus, the lowest (C) possible temperatures, is (D) unattainable in practice.

Relative Pronouns that Refer to Persons

Remember that both *who* and *whom* are used to refer to persons. *Who* is used as the subject of a sentence or a clause. *Whom* is used as the complement of a sentence or a clause. *Whom* is often used after a preposition as the object of the preposition.

	who	V	
Everyone	who	took	the tour was impressed by the paintings

Avoid using *whom* as the subject of a verb.

	whom	S	V	
He was the only American	whom	I	saw	at the conference

Avoid using *who* instead of *whom* before a subject and a verb.

EXAMPLES

INCORRECT: I asked him who he was calling.
CORRECT: I asked him whom he was calling.

NCORRECT: Did you meet the girl whom was chosen Homecoming Queen?
CORRECT: Did you meet the girl who was chosen Homecoming Queen?

NCORRECT: He didn't know who he would take to the party.
CORRECT: He didn't know whom he would take to the party.

NCORRECT: I know the candidate whom was elected.
CORRECT: I know the candidate who was elected.

NCORRECT: There is often disagreement as to whom is the better student, Bob or Ellen.
CORRECT: There is often disagreement as to who is the better student, Bob or Ellen.

EXERCISES

Part A: Choose the correct answer.

In a parliamentary system, it is not the monarch but the prime minister __________.
(A) whom the real power
(B) who has the real power
(C) whom has the real power
(D) who the real power

Part B: Choose the incorrect word or phrase and correct it.

The Pilgrims were 102 English emigrants whom (A), after arriving (B) on the Mayflower, became (C) the first (D) European settlers in New England.

50 Reflexive Pronouns

Remember that reflexive pronouns may be used when both the subject and the complement refer to the same person or thing. Reflexive pronouns are used as the complement of a sentence or a clause or as the object of a preposition. The following are reflexive pronouns:

myself	*ourselves*
yourself	*yourselves*
himself	*themselves*
herself	
itself	

S	V	pronoun (reflexive)
Some language learners	can correct	themselves

Avoid using object pronouns or possessive pronouns instead of reflexive pronouns.

EXAMPLES

NCORRECT: Be careful or you will hurt to you.
CORRECT: Be careful or you will hurt yourself.

INCORRECT: A child can usually feed self by the age of six months.
CORRECT: A child can usually feed himself by the age of six months.

INCORRECT: I had to teach me to swim.
CORRECT: I had to teach myself to swim.

INCORRECT: Help you to whatever you like.
CORRECT: Help yourself to whatever you like.

INCORRECT: An oven that cleans its is very handy.
CORRECT: An oven that cleans itself is very handy.

EXERCISES

Part A: Choose the correct answer.

The jaw structure of a snake permits it to eat and digest animals much larger than ________.

(A) it
(B) itself
(C) its
(D) it has

Part B: Choose the incorrect word or phrase and correct it.

According to (A) the Fifth Amendment to the U.S. Constitution, no (B) person should be compelled (C) to be a witness against him own (D).

Reciprocal Pronouns

Remember that the reciprocal pronoun phrase *each other* may be used when the plural subject and complement refer to the same persons or things, and they are performing a reciprocal (mutual) act.

S	V	pronoun (reciprocal)	
My sister and I	visit	each other	about once a week

Remember that *each other* is used to express mutual acts for all persons. *One another* is also correct.

EXAMPLES

INCORRECT: Family members love to each other.
CORRECT: Family members love each other.

INCORRECT: Let's meet each to the other after class.
CORRECT: Let's meet each other after class.

INCORRECT: It is considered cheating when students help each the other one on tests or quizzes.
CORRECT: It is considered cheating when students help each other on tests or quizzes.

NCORRECT: Jack and Sandra aren't dating one to the other any more.
CORRECT: Jack and Sandra aren't dating each other any more.

NCORRECT: They will never find each another at this crowded airport.
CORRECT: They will never find each other at this crowded airport.

EXERCISES

Part A: Choose the correct answer.

Business partners can usually sell their mutually owned property without consulting _________ unless they have agreed to a separate contract.
(A) other
(B) other one
(C) one the other
(D) each other

Part B: Choose the incorrect word or phrase and correct it.

The twinkling lights of the firefly are (A) signals so that (B) the male and female of the species can find (C) each to the other (D).

CUMULATIVE REVIEW EXERCISE FOR PRONOUNS

DIRECTIONS: Some of the sentences in this exercise are correct. Some are incorrect. First, find the correct sentences, and mark them with a check (√). Then find the incorrect sentences, and correct them. Check your answers using the key on pages 530–531.

1. College students like to entertain themselves by playing Frisbee, a game of catch played with a plastic disk instead of a ball.
2. The final member of the Bach family, Dr. Otto Bach, died in 1893, taking with he the musical genius that had entertained Germany for two centuries.
3. When recessive genes combine with each the other one, a child with blue eyes can be born to parents both of whom have brown eyes.
4. Almost all of the people who ultimately commit suicide have made a previous unsuccessful attempt to kill themselves or have threatened to do so.
5. Officials at a college or university must see a student's transcripts and financial guarantees prior to them issuing him or her a form I-20.
6. Through elected officials, a representative democracy includes citizens like you and I in the decision-making process.
7. It was her, Anne Sullivan, who stayed with Helen Keller for fifty years, teaching and encouraging her student.

8. To appreciate what the hybrid corn breeder does, it is necessary to understand how corn reproduces its.

9. Most foreign students realize that it is important for they to buy health insurance while they are living in the United States, because hospital costs are very high.

10. Top management in a firm is usually interpreted to mean the president and the vice-presidents that report to him or her.

11. The barnacle produces glue and attaches itself to ship bottoms and other places.

12. Peers are people of the same general age and educational level with whom an individual associates.

13. When an acid and a base neutralize one the other, the hydrogen from the acid and the oxygen from the base join to form water.

14. About two thirds of the world is inhabited by people which are severely undernourished.

15. In order for a caller to charge a call from another location to his home telephone number, the operator insists on him using a credit card or waiting until someone at the home number can verify that charges will be paid.

Problems with Nouns

You have probably learned that "a noun is the name of a person, place, or thing." Nouns perform several functions in English, but "naming" is clearly the most important.

There are two basic classifications of nouns in English. In some grammar books, they are called *count nouns* and *noncount nouns.* In other grammar books, they are called *count nouns* and *mass nouns.* In still other grammar books, they are called *countable* and *uncountable* nouns.

All of these names are very confusing because, of course, everything can be counted. The problem is *how* to count it. And, in that respect, the two classifications of nouns are very different.

Count or countable nouns have both singular and plural forms. They are used in agreement with singular or plural verbs. In contrast, mass or noncount, uncountable nouns have only one form. They are used in agreement with singular verbs.

Often count or countable nouns are individual persons, places, or things that can be seen and counted individually. Often mass, noncount, or uncountable nouns are substances and ideas that are shapeless by nature and cannot be seen and counted individually.

But it is not always logic that determines whether a noun is count or noncount. Sometimes it is simply a grammatical convention—that is, a category that people agree to use in their language. Both beans and rice have small parts that would be difficult but not impossible to count. But beans is considered a count noun and rice is considered a noncount noun. Why? Because it is a grammatical convention.

Count Nouns

Remember that *count nouns* have both singular and plural forms. Plural numbers can precede *count nouns* but not *noncount* nouns.

There are several categories of *count nouns* that can help you organize your study. Some of them are listed here.

1. Names of persons, their relationships, and their occupations:
   one boy *two boys*
   one friend *two friends*
   one student *two students*

2. Names of animals, plants, insects:
   one dog *two dogs*
   one flower *two flowers*
   one bee *two bees*

3. Names of things with a definite, individual shape:
   one car *two cars*
   one house *two houses*
   one room *two rooms*

4. Units of measurement:
   one inch *two inches*
   one pound *two pounds*
   one degree *two degrees*

5. Units of classification in society:
   one family *two families*
   one country *two countries*
   one language *two languages*

6. Containers of noncount solids, liquids, pastes, and gases:
   one bottle *two bottles*
   one jar *two jars*
   one tube *two tubes*

7. A limited number of abstract concepts:
   one idea *two ideas*
   one invention *two inventions*
   one plan *two plans*

Number (plural)	Noun (count-plural)
sixty	years

Avoid using a singular *count noun* with a plural number.

EXAMPLES

INCORRECT: We have twenty dollar left.
CORRECT: We have twenty dollars left.

INCORRECT: I hope that I can lose about five pound before summer.
CORRECT: I hope that I can lose about five pounds before summer.

INCORRECT: Several of the people in this class speak three or four language.
CORRECT: Several of the people in this class speak three or four languages.

INCORRECT: The temperature has risen ten degree in two hours.
CORRECT: The temperature has risen ten degrees in two hours.

INCORRECT: The teacher has ordered two book, but they aren't in at the bookstore.
CORRECT: The teacher has ordered two books, but they aren't in at the bookstore.

EXERCISES

Part A: Choose the correct answer.

A desert receives less than twenty-five _________ of rainfall every year.
(A) centimeter
(B) a centimeter
(C) centimeters
(D) of centimeters

Part B: Choose the incorrect word or phrase and correct it.

In 1950 (A) it was naively (B) predicted that eight or ten computer (C) would be sufficient to handle (D) all of the scientific and business needs in the United States.

Noncount Nouns

Remember that *noncount* nouns have only one form. They are used in agreement with singular verbs. The word *the* does not precede them.

There are categories of *noncount* nouns that can help you organize your study. Some of them are listed here.

1. Food staples that can be purchased in various forms:
   bread
   meat
   butter
2. Construction materials that can change shape, depending on what is made:
   wood
   iron
   grass

3. Liquids that can change shape, depending on the shape of the container:
   oil
   tea
   milk

4. Natural substances that can change shape, depending on natural laws:
   steam, water, ice
   smoke, ashes
   oxygen

5. Substances with many small parts:
   rice
   sand
   sugar

6. Groups of things that have different sizes and shapes:
   clothing *(a coat, a shirt, a sock)*
   furniture *(a table, a chair, a bed)*
   luggage *(a suitcase, a trunk, a box)*

7. Languages:
   Arabic
   Japanese
   Spanish

8. Abstract concepts, often with endings *-ness, -ance, -ence, -ity:*
   beauty
   ignorance
   peace

9. Most *-ing* forms:
   learning
   shopping
   working

noun (noncount)	verb (singular)	
Friendship	is	important

Avoid using *the* before a *noncount* noun. Avoid using a plural verb with a noncount noun.

Examples

INCORRECT: The happiness means different things to different people.
CORRECT: Happiness means different things to different people.

INCORRECT: Toshi speaks the Japanese at home.
CORRECT: Toshi speaks Japanese at home.

INCORRECT: Bread are expensive in the grocery store on the corner.
CORRECT: Bread is expensive in the grocery store on the corner.

INCORRECT: I like my tea with the milk.
CORRECT: I like my tea with milk.

INCORRECT: If you open the door, airs will circulate better.
CORRECT: If you open the door, air will circulate better.

EXERCISES

Part A: Choose the correct answer.

_________ at 212 degrees F. and freezes at 32 degrees F.

(A) Waters boils
(B) The water boils
(C) Water boils
(D) Waters boil

Part B: Choose the incorrect word or phrase and correct it.

<u>The religion</u> (A) attempts <u>to clarify</u> (B) <u>mankind's</u> (C) relationship with a <u>superhuman power.</u> (D)

Nouns with Count and Noncount Meanings

Remember that some nouns may be used as *count* or as *noncount* nouns depending on their meanings. Materials and abstract concepts are *noncount* nouns, but they may be used as *count* nouns to express specific meanings.

Count noun	Specific meaning	Noncount noun	General meaning
an agreement agreements	an occasion or a document	agreement	abstract concept all agreements
a bone bones	a part of a skeleton	bone	construction material
a business businesses	a company	business	abstract concept all business transactions
a cloth cloths	a piece of cloth	cloth	construction material
a decision decisions	an occasion	decision	abstract concept all decisions
an education educations	a specific person's	education	abstract concept all education
a fire fires	an event	fire	material
a glass glasses	a container	glass	construction material

a history histories	a historical account	history	abstract concept all history
an honor honors	an occasion or an award	honor	abstract concept all honor
a language languages	a specific variety	language	abstract concept all languages
a life lives	a specific person's	life	abstract concept all life
a light lights	a lamp	light	the absence of darkness
a noise noises	a specific sound	noise	abstract concept all sounds
a pain pains	a specific occasion	pain	abstract concept all pain
a paper papers	a document or sheet	paper	construction material
a pleasure pleasures	a specific occasion	pleasure	abstract concept all pleasure
a silence silences	a specific occasion	silence	abstract concept all silence
a space spaces	a blank	space	the universe
a stone stones	a small rock	stone	construction material
a success successes	an achievement	success	abstract concept all success
a thought thoughts	an idea	thought	abstract concept all thought
a time times	a historical period or moment	time	abstract concept all time
a war wars	a specific war	war	the general act of war all wars
a work works	an artistic creation	work	employment abstract concept all work

	a document	
I have	a paper	due Monday

	construction material	
Let's use	paper	to make the present

Avoid using *count* nouns with specific meanings to express the general meanings of *noncount* nouns.

EXAMPLES

INCORRECT: Dr. Bradley will receive special honor at the graduation.
CORRECT: Dr. Bradley will receive a special honor at the graduation. (an award)

INCORRECT: She needs to find a work.
CORRECT: She needs to find work. (employment)

INCORRECT: My neighbor dislikes a noise.
CORRECT: My neighbor dislikes noise. (all sounds)

INCORRECT: We need glass for the juice.
CORRECT: We need a glass for the juice.
or
We need glasses for the juice. (containers)

INCORRECT: A war is as old as mankind.
CORRECT: War is as old as mankind. (the act of war)

EXERCISES

Part A: Choose the correct answer.

It is generally believed that an M.B.A. degree is good preparation for a career in ________.

(A) a business
(B) business
(C) businesses
(D) one business

Part B: Choose the incorrect word or phrase and correct it.

A space is the last frontier for man to conquer.
(A) (B) (C) (D)

Count and Noncount Nouns with Similar Meanings

Remember that there are pairs of nouns with similar meanings, but one is a *count* noun and the other is a *noncount* noun.

Count noun	Noncount noun
a climate climates	weather
a laugh laughs	laughter
a human being human beings	humanity
a job jobs	work
a machine machines	machinery
a man men	mankind; man
a person persons	people
a snowflake snowflakes	snow
a sunbeam sunbeams	sunlight; sunshine
a traffic jam traffic jams	traffic

	a	noun (count)	
The shape of	a	snowflake	is unique

Avoid using *a* with a *noncount* noun instead of a singular *count* noun.

EXAMPLES

INCORRECT: California has a good weather.
CORRECT: California has good weather.
or
California has a good climate.

INCORRECT: A laughter is the best medicine.
CORRECT: Laughter is the best medicine.
or
A laugh is the best medicine.

INCORRECT: We are late because we got stuck in a traffic.
CORRECT: We are late because we got stuck in traffic.
or
We are late because we got stuck in a traffic jam.

INCORRECT: A machinery in the factory needs to be fixed.
CORRECT: Machinery in the factory needs to be fixed.
or
A machine in the factory needs to be fixed.

INCORRECT: We are supposed to have a sunshine this weekend.
CORRECT: We are supposed to have sunshine this weekend.

EXERCISES

Part A: Choose the correct answer.

Unemployment compensation is money to support an unemployed person while he or she is lookir for __________.

(A) job
(B) a job
(C) works
(D) a work

Part B: Choose the incorrect word or phrase and correct it.

It is believed that a people (A) could live (B) on Mars (C) with little life support because the atmosphere is sim ilar to that (D) of Earth.

Noncount Nouns that Are Count Nouns in Other Languages

Remember, many nouns that are *count* nouns in other languages may be *noncount* nouns English. Some of the most troublesome have been listed for you on the following page.

advice	*homework*	*money*	*poetry*
anger	*ignorance*	*music*	*poverty*
courage	*information*	*news*	*progress*
damage	*knowledge*	*patience*	
equipment	*leisure*	*permission*	
fun	*luck*		

	Ø	Noun (noncount)
Did you do your		homework?

Avoid using *a* or *an* before *noncount* nouns.

EXAMPLES

INCORRECT: Do you have an information about it?
CORRECT: Do you have <u>information</u> about it?

INCORRECT: Counselors are available to give you an advice before you register for your classes.
CORRECT: Counselors are available to give you <u>advice</u> before you register for your classes.

INCORRECT: George had a good luck when he first came to State University.
CORRECT: George had good <u>luck</u> when he first came to State University.

INCORRECT: A news was released about the hostages.
CORRECT: <u>News</u> was released about the hostages.

INCORRECT: Did you get a permission to take the placement test?
CORRECT: Did you get <u>permission</u> to take the placement test?

EXERCISES

Part A: Choose the correct answer.

Fire-resistant materials are used to retard ________ of modern aircraft in case of accidents.

(A) a damage to the passenger cabin
(B) that damages to the passenger cabin
(C) damage to the passenger cabin
(D) passenger cabin's damages

Part B: Choose the incorrect word or phrase and correct it.

<u>A progress</u> (A) <u>has been made</u> (B) toward <u>finding</u> (C) <u>a cure</u> (D) for AIDS.

Singular and Plural Expressions of Noncount Nouns

Remember that the following singular and plural expressions are idiomatic:

a piece of advice	*two pieces of advice*
a piece of bread	*two pieces of bread*
a piece of equipment	*two pieces of equipment*
a piece of furniture	*two pieces of furniture*
a piece of information	*two pieces of information*
a piece of jewelry	*two pieces of jewelry*
a piece of luggage	*two pieces of luggage*
a piece of mail	*two pieces of mail*
a piece of music	*two pieces of music*
a piece of news	*two pieces of news*
a piece of toast	*two pieces of toast*
a loaf of bread	*two loaves of bread*
a slice of bread	*two slices of bread*
an ear of corn	*two ears of corn*
a bar of soap	*two bars of soap*
a bolt of lightning	*two bolts of lightning*
a clap of thunder	*two claps of thunder*
a gust of wind	*two gusts of wind*

	a	singular	of	noun (noncount)
A folk song is	a	piece	of	popular music

	number	plural	of	noun (noncount)
I ordered	twelve	bars	of	soap

Avoid using the noncount noun without the singular or plural idiom to express a singular or plural.

EXAMPLES

INCORRECT: A mail travels faster when the zip code is indicated on the envelope.
CORRECT: A piece of mail travels faster when the zip code is indicated on the envelope.

INCORRECT: There is a limit of two carry-on luggages for each passenger.
CORRECT: There is a limit of two pieces of carry-on luggage for each passenger.

INCORRECT: Each furniture in this display is on sale for half price.
CORRECT: Each piece of furniture in this display is on sale for half price.

INCORRECT: I'd like a steak, a salad, and a corn's ear with butter.
CORRECT: I'd like a steak, a salad, and an ear of corn with butter.

INCORRECT: The Engineering Department purchased a new equipment to simulate conditions in outer space.

CORRECT: The Engineering Department purchased a new piece of equipment to simulate conditions in outer space.

EXERCISES

Part A: Choose the correct answer.

Hybrids have one more _________ per plant than the other varieties.

(A) corns
(B) ear of corn
(C) corn ears
(D) corn's ears

Part B: Choose the incorrect word or phrase and correct it.

A few tiles on *Skylab* were the only equipments that failed to perform well in outer space.
(A) (B) (C) (D)

Classifications—*Kind* and *Type*

Remember that *kind* and *type* express classification.

	kinds types	of	noun (plural count) (noncount)
Cable TV has many different Dr. Parker gives several	kinds types	of of	shows homework

one	kind type	of	noun (singular count) (noncount)	
One One	kind type	of of	show homework	is news is a lab report

Avoid using *kind of* and *type of* with a plural count noun. Avoid using *kind* and *type* without *of*.

EXAMPLES

INCORRECT: There are four kind of Coke now.

CORRECT: There are four kinds of Coke now.

INCORRECT: We saw several kind of birds at the wildlife preserve.

CORRECT: We saw several kinds of birds at the wildlife preserve.

INCORRECT: This exam has two types problems.
CORRECT: This exam has <u>two types of problems</u>.

INCORRECT: Are you looking for a special kinds of car?
CORRECT: Are you looking for <u>a special kind of car</u>?

INCORRECT: I only know how to run one type a computer program.
CORRECT: I only know how to run <u>one type of computer program</u>.

EXERCISES

Part A: Choose the correct answer.

According to estimates by some botanists, there are __________ of plants.
(A) seven thousand type
(B) seven thousand types
(C) type of seven thousand
(D) types seven thousand

Part B: Choose the incorrect word or phrase and correct it.

One <u>kinds of tool</u> (A) that <u>was</u> (B) popular during the Stone Age <u>was</u> (C) a flake, used <u>for cutting</u> (D) and scraping

Infinitive and *-ing* Subjects

Remember that either an infinitive or an *-ing* form may be used as the subject of a sentence or clause.

S (infinitive)	V	
To read a foreign language	is	even more difficult

S (*-ing*)	V	
Reading quickly and well	requires	practice

Avoid using a verb word instead of an infinitive or an *-ing* form in the subject. Avoid using *to* with a *-ing* form.

EXAMPLES

INCORRECT: To working provides people with personal satisfaction as well as money.
CORRECT: <u>To work</u> provides people with personal satisfaction as well as money.
or
<u>Working</u> provides people with personal satisfaction as well as money.

INCORRECT: The sneeze spreads germs.
CORRECT: To sneeze spreads germs.
or
Sneezing spreads germs.

INCORRECT: Shoplift is considered a serious crime.
CORRECT: To shoplift is considered a serious crime.
or
Shoplifting is considered a serious crime.

INCORRECT: The rest in the afternoon is a custom in many countries.
CORRECT: To rest in the afternoon is a custom in many countries.
or
Resting in the afternoon is a custom in many countries.

INCORRECT: To exercising makes most people feel better.
CORRECT: To exercise makes most people feel better.
or
Exercising makes most people feel better.

EXERCISES

Part A: Choose the correct answer.

_________ trees is a custom that many people engage in to celebrate Arbor Day.
(A) The plant
(B) Plant
(C) Planting
(D) To planting

Part B: Choose the incorrect word or phrase and correct it.

Spell (A) correctly (B) is easy with the aid of a number of word processing (C) programs for personal computers (D).

Qualifying Phrases with *-ing* Nouns

Remember that an *-ing* form may be used as a noun. In some grammar books, this *-ing* form is called a gerund. Remember that *-ing* forms are usually noncount nouns and that noncount nouns are not preceded by *the* unless followed by a qualifying phrase.

We have already classified most *-ing* forms as *noncount* nouns, but there is one pattern in which *the* is used with a *noncount -ing* noun. When a prepositional phrase qualifies the noun, that is, adds specific information, *the* may be used with an *-ing* noun subject.

the	*-ing*	qualifying phrase of noun	
The	reading	of technical material	requires knowledge of technical terms

EXAMPLES

INCORRECT: Correcting of errors in a language class can be embarrassing.
CORRECT: The correcting of errors in a language class can be embarrassing.

INCORRECT: Writing of letters is an art.
CORRECT: The writing of letters is an art.

INCORRECT: Winning of prizes is not as important as playing well.
CORRECT: The winning of prizes is not as important as playing well.

INCORRECT: Sending of electronic mail (e-mail) is now common.
CORRECT: The sending of electronic mail (e-mail) is now common.

INCORRECT: Singing of Christmas carols is an old tradition.
CORRECT: The singing of Christmas carols is an old tradition.

EXERCISES

Part A: Choose the correct answer.

_________ is not a new idea.

(A) The planning of cities
(B) Cities to plan them
(C) Plan cities
(D) To planning cities

Part B: Choose the incorrect word or phrase and correct it.

Writing of (A) instructions for (B) computers is called (C) computer programming (D).

Nominal *That* Clause

Remember that sometimes the subject of a verb is a single noun. Other times it is a long noun phrase or a long noun clause.

One example of a long noun clause is the *nominal that* clause. Like all clauses, the *nominal that* clause has a subject and verb. The *nominal that* clause functions as the main subject of the main verb which follows it.

Nominal *that* clause S	V	
That vitamin C prevents colds	is	well known

EXAMPLES

INCORRECT: That it is that she has known him for a long time influenced her decision.
CORRECT: That she has known him for a long time influenced her decision.

INCORRECT: It is that we need to move is sure.
CORRECT: That we need to move is sure.

INCORRECT: Is likely that the library is closed.
CORRECT: That the library is closed is likely.

INCORRECT: She will win is almost certain.
CORRECT: That she will win is almost certain.

INCORRECT: That is not fair seems obvious.
CORRECT: That it is not fair seems obvious.

EXERCISES

Part A: Choose the correct answer.

_________ migrate long distances is well documented.

(A) That it is birds
(B) That birds
(C) Birds that
(D) It is that birds

Part B: Choose the incorrect word or phrase and correct it.

That it is (A) the moon influences only one kind (B) of tide is not generally (C) known (D).

CUMULATIVE REVIEW EXERCISE FOR NOUNS

DIRECTIONS: Some of the sentences in this exercise are correct. Some are incorrect. First, find the correct sentences, and mark them with a check (√). Then find the incorrect sentences, and correct them. Check your answers using the key on pages 531–532.

1. Tuition at state universities has risen by one hundred fifty dollar.
2. Although polyester was very popular and is still used in making clothing, cloths made of natural fibers is more fashionable today.
3. The peace in the world is the goal of the United Nations.
4. Dam is a wall constructed across a valley to enclose an area in which water is stored.
5. The light travels in a straight line.
6. To hitchhike in the United States is very dangerous.

7. The ptarmigan, like a large number of Arctic animal, is white in winter and brown in summer.

8. Even children in elementary school are assigned homeworks.

9. Spirituals were influenced by a music from the African coast.

10. The stare at a computer screen for long periods of time can cause severe eyestrain.

11. There are two kind of major joints in the body of a vertebrate, called the hinge joint and the ball and socket joint.

12. That an earthquake of magnitude eight on the Richter Scale occurs once every five or ten years.

13. Art of colonial America was very functional, consisting mainly of useful objects such as furniture and household utensils.

14. To producing one ton of coal it may be necessary to strip as much as thirty tons of rock.

15. A mail that is postmarked on Monday before noon and sent express can be delivered the next day anywhere in the United States.

Problems with Adjectives

Adjectives and adjective phrases describe nouns. They may be used to describe *quantity* (number or amount); *sufficiency* (number or amount needed); *consecutive order* (order in a sequence); *quality* (appearance); and *emphasis* (importance or force.)

Most adjectives and adjective phrases have only one form in English. They do not change forms to agree with the nouns they describe.

Problems with Determiners

Determiners are a special kind of adjective. Like other adjectives, determiners describe nouns. But unlike other adjectives, determiners must agree with the nouns they describe. In other words, you must know whether the noun is a singular count noun, a plural count noun, or a noncount noun before you can choose the correct determiner. The noun *determines* which adjective form you use.

Determiners—*A* and *An*

Remember that both *a* and *an* mean *one.* They are used before singular count nouns. *A* is used before words that begin with a consonant sound. *An* is used before words that begin with a vowel sound.

A	consonant sound	
A	*f*oreign student	must have an I-20 form

An	vowel sound	
An	*i*nternational student	must have an I-20 form

Avoid confusing vowel and consonant spellings with vowel and consonant sounds. *U* is a vowel spelling, but it has the consonant sound *Y* in words like *use, universal, usual*, etc. *H* is a consonant spelling that has a vowel sound in words like *hour* and *honor*, but not in words like *history* and *horror.*

EXAMPLES

INCORRECT: It is a big decision to choose an university.
CORRECT: It is a big decision to choose a university.

INCORRECT: Do you have an use for this empty box?
CORRECT: Do you have a use for this empty box?

INCORRECT: Chemistry 100H is a honors section.
CORRECT: Chemistry 100H is an honors section.

INCORRECT: Let's just wait an year or two before we get married.
CORRECT: Let's just wait a year or two before we get married.

INCORRECT: I'll call you back in a hour.
CORRECT: I'll call you back in an hour.

EXERCISES

Part A: Choose the correct answer.

Sunspots are known to cause ________ enormous increase in the intensity of the sun's electromagnetic radiation.

(A) an
(B) a
(C) some
(D) one

Part B: Choose the incorrect word or phrase and correct it.

Although almost all insects have six legs, a immature insect may not have any.
(A) almost all (B) have (C) a (D) may not have any

Noncount Nouns with Qualifying Phrases—*The*

Remember, *the* is used with count nouns. You have also learned that *the* can be used before an *-ing* noun that is followed by a qualifying phrase.

In addition, *the* can be used before a noncount noun with a qualifying phrase.

The	noncount noun	Qualifying Phrase	
The	art	of the Middle Ages	is on display

EXAMPLES

INCORRECT: Poetry of Carl Sandburg is being read at the student union on Friday.
CORRECT: The poetry of Carl Sandburg is being read at the student union on Friday.

INCORRECT: Poverty of people in the rural areas is not as visible as that of people in the city.
CORRECT: The poverty of people in the rural areas is not as visible as that of people in the city.

INCORRECT: Science of genetic engineering is not very old.
CORRECT: The science of genetic engineering is not very old.

INCORRECT: History of this area is interesting.
CORRECT: The history of this area is interesting.

INCORRECT: Work of many people made the project a success.
CORRECT: The work of many people made the project a success.

EXERCISES

Part A: Choose the correct answer.

_________ of Country-Western singers may be related to old English ballads.
(A) The music
(B) Music
(C) Their music
(D) Musics

Part B: Choose the incorrect word or phrase and correct it.

Philosophy (A) of the ancient Greeks has been preserved (B) in the scholarly writing (C) of Western civilization (D).

Ø Meaning *All*

Remember that no article (Ø) before a noncount or a plural count noun has the same meaning as *all*.

all Ø	noun (noncount)	verb (singular)	
All	art Art	is is	interesting interesting

all Ø	noun (count-plural)	verb (plural)	
All	trees Trees	prevent prevent	erosion erosion

Avoid using *the* before the noun to express *all*.

EXAMPLES

INCORRECT: The dormitories are noisy.
CORRECT: Dormitories are noisy.
(all dormitories)

INCORRECT: The convenience stores have high prices.
CORRECT: Convenience stores have high prices.
(all convenience stores)

INCORRECT: I like the music.
CORRECT: I like music.
(all music)

INCORRECT: The mathematics is easy for me.
CORRECT: Mathematics is easy for me.
(all mathematics)

INCORRECT: Professor Collins is an expert in the microbiology.
CORRECT: Professor Collins is an expert in microbiology.
(all microbiology)

EXERCISES

Part A: Choose the correct answer.

_________ is an ancient source of energy.

(A) The wind
(B) Winds
(C) Wind
(D) A wind

Part B: Choose the incorrect word or phrase and correct it.

The soil (A) is (B) composed (C) of a mixture of organic matter called (D) humus and inorganic matter derived from rocks.

No Meaning *Not Any*

Remember that *no* means *not any.* It may be used with a singular or plural count noun or with a non count noun.

no	noun (count singular) noun (count plural)	verb (singular) verb (plural)
No No	tree trees	grows above the tree line grow above the tree line

no	noun (noncount)	verb (singular)	
No	art	is	on display today

Avoid using the negatives *not* or *none* instead of *no.* Avoid using a singular verb with a plural count noun.

Examples

INCORRECT: There is not reason to worry.
CORRECT: There is no reason to worry.

INCORRECT: None news is good news.
CORRECT: No news is good news.

INCORRECT: We have not a file under the name Wagner.
CORRECT: We have no file under the name Wagner.

INCORRECT: None of cheating will be tolerated.
CORRECT: No cheating will be tolerated.

INCORRECT: Bill told me that he has none friends.
CORRECT: Bill told me that he has no friends.

EXERCISES

Part A: Choose the correct answer.

At Woolworth's first five-and-ten-cent store, __________ more than a dime.

(A) neither items cost
(B) items not cost
(C) items none costing
(D) no item cost

Part B: Choose the incorrect word or phrase and correct it.

Some religions <u>have</u> (A) <u>none</u> (B) deity but <u>are</u> (C) philosophies that function <u>instead of religions</u> (D).

PROBLEM 66

One of the and *Some of the*

Remember that *one* means one of a group. *Some* means several of a group.

one of the	noun (count plural)	verb (singular)	
One of the	trees	is	dead

some of the	noun (count plural)	verb (plural)	
Some of the	trees	are	dead

some of the	noun (noncount)	verb (singular)	
Some of the	art	is	in the museum

Avoid using *one of the* or *some of the* with a singular count noun or *one of the* with a noncount noun. Avoid using a plural verb with *one of the.*

EXAMPLES

INCORRECT: Some of the parking space at the back are empty.
CORRECT: <u>Some of the</u> <u>parking spaces</u> at the back <u>are</u> empty.

INCORRECT: One of the major field of study that Laura is considering is nursing.
CORRECT: <u>One of the</u> <u>major fields</u> of study that Laura is considering <u>is</u> nursing.

INCORRECT: One of my friends are in the hospital.
CORRECT: <u>One of my</u> <u>friends</u> <u>is</u> in the hospital.

INCORRECT: You should save some of the moneys.
CORRECT: You should save <u>some of the</u> <u>money</u>.

INCORRECT: One of the best reason to eat vegetables is to add fiber to your diet.
CORRECT: One of the best reasons to eat vegetables is to add fiber to your diet.

EXERCISES

Part A: Choose the correct answer.

One of __________ of the late Middle Ages was Saint Thomas Aquinas, a scholar who studied under Albertus Magnus.

(A) the thinkers who was great
(B) the great thinker
(C) the greatest thinkers
(D) who thought greatly

Part B: Choose the incorrect word or phrase and correct it.

One of the primary cause (A) of accidents in coal mines (B) is (C) the accumulation of gas (D).

Few and *Little*

Remember that *few* and *little* have the same meaning, but *few* is used before plural count nouns and *little* is used before noncount nouns.

few	noun (count)	
Few	reference books	may be checked out

Avoid using a noncount noun instead of a count noun after *few*.

	little	noun (noncount)
Before he came to the U.S., he had done	little	traveling

Avoid using a count noun instead of a noncount noun after *little*.

EXAMPLES

INCORRECT: Professor Stone keeps little chairs in his office because he doesn't have room for many.
CORRECT: Professor Stone keeps few chairs in his office because he doesn't have room for many.

INCORRECT: John has very little friends.
CORRECT: John has very few friends.

INCORRECT: There is few time to waste.
CORRECT: There is little time to waste.

INCORRECT: My brother used to help me a lot, but now he gives me few advice.
CORRECT: My brother used to help me a lot, but now he gives me <u>little</u> <u>advice</u>.

INCORRECT: He had to balance his account very carefully because he had few money.
CORRECT: He had to balance his account very carefully because he had <u>little</u> <u>money</u>.

EXERCISES

Part A: Choose the correct answer.

Although southern California is densely populated, __________ live in the northern part of the state.

(A) a little people
(B) a few the people
(C) few people
(D) a little of people

Part B: Choose the incorrect word or phrase and correct it.

Unless <u>one</u> (A) subscribes to a large metropolitan newspaper <u>such as</u> (B) the *Wall Street Journal*, or the *Washington Post*, <u>one</u> (C) will find very <u>few news</u> (D) from abroad.

Much and *Many*

Remember that *many* and *much* have the same meaning, but *many* is used before plural count nouns and *much* is used before noncount nouns.

	many	noun (count—plural)	
There are	many	television programs	for children on Saturday

Avoid using a noncount noun instead of a plural count noun after *many*.

	much	noun (noncount)
We don't have	much	information

Avoid using a count noun instead of a noncount noun after *much*.

EXAMPLES

INCORRECT: The letter was short because there wasn't many news.
CORRECT: The letter was short because there wasn't <u>much</u> <u>news</u>.

INCORRECT: Peter and Carol don't have much children.
CORRECT: Peter and Carol don't have <u>many</u> <u>children</u>.

INCORRECT: How much years have you been living in Texas?
CORRECT: How <u>many years</u> have you been living in Texas?

INCORRECT: He always has much problems with his teeth.
CORRECT: He always has <u>many problems</u> with his teeth.

INCORRECT: I think that there is too many violence on TV.
CORRECT: I think that there is too <u>much violence</u> on TV.

EXERCISES

Part A: Choose the correct answer.

Although the Ojibwa Indians fought frequently with the Sioux, they didn't have ______ with early white settlers.
(A) much contact
(B) lots contact
(C) many contact
(D) large contact

Part B: Choose the incorrect word or phrase and correct it.

<u>Many</u> (A) heavy work that was once <u>done</u> (B) <u>by hand</u> (C) can now be done more <u>easily</u> (D) with the help of compressed air.

A Little and *Little* *A Few* and *Few*

Remember this story in English:

There were two men. Each man had half a cup of happiness. One man said, "How sad! I have *little* happiness." The other man said, "How wonderful! I have *a little* happiness." The difference between *little* and *a little* is the point of view. *Little* or *few* means not a lot. *A little* or *a few* means some.

	a little little	noun (noncount)
We have We have	a little little	time time

	a few few	noun (count—plural)
We made We made	a few few	mistakes mistakes

EXAMPLES

INCORRECT: Give me little butter, please.
CORRECT: Give me a little butter, please.
(some)

INCORRECT: We have a little news about the plane crash.
CORRECT: We have little news about the plane crash.
(not much)

INCORRECT: There are few tickets left for the concert.
CORRECT: There are a few tickets left for the concert.
(some)

INCORRECT: A few people in my apartment building are friendly.
CORRECT: Few people in my apartment building are friendly.
(not many)

INCORRECT: She speaks a little French.
CORRECT: She speaks little French.
(not much)

Note: All of the sentences in this problem are grammatically correct, but only the sentences marked correct express the meanings in parentheses.

EXERCISES

Part A: Choose the correct answer.

__________ is currently available to researchers and physicians who study and treat acromegaly, a glandular disorder characterized by enlargement and obesity.

(A) The little information
(B) Few information
(C) Little information
(D) A few information

Part B: Choose the incorrect word or phrase and correct it.

When there is (A) a few (B) money remaining after all expenses have been paid (C), we say that a small economic surplus or profit has been created (D).

Only a Few and *Only a Little*

Remember that *only a few* and *only a little* have the same meaning, but *only a few* is used before a plural count noun and *only a little* is used before a noncount noun.

only	a few	noun (count—plural)	
Only	a few	dollars	have been budgeted for supplies

Avoid using *few* instead of *a few* after *only*.

	only	a little	noun (noncount)	
We have	only	a little	homework	for Monday

Avoid using *little* instead of *a little* after *only*.

EXAMPLES

INCORRECT: Only a little students are lazy.
CORRECT: Only a few students are lazy.

INCORRECT: Tom took only few pictures.
CORRECT: Tom took only a few pictures.

INCORRECT: We will need only a few food for the picnic.
CORRECT: We will need only a little food for the picnic.

INCORRECT: Only few people were at the reception.
CORRECT: Only a few people were at the reception.

INCORRECT: The advisor makes only few exceptions to the rules regarding prerequisites.
CORRECT: The advisor makes only a few exceptions to the rules regarding prerequisites.

EXERCISES

Part A: Choose the correct answer.

__________ can be grown on arid land.
(A) Only a few crops
(B) Only few crop
(C) Only a little crops
(D) Only little crop

Part B: Choose the incorrect word or phrase and correct it.

Only a little (A) early scientists, among (B) them (C) Bacon, Copernicus, and Bruno, believed that the principles (D) underlying the physical world could be discovered and understood through careful observation and analysis.

A Large (Small) Number of and a Large (Small) Amount of

Remember that *a large (small) number of* and *a large (small) amount of* have the same meaning, but *a large (small) number of* is used before a plural count noun and *a large (small) amount of* is used before a noncount noun.

A large/small number of	noun (count—plural)	
A large number of	students	from other countries attend State University

A large/small amount of	noun (noncount)	
A small amount of	rain	is expected tomorrow

Avoid using *number* with noncount nouns and *amount* with count nouns.

EXAMPLES

INCORRECT: You will just need a small number of clothing to go to college because the lifestyle is very informal.
CORRECT: You will just need a small amount of clothing to go to college because the lifestyle is very informal.

INCORRECT: There are a small amount of Chinese restaurants in the city.
CORRECT: There are a small number of Chinese restaurants in the city.

INCORRECT: We don't have time for a large amount of interruptions.
CORRECT: We don't have time for a large number of interruptions.

INCORRECT: The lab has a large number of equipment.
CORRECT: The lab has a large amount of equipment.

INCORRECT: A small amount of families own most of the land here.
CORRECT: A small number of families own most of the land here.

EXERCISES

Part A: Choose the correct answer.

Only __________ of the breeds of cattle have been brought to the United States.
(A) a small amount
(B) a little amount
(C) a small number
(D) a little number

Part B: Choose the incorrect word or phrase and correct it.

The amount (A) of books in the Library of Congress (B) is (C) more than (D) 58 million volumes.

PROBLEM 72

Almost All of the and Most of the

Remember that *almost all of the* and *most of the* mean all except a few, but *almost all of the* includes more.

almost all (of the) most (of the)	noun (count—plural)	verb (plural)	
Almost all (of the) Most (of the)	trees in our yard trees	are are	oaks oaks

almost all (of the) most (of the)	noun (noncount)	verb (singular)
Almost all (of the) Most (of the)	art by R. C. Gorman art by R. C. Gorman	is expensive is expensive

Avoid using *almost* without *all* or *all of the.* Avoid using *most of* without *the.*

EXAMPLES

INCORRECT: Almost the states have a sales tax.
CORRECT: Almost all of the states have a sales tax.

or

Almost all states have a sales tax.

or

Most of the states have a sales tax.

or

Most states have a sales tax.

INCORRECT: Most of teachers at State University care about their students' progress.
CORRECT: Almost all of the teachers at State University care about their students' progress.

or

Almost all teachers at State University care about their students' progress.

or

Most of the teachers at State University care about their students' progress.

or

Most teachers at State University care about their students' progress.

INCORRECT: My cousin told me that most of people who won the lottery got only a few dollars, not the grand prize.
CORRECT: My cousin told me that almost all of the people who won the lottery got only a few dollars, not the grand prize.

or

My cousin told me that almost all people who won the lottery got only a few dollars, not the grand prize.

or

My cousin told me that most of the people who won the lottery got only a few dollars, not the grand prize.

or

My cousin told me that most people who won the lottery got only a few dollars, not the grand prize.

INCORRECT: Most the dictionaries have information about pronunciation.
CORRECT: Almost all of the dictionaries have information about pronunciation.

or

Almost all dictionaries have information about pronunciation.

or

Most of the dictionaries have information about pronunciation.

or

Most dictionaries have information about pronunciation.

INCORRECT: Is it true that most Americans watches TV every night?
CORRECT: It is true that almost all of the Americans watch TV every night?

or

Is it true that almost all Americans watch TV every night?

or

Is it true that most of the Americans watch TV every night?

or

Is it true that most Americans watch TV every night?

EXERCISES

Part A: Choose the correct answer.

__________ fuel that is used today is a chemical form of solar energy.

(A) Most of
(B) The most
(C) Most
(D) Almost the

Part B: Choose the incorrect word or phrase and correct it.

Almost (A) the plants known to us (B) are made up of a great many cells, (C) specialized to perform (D) different tasks.

PROBLEMS WITH OTHER ADJECTIVES

Besides determiners that express number and amount, there are adjectives and adjective-related structures that express *sufficiency*, *consecutive order*, *quality*, and *emphasis*.

Adjectives usually do not change to agree with the noun that they modify.

Sufficiency—*Enough* with Nouns

Remember that *enough* means sufficient. It can be used before or after a plural count noun or a noncount noun.

			noun (count—plural) noun (noncount)
We	have	enough	tickets
We	have	enough	time

		noun (count—plural) noun (noncount)	enough
We	have	tickets	enough
We	have	time	enough

Avoid using *as* and *the* with *enough*. Avoid using a singular count noun instead of a plural count noun.

EXAMPLES

INCORRECT: There aren't enough car for all of us to go.
CORRECT: There aren't enough cars for all of us to go.
or
There aren't cars enough for all of us to go.

INCORRECT: Without enough the sleep, you won't be able to do well on the examination.
CORRECT: Without enough sleep, you won't be able to do well on the examination.
or
Without sleep enough, you won't be able to do well on the examination.

INCORRECT: Do we have hamburgers enough as for the party?
CORRECT: Do we have enough hamburgers for the party?
or
Do we have hamburgers enough for the party?

CORRECT: Virginia doesn't have the enough information to make a decision.
CORRECT: Virginia doesn't have <u>enough</u> <u>information</u> to make a decision.

or

Virginia doesn't have <u>information</u> <u>enough</u> to make a decision.

CORRECT: I need to buy a lamp because I don't have enough the light in my room.
CORRECT: I need to buy a lamp because I don't have <u>enough</u> <u>light</u> in my room.

or

I need to buy a lamp because I don't have <u>light</u> <u>enough</u> in my room.

XERCISES

art A: Choose the correct answer.

When your body does not get ________, it cannot make the glucose it needs.
(A) enough food
(B) food as enough
(C) food enoughly
(D) enough the food

art B: Choose the incorrect word or phrase and correct it.

<u>As soon</u> (A) as the company has <u>as enough earnings</u> (B) <u>to make up for</u> (C) a bad year, the stockholders of cumulative preferred stock receive dividends for the bad year <u>as well</u> (D) as for the good year.

Sufficiency—*Enough* with Adjectives

Remember that *enough* with adjectives means sufficiently.

S	V	adjective	enough	infinitive	
It	is	warm	enough	to go	swimming

S	V	not	adjective	enough	infinitive	
It	is	not	warm	enough	to go	swimming

Avoid using *enough* before the adjective instead of after it. Avoid using *as* between *enough* and the nfinitive.

EXAMPLES

NCORRECT: Her little car isn't big enough as to seat more than two people comfortably.
CORRECT: Her little car isn't <u>big enough</u> to seat more than two people comfortably.

INCORRECT: That excuse isn't enough good.
CORRECT: That excuse isn't good enough.

INCORRECT: He should be as strong enough to get out of bed in a few days.
CORRECT: He should be strong enough to get out of bed in a few days.

INCORRECT: Billy isn't enough old to enlist in the army.
CORRECT: Billy isn't old enough to enlist in the army.

INCORRECT: His score on the exam was enough good to qualify him for a graduate program.
CORRECT: His score on the exam was good enough to qualify him for a graduate program.

EXERCISES

Part A: Choose the correct answer.

The definitions for "gram calories" or "calories" are ___________ for most engineering work.

(A) accurate as enough
(B) enough accurate
(C) accurate enough
(D) as accurate enough

Part B: Choose the incorrect word or phrase and correct it.

Most large corporations provide pension plans for their employees so that (A) they will be secure enough than (B) to live (C) comfortably (D) during their retirement.

Consecutive Order—*One, Another, the Other*

Remember that *one*, *another*, and *the other* are used before or instead of singular count nouns. When they are used before singular count nouns, they are adjectives. When they are used instead of singular count nouns, they are pronouns.

One, another, and *the other* organize three nouns consecutively. *One* and *the other* organize two nouns consecutively. *One* means the first one mentioned. *Another* means one more in addition to the first one mentioned. *The other* means the one remaining.

1 one	count noun (singular)		2 another	count noun (singular)	
One	movie	starts at five,	another	movie	starts at seven, and

3 the other	count noun (singular)	
the other	movie	starts at nine

1 one	count noun (singular)		2 another		3 the other	
One	bus	leaves at two,	another	at six, and	the other	at ten

EXAMPLES

INCORRECT: One of my roommates studies engineering, another studies business, and the another studies computer science.
CORRECT: One of my roommates studies engineering, another (roommate) studies business, and the other (roommate) studies computer science.

INCORRECT: One problem is finding an apartment, another is furnishing it, and other is getting the utilities turned on.
CORRECT: One problem is finding an apartment, another (problem) is furnishing it, and the other (problem) is getting the utilities turned on.

INCORRECT: Of the three busiest vacation areas in the United States, one is Disney World, one another is New York City, and the other is Washington, D.C.
CORRECT: Of the three busiest vacation areas in the United States, one (area) is Disney World, another (area) is New York City, and the other (area) is Washington, D.C.

INCORRECT: There are three major restaurant chains near the campus that specialize in fast-food hamburgers: one is McDonald's, another is Wendy's, and the another one is Burger King.
CORRECT: There are three major restaurant chains near the campus that specialize in fast-food hamburgers: one (restaurant) is McDonald's, another (restaurant) is Wendy's, and the other (restaurant) is Burger King.

INCORRECT: One English proficiency test is the TOEFL and other is the Michigan Test of English Language Proficiency.
CORRECT: One English proficiency test is the TOEFL and the other (test) is the Michigan Test of English Language Proficiency.

EXERCISES

Part A: Choose the correct answer.

There are three kinds of solar eclipses: one is total, another is annular, and ________.

(A) the another is partial
(B) the partial is other
(C) other is partial
(D) the other is partial

Part B: Choose the incorrect word or phrase and correct it.

One of the most popular major fields of study for foreign scholars (A) in the United States (B) is (C) business and the another (D) is engineering.

Consecutive Order—*Some, Other, the Other*
Some, Others, the Others (the Rest)

Remember that *some*, *other*, and *the other* are used before plural count nouns. They are adjectives.

1 Some	count noun (plural)		2 other	count noun (plural)	
Some	houses	are for rent,	other	houses	are for sale, and
3 the other the rest of the		count noun (plural)			
the other the rest of the		houses		are empty	

Some, *others*, and *the others* (*the rest*) are used instead of plural count nouns. They are pronouns.

1 Some	count noun (plural)		2 others	
Some Some	schools schools	are universities, are universities,	others others	are colleges, and are colleges, and
3 the others the rest				
the others the rest			are junior colleges are junior colleges	

Avoid using *another* instead of *other*. Avoid using *rest of* or *rest* instead of *the rest of the* or *the rest*.

Examples

INCORRECT: Some of these T-shirts are red, others are blue, and rest are white.
CORRECT: Some of these T-shirts are red, others are blue, and the rest are white.

INCORRECT: Some of our friends are from the Middle East, the others are from the Far East, and the rest are from Latin America.
CORRECT: Some of our friends are from the Middle East, others are from the Far East, and the rest are from Latin America.

INCORRECT: Some people finish a bachelor's degree in four years and other take five years.
CORRECT: Some people finish a bachelor's degree in four years and other people take five years.

INCORRECT: Some of the home computer models on sale have 1.5GB, other models have 2.5GB, and the rest of models have 4GB hard drives.

CORRECT: Some of the home computer models on sale have 1.5GB, other models have 2.5GB, and the rest of the models have 4GB hard drives.

INCORRECT: Some applicants want student visas, other applicants want resident visas, and the others applicants want tourist visas.

CORRECT: Some applicants want student visas, other applicants want resident visas, and the other applicants want tourist visas.

EXERCISES

Part A: Choose the correct answer.

Some plants are annuals; __________ are biennials; the rest are perennials.

(A) some another
(B) another
(C) others
(D) other

Part B: Choose the incorrect word or phrase and correct it.

In experiments with large numbers (A) of animals crowded in small cages, some have not been affected, but the rest of (B) have shown (C) all of the symptoms (D) associated with stress and mental illness.

Numerical Order

Remember that *the* is used with an ordinal number before a singular count noun to express numerical order. A cardinal number is used after a singular count noun to express numerical order.

Remember that the following are ordinal numbers:

first	*sixth*	*eleventh*	*sixteenth*
second	*seventh*	*twelfth*	*seventeenth*
third	*eighth*	*thirteenth*	*eighteenth*
fourth	*ninth*	*fourteenth*	*nineteenth*
fifth	*tenth*	*fifteenth*	*twentieth*

	the	ordinal number	count noun (singular)	
I am outlining	the	sixth	chapter	in my notebook

Avoid using *the* before the noun instead of before the ordinal number. Avoid using a cardinal instead of an ordinal number.

Remember that the following are cardinal numbers:

one	*six*	*eleven*	*sixteen*
two	*seven*	*twelve*	*seventeen*
three	*eight*	*thirteen*	*eighteen*
four	*nine*	*fourteen*	*nineteen*
five	*ten*	*fifteen*	*twenty*

	count noun (singular)	cardinal number	
I am outlining	chapter	six	in my notebook

Avoid using *the* before the cardinal number or before the noun. Avoid using an ordinal number instead of a cardinal number.

EXAMPLES

INCORRECT: Flight 656 for Los Angeles is now ready for boarding at the concourse seven.
CORRECT: Flight 656 for Los Angeles is now ready for boarding at concourse seven.

INCORRECT: We left before the beginning of act third.
CORRECT: We left before the beginning of the third act.
or
We left before the beginning of act three.

INCORRECT: Your tickets are for gate the tenth, section B.
CORRECT: Your tickets are for gate ten, section B.

INCORRECT: Look in volume second of the *Modern Medical Dictionary.*
CORRECT: Look in the second volume of the *Modern Medical Dictionary.*
or
Look in volume two of the *Modern Medical Dictionary.*

INCORRECT: The New York–Washington train is arriving on track the fourth.
CORRECT: The New York–Washington train is arriving on track four.

EXERCISES

Part A: Choose the correct answer.

_________ planet from the sun, Mars has a year of 687 days.
(A) The fourth
(B) The four
(C) Four
(D) Fourth

Part B: Choose the incorrect word or phrase and correct it.

Labor Day (A) is always celebrated (B) on first (C) Monday in September. (D)

Nouns that Function as Adjectives

Remember that when two nouns occur together, the first noun describes the second noun; that is, the first noun functions as an adjective. Adjectives do not change form, singular or plural.

	noun	noun
All of us are foreign	language	teachers

Avoid using a plural form for the first noun even when the second noun is plural. Avoid using a possessive form for the first noun.

EXAMPLES

INCORRECT: May I borrow some notebooks paper?
CORRECT: May I borrow some notebook paper?

INCORRECT: All business' students must take the Graduate Management Admission Test.
CORRECT: All business students must take the Graduate Management Admission Test.

INCORRECT: I forgot their telephone's number.
CORRECT: I forgot their telephone number.

INCORRECT: There is a sale at the shoes store.
CORRECT: There is a sale at the shoe store.

INCORRECT: Put the mail on the hall's table.
CORRECT: Put the mail on the hall table.

EXERCISES

Part A: Choose the correct answer.

________ is cheaper for students who maintain a B average because they are a better risk than average or below-average students.

(A) Automobile's insurance
(B) Insurance of automobiles
(C) Automobile insurance
(D) Insurance automobile

Part B: Choose the incorrect word or phrase and correct it.

Sex's education (A) is instituted to help the student understand (B) the process of maturation, to eliminate anxieties (C) related (D) to development, to learn values, and to prevent disease.

Hyphenated Adjectives

Remember that it is common for a number to appear as the first in a series of hyphenated adjec tives. Each word in a hyphenated adjective is an adjective and does not change form, singular or plura

	a	adjective	—	adjective	noun
Agriculture 420 is	a	five	—	hour	class

a	adjective	—	adjective	—	adjective	noun	
A	sixty	—	year	—	old	employee	may retire

Avoid using a plural form for any of the adjectives joined by hyphens even when the noun that fol lows is plural.

Examples

INCORRECT: A three-minutes call anywhere in the United States costs less than a dollar when you dia it yourself.
CORRECT: A three-minute call anywhere in the United States costs less than a dollar when you dial it yourself.

INCORRECT: They have a four-months-old baby.
CORRECT: They have a four-month-old baby.

INCORRECT: Can you make change for a twenty-dollars bill?
CORRECT: Can you make change for a twenty-dollar bill?

INCORRECT: A two-doors car is cheaper than a four-doors model.
CORRECT: A two-door car is cheaper than a four-door model.

INCORRECT: I have to write a one-thousand-words paper this weekend.
CORRECT: I have to write a one-thousand-word paper this weekend.

Exercises

Part A: Choose the correct answer.

The evolution of vertebrates suggests development from a very simple heart in fish to a ________ in man.

(A) four-chamber heart
(B) four-chambers heart
(C) four-chamber hearts
(D) four-chamber's heart

Part B: Choose the incorrect word or phrase and correct it.

The MX <u>is</u> <u>a four-stages</u> rocket with <u>an 8000</u>-mile range, <u>larger than</u> that of the Minuteman.
(A) (B) (C) (D)

Adjectives Ending in *-ed* and *-ing*

Remember that an *-ing* noun that functions as an adjective usually expresses cause. It is derived from an active verb. An *-ed* adjective usually expresses result. It is derived from a passive verb.

	-ed adjective	(by someone or something)
The audience is	thrilled	(by the concert)

	-ing adjective	(to someone or something)
The concert is	thrilling	(to the audience)

Examples

INCORRECT: We were surprising by the results of the test.
CORRECT: We were <u>surprised</u> by the results of the test.
(The results were surprising.)

INCORRECT: This desk is disorganizing.
CORRECT: This desk is <u>disorganized</u>.

INCORRECT: What an interested idea!
CORRECT: What an <u>interesting</u> idea!
(We are interested.)

INCORRECT: Drug abuse is increasing at an alarmed rate.
CORRECT: Drug abuse is increasing at an <u>alarming</u> rate.
(We are alarmed.)

INCORRECT: The petition has been signed by concerning citizens.
CORRECT: The petition has been signed by <u>concerned</u> citizens.

Exercises

Part A: Choose the correct answer.

The *Canterbury Tales*, written about 1386, is as alive and ________ today as it was nearly 600 years ago.

(A) appealed
(B) appeal
(C) appealing
(D) the appeal of

Part B: Choose the incorrect word or phrase and correct it.

It is not surprised (A) that the Arabs, who (B) possessed (C) a remarkable gift for astronomy, mathematics, and geometry, were (D) also skillful mapmakers.

Cause-and-Result—*So*

Remember that *so* is used before an adjective or an adverb followed by *that*. The *so* clause expresses cause. The *that* clause expresses result.

CAUSE				RESULT			
S	V	so	adverb adjective	that	S	V	
She	got up	so	late	that	she	missed	her bus
The music	was	so	loud	that	we	couldn't talk	

Avoid using *as* or *too* instead of *so* in clauses of cause. Avoid using *as* instead of *that* in clauses of result.

EXAMPLES

INCORRECT: He is so slow as he never gets to class on time.
CORRECT: He is so slow that he never gets to class on time.

INCORRECT: This suitcase is as heavy that I can hardly carry it.
CORRECT: This suitcase is so heavy that I can hardly carry it.

INCORRECT: We arrived so late as Professor Baker had already called the roll.
CORRECT: We arrived so late that Professor Baker had already called the roll.

INCORRECT: He drives so fast as no one likes to ride with him.
CORRECT: He drives so fast that no one likes to ride with him.

INCORRECT: Preparing frozen foods is too easy that anyone can do it.
CORRECT: Preparing frozen foods is so easy that anyone can do it.

EXERCISES

Part A: Choose the correct answer.

Oil paints are __________ they have become the most popular painter's colors.

(A) so versatile and durable that
(B) so versatile and durable than
(C) such versatile and durable as
(D) such versatile and durable

art B: Choose the incorrect word or phrase and correct it.

By the mid-nineteenth century, land was such expensive in large cities that architects began to
(A) (B)
conserve space by designing skyscrapers.
(C) (D)

Cause-and-Result—*Such*

Remember that the *such* clause expresses cause and the *that* clause expresses result.

CAUSE						RESULT		
S	V	such	a	adjective	count noun (singular)	that	S	V
It	was	such	a	hot	day	that	we	went out
				or				
S	V	so	adjective	a	count noun (singular)	that	S	V
It	was	so	hot	a	day	that	we	went out

Avoid using *so* instead of *such* before *a*. Avoid omitting *a* from the patterns.

CAUSE					RESULT			
S	V	such	adjective	count noun (plural) noun (noncount)	that	S	V	
These	are	such	long	assignments	that	I	can't finish	them
This	is	such	good	news	that	I	will call	them

Avoid using *so* instead of *such.*

XAMPLES

NCORRECT: It was so interesting book that he couldn't put it down.
CORRECT: It was such an interesting book that he couldn't put it down.

or

It was so interesting a book that he couldn't put it down.

INCORRECT: She is such nice girl that everyone likes her.
CORRECT: She is <u>such a nice girl</u> that everyone likes her.
or
She is <u>so nice a girl</u> that everyone likes her.

INCORRECT: We had so a small lunch that I am hungry already.
CORRECT: We had <u>such a small lunch</u> that I am hungry already.
or
We had <u>so small a lunch</u> that I am hungry already.

INCORRECT: That so many advances have been made in so short time is the most valid argument for retaining the research unit.
CORRECT: That so many advances have been made in <u>such a short time</u> is the most valid argument for retaining the research unit.
or
That so many advances have been made in <u>so short a time</u> is the most valid argument for retaining the research unit.

INCORRECT: It is so nice weather that I would like to go to the beach.
CORRECT: It is <u>such nice weather</u> that I would like to go to the beach.

EXERCISES

Part A: Choose the correct answer.

Water is __________ that it generally contains dissolved materials in greater or lesser amounts.

(A) such an excellent solvent
(B) such excellent a solvent
(C) such a excellent solvents
(D) a such excellent solvent

Part B: Choose the incorrect word or phrase and correct it.

Albert Einstein was <u>such brilliant a scientist</u> (A) that <u>many of his colleagues</u> (B) had to <u>study</u> (C) for <u>several years</u> (D) in order to form opinions about his theories.

Excess—*Too*

Remember that *too* means excessively. The *too* clause expresses cause. The infinitive expresses result.

CAUSE			RESULT
	too	adjective	infinitive
This tea is	too	hot	to drink

Avoid using *so* or *such a* instead of *too* before an adjective when an infinitive follows.

EXAMPLES

INCORRECT: The top shelf in the cupboard is so high for me to reach.
CORRECT: The top shelf in the cupboard is too high for me to reach.

INCORRECT: Ralph is such a young to retire.
CORRECT: Ralph is too young to retire.

INCORRECT: This brand is too expensive for buy.
CORRECT: This brand is too expensive to buy.

INCORRECT: He always plays his stereo so loud (to enjoy).
CORRECT: He always plays his stereo too loud (to enjoy).

INCORRECT: It is too cold go swimming.
CORRECT: It is too cold to go swimming.

EXERCISES

Part A: Choose the correct answer.

The tiny pictures on microfilm are __________ small to be read with the naked eye.
(A) so
(B) too
(C) much
(D) such

Part B: Choose the incorrect word or phrase and correct it.

Mercury is not often visible because it is so near the sun to be seen.
(A) (B) (C) (D)

Emphasis—*Very*

Remember that *very* is used for emphasis. *Very* does not usually introduce a clause or infinitive that expresses result.

			very	adjective	Ø
This	tea	is	very	hot	

Avoid using *too* or *so* instead of *very* when there is no clause of result.

Note: In conversational English, you will often hear *so* instead of *very*, but this is not correct in the kind of formal, written English found on the TOEFL.

EXAMPLES

INCORRECT: We went out to eat because we were too hungry.
CORRECT: We went out to eat because we were very hungry.

INCORRECT: This dorm has too small rooms.
CORRECT: This dorm has very small rooms.

INCORRECT: New York is so big, and I am not used to it.
CORRECT: New York is very big, and I am not used to it.

INCORRECT: Last month we had a too high electric bill.
CORRECT: Last month we had a very high electric bill.

INCORRECT: Darlene says that the courts are so lenient.
CORRECT: Darlene says that the courts are very lenient.

EXERCISES

Part A: Choose the correct answer.

Young rivers have no flood plains and their valleys are ________.
(A) very narrow
(B) too narrow
(C) so narrow
(D) narrowly

Part B: Choose the incorrect word or phrase and correct it.

The smallest (A) of the apes, the gibbon is distinguished by (B) its (C) too long (D) arms.

PROBLEM 85 Adjectives with Verbs of the Senses

Remember that an adjective, not an adverb, is used after verbs of the senses. The following verbs are examples of verbs of the senses:

feel *sound*
look *taste*
smell

S	V (senses)	adjective	
I	felt	bad	about the mistake

Avoid using an adverb instead of an adjective after verbs of the senses.

EXAMPLES

INCORRECT: We love to go to the country in the spring because the wild flowers smell so sweetly.
CORRECT: We love to go to the country in the spring because the wild flowers smell so sweet.

INCORRECT: Although the medicine tastes badly, it seems to help my condition.
CORRECT: Although the medicine tastes bad, it seems to help my condition.

INCORRECT: The meal tasted well.
CORRECT: The meal tasted good.

INCORRECT: The music sounds sweetly and soothing.
CORRECT: The music sounds sweet and soothing.

INCORRECT: When he complained that the food tasted badly, the waiter took it back to the kitchen and brought him something else.
CORRECT: When he complained that the food tasted bad, the waiter took it back to the kitchen and brought him something else.

EXERCISES

Part A: Choose the correct answer.

If one is suffering from a psychosomatic illness, that is, a disease contributed to by mental anxiety, one may still feel very ________.

(A) badly
(B) bad
(C) worsely
(D) worser

Part B: Choose the incorrect word or phrase and correct it.

It has been proven (A) that when a subject identifies a substance as tasting well (B), he (C) is often associating (D) the taste with the smell.

CUMULATIVE REVIEW EXERCISE FOR ADJECTIVES AND ADJECTIVE-RELATED STRUCTURES

DIRECTIONS: Some of the sentences in this exercise are correct. Some are incorrect. First, find the correct sentences, and mark them with a check (√). Then find the incorrect sentences, and correct them. Check your answers using the key on page 532.

1. Today's modern TV cameras require only a few light as compared with earlier models.
2. Diamonds that are not good enough to be made into gems are used in industry for cutting and drilling.
3. Cane sugar contains not vitamins.
4. Humorist Will Rogers was brought up on a cattle ranch in the Oklahoma Indian territory, but the life of a cowboy was not excited enough for him.
5. One of the most distinctive features of Islamic architecture is the arch.
6. It is impossible to view Picasso's *Guernica* without feeling badly about the fate of the people portrayed.
7. The Erie was so large a canal that more than eighty locks and twenty aqueducts were required.
8. An usual treatment for the flu is to drink plenty of liquids.

9. The United States did not issue any stamps until 1847 when one was printed for use east of the Mississippi and one another for use west of the Mississippi.

10. Red corpuscles are so numerous that a thimbleful of human's blood would contain almost ten thousand million of them.

11. The Malay Archipelago is the world's largest group of islands, forming a ten-thousand-islands chain.

12. Some property of lead are its softness and its resistance.

13. Aristotle is considered the father of the logic.

14. Metals such as iron and magnesium are quite common, but are mostly found in silicates, making them so expensive to extract.

15. History of the war in Vietnam is just being written.

Problems with Comparatives

Nouns may be compared for exact or general *similarity* or *difference.* They may also be compared for similar or different *qualities* or *degrees,* more or less, of specific qualities. In addition, they may be compared to *estimates.*

Exact Similarity—*the Same as* and *the Same*

Remember that *the same as* and *the same* have the same meaning, but *the same as* is used between the two nouns compared, and *the same* is used after the two nouns or a plural noun.

noun		the same as	noun
This coat	is	the same as	that one

noun		noun		the same
This coat	and	that one	are	the same

noun (plural)		the same
These coats	are	the same

Avoid using *to* and *like* instead of *as.* Avoid using *the same* between the two nouns compared.

EXAMPLES

INCORRECT: That car is almost the same like mine.
CORRECT: That car is almost the same as mine.

or

That car and mine are almost the same.

INCORRECT: My briefcase is exactly the same that yours.
CORRECT: My briefcase is exactly the same as yours.

or

My briefcase and yours are exactly the same.

INCORRECT: Is your book the same to mine?
CORRECT: Is your book the same as mine?

or

Are your book and mine the same?

INCORRECT: Are this picture and the one on your desk same?
CORRECT: Are this picture and the one on your desk the same?

or

Is this picture the same as the one on your desk?

INCORRECT: The teacher gave Martha a failing grade on her composition because it was the same a composition he had already read.
CORRECT: The teacher gave Martha a failing grade on her composition because it was the same as a composition he had already read.

or

The teacher gave Martha a failing grade on her composition because it and a composition he had already read were the same.

EXERCISES

Part A: Choose the correct answer.

Although we often use "speed" and "velocity" interchangeably, in a technical sense, "speed" is not always _________ "velocity."

(A) alike
(B) the same as
(C) similar
(D) as

Part B: Choose the incorrect word or phrase and correct it.

When two products are basically (A) the same as, (B) advertising (C) can influence (D) the public's choice.

General Similarity—*Similar to* and *Similar*

Remember that *similar to* and *similar* have the same meaning, but *similar to* is used between the two nouns compared, and *similar* is used after the two nouns or a plural noun.

noun		similar to	noun
This coat	is	similar to	that one

noun		noun		similar
This coat	and	that one	are	similar

noun (plural)		similar
These coats	are	similar

Avoid using *as* instead of *to.* Avoid using *similar to* after the two nouns or a plural noun.

EXAMPLES

INCORRECT: I would really like to have a stereo that is similar the one on display.
CORRECT: I would really like to have a stereo that is similar to the one on display.

or

The stereo that I would like to have and the one on display are similar.

INCORRECT: My roommate's values and mine are similar to in spite of our being from different countries.
CORRECT: My roommate's values are similar to mine in spite of our being from different countries.

or

My roommate's values and mine are similar in spite of our being from different countries.

INCORRECT: Cliff's glasses are similar like yours, but his cost a lot less.
CORRECT: Cliff's glasses are similar to yours, but his cost a lot less.

or

Cliff's glasses and yours are similar, but his cost a lot less.

INCORRECT: That joke is similar as a joke that I heard.
CORRECT: That joke is similar to a joke that I heard.

or

That joke and a joke that I heard are similar.

INCORRECT: All of the other departments are similar this one.
CORRECT: All of the other departments are similar to this one.

or

All of the other departments and this one are similar.

EXERCISES

Part A: Choose the correct answer.

The vegetation in temperate zones all around the world is __________ .

(A) similar
(B) like
(C) same
(D) as

Part B: Choose the incorrect word or phrase and correct it.

The medical problems of parents and <u>their</u> (A) children tend <u>to be</u> (B) very <u>similar to</u> (C) <u>because of</u> (D) the hereditary nature of many diseases.

PROBLEM 88

General Similarity—*Like* and *Alike*

Remember that *like* and *alike* have the same meaning, but *like* is used between the two nouns compared, and *alike* is used after the two nouns or a plural noun.

noun		like	noun
This coat	is	like	that one

noun		noun		alike
This coat	and	that one	are	alike

noun (plural)		alike
These coats	are	alike

Avoid using *as* instead of *like*. Avoid using *like* after the two nouns compared.

EXAMPLES

INCORRECT: The weather feels as spring.
CORRECT: The weather feels <u>like</u> <u>spring</u>.

INCORRECT: These suits are like.
CORRECT: This suit is <u>like</u> <u>that suit</u>.

or

These suits are <u>alike</u>.

INCORRECT: Your recipe for chicken is like to a recipe that my mother has.
CORRECT: Your recipe for chicken is like a recipe that my mother has.
or
Your recipe for chicken and a recipe that my mother has are alike.

INCORRECT: I want to buy some shoes same like the ones I have on.
CORRECT: I want to buy some shoes like the ones I have on.
or
The shoes I want to buy and the shoes I have on are alike.

INCORRECT: Anthony and his brother don't look like.
CORRECT: Anthony doesn't look like his brother.
or
Anthony and his brother don't look alike.

EXERCISES

Part A: Choose the correct answer.

Although they are smaller, chipmunks are ________ most other ground squirrels.
(A) like to
(B) like as
(C) like
(D) alike

Part B: Choose the incorrect word or phrase and correct it.

The first (A) living structures to appear (B) on Earth thousands of years ago (C) were alike (D) viruses.

Specific Similarity—Quality Nouns

Remember that a quality noun is used in comparisons of a specific characteristic.

The following are examples of quality nouns:

age	*height*	*price*	*style*
color	*length*	*size*	*weight*

noun	V	the same	noun (quality)	as	noun
She	is	the same	age	as	John

Avoid using *to*, *than*, or *like* instead of *as*. Avoid using a quality adjective instead of a quality noun after *the same*.

EXAMPLES

INCORRECT: I want to buy a pair of shoes the same style like these I'm wearing.
CORRECT: I want to buy a pair of shoes the same style as these I'm wearing.

INCORRECT: This is not the same big as the rest of the apartments.
CORRECT: This is not the same size as the rest of the apartments.

INCORRECT: The gold chain that Edith saw is same weight as yours.
CORRECT: The gold chain that Edith saw is the same weight as yours.

INCORRECT: Please cut my hair the same length like the style in this magazine.
CORRECT: Please cut my hair the same length as the style in this magazine.

INCORRECT: Is this thread the same color the cloth?
CORRECT: Is this thread the same color as the cloth?

EXERCISES

Part A: Choose the correct answer.

Some retirement communities will not sell property to new residents unless they are about ________ the rest of the residents.

(A) the same age
(B) the same old
(C) the same age as
(D) the same old as

Part B: Choose the incorrect word or phrase and correct it.

The bodies of cold-blooded animals (A) have (B) the same temperature (C) their surroundings, but those of warm-blooded animals do not (D).

PROBLEM 90 Specific Similarity—Quality Adjectives

Remember that a quality adjective is used in comparisons of a specific characteristic.

The following are examples of quality adjectives:

big	*expensive*	*light*	*small*
cheap	*hard*	*little*	*tall*
clear	*heavy*	*long*	*young*
cold	*hot*	*old*	
easy	*large*	*short*	

noun	V	as	adjective (quality)	as	noun
She	is	as	old	as	John

Avoid using *to, than*, or *like* instead of *as*. Avoid using a quality noun instead of a quality adjective after *as*.

EXAMPLES

INCORRECT: Mary's job is as hard than Bill's.
CORRECT: Mary's job is as hard as Bill's.

INCORRECT: Miss Jones' English is not as clear than Dr. Baker's.
CORRECT: Miss Jones' English is not as clear as Dr. Baker's.

INCORRECT: He is not as tall like his brother.
CORRECT: He is not as tall as his brother.

INCORRECT: The meat at the supermarket is not as expensive that the meat at a butcher shop.
CORRECT: The meat at the supermarket is not as expensive as the meat at a butcher shop.

INCORRECT: College Station is not as big Austin.
CORRECT: College Station is not as big as Austin.

EXERCISES

Part A: Choose the correct answer.

Although the name was not popularized until the Middle Ages, engineering ________ civilization.

(A) as old as
(B) is as old as
(C) that is old as
(D) as old as that

Part B: Choose the incorrect word or phrase and correct it.

Despite (A) its (B) smaller size (C), the Indian Ocean is as deep (D) the Atlantic Ocean.

General Difference—*Different from* and *Different*

Remember that *different from* and *different* have the same meaning, but *different from* is used between the two nouns compared, and *different* is used after the two nouns or a plural noun.

noun		different from	noun
This coat	is	different from	that one

noun		noun		different
This coat	and	that one	are	different

noun (plural)		different
These coats	are	different

Avoid using *to* and *than* instead of *from.* Avoid using *different* between the two nouns compared.

EXAMPLES

INCORRECT: Although they are both weekly news magazines, *Time* and *Newsweek* are different from in several ways.

CORRECT: Although they are both weekly news magazines, *Time is* different from *Newsweek* in several ways.

or

Although they are both weekly news magazines, *Time* and *Newsweek* are different in several ways.

INCORRECT: The watch in the window is a little different this one.

CORRECT: The watch in the window is a little different from this one.

or

The watch in the window and this one are a little different.

INCORRECT: Long distance telephone rates for daytime hours are different than rates for nighttime hours.

CORRECT: Long distance telephone rates for daytime hours are different from rates for nighttime hours.

or

Long distance telephone rates for daytime hours and rates for nighttime hours are different.

INCORRECT: A nursery school is different a day care center.

CORRECT: A nursery school is different from a day care center.

or

A nursery school and a day care center are different.

INCORRECT: The tour packages that we offer are different than most tours.

CORRECT: The tour packages that we offer are different from most tours.

or

The tour packages that we offer and most tours are different.

EXERCISES

Part A: Choose the correct answer.

The works of Picasso were quite __________ during various periods of his artistic life.

(A) differ
(B) different
(C) different from
(D) different than

Part B: Choose the incorrect word or phrase and correct it.

Although business practices have been applied (A) successfully (B) to agriculture, farming (C) is different (D) other industries.

General Difference—*to Differ from*

Remember that *differ* is a verb and must change forms to agree with the subject.

	DIFFER	from	
This one	differs	from	the rest

Avoid using BE with *differ*. Avoid using *than*, *of*, or *to* after *differ*.

EXAMPLES

INCORRECT: Sharon is different of other women I know.
CORRECT: Sharon is different from other women I know.
or
Sharon differs from other women I know.

INCORRECT: Do you have anything a little different to these?
CORRECT: Do you have anything a little different from these?
or
Do you have anything that differs a little from these?

INCORRECT: The campus at State University different from that of City College.
CORRECT: The campus at State University differs from that of City College.
or
The campus at State University is different from that of City College.

INCORRECT: Jayne's apartment is very differs from Bill's even though they are in the same building.
CORRECT: Jayne's apartment is very different from Bill's even though they are in the same building.
or
Jayne's apartment differs from Bill's even though they are in the same building.

INCORRECT: Customs differ one region of the country to another.
CORRECT: Customs differ from one region of the country to another.
or
Customs are different from one region of the country to another.

Exercises

Part A: Choose the correct answer.

Modern blimps like the famous Goodyear blimps _________ the first ones in that they are filled with helium instead of hydrogen.

(A) differ from
(B) different from
(C) is different from
(D) different

Part B: Choose the incorrect word or phrase and correct it.

Crocodiles (A) different from (B) alligators in that they have pointed snouts (C) and long lower teeth that stick out when their mouths are closed (D).

Comparative Estimates—Multiple Numbers

Remember that the following are examples of multiple numbers:

half	*four times*
twice	*five times*
three times	*ten times*

	multiple	as	much many	as	
Fresh fruit costs	twice	as	much	as	canned fruit
We have	half	as	many	as	we need

Avoid using *so* instead of *as* after a multiple. Avoid using *more than* instead of *as much as* or *as many as.* Avoid using the multiple after *as much* and *as many.*

Examples

INCORRECT: This one is prettier, but it costs twice more than the other one.
CORRECT: This one is prettier, but it costs twice as much as the other one.

INCORRECT: The rent at College Apartments is only half so much as you pay here.
CORRECT: The rent at College Apartments is only half as much as you pay here.

INCORRECT: Bob found a job that paid as much twice as he made working at the library.
CORRECT: Bob found a job that paid twice as much as he made working at the library.

INCORRECT: The price was very reasonable; I would gladly have paid three times more than he asked.
CORRECT: The price was very reasonable; I would gladly have paid three times as much as he asked.

INCORRECT: We didn't buy the car because they wanted as much twice as it was worth.
CORRECT: We didn't buy the car because they wanted <u>twice as much as</u> it was worth.

EXERCISES

Part A: Choose the correct answer.

After the purchase of the Louisiana Territory, the United States had ________ it had previously owned.

(A) twice more land than
(B) two times more land than
(C) twice as much land as
(D) two times much land than

Part B: Choose the incorrect word or phrase and correct it.

With American prices for sugar at three times <u>as much</u> (A) the world price, manufacturers <u>are</u> (B) beginning <u>to use</u> (C) fructose blended with pure sugar, <u>or</u> (D) sucrose.

Comparative Estimates—*More Than* and *Less Than*

Remember that *more than* or *less than* is used before a specific number to express an estimate that may be a little more or a little less than the number.

	more than	number	
Steve has	more than	a thousand	coins in his collection

	less than	number	
Andy has	less than	a dozen	coins in his pocket

Avoid using *more* or *less* without *than* in estimates. Avoid using *as* instead of *than*.

EXAMPLES

INCORRECT: More one hundred people came to the meeting.
CORRECT: <u>More than one hundred</u> people came to the meeting.

INCORRECT: We have lived in the United States for as less than seven years.
CORRECT: We have lived in the United States for <u>less than seven</u> years.

INCORRECT: The main library has more as one million volumes.
CORRECT: The main library has <u>more than one million</u> volumes.

INCORRECT: A new shopping center on the north side will have five hundred shops more than.
CORRECT: A new shopping center on the north side will have more than five hundred shops.

INCORRECT: There are most than fifty students in the lab, but only two computers.
CORRECT: There are more than fifty students in the lab, but only two computers.

EXERCISES

Part A: Choose the correct answer.

In the Great Smoky Mountains, one can see __________ 150 different kinds of trees.
(A) more than
(B) as much as
(C) up as
(D) as many to

Part B: Choose the incorrect word or phrase and correct it.

Pelé scored more as (A) 1280 goals during his career, (B) gaining (C) a reputation as the best (D) soccer player of all time.

Comparative Estimates—*As Many As*

Remember that *as many as* is used before a specific number to express an estimate that does not exceed the number.

	as many as	number	
We should have	as many as	five hundred	applications

Avoid using *as many* instead of *as many as.* Avoid using *much* instead of *many* before a specific number.

Note: Comparative estimates with *as much as* are also used before a specific number that refers to weight, distance, or money. For example, *as much as* ten pounds, *as much as* two miles, or *as much as* twenty dollars.

EXAMPLES

INCORRECT: We expect as much as thirty people to come.
CORRECT: We expect as many as thirty people to come.

INCORRECT: There are as many fifteen thousand students attending summer school.
CORRECT: There are as many as fifteen thousand students attending summer school.

INCORRECT: The children can see as much as twenty-five baby animals in the nursery at the zoo.
CORRECT: The children can see as many as twenty-five baby animals in the nursery at the zoo.

INCORRECT: Many as ten planes have sat in line waiting to take off.
CORRECT: As many as ten planes have sat in line waiting to take off.

INCORRECT: State University offers as much as two hundred major fields of study.
CORRECT: State University offers as many as two hundred major fields of study.

EXERCISES

Part A: Choose the correct answer.

It has been estimated that _______ one hundred thousand men participated in the gold rush of 1898.

(A) approximate
(B) until
(C) as many as
(D) more

Part B: Choose the incorrect word or phrase and correct it.

It is generally accepted that the common cold is caused (A) by (B) as much as (C) forty strains of viruses that (D) may be present in the air at all times.

Degrees of Comparison—Comparative Adjectives

Remember that two- and three-syllable adjectives form the comparative by using *more* or *less* before the adjective form. One-syllable adjectives form the comparative by using *-er* after the form. Two-syllable adjectives which end in *y* form the comparative by changing the *y* to *i* and adding *-er.*

	more (less) adjective (two + syllables) adjective *-er* (one syllable) adjective *-er* (two + syllables ending in *-y*)	than	
An essay test is	more difficult	than	an objective test
An essay test is	harder	than	an objective test
An essay test is	easier	than	an objective test

Avoid using *as* or *that* instead of *than.* Avoid using both *more* and an *-er* form.

EXAMPLES

INCORRECT: This room is more spacious as the other one.
CORRECT: This room is more spacious than the other one.

INCORRECT: The bill which we received was more higher than the estimate.
CORRECT: The bill which we received was higher than the estimate.

INCORRECT: Eileen has been more happy lately than she was when she first came.
CORRECT: Eileen has been happier lately than she was when she first came.

INCORRECT: The books for my engineering course are expensive the books for my other courses.
CORRECT: The books for my engineering course are more expensive than the books for my other courses.

INCORRECT: The climate here is more milder than that of New England.
CORRECT: The climate here is milder than that of New England.

EXERCISES

Part A: Choose the correct answer.

The Disney Amusement Park in Japan is _________ Florida or California.
(A) the largest than the ones in
(B) larger than the ones in
(C) larger the ones in
(D) the largest of the ones

Part B: Choose the incorrect word or phrase and correct it.

The diesel engine that (A) runs on oil is (B) efficient (C) than most other engines because (D) it converts more of the useful energy stored up in the fuel.

PROBLEM 97 Degrees of Comparison—Superlative Adjectives

Remember that superlatives are used to compare more than two.

	the	most (least) adjective (two + syllables) adjective *-est* (one syllable) adjective *-est* (two + syllables ending in *-er*)
An essay test is	the	most difficult
An essay test is	the	hardest
An essay test is	the	trickiest

Avoid using a comparative *-er* form when three or more are compared.

EXAMPLES

INCORRECT: She is more prettier than all of the girls in our class.
CORRECT: She is the prettiest of all of the girls in our class.

INCORRECT: New York is the larger of all American cities.
CORRECT: New York is the largest of all American cities.

INCORRECT: Of all of the candidates, Alex is probably the less qualified.
CORRECT: Of all of the candidates, Alex is probably the least qualified.

INCORRECT: Although there are a number of interesting findings, a most significant results are in the abstract.

CORRECT: Although there are a number of interesting findings, the most significant results are in the abstract.

INCORRECT: In my opinion, the more beautiful place in Oregon is Mount Hood.

CORRECT: In my opinion, the most beautiful place in Oregon is Mount Hood.

EXERCISES

Part A: Choose the correct answer.

The blue whale is __________ known animal, reaching a length of more than one hundred feet.

(A) the large
(B) the larger
(C) the largest
(D) most largest

Part B: Choose the incorrect answer and correct it.

The more important theorem of all in plane geometry is the Pythagorean Theorem.
(A) (B) (C)(D)

Degrees of Comparison—Irregular Adjectives

Remember that some very common adjectives have irregular forms. Some of them are listed here for you.

Adjective	*Comparative—to compare two*	*Superlative—to compare three or more*
bad	*worse*	*the worst*
far	*farther*	*the farthest*
	further	*the furthest*
good	*better*	*the best*
little	*less*	*the least*
many	*more*	*the most*
much	*more*	*the most*

	irregular comparative	than	
This ice cream is	better	than	the other brands

	irregular superlative	
This ice cream is	the best	of all

Avoid using a regular form instead of an irregular form for these adjectives.

EXAMPLES

INCORRECT: The lab is more far from the bus stop than the library.
CORRECT: The lab is farther from the bus stop than the library.
or
The lab is further from the bus stop than the library.

INCORRECT: The badest accident in the history of the city occurred last night on the North Freeway.
CORRECT: The worst accident in the history of the city occurred last night on the North Freeway.

INCORRECT: These photographs are very good, but that one is the better of all.
CORRECT: These photographs are very good, but that one is the best of all.

INCORRECT: Please give me much sugar than you did last time.
CORRECT: Please give me more sugar than you did last time.

INCORRECT: This composition is more good than your last one.
CORRECT: This composition is better than your last one.

EXERCISES

Part A: Choose the correct answer.

________ apples are grown in Washington State.
(A) Best
(B) The most good
(C) The best
(D) The better

Part B: Choose the incorrect word or phrase and correct it.

Because (A) a felony is more bad (B) than a misdemeanor, the punishment is more severe (C), and often includes a jail sentence as well as (D) a fine.

Degrees of Comparison—Comparative Adverbs

Remember that adverbs also have a comparative form to compare two verb actions and a superlative form to compare three or more verb actions.

	more adverb (two + syllables) less adverb (two + syllables) adverb *-er* (one syllable)	than	
We finished the test	more rapidly	than	Mark
We finished the test	less rapidly	than	Mark
We finished the test	faster	than	Mark

	the most adverb (two + syllables) the least adverb (two + syllables) adverb *-est* (one syllable)	
We finished the test We finished the test We finished the test	the most rapidly the least rapidly the fastest	of all of all of all

Avoid using *-er* with adverbs of more than one syllable even when they end in *-ly*.

EXAMPLES

INCORRECT: Professor Tucker was pleased because our group approached the project more scientifically the others.
CORRECT: Professor Tucker was pleased because our group approached the project more scientifically than the others.

INCORRECT: This train always leaves late than the time on the schedule.
CORRECT: This train always leaves later than the time on the schedule.

INCORRECT: The students in Dr. Neal's class complained the most bitter about the grading system.
CORRECT: The students in Dr. Neal's class complained the most bitterly about the grading system.

INCORRECT: I wish we could see each other more frequenter.
CORRECT: I wish we could see each other more frequently.

INCORRECT: He drives more fast than she does.
CORRECT: He drives faster than she does.

EXERCISES

Part A: Choose the correct answer.

Many chemicals react __________ in acid solutions.
(A) more quick
(B) more quickly
(C) quicklier
(D) as quickly more

Part B: Choose the incorrect word or phrase and correct it.

Quality control studies show that employees work the most efficient (A) when they are involved in (B) the total operation rather than in (C) only one part of it (D).

Double Comparatives

Remember that when two comparatives are used together, the first comparative expresses cause and the second comparative expresses result. A comparative is *more* or *less* with an adjective, or an adjective with *-er*.

CAUSE				RESULT			
The	comparative	S	V,	the	comparative	S	V
The	more	you	review,	the	easier	the patterns	will be

Avoid using *as* instead of *the*. Avoid using the **incorrect** form ~~*lesser*~~. Avoid omitting *the*. Avoid omit-g *-er* from the adjective.

XAMPLES

CORRECT: The more you study during the semester, the lesser you have to study the week before exams.
CORRECT: The more you study during the semester, the less you have to study the week before exams.

CORRECT: The faster we finish, the soon we can leave.
CORRECT: The faster we finish, the sooner we can leave.

CORRECT: The less one earns, the lesser one must pay in income taxes.
CORRECT: The less one earns, the less one must pay in income taxes.

CORRECT: The louder he shouted, less he convinced anyone.
CORRECT: The louder he shouted, the less he convinced anyone.

CORRECT: The more you practice speaking, the well you will do it.
CORRECT: The more you practice speaking, the better you will do it.

XERCISES

art A: Choose the correct answer.

It is generally true that the lower the stock market falls, __________ .

(A) higher the price of gold rises
(B) the price of gold rises high
(C) the higher the price of gold rises
(D) rises high the price of gold

art B: Choose the incorrect word or phrase and correct it.

The higher the solar activity, the intense (A) the auroras (B) or polar light displays in the skies near (C) the Earth's geomagnetic poles (D).

Illogical Comparatives—General Similarity and Difference

Remember that comparisons must be made with logically comparable nouns. You can't compare *the climate* in the North with *the South*. You must compare *the climate* in the North with *the climate* in the South.

Remember that *that of* and *those of* are used instead of repeating a noun to express a logical comparative. An example with *different from* appears below.

noun (singular)		different	from	that	
Football in the U.S.	is	different	from	that	in other countries

noun (plural)		different	from	those	
The rules	are	different	from	those	of soccer

Avoid omitting *that* and *those.* Avoid using *than* instead of *from* with *different.*

EXAMPLES

INCORRECT: The food in my country is very different than that in the United States.
CORRECT: The food in my country is very different from that in the United States.

INCORRECT: The classes at my university are very different from State University.
CORRECT: The classes at my university are very different from those at State University.

INCORRECT: The English that is spoken in Canada is similar to the United States.
CORRECT: The English that is spoken in Canada is similar to that of the United States.

INCORRECT: Drugstores here are not like at home.
CORRECT: Drugstores here are not like those at home.

INCORRECT: The time in New York City differs three hours from Los Angeles.
CORRECT: The time in New York City differs three hours from that of Los Angeles.

EXERCISES

Part A: Choose the correct answer.

One's fingerprints are ________.
(A) different from those of any other person
(B) different from any other person
(C) different any other person
(D) differs from another person

Part B: Choose the incorrect word or phrase and correct it.

Perhaps the colonists were looking for (A) a climate like England, (B) when they decided to settle (C) the North American continent instead of (D) the South American continent.

Illogical Comparatives—Degrees

Remember that comparisons must be made with logically comparable nouns.

noun (singular)		more + adjective adjective *-er*	than	that	
The climate in the North	is	more severe	than	that	of the South
The climate in the North	is	colder	than	that	of the South

noun (plural)		more + adjective adjective *-er*	than	those	
The prices	are	more expensive	than	those	at a discount store
The prices	are	higher	than	those	at a discount store

Avoid omitting *that* and *those.*

EXAMPLES

INCORRECT: Her qualifications are better than any other candidate.
CORRECT: Her qualifications are better than those of any other candidate.

INCORRECT: Professor Baker's class is more interesting than Professor Williams.
CORRECT: Professor Baker's class is more interesting than that of Professor Williams.

INCORRECT: The audience is much larger than last year's concert.
CORRECT: The audience is much larger than that of last year's concert.

INCORRECT: The rooms in the front are much noisier than the back.
CORRECT: The rooms in the front are much noisier than those in the back.

INCORRECT: The interest on savings accounts at City Bank are higher than Bank Plus.
CORRECT: The interest on savings accounts at City Bank are higher than that of Bank Plus.

EXERCISES

Part A: Choose the correct answer.

The total production of bushels of corn in the United States is ________ all other cereal crops combined.

(A) more as
(B) more than that of
(C) more of
(D) more that

Part B: Choose the incorrect word or phrase and correct it.

Because (A) there were so few women (B) in the early Western states, the freedom and rights of Western women were more extensive (C) than Eastern ladies (D).

CUMULATIVE REVIEW EXERCISE FOR COMPARATIVES

DIRECTIONS: Some of the sentences in this exercise are correct. Some are incorrect. First, find the correct sentences, and mark them with a check (√). Then find the incorrect sentences, and correct them. Check your answers using the key on page 533.

1. One object will not be the same weight than another object because the gravitational attraction differs from place to place on the Earth's surface.
2. An identical twin is always the same sex as his or her twin because they develop from the same zygote.
3. As many 100 billion stars are in the Milky Way.
4. Compared with numbers fifty years ago, there are twice more students in college today.
5. The valuablest information we currently have on the ocean floors is that which was obtained by oceanographic satellites such as *Seasat.*
6. The oxygen concentration in the lungs is higher than the blood.
7. Since the Earth is spherical, the larger the area, the worser the distortion on a flat map.
8. The eyes of an octopus are remarkably similar to those of a human being.
9. The terms used in one textbook may be different another text.
10. During very cold winters, residential utility bills are as high sixteen hundred dollars a month in New England.
11. When the ratio of gear teeth is five:one, the small gear rotates five times as fast as the large gear.
12. Although lacking in calcium and vitamin A, grains have most carbohydrates than any other food.
13. The more narrow the lens diameter, the more great the depth of field.
14. No fingerprint is exactly alike another.
15. There is disagreement among industrialists as to whether the products of this decade are inferior to the past.

Problems with Prepositions

Prepositions are words or phrases that clarify relationships. Prepositions are usually followed by nouns and pronouns. Sometimes the nouns are *-ing* form nouns.

Prepositions are also used in idioms.

Place—*Between* and *Among*

Remember that *between* and *among* have the same meaning, but *between* is used with two nouns and *among* is used with three or more nouns or a plural noun.

	between	noun 1		noun 2
The work is distributed	between	the secretary	and	the receptionist

	among	noun 1	noun 2		noun 3
The rent payments are divided	among	Don,	Bill,	and	Gene

Avoid using *between* with three or more nouns or a plural noun.

EXAMPLES

INCORRECT: The choice is between a vanilla, chocolate, and strawberry ice cream cone.
CORRECT: The choice is among a vanilla, chocolate, and strawberry ice cream cone.

INCORRECT: Rick and his wife can usually solve their problems among them.
CORRECT: Rick and his wife can usually solve their problems between them.

INCORRECT: Profits are divided between the stockholders of the corporation.
CORRECT: Profits are divided among the stockholders of the corporation.

INCORRECT: The votes were evenly divided among the Democratic candidate and the Republican candidate.
CORRECT: The votes were evenly divided between the Democratic candidate and the Republican candidate.

INCORRECT: The property was divided equally among his son and daughter.
CORRECT: The property was divided equally between his son and daughter.

EXERCISES

Part A: Choose the correct answer.

Although it is difficult __________, a frog is more likely to be smooth and wet, and a toad rough and dry.
(A) distinguishing among a frog and a toad
(B) distinguish a frog and a toad
(C) between a frog and a toad distinguish
(D) to distinguish between a frog and a toad

Part B: Choose the incorrect word or phrase and correct it.

In a federal form of government like (A) that of the United States, (B) power is divided (C) between (D) the legislative, executive, and judicial branches.

Place—*In, On, At*

Remember that *in*, *on*, and *at* have similar meanings, but they are used with different kinds of places. In general, *in* is used before large places; *on* is used before middle-sized places; and *at* is used before numbers in addresses. Finally, *in* is used again before very small places.

in	on	at	in
COUNTRY	*STREET*	*NUMBER*	*a corner (of a room)*
STATE	*STREET CORNER*		*a room*
PROVINCE	*COAST*		*a building*
COUNTY	*RIVER*		*a park*
CITY	*a ship*		*a car*
	a train		*a boat*
	a plane		

	in	COUNTRY	in	STATE	in	CITY
We live	in	the United States	in	North Carolina	in	Jacksonville

on	COAST	on	RIVER	at	NUMBER
on	the East Coast	on	New River	at	2600 River Road

Avoid using *in* instead of *on* for streets and other middle-sized places.

EXAMPLES

INCORRECT: Cliff can live on Yellowstone National Park because he is a park ranger.
CORRECT: Cliff can live <u>in</u> <u>Yellowstone National Park</u> because he is a park ranger.

INCORRECT: Is Domino's Pizza in Tenth Street?
CORRECT: Is Domino's Pizza <u>on</u> <u>Tenth Street</u>?

INCORRECT: The apartments at the Hudson River are more expensive than the ones across the street.
CORRECT: The apartments <u>on</u> <u>the Hudson River</u> are more expensive than the ones across the street.

INCORRECT: We are going to stay overnight on Chicago.
CORRECT: We are going to stay overnight <u>in</u> <u>Chicago</u>.

INCORRECT: Let's take our vacation in the coast instead of in the mountains.
CORRECT: Let's take our vacation <u>on</u> <u>the coast</u> instead of in the mountains.

EXERCISES

Part A: Choose the correct answer.

__________ of the United States from southern New Hampshire in the north to Virginia in the south, a vast urban region has been defined as a megalopolis, that is, a cluster of cities.

(A) On the northeastern seaboard
(B) It is in the northeastern seaboard
(C) That the northeastern seaboard
(D) At the northeastern seaboard

Part B: Choose the incorrect word or phrase and correct it.

<u>Many</u> of the famous <u>advertising</u> offices are <u>located</u> <u>in</u> Madison Avenue.
(A) (B) (C) (D)

Time—*In, On, At*

Remember that *in, on,* and *at* have similar meanings, but they are used with different times. In general, *in* is used before large units of time; *on* is used before middle-sized units of time; and *at* is used before numbers in clock time.

Idiomatic phrases such as *in the morning, in the afternoon, in the evening, at night, at noon,* must be learned individually like vocabulary.

in YEAR *on DAY* *at TIME*
MONTH *DATE*

	in	YEAR	in	MONTH	on	DAY	at	TIME
Lilly was born	in	1919	in	December	on	Sunday	at	7:00

Avoid using *in* before days and dates.

EXAMPLES

INCORRECT: I would rather take classes on the afternoon.
CORRECT: I would rather take classes <u>in</u> <u>the afternoon</u>.

INCORRECT: Gloria has a part-time job in the night.
CORRECT: Gloria has a part-time job <u>at</u> <u>night</u>.

INCORRECT: The rainy season begins on July.
CORRECT: The rainy season begins in July.

INCORRECT: The graduation is in May 20.
CORRECT: The graduation is on May 20.

INCORRECT: We came to the United States on 1997.
CORRECT: We came to the United States in 1997.

EXERCISES

Part A: Choose the correct answer.

Most stores in large American cities close _______ five or six o'clock on weekdays, but the malls in the suburbs stay open much later.

(A) at
(B) in
(C) on
(D) until

Part B: Choose the incorrect word or phrase and correct it.

Accountants (A) are always busiest on April (B) because both federal and (C) state taxes are due on the fifteenth (D).

Addition—*Besides*

Remember that *besides* means *in addition to. Beside* means *near.*

besides	noun adjective	
Besides	our dog,	we have two cats and a canary
Besides	white,	we stock green and blue

	beside	noun
We sat	beside	the teacher

Avoid using *beside* instead of *besides* to mean *in addition.*

EXAMPLES

INCORRECT: Beside Marge, three couples are invited.
CORRECT: Besides Marge, three couples are invited.

INCORRECT: Beside Domino's, four other pizza places deliver.
CORRECT: Besides Domino's, four other pizza places deliver.

INCORRECT: To lead a well-balanced life, you need to have other interests beside studying.
CORRECT: To lead a well balanced life, you need to have other interests besides studying.

INCORRECT: Beside taxi service, there isn't any public transportation in town.
CORRECT: Besides taxi service, there isn't any public transportation in town.

INCORRECT: Janice has lots of friends beside her roommate.
CORRECT: Janice has lots of friends besides her roommate.

EXERCISES

Part A: Choose the correct answer.

__________ a mayor, many city governments employ a city manager.

(A) Beside
(B) Besides
(C) And
(D) Also

Part B: Choose the incorrect word or phrase and correct it.

To receive (A) a degree from an American university, one must take many courses beside (B) those (C) in one's (D) major field.

Exception—*But* and *Except*

Remember that when it is used as a preposition, *but* means *except*.

	but except	noun	
All of the students All of the students	but except	the seniors the seniors	will receive their grades will receive their grades

Avoid using *exception, except to,* or *excepting* instead of *except.*

EXAMPLES

INCORRECT: All of the group exception Barbara went to the lake.
CORRECT: All of the group but Barbara went to the lake.
or
All of the group except Barbara went to the lake.

INCORRECT: You can put everything but for those silk blouses in the washer.
CORRECT: You can put everything but those silk blouses in the washer.
or
You can put everything except those silk blouses in the washer.

INCORRECT: Everyone except to Larry wants sugar in the tea.
CORRECT: Everyone but Larry wants sugar in the tea.
or
Everyone except Larry wants sugar in the tea.

INCORRECT: No one excepting Kathy knows very much about it.
CORRECT: No one but Kathy knows very much about it.
or
No one except Kathy knows very much about it.

INCORRECT: The mail comes at ten o'clock every day not Saturday.
CORRECT: The mail comes at ten o'clock every day but Saturday.
or
The mail comes at ten o'clock every day except Saturday.

EXERCISES

Part A: Choose the correct answer.

Everyone _________ albinos has a certain amount of pigment in the skin to add color.
(A) but
(B) that
(C) without
(D) not

Part B: Choose the incorrect word or phrase and correct it.

There are (A) no (B) pouched animals in the United States (C) but only (D) the opossum.

Replacement—*Instead of* and *Instead*

Remember that *instead of* and *instead* both mean *in place of*, but *instead of* is used before a noun adjective, or adverb, and *instead* is used at the end of a sentence or a clause to refer to a noun, adjective, or adverb that has already been mentioned.

	noun adjective adverb	instead of	noun adjective adverb	
We went to You should be Treat the dog	Colorado firm gently	instead of instead of instead of	abroad patient roughly	on our vacation this year in this case

Avoid using *instead* without *of.*

	noun adjective adverb	instead
We went to	Colorado	instead
You should be	firm	instead
Treat the dog	gently	instead

Avoid using *instead* before a noun.

XAMPLES

NCORRECT: Bob's father wanted him to be an engineer instead a geologist.
CORRECT: Bob's father wanted him to be an engineer instead of a geologist.
or
Bob's father wanted him to be an engineer instead.

NCORRECT: Could I have rice instead potatoes, please?
CORRECT: Could I have rice instead of potatoes, please?
or
Could I have rice instead, please?

NCORRECT: Paula's problem is that she likes to go to movies stead of to class.
CORRECT: Paula's problem is that she likes to go to movies instead of to class.
or
Paula's problem is that she likes to go to movies instead.

NCORRECT: We chose Terry instead from Gene as our representative.
CORRECT: We chose Terry instead of Gene as our representative.
or
We chose Terry instead.

NCORRECT: It is important to eat well at lunchtime in place buying snacks from vending machines.
CORRECT: It is important to eat well at lunchtime instead of buying snacks from vending machines.
or
It is important to eat well at lunchtime instead.

XERCISES

art A: Choose the correct answer.

John Dewey advocated teaching methods that provided experiences for students to participate in __________ material for them to memorize.

(A) instead of
(B) not only
(C) although
(D) contrasting

art B: Choose the incorrect word or phrase and correct it.

Sharks differ from (A) other fish (B) in that their skeletons are made (C) of cartilage instead (D) bone.

Example—*Such as*

Remember that *such as* means for example.

	such as	noun (example)	
Some birds	such as	robins and cardinals	spend the winter in the North

Avoid using *such* or *as such* instead of *such as.*

EXAMPLES

INCORRECT: By using coupons, you can get a discount on a lot of things, such groceries, toiletries, and household items.

CORRECT: By using coupons, you can get a discount on a lot of things, such as groceries, toiletrie and household items.

INCORRECT: Taking care of pets as such dogs and cats can teach children lessons in responsibility.

CORRECT: Taking care of pets such as dogs and cats can teach children lessons in responsibility.

INCORRECT: Magazines such *Time, Newsweek,* and *U.S. News and World Report* provide the reader with a pictorial report of the week's events.

CORRECT: Magazines such as *Time, Newsweek,* and *U.S. News and World Report* provide the reade with a pictorial report of the week's events.

INCORRECT: Jobs at fast-food restaurants for such as McDonald's or Taco Bell are often filled by students.

CORRECT: Jobs at fast-food restaurants such as McDonald's or Taco Bell are often filled by students.

INCORRECT: A metal detector buzzes not only when firearms are located but also when smaller met objects as keys and belt buckles are found.

CORRECT: A metal detector buzzes not only when firearms are located but also when smaller met objects such as keys and belt buckles are found.

EXERCISES

Part A: Choose the correct answer.

Some forms of mollusks are extremely useful as food, especially the bivalves __________ oyste clams, and scallops.

(A) such
(B) such as
(C) as
(D) so

Part B: Choose the incorrect word or phrase and correct it.

Urban consumers have formed (A) co-operatives to provide (B) themselves (C) with necessities such (D) groceries, household appliances, and gasoline at a lower cost.

110 Condition and Unexpected Result—*Despite* and *in Spite of*

Remember that *despite* and *in spite of* have the same meaning. They introduce a contradiction in a sentence or clause of cause-and-result.

Despite	noun,	
Despite	his denial,	we knew that he was guilty
	or	
In spite of	noun,	
In spite of	his denial,	we knew that he was guilty

Avoid using *of* with *despite.* Avoid omitting *of* after *in spite.*

EXAMPLES

INCORRECT: Despite of the light rain, the baseball game was not canceled.
CORRECT: Despite the light rain, the baseball game was not canceled.
or
In spite of the light rain, the baseball game was not canceled.

INCORRECT: Dick and Sarah are still planning to get married despite of their disagreement.
CORRECT: Dick and Sarah are still planning to get married despite their disagreement.
or
Dick and Sarah are still planning to get married in spite of their disagreement.

INCORRECT: In spite the interruption, she was still able to finish her assignment before class.
CORRECT: Despite the interruption, she was still able to finish her assignment before class.
or
In spite of the interruption, she was still able to finish her assignment before class.

INCORRECT: Despite of their quarrel, they are very good friends.
CORRECT: Despite their quarrel, they are very good friends.
or
In spite of their quarrel, they are very good friends.

INCORRECT: In spite the delay, they arrived on time.
CORRECT: Despite the delay, they arrived on time.
or
In spite of the delay, they arrived on time.

EXERCISES

Part A: Choose the correct answer.

__________ under Chief Tecumseh, the Shawnees lost most of their lands to whites and were move into territories.

(A) In spite of resistance
(B) In spite resistance
(C) Spite of resistance
(D) Spite resistance

Part B: Choose the incorrect word or phrase and correct it.

Despite of (A) the fact that backgammon is easy to learn, it (B) is as difficult to play (C) as chess (D).

Cause—*Because of* and *Because*

Remember that *because of* is a prepositional phrase. It introduces a noun or a noun phrase. *Because* is a conjunction. It introduces a clause with a subject and a verb.

	because	S	V
They decided to stay at home	because	the weather	was bad

or

	because of	noun
They decided to stay at home	because of	the weather

Avoid using *because of* before a subject and verb. Avoid using *because* before a noun which is no followed by a verb.

EXAMPLES

INCORRECT: Classes will be canceled tomorrow because a national holiday.
CORRECT: Classes will be canceled tomorrow <u>because</u> <u>it is</u> a national holiday.

or

Classes will be canceled tomorrow <u>because of</u> <u>a national holiday</u>.

INCORRECT: She was absent because of her cold was worse.
CORRECT: She was absent <u>because</u> <u>her cold was</u> worse.

or

She was absent <u>because of</u> <u>her cold</u>.

INCORRECT: John's family is very happy because his being awarded a scholarship.
CORRECT: John's family is very happy because he has been awarded a scholarship.
or
John's family is very happy because of his being awarded a scholarship.

INCORRECT: She didn't buy it because of the price was too high.
CORRECT: She didn't buy it because the price was too high.
or
She didn't buy it because of the price.

INCORRECT: It was difficult to see the road clearly because the rain.
CORRECT: It was difficult to see the road clearly because it was raining.
or
It was difficult to see the road clearly because of the rain.

EXERCISES

Part A: Choose the correct answer.

_________ in the cultivation of a forest, trees need more careful planning than any other crop does.

(A) Because the time and area involved
(B) For the time and area involving
(C) Because of the time and area involved
(D) As a cause of the time and area involved

Part B: Choose the incorrect word or phrase and correct it.

Many roads and railroads were built (A) in the 1880s (B) because of (C) the industrial cities needed a network to link (D) them with sources of supply.

Cause—*From*

Remember that *from* means caused by. It is usually used after adjectives.

	adjective	from	noun *-ing* noun	
The chairs are	wet	from	the rain	
The chairs are	wet	from	sitting	out in the rain

Avoid using *for* before the *-ing* noun.

EXAMPLES

INCORRECT: Be careful not to get sunburned from stay out on the beach too long.
CORRECT: Be careful not to get sunburned <u>from</u> <u>staying</u> out on the beach too long.

INCORRECT: We felt sleepy all day for watching television so late last night.
CORRECT: We felt sleepy all day <u>from</u> <u>watching</u> television so late last night.

INCORRECT: Joe is going to get sick to study too much.
CORRECT: Joe is going to get sick <u>from</u> <u>studying</u> too much.

INCORRECT: If you go early, you will just get nervous to waiting.
CORRECT: If you go early, you will just get nervous <u>from</u> <u>waiting.</u>

INCORRECT: The car is really hot from to sit in the sun all day.
CORRECT: The car is really hot <u>from</u> <u>sitting</u> in the sun all day.

EXERCISES

Part A: Choose the correct answer.

It is now believed that some damage to tissues may result __________ them to frequent X-rays.
(A) the exposing
(B) from exposure
(C) from exposing
(D) expose

Part B: Choose the incorrect word or phrase and correct it.

<u>Many</u> (A) of the problems associated with aging <u>such as</u> (B) disorientation and irritability <u>may result</u> (C) <u>from to eat</u> (D) an unbalanced diet.

Purpose—*For*

Remember that *for* is used before a noun to express purpose for a tool or instrument. Some nouns are *-ing* forms.

	noun (instrument)	for	noun *-ing* noun	
This is a good	book	for	research	
This is a good	book	for	researching	the topic

Avoid using *for to* before the *-ing* noun.

Note: The infinitive is the most common way to express purpose. The infinitive can be used in all situations. *For* with an *-ing* form is usually limited to situations in which there is an instrument named.

EXAMPLES

INCORRECT: I bought a trunk for to store my winter clothes.
CORRECT: I bought a trunk for storing my winter clothes.
or
I bought a trunk to store my winter clothes.

INCORRECT: She has a CB radio in her car to emergencies.
CORRECT: She has a CB radio in her car for emergencies.
or
She has a CB radio in her car to help in emergencies.

INCORRECT: Each room has its own thermostat for to control the temperature.
CORRECT: Each room has its own thermostat for controlling the temperature.
or
Each room has its own thermostat to control the temperature.

INCORRECT: Sam needs another VCR for copy videotapes.
CORRECT: Sam needs another VCR for copying videotapes.
or
Sam needs another VCR to copy videotapes.

INCORRECT: Why don't you use the microscope in the lab for to examine the specimen?
CORRECT: Why don't you use the microscope in the lab for examining the specimen?
or
Why don't you use the microscope in the lab to examine the specimen?

EXERCISES

Part A: Choose the correct answer.

The most exact way known to science __________ the age of artifacts is based on the radioactivity of certain minerals.

(A) for to determine
(B) for determine
(C) for determining
(D) to determining

Part B: Choose the incorrect word or phrase and correct it.

George Ellery Hale and his (A) colleagues designed the two-hundred-inch (B) telescope on Mount Palomar (C) study (D) the structure of the universe.

Means—*By*

Remember that *by* expresses means.
A phrase with *by* answers the question *how?*

Avoid using an infinitive instead of an *-ing* form.

	by	*-ing*	
This report was written	by	programming	a computer

EXAMPLES

INCORRECT: You can win by to practice.
CORRECT: You can win by practicing.

INCORRECT: Make a reservation for calling our 800 number.
CORRECT: Make a reservation by calling our 800 number.

INCORRECT: Beverly lost weight for hiking.
CORRECT: Beverly lost weight by hiking.

INCORRECT: Gloria made a lot of friends to working in the cafeteria.
CORRECT: Gloria made a lot of friends by working in the cafeteria.

INCORRECT: Choose the correct answer for marking the letter that corresponds to it on the answer sheet.
CORRECT: Choose the correct answer by marking the letter that corresponds to it on the answer sheet.

EXERCISES

Part A: Choose the correct answer.

Ladybugs are brightly colored beetles that help farmers by ______________.
(A) eat other insects
(B) to eat other insects
(C) eating other insects
(D) other insect's eating

Part B: Choose the incorrect word or phrase and correct it.

The government raises (A) money to operate (B) by tax (C) cigarettes, liquor, gasoline, tires, and telephone calls. (D)

Time Limit—*From, To*

Remember that *from* introduces a time and *to* sets a limit.

	from	time	to	limit
The group was popular	from	the 1980s	to	the 1990s

Avoid using *for* instead of *from* and instead of *to*.

EXAMPLES

INCORRECT: I need you to baby-sit from six o'clock and ten-thirty.
CORRECT: I need you to baby-sit from six o'clock to ten-thirty.

INCORRECT: The class is scheduled for January 15 to May 7.
CORRECT: The class is scheduled from January 15 to May 7.

INCORRECT: You could have a room from Monday and Friday, but we are booked over the weekend.
CORRECT: You could have a room from Monday to Friday, but we are booked over the weekend.

INCORRECT: She was a student here to 1990 to 1995.
CORRECT: She was a student here from 1990 to 1995.

INCORRECT: The ticket is valid from June and September.
CORRECT: The ticket is valid from June to September.

EXERCISES

Part A: Choose the correct answer.

The Copper Age lasted______, after which bronze was introduced.
(A) from about 5000 B.C. to about 3700 B.C.
(B) about from 5000 B.C. and about 3700 B.C.
(C) for about 5000 B.C. to 3700 B.C. about
(D) about 5000 B.C. to about 3700 B.C.

Part B: Choose the incorrect word or phrase and correct it.

Led by Daniel Webster (A), the Whig party was one of (B) the two major political powers (C) in the United States from 1834 and 1852 (D).

CUMULATIVE REVIEW EXERCISE FOR PREPOSITIONS

DIRECTIONS: Some of the sentences in this exercise are correct. Some are incorrect. First, find the correct sentences, and mark them with a check (√). Then find the incorrect sentences, and correct them. Check your answers using the key on pages 533–534.

1. It is possible to find the weight of anything that floats for weighing the water that it displaces.

2. Metals such copper, silver, iron, and aluminum are good conductors of electricity.

3. The Mother Goose nursery rhymes have been traced back to a collection that appeared in England on 1760.

4. In making a distinction between butterflies and moths, it is best to examine the antennae.

5. None of the states but for Hawaii is an island.

6. Beside copper, which is the principal metal produced, gold, silver, lead, zinc, iron, and uranium are mined in Utah.

7. This year, beside figuring standard income tax, taxpayers might also have to compute alternative minimum tax.

8. Jet engines are used instead piston engines for almost all but the smallest aircraft.

9. Trained athletes have slower heart rates because of their hearts can pump more blood with every beat.

10. Tools as such axes, hammerstones, sickles, and awls were made by Paleolithic man using a method called pressure flaking.

11. Despite of some opposition, many city authorities still fluoridate water to prevent tooth decay.

12. The White House is on 1700 Pennsylvania Avenue.

13. Ice skating surfaces can be made of interlocking plastic squares instead of ice.

14. In supply-side economics, a balanced budget results from to reduce government spending.

15. All of the Native Americans but the Sioux were defeated by the European settlers.

Problems with Conjunctions

Conjunctions are words or phrases that clarify relationships between clauses. "Conjoin" means "to join together."

PROBLEMS WITH CORRELATIVE CONJUNCTIONS

Correlative conjunctions are pairs that are used together. They often express inclusion or exclusion.

Correlative conjunctions must be followed by the same grammatical structures; in other words, you must use parallel structures after correlative conjunctions.

Correlative Conjunctions—Inclusives *both . . . and*

Remember that *both . . . and* are correlative conjunctions. They are used together to include two parallel structures (two nouns, adjectives, verbs, adverbs).

	both	parallel structure	and	parallel structure	
	Both	Dr. Jones	and	Miss Smith	spoke
The lecture was	both	interesting	and	instructive	

Avoid using *as well as* instead of *and* with *both.* Avoid using *both . . . and* for more than two parallel structures.

EXAMPLES

INCORRECT: She speaks both English as well as Spanish at home.
CORRECT: She speaks both English and Spanish at home.

INCORRECT: Virginia opened and a savings account and a checking account.
CORRECT: Virginia opened both a savings account and a checking account.

INCORRECT: The weather on Sunday will be both sunny, warmer also.
CORRECT: The weather on Sunday will be both sunny and warmer.

INCORRECT: We can use the bike both to ride to school also go to the grocery store.
CORRECT: We can use the bike both to ride to school and to go to the grocery store.

INCORRECT: The party will celebrate both our finishing the term as well your getting a new job.
CORRECT: The party will celebrate both our finishing the term and your getting a new job.

EXERCISES

Part A: Choose the correct answer.

The belief in life after death is prevalent in both primitive societies _________ advanced cultures.

(A) and
(B) and in
(C) and also
(D) also

Part B: Choose the incorrect word or phrase and correct it.

Both viruses also (A) genes are (B) made from nucleoproteins, the essential chemicals with which living (C) matter duplicates itself (D).

Correlative Conjunctions—Inclusives *both . . . and . . . as well as*

Remember that *both . . . and . . . as well as* are correlative conjunctions. They must be used in sequence to include two or three parallel structures (nouns, adjectives, verbs, adverbs).

	parallel structure	as well as	parallel structure
He enjoys playing	basketball	as well as	football
He is	intelligent	as well as	athletic

	(both)	parallel structure	and	parallel structure	as well as	parallel structure
He enjoys playing	both	soccer	and	baseball	as well as	tennis
He is	both	intelligent	and	artistic	as well as	athletic

Avoid using *as well* instead of *as well as.*

EXAMPLES

INCORRECT: Both Mary, Ellen, and Jean are going on the tour.
CORRECT: Both Mary and Ellen as well as Jean are going on the tour.

INCORRECT: My fiancé is both attractive and intelligent as well considerate.
CORRECT: My fiancé is both attractive and intelligent as well as considerate.

INCORRECT: There are snacks both in the refrigerator and in the oven as well on the table.
CORRECT: There are snacks both in the refrigerator and in the oven as well as on the table.

INCORRECT: To reach your goal, you must plan and work as well dream.
CORRECT: To reach your goal, you must plan and work as well as dream.

INCORRECT: We will keep in touch by both writing both calling and visiting each other.
CORRECT: We will keep in touch by both writing and calling as well as visiting each other.

EXERCISES

Part A: Choose the correct answer.

The terrain in North Carolina includes both the Highlands and the Coastal Plain, ________ the Piedmont Plateau between them.

(A) as well as
(B) also
(C) and too
(D) and so

Part B: Choose the incorrect word or phrase and correct it.

Agronomists study (A) crop disease, (B) selective breeding, crop rotation, and climatic factors, as well (C) soil content and (D) erosion.

Correlative Conjunctions—Inclusives *not only . . . but also*

Remember that *not only . . . but also* are correlative conjunctions. They are used together to include two parallel structures (two nouns, adjectives, verbs, adverbs).

	not only	parallel structure	but also	parallel structure
One should take	not only	cash	but also	traveler's checks
Checks are	not only	safer	but also	more convenient

Avoid using *only not* instead of *not only.* Avoid using *but* instead of *but also.* Avoid using the incorrect pattern:

not only	parallel structure	but	parallel structure	also
not only	cash safer	but but	traveler's checks more convenient	also also

EXAMPLES

INCORRECT: The program provides only not theoretical classes but also practical training.
CORRECT: The program provides not only theoretical classes but also practical training.

INCORRECT: The new models are not only less expensive but more efficient also.
CORRECT: The new models are not only less expensive but also more efficient.

INCORRECT: The objective is not to identify the problem but also to solve it.
CORRECT: The objective is not only to identify the problem but also to solve it.

INCORRECT: Not only her parents but her brothers and sisters also live in Wisconsin.
CORRECT: Not only her parents but also her brothers and sisters live in Wisconsin.

INCORRECT: To complete his physical education credits, John took not only swimming also golf.
CORRECT: To complete his physical education credits, John took not only swimming but also golf.

EXERCISES

Part A: Choose the correct answer.

Amniocentesis can be used not only to diagnose fetal disorders __________ the sex of the unborn child with 95 percent accuracy.

(A) but determining
(B) but also determining
(C) but to determine
(D) but also to determine

Part B: Choose the incorrect word or phrase and correct it.

The deadbolt is the best (A) lock for entry doors because (B) it is not only (C) inexpensive but installation is easy. (D)

Correlative Conjunctions—Exclusives *not . . . but*

Remember that *not. . . but* are correlative conjunctions. They are used together to exclude the structure that follows *not* (noun, adjective, verb, adverb) and include the structure that follows *but.*

	not	noun adjective	but	noun adjective
The largest university is The school color is	not not	Minnesota blue	but but	Ohio State red

Avoid using *only* instead *of but.*

EXAMPLES

INCORRECT: According to the coroner, she died not of injuries sustained in the accident, only of a heart attack.
CORRECT: According to the coroner, she died not of injuries sustained in the accident but of a heart attack.

INCORRECT: The office that I was assigned was not large and cheerful but only small and dark.
CORRECT: The office that I was assigned was not large and cheerful but small and dark.

INCORRECT: To judge your friends, you should not listen to what they say only observe what they do.
CORRECT: To judge your friends, you should not listen to what they say but observe what they do.

INCORRECT: Jill could make herself understood if she spoke not louder but only more slowly.
CORRECT: Jill could make herself understood if she spoke not louder but more slowly.

INCORRECT: It is not the money only the principle that makes me angry.
CORRECT: It is not the money but the principle that makes me angry.

EXERCISES

Part A: Choose the correct answer.

It is usually ________ lava but gas that kills people during volcanic eruptions.
(A) not only
(B) not
(C) neither
(D) no

Part B: Choose the incorrect word or phrase and correct it.

Before (A) the invention of the musical staff, people passed musical compositions on to each other (B) not by writing them down but also (C) by remembering them (D).

PROBLEMS WITH OTHER CONJUNCTIONS

Affirmative Agreement—*So* and *Too*

Remember that *so, too,* and *also* have the same meaning, but *so* is used before auxiliary verbs and *too* and *also* are used after auxiliary verbs.

S	MODAL HAVE V Be	verb word participle *-ing*		and	so	MODAL HAVE DO BE	S
My wife	will	talk	to him	and	so	will	I
My wife	has	talked	about it,	and	so	have	I
My wife	talked			and	so	did	I
My wife	is	talking		and	so	am	I

S	MODAL HAVE V Be	verb word participle *-ing*		and	S	MODAL HAVE DO BE	also too
My wife	will	talk	to him	and	I	will	too
My wife	has	talked	about it,	and	I	have	too
My wife	talked			and	I	did	too
My wife	is	talking		and	I	am	too

Avoid using *also* instead of *so*.

EXAMPLES

INCORRECT: We are going to the concert, and so do they.

CORRECT: We are going to the concert, and so are they.

or

We are going to the concert, and they are too.

or

We are going to the concert, and they are also.

INCORRECT: He likes to travel, and so is she.
CORRECT: He likes to travel, and so does she.
or
He likes to travel, and she does too.
or
He likes to travel, and she does also.

INCORRECT: I am worried about it, and also is he.
CORRECT: I am worried about it, and so is he.
or
I am worried about it, and he is too.
or
I am worried about it, and he is also.

INCORRECT: Mary wants to go home, and so want we.
CORRECT: Mary wants to go home, and so do we.
or
Mary wants to go home, and we do too.
or
Mary wants to go home, and we do also.

INCORRECT: She took pictures, and I did so.
CORRECT: She took pictures, and so did I.
or
She took pictures, and I did too.
or
She took pictures, and I did also.

EXERCISES

Part A: Choose the correct answer.

Technically, glass is a mineral and ________________.

(A) water so
(B) water is so
(C) so is water
(D) so water is

Part B: Choose the incorrect word or phrase and correct it.

Some birds (A) can travel at speeds approaching one hundred miles an hour (B), and a few land animals (C) can so (D).

Negative Agreement—*Neither* and *Either*

Remember that *neither* and *either* have the same meaning, but *neither* is used before auxiliary verbs and *either* is used after auxiliary verbs and *not.*

S	MODAL HAVE DO BE not	verb word participle verb word -*ing* form,	and	neither	MODAL HAVE DO BE	S
My roommate	won't	go,	and	neither	will	I
My roommate	hasn't	gone,	and	neither	have	I
My roommate	doesn't	go,	and	neither	do	I
My roommate	isn't	going,	and	neither	am	I

Avoid using *either* instead of *neither.* Avoid using the subject before *BE, DO, HAVE,* or the modal in a clause with *neither.*

S	MODAL HAVE DO BE not	verb word participle verb word -*ing* form	and	S	MODAL HAVE DO BE not	either
My roommate	won't	go,	and	I	won't	either
My roommate	hasn't	gone,	and	I	haven't	either
My roommate	doesn't	go,	and	I	don't	either
My roommate	isn't	going,	and	I	'm not	either

Avoid using *neither* instead of *either.*

EXAMPLES

INCORRECT: She hasn't finished the assignment yet, and neither I have.
CORRECT: She hasn't finished the assignment yet, and neither have I.
or
She hasn't finished the assignment yet, and I haven't either.

INCORRECT: I didn't know the answer, and he didn't neither.
CORRECT: I didn't know the answer, and neither did he.
or
I didn't know the answer, and he didn't either.

INCORRECT: If Jane won't go to the party, either will he.
CORRECT: If Jane won't go to the party, neither will he.
or
If Jane won't go to the party, he won't either.

INCORRECT: She is not in agreement, and neither do I.
CORRECT: She is not in agreement, and neither am I.
or
She is not in agreement, and I'm not either.

INCORRECT: He won't be here today, and either his sister will.
CORRECT: He won't be here today, and neither will his sister.
or
He won't be here today, and his sister won't either.

EXERCISES

Part A: Choose the correct answer.

Although they are both grown in the United States and exported abroad, corn is not native to America and winter wheat ____________.

(A) is neither
(B) isn't either
(C) isn't neither
(D) is either

Part B: Choose the incorrect word or phrase and correct it.

<u>According</u> (A) to <u>many educators</u> (B), television should not <u>become</u> (C) a replacement for good teachers, and neither <u>are</u> (D) computers.

Planned Result—*So That*

Remember that *so that* introduces a clause of planned result.

S	V		so that	S	V	
He	is studying	hard	so that	he	can pass	his exams

Avoid using *so* instead of *so that* as a purpose connector in written English.
Note: In spoken English, *so* instead of *so that* is often used. In written English, *so that* is preferred.

EXAMPLES

INCORRECT: He borrowed the money so he could finish his education.
CORRECT: He borrowed the money <u>so that</u> he could finish his education.

INCORRECT: Larry took a bus from New York to California so he could see the country.
CORRECT: Larry took a bus from New York to California <u>so that</u> he could see the country.

INCORRECT: Many men join fraternities so they will be assured of group support.
CORRECT: Many men join fraternities <u>so that</u> they will be assured of group support.

INCORRECT: Don't forget to register this week so you can vote in the election.
CORRECT: Don't forget to register this week <u>so that</u> you can vote in the election.

INCORRECT: Every student needs a social security number so he can get a university identification card made.
CORRECT: Every student needs a social security number <u>so that</u> he can get a university identification card made.

EXERCISES

Part A: Choose the correct answer.

A communications satellite orbits the Earth at the same rate that the Earth revolves ________ over a fixed point on the surface.

(A) so it can remain
(B) so that it can remain
(C) it can remain
(D) so can remain

Part B: Choose the incorrect word or phrase and correct it.

The function of pain is to warn (A) the individual of danger so (B) he (C) can take action to avoid more serious (D) damage.

Future Result—*When*

Remember that *when* introduces a clause of condition for future result.

RESULT		CONDITION		
S	V (present) V (will + verb word)	when	S	V (present)
The temperature	drops	when	the sun	sets
The temperature	will drop	when	the sun	sets

Avoid using *will* instead of a present verb after *when.*

EXAMPLES

INCORRECT: I will call you when I will return from my country.
CORRECT: I will call you when I return from my country.

INCORRECT: Marilyn plans to work in her family's store when she will get her M.B.A.
CORRECT: Marilyn plans to work in her family's store when she gets her M.B.A.

INCORRECT: He will probably buy some more computer software when he will get paid.
CORRECT: He will probably buy some more computer software when he gets paid.

INCORRECT: She will feel a lot better when she will stop smoking.
CORRECT: She will feel a lot better when she stops smoking.

INCORRECT: When Gary will go to State University, he will be a teaching assistant.
CORRECT: When Gary goes to State University, he will be a teaching assistant.

EXERCISES

Part A: Choose the correct answer.

Bacterial spores germinate and sprout _________ favorable conditions of temperature and food supply.

(A) when encountering of
(B) when they encounter
(C) when they will encounter
(D) when the encounter of

Part B: Choose the incorrect word or phrase and correct it.

In <u>most states</u> (A) insurance agents <u>must pass</u> (B) an examination <u>to be licensed</u> (C) when they <u>will complete</u> (D) their training.

Indirect Questions

Remember that question words can be used as conjunctions. Question words introduce a clause of indirect question.

Question words include the following:

who	*why*
what	*how*
what time	*how long*
when	*how many*
where	*how much*

S	V	question word	S	V
I	don't remember	what	her name	is

V	S		question word	S	V
Do	you	remember	what	her name	is?

Avoid using *do, does,* or *did* after the question word. Avoid using the verb before the subject after the question word.

EXAMPLES

INCORRECT: I didn't understood what did he say.
CORRECT: I didn't understand <u>what</u> <u>he</u> <u>said</u>.

INCORRECT: Do you know how much do they cost?
CORRECT: Do you know <u>how much</u> <u>they</u> <u>cost</u>?

NCORRECT: I wonder when is her birthday.
CORRECT: I wonder when her birthday is.

NCORRECT: Could you please tell me where is the post office?
CORRECT: Could you please tell me where the post office is?

NCORRECT: Can they tell you what time does the movie start?
CORRECT: Can they tell you what time the movie starts?

EXERCISES

Part A: Choose the correct answer.

Recently, there have been several outbreaks of disease like legionnaire's syndrome, and doctors don't know ______________.

(A) what is the cause
(B) the cause is what
(C) is what the cause
(D) what the cause is

Part B: Choose the incorrect word or phrase and correct it.

In Ground Control Approach, the air traffic controller (A) informs (B) the pilot how far is the plane (C) from the touchdown point (D).

PROBLEM 125 Question Words with *-ever*

Remember that *-ever* means *any. Whoever* and *whomever* mean anyone; *whatever* means anything; *wherever* means anywhere; *whenever* means any time; *however* means any way.

The *-ever* words may be used as conjunctions to introduce clauses.

S	V		-ever	S	V
I	agree	with	whatever	you	decide

Avoid using *any* instead of *-ever.* Avoid using *-ever* before instead of after the question word.

EXAMPLES

INCORRECT: We can leave ever when Donna is ready.
CORRECT: We can leave whenever Donna is ready.

INCORRECT: Order any what you like.
CORRECT: Order whatever you like.

INCORRECT: The representative will vote for whom the membership supports.
CORRECT: The representative will vote for whomever the membership supports.

INCORRECT: Feel free to present your projects ever how you wish.
CORRECT: Feel free to present your projects <u>however</u> <u>you</u> <u>wish</u>.

INCORRECT: I can meet with you ever you have the time.
CORRECT: I can meet with you <u>whenever</u> <u>you</u> <u>have</u> the time.

EXERCISES

Part A: Choose the correct answer.

Blue-green algae are found __________ there is ample moisture.
(A) wherever
(B) ever where
(C) ever
(D) there ever

Part B: Choose the incorrect word or phrase and correct it.

<u>Ever</u> (A) the Senate <u>passes</u> (B) a bill, a messenger takes it to the House of Representatives, delivers it to the Speaker of the House, and <u>bows</u> (C) <u>deeply</u> (D) from the waist.

CUMULATIVE REVIEW EXERCISE FOR CONJUNCTIONS

<u>DIRECTIONS</u>: Some of the sentences in this exercise are correct. Some are incorrect. First, find the correct sentences, and mark them with a (√). Then find the incorrect sentences, and correct them. Check your answers using the key on pages 534–535.

1. Foreign students who are making a decision about which school to attend may not know exactly where the choices are located.
2. Now, classes taught by television are equipped with boom microphones in the classrooms so students can stop the action, ask their questions, and receive immediate answers.
3. The Colosseum received its name not for its size but for a colossally large statue of Nero near it.
4. A wind instrument is really just a pipe arranged so air can be blown into it at one end.
5. It is very difficult to compute how much does an item cost in dollars when one is accustomed to calculating in another monetary system.
6. Adolescence, or the transitional period between childhood and adulthood, is not only a biological concept but a social concept.
7. Light is diffused when it will strike a rough surface.
8. The koala bear is not a bear at all, but a marsupial.

9. Ferns will grow wherever the soil is moist and the air is humid.

0. Although most rocks contain several minerals, limestone contains only one and marble is too.

1. Learners use both visual and auditory as well that analytical means to understand a new language.

2. In a recent study, many high school students did not know where were important geographical entities on the map of the United States.

3. It is not only lava but poisonous gases also that cause destruction and death during the eruption of a volcano.

4. Until recently West Point did not admit women and neither Annapolis.

5. The Federal Trade Commission may intervene whenever unfair business practices, particularly monopolies, are suspected.

Problems with Adverbs and Adverb-Related Structures

Adverbs and adverb phrases add information to sentences. They add information about *manner*, hat is, how something is done; *frequency* or how often; *time* and *date* or when; and *duration* of time or ow long.

Adverbs of Manner

Remember that adverbs of manner describe the manner in which something is done. They answer he question, *how?* Adverbs of manner usually end in *-ly*.

S	V	adverb (manner)	
The class	listened	attentively	to the lecture

Avoid using an adjective instead of an adverb of manner. Avoid using an adverb of manner between he two words of an infinitive.

XAMPLES

NCORRECT: After only six months in the United States, Jack understood everyone perfect.
CORRECT: After only six months in the United States, Jack understood everyone <u>perfectly</u>.

NCORRECT: Please do exact as your doctor says.
CORRECT: Please do <u>exactly</u> as your doctor says.

INCORRECT: From the top of the Empire State Building, tourists are able to clearly see New York.
CORRECT: From the top of the Empire State Building, tourists are able to see New York clearly.

INCORRECT: Broad speaking, curriculum includes all experiences which the student may have within the environment of the school.
CORRECT: Broadly speaking, curriculum includes all experiences which the student may have within the environment of the school.

INCORRECT: Passengers travel comfortable and safely in the new jumbo jets.
CORRECT: Passengers travel comfortably and safely in the new jumbo jets.

EXERCISES

Part A: Choose the correct answer.

A symbol of the ancient competition, the Olympic flame burns ________ throughout the games.

(A) in a continuous way
(B) continuous
(C) continuously
(D) continual

Part B: Choose the incorrect word or phrase and correct it.

Although the "Lake Poets" Wordsworth, Coleridge, and Southey were friends, they (A) did not really form a group since Southey's style differed wide (B) from (C) that of the other two (D).

Adverbs of Manner—*Fast, Late,* and *Hard*

Remember that although most adverbs of manner end in -ly, *fast, late,* and *hard* do not have *-ly* endings.

S	V		fast
This medication	relieves	headaches	fast

S	V		late	
My roommate	returned	home	late	last night

S	V	hard
The team	played	hard

Avoid using the **incorrect** forms ~~*fastly*~~ and ~~*lately*~~ and ~~*hardly*~~.

Note: *Lately* and *hardly* are not adverb forms of *late* and *hard*. *Lately* means recently. *Hardly* means almost not at all.

EXAMPLES

INCORRECT: Helen types fastly and efficiently.
CORRECT: Helen types fast and efficiently.

INCORRECT: The plane is scheduled to arrive lately because of bad weather.
CORRECT: The plane is scheduled to arrive late because of bad weather.

INCORRECT: Although he tried as hardly as he could, he did not win the race.
CORRECT: Although he tried as hard as he could, he did not win the race.

INCORRECT: When students register lately for classes, they must pay an additional fee.
CORRECT: When students register late for classes, they must pay an additional fee.

INCORRECT: First class mail travels as fastly as airmail now.
CORRECT: First class mail travels as fast as airmail now.

EXERCISES

Part A: Choose the correct answer.

When a woman becomes pregnant ____________ in life, she encounters additional risks in delivering a healthy baby.

(A) lately
(B) lateness
(C) latest
(D) late

Part B: Choose the incorrect word or phrase and correct it.

Overseas telephone service has been expanding (A) fastly (B) since its inauguration in 1927 (C) when a radio circuit was established (D) between New York and London.

Sometime and *Sometimes*

Remember that *sometime* means at some time in the indefinite future. *Sometimes* means occasionally.

Sometime is usually used after a verb. *Sometimes* is usually used at the beginning or end of a sentence or a clause.

Sometime answers the question, *when? Sometimes* answers the question, *how often?*

S	V		no specific date in the future sometime
My family	will call	me long distance	sometime

occasionally sometimes	S	V	
Sometimes	my family	calls	me long distance

Avoid using *sometimes* instead of *sometime* to express an indefinite time in the future.

EXAMPLES

INCORRECT: Let's have lunch sometimes.
CORRECT: Let's have lunch sometime.
(no specific date in the future)

INCORRECT: It is cool now, but sometime it gets very warm here.
CORRECT: It is cool now, but sometimes it gets very warm here.
(occasionally)

INCORRECT: Janet would like to travel sometimes, but right now she has to finish her degree.
CORRECT: Janet would like to travel sometime, but right now she has to finish her degree.
(no specific date in the future)

INCORRECT: Why don't you call me sometimes?
CORRECT: Why don't you call me sometime?
(no specific date in the future)

INCORRECT: Sometime car manufacturers must recall certain models because of defects in design.
CORRECT: Sometimes car manufacturers must recall certain models because of defects in design.
(occasionally)

EXERCISES

Part A: Choose the correct answer.

_____________ on clear days one can see the snowcap of Mount Rainier from Seattle.

(A) Sometime
(B) Some
(C) Sometimes
(D) Somestime

Part B: Choose the incorrect word or phrase and correct it.

Sometime (A) several nations (B) become (C) partners in a larger political state, as for example, (D) the four nations joined in the United Kingdom of Great Britain and Northern Ireland.

Negative Emphasis

Remember that negatives include phrases like *not one, not once, not until, never, never again, only rarely,* and *very seldom.* Negatives answer the question, *how often?* They are used at the beginning of a statement to express emphasis. Auxiliaries must agree with verbs and subjects.

negative	auxiliary	S	V	
Never	have	I	seen	so much snow

Avoid using a subject before the auxiliary in this pattern.

Examples

INCORRECT: Never again they will stay in that hotel.
CORRECT: Never again will they stay in that hotel.

INCORRECT: Only rarely an accident has occurred.
CORRECT: Only rarely has an accident occurred.

INCORRECT: Very seldom a movie can hold my attention like this one.
CORRECT: Very seldom can a movie hold my attention like this one.

INCORRECT: Not one paper she has finished on time.
CORRECT: Not one paper has she finished on time.

INCORRECT: Not once Steve and Jan have invited us to their house.
CORRECT: Not once have Steve and Jan invited us to their house.

Exercises

Part A: Choose the correct answer.

Not until the Triassic Period ________________ .

(A) the first primitive mammals did develop
(B) did the first primitive mammals develop
(C) did develop the first primitive mammals
(D) the first primitive mammals develop

Part B: Chose the incorrect word or phrase and correct it.

Only rarely wins the same major league baseball team the World Series two years in a row.
(A) Only (B) wins the same major league baseball team (C) two years (D) in a row

Introductory Adverbial Modifiers—*Once*

Remember that *once* means at one time in the past. *Once* answers the question, *when? Once* is often used as an introductory adverbial modifier. It modifies the main subject that follows the clause.

once	noun	,	S	V	
Once	a salesman	,	Pete	has been promoted	to district manager

Avoid using *that* before *once.*

EXAMPLES

INCORRECT: That once a student at State University, he is now an engineer for an American company.
CORRECT: Once a student at State University, he is now an engineer for an American company.

INCORRECT: Once that a clerk in a grocery store, Helen is now a policewoman.
CORRECT: Once a clerk in a grocery store, Helen is now a policewoman.

INCORRECT: That once a citizen of Ireland, he is now applying for permanent residency in Canada.
CORRECT: Once a citizen of Ireland, he is now applying for permanent residency in Canada.

INCORRECT: It was once Republicans, we usually vote for Democratic candidates now.
CORRECT: Once Republicans, we usually vote for Democratic candidates now.

INCORRECT: That once an avid soccer fan, he is now becoming more interested in American football.
CORRECT: Once an avid soccer fan, he is now becoming more interested in American football.

EXERCISES

Part A: Choose the correct answer.

__________ a novelty in American retailing, fixed prices are now universal in sales.

(A) It was once
(B) Once it was
(C) That once
(D) Once

Part B: Choose the incorrect word or phrase and correct it.

That once (A) a talented child actress, Shirley Temple Black has established herself (B) as a career diplomat, serving (C) both as a representative in the United Nations and (D) as an ambassador abroad.

Introductory Adverbial Modifiers—*While*

Remember that *while* means at the same time. *While* answers the question *when?* It is often used as an introductory adverbial modifier. It modifies the main subject that follows the clause.

When can also mean at the same time, but *when* must be used before a subject and a verb in the same clause.

while	noun	,	S	V	
While	a salesman	,	Pete	traveled	a lot

while when	S	V		,	S	V	
While	he	was	a salesman	,	Pete	traveled	a lot
When	he	was	a salesman	,	Pete	traveled	a lot

Avoid using *when* instead of *while* without a subject and verb in the same clause.

EXAMPLES

INCORRECT: When in Washington, D.C., they saw the Capitol Building where Congress meets.
CORRECT: While (tourists) in Washington, D.C., they saw the Capitol Building where Congress meets.

or

While they were (tourists) in Washington, D.C., they saw the Capitol Building where Congress meets.

or

When they were (tourists) in Washington, D.C., they saw the Capitol Building where Congress meets.

INCORRECT: I was very homesick when a student abroad.
CORRECT: I was very homesick while a student abroad.

or

I was very homesick while I was a student abroad

or

I was very homesick when I was a student abroad.

INCORRECT: When still a teaching assistant, he was doing important research.
CORRECT: While still a teaching assistant, he was doing important research.

or

While he was still a teaching assistant, he was doing important research.

or

When he was still a teaching assistant, he was doing important research.

INCORRECT: According to the newspapers he accepted bribes when a high official of the government.

CORRECT: According to the newspaper, he accepted bribes while a high official of the government.

or

According to the newspaper, he accepted bribes while he was a high official of the government.

or

According to the newspaper, he accepted bribes when he was a high official of the government.

INCORRECT: While she on vacation, she bought gifts for her family.

CORRECT: While (a visitor) on vacation, she bought gifts for her family.

or

While she was (a visitor) on vacation, she bought gifts for her family.

or

When she was (a visitor) on vacation, she bought gifts for her family.

EXERCISES

Part A: Choose the correct answer.

_________ a bridge builder, Gustav Eiffel designed the Eiffel Tower for the Paris Exposition of 1889.

(A) While
(B) When
(C) It was when
(D) It while was

Part B: Choose the incorrect word or phrase and correct it.

When (A) a child, Barbara Mandrell played (B) the guitar, banjo, and saxophone in her family's band, but in 1981 (C) she was named (D) Entertainer of the Year for her singing, and she has continued her successful vocal career for several decades.

No Longer

Remember that *no longer* means not any more. *No longer* is often used between the auxiliary verb and the main verb.

No longer answers the question, *when?*

S	V (auxiliary)	no longer	V (main)	
I	can	no longer	see	without my glasses

Avoid using *not* and *none* instead of *no.*

EXAMPLES

INCORRECT: We can not longer tolerate living with Terry.
CORRECT: We can <u>no longer</u> tolerate living with Terry.

INCORRECT: Brad none longer works here.
CORRECT: Brad <u>no longer</u> works here.

INCORRECT: Since she talked with her advisor, she is not longer interested in majoring in political science.
CORRECT: Since she talked with her advisor, she is <u>no longer</u> interested in majoring in political science.

INCORRECT: The person you are trying to reach is no long at this telephone number.
CORRECT: The person you are trying to reach is <u>no longer</u> at this telephone number.

INCORRECT: Although they used to write each other every day, they are not longer exchanging letters.
CORRECT: Although they used to write each other every day, they are <u>no longer</u> exchanging letters.

EXERCISES

Part A: Choose the correct answer.

According to communications theory, after the message leaves the sender, he ________ controls it.
(A) not longer
(B) none longer
(C) longer doesn't
(D) no longer

Part B: Choose the incorrect word or phrase and correct it.

Ghost towns <u>like</u> (A) Rhyolite, Nevada, are communities that are <u>not longer</u> (B) inhabited <u>because</u> (C) changes in economic conditions have caused the people <u>to move</u> (D) elsewhere.

Duration—*For* and *Since*

Remember that *for* is used before a quantity of time. *For* expresses duration. *For* answers the question, *how long? Since* is used before a specific time. *Since* expresses duration too, but *since* answers the question, *beginning when?*

Remember that a quantity of time may be several days—a month, two years, etc. A specific time may be Wednesday, July, 1960, etc. You will notice that the structure *HAVE* and a participle is often used with adverbs of duration.

S	HAVE	participle		for	quantity of time
She	has	been	in the U.S.	for	six months

S	HAVE	participle		since	specific time
She	has	been	in the U.S.	since	June

Avoid using *for* before specific times. Avoid using *before* after HAVE and a participle.

EXAMPLES

INCORRECT: Mary has been on a diet since three weeks.
CORRECT: Mary has been on a diet <u>for</u> <u>three weeks.</u>

INCORRECT: She has been living here before April.
CORRECT: She has been living here <u>since</u> <u>April</u>.

INCORRECT: We haven't seen him since almost a year.
CORRECT: We haven't seen him <u>for</u> <u>almost a year</u>.

INCORRECT: We have known each other before 1974.
CORRECT: We have known each other <u>since</u> <u>1974</u>.

INCORRECT: He has studied English since five years.
CORRECT: He has studied English <u>for</u> <u>five years</u>.

EXERCISES

Part A: Choose the correct answer.

Penguins, the most highly specialized of all aquatic birds, may live _______ twenty years.

(A) before
(B) since
(C) for
(D) from

Part B: Choose the incorrect word or phrase and correct it.

Because national statistics on crime have only been kept <u>for 1930,</u> (A) <u>it</u> (B) is not possible <u>to make</u> (C) judgments about crime <u>during the early years</u> (D) of the nation.

Dates

Remember that there is an expected pattern for dates of the month. Dates answer the question *when?*

	the	ordinal number		of	month
Valentine's Day is on	the	fourteenth		of	February

	Ø	month	ordinal number
Valentine's Day is on		February	fourteenth

Avoid using a cardinal number instead of an ordinal number.

EXAMPLES

INCORRECT: I have an appointment on the five of June at three o'clock.
CORRECT: I have an appointment on the fifth of June at three-o'clock.
or
I have an appointment on June fifth at three o'clock.

INCORRECT: School starts on sixteen September this year.
CORRECT: School starts on the sixteenth of September this year.
or
School starts on September sixteenth this year.

INCORRECT: Her birthday is second December.
CORRECT: Her birthday is the second of December.
or
Her birthday is December second.

INCORRECT: Please change my reservation to the ten of November.
CORRECT: Please change my reservation to the tenth of November.
or
Please change my reservation to November tenth.

INCORRECT: Independence Day in the United States is the four of July.
CORRECT: Independence Day in the United States is the fourth of July.
or
Independence Day in the United States is July fourth.

EXERCISES

Part A: Choose the correct answer.

Memorial Day, a holiday set aside to remember those who have died, is usually celebrated on ______.

(A) thirtieth May
(B) the thirtieth May
(C) May thirty
(D) the thirtieth of May

Part B: Choose the incorrect word or phrase and correct it.

On the fourth July (A) in 1884, the Statue of Liberty was presented (B) formally (C) by the people of France (D) to the people of the United States.

Pseudocomparatives

Remember that although *as high as* and *as soon as* appear to be comparatives, they are adverbia idioms. *As high as* introduces a limit of height or cost. It answers the question, *how high* or *how muc* (money)? *As soon as* introduces a limit of time. It answers the question, *when?*

	as high as	
The price of a haircut runs	as high as	fifty dollars

S	will	verb word		as soon as when	S	V (present)
He	will	go	home	as soon as	he	graduates

Avoid using *to* instead of *as.* Avoid using *will* and a verb word instead of a present verb after *as soon a*

EXAMPLES

INCORRECT: I plan to move as soon as I will find another apartment.
CORRECT: I plan to move as soon as I find another apartment.

INCORRECT: Since taxi fare from the airport may run as high to twenty dollars, I suggest that you tak a limousine.
CORRECT: Since taxi fare from the airport may run as high as twenty dollars, I suggest that you tak a limousine.

INCORRECT: She will call you back as soon as she will finish dinner.
CORRECT: She will call you back as soon as she finishes dinner.

INCORRECT: The cost of one day in an average hospital can run as high to $2000.
CORRECT: The cost of one day in an average hospital can run as high as $2000.

INCORRECT: Your application will be considered as soon as your file will be complete.
CORRECT: Your application will be considered as soon as your file is complete.

EXERCISES

Part A: Choose the correct answer.

In Xerox printing, the ink becomes fused to the paper as soon as ______________.
(A) the paper heated
(B) the paper is heated
(C) heats the paper
(D) heating the paper

Part B: Choose the incorrect word or phrase and correct it.

Alcoholic beverages vary <u>widely</u> (A) in content, ranging <u>from</u> (B) only 2 or 3 percent for some light beers to <u>as high to</u> (C) 60 percent <u>for</u> (D) some vodkas and brandies.

136 Generalization—*As a Whole* and *Wholly*

Remember that *as a whole* means generally. *Wholly* means completely. *As a whole* is often used at the beginning of a sentence or a clause. *Wholly* is often used after the auxiliary or main verb.

generally as a whole	S	V	
As a whole	the news	is	correct

S	V	completely wholly	
The news	is	wholly	correct

Avoid using *wholly* instead of *as a whole* at the beginning of a sentence or clause to mean generally. Avoid using *as whole* instead of *as a whole.*

EXAMPLES

INCORRECT: Wholly, we are in agreement.
CORRECT: <u>As a whole,</u> we are in agreement.
(generally)

INCORRECT: The house and all of its contents was as a whole consumed by the fire.
CORRECT: The house and all of its contents was <u>wholly</u> consumed by the fire.
(completely)

INCORRECT: The teams are not rated equally, but, wholly, they are evenly matched.
CORRECT: The teams are not rated equally, but, <u>as a whole,</u> they are evenly matched.
(generally)

INCORRECT: Wholly, Dan's operation proved to be successful.
CORRECT: <u>As a whole,</u> Dan's operation proved to be successful.
(generally)

INCORRECT: As whole, people try to be helpful to tourists.
CORRECT: <u>As a whole,</u> people try to be helpful to tourists.
(generally)

EXERCISES

Part A: Choose the correct answer.

__________ the Gulf Stream is warmer than the ocean water surrounding it.

(A) Wholly
(B) Whole
(C) As a whole
(D) A whole as

Part B: Choose the incorrect word or phrase and correct it.

Although <u>there are</u> (A) exceptions, <u>as whole</u> (B), the male of the bird species is <u>more</u> (C) <u>brilliantly</u> (D) colored.

CUMULATIVE REVIEW EXERCISE FOR ADVERBS AND ADVERB-RELATED STRUCTURES

<u>DIRECTIONS</u>: Some of the sentences in this exercise are correct. Some are incorrect. First, find the correc sentences and mark them with a (√). Then find the incorrect sentences, and correct them. Check you answers using the key on page 535.

1. Not once Lincoln has been painted smiling.

2. The first *Skylab* crew was launched on twenty-fifth May, 1973.

3. Wholly, artificial insemination has contributed to the quality of maintaining dairy herds.

4. Thor Heyerdahl worked diligent to prove his theory of cultural diffusion.

5. The Navajos have lived in Arizona for almost one thousand years.

6. That once a serious problem, measles can now be prevented by a vaccine.

7. Because the British fleet arrived lately off the Yorktown Peninsula, the French were able to contro the seas, thereby aiding the United States during the Revolution.

8. When the chemicals inside a cell not longer produce ions, the cell stops functioning.

9. The common goldfish may live as long twenty-five years.

10. When a mechanic working at odd jobs, Elisha Otis invented the elevator.

11. Sometimes students fail to score well on examinations because they are too nervous to concentrate

12. Alligators are no longer on the endangered species list.

13. The standard for atomic weight has been provided by the carbon isotope C12 since 1961.

14. That it was once a busy mining settlement, Virginia City is now a small town with a population o one thousand people.

15. Not until the late Middle Ages glass did become a major construction material.

Problems with Sentences and Clauses

Sentences and Clauses

Remember that a main clause, also called an independent clause, can function as a separate sentence. A subordinate clause, also called a dependent clause, must be attached to a main clause. A dependent clause is often marked with the clause marker *that.*

SENTENCE		
Main Clause (Sentence)	Clause Marker - - - - - - - - - - -	Dependent Clause
We were glad	that	the box came

Avoid using the clause marker with dependent clauses as sentences. Avoid using the clause marker *that* with a sentence that has no dependent clause following it.

Examples

INCORRECT: Utensils and condiments that are found on the table by the door.
CORRECT: <u>Utensils and condiments</u> <u>are found</u> on the table by the door.

INCORRECT: During final exam week, that the library when opening all night.
CORRECT: During final exam week, <u>the library</u> <u>is open</u> all night.

INCORRECT: The weather that is very rainy this time of year.
CORRECT: <u>The weather</u> <u>is</u> very rainy this time of year.

INCORRECT: All of the dorms that are located on East Campus.
CORRECT: All of the <u>dorms</u> <u>are located</u> on East Campus.

INCORRECT: During our vacation, that we suspended the newspaper delivery.
CORRECT: During our vacation, <u>we</u> <u>suspended</u> the newspaper delivery.

Exercises

Part A: Choose the correct answer.

Of all the cities in Texas, ________.
(A) that San Antonio is probably the most picturesque
(B) San Antonio is probably the most picturesque
(C) probably San Antonio the most picturesque
(D) the most picturesque probably that San Antonio

Part B: Choose the incorrect word or phrase and correct it.

<u>Thunder</u> <u>that</u> is audible from distances as far away <u>as</u> ten <u>miles</u>.
(A) (B) (C) (D)

Clause-Marker Subjects

Remember that some dependent clauses may come in the middle of a main clause. In many of these dependent clauses, the clause marker is the subject of the dependent clause, for example, the clause-marker *which.*

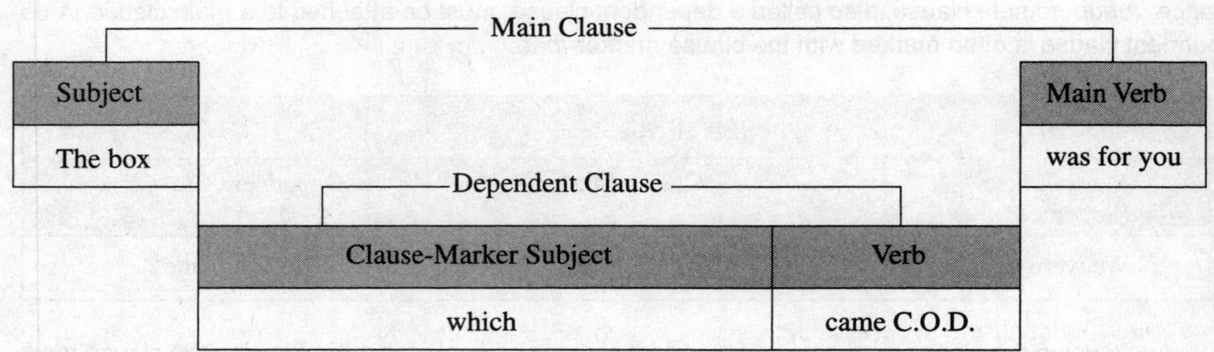

Avoid using a clause-marker subject without a verb or a verb without a clause-marker subject in dependent clauses of this type.

EXAMPLES

INCORRECT: The concert, is scheduled for Friday, has been canceled.
CORRECT: The concert, which is scheduled for Friday, has been canceled.

INCORRECT: Asking questions, which essential in learning a language, can be difficult for beginners.
CORRECT: Asking questions, which is essential in learning a language, can be difficult for beginners.

INCORRECT: My suitcases, which they are now at the city airport, have been located.
CORRECT: My suitcases, which are now at the city airport, have been located.

INCORRECT: The telephone number, which number I wrote down, is for the hotel.
CORRECT: The telephone number, which is written down, is for the hotel.

INCORRECT: The flowers, which were just delivering, are from Steve.
CORRECT: The flowers, which were just delivered, are from Steve.

EXERCISES

Part A: Choose the correct answer.

The Good Earth, _______, is a novel set in China.

(A) which by Pearl Buck
(B) which was written by Pearl Buck
(C) was written by Pearl Buck
(D) Pearl Buck being the one who wrote it

Part B: Choose the incorrect word or phrase and correct it.

Quasars, which (A) relatively small objects, emit (B) an enormous amount (C) of energy (D).

139 Verbs in Dependent Clauses

Remember that both main clauses and dependent clauses must have their own verbs.

Main Clause	Clause Marker - - - - - - - - - - Dependent Clause		
S V	that	S	V
It is good	that	the box	arrived on time

Avoid deleting the verb in a dependent clause, or using an *-ing* form instead of a verb in the dependent clause.

Examples

INCORRECT: It is a shame that you missing the movie.
CORRECT: It is a shame that you missed the movie.

INCORRECT: She knows that mistakes in grammar occasionally.
CORRECT: She knows that she makes mistakes in grammar occasionally.

INCORRECT: He said that going was he wanted.
CORRECT: He said that he wanted to go.

INCORRECT: I noticed that Mary's absence today.
CORRECT: I noticed that Mary was absent today.

INCORRECT: The experiment proved that less water for the plants.
CORRECT: The experiment proved that the plants needed less water.

Exercises

Part A: Choose the correct answer.

Most beekeepers have observed________at the approach of a thunderstorm.

(A) enraging the bees
(B) that bees become enraged
(C) that bees enraging
(D) become enraged the bees

Part B: Choose the incorrect word or phrase and correct it.

Most (A) modern observatories contain (B) telescopes that scientists using (C) as cameras to take (D) photographs of remote galaxies.

Adjective Clauses

Remember that in some dependent clauses, called adjective clauses, the clause marker refers to and modifies the object of the main clause.

Main Clause			Clause Marker - - - Dependent Clause		
S	V		that	S	V
These boxes	are	the ones	that	we	ordered

Avoid adjective clauses without a subject or without a verb.

EXAMPLES

INCORRECT: This is the way that coming the last time.
CORRECT: This is the way that we came the last time.

INCORRECT: These are the ones that bought.
CORRECT: These are the ones that I bought.

INCORRECT: This book is the one that our class.
CORRECT: This book is the one that our class used.

INCORRECT: These are the assignments that our teacher giving us.
CORRECT: These are the assignments that our teacher gave us.

INCORRECT: There are some things that don't understand about living in the United States.
CORRECT: There are some things that I don't understand about living in the United States.

EXERCISES

Part A: Choose the correct answer.

Culture influences the way_______.
(A) viewing the world
(B) that we view the world
(C) the world view
(D) is the view of the world

Part B: Choose the incorrect word or phrase and correct it.

Of all the reference materials, the encyclopedia is the one that most people using.
(A) (B) (C) (D)

CUMULATIVE REVIEW EXERCISE FOR SENTENCES AND CLAUSES

<u>DIRECTIONS</u>: Some of the sentences in this exercise are correct. Some are incorrect. First, find the correct sentences, and mark them with a check (√). Then find the incorrect sentences, and correct them. Check your answers using the key on page 536.

1. Since 1927, that the Academy Awards have been given for outstanding contributions to the film industry.

2. The Guggenheim Museum is cast in concrete with a smooth finish and curving walls that offer a unique backdrop for the art exhibited there.

3. Solar panels that convert sunlight into electricity are still not being exploited fully.

4. During a total eclipse of the sun that the Earth moving into the shadow of the moon.

5. Founded by John Smith, that Jamestown became the first successful English colony in America.

6. A chameleon is a tree lizard that can change colors in order to conceal itself in the vegetation.

7. Many of the names of cities in California that are adapted from the Spanish language because of the influence of early missionaries and settlers from Spain.

8. The oceans, which cover two thirds of the Earth's surface, are the object of study for oceanographers.

9. Sports heroes in the United States earn salaries that they are extraordinarily high in comparison with those of most other occupations.

10. The atoms of elements that joining together to form compounds or molecules.

11. Rafts made from the trunks of trees may have been the earliest vehicles.

12. The idea of a set which is the most fundamental concept in mathematics.

13. Water that has had the minerals removed is called "soft" water.

14. A feeling of superiority based on pride in cultural achievements and characteristics that calling ethnocentrism.

15. Skeletal muscles are voluntary muscles which are controlled directly by the nervous system.

STYLE

Style is a general term that includes elements larger than a single grammatical pattern or structure. In most grammar books, *style* means *sentence structure*—that is, how the parts of a sentence relate to each other.

Some of the most important elements of style are summarized in this review section.

Problems with Point of View

Point of view means maintaining the correct sequence of verb tenses and time phrases in a sentence.

Point of View—Verbs

In all patterns, maintain a point of view, either present or past.
Avoid changing from present to past tense, or from past to present tense in the same sentence.

EXAMPLES

INCORRECT: He was among the few who want to continue working on the project.
CORRECT: He is among the few who want to continue working on the project.
or
He was among the few who wanted to continue working on the project.

INCORRECT: It is an accepted custom for a man to open the door when he accompanied a woman.
CORRECT: It is an accepted custom for a man to open the door when he accompanies a woman.
or
It was an accepted custom for a man to open the door when he accompanied a woman.

INCORRECT: She closed the door and hurries away to class.
CORRECT: She closes the door and hurries away to class.
or
She closed the door and hurried away to class.

INCORRECT: We receive several applications a day and with them had been copies of transcripts and degrees.
CORRECT: We receive several applications a day and with them are copies of transcripts and degrees.
or
We received several applications a day and with them were copies of transcripts and degrees.

INCORRECT: Mr. Davis tried to finish his research, but he found only part of the information that he needs.

CORRECT: Mr. Davis <u>tries</u> to finish his research, but he <u>finds</u> only part of the information that he <u>needs</u>.

or

Mr. Davis <u>tried</u> to finish his research, but he <u>found</u> only part of the information that he <u>needed</u>.

EXERCISES

Part A: Choose the correct answer.

The first transistor was basically a small chip made of germanium onto one surface of which two pointed wire contacts __________ side by side.

(A) are made
(B) made
(C) were made
(D) making

Part B: Choose the incorrect word or phrase and correct it.

<u>Because</u> (A) early balloons were at the mercy of <u>shifting</u> (B) winds, they <u>are</u> (C) not considered a practical means of transportation <u>until the 1850s</u> (D).

Point of View—Reported Speech

Some verbs are used to report past events.
Remember that the following verbs are used as the first past verb in the pattern below:

asked	*knew*	*said*
believed	*remembered*	*thought*
forgot	*reported*	*told*

S	V (past)	that	S	V (past)	
He	said	that	he	was	sorry

Avoid using a present verb after *that* in the pattern.
Note: When the reported sentence deals with a general truth, then a present verb may be used after *that* in the pattern. For example, *in the early 1500s, some sailors believed that the world* is *round.* If current knowledge supersedes a formerly accepted truth, then the past verb is retained. For example, *in the early 1500s, many sailors believed that the world* was *flat.*

EXAMPLES

INCORRECT: I thought that he is coming today.
CORRECT: I <u>thought</u> that he <u>was</u> coming today.

INCORRECT: A research scientist at State University reported that he finds a blood test to diagnose cancer.
CORRECT: A research scientist at State University reported that he found a blood test to diagnose cancer.

INCORRECT: When she told us that everything is ready, we went into the dining room and seated ourselves.
CORRECT: When she told us that everything was ready, we went into the dining room and seated ourselves.

INCORRECT: They asked him if he will help us.
CORRECT: They asked him if he would help us.

INCORRECT: Professor Baker told his class that there 10,000 species of ferns.
CORRECT: Professor Baker told his class that there are 10,000 species of ferns.
(A general truth by current scientific standards.)

EXERCISES

Part A: Choose the correct answer.

Ancient people believed that __________ with a sun and a moon rotating around it.

(A) the earth was the center of the universe
(B) the earth is the center of the universe
(C) the center of the universe is earth
(D) the universe has earth at the center

Part B: Choose the incorrect word or phrase and correct it.

William Faulkner, a famous novelist from Mississippi, said that it is (A) not possible to understand (B) the South (C) unless you (D) were born there.

Point of View—Verbs and Adverbs

In all patterns, avoid using past adverbs with verbs in the present tense.

EXAMPLES

INCORRECT: Between one thing and another, Charles does not finish typing his paper last night.
CORRECT: Between one thing and another, Charles did not finish typing his paper last night.

INCORRECT: In 1990, according to statistics from the Bureau of Census, the population of the United States is 250,000,000.
CORRECT: In 1990, according to statistics from the Bureau of Census, the population of the United States was 250,000,000.

INCORRECT: We do not receive mail yesterday because it was a holiday.
CORRECT: We did not receive mail yesterday because it was a holiday.

INCORRECT: Mary does not finish her homework in time to go with us to the football game yesterday afternoon.

CORRECT: Mary did not finish her homework in time to go with us to the football game yesterday afternoon.

INCORRECT: Although there are only two hundred foreign students studying at State University in 1990, there are more than five hundred now.

CORRECT: Although there were only two hundred foreign students studying at State University in 1990, there are more than five hundred now.

EXERCISES

Part A: Choose the correct answer.

Iron__________ for weapons and tools in the Bronze Age following the Stone Age.

(A) is generally used
(B) generally used
(C) was generally used
(D) used generally

Part B: Choose the incorrect word or phrase and correct it.

The Nineteenth Amendment (A) to the Constitution gives (B) women the right to vote (C) in the elections (D) of 1920.

Point of View—Activities of the Dead

In all patterns, avoid using present verbs to refer to activities of the dead.

EXAMPLES

INCORRECT: Just before he died, my friend who writes poetry published his first book.
CORRECT: Just before he died, my friend who wrote poetry published his first book.

INCORRECT: Professor Ayers was so punctual that until the day he died, he always arrives in class just as the bell rings.
CORRECT: Professor Ayers was so punctual that until the day he died, he always arrived in class just as the bell rang.

INCORRECT: Before he died, the man who lives across the street used to help me with my English.
CORRECT: Before he died, the man who lived across the street used to help me with my English.

INCORRECT: A short time before he died, the old man has written a will, leaving his entire estate to his brother.
CORRECT: A short time before he died, the old man had written a will, leaving his entire estate to his brother.

INCORRECT: Until the day she died, the lady who lives next door visited me every evening.
CORRECT: Until the day she died, the lady who lived next door visited me every evening.

EXERCISES

Part A: Choose the correct answer.

From 1926 until her death, Margaret Mead___________ New York's American Museum of Natural History.

(A) was associated with
(B) associates with
(C) is associated with
(D) associated

Part B: Choose the incorrect word or phrase and correct it.

Before dinosaurs <u>became</u> (A) extinct, plant life <u>is</u> (B) <u>very</u> (C) <u>different</u> (D) on Earth.

CUMULATIVE REVIEW EXERCISE FOR POINT OF VIEW

DIRECTIONS: Some of the sentences in this exercise are correct. Some are incorrect. First, find the correct sentences, and mark them with a check (√). Then find the incorrect sentences and correct them. Check your answers using the key on pages 536–537.

1. Until she died at the age of forty, Marilyn Monroe is the most glamorous star in Hollywood.
2. American colleges do not have very many foreign students learning English full time before 1970.
3. Ted Kennedy told the American people that he could not run for president for personal reasons.
4. George Washington Carver was one of the first educators who try to establish schools of higher education for blacks.
5. Before the 1920s, no women will have voted in national elections in the United States.
6. Styles that have been popular in the 1940s have recently reappeared in high-fashion boutiques.
7. Since his murder, John Lennon has become a legend among those who had been his fans.
8. When Lyndon Johnson became president in 1963, he had already served in politics for thirty-two years.
9. Early TV programs like the "Arthur Godfrey Show" are beginning as radio programs.
10. Dr. Howard Evans of Colorado State University reported that insects solve the food shortage if we could adjust to eating them.
11. The year that James Smithson died, he was leaving a half million dollars to the United States government to found the Smithsonian Institute.
12. Mary Decker said that she ran every day to train for the Olympics.

13. A liquid crystal is among the few unstable molecular arrangements that are on the borderline between solids and liquids and whose molecules were easily changed from one to the other.

14. The chestnut tree used to be an important species in the Eastern forests of the United States until a blight kills a large number of trees.

15. The Cincinnati Reds win the championship several years ago.

Problems with Agreement

Agreement means selecting subjects that agree in person and number with verbs, and selecting pronouns that agree in person and number with reference nouns and other pronouns.

Agreement—Modified Subject and Verb

In all patterns, there must be agreement of subject and verb.
Avoid using a verb that agrees with the modifier of a subject instead of with the subject itself.

Examples

INCORRECT: His knowledge of languages and international relations aid him in his work.
CORRECT: His <u>knowledge</u> of languages and international relations <u>aids</u> him in his work.

INCORRECT: The facilities at the new research library, including an excellent microfilm file, is among the best in the country.
CORRECT: The <u>facilities</u> at the new research library, including an excellent microfilm file, <u>are</u> among the best in the country.

INCORRECT: All trade between the two countries were suspended pending negotiation of a new agreement.
CORRECT: All <u>trade</u> between the two countries <u>was</u> suspended pending negotiation of a new agreement.

INCORRECT: The production of different kinds of artificial materials are essential to the conservation of our natural resources.
CORRECT: The <u>production</u> of different kinds of artificial materials <u>is</u> essential to the conservation of our natural resources.

INCORRECT: Since the shipment of supplies for our experiments were delayed, we will have to reschedule our work.
CORRECT: Since the <u>shipment</u> of supplies for our experiments <u>was</u> delayed, we will have to reschedule our work.

Exercises

Part A: Choose the correct answer.

Groups of tissues, each with its own function, ___________ in the human body.

(A) it makes up the organs
(B) make up the organs
(C) they make up the organs
(D) makes up the organs

Part B: Choose the incorrect word or phrase and correct it.

The Zoning Improvement Plan, better known as (A) zip codes, enable (B) postal clerks to speed (C) the routing of an (D) ever-increasing volume of mail.

Agreement—Subject with Accompaniment and Verb

Remember that there must be agreement of subject and verb. In all patterns, avoid using a verb that agrees with a phrase of accompaniment instead of with the subject itself.

Examples

INCORRECT: The guest of honor, along with his wife and two sons, were seated at the first table.
CORRECT: The guest of honor, along with his wife and two sons, was seated at the first table.

INCORRECT: The ambassador, with his family and staff, invite you to a reception at the embassy on Tuesday afternoon at five o'clock.
CORRECT: The ambassador, with his family and staff, invites you to a reception at the embassy on Tuesday afternoon at five o'clock.

INCORRECT: Mary, accompanied by her brother on the piano, were very well received at the talent show.
CORRECT: Mary, accompanied by her brother on the piano, was very well received at the talent show.

INCORRECT: Senator Davis, with his assistant and his press secretary, are scheduled to arrive in New York today.
CORRECT: Senator Davis, with his assistant and his press secretary, is scheduled to arrive in New York today.

INCORRECT: Bruce Springsteen, accompanied by the E. Street Band, are appearing in concert at the Student Center on Saturday night.
CORRECT: Bruce Springsteen, accompanied by the E. Street Band, is appearing in concert at the Student Center on Saturday night.

EXERCISES

Part A: Choose the correct answer.

Thor Heyerdahl, accompanied by the crew of the *Kon Tiki*, __________ in order to prove his theories of cultural diffusion.

(A) have sailed specifically charted courses
(B) sailing specifically charted courses
(C) has sailed specifically charted courses
(D) they sail specifically charted courses

Part B: Choose the incorrect word or phrase and correct it.

The high protein content of various strains of alfalfa plants, along with the characteristically (A) long root system that enables (B) them to survive long droughts, make (C) them particularly (D) valuable in arid countries.

Agreement—Subject with Appositive and Verb

Remember that there must be agreement of subject and verb. An appositive is a word or phrase that follows a noun and defines it. An appositive usually has a comma before it and a comma after it.

In all patterns, avoid using a verb that agrees with words in the appositive after a subject instead of with the subject itself.

EXAMPLES

INCORRECT: The books, an English dictionary and a chemistry text, was on the shelf yesterday.
CORRECT: The books, an English dictionary and a chemistry text, were on the shelf yesterday.

INCORRECT: Three swimmers from our team, Paul, Ed, and Jim, is in competition for medals.
CORRECT: Three swimmers from our team, Paul, Ed, and Jim, are in competition for medals.

INCORRECT: Several pets, two dogs and a cat, needs to be taken care of while we are gone.
CORRECT: Several pets, two dogs and a cat, need to be taken care of while we are gone.

INCORRECT: State University, the largest of the state-supported schools, have more than 50,000 students on main campus.
CORRECT: State University, the largest of the state-supported schools, has more than 50,000 students on main campus.

INCORRECT: This recipe, an old family secret, are an especially important part of our holiday celebrations.
CORRECT: This recipe, an old family secret, is an especially important part of our holiday celebrations.

EXERCISES

Part A: Choose the correct answer.

Cupid, one of the ancient Roman gods, ________.

(A) were a little winged child
(B) representing as a little winged child
(C) was represented as a little winged child
(D) a little winged child

Part B: Choose the incorrect word or phrase and correct it.

Columbus, Ohio, the capital of the state, are (A) not only the largest (B) city in Ohio but also (C) a typical metropolitan area, often used (D) in market research.

Agreement—Verb-Subject Order

There and *here* introduce verb-subject order. The verb agrees with the subject following it.

there	V	S
There	are	the results of the election

here	V	S
Here	is	the result of the election

Avoid using a verb that does not agree with the subject.

EXAMPLES

INCORRECT: There was ten people in line already when we arrived.
CORRECT: There were ten people in line already when we arrived.

INCORRECT: There have been very little rain this summer.
CORRECT: There has been very little rain this summer.

INCORRECT: Here are their house.
CORRECT: Here is their house.

INCORRECT: There has been several objections to the new policy.
CORRECT: There have been several objections to the new policy.

INCORRECT: I think that there were a problem.
CORRECT: I think that there was a problem.

Exercises

Part A: Choose the correct answer.

In a suspension bridge________ that carry one or more flexible cables firmly attached at each end.

(A) there is two towers on it
(B) there are two towers
(C) two towers there are
(D) towers there are two

Part B: Choose the incorrect word or phrase and correct it.

<u>There is</u> (A) about 600 schools <u>in the United States</u> (B) that <u>use</u> (C) the Montessori method <u>to encourage</u> (D) individual initiative.

Agreement—Indefinite Subject and Verb

Remember that the following subjects require a singular verb:

anyone	*either*	*neither*	*what*
anything	*everyone*	*no one*	*whatever*
each	*everything*	*nothing*	*whoever*

The following subjects require either a singular or a plural verb depending on a qualifying phrase or other context from the sentence:

all
any
some
the rest

Avoid using plural verbs with singular subjects, and singular verbs with plural subjects.

Examples

INCORRECT: Everyone who majors in architecture and fine arts study History of Art 450.
CORRECT: <u>Everyone</u> who majors in architecture and fine arts <u>studies</u> History of Art 450.

INCORRECT: Either of these buses go past the university.
CORRECT: <u>Either</u> of these buses <u>goes</u> past the university.

INCORRECT: Anyone who wish to participate in the state lottery may do so by purchasing a ticket at a store that displays the official lottery seal.
CORRECT: <u>Anyone who</u> <u>wishes</u> to participate in the state lottery may do so by purchasing a ticket at a store that displays the official lottery seal.

INCORRECT: Neither Canada nor Mexico require that citizens of the United States have passports.
CORRECT: <u>Neither</u> Canada nor Mexico <u>requires</u> that citizens of the United States have passports.

INCORRECT: The first two problems are very difficult, but the rest is easy.
CORRECT: The first two problems are very difficult, but <u>the rest (of the problems)</u> <u>are</u> easy.

EXERCISES

Part A: Choose the correct answer.

Each of the radioisotopes produced artificially __________ its own distinct structure.

(A) have
(B) has
(C) having
(D) have had

Part B: Choose the incorrect word or phrase and correct it.

Everyone <u>who</u> (A) has traveled across the United States <u>by</u> (B) car, train, or bus <u>are</u> (C) surprised to see <u>such a large expanse</u> (D) of territory with such variation among the lifestyles of the people.

Agreement—Collective Subject and Verb

Remember that the following collective subjects agree with singular verbs:

audience	*faculty*	*police*	*variety*
band	*family*	*public*	*2, 3, 4, . . . dollars*
chorus	*group*	*series*	*2, 3, 4, . . . miles*
class	*majority*	*staff*	
committee	*orchestra*	*team*	

Remember that the following subject agrees with a plural verb:

people

Avoid using plural verbs with singular subjects and singular verbs with plural subjects.

Note: In certain cases, to express the separate nature of individuals in a group, the writer may use a plural verb with the collective subjects.

EXAMPLES

INCORRECT: Twenty dollars are the price.
CORRECT: <u>Twenty dollars</u> <u>is</u> the price.

INCORRECT: Many people is coming to the graduation.
CORRECT: <u>Many people</u> <u>are coming</u> to the graduation.

INCORRECT: An audience usually do not applaud in a church.
CORRECT: <u>An audience</u> usually <u>does not applaud</u> in a church.

INCORRECT: Four miles are the distance to the office.
CORRECT: <u>Four miles</u> <u>is</u> the distance to the office.

INCORRECT: The staff are meeting in the conference room.
CORRECT: <u>The staff</u> <u>is meeting</u> in the conference room.

EXERCISES

Part A: Choose the correct answer.

A good team ______________ of both recruiting and coaching as well as performing.

(A) is a result
(B) it is a result
(C) resulting
(D) result it

Part B: Choose the incorrect word or phrase and correct it.

Because entertaining is such a competitive business, a group of singers or musicians needing a
(A) (B) (C)
manager to help market the music.
(D)

Agreement—Noun and Pronoun

In all patterns, there must be agreement of noun and pronoun.
Avoid using a pronoun that does not agree in number with the noun to which it refers.

EXAMPLES

INCORRECT: If you want to leave a message for Mr. and Mrs. Carlson, I will be glad to take them.
CORRECT: If you want to leave a message for Mr. and Mrs. Carlson, I will be glad to take it.

INCORRECT: Al is interested in mathematics and their applications.
CORRECT: Al is interested in mathematics and its applications.

INCORRECT: It is easier to talk about a problem than to resolve them.
CORRECT: It is easier to talk about a problem than to resolve it.

INCORRECT: Although their visas will expire in June, they can have it extended for three months.
CORRECT: Although their visas will expire in June, they can have them extended for three months.

INCORRECT: In spite of its small size, these cameras take very good pictures.
CORRECT: In spite of their small size, these cameras take very good pictures.

EXERCISES

Part A: Choose the correct answer.

A college bookstore that sells used textbooks stocks ______ along with the new ones on the shelf under the course title.

(A) its
(B) their
(C) a
(D) them

Part B: Choose the incorrect word or phrase and correct it.

Magnesium, <u>the lightest</u> (A) of our structural metals, has an important place <u>among</u> (B) common engineering materials <u>because of</u> (C) <u>their</u> (D) weight.

Agreement—Subject and Possessive Pronouns

In all patterns, there must be agreement of subject pronoun and possessive pronouns that refer to the subject.

Subject Pronouns	Possessive Pronouns
I	*my*
you	*your*
he	*his*
she	*her*
it	*its*
we	*our*
you	*your*
they	*their*

Remember that *it* refers to a small baby. Avoid using *it's* instead of *its* as a possessive pronoun. *It's* means *it is*.

EXAMPLES

INCORRECT: Those of us who are over fifty years old should get their blood pressure checked regularly.
CORRECT: <u>Those of us</u> who are over fifty years old should get <u>our</u> blood pressure checked regularly.

INCORRECT: Our neighbors know that when they go on vacation, we will get its mail for them.
CORRECT: Our neighbors know that when <u>they</u> go on vacation, we will get <u>their</u> mail for them.

INCORRECT: A mother who works outside of the home has to prepare for emergencies when she cannot be there to take care of your sick child.
CORRECT: A mother who works outside of the home has to prepare for emergencies when <u>she</u> cannot be there to take care of <u>her</u> sick child.

INCORRECT: Wine tends to lose their flavor when it has not been properly sealed.
CORRECT: Wine tends to lose <u>its</u> flavor when <u>it</u> has not been properly sealed.

INCORRECT: Optional equipment on a car can add several hundred dollars to it's resale value when you trade it in.
CORRECT: Optional equipment on a car can add several hundred dollars to <u>its</u> resale value when you trade <u>it</u> in.

EXERCISES

Part A: Choose the correct answer.

The television programs we allow ___________ to watch influence their learning.
(A) a children
(B) our children
(C) our child
(D) their childs

Part B: Choose the incorrect word or phrase and correct it.

Although maple trees are <u>among</u> (A) the most colorful varieties <u>in the fall,</u> (B) they lose <u>its</u> (C) leaves <u>sooner than</u> (D) oak trees.

PROBLEM 13 Agreement—Impersonal Pronouns

In all patterns, there must be agreement of impersonal pronouns in a sentence.

Remember that for formal writing, it is necessary to continue using the impersonal pronoun *one* throughout a sentence. For more informal writing, *he* or *his* may be used instead of *one* or *one's* to refer to a previous use of the pronoun *one*.

Avoid using *you, your, they,* or *their* to refer to the impersonal pronoun *one.*

EXAMPLES

INCORRECT: At a large university, one will almost always be able to find a friend who speaks your language.

CORRECT: At a large university, <u>one</u> will almost always be able to find a friend who speaks <u>one's</u> language.

or

At a large university, <u>one</u> will almost always be able to find a friend who speaks <u>his</u> language.

INCORRECT: If one knew the facts, you would not be so quick to criticize.

CORRECT: If <u>one</u> knew the facts, <u>one</u> would not be so quick to criticize.

or

If <u>one</u> knew the facts, <u>he</u> would not be so quick to criticize.

INCORRECT: In order to graduate, one must present their thesis thirty days prior to the last day of classes.

CORRECT: In order to graduate, <u>one</u> must present <u>one's</u> thesis thirty days prior to the last day of classes.

or

In order to graduate, <u>one</u> must present <u>his</u> thesis thirty days prior to the last day of classes.

INCORRECT: Regardless of one's personal beliefs, you have the responsibility to report the facts as impartially as possible.

CORRECT: Regardless of <u>one's</u> personal beliefs, <u>one</u> has the responsibility to report the facts as impartially as possible.

or

Regardless of <u>one's</u> personal beliefs, <u>he</u> has the responsibility to report the facts as impartially as possible.

INCORRECT: If one does not work hard, you cannot expect to succeed.

CORRECT: If <u>one</u> does not work hard, <u>one</u> cannot expect to succeed.

or

If <u>one</u> does not work hard, <u>he</u> cannot expect to succeed.

EXERCISES

Part A: Choose the correct answer.

The more hemoglobin one has, the more oxygen is carried to __________ cells.

(A) one
(B) its
(C) their
(D) one's

Part B: Choose the incorrect word or phrase and correct it.

One can only live without water <u>for</u> (A) about ten days <u>because</u> (B) almost 60 percent of <u>their</u> (C) body <u>is</u> (D) water.

PROBLEM 14 Agreement —Subject and Appositive

In all patterns, there must be agreement of the subject and the appositive, an explanatory phrase that follows the subject.

Avoid using a noun or pronoun in the appositive that does not agree in number with the subject to which it refers.

EXAMPLES

INCORRECT: The people in my class, mostly international student, are very friendly.

CORRECT: <u>The people</u> in my class, mostly international <u>students</u>, are very friendly.

INCORRECT: The final exam, essay tests, will be given during the last week of classes.

CORRECT: <u>The final exam</u>, an essay <u>test</u>, will be given during the last week of classes.

INCORRECT: We didn't sleep because of Jan's dog, a little poodle puppy that missed their mother.

CORRECT: We didn't sleep because of <u>Jan's dog</u>, a little poodle <u>puppy</u> that missed <u>its</u> mother.

INCORRECT: I haven't seen my cousins, now a young woman, for many years.

CORRECT: I haven't seen <u>my cousins</u>, now <u>young women</u>, for many years.

INCORRECT: The notes that I took, some of it with extensive drawings, are missing from my folder.

CORRECT: <u>The notes</u> that I took, some of <u>them</u> with extensive drawings, are missing from my folder.

EXERCISES

Part A: Choose the correct answer.

Clones,________, are genetically homogeneous.

(A) plant growing from a single specimen
(B) that a plant grown from a single specimen
(C) plants grown from a single specimen
(D) from a single specimen, plants

Part B: Choose the incorrect word or phrase and correct it.

The Gray Wolf, a species reintroduced (A) into their native habitat (B) in Yellowstone National Park, has begun (C) to breed naturally (D) there.

CUMULATIVE REVIEW EXERCISE FOR AGREEMENT

DIRECTIONS: Some of the sentences in this exercise are correct. Some are incorrect. First, find the correct sentences, and mark them with a check (√). Then find the incorrect sentences, and correct them. Check your answers using the key on pages 537–538.

1. Thirty-five thousand dollars are the average income for a four-person family living in a medium-sized community in the United States.
2. Mary Ovington, along with a number of journalists and social workers, were instrumental in establishing the Negro National Committee, now called the NAACP.
3. Fossils show that early people was only four feet six inches tall on the average.
4. Each of the Medic Alert bracelets worn by millions of Americans who suffer from diabetes and drug allergic reactions is individually engraved with the wearer's name.
5. The Yon Ho, which is still in use today and is recognized as one of the world's great canals, date from the sixth century.
6. Since the Federal Deposit Insurance Corporation started guaranteeing bank accounts of $100,000 or less, there is no reason for small investors to fear losing their savings.
7. One hundred eighty-six thousand miles per second are the speed of light.
8. It is believed that dodo birds forgot how to fly and eventually became extinct because there was no natural enemies on the island of Mauritius, where they lived.
9. Several arid areas in Arizona has been irrigated and reclaimed for cultivation.
10. The nucleus of a human cell, except those of eggs and sperm, contain forty-six thread-like structures called chromosomes.
11. In spite of its fragile appearance, a newborn infant is extremely sturdy.

12. The ozone layer, eight to thirty miles above the Earth, protect us from too many ultraviolet rays.

13. Although amendments have been added, not once has the American Constitution been changed.

14. Michael Jackson, with members of his band, travel to key cities to give concerts and make publi appearances.

15. Over 90 percent of the world's population now uses the metric system.

Problems with Introductory Verbal Modifiers

Introductory verbal modifiers introduce and modify the subject and verb in the main clause of the sentence. They can be *-ing* forms, *-ed* forms, or infinitives. They are usually separated from the main clause by a comma.

Verbal Modifiers— *-ing* and *-ed* Forms

-ing forms and *-ed* forms may be used as verbals. Verbals function as modifiers.

An introductory verbal modifier with *-ing* or *-ed* should immediately precede the noun it modifies. Otherwise, the relationship between the noun and the modifier is unclear, and the sentence is illogical.

Avoid using a noun immediately after an introductory verbal phrase which may not be logically modified by the phrase.

EXAMPLES

INCORRECT: After graduating from City College, Professor Baker's studies were continued at State University, where he received his Ph.D. in English.
CORRECT: After graduating from City College, Professor Baker continued his studies at State University, where he received his Ph.D. in English.

INCORRECT: Returning to her room, several pieces of jewelry were missing.
CORRECT: Returning to her room, she found that several pieces of jewelry were missing.

INCORRECT: Having been delayed by heavy traffic, it was not possible for her to arrive on time.
CORRECT: Having been delayed by heavy traffic, she arrived late.

INCORRECT: Accustomed to getting up early, the new schedule was not difficult for him to adjust to.
CORRECT: Accustomed to getting up early, he had no difficulty adjusting to the new schedule.

INCORRECT: After finishing his speech, the audience was invited to ask questions.
CORRECT: After finishing his speech, he invited the audience to ask questions.

EXERCISES

Part A: Choose the correct answer.

__________ air traffic controllers guide planes through conditions of near zero visibility.

(A) They talk with pilots and watch their approach on radar,
(B) Talking with pilots and watching their approach on radar,
(C) Talk with pilots and watch their approach on radar,
(D) When they talked with pilots and watched their approach on radar,

Part B: Choose the incorrect word or phrase and correct it.

Have designed (A) his own plane, *The Spirit of St. Louis,* Lindbergh flew (B) from Roosevelt Field in New York across the ocean to (C) Le Bourget Field outside Paris (D).

Verbal Modifiers—Infinitives of Purpose to Introduce Instructions

An infinitive that expresses purpose may be used as an introductory verbal modifier. Remember that a verb word follows the infinitive. The verb word expresses a manner to accomplish the purpose.

Avoid using a noun or *to* with an *-ing* form instead of the infinitive of purpose. Avoid using an *-ing* form or a passive construction after an introductory verbal modifier.

EXAMPLES

INCORRECT: To protect yourself from dangerous exposure to the sun's rays, using a sun screen.
CORRECT: To protect yourself from dangerous exposure to the sun's rays, use a sun screen.

INCORRECT: Prepare for the TOEFL, study thirty minutes every day for several months.
CORRECT: To prepare for the TOEFL, study thirty minutes every day for several months.

INCORRECT: In order to take advantage of low air fares, to buy your tickets well in advance.
CORRECT: In order to take advantage of low air fares, buy your tickets well in advance.

INCORRECT: To taking action pictures, always use a high-speed film.
CORRECT: To take action pictures, always use a high-speed film.

INCORRECT: The send letters and packages from the United States overseas, use Global Mail or DHL Delivery.
CORRECT: To send letters and packages from the United States overseas, use Global Mail or DHL Delivery.

EXERCISES

Part A: Choose the correct answer.

To relieve pressure in the skull,______________ into the blood.

(A) you will inject a strong solution of pure glucose
(B) to inject a strong solution of pure glucose
(C) a strong solution of glucose will inject purely
(D) inject a strong solution of pure glucose

Part B: Choose the incorrect word or phrase and correct it.

To estimate how much it will cost (A) to build (B) a home, finding (C) the total square footage of the house and multiply by cost (D) per square foot.

CUMULATIVE REVIEW EXERCISE FOR INTRODUCTORY VERBAL MODIFIERS

DIRECTIONS: Some of the sentences in this exercise are correct. Some are incorrect. First, find the correct sentences, and mark them with a check (√). Then find the incorrect sentences, and correct them. Check your answers using the key on pages 538–539.

1. Having ruled since the sixth century, the present emperor of Japan has a long and noble tradition.
2. Built on 230 acres, the palace of Versailles is one of the showplaces of France.
3. Believing that true emeralds could not be broken, Spanish soldiers in Pizarro's expedition to Peru tested the jewels they found by pounding them with hammers.
4. Adopted as the laws of the former British colonies after the Revolutionary War, Canada was invited to become a member of the Confederation under the Articles of Confederation.
5. After surrendering in 1886 and being imprisoned in Florida and Alabama, the Apache chief Geronimo became a farmer and lived out his life on a military reservation in Oklahoma.
6. While hibernating, the respiration of animals decreases.
7. To improve the study of chemical reactions, the introduction of effective quantitative methods by Lavoisier.
8. Migrating in a wedge formation, a goose conserves energy by flying in the air currents created by the goose ahead of it.
9. Invented in China about 105 A.D., paper was manufactured in Baghdad and later in Spain four hundred years before the first English paper mill was founded.
10. After lasting for six centuries, it has never been explained why the Mayan culture collapsed.
11. Wounded by an assassin's bullet while he was watching a play at the Ford Theater, death came to Lincoln a few hours after being shot.
12. While viewing objects under a microscope, Robert Hooke discovered that all living things were made up of cells.
13. Located in San Francisco Bay and nicknamed the "Rock," dangerous criminals were once incarcerated on Alcatraz Island.

4. Having calculated the length of time for the first voyages to the moon, Kepler wrote that passengers would have to be drugged.

5. To prepare the fields for planting and irrigation, farmers use laser beams.

Problems with Parallel Structure

Parallel structure means expressing ideas of equal importance with the same grammatical tructures.

Parallel Structure—In a Series

In all patterns, ideas of equal importance should be expressed by the same grammatical structure. Avoid expressing ideas in a series with different structures.

XAMPLES

NCORRECT: Jane is young, enthusiastic, and she has talent.
CORRECT: Jane is young, enthusiastic, and talented.

NCORRECT: We learned to read the passages carefully and underlining the main ideas.
CORRECT: We learned to read the passages carefully and to underline the main ideas.

NCORRECT: The duties of the new secretary are to answer the telephone, to type letters, and book keeping.
CORRECT: The duties of the new secretary are to answer the telephone, to type letters, and to do the bookkeeping.

NCORRECT: The patient's symptoms were fever, dizziness, and his head hurt.
CORRECT: The patient's symptoms were fever, dizziness, and headaches.

NCORRECT: Professor Williams enjoys teaching and to write.
CORRECT: Professor Williams enjoys teaching and writing.

XERCISES

art A: Choose the correct answer.

In a hot, sunny climate, man acclimatizes by eating less, drinking more liquids, wearing lighter clothing, and ____________________.

(A) skin changes that darken
(B) his skin may darken
(C) experiencing a darkening of the skin
(D) darkens his skin

Part B: Choose the incorrect word or phrase and correct it.

The aims of the European Economic Community are (A) to eliminate tariffs between member countries; developing (B) common policies for agriculture, labor, welfare, trade, and transportation (C); and to abolish (D) trusts and cartels.

Parallel Structure—After Correlative Conjunctions

Remember that ideas of equal importance are introduced by correlative conjunctions:

both...and
not only...but also

Avoid expressing ideas after correlative conjunctions with different structures.

EXAMPLES

INCORRECT: She is not only famous in the United States but also abroad.
CORRECT: She is famous not only in the United States but also abroad.

INCORRECT: The exam tested both listening and to read.
CORRECT: The exam tested both listening and reading.

INCORRECT: He is not only intelligent but also he is creative.
CORRECT: He is not only intelligent but also creative.

INCORRECT: Flying is not only faster but also it is safer than traveling by car.
CORRECT: Flying is not only faster but also safer than traveling by car.

INCORRECT: John registered for both Electrical Engineering 500 and to study Mathematics 390.
CORRECT: John registered for both Electrical Engineering 500 and Mathematics 390.

EXERCISES

Part A: Choose the correct answer.

Both historically and __________, Ontario is the heartland of Canada.

(A) in its geography
(B) geographically
(C) also its geography
(D) geography

Part B: Choose the incorrect word or phrase and correct it.

The cacao bean was cultivated (A) by the Aztecs (B) not only to drink (C) but also (D) currency.

CUMULATIVE REVIEW EXERCISE FOR PARALLEL STRUCTURE

DIRECTIONS: Some of the sentences in this exercise are correct. Some are incorrect. First, find the correct sentences, and mark them with a check (√). Then find the incorrect sentences, and correct them. Check your answers using the key on page 539.

1. We are indebted to the Arabs not only for reviving Greek works but also they introduced useful ideas from India.

2. A century ago in America, all postal rates were determined not by weighing the mail but measuring the distance that the mail had to travel.

3. The four basic elements that make up all but 1 percent of terrestrial matter include carbon, hydrogen, nitrogen, and oxygen is also.

4. The three thousand stars visible to the naked eye can be seen because they are either extremely bright or they are relatively close to the Earth.

5. George Kaufman distinguished himself as a newspaperman, a drama critic, and he was a successful playwright.

6. To apply for a passport, fill out the application form, attach two recent photographs, and taking it to your local passport office.

7. Shakespeare was both a writer and he acted.

8. To save on heating and finding cheaper labor are two of the most common reasons that companies give for moving from the Midwest to the South.

9. Both plants and animals have digestive systems, respiratory systems, and reproduce.

10. Pollution control involves identifying the sources of contamination, development improved or alternative technologies and sources of raw material, and persuading industries and citizens to adopt them either voluntarily or legally.

11. Tobacco was considered a sacred plant, and it was used to indicate friendship and concluded peace negotiations between Native Americans and whites.

12. The kidneys both eliminate water and salt.

13. A person who purchases a gun for protection is six times more likely to kill a friend or relative than killing an intruder.

14. The Brooklyn Bridge was remarkable not only for the early use of the pneumatic caisson but also for the introduction of steel wire.

15. Microwaves are used for cooking, for telecommunications, and also medical diagnosis is made from them.

Problems with Redundancy

Redundancy means using more words than necessary.

Redundancy—Unnecessary Phrases

In all patterns, prefer simple, direct sentences to complicated, indirect sentences. Find the Subjec Verb-Complement-Modifier, and determine whether the other words are useful or unnecessary.

S	V	C	M
Lee	learned	English	quickly

Avoid using an adjective with such phrases as *in character* or *in nature*.

Avoid using the redundant pattern instead of an adverb such as *quickly.*

in a	adjective	manner
~~in a~~	~~quick~~	~~manner~~

EXAMPLES

INCORRECT: The key officials who testified before the Senate committee responded in a manner that was evasive.
CORRECT: The key officials who testified before the Senate committee responded evasively.

INCORRECT: Mr. Davis knows a great deal in terms of the condition of the situation.
CORRECT: Mr. Davis knows a great deal about the situation.

INCORRECT: It was a problem which was very difficult in character and very delicate in nature.
CORRECT: The problem was difficult and delicate.

INCORRECT: The disease was very serious in the nature of it.
CORRECT: The disease was very serious.

INCORRECT: Mary had always behaved in a responsible manner.
CORRECT: Mary had always behaved responsibly.

EXERCISES

Part A: Choose the correct answer.

Waitresses and waiters who serve __________ deserve at least a 20 percent tip.

(A) in a courteous manner
(B) courteously
(C) with courtesy in their manner
(D) courteous

Part B: Choose the incorrect word or phrase and correct it.

Hummingbirds move <u>their</u> wings so <u>rapid a way</u> that they appear <u>to be hanging</u> <u>in the air</u>.
(A) (B) (C) (D)

Redundancy—Repetition of Words with the Same Meaning

In all patterns, avoid using words with the same meaning consecutively in a sentence.

EXAMPLES

INCORRECT: The money that I have is sufficient enough for my needs.
CORRECT: The money that I have is <u>sufficient</u> for my needs.

INCORRECT: Bill asked the speaker to repeat again because he had not heard him the first time.
CORRECT: Bill asked the speaker <u>to repeat</u> because he had not heard him the first time.

INCORRECT: The class advanced forward rapidly.
CORRECT: The class <u>advanced</u> rapidly.

INCORRECT: She returned back to her hometown after she had finished her degree.
CORRECT: She <u>returned</u> to her hometown after she had finished her degree.

INCORRECT: I am nearly almost finished with this chapter.
CORRECT: I am <u>nearly</u> finished with this chapter.
or
I am <u>almost</u> finished with this chapter.

EXERCISES

Part A: Choose the correct answer.

Famous for his __________ punctuation, typography, and language, Edward Estlin Cummings published his collected poems in 1954.

(A) new innovations for
(B) innovations in
(C) newly approached
(D) innovations newly approached in

Part B: Choose the incorrect word or phrase and correct it.

The idea of a submarine is <u>an old ancient one,</u> dating from <u>as early as</u> <u>the fifteenth century</u> when Drebbel and Da Vinci <u>made</u> preliminary drawings.
(A) (B) (C) (D)

Redundancy—Repetition of Noun by Pronoun

In all patterns, avoid using a noun and the pronoun that refers to it consecutively in a sentence. Avoid using a pronoun after the noun it refers to, and *that.*

EXAMPLES

INCORRECT: My teacher he said to listen to the news on the radio in order to practice listening comprehension.
CORRECT: My teacher said to listen to the news on the radio in order to practice listening comprehension.

INCORRECT: Steve he plans to go into business with his father.
CORRECT: Steve plans to go into business with his father.

INCORRECT: My sister she found a store that imported food from our country.
CORRECT: My sister found a store that imported food from our country.

INCORRECT: Hospitalization that it covers room, meals, nursing, and additional hospital expenses such as lab tests, X-rays, and medicine.
CORRECT: Hospitalization covers room, meals, nursing, and additional hospital expenses such as lab tests, X-rays, and medicine.

INCORRECT: Anne she wants to visit Washington, D.C., before she goes home.
CORRECT: Anne wants to visit Washington, D.C., before she goes home.

EXERCISES

Part A: Choose the correct answer.

A perennial is____________ for more than two years, such as trees and shrubs.
(A) any plant that it continues to grow
(B) any plant it continuing to grow
(C) any plant that continues to grow
(D) any plant continuing growth

Part B: Choose the incorrect word or phrase and correct it.

Advertising it (A) provides (B) most of the income (C) for magazines, newspapers, radio, and television in the United States (D) today.

CUMULATIVE REVIEW EXERCISE FOR REDUNDANCY

DIRECTIONS: Some of the sentences in this exercise are correct. Some are incorrect. First, find the correct sentences, and mark them with a check (√). Then find the incorrect sentences, and correct them. Check your answers using the key on page 540.

1. Many dentists now say that plaque can cause damage of a more serious nature and degree to teeth than cavities.

2. The most common name in the world it is Mohammad.

3. The idea for the Monroe Doctrine was originally first proposed not by Monroe but by the British Secretary for Foreign Affairs, George Canning.

4. That comets' tails are caused by solar wind it is generally accepted.

5. One hundred thousand earthquakes are felt every year, one thousand of which cause severe serious damage.

6. Irving Berlin, America's most prolific songwriter, he never learned to read or write music.

7. The corporation, which is by far the most influential form of business ownership, is a comparatively new innovation.

8. That the Earth and the moon formed simultaneously at the same time is a theory that accounts for the heat of the early atmosphere surrounding the Earth.

9. The longest mountain range, the Mid-Atlantic Range, is not hardly visible because most of it lies under the ocean.

10. The Navajo language was used in a successful manner as a code by the United States in World War II.

11. One of the magnificent Seven Wonders of the Ancient World was the enormous large statue known as the Colossus of Rhodes.

12. It is the first digit that appears on any zip code that it refers to one of ten geographical areas in the United States.

13. Limestone formations growing downward from the roofs of caves that they are stalactites.

14. All matter is composed of molecules or atoms that are in motion in a constant way.

15. The fact that the Earth rotates wasn't known until the years of the 1850s.

Problems with Word Choice

Word choice means choosing between similar words to express precise meanings.

Transitive and Intransitive Verbs—*Raise* and *Rise*

A transitive verb is a verb that takes a complement. An intransitive verb is a verb that does not take a complement.

The following pairs of verbs can be confusing. Remember that *raise* is a transitive verb; it takes a complement. *Rise* is an intransitive verb; it does not take a complement.

Transitive			Intransitive		
Verb word	*Past*	*Participle*	*Verb word*	*Past*	*Participle*
raise	*raised*	*raised*	*rise*	*rose*	*risen*

Remember that *to raise* means to move to a higher place or to cause to rise. *To rise* means to go up or to increase.

Raise and rise are also used as nouns. A *raise* means an increase in salary. A *rise* means an increase in price, worth, quantity, or degree.

S	RAISE	C	M
Heavy rain	raises	the water level of the reservoir	every spring
Heavy rain	raised	the water level of the reservoir	last week

S	RISE	C	M
The water level	rises		when it rains every spring
The water level	rose		when it rained last week

Examples

INCORRECT: The cost of living has raised 3 percent in the past year.
CORRECT: The cost of living has risen 3 percent in the past year.

INCORRECT: The flag is risen at dawn by an honor guard.
CORRECT: The flag is raised at dawn by an honor guard.
(An honor guard raises the flag.)

INCORRECT: Kay needs to rise her grades if she wants to get into graduate school.
CORRECT: Kay needs to raise her grades if she wants to get into graduate school.

INCORRECT: The landlord has risen the rent.
CORRECT: The landlord has raised the rent.

INCORRECT: The smoke that is raising from that oil refinery is black.
CORRECT: The smoke that is rising from that oil refinery is black.

EXERCISES

Part A: Choose the correct answer.

The average elevation of the Himalayas is twenty thousand feet, and Mount Everest ________ to more than twenty-nine thousand feet at its apex.

(A) raises
(B) rises
(C) roses
(D) arises

Part B: Choose the incorrect word or phrase and correct it.

When the temperature is risen (A) to the burning point (B) without a source of escape for the heat (C), spontaneous combustion occurs (D).

Transitive and Intransitive Verbs—*Lay* and *Lie*

Remember that *lay* is a transitive verb; it takes a complement. *Lie* is an intransitive verb; it does not take a complement.

Transitive			Intransitive		
Verb word	*Past*	*Participle*	*Verb word*	*Past*	*Participle*
lay	*laid*	*laid*	*lie*	*lay*	*lain*

Remember that *to lay* means to put, to place, or to cause to lie. *To lie* means to recline or to occupy a place.

The past form of the verb *to lie* is *lay*.

S	LAY	C	M
The postman	lays	the mail	on the table every day
The postman	laid	the mail	on the table yesterday

S	LIE	C	M
He	lies		on the sofa to rest every day after work
He	lay		on the sofa to rest yesterday after work

Examples

INCORRECT: Her coat was laying on the chair.
CORRECT: Her coat was lying on the chair.

INCORRECT: I have lain your notebook on the table by the door so that you won't forget it.
CORRECT: I have laid your notebook on the table by the door so that you won't forget it.

INCORRECT: Key West lays off the coast of Florida.
CORRECT: Key West lies off the coast of Florida.

INCORRECT: Why don't you lay down for awhile?
CORRECT: Why don't you lie down for awhile?

INCORRECT: Linda always forgets where she lies her glasses.
CORRECT: Linda always forgets where she lays her glasses.

Exercises

Part A: Choose the correct answer.

The geographic position of North America, ______________ in the early days of the European settlement.

(A) laying between the Atlantic and the Pacific Oceans, isolating it
(B) isolating it as it laid between the Atlantic and the Pacific Oceans
(C) lying between the Atlantic and the Pacific Oceans, isolated it
(D) isolating it between the Atlantic and the Pacific Oceans as it was layed

Part B: Choose the incorrect word or phrase and correct it.

Melanin, a pigment that lays (A) under the skin, is (B) responsible for skin color, including the variations that occur (C) among (D) different races.

Transitive and Intransitive Verbs—*Set* and *Sit*

Remember that *set* is a transitive verb; it takes a complement. *Sit* is an intransitive verb; it does not take a complement.

Transitive			Intransitive		
Verb word	*Past*	*Participle*	*Verb word*	*Past*	*Participle*
set	*set*	*set*	*sit*	*sat*	*sat*

Remember that *to set* means to put, to place, or to cause to sit. *To sit* means to occupy a place on a chair or a flat surface.

S	SET	C	M
The students	set	the lab equipment	on the table every class
The students	set	the lab equipment	on the table last class period

S	SIT	C	M
The equipment	sits		on the table every class
The equipment	sat		on the table last class period

EXAMPLES

INCORRECT: Please sit the telephone on the table by the bed.
CORRECT: Please set the telephone on the table by the bed.

INCORRECT: Won't you set down?
CORRECT: Won't you sit down?

INCORRECT: Their house sets on a hill overlooking a lake.
CORRECT: Their house sits on a hill overlooking a lake.

INCORRECT: Let's sit your suitcases out of the way.
CORRECT: Let's set your suitcases out of the way.

INCORRECT: Terry has set there waiting for us for almost an hour.
CORRECT: Terry has sat there waiting for us for almost an hour.

EXERCISES

Part A: Choose the correct answer.

When Jacqueline Kennedy was first lady, she collected many beautiful antiques and ______________ them among the original pieces in the White House.

(A) sat
(B) set
(C) sit
(D) sits

Part B: Choose the incorrect word or phrase and correct it.

Hyde Park, the family estate of Franklin D. Roosevelt, sets on top of a bluff overlooking
(A) (B) (C)
the Hudson River.
(D)

Similar Verbs—*Tell* and *Say*

Verb word	Past	Participle	Verb word	Past	Participle
tell	*told*	*told*	*say*	*said*	*said*

Remember that *to tell* and *to say* have similar meanings, but *tell* is often used before complements, especially persons. *To say* is not used before complements that are persons. *To say* is usually followed by a clause introduced by *that.*

S	TELL	C	M
The teacher The teacher	tells told	us us	how to do it how to do it

S	SAY	C	M
The teacher The teacher	says said		that we are making progress that we were making progress

Examples

INCORRECT: Jayne said him that she would meet us here.
CORRECT: Jayne told him that she would meet us here.

INCORRECT: Margaret told that she would call before she came.
CORRECT: Margaret said that she would call before she came.

INCORRECT: Randy says a lot of jokes and funny stories.
CORRECT: Randy tells a lot of jokes and funny stories.

INCORRECT: I have said the truth.
CORRECT: I have told the truth.

INCORRECT: The girls told (that) they were hungry.
CORRECT: The girls said that they were hungry.

Exercises

Part A: Choose the correct answer.

In his inaugural speech, John Kennedy ______________ that we should not ask what our country could do for us but what we could do for our country.

(A) said
(B) told
(C) did
(D) got

Part B: Choose the incorrect word or phrase and correct it.

Before television became so popular (A), Americans used to entertain (B) each other (C) in the evening by playing games, saying (D) stories, and singing songs.

Similar Verbs—*Let* and *Leave*

Verb word	Past	Participle	Verb word	Past	Participle
let	*let*	*let*	*leave*	*left*	*left*

Remember that *to let* and *to leave* have similar sounds, but not similar meanings. *To let* means to allow or to permit. *To leave* means to let someone or something remain. *To leave* also means to depart or to go.

S	LET	C	M
Their mother	lets	them	stay up late every night
Their mother	let	them	stay up late last night

S	LEAVE	C	M
She	leaves	her briefcase	at the office every day
She	left	her briefcase	at the office yesterday

EXAMPLES

INCORRECT: Although her doctor allowed her family to visit her, he wouldn't leave anyone else go into her room.
CORRECT: Although her doctor allowed her family to visit her, he wouldn't let anyone else go into her room.

INCORRECT: You can let your car in long-term parking until you come back.
CORRECT: You can leave your car in long-term parking until you come back.

INCORRECT: Professor Baker wouldn't leave us use our dictionaries during the test.
CORRECT: Professor Baker wouldn't let us use our dictionaries during the test.

INCORRECT: Just let the paper in my mailbox.
CORRECT: Just leave the paper in my mailbox.

INCORRECT: Just let your coats on the racks in the hall.
CORRECT: Just leave your coats on the racks in the hall.

EXERCISES

Part A: Choose the correct answer.

Although blood__________ a residue in urine and stool samples, it cannot always be detected without the aid of a microscope.

(A) let
(B) leave
(C) leaves
(D) lets

Part B: Choose the incorrect word or phrase and correct it.

To assure (A) the safety of those workers who (B) must handle radioactive material, the employer should not leave (C) them enter (D) contaminated areas without protective clothing.

Similar Verbs—*Borrow* and *Lend*

Verb word	Past	Participle	Verb word	Past	Participle
borrow	*borrowed*	*borrowed*	*lend*	*lent*	*lent*

Remember that *to borrow* and *to lend* have related meanings. *To borrow* means to take and give back. It is often followed by the word *from. To lend* means to give and take back. It is often followed by the word *to.*

S	BORROW	C	M
Karen's father	borrows	money	from the bank every term
Karen's father	borrowed	money	from the bank last term

S	LEND	C	M
The bank	lends	money	to Karen's father every term
The bank	lent	money	to Karen's father last term

EXAMPLES

INCORRECT: Stan had an accident while he was driving the car that his cousin had borrowed him.
CORRECT: Stan had an accident while he was driving the car that his cousin had lent him.

INCORRECT: Would you please borrow me your pen?
CORRECT: Would you please lend me your pen?

INCORRECT: Can I lend this dictionary for a few minutes while I check my composition?
CORRECT: Can I borrow this dictionary for a few minutes while I check my composition?

INCORRECT: She lent my key to get into the apartment, and lost it.
CORRECT: She borrowed my key to get into the apartment, and lost it.

INCORRECT: Thank you for borrowing me your umbrella.
CORRECT: Thank you for lending me your umbrella.

EXERCISES

Part A: Choose the correct answer.

Countries may ____________ the World Bank for development projects.
(A) borrow large sums of money from
(B) lend large sums of money from
(C) borrow large sums of money
(D) lend large sums of money

Part B: Choose the incorrect word or phrase and correct it.

Either a savings and loan company or (A) a bank can borrow (B) money to those people who (C) want to buy (D) a home.

Similar Verbs—*Make* and *Do*

Verb word	Past	Participle	Verb word	Past	Participle
do	*did*	*done*	*make*	*made*	*made*

Remember that *to do* and *to make* have similar meanings, but *do* is often used before complements that describe work and chores. *To make* is often used before complements that are derived from verbs.

DO an assignment	*MAKE an agreement*	*(to agree)*
the dishes	*an announcement*	*(to announce)*
a favor	*an attempt*	*(to attempt)*
homework	*a decision*	*(to decide)*
the laundry	*a discovery*	*(to discover)*
a paper	*an offer*	*(to offer)*
research	*a profit*	*(to profit)*
work	*a promise*	*(to promise)*

S	DO	C	M
We	do	our homework	before class every day
We	did	our homework	before class yesterday

S	MAKE	C	M
We	make	an agreement	with each other every semester
We	made	an agreement	with each other last semester

EXAMPLES

INCORRECT: I really don't mind making the homework for this class.
CORRECT: I really don't mind doing the homework for this class.

INCORRECT: Did you do a mistake?
CORRECT: Did you make a mistake?

INCORRECT: Please make me a favor.
CORRECT: Please do me a favor.

INCORRECT: Are they doing progress on the new road?
CORRECT: Are they making progress on the new road?

INCORRECT: Have you done any interesting discoveries while you were doing your research?
CORRECT: Have you made any interesting discoveries while you were doing your research?

EXERCISES

Part A: Choose the correct answer.

The president usually ______________ unless his press secretary approves it.
(A) doesn't do a statement
(B) doesn't make a statement
(C) doesn't statement
(D) no statement

Part B: Choose the incorrect word or phrase and correct it.

A one hundred-horsepower tractor can make the work of a large number of horses.

(A) (B) (C) (D)

Prepositional Idioms

Prefer these idioms	Avoid these errors
accede to	accede on, by
according to	according
approve of	approve for
ashamed of	ashamed with
bored with	bored of

capable of	capable to
compete with	compete together
composed of	composed from
concerned with	concerned of
conscious of	conscious for
depend on	depend in, to
effects on	effects in
equal to	equal as
except for	excepting for
from now on	after now on
from time to time	for, when time to time
frown on	frown to
glance at, through	glance
incapable of	incapable to
in conflict	on conflict
inferior to	inferior with
in the habit of	in the habit to
in the near future	at the near future
knowledge of	knowledge on
near; next to	near to
of the opinion	in opinion
on top of	on top
opposite	opposite over
prior to	prior
regard to	regard of
related to	related with
respect for	respect of
responsible for	responsible
similar to	similar as
since	ever since
until	up until
with regard to	with regard of

EXAMPLES

INCORRECT: Excepting for the Gulf Coast region, most of the nation will have very pleasant weather tonight and tomorrow.

CORRECT: Except for the Gulf Coast region, most of the nation will have very pleasant weather tonight and tomorrow.

INCORRECT: In recent years, educators have become more concerned of bilingualism.
CORRECT: In recent years, educators have become more <u>concerned with</u> bilingualism.

INCORRECT: He always does what he pleases, without regard of the rules and regulations.
CORRECT: He always does what he pleases, without <u>regard to</u> the rules and regulations.

INCORRECT: The bank opposite over the university isn't open on Saturdays.
CORRECT: The bank <u>opposite</u> the university isn't open on Saturdays.

INCORRECT: The customs of other countries are not inferior with those of our own country.
CORRECT: The customs of other countries are not <u>inferior to</u> those of our own country.

EXERCISES

Part A: Choose the correct answer.

_______________ discovery of insulin, it was not possible to treat diabetes.

(A) Prior to the
(B) Prior
(C) The prior
(D) To prior

Part B: Choose the incorrect word or phrase and correct it.

<u>The price</u> (A) of gold <u>depends in</u> (B) <u>several factors,</u> (C) including supply and demand <u>in relation to</u> (D) the value of the dollar.

Parts of Speech

Although it is usually very easy to identify the parts of speech, word families can be confusing. Word families are groups of words with similar meanings and spellings. Each word in the family is a different part of speech. For example, *agreement* is a noun; *agreeable* is an adjective; to *agree* is a verb.

The endings of words can help you identify the part of speech.

Nouns Derived from Verbs

Verb	Ending	Noun
store	*-age*	*storage*
accept	*-ance*	*acceptance*
insist	*-ence*	*insistence*
agree	*-ment*	*agreement*
authorize	*-sion/-tion*	*authorization*

Nouns Derived from Adjectives

Adjective	Ending	Noun
convenient	*-ce*	*convenience*
redundant	*-cy*	*redundancy*
opposite	*-tion*	*opposition*
soft	*-ness*	*softness*
durable	*-ty*	*durability*

Adjectives Derived from Nouns

Noun	Ending	Adjective
possibility	*-able/-ible*	*possible*
intention	*-al*	*intentional*
distance	*-ant*	*distant*
frequency	*-ent*	*frequent*
juice	*-y*	*juicy*

Adverbs Derived from Adjectives

Adjective	Ending	Adverb
efficient	*-ly*	*efficiently*

EXAMPLES

INCORRECT: The agreeing is not legal unless everyone signs his name.
CORRECT: The <u>agreement</u> is not legal unless everyone signs his name.

INCORRECT: Even young children begin to show able in mathematics.
CORRECT: Even young children begin to show <u>ability</u> in mathematics.

INCORRECT: Arranging have been made for the funeral.
CORRECT: <u>Arrangements</u> have been made for the funeral.

INCORRECT: A free educating is guaranteed to every citizen.
CORRECT: A free <u>education</u> is guaranteed to every citizen.

INCORRECT: The develop of hybrids has increased yields.
CORRECT: The <u>development</u> of hybrids has increased yields.

EXERCISES

Part A: Choose the correct answer.

Unless protected areas are established, the Bengal tiger, the blue whale, and the California condor face_________ of extinction.

(A) possible
(B) the possibility
(C) to be possible
(D) possibly

Part B: Choose the incorrect word or phrase and correct it.

<u>Because</u> (A) blood from different individuals may <u>different</u> (B) in the type of antigen on the surface of the red cells and the type of antibody in the plasma, a dangerous reaction <u>can occur</u> (C) between the donor <u>and</u> (D) recipient in a blood transfusion.

CUMULATIVE REVIEW EXERCISE FOR WORD CHOICE

DIRECTIONS: Some of the sentences in this exercise are correct. Some are incorrect. First, find the correct sentences, and mark them with a check (√). Then find the incorrect sentences, and correct them. Check your answers using the key on pages 540–541.

1. The manage of a small business requires either education or experience in sales and accounting.

2. Because of the traffic in ancient Rome, Julius Caesar would not let anyone use a wheeled vehicle on the streets during the day.

3. Occasionally dolphins need to raise to the surface of the water to take in oxygen.

4. Thomas Jefferson's home, which he designed and built, sets on a hill overlooking the Virginia countryside.

5. Once, the gold reserve of the United States Treasury was saved when J.P. Morgan, then the richest man in America, borrowed more than fifty million dollars' worth of gold to the federal government.

6. Dreams may be the expression of fears and desires that we are not conscious of during our waking hours.

7. Ice has the same hard as concrete.

8. We might never have heard about Daniel Boone had he not told a schoolmaster his stories about the frontier.

9. Terrorists are capable to hijacking planes and taking hostages in spite of security at international airports.

10. It is not the TOEFL but the academic preparation of students that is the best indicator of their successfully.

11. Some business analysts argue that the U.S. automobile industry is suffering because Congress will not impose heavier import duties, but others say that the cars themselves are inferior with the foreign competition.

12. Lotteries are used to rise money for the states that sponsor them.

13. When a human being gets hurt, the brain excretes a chemical called enkaphalin to numb the painful.

14. Benjamin Franklin told that the turkey should be our national bird.

15. The prime rate is the rate of interest that a bank will charge when it lends money to its best clients.

TYPES OF QUESTIONS

Multiple-Choice Questions

All of the questions on both the Paper-Based TOEFL and the Computer-Based TOEFL are multiple-choice. There are no computer-assisted questions with special directions.

Although the structure questions in this book are numbered, and the answer choices are lettered A, B, C, and D, the same questions on the CD-ROM that is available to supplement the book are not numbered and lettered. You need the numbers and letters in the book to refer to the Answer Key, the Explanatory Answers, and the Transcript for the Listening section. On the CD-ROM, you can refer to other chapters by clicking on the screen. The questions on the CD-ROM are like those on the Computer-Based TOEFL.

Paper-Based TOEFL

1. If water is heated to 121 degrees F, _________ as steam.
   (A) it will boil and escape
   (B) it is boiling and escaping
   (C) it boil and escape
   (D) it would boil and escape

2. If <u>water</u> (A) freezes, <u>it</u> (B) <u>has become</u> (C) <u>a</u> (D) solid.

Answer Sheet

1. ● Ⓑ Ⓒ Ⓓ
2. Ⓐ Ⓑ ● Ⓓ

Computer-Based TOEFL

If water is heated to 121 degrees F, _________ as steam.

● it will boil and escape
○ it is boiling and escaping
○ it boil and escape
○ it would boil and escape

If <u>water</u> freezes, <u>it</u> <u>has become</u>

<u>a</u> solid.

Computer Tutorial for the Structure Section

In order to succeed on the Computer-Based TOEFL, you must understand the computer vocabulary used for the test, and you must be familiar with the icons on the computer screens that you will see on the test. First, review the vocabulary that you learned in the Tutorial for Section 1 on page 61. The same vocabulary is used for Section 2. Then study the computer screens in this Tutorial.

Testing Tools: Review of Vocabulary, Icons, and Keys

The following words are from the list of general vocabulary for the Computer-Based TOEFL introduced in the previous chapter. Using the word list, fill in the blanks in the ten sentences.

Arrow	**Help (Question mark)**	**Next**
Click	**Icon**	**Oval**
Confirm Answer	**Mouse**	**Time (Clock)**
Dismiss Directions	**Mouse Pad**	

1. A ________ is a small control with a button on it.

2. A ________ is a rectangular pad where you move the mouse.

3. An ________ is a marker on the screen that shows you where you are moving on the computer.

4. To ________ is to depress the button on the mouse. You ________ the mouse to make changes on the screen.

5. An ________ is a small picture or word or phrase in a box. Move the arrow to the ________ to tell the computer what to do.

6. Click on ________ to remove the directions from the screen.

7. Click on an ________ to choose an answer to one of the multiple-choice questions.

8. Click on ________, then click on ________ to see the next question.

9. Click on ________ to see a list of the icons and directions.

10. Click on ________ to hide or show the time you have left to finish the section of the test you are working on.

Computer Screens for Section 2

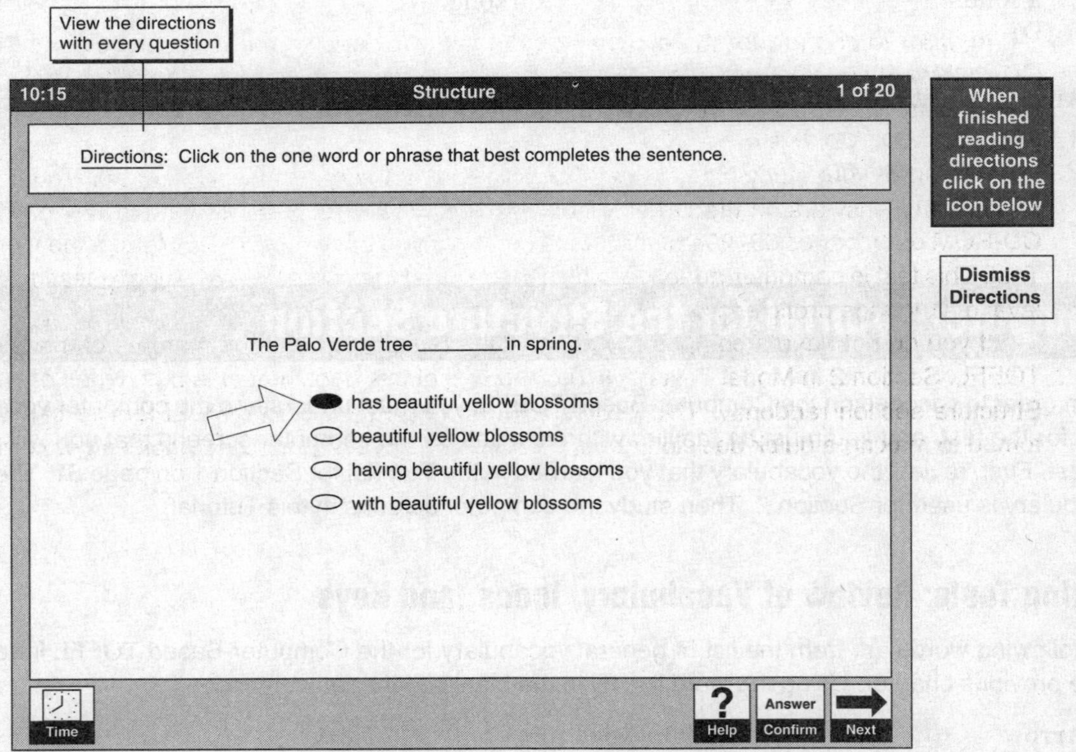
View the directions with every question
10:15
Structure
1 of 20
When finished reading directions click on the icon below
Directions: Click on the one word or phrase that best completes the sentence.
Dismiss Directions
The Palo Verde tree ________ in spring.
has beautiful yellow blossoms
beautiful yellow blossoms
having beautiful yellow blossoms
with beautiful yellow blossoms
Time
?
Help
Answer
Confirm
Next

TIP: There are only two types of questions in Section 2. After you have read and understood the directions for both types of questions in this Tutorial, you will not need to read the top part of the screen every time.

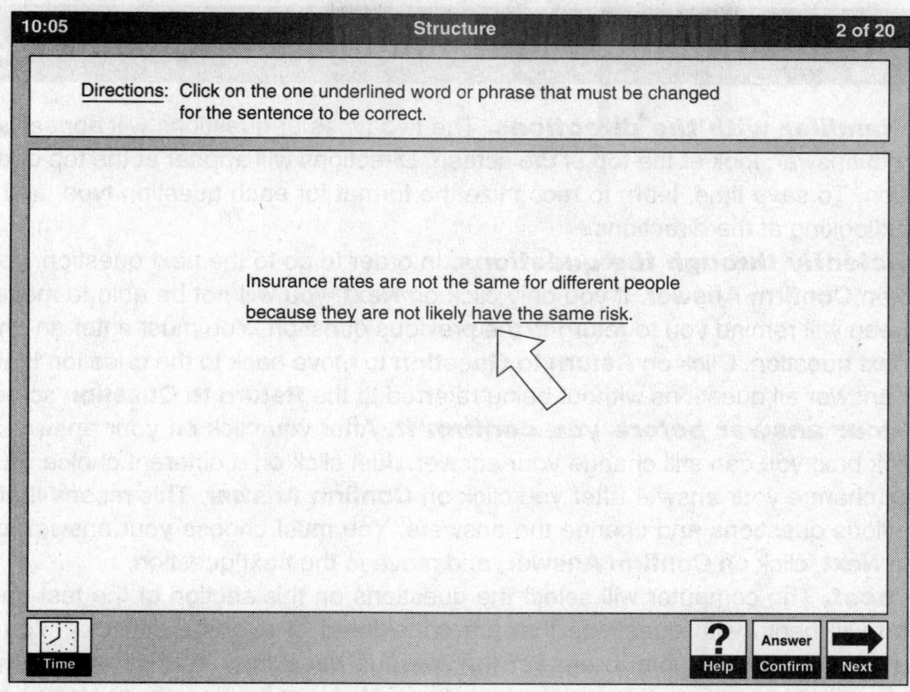

TIP: Be sure to click on **Next** before you click on **Answer Confirm.** If you do not click on these two icons in the correct order, the next question will not appear.

Simulations for Section 2

In order to prepare for the experience that you will have on the Computer-Based TOEFL, use the CD-ROM that supplements this book. Locate the Structure section on the Model Tests. The computer will simulate the Structure section on the Computer-Based TOEFL. These Model Tests are computer-assisted.

As part of your study plan, be sure to review all of the questions in all of the Model Tests. Use the Explanatory Answers on the CD-ROM or on pages 553–616. Refer to the Review of Structure on the CD-ROM or on pages 69–294 of this book. Finally, if you have the CD-ROM, take the Cumulative Model Test. This test is computer-adaptive, which means that the computer will select questions for you at your level of language proficiency.

If you do not have a computer, you can still simulate some of the features of the Computer-Based TOEFL. Section 2 in Model Tests 1–8 in Chapter 7 of this book presents both types of questions for the Structure section randomly. This is different from the Paper-Based TOEFL. You can become accustomed to making a quick decision about the kind of answer required—completion or correction.

Advice for the Structure Section: Computer-Based TOEFL

Become familiar with the directions. The two types of questions will appear at random. If you forget how to answer, look at the top of the screen. Directions will appear at the top of every screen for each question. To save time, learn to recognize the format for each question type, and be ready to respond without looking at the directions.

Move efficiently through the questions. In order to go to the next question, you must click on **Next** and then **Confirm Answer**. If you only click on **Next**, you will not be able to move to the next question. A screen will remind you to return to the previous question. You must enter an answer before you go to the next question. Click on **Return to Question** to move back to the question that you did not answer. Try to answer all questions without being referred to the **Return to Question** screen.

Change your answer before you confirm it. After you click on your answer and see the dark oval or dark box, you can still change your answer. Just click on a different choice. But remember that you cannot change your answer after you click on **Confirm Answer**. This means that you cannot go back to previous questions and change the answers. You must choose your answer, click on your choice, click on **Next**, click on **Confirm Answer**, and move to the next question.

Do your best. The computer will select the questions on this section of the test based on your responses. You will begin with questions that are considered of average difficulty. You will receive easier questions if you are not able to answer the average questions. You will receive more difficult questions if you are able to answer the average questions. You receive more points for the more difficult questions. Just do your best, and you will receive the most points for your level of structure ability.

Understand the Help screen. The **Help** screen has a question mark on it. It is mostly designed to repeat directions. Be careful. You can waste a lot of time on this screen. If you click on **Help** and you want to go back to the question you were answering, look at the box in the bottom right corner. Click on **Return to Where I Was.**

Get help from the test administrator. If you think that your computer is not performing correctly, notify one of the test administrators immediately. There should be several in the room. They cannot help you with the answers on the TOEFL, but they can help you use the computer. That is why they are there. Tell the administrator, "Excuse me. My computer won't ________ ." Show the administrator the problem on the computer.

Stay focused. There is only one test question on the screen at any time. Focus on it. If you need to rest your eyes or your neck muscles, don't look around at other people. Look down at your lap with your eyes closed. Then look up at the ceiling with your eyes closed. Then return to the question. Remember that you cannot return to previous questions, so give each question your full attention while it is on the screen. Then, get ready to focus on the next question.

REVIEW OF SECTION 3: READING

Overview of the Reading Section

QUICK COMPARISON
PAPER-BASED TOEFL AND COMPUTER-BASED TOEFL
SECTION 3

Paper-Based TOEFL Reading Comprehension	*Computer-Based TOEFL Reading*
There are five reading passages with an average of ten questions after each passage.	There are three to six reading passages with an average of six to ten questions after each passage.
There are fifty questions.	There are between forty-four and fifty-five questions.
Everyone taking the TOEFL answers the same questions.	The computer does not select questions at your level of language proficiency. You will have the same questions as others who take the same form of the test.
There are no pictures or visual cues.	There may be pictures in the questions that refer to the content of the reading passage.
All of the questions are multiple-choice.	Most of the questions are multiple-choice, but some of the questions have special directions.
Every question has only one answer.	Some of the questions have two answers.
You answer on a paper answer sheet, filling in ovals marked (A), (B), (C), and (D).	You click on the screen in the oval that corresponds to the answer you have chosen, or you follow the directions on the screen.
You have fifty-five minutes to complete the section.	You have seventy to ninety minutes to complete the section.
You can return to previous passages and questions, erase, and change answers on your answer sheet.	You can return to previous passages and questions, change answers, and answer questions you have left blank.
You may not take notes.	You may not take notes.

Directions for Section 3

Computer-Based TOEFL

The directions for the Computer-Based TOEFL are reprinted with the permission of Educational Testing Service (ETS) from the official *Information Bulletin* for the Computer-Based TOEFL.

This section measures the ability to read and understand short passages similar in topic and style to those that students are likely to encounter in North American universities and colleges. This section contains reading passages and questions about the passages. There are several different types of questions in this section.

In the Reading section, you will first have the opportunity to read the passage.

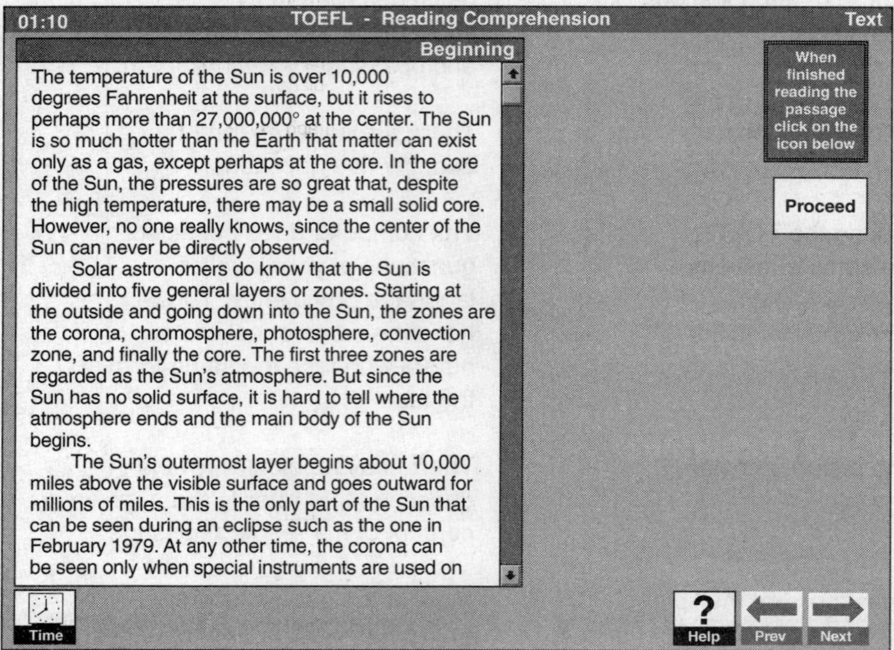

You will use the scroll bar to view the rest of the passage.

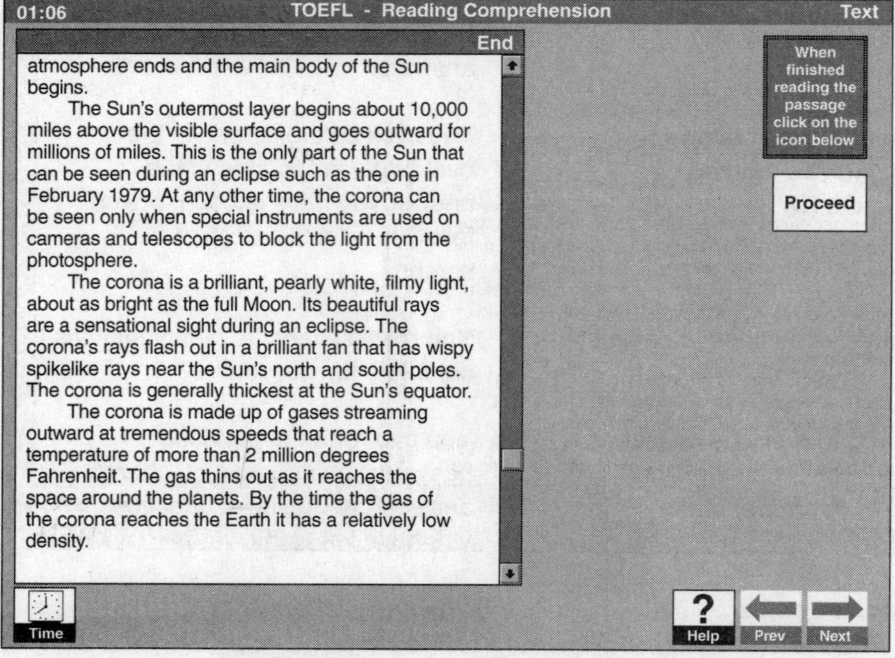

When you have finished reading the passage, you will use the mouse to click on **Proceed**. Then the questions about the passage will be presented. You are to choose the one best answer to each question. Answer all questions about the information in a passage on the basis of what is stated or implied in that passage.

Most of the questions will be multiple-choice questions. To answer these questions, you will click on a choice below the question. Here is an example.

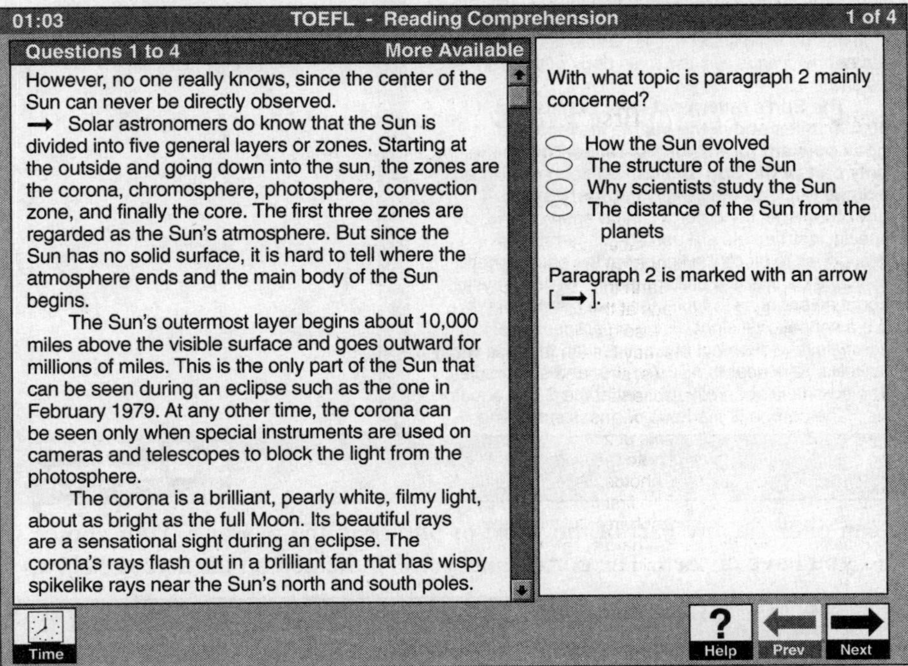

The oval darkens to show which answer you have chosen. To choose a different answer, click on a different oval. The correct answer is indicated on the screen below.

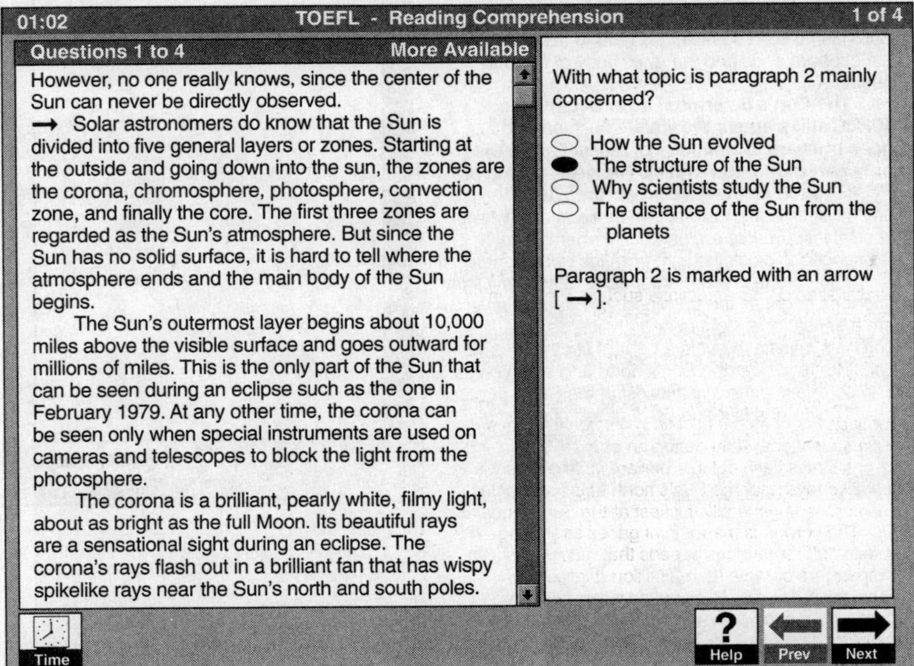

You will see the next question after you click on **Next**. To answer some questions, you will click on a word or phrase. Here is an example.

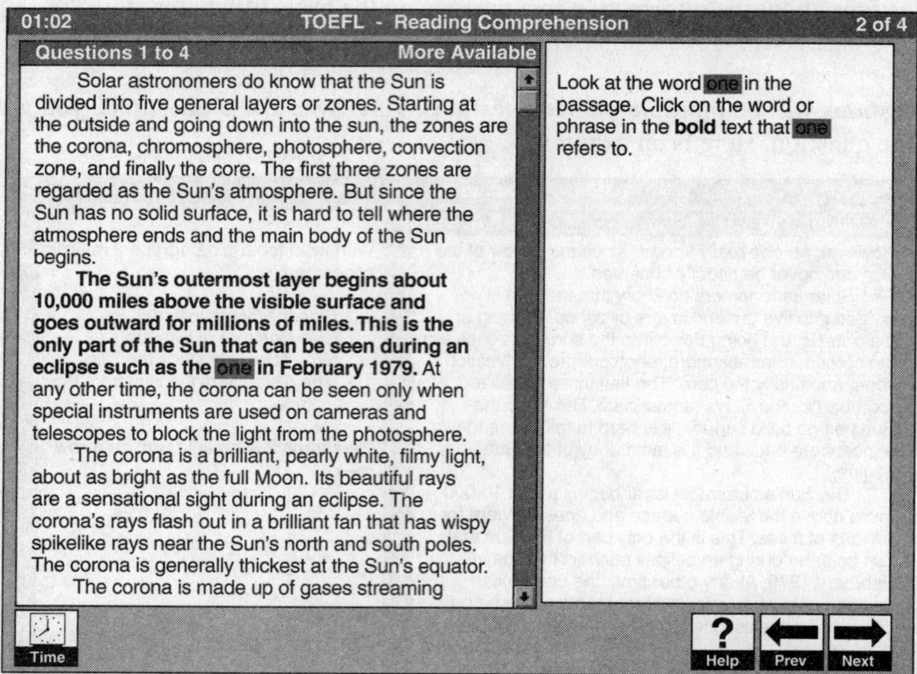

To answer, you can click on any part of the word or phrase in the passage. Your choice will darken to show which word you have chosen. The correct answer is indicated on the screen below.

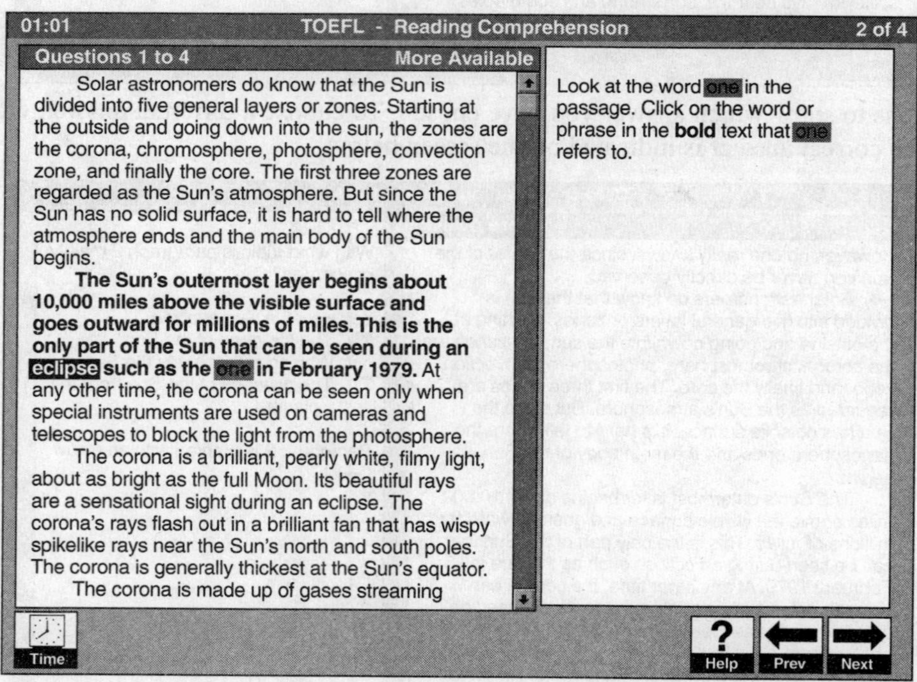

You will see the next question after you click on **Next**. To answer some questions, you will click on a sentence in the passage. Here is an example.

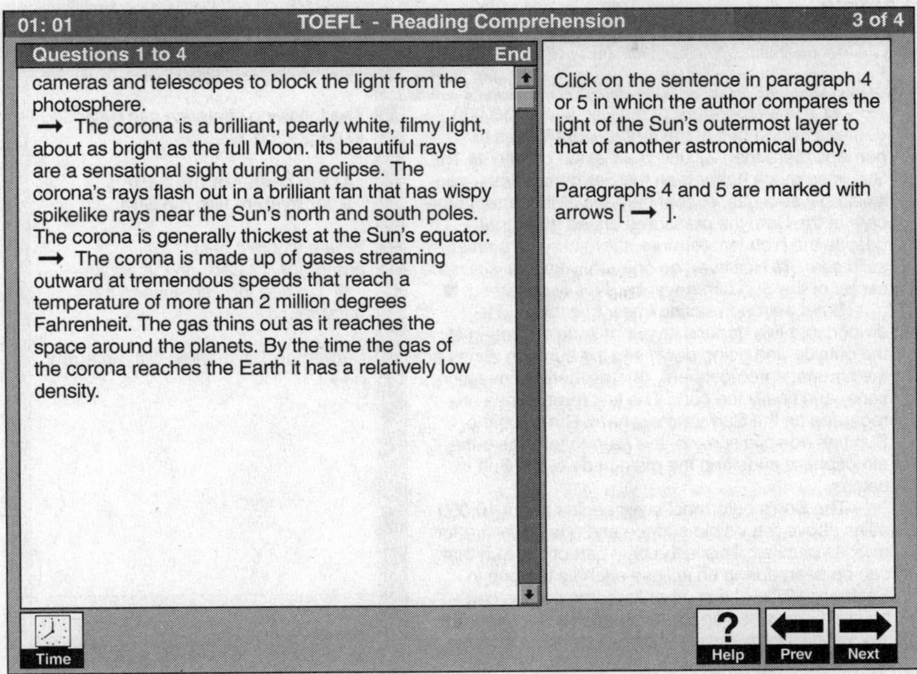

You can click on any part of the sentence in the passage. The sentence will darken to show which answer you have chosen. The correct answer is indicated below.

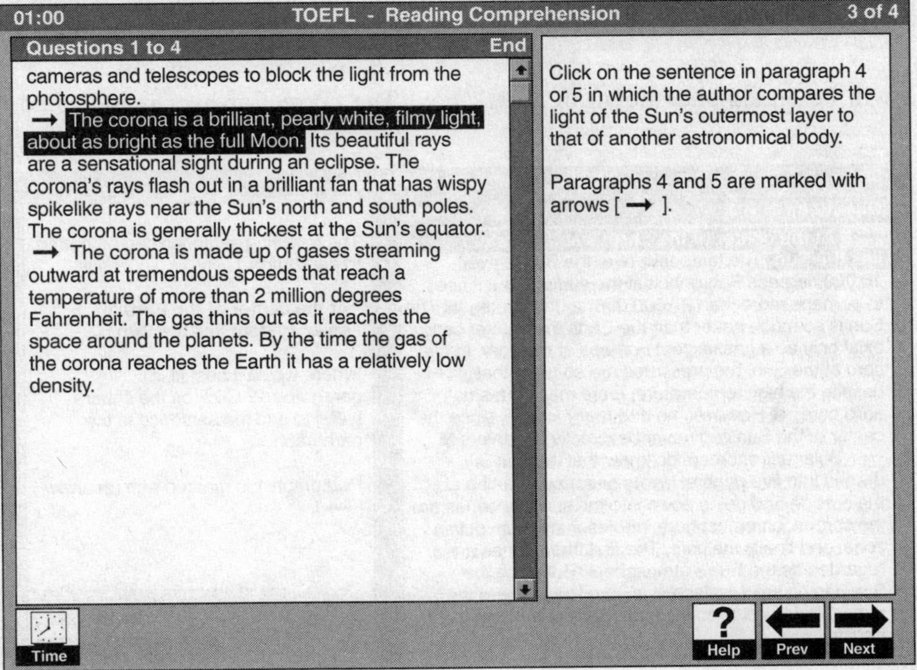

You will see the next question after you click on **Next**.

To answer some questions, you will click on a square to add a sentence to the passage.

Here is an example.

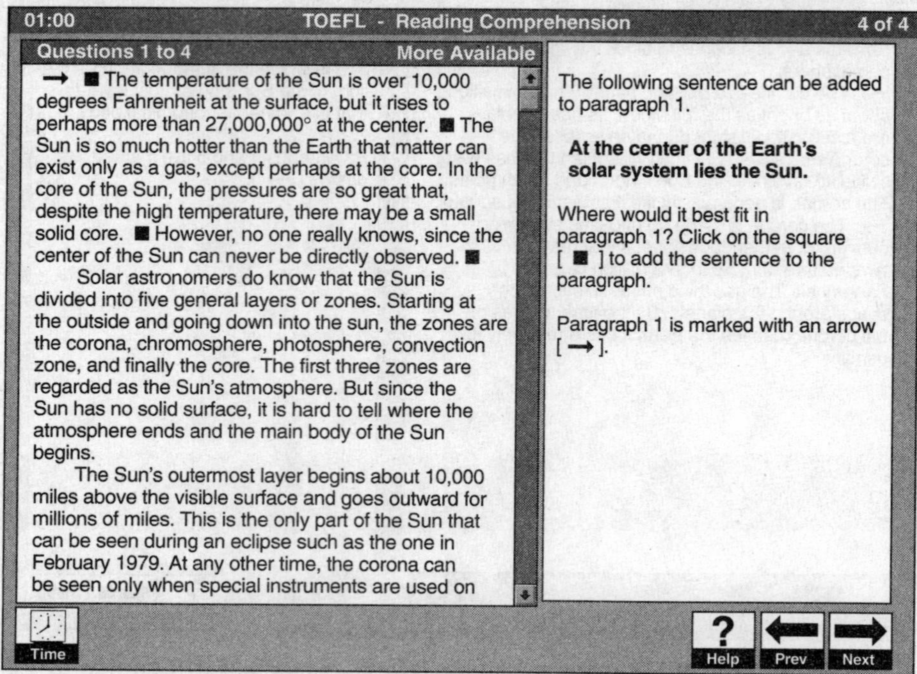

When you click on a square, the sentence will appear in the passage at the place you have chosen. You can see if this is the best place to add the sentence, and you can click on another square to change your answer.

The sentence will be added and shown in a dark box. The correct answer is indicated on the screen below.

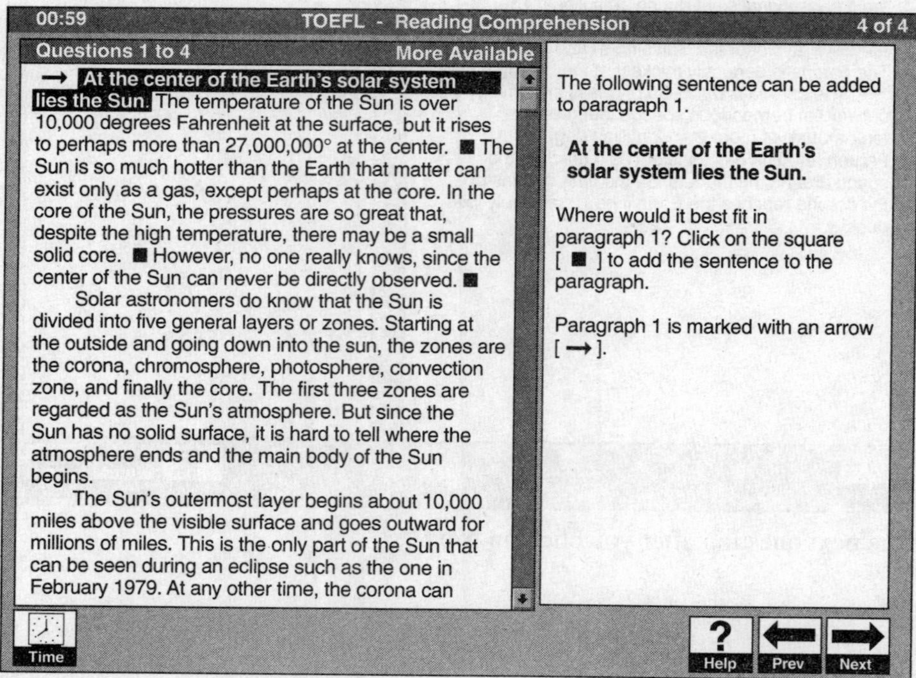

Review of Problems and Questions for the Reading Section

This Review can be used to prepare for both the Paper-Based TOEFL and the Computer-Based TOEFL. For the most part, the same types of problems are tested on both the Paper-Based TOEFL and the Computer-Based TOEFL. Most of the questions on both the Paper-Based TOEFL and the Computer-Based TOEFL are multiple-choice.

Some of the questions on the Computer-Based TOEFL are computer-assisted. Although the computer-assisted questions in this book are numbered, and the answer choices are lettered A, B, C, and D, the same questions on the CD-ROM that supplements the book are not numbered and lettered. You need the numbers and letters in the book to refer to the Answer Key, the Explanatory Answers, and the Transcript for the Listening section. On the CD-ROM, you can refer to other chapters by clicking on the screen. The CD-ROM and the following examples are like those on the Computer-Based TOEFL. The computer-assisted questions have special directions on the screen.

TYPES OF PROBLEMS

Problems like those in this Review frequently appear on Section 3 of the TOEFL.
To prepare for Section 3 of the TOEFL, study the problems in this chapter.

Reading Comprehension

1 Previewing
2 Reading for Main Ideas
3 Using Contexts for Vocabulary
4 Scanning for Details
5 Making Inferences
6 Identifying Exceptions
8 Referring to the Passage

Previewing

Research shows that it is easier to understand what you are reading if you begin with a general idea of what the passage is about. Previewing helps you form a general idea of the topic in your mind.

To preview, read the first sentence of each paragraph and the last sentence of the passage. You should do this as quickly as possible. Remember, you are not reading for specific information, but for an impression of the *topic.*

EXERCISE

DIRECTIONS: Preview the following passage. Focus on the first sentence in each paragraph and the last sentence of the passage. Can you identify the topic? Check your answer using the key on page 542.

A black hole is a region of space created by the total gravitational collapse of matter. It is so intense that nothing, not even light or radiation, can escape. In other words, it is a one-way surface through which matter can fall inward but cannot emerge.

Some astronomers believe that a black hole may be formed when a large star collapses inward from its own weight. So long as they are emitting heat and light into space, stars support themselves against their own gravitational pull with the outward thermal pressure generated by heat from nuclear reactions deep in their interiors. But if a star eventually exhausts its nuclear fuel, then its unbalanced gravitational attraction could cause it to contract and collapse. Furthermore, it could begin to pull in surrounding matter, including nearby comets and planets, creating a black hole.

Reading for Main Ideas

By previewing, you can form a general idea of what a reading passage is about; that is, you identify the *topic.* By reading for main ideas, you identify the point of view of the author—that is, what the writer's *thesis* is. Specifically, what does the author propose to write about the topic? If you could reduce the reading to one sentence, what would it be?

Questions about the main idea can be worded in many ways. For example, the following questions are all asking for the same information: (1) What is the main idea? (2) What is the subject? (3) What is the topic? (4) What would be a good title?

EXERCISE

DIRECTIONS: The main idea usually occurs at the beginning of a reading passage. Look at the first two sentences in the following passage. Can you identify the main idea? What would be a good title for this passage? Check your answers using the key on page 542.

For more than a century, despite attacks by a few opposing scientists, Charles Darwin's theory of evolution by natural selection has stood firm. Now, however, some respected biologists are beginning to question whether the theory accounts for major developments such as the shift from water to land habitation. Clearly, evolution has not proceeded steadily but has progressed by radical advances. Recent research in molecular biology, particularly in the study of DNA, provides us with a new possibility. Not only environmental change but also genetic codes in the underlying structure of DNA could govern evolution.

Using Contexts for Vocabulary

Before you can use a context, you must understand what a context is. In English, a context is the combination of vocabulary and grammar that surrounds a word. Context can be a sentence or a paragraph or a passage. Context helps you make a general *prediction* about meaning. If you know the general meaning of a sentence, you also know the general meaning of the words in the sentence.

Making predictions from contexts is very important when you are reading a foreign language. In this way, you can read and understand the meaning of a passage without stopping to look up every new word in a dictionary. On an examination like the TOEFL, dictionaries are not permitted in the room.

EXERCISE

DIRECTIONS: Read the following passage, paying close attention to the underlined words. Can you understand their meanings from the context without using a dictionary? Check your answers using the key on page 542.

At the age of sixty-six, Harland Sanders had to auction off everything he owned in order to pay his debts. Once the successful proprietor of a large restaurant, Sanders saw his business suffer from the construction of a new freeway that bypassed his establishment and rerouted the traffic that had formerly passed.

With an income of only $105 a month in Social Security, he packed his car with a pressure cooker, some chickens, and sixty pounds of the seasoning that he had developed for frying chicken. He stopped at restaurants, where he cooked chicken for owners to sample. If they liked it, he offered to show them how to cook it. Then he sold them the seasoning and collected a royalty of four cents on each chicken they cooked. The rest is history. Eight years later, there were 638 Kentucky Fried Chicken franchises, and Colonel Sanders had sold his business again—this time for over two million dollars.

Scanning for Details

After reading a passage on the TOEFL, you will be expected to answer six to ten questions. Most of them are multiple-choice. First, read a question and find the important content words. Content words are usually nouns, verbs, or adjectives. They are called content words because they contain the content or meaning of a sentence.

Next, let your eyes travel quickly over the passage for the same content words or synonyms of the words. This is called *scanning.* By scanning, you can find a place in the reading passage where the answer to a question is found. Finally, read those specific sentences carefully and choose the answer that corresponds to the meaning of the sentences you have read.

EXERCISE

DIRECTIONS: First, read the following passage. Then, read the questions after the reading passage, and look for the content words. Finally, scan the passage for the same words or synonyms. Can you answer the questions? Check your answers using the key on pages 542–543.

To prepare for a career in engineering, a student must begin planning in high school. Mathematics and science should form the core curriculum. For example, in a school where sixteen credit hours are required for high school graduation, four should be in mathematics, one each in chemistry, biology, and physics. The remaining credits should include four in English and at least three in the humanities and social sciences. The average entering freshman in engineering should have achieved at least a 2.5 grade point average on a 4.0 scale in his or her high school. Although deficiencies can be corrected during the first year, the student who needs additional work should expect to spend five instead of four years to complete a degree.

1. What is the average grade point for an entering freshman in engineering?

2. When should a student begin planning for a career in engineering?

3. How can a student correct deficiencies in preparation?

4. How many credits should a student have in English?

5. How many credits are required for a high school diploma?

Making Inferences

Sometimes, in a reading passage, you will find a direct statement of fact. That is called evidence. But other times, you will not find a direct statement. Then you will need to use the evidence you have to make an inference. An *inference* is a logical conclusion based on evidence. It can be about the passage itself or about the author's viewpoint.

EXERCISE

DIRECTIONS: First, read the following passage. Then, read the questions after the passage, and make inferences. Can you find the evidence for your inference in the reading passage? Check your answers using the key on page 543.

When an acid is dissolved in water, the acid molecule divides into two parts, a hydrogen ion and another ion. An ion is an atom or a group of atoms that has an electrical charge. The charge can be either positive or negative. If hydrochloric acid is mixed with water, for example, it divides into hydrogen ions and chlorine ions.

A strong acid ionizes to a great extent, but a weak acid does not ionize so much. The strength of an acid, therefore, depends on how much it ionizes, not on how many hydrogen ions are produced. It is interesting that nitric acid and sulfuric acid become greatly ionized whereas boric acid and carbonic acid do not.

1. What kind of acid is sulfuric acid?
2. What kind of acid is boric acid?

PROBLEM 6 Identifying Exceptions

After reading a passage on the TOEFL, you will be asked to select from four possible answers the one that is NOT mentioned in the reading.

Use your scanning skills to locate related words and phrases in the passage and the answer choices.

EXERCISE

DIRECTIONS: First, read the following passage. Then, read the question after the reading passage. Last, scan the passage again for related words and phrases. Try to eliminate three of the choices. Check your answer using the key on pages 543–544.

All music consists of two elements—expression and design. Expression is inexact and subjective and may be enjoyed in a personal or instinctive way. Design, on the other hand, is exact and must be analyzed objectively in order to be understood and appreciated. The folk song, for example, has a definite musical design that relies on simple repetition with a definite beginning and ending. A folk song generally consists of one stanza of music repeated for each stanza of verse.

Because of their communal, and usually uncertain origin, folk songs are often popular verse set to music. They are not always recorded and tend to be passed on in a kind of musical version of oral history. Each singer revises and perfects the song. In part as a consequence of this continuous revision process, most folk songs are almost perfect in their construction and design. A particular singer's interpretation of the folk song may provide an interesting expression, but the simple design that underlies the song itself is stable and enduring.

1. All of the following are true of a folk song EXCEPT
   (A) there is a clear start and finish
   (B) the origin is often not known
   (C) the design may change in the interpretation
   (D) simple repetition is characteristic of its design

Locating References

After reading a passage on the TOEFL, you will be asked to find the antecedent of a pronoun. An antecedent is a word or phrase to which a pronoun refers. Usually, you will be given a pronoun such as "it," "its," "them," or "their," and you will be asked to locate the reference word or phrase in the passage.

First, find the pronoun in the passage. Then read the sentence using the four answer choices in place of the pronoun. The meaning of the sentence in the context of the passage will not change when you substitute the correct antecedent.

EXERCISE

DIRECTIONS: First, find the pronoun in the following passage. Next, start reading several sentences before the sentence in which the pronoun is found, and continue reading several sentences after it. Then, substitute the words or phrases in the answer choices. Which one does not change the meaning of the sentence? Check your answer using the key on page 544.

The National Road, also known as the Cumberland Road, was constructed in the early 1800s to provide transportation between the established commercial areas of the East and Northwest Territory. By 1818, the road had reached Wheeling, West Virginia, 130 miles from its point of origin in Cumberland, Maryland. The cost was a monumental thirteen thousand dollars per mile.

Upon reaching the Ohio River, the National Road became one of the major trade routes to the western states and territories, providing Baltimore with a trade advantage over neighboring cities. In order to compete, New York state authorized the construction of the Erie Canal, and Philadelphia initiated a transportation plan to link it with Pittsburgh. Towns along the rivers, canals, and the new National Road became important trade centers.

1. The word its refers to
(A) the Northwest Territory
(B) 1818
(C) the road
(D) Wheeling, West Virginia

Referring to the Passage

After reading the passage on the TOEFL, you will be asked to find certain information in the passage, and identify it by line number or paragraph.

First, read the question. Then refer to the line numbers and paragraph numbers in the answer choices to scan for the information in the question.

EXERCISE

DIRECTIONS: First, read the following passage. Then, refer back to the passage. Can you find the correct reference? Check your answer using the key on page 544.

In September of 1929, traders experienced a lack of confidence in the stock market's ability to continue its phenomenal rise. Prices fell. For many inexperienced investors, the drop produced a panic. They had all their money tied up in the market, and they were pressed to sell before the prices fell even lower. Sell orders were coming in so fast that the ticker tape at the New York Stock Exchange could not accommodate all the transactions.

To try to reestablish confidence in the market, a powerful group of New York bankers agreed to pool their funds and purchase stock above current market values. Although the buy orders were minimal, they were counting on their reputations to restore confidence on the part of the smaller investors, thereby affecting the number of sell orders. On Thursday, October 24, Richard Whitney, the Vice President of the New York Stock Exchange and a broker for the J.P. Morgan Company, made the effort on their behalf. Initially, it appeared to have been successful, then, on the following Tuesday, the crash began again and accelerated. By 1932, stocks were worth only twenty percent of their value at the 1929 high. The results of the crash had extended into every aspect of the economy, causing a long and painful depression, referred to in American history as the Great Depression.

1. Where in the passage does the author refer to the reason for the stock market crash?

2. Where in the passage does the author suggest that there was a temporary recovery in the stock market?

CUMULATIVE REVIEW EXERCISE FOR READING COMPREHENSION

Read the following passage, using the skills you have learned. Preview, read for main ideas, and use contexts for vocabulary. To read faster, read phrases instead of words. Then, answer the questions that follow the passage. Scan for details and evidence. Make inferences.

The computer-based version of this reading passage is best viewed on the CD-ROM that supplements this book. Scroll through the passage, using the skills that you have learned. Check your answers on the screen. If you do not have a computer, then use the print version shown with the following computer-assisted questions.

Although each baby has an individual schedule of development, general patterns of growth have been observed. Three periods of development have been identified, including early infancy, which extends from the first to the sixth month; middle infancy, from the sixth to the ninth month; and late infancy, from the ninth to the fifteenth month. Whereas the newborn is concerned with his or her inner world and responds primarily to hunger and pain, in early infancy the baby is already aware of the surrounding world. During the second month, many infants are awake more and can raise their heads to look at things. They also begin to smile at people. By four months, the baby is searching for things but not yet grasping them with its hands. It is also beginning to be wary of strangers and may scream when a visiting relative tries to pick it up. By five months, the baby is grabbing objects and putting them into its mouth. Some babies are trying to feed themselves with their hands.

In middle infancy, the baby concentrates on practicing a great many speech sounds. It loves to imitate actions and examine interesting objects. At about seven months, it begins to crawl, a skill that it masters at the end of middle infancy.

In late infancy, the baby takes an interest in games, songs, and even books. Progress toward walking moves through standing, balancing, bouncing in place, and walking with others. As soon as the baby walks well alone, it has passed from infancy into the active toddler stage.

TYPES OF QUESTIONS

Multiple-Choice Questions

Paper-Based TOEFL

1. What does this passage mainly discuss?
   (A) Growth in early infancy
   (B) The active toddler stage
   (C) How a baby learns to walk
   (D) The developmental stages of infancy

2. The word "primarily" in line 9 could best be replaced by
   (A) often
   (B) naturally
   (C) for the most part
   (D) in a loud way

3. According to this reading passage, what would a six-month-old baby like to do?
   (A) Smile at people
   (B) Crawl on the floor
   (C) Imitate actions
   (D) Play simple games

4. A baby in late infancy would be able to do all of the following EXCEPT
   (A) make many speech sounds
   (B) walk well alone
   (C) show interest in games
   (D) imitate actions

Answer Sheet

1. Ⓐ Ⓑ Ⓒ ●
2. Ⓐ Ⓑ ● Ⓓ
3. Ⓐ Ⓑ ● Ⓓ
4. Ⓐ ● Ⓒ Ⓓ

Computer-Based TOEFL

What does this passage mainly discuss?
- ○ Growth in early infancy
- ○ The active toddler stage
- ○ How a baby learns to walk
- ● The developmental stages of infancy

The word **primarily** could best be replaced by
- ○ often
- ○ naturally
- ● for the most part
- ○ in a loud way

According to this reading passage, what would a six-month-old baby like to do?
- ○ Smile at people
- ○ Crawl on the floor
- ● Imitate actions
- ○ Play simple games

A baby in late infancy would be able to do all of the following EXCEPT
- ○ make many speech sounds
- ● walk well alone
- ○ show interest in games
- ○ imitate actions

Computer-Assisted Questions

Location Questions

On some of the computer-assisted questions, you will be asked to locate information in the passage. These questions are like the multiple-choice questions on the Paper-Based TOEFL where you must locate information by identifying the line numbers in the passage. On the computer-assisted questions, you must click on the sentence or paragraph in the passage.

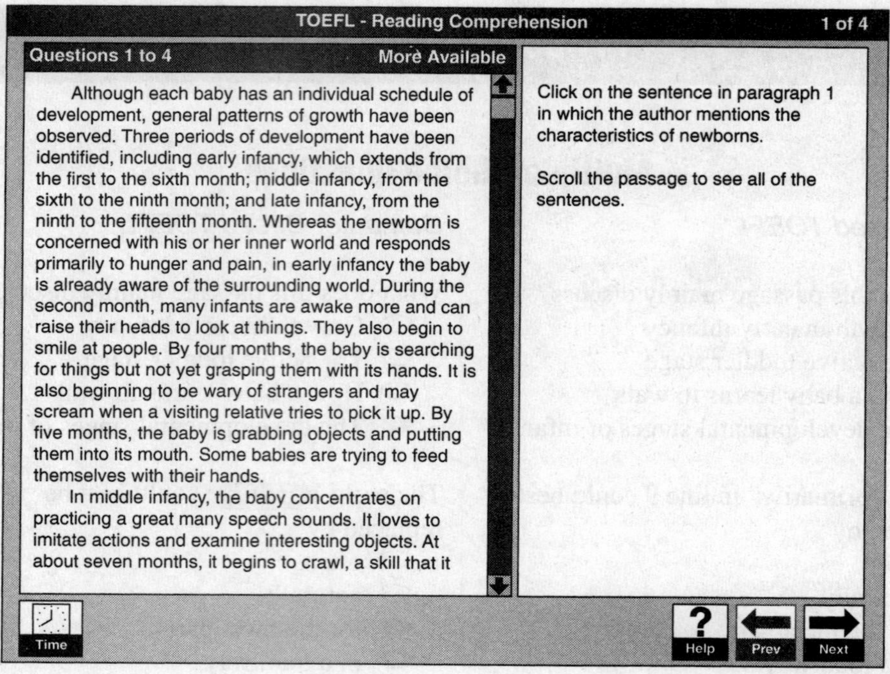
TOEFL - Reading Comprehension
1 of 4
Questions 1 to 4
More Available
Although each baby has an individual schedule of development, general patterns of growth have been observed. Three periods of development have been identified, including early infancy, which extends from the first to the sixth month; middle infancy, from the sixth to the ninth month; and late infancy, from the ninth to the fifteenth month. Whereas the newborn is concerned with his or her inner world and responds primarily to hunger and pain, in early infancy the baby is already aware of the surrounding world. During the second month, many infants are awake more and can raise their heads to look at things. They also begin to smile at people. By four months, the baby is searching for things but not yet grasping them with its hands. It is also beginning to be wary of strangers and may scream when a visiting relative tries to pick it up. By five months, the baby is grabbing objects and putting them into its mouth. Some babies are trying to feed themselves with their hands.
In middle infancy, the baby concentrates on practicing a great many speech sounds. It loves to imitate actions and examine interesting objects. At about seven months, it begins to crawl, a skill that it
Click on the sentence in paragraph 1 in which the author mentions the characteristics of newborns.
Scroll the passage to see all of the sentences.
Time
Help
Prev
Next

Synonyms

On some of the computer-assisted questions, you will be asked to locate synonyms in the reading passage. You must click on the word or phrase in the passage.

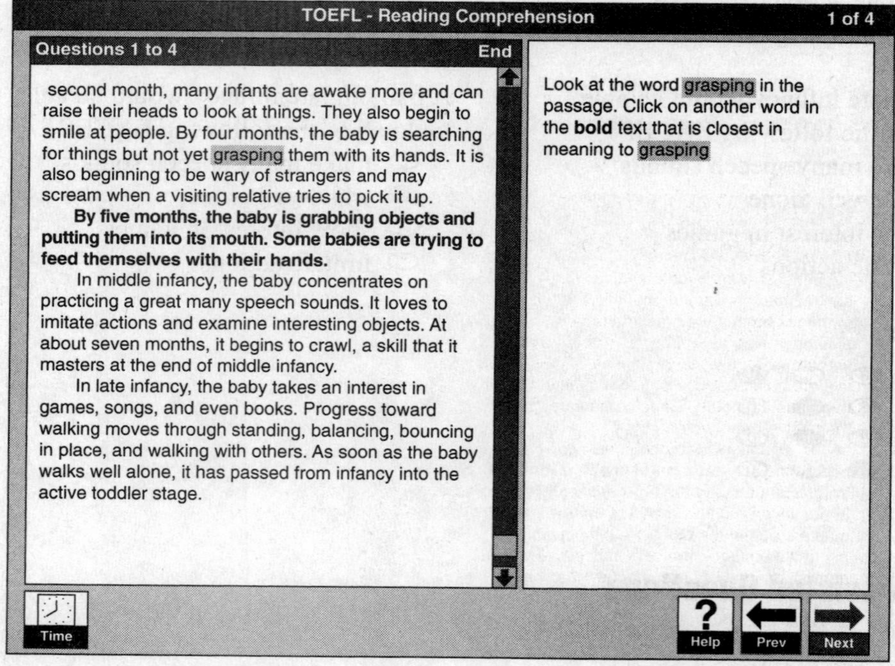
TOEFL - Reading Comprehension
1 of 4
Questions 1 to 4
End
second month, many infants are awake more and can raise their heads to look at things. They also begin to smile at people. By four months, the baby is searching for things but not yet grasping them with its hands. It is also beginning to be wary of strangers and may scream when a visiting relative tries to pick it up.
By five months, the baby is grabbing objects and putting them into its mouth. Some babies are trying to feed themselves with their hands.
In middle infancy, the baby concentrates on practicing a great many speech sounds. It loves to imitate actions and examine interesting objects. At about seven months, it begins to crawl, a skill that it masters at the end of middle infancy.
In late infancy, the baby takes an interest in games, songs, and even books. Progress toward walking moves through standing, balancing, bouncing in place, and walking with others. As soon as the baby walks well alone, it has passed from infancy into the active toddler stage.
Look at the word grasping in the passage. Click on another word in the bold text that is closest in meaning to grasping
Time
Help
Prev
Next

Paraphrased Sentences

On some of the computer-assisted questions, you will be asked to identify paraphrases of sentences in the passage.

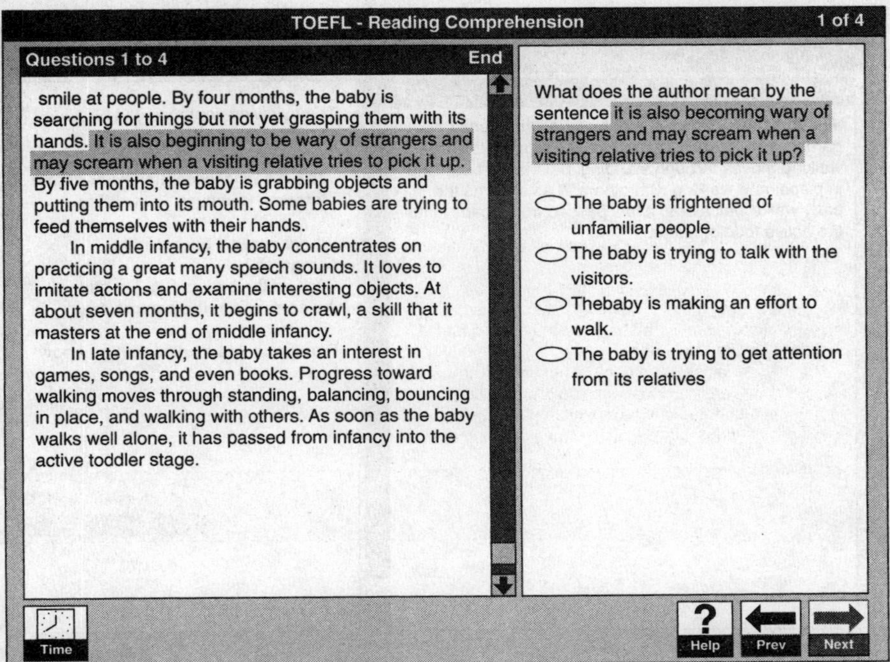
TOEFL - Reading Comprehension
1 of 4
Questions 1 to 4
End
smile at people. By four months, the baby is searching for things but not yet grasping them with its hands. It is also beginning to be wary of strangers and may scream when a visiting relative tries to pick it up. By five months, the baby is grabbing objects and putting them into its mouth. Some babies are trying to feed themselves with their hands.
In middle infancy, the baby concentrates on practicing a great many speech sounds. It loves to imitate actions and examine interesting objects. At about seven months, it begins to crawl, a skill that it masters at the end of middle infancy.
In late infancy, the baby takes an interest in games, songs, and even books. Progress toward walking moves through standing, balancing, bouncing in place, and walking with others. As soon as the baby walks well alone, it has passed from infancy into the active toddler stage.
What does the author mean by the sentence it is also becoming wary of strangers and may scream when a visiting relative tries to pick it up?
The baby is frightened of unfamiliar people.
The baby is trying to talk with the visitors.
Thebaby is making an effort to walk.
The baby is trying to get attention from its relatives
Time
?
Help
Prev
Next

Reference Questions

On some of the computer-assisted questions, you will be asked to locate the nouns to which pronouns refer. These questions are like the multiple-choice questions on the Paper-Based TOEFL where you must choose the noun from four answer choices. On the computer-assisted questions, you must find the noun and click on it in the passage.

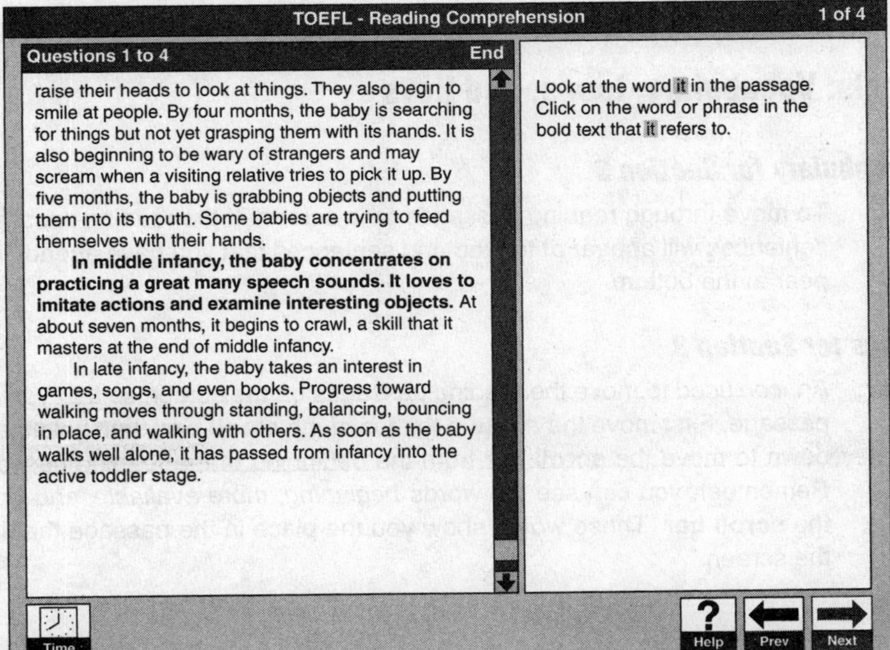
TOEFL - Reading Comprehension
1 of 4
Questions 1 to 4
End
raise their heads to look at things. They also begin to smile at people. By four months, the baby is searching for things but not yet grasping them with its hands. It is also beginning to be wary of strangers and may scream when a visiting relative tries to pick it up. By five months, the baby is grabbing objects and putting them into its mouth. Some babies are trying to feed themselves with their hands.
In middle infancy, the baby concentrates on practicing a great many speech sounds. It loves to imitate actions and examine interesting objects. At about seven months, it begins to crawl, a skill that it masters at the end of middle infancy.
In late infancy, the baby takes an interest in games, songs, and even books. Progress toward walking moves through standing, balancing, bouncing in place, and walking with others. As soon as the baby walks well alone, it has passed from infancy into the active toddler stage.
Look at the word it in the passage. Click on the word or phrase in the bold text that it refers to.
Time
?
Help
Prev
Next

Sentence Insertion Questions

On some of the computer-assisted questions, you will be asked to locate the most logical place in the passage where a sentence could be inserted. You will have several options marked with a square (■) in the passage.

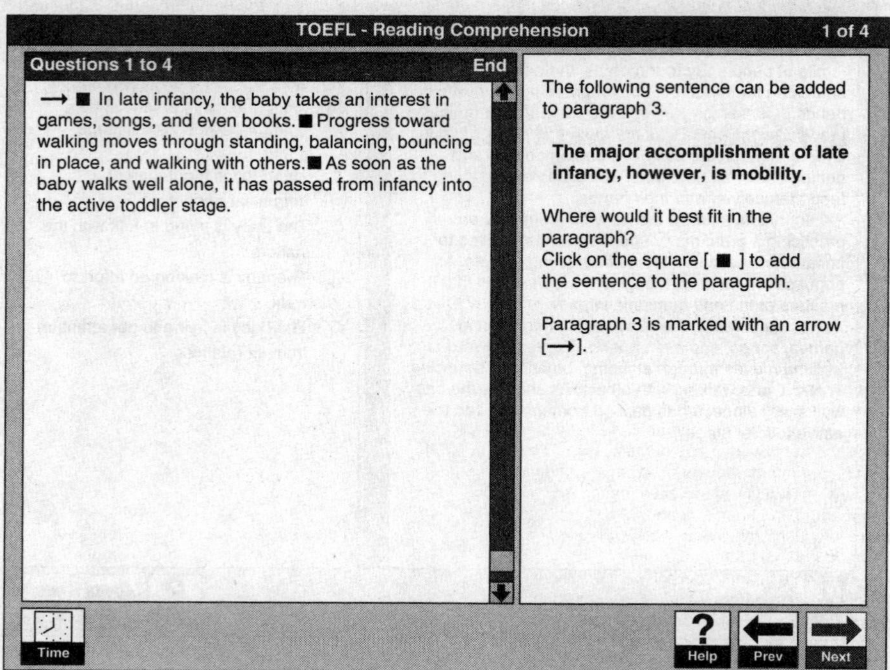
TOEFL - Reading Comprehension
1 of 4
Questions 1 to 4
End
→ ■ In late infancy, the baby takes an interest in games, songs, and even books. ■ Progress toward walking moves through standing, balancing, bouncing in place, and walking with others. ■ As soon as the baby walks well alone, it has passed from infancy into the active toddler stage.
The following sentence can be added to paragraph 3.
The major accomplishment of late infancy, however, is mobility.
Where would it best fit in the paragraph?
Click on the square [■] to add the sentence to the paragraph.
Paragraph 3 is marked with an arrow [→].
Time
Help
Prev
Next

Computer Tutorial for the Reading Section

Testing Tools: Vocabulary, Icons, and Keys

Specific Vocabulary for Section 3

Scroll To move through reading passages on a screen. If the reading passage is long, new sentences will appear at the top and sentences that you have already read will disappear at the bottom.

Specific Icons for Section 3

Scroll Bar An *icon* used to move the reading passages on the screen so that you can see a long passage. First move the *arrow* to the top of the **scroll bar**; then hold the *mouse button* down to move the **scroll bar** from the beginning of the reading passage to the end. Remember, you can see the words *beginning*, *more available*, and *end* at the top of the **scroll bar**. These words show you the place in the passage that is displayed on the screen.

Proceed An *icon* at the bottom of the screen with the reading passage. *Click* on **Proceed** after you have read the passage in order to see the first question. Remember, you cannot use **Proceed** until you have scrolled down to the end of the passage.

Previous An *icon* at the bottom of the screen with the questions. *Click* on **Previous** to see the previous question.

Computer Screens for Section 3

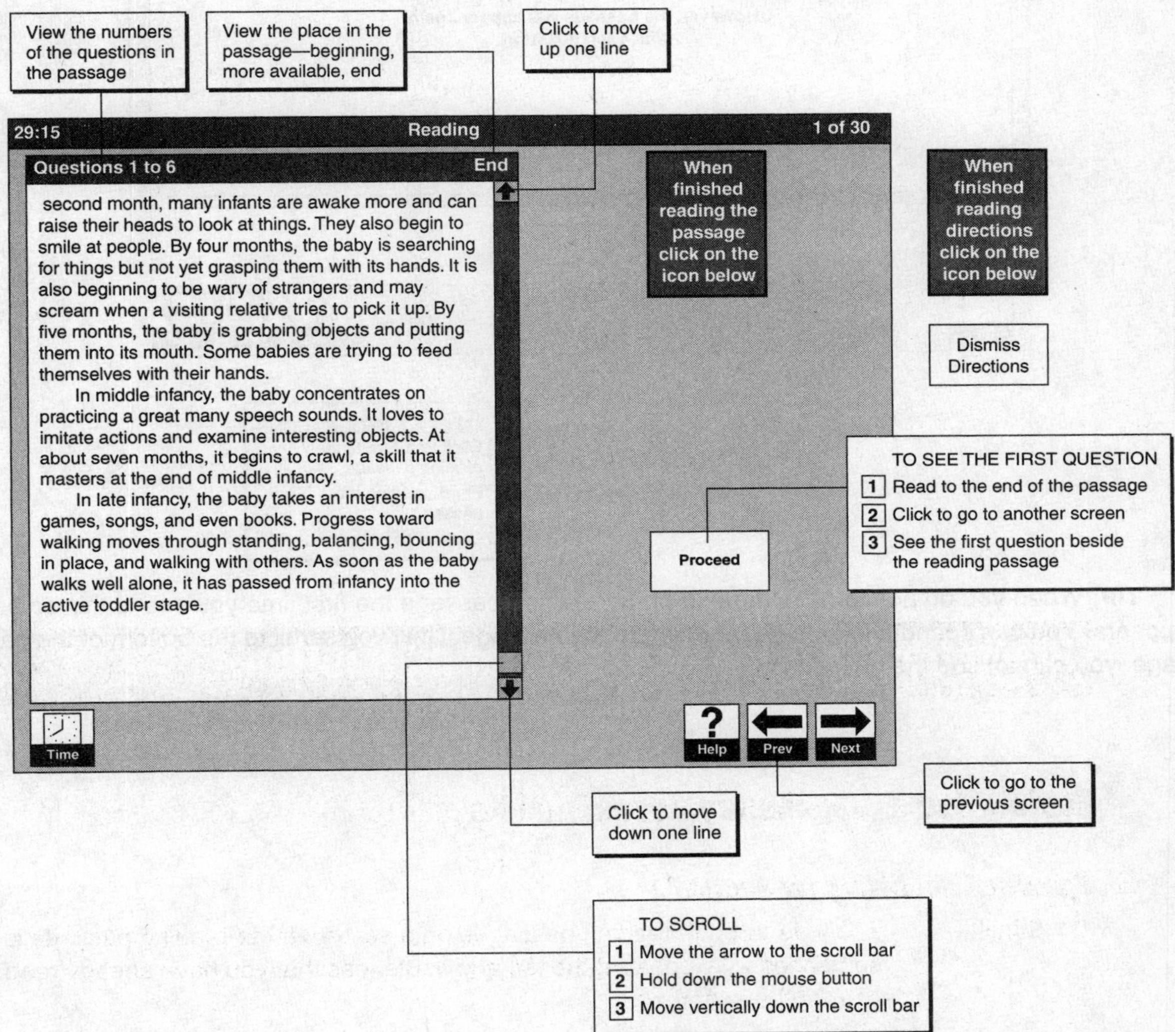
View the numbers of the questions in the passage
View the place in the passage—beginning, more available, end
Click to move up one line
29:15
Reading
1 of 30
Questions 1 to 6
End
second month, many infants are awake more and can raise their heads to look at things. They also begin to smile at people. By four months, the baby is searching for things but not yet grasping them with its hands. It is also beginning to be wary of strangers and may scream when a visiting relative tries to pick it up. By five months, the baby is grabbing objects and putting them into its mouth. Some babies are trying to feed themselves with their hands.
In middle infancy, the baby concentrates on practicing a great many speech sounds. It loves to imitate actions and examine interesting objects. At about seven months, it begins to crawl, a skill that it masters at the end of middle infancy.
In late infancy, the baby takes an interest in games, songs, and even books. Progress toward walking moves through standing, balancing, bouncing in place, and walking with others. As soon as the baby walks well alone, it has passed from infancy into the active toddler stage.
When finished reading the passage click on the icon below
When finished reading directions click on the icon below
Dismiss Directions
TO SEE THE FIRST QUESTION
1 Read to the end of the passage
2 Click to go to another screen
3 See the first question beside the reading passage
Proceed
Time
Help
Prev
Next
Click to go to the previous screen
Click to move down one line
TO SCROLL
1 Move the arrow to the scroll bar
2 Hold down the mouse button
3 Move vertically down the scroll bar

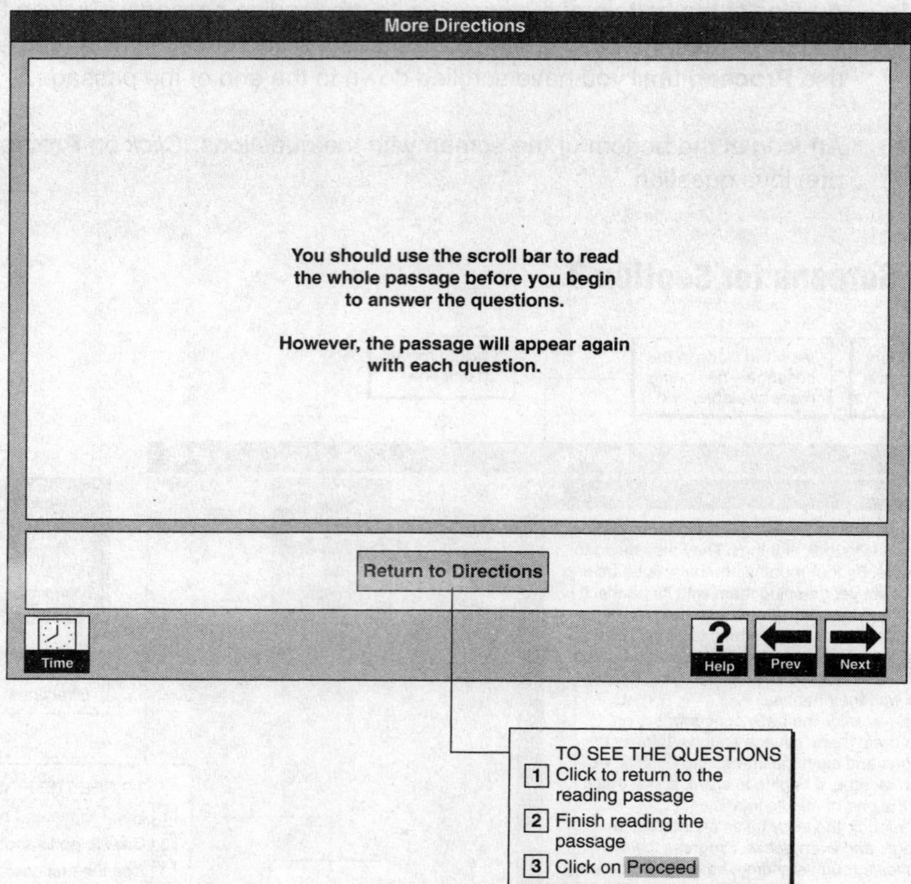

TIP: When you do not scroll to the end of the reading passage the first time you see it, this screen appears. You can spend a lot of time returning to the passage. Until you scroll to the bottom of the passage, you cannot see the questions.

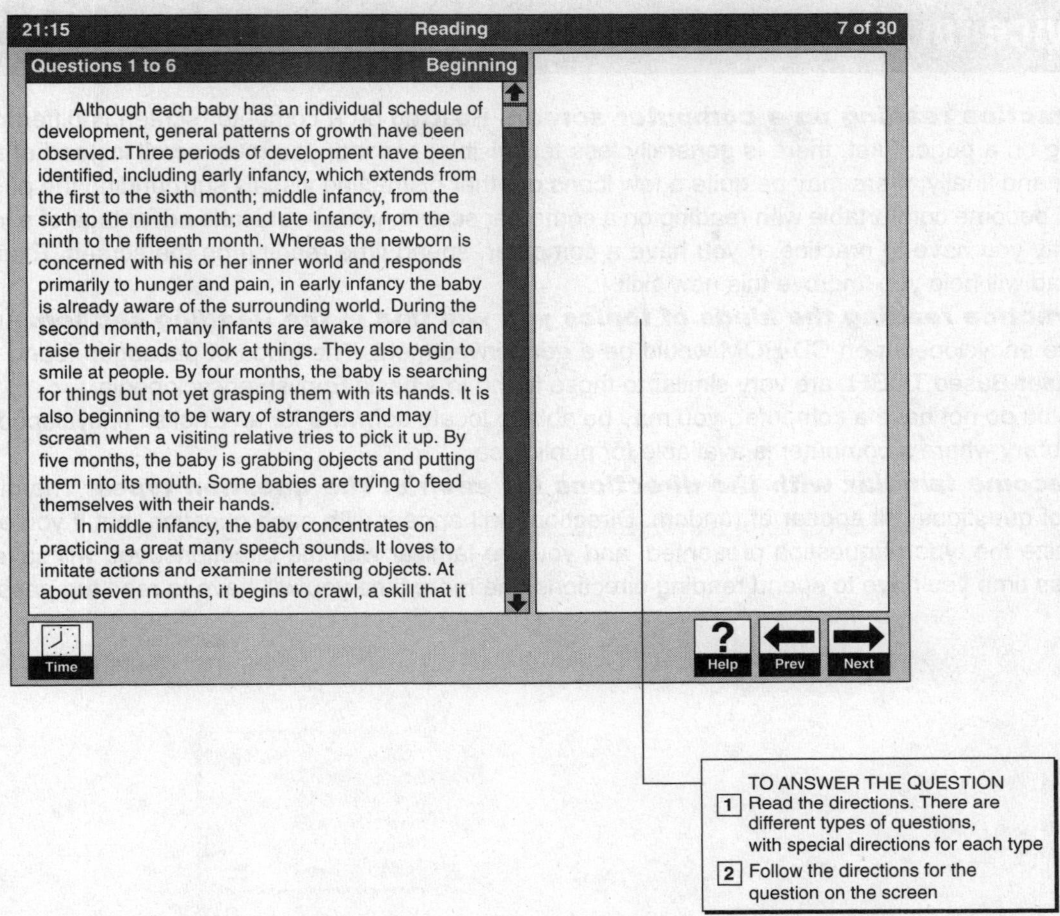
21:15
Reading
7 of 30
Questions 1 to 6
Beginning
Although each baby has an individual schedule of development, general patterns of growth have been observed. Three periods of development have been identified, including early infancy, which extends from the first to the sixth month; middle infancy, from the sixth to the ninth month; and late infancy, from the ninth to the fifteenth month. Whereas the newborn is concerned with his or her inner world and responds primarily to hunger and pain, in early infancy the baby is already aware of the surrounding world. During the second month, many infants are awake more and can raise their heads to look at things. They also begin to smile at people. By four months, the baby is searching for things but not yet grasping them with its hands. It is also beginning to be wary of strangers and may scream when a visiting relative tries to pick it up. By five months, the baby is grabbing objects and putting them into its mouth. Some babies are trying to feed themselves with their hands.
In middle infancy, the baby concentrates on practicing a great many speech sounds. It loves to imitate actions and examine interesting objects. At about seven months, it begins to crawl, a skill that it
Time
Help
Prev
Next
TO ANSWER THE QUESTION
1 Read the directions. There are different types of questions, with special directions for each type
2 Follow the directions for the question on the screen

TIP: The answer to the question on the right side of the screen is always found in the part of the passage visible on the left side of the screen. You usually do not have to scroll through the passage to find the answer.

Simulations for Section 3

In order to prepare for the experience that you will have on the Computer-Based TOEFL, you can use the CD-ROM that supplements this book. Locate the Reading section on the Model Tests. The computer will simulate the Reading section on the Computer-Based TOEFL. These model tests are computer-assisted. The Reading section of the Computer-Based TOEFL is not computer-adaptive.

As part of your study plan, be sure to review all of the questions in all of the Model Tests. Use the Explanatory Answers on the CD-ROM or on pages 553–616.

If you do not have a computer, you can still simulate some of the features of the Computer-Based TOEFL. Section 3 of Model Tests 1–8 in Chapter 7 of this book is printed in two columns to give you the same kind of visual impression that you will have when you read from a computer screen. The on-screen directions for computer-assisted questions are also printed in the book.

Advice for the Reading Section: Computer-Based TOEFL

Practice reading on a computer screen. Reading on a computer screen is different from reading on a page. First, there is generally less text visible; second, you must scroll instead of turning pages; and finally, there may be quite a few icons or other distracting visuals surrounding the passage.

To become comfortable with reading on a computer screen, you should take advantage of every opportunity you have to practice. If you have a computer, spend time reading on the screen. Everything you read will help you improve this new skill.

Practice reading the kinds of topics you will find in the Reading section. An inexpensive encyclopedia on CD-ROM would be a good investment. The kinds of passages found on the Computer-Based TOEFL are very similar to those found in a basic English encyclopedia.

If you do not have a computer, you may be able to locate software for an English encyclopedia at a local library where a computer is available for public use.

Become familiar with the directions for each of the question types. The different types of questions will appear at random. Directions will appear with each question, but if you already recognize the type of question presented, and you are familiar with the directions, you will save time. The less time you have to spend reading directions, the more time you will have to read the passages.

REVIEW OF WRITING ESSAYS

Overview of the Writing Section

QUICK COMPARISON
PAPER-BASED TOEFL AND COMPUTER-BASED TOEFL
ESSAY

Paper-Based TOEFL *Test of Written English*	*Computer-Based TOEFL* *Writing*
The essay, also called the Test of Written English (TWE), is offered five times each year. You must select a TOEFL test date when the TWE is scheduled if you need an essay score.	The essay is required as part of every TOEFL. You must write the essay as the last part of your TOEFL examination.
When you register for the TOEFL on one of the dates when the TWE is offered, you do not have to register separately for the TWE. It is offered at no additional cost.	When you register for the TOEFL, you are automatically registered for the Writing section. It is offered at no additional cost.
There is only one topic for each essay.	There is only one topic for each essay.
Everyone taking the TOEFL writes an essay on the same topic.	The computer selects a topic for you. It may not be the same topic that is selected for someone else taking the TOEFL that day.
You do not know any of the topics for the essay.	All of the topics for the essay are published in the *TOEFL Information Bulletin* for Computer-Based Testing free of charge from ETS. They are also listed on the ETS web site at www.toefl.org.
Most of the topics ask you to agree or disagree with a statement or to express an opinion.	Most of the topics ask you to agree or disagree with a statement or to express an opinion.
There are three types of topics commonly used on the TWE:	There are three types of topics commonly used on the Writing Section:
1. *Argument.* Argue both sides of an issue, and take a position.	1. *Argument.* Argue both sides of an issue, and take a position.
2. *Persuasion.* Agree or disagree with a statement, and support your opinion.	2. *Persuasion.* Agree or disagree with a statement, and support your opinion.

3. *Extension.* Based on several examples that support an argument, choose another example, and give reasons for the choice.

The topics are very general and do not require any specialized knowledge of the subject to answer them.

You have thirty minutes to complete the essay.

You handwrite your essay on paper provided in the test materials.

You have one page to organize your essay. This page is not graded. You may organize in any way that is helpful to you—notes, a list, an outline, or a drawing. You may use your first language on this page.

Your essay will not be scored for neatness, but the readers must be able to understand what you have written.

You should write about 300–500 words, or three to five short paragraphs.

A scale from 1 to 6 is used to grade the essay.

The scale is printed on page 325.

Your essay will be scored by two professional teachers, reading independently. When the two scores differ by more than one point, a third teacher will read and score your essay.

3. *Extension.* Based on several examples that support an argument, choose another example, and give reasons for the choice.

The topics are very general and do not require any specialized knowledge of the subject to answer them.

You have thirty minutes to complete the essay.

You can choose to handwrite your essay on paper or type it on the computer.

You have one page to organize your essay. This page is not graded. You may organize in any way that is helpful to you—notes, a list, an outline, or a drawing. You may use your first language on this page.

Your essay will not be scored for neatness, but the readers must be able to understand what you have written.

You should write about 300–500 words, or three to five short paragraphs.

A scale from 1 to 6 is used to grade the essay.

The scale is printed on page 325.

Your essay will be scored by two professional teachers, reading independently. When the two scores differ by more than one point, a third teacher will read and score your essay.

The score is reported separately from the TOEFL score. It will not be included in the computation of the total TOEFL score and will not affect your score on the multiple-choice TOEFL.

The score is combined with the score on the Structure section. It will be factored in the section score at 50 percent.

Directions for the Essay

Computer-Based TOEFL

The directions for the Computer-Based TOEFL are reprinted with the permission of Educational Testing Service (ETS) from the official *Information Bulletin* for the Computer-Based TOEFL.

In this section, you will have an opportunity to demonstrate your ability to write in English. This includes the ability to generate and organize ideas, to support those ideas with examples or evidence, and to compose in standard written English in response to an assigned topic.

On the day of the test, an essay topic will be given to you. You will have 30 minutes to write your essay on that topic. Before the topic is presented, you must choose whether to type your essay on the computer or to handwrite your essay on the paper essay answer sheet provided.

Scratch paper will be given to you for making notes. However, only your response handwritten on the essay answer sheet or typed in the essay box on the computer will be scored.

The essay topic will be presented to you on the computer screen. The essay screen will be similar to this:

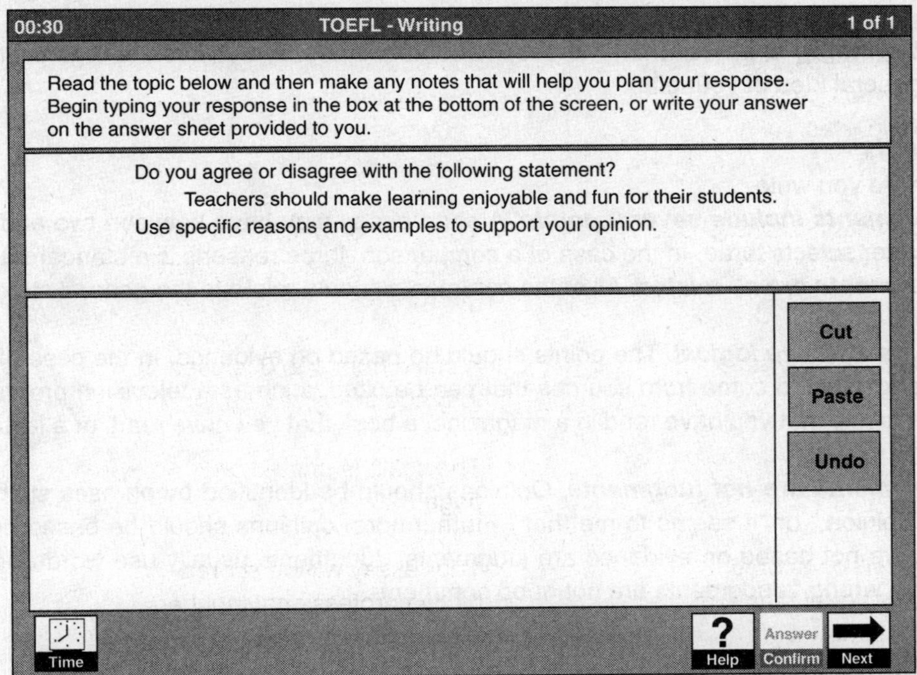

You can click on **Next** and **Confirm Answer** to end the Writing section at any time. At the end of 30 minutes the computer will automatically end the section.

Review of Strategies and Topics for the Writing Section

This Review can be used to prepare for both the Paper-Based TOEFL and the Computer-Based TOEFL. For the most part, the same types of topics are tested on both the Paper-Based TOEFL and the Computer-Based TOEFL. The essays on both the Paper-Based TOEFL and the Computer-Based TOEFL are scored using the same scale.

Three Steps for Writing Short Essays

There are three steps that most good writers follow in organizing their writing. You should use these steps when you write a short essay. First, tell your reader what you are going to write. Second, write it. Third, tell your reader what you wrote.

To look at these steps another way, your essay should have three parts:

1. A good beginning
2. Several good comments
3. A good ending

In this review of writing, we will discuss and give examples of the three parts of a short essay, using the types of topics that you will find on the TOEFL.

A Good Beginning

This is where you tell the reader what you are going to write. A good beginning has certain requirements.

A good beginning is short. Two or three sentences is enough to tell your reader how you plan to approach the topic.

A good beginning is direct. In the case of a comparison, state both sides of the argument in your first sentence. In a short composition, you don't have enough time for indirect approaches.

A good beginning is an outline. The second sentence usually outlines the organization. It gives the reader a general idea of your plan.

Good Comments

This is where you write.

Good comments include several points. A short essay may have between two and five points. Usually, the writer selects three. In the case of a comparison, three reasons is a standard argument.

Good comments are all related. All of the comments should relate to the general statement in the first sentence.

Good comments are logical. The points should be based on evidence. In the case of a comparison, the evidence should come from sources that can be cited, such as a television program that you have seen, an article that you have read in a magazine, a book that you have read, or a lecture that you have heard.

Good comments are not judgments. Opinions should be identified by phrases such as, "in my view," "in my opinion," or "it seems to me that." Furthermore, opinions should be based on evidence. Opinions that are not based on evidence are judgments. Judgments usually use words like "good" or "bad," "right" or "wrong." Judgments are not good comments.

A Good Ending

This is where you tell the reader what you wrote.

A good ending is a summary. The last sentence is similar to the first sentence. In a short essay, a good ending does not add new information. It does not introduce a new idea.

A good ending is not an apology. A good ending does not apologize for not having said enough, for not having had enough time, or for not using good English.

Scoring Scale for the Essay

The essay is scored on a scale of 1 to 6. A score between two points on the scale—5.5, 4.5, 3.5, 2.5, 1.5—can also be reported. The following guidelines are used by evaluators:

6 shows consistent proficiency	• Is well organized • Addresses the topic • Includes examples and details • Has few errors in grammar and vocabulary
5 shows inconsistent proficiency	• Is well organized • Addresses the topic • Includes fewer examples and details • Has more errors in grammar and vocabulary
4 shows minimal proficiency	• Is adequately organized • Addresses most of the topic • Includes some examples and details • Has errors in grammar and vocabulary that occasionally confuse meaning
3 shows developing proficiency	• Is inadequately organized • Addresses part of the topic • Includes few examples and details • Has many errors in grammar and vocabulary that confuse meaning
2 shows little proficiency	• Is disorganized • Does not address the topic • Does not include examples and details • Has many errors in grammar and vocabulary that consistently confuse meaning
1 shows no proficiency	• Is disorganized • Does not address the topic • Does not include examples and details • Has so many errors in grammar and vocabulary that meaning is not communicated
0 shows no comprehension	• Does not write an essay • Writes an essay on a different topic

Example Essay

The following example essay would receive a score of 6. It is well organized, it addresses the topic, it includes examples and details, and it has some but not many errors in grammar and vocabulary.

Read and study this example essay before you complete the Model Tests.

Some students in the United States work while they are earning their degrees in college; others receive support from their families. How should a student's education be supported? Argue both sides of the issue and defend your position.

Notes

friends praise initiative

WORK

future employers be impressed

student satisfaction

friends praise efforts for family

FAMILY

future employees not expect

every family member benefit society

Some students in the United States work while they are earning their degrees; others receive support from their families. Both approaches have advantages and disadvantages. In this essay, I will name some of the advantages of each approach, and I will argue in favor family support.

In a society where independence and individual accomplishment are value, a student who earned his degree by working would be greatly admired. Friends would praise him for his initiative and perseverence. Future employers might be impressed by his work record. He might derive greater satisfaction from his personal investment in it.

On the other hand, in a society where cooperation and family dependence are value, a student who received support would be better understood. Friends would praise him for his efforts on behalf of his family. Future employers would not expect a work record from a student. He might feel greater responsibility toward others in his family because the accomplishment was shared.

Thus, not one but every family member would assured some opportunity or benefit.

For my part, I must argue in favor of family support. While I study at an American University, my older brother will send me money every month. When I finish my degree and find a good job, I will send my younger sister to a school or university. It may not be a better way, but it is the way that my society rewards.

Evaluator's Comments

This writing sample is well organized with a good topic sentence and good support statements. It addresses the question, and does not digress from the topic. There is a logical progression of ideas and excellent language proficiency, as evidenced by a variety of grammatical structures and appropriate vocabulary. There are only a few grammatical errors that have been corrected below:

Line 7	in favor of
Line 9	are valued
Lines 18–19	are valued
Line 28	would be assured

SCORE: 6

Computer Tutorial for the Writing Section

Testing Tools: Vocabulary, Icons, and Keys

Specific Vocabulary for the Essay

Text All printed material on the screen. **Text** can refer to a word, a sentence, a paragraph, several paragraphs, or an essay.

Cursor The line that shows you where you can begin typing. When you move the *mouse,* the **cursor** appears. You can move the **cursor** on your essay by moving the *mouse* on your *mouse pad.*

Blinking Flashing on and off. The *cursor* is usually **blinking** to help you see it.

Highlight To select *text* in your essay that you want to edit. To **highlight**, move the *cursor* to the beginning of the place in your essay that you want to change. Hold down the mouse button and move to the end of the place in your essay that you want to change. Release the mouse button. The **highlighted** *text* should be shaded.

Keys The individual buttons on the keyboard used for typing and editing your essay.

Keys for the Essay

Arrow Keys Keys that let you move around in your essay. There is an **up arrow, down arrow, left arrow,** and **right arrow**. They are found between the letters and the numbers on the keyboard. Use the **arrow keys** to move up, down, left, or right.

Page Up, Page Down Keys that let you see your essay if it is longer than the screen. The **Page Up** and **Page Down** keys are above the *arrow keys* on the keyboard. Use **Page Up** to scroll to the beginning of your essay. Use **Page Down** to scroll to the end of your essay.

Backspace A key that moves you back one space at a time. Use the **Backspace** key to erase *text* from right to left.

Space Bar The long key at the bottom of the keyboard. Use the **Space Bar** two or three times to indent a paragraph. Remember, the *Tab* key does not function on your keyboard.

Icons for the Essay

Cut An example of an *icon.* After you *highlight* the text you want to delete or move, click on **Cut**. The text will disappear. Use the **Cut** icon to delete text or as the first step in moving text.

Paste An example of an *icon.* After you *cut* text, you can move the *cursor* to the place in the essay where you want to insert the text, and click on **Paste**. The text you *highlighted* will appear. Use the **Paste** icon as the second step in moving text.

Undo An example of an *icon.* It lets you change your mind. For example, if you move a sentence, and then you want to move it back to the original place in your essay, click on **Undo**. **Undo** will return whatever you did last back to the way it looked before you made the change. Remember, **Undo** will only return your last change, not several changes.

Keyboard for the Essay

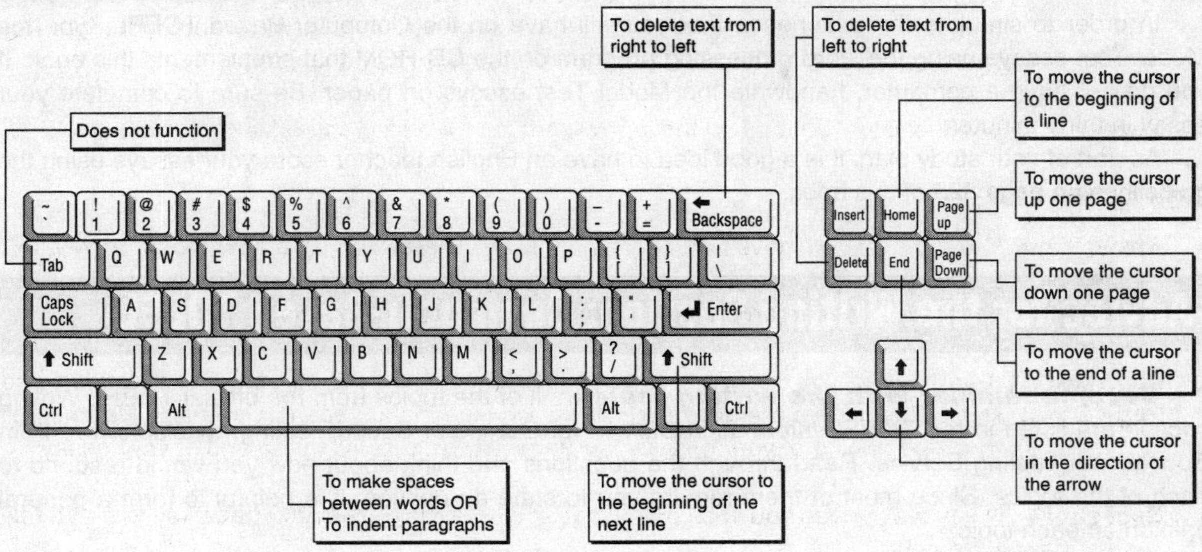

TIP: If you click the mouse, you can delete text. You may even delete your essay! If this happens, click on **Undo** immediately.

Computer Screen for the Essay

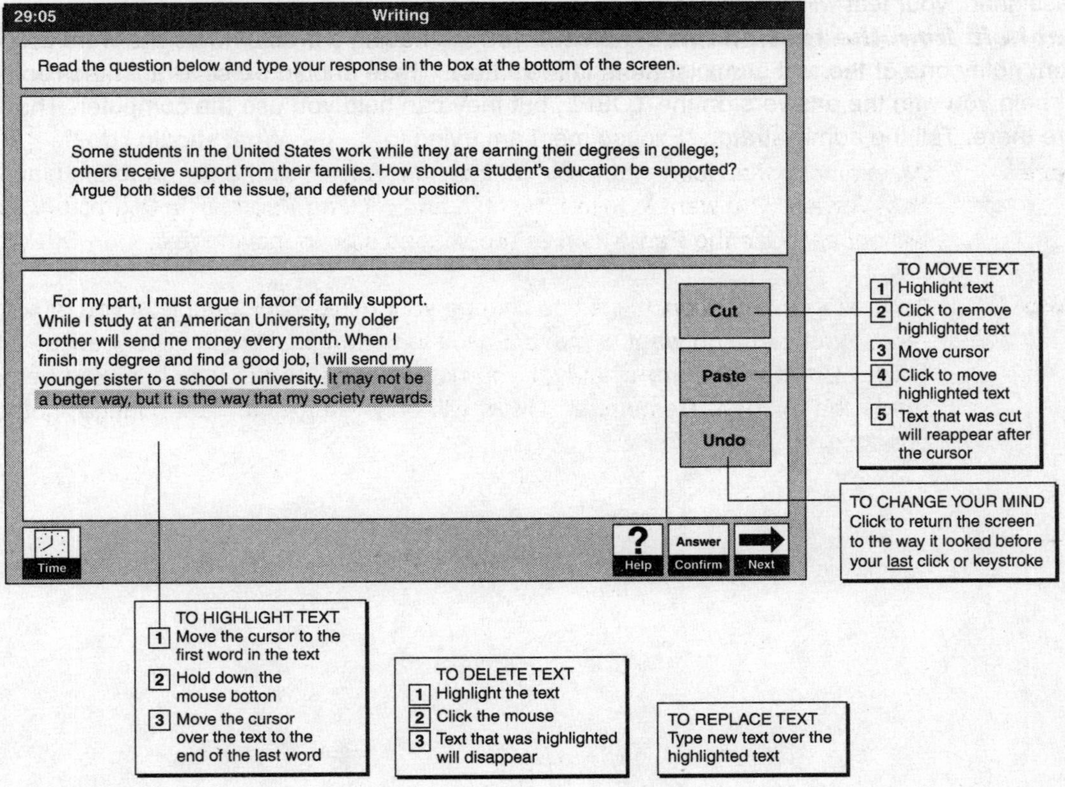

TIP: Be sure that you have completed the essay to your satisfaction before you click on **Answer Confirm.** After you click on **Answer Confirm**, you cannot continue writing or editing your essay.

Simulations for the Essay

In order to simulate the experience that you will have on the Computer-Based TOEFL, type the Model Test essays using the word processing program on the CD-ROM that supplements this book. If you do not have a computer, handwrite the Model Test essays on paper. Be sure to complete your essay in thirty minutes.

As part of your study plan, it is a good idea to have an English teacher score your essays using the guidelines on page 325 of this book.

Advice for the Writing Section: Computer-Based TOEFL

Become familiar with the writing topics. All of the topics from the official TOEFL Writing section are listed in the *TOEFL Information Bulletin* for Computer-Based Testing, available free from Educational Testing Service. Read through the questions and think about how you would respond to each of the topics. Since most of them require you to state an opinion, it is helpful to form a general opinion on each topic.

Decide whether you will handwrite or type your essay. The word processing program for the computer is very simple. If you know how to use Windows, it should be easy for you to adjust. But if you feel uncomfortable using the computer to write the essay, you may choose to handwrite it. By making your decision before you take the TOEFL, you will not waste time thinking about the way you will complete your test. You can use every minute to organize and write the essay.

Write on the topic you are assigned. If you write on a topic other than the one you have been assigned, your test will not be scored.

Get help from the test administrator. If you are having a problem with the word processing program, notify one of the test administrators immediately. There should be several in the room. They cannot help you with the answers on the TOEFL, but they can help you use the computer. That is why they are there. Tell the administrator, "Excuse me. I am trying to _____. What should I do?"

TOEFL MODEL TESTS

There are two types of Model Tests to help you prepare for the TOEFL. The questions on Model Tests 1–8 are like those that frequently appear on the Computer-Based TOEFL. The questions on the Cumulative Model Test are also like those that frequently appear on the Computer-Based TOEFL.

The difference between Model Tests 1–8 and the Cumulative Model Test is that Model Tests 1–8 are simulations of a Computer-Based TOEFL. A simulation is an experience that is similar, but not exactly the same. On these Model Tests, you will see the same types of questions, and you will answer them in the same way that you will on the actual Computer-Based TOEFL that you take, but the computer will not be selecting questions for you at your level of language proficiency. These Model Tests are computer-assisted, but not computer-adaptive. On the Cumulative Model Test, you will see the same types of questions, and you will answer them in the same way that you will on the actual Computer-Based TOEFL. In addition, the computer will be selecting questions for you at your level of language proficiency. This Model Test is computer-adaptive. Both types of Model Tests are found on the CD-ROM that supplements this book.

First, take Model Tests 1–8 and study the Explanatory Answers. Then, take the Cumulative Model Test (computer-adaptive) and repeat it until you are answering correctly at least 80 percent of the time.

How to Answer Questions for Model Tests 1–8

If you use the CD-ROM to take the Model Tests, you will not need to write in your book. If you do not have access to a computer, mark your responses to Model Tests 1–8 directly on the tests in the book.

For multiple-choice questions that require you to choose one answer, fill in the oval of the letter that corresponds to the answer you have chosen.

The Palo Verde tree ________ in spring.

Ⓐ has beautiful yellow blossoms
Ⓑ beautiful yellow blossoms
Ⓒ having beautiful yellow blossoms
Ⓓ with beautiful yellow blossoms

The Palo Verde tree ________ in spring.

● has beautiful yellow blossoms
Ⓑ beautiful yellow blossoms
Ⓒ having beautiful yellow blossoms
Ⓓ with beautiful yellow blossoms

For questions that require you to choose two answers, mark an X in the squares that correspond to the answers you have chosen.

According to the professor, what was the Hemingway style?

Click on two answers

[A] Powerful descriptions
[B] Imaginative details
[C] Short sentences
[D] Difficult symbolism

According to the professor, what was the Hemingway style?

Click on two answers

[X] Powerful descriptions
[B] Imaginative details
[X] Short sentences
[D] Difficult symbolism

For questions that require you to click on sentences to move them into categories on charts, write letters on the charts that correspond to the sentences you have chosen.

How did Hemingway use his experience in different novels?

Click on the sentence.
Then click on the space where it belongs.
Use each sentence only once.

[A] He was fishing in the Gulf of Mexico.
[B] He was driving an ambulance in Italy.
[C] He was working as a newspaper reporter in Paris.

How did Hemingway use his experience in different novels?

Click on the sentence.
Then click on the space where it belongs.
Use each sentence only once.

[A] He was fishing in the Gulf of Mexico.
[B] He was driving an ambulance in Italy.
[C] He was working as a newspaper reporter in Paris.

The Sun Also Rises	A Farewell to Arms	The Old Man and the Sea

The Sun Also Rises	A Farewell to Arms	The Old Man and the Sea
C	B	A

For questions that require you to put events in order, write letters in the numbered boxes that correspond to the sequence you have chosen.

The professor briefly describes Hemingway's life as an author. Summarize the biographical data by putting the events in order.

Click on the sentence.
Then click on the space where it belongs.
Use each sentence only once.

[A] Hemingway wrote about his experiences as an ambulance driver during the war.
[B] Hemingway received the Nobel Prize for literature.
[C] Hemingway published *The Old Man and the Sea.*
[D] Hemingway was a newspaper reporter in Paris.

1	
2	
3	
4	

The professor briefly describes Hemingway's life as an author. Summarize the biographical data by putting the events in order.

Click on the sentence.
Then click on the space where it belongs.
Use each sentence only once.

[A] Hemingway wrote about his experiences as an ambulance driver during the war.
[B] Hemingway received the Nobel Prize for literature.
[C] Hemingway published *The Old Man and the Sea.*
[D] Hemingway was a newspaper reporter in Paris.

1	D
2	A
3	C
4	B

For questions that require you to click on a word or phrase, circle the word or phrase in the passage.

Look at the word one in the passage. Click on the word or phrase in the bold text that one refers to.

Solar astronomers do know that the sun is divided into five general layers or zones. Starting at the outside and going down into the sun, the zones are the corona, chromosphere, photosphere, convection zone, and finally the core. The first three zones are regarded as the sun's atmosphere. But since the sun has no solid surface, it is hard to tell where the atmosphere ends and the main body of the sun begins.

The sun's outermost layer begins about 10,000 miles above the visible surface and goes outward for millions of miles.This is the only part of the sun that can be seen during an eclipse such as the one in February 1979. At any other time, the corona can be seen only when special instruments are used on cameras and telescopes to block the light from the photosphere.

The corona is a brilliant, pearly white, filmy light, about as bright as the full moon. Its beautiful rays are a sensational sight during an eclipse. The corona's rays flash out in a brilliant fan that has wispy spikelike rays near the sun's north and south poles. The corona is generally thickest at the sun's equator.

The corona is made up of gases streaming

Look at the word one in the passage. Click on the word or phrase in the bold text that one refers to.

Solar astronomers do know that the sun is divided into five general layers or zones. Starting at the outside and going down into the sun, the zones are the corona, chromosphere, photosphere, convection zone, and finally the core. The first three zones are regarded as the sun's atmosphere. But since the sun has no solid surface, it is hard to tell where the atmosphere ends and the main body of the sun begins.

The sun's outermost layer begins about 10,000 miles above the visible surface and goes outward for millions of miles.This is the only part of the sun that can be seen during an eclipse such as the one in February 1979. At any other time, the corona can be seen only when special instruments are used on cameras and telescopes to block the light from the photosphere.

The corona is a brilliant, pearly white, filmy light, about as bright as the full moon. Its beautiful rays are a sensational sight during an eclipse. The corona's rays flash out in a brilliant fan that has wispy spikelike rays near the sun's north and south poles. The corona is generally thickest at the sun's equator.

The corona is made up of gases streaming

For questions that require you to click on a sentence, circle the sentence in the passage.

Click on the sentence in paragraph 4 or 5 in which the author compares the light of the sun's outermost layer to that of another astronomical body.

Paragraphs 4 and 5 are marked with arrows [→]

cameras and telescopes to block the light from the photosphere.

→ The corona is a brilliant, pearly white, filmy light, about as bright as the full moon. Its beautiful rays are a sensational sight during an eclipse. The corona's rays flash out in a brilliant fan that has wispy spikelike rays near the sun's north and south poles. The corona is generally thickest at the sun's equator.

→ The corona is made up of gases streaming outward at tremendous speeds that reach a temperature of more than 2 million degrees Fahrenheit. The gas thins out as it reaches the space around the planets. By the time the gas of the corona reaches the Earth it has a relatively low density.

Click on the sentence in paragraph 4 or 5 in which the author compares the light of the sun's outermost layer to that of another astronomical body.

Paragraphs 4 and 5 are marked with arrows [→]

cameras and telescopes to block the light from the photosphere.

→ The corona is a brilliant, pearly white, filmy light, about as bright as the full moon. Its beautiful rays are a sensational sight during an eclipse. The corona's rays flash out in a brilliant fan that has wispy spikelike rays near the sun's north and south poles. The corona is generally thickest at the sun's equator.

→ The corona is made up of gases streaming outward at tremendous speeds that reach a temperature of more than 2 million degrees Fahrenheit. The gas thins out as it reaches the space around the planets. By the time the gas of the corona reaches the Earth it has a relatively low density.

For questions that require you to add a sentence, circle the square [■] where the sentence is to be inserted.

The following sentence can be added to paragraph 1.

At the center of the Earth's solar system lies the sun.

Where would it best fit in paragraph 1? Click on the square [■] to add the sentence to the paragraph.

Paragraph 1 is marked with an arrow [→].

→ ■ The temperature of the sun is over 10,000 degrees Fahrenheit at the surface, but it rises to perhaps more than 27,000,000° at the center. ■The sun is so much hotter than the Earth that matter can exist only as a gas, except perhaps at the core. In the core of the sun, the pressures are so great that, despite the high temperature, there may be a small solid core. ■However, no one really knows, since the center of the sun can never be directly observed. ■ .

Solar astronomers do know that the sun is divided into five general layers or zones. Starting at the outside and going down into the sun, the zones are the corona, chromosphere, photosphere, convection zone, and finally the core. The first three zones are regarded as the sun's atmosphere. But since the sun has no solid surface, it is hard to tell where the atmosphere ends and the main body of the sun begins.

The sun's outermost layer begins about 10,000 miles above the visible surface and goes outward for millions of miles. This is the only part of the sun that can be seen during an eclipse such as the one in

The following sentence can be added to paragraph 1.

At the center of the Earth's solar system lies the sun.

Where would it best fit in paragraph 1? Click on the square [■] to add the sentence to the paragraph.

Paragraph 1 is marked with an arrow [→].

→(■)The temperature of the sun is over 10,000 degrees Fahrenheit at the surface, but it rises to perhaps more than 27,000,000° at the center. ■The sun is so much hotter than the Earth that matter can exist only as a gas, except perhaps at the core. In the core of the sun, the pressures are so great that, despite the high temperature, there may be a small solid core. ■However, no one really knows, since the center of the sun can never be directly observed. ■

Solar astronomers do know that the sun is divided into five general layers or zones. Starting at the outside and going down into the sun, the zones are the corona, chromosphere, photosphere, convection zone, and finally the core. The first three zones are regarded as the sun's atmosphere. But since the sun has no solid surface, it is hard to tell where the atmosphere ends and the main body of the sun begins.

The sun's outermost layer begins about 10,000 miles above the visible surface and goes outward for millions of miles. This is the only part of the sun that can be seen during an eclipse such as the one in

Model Test 1
Computer-Assisted TOEFL

Section 1: Listening

The Listening section of the test measures the ability to understand conversations and talks in English. You will use headphones to listen to the conversations and talks. While you are listening, pictures of the speakers or other information will be presented on your computer screen. There are two parts to the Listening section, with special directions for each part.

On the day of the test, the amount of time you will have to answer all of the questions will appear on the computer screen. The time you spend listening to the test material will not be counted. The listening material and questions about it will be presented only one time. You will not be allowed to take notes or have any paper at your computer. You will both see and hear the questions before the answer choices appear. You can take as much time as you need to select an answer; however, it will be to your advantage to answer the questions as quickly as possible. You may change your answer as many times as you want before you confirm it. After you have confirmed an answer, you will not be able to return to the question.

Before you begin working on the Listening section, you will have an opportunity to adjust the volume of the sound. You will not be able to change the volume after you have started the test.

QUESTION DIRECTIONS — Part A

In Part A of the Listening section, you will hear short conversations between two people. In some of the conversations, each person speaks only once. In other conversations, one or both of the people speak more than once. Each conversation is followed by one question about it.

Each question in this part has four answer choices. You should click on the best answer to each question. Answer the questions on the basis of what is stated or implied by the speakers.

1. What is the man's problem?

Ⓐ He doesn't mind the traffic.
Ⓑ He takes the bus to school.
Ⓒ He has to stand on the bus if he takes it to school.
Ⓓ He wants to ride to school with the woman.

2. What does the man mean?

Ⓐ The woman should not consider her advisor in the decision.
Ⓑ The woman should not take Dr. Sullivan's section.
Ⓒ The woman's advisor will not be offended.
Ⓓ The woman should not take a physics course.

3. What does the woman imply?

Ⓐ She is not interested in the man.
Ⓑ She does not like lectures.
Ⓒ She would go out with the man on another occasion.
Ⓓ She would rather stay at home.

4. What does the woman mean?

Ⓐ The bike is in good condition.
Ⓑ The man needs to replace the bike.
Ⓒ The bike is missing.
Ⓓ It is a new bike.

5. What does the man want to drink?

Ⓐ Something cold.
Ⓑ Coffee.
Ⓒ Tea.
Ⓓ Both coffee and tea.

6. What does the man suggest the woman do?

(A) Ask directions.
(B) Walk to the shopping center.
(C) Take a taxi.
(D) Wait for the bus.

7. What can be inferred about the man?

(A) He does not plan to study.
(B) He has a very busy schedule.
(C) He is lost.
(D) He has not registered yet.

8. What does the man mean?

(A) He does not want to listen to the radio.
(B) He has changed his opinion about turning on the radio.
(C) The radio will not bother him.
(D) The radio is not working very well.

9. What does the woman suggest Anna do?

(A) Stop worrying.
(B) Go out more.
(C) Talk to a friend.
(D) Get counseling.

10. What does the man mean?

(A) He prefers to talk another time.
(B) He wants the woman to go away.
(C) He would like the woman to continue.
(D) He doesn't know what to think.

11. What will the man probably do?

(A) Accept the woman's apology.
(B) Allow the woman to go ahead of him.
(C) Apologize to the woman.
(D) Go to the front of the line.

12. What does the woman imply?

(A) The neighbors have parties often.
(B) She does not like her neighbors.
(C) The neighbors' party is disturbing her.
(D) She will not be invited to the neighbors' party.

13. What had the man assumed?

(A) Dr. Franklin is not very understanding.
(B) The extension was a very bad idea.
(C) She is sorry that the man was denied his request.
(D) The professor's answer is not surprising.

14. What problem do the man and woman have?

(A) They do not have a telephone.
(B) They are late.
(C) They have been left.
(D) They got lost.

15. What is the woman probably going to do?

(A) Pay the rent for half a month.
(B) Help the man move.
(C) Stay where she is living until the 15th.
(D) Move out of the apartment.

16. What had the man assumed about MaryAnne?

(A) She had already taken the test.
(B) She did not want to take classes.
(C) She had not taken the placement test.
(D) She would take the math classes later.

17. What does the man mean?

(A) The plan is to remain in the class.
(B) It is not comfortable in the classroom.
(C) He has been absent because he was sick.
(D) The weather has been very bad.

QUESTION DIRECTIONS — Part B

In Part B of the Listening section, you will hear several longer conversations and talks. Each conversation or talk is followed by several questions. The conversations, talks, and questions will not be repeated.

The conversations and talks are about a variety of topics. You do not need special knowledge of the topics to answer the questions correctly. Rather, you should answer each question on the basis of what is stated or implied by the speakers in the conversations or talks.

For most of the questions, you will need to click on the best of four possible answers. Some questions will have special directions. The special directions will appear in a box on the computer screen.

18. What is Mike's problem?

Ⓐ He was late arriving at registration.
Ⓑ He needs an advisor's signature on a course request form.
Ⓒ He is not doing well in the class because it is so large.
Ⓓ He must have the permission of the instructor to enroll in a class.

19. What does Mike want Professor Day to do?

Ⓐ Help him with the class.
Ⓑ Explain some technical vocabulary.
Ⓒ Give him special permission to take the class.
Ⓓ Take a form to the registration area.

20. What does Mike say about graduation?

Ⓐ He has planned to graduate in the fall.
Ⓑ He has to take Professor Day's class in order to graduate.
Ⓒ He needs the professor to sign his application for graduation.
Ⓓ He does not have enough credits for graduation.

21. What does Professor Day decide to do?

Ⓐ Enroll Mike in the class next year.
Ⓑ Allow Mike to take the class this term.
Ⓒ Give Mike permission to graduate without the class.
Ⓓ Register Mike for another class.

22. What is MUZAK?

Ⓐ A slow, soft song.
Ⓑ Music in restaurants.
Ⓒ Background music.
Ⓓ A pleasant addition to the environment.

23. What is the average increase in productivity when MUZAK is introduced?

Ⓐ Thirteen percent.
Ⓑ Five to ten percent.
Ⓒ One hundred percent.
Ⓓ Thirty percent.

24. What is stimulus progression?

Ⓐ Background music that is low in stimulus value.
Ⓑ Upbeat music that stimulates sales.
Ⓒ Music engineered to reduce stress.
Ⓓ Music that starts slow and gets faster at times of the day when people get tired.

25. How does MUZAK influence sales in supermarkets?

Ⓐ It can cause shoppers to go through the line faster.
Ⓑ It can cause shoppers to buy thirty percent more or less.
Ⓒ It can cause shoppers to walk slower and buy more.
Ⓓ It does not influence sales.

26. What is this announcement mainly about?

Ⓐ The "Sun-Up Semester" program.
Ⓑ The Community College campus.
Ⓒ Video telecourses.
Ⓓ Technology for distance learning.

27. Why does the speaker mention the "Sun-Up Semester"?

Ⓐ To clarify how to register.
Ⓑ To advertise the college.
Ⓒ To provide a listing of courses.
Ⓓ To give students an alternative to video tapes.

28. How can students register for a course?

Ⓐ They should come to campus.
Ⓑ They can call the Community College.
Ⓒ They must contact the instructor.
Ⓓ They can use computers.

29. How can students contact the instructor?

Ⓐ By using e-mail.
Ⓑ By calling KCC-TV.
Ⓒ By writing letters.
Ⓓ By making video tapes.

30. What is the main topic of this conversation?

Ⓐ The woman's health.
Ⓑ The woman's grades.
Ⓒ The man's joke.
Ⓓ The man's stress.

31. What was the woman's problem?

Ⓐ She was taking too many classes.
Ⓑ She was very tired because she studied too late.
Ⓒ She had been ill last semester.
Ⓓ She may have to withdraw from school this semester.

32. Why is mono called the "college disease"?

Ⓐ Many students get mono while they are in college.
Ⓑ If one student gets mono, the whole college becomes infected.
Ⓒ It is a joke about college students that the woman tells.
Ⓓ The disease was first identified on a college campus.

33. What advice does the woman give the man?

Ⓐ Drop out of school for a semester and return later.
Ⓑ Study harder to learn all the lessons this semester.
Ⓒ Take fewer hours each semester and add one semester to the program.
Ⓓ Add extra classes to the program even if it requires another semester.

34. What central theme does the lecture examine?

Ⓐ The relationship between language and culture.
Ⓑ The culture of Hopi society.
Ⓒ Native American cultures.
Ⓓ The life of Benjamin Lee Whorf.

35. Which languages did Whorf use in his research?

Ⓐ European languages.
Ⓑ South American languages.
Ⓒ Native American languages.
Ⓓ Computer languages.

36. According to the lecturer, what is linguistic relativity?

Ⓐ All languages are related.
Ⓑ All Native American languages are related.
Ⓒ Language influences the manner in which an individual understands reality.
Ⓓ Language and culture are not related.

37. What is another name for linguistic relativity?

Ⓐ The Sapir Hypothesis.
Ⓑ The Sapir-Whorf Hypothesis.
Ⓒ The Sapir-Whorf-Boas Hypothesis.
Ⓓ The American Indian Model of the Universe.

38. What is the topic of this discussion?

Ⓐ Air pollution.
Ⓑ Acid rain.
Ⓒ Fossil fuels.
Ⓓ The Great Lakes.

39. What is acid rain?

Ⓐ Precipitation that is polluted by sulfuric acid and nitric acid.
Ⓑ Rain that falls after a long period of severe drought.
Ⓒ Large concentrations of acid in the soil around the Great Lakes.
Ⓓ Water vapor that is mixed with a high concentration of sulfur.

40. In which two ways has the environment been damaged along the Great Lakes?

Click on 2 answers.

[A] The air now contains dangerous levels of carbon monoxide.
[B] Weather patterns have been disturbed.
[C] Water resources have been polluted.
[D] The soil has been depleted of nutrients.

41. What are the conditions of the Air Quality Accord?

(A) Companies in the United States must control pollution that could affect Canadian resources.
(B) There are limits placed on the quantity of acidic deposits that can cross the border.
(C) Governments and agencies will regulate automobile emissions.
(D) Fuels cannot contain any sulfur near the border.

42. What is the topic of this lecture?

(A) Three major types of bacteria.
(B) How microscopic organisms are measured.
(C) How bacteria is used for research in genetics.
(D) Diseases caused by bacteria.

43. Which two characteristics are common in bacteria?

Click on 2 answers.

[A] They have one cell.
[B] They are harmful to humans.
[C] They reproduce quickly.
[D] They die when exposed to air.

44. Which of the following slides contain cocci bacteria?

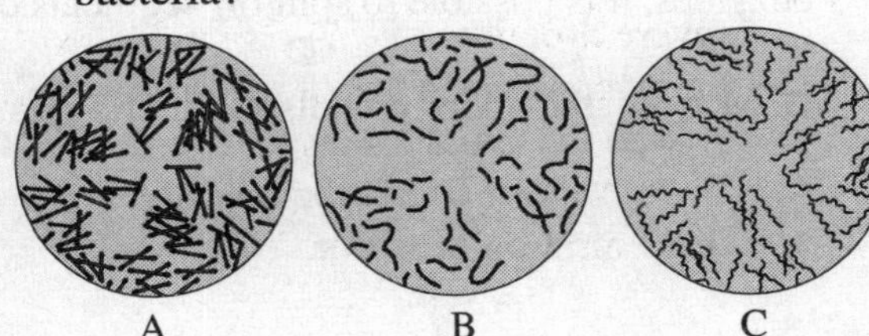

45. Why are bacteria being used in the research study at the University?

(A) Bacteria have unusual cell formations.
(B) Bacteria live harmlessly on the skin, mouth, and intestines.
(C) Bacteria are similar to other life forms.
(D) Bacteria cause many diseases in humans.

46. What is the purpose of this conversation?

(A) The man needs help changing his schedule.
(B) The man is looking for a job in the morning.
(C) The man is trying to get a student loan.
(D) The man is changing his major to sociology.

47. Why does the man need to take at least twelve hours?

(A) He wants to graduate as soon as possible.
(B) He must be a full-time student to qualify for his loan.
(C) His advisor insists that he study full time.
(D) All the courses are required.

48. Why does the man prefer Sociology 560?

(A) It is a required course.
(B) It is offered in the afternoon.
(C) It is taught by Dr. Brown.
(D) It is a sociology class.

49. What will Dr. Kelly do?

(A) Help the man withdraw from school.
(B) Change the man's class schedule.
(C) Give the man a student loan.
(D) Change the man's major.

50. What will the man probably do after the conversation?

(A) Go to Dr. Brown's office.
(B) See Dr. Brown in class.
(C) Call Dr. Brown.
(D) Send the form to Dr. Brown.

Section 2: Structure

This section measures the ability to recognize language that is appropriate for standard written English. There are two types of questions in this section.

In the first type of question, there are incomplete sentences. Beneath each sentence, there are four words or phrases. You will choose the one word or phrase that best completes the sentence.

Clicking on a choice darkens the oval. After you click on **Next** and **Confirm Answer**, the next question will be presented.

The second type of question has four underlined words or phrases. You will choose the one underlined word or phrase that must be changed for the sentence to be correct.

Clicking on an underlined word or phrase will darken it. After you click on **Next** and **Confirm Answer**, the next question will be presented.

1. Justice Sandra Day O'Connor was ------- to serve on the U.S. Supreme Court.

   (A) the woman who first
   (B) the first woman
   (C) who the first woman
   (D) the first and a woman

2. North Carolina is well known not only for the Great Smoky Mountains National Park -------- for the Cherokee settlements.

   (A) also
   (B) and
   (C) but also
   (D) because of

3. If biennials were planted this year, they will be (A) likely (B) to bloom (C) next year (D).

4. The value of the dollar (A) declines (B) as (C) the rate of inflation raises (D).

5. General Grant had General Lee -------- him at Appomattox to sign the official surrender of the Confederate forces.

   (A) to meet
   (B) met
   (C) meet
   (D) meeting

6. Anthropologists assert that many of the early Native Americans who lived on the Plains did not engage in planting crops but (A) to hunt (B), living (C) primarily (D) on buffalo meat.

7. The differential attractions of the sun and the moon have (A) a direct effect in (B) the rising (C) and falling of (D) the tides.

8. ------- both men and women have often achieved their career ambitions by midlife, many people are afflicted by at least a temporary period of dissatisfaction and depression.

   (A) Because
   (B) So
   (C) A
   (D) Who

9. With special enzymes that are call (A) restriction enzymes, it is possible to split off (B) segments of DNA from (C) the donor (D) organism.

10. Because of [A] the movement of a glacier, the form [B] of [C] the Great Lakes was very slow [D].

11. -------- small specimen of the embryonic fluid is removed from a fetus, it will be possible to determine whether the baby will be born with birth defects.

(A) A
(B) That a
(C) If a
(D) When it is a

12. To generate income, magazine publishers must decide whether to increase the subscription price or -------- .

(A) to sell advertising
(B) if they should sell advertising
(C) selling advertising
(D) sold advertising

13. If [A] it receives enough [B] rain at the proper time, hay will grow [C] quickly, as [D] grass.

14. *Psychology Today* is [A] interesting [B], informative, and it is [C] easy to read [D].

15. Before [A] she died, Andrew Jackson's daughter, who [B] lives [C] in the family mansion, used to take [D] tourists through her home.

16. If it -------- more humid in the desert of the Southwest, the hot temperatures would be unbearable.

(A) be
(B) is
(C) was
(D) were

17. -------- Java Man, who lived before the first Ice Age, is the first manlike animal.

(A) It is generally believed that
(B) Generally believed it is
(C) Believed generally is
(D) That is generally believed

18. It is essential that the temperature is not [A] elevated to a point [B] where the substance formed may become [C] unstable and decompose into its [D] constituent elements.

19. John Philip Sousa, who [A] many [B] people consider the greatest [C] composer of marches, wrote his music during the era known as [D] the Gay 90s.

20. For the investor who -------- money, silver or bonds are good options.

(A) has so little a
(B) has very little
(C) has so few
(D) has very few

21. Although it [A] can be derived from [B] oil, coal, and tar, kerosene is usually produced [C] by refine [D] it from petroleum.

22. Aeronomy is [A] the study [B] of the earth's [C] upper atmosphere, which includes their [D] composition, temperature, density, and chemical reactions.

23. The purpose of [A] the United Nations, broad speaking, [B] is [C] to maintain peace and security and to encourage [D] respect for human rights.

24. Of all the cereals, rice is the one ------- food for more people than any of the other grain crops.

(A) it provides
(B) that providing
(C) provides
(D) that provides

25. Although Congressional representatives and senators may serve an unlimited number of <u>term</u> (A), the president <u>is limited</u> (B) to two, <u>for a total</u> (C) <u>of eight years</u> (D).

Section 3: Reading

This section measures the ability to read and understand short passages similar in topic and style to those that students are likely to encounter in North American universities and colleges. This section contains reading passages and questions about the passages. There are several different types of questions in this section.

In the Reading section, you will first have the opportunity to read the passage.

You will use the scroll bar to view the rest of the passage.

When you have finished reading the passage, you will use the mouse to click on **Proceed**. Then the questions about the passage will be presented. You are to choose the one best answer to each question. Answer all questions about the information in a passage on the basis of what is stated or implied in that passage.

Most of the questions will be multiple-choice questions. To answer these questions you will click on a choice below the question.

To answer some questions, you will click on a word or phrase.

To answer some questions, you will click on a sentence in the passage.

To answer some questions, you will click on a square to add a sentence to the passage.

It has long been known that when the green parts of plants are exposed to light under suitable conditions of temperature and moisture, carbon dioxide is absorbed by the plant from the atmospheric CO_2, and oxygen is released into the air. This exchange of gases in plants is the opposite of the process that occurs in respiration. In this plant process, which is called photosynthesis, carbohydrates are synthesized in the presence of light from carbon dioxide and water by specialized structures in the cytoplasm of plant cells called chloroplasts. These chloroplasts contain not only two types of light-trapping green chlorophyll but also a vast array of protein substances called enzymes. In most plants, the water required by the photosynthesis process is absorbed from the soil by the roots and translocated through the xylem of the root and stem to the chlorophyll-laden leaves. Except for the usually small percentage used in respiration, the oxygen released in the process diffuses out of the leaf into the atmosphere through stomates. In simple terms, carbon dioxide is the fuel, and oxygen is the product of the chemical reaction. For each molecule of carbon dioxide used, one molecule of oxygen is released. Here is a summary chemical equation for photosynthesis:

$$6CO_2 + 6H_2O \rightarrow C_6H_{12}O_6 + 6O_2$$

As a result of this process, radiant energy from the sun is stored as chemical energy. In turn, the chemical energy is used to decompose carbon dioxide and water. The products of their decomposition are recombined into a new compound, which successively builds up into the more and more complex substances that comprise the plant. These organic substances, that is, the sugars, starches, and cellulose, all belong to the class of organic molecules. In other words, the process of photosynthesis can be understood as an enzyme-induced chemical change from carbon dioxide and water into the simple sugar glucose. This carbohydrate, in turn, is utilized by the plant to generate other forms of energy, such as the long chains of plant cells or polymers that comprise the cellular structures of starches or cellulose. Many intermediate steps are involved in the production of a simple sugar or starch. At the same time, a balance of gases is preserved in the atmosphere by the process of photosynthesis.

1. Which title best expresses the ideas in this passage?

Ⓐ A Chemical Equation
Ⓑ The Process of Photosynthesis
Ⓒ The Parts of Vascular Plants
Ⓓ The Production of Sugar

2. The combination of carbon dioxide and water to form sugar results in an excess of

Ⓐ water
Ⓑ oxygen
Ⓒ carbon
Ⓓ chlorophyll

3. Which process is the opposite of photosynthesis?

Ⓐ Decomposition
Ⓑ Synthesization
Ⓒ Diffusion
Ⓓ Respiration

4. In photosynthesis, energy from the sun is

Ⓐ changed to chemical energy
Ⓑ conducted from the xylem to the leaves of green plants
Ⓒ not necessary to the process
Ⓓ released one to one for each molecule of carbon dioxide used

5. Click on the sentence in paragraph 1 that describes how oxygen is released into the atmosphere.

Paragraph 1 is marked with an arrow (→).

Beginning

→ It has long been known that when the green parts of plants are exposed to light under suitable conditions of temperature and moisture, carbon dioxide is absorbed by the plant from the atmospheric CO_2, and oxygen is released into the air. This exchange of gases in plants is the opposite of the process that occurs in respiration. In this plant process, which is called photosynthesis, carbohydrates are synthesized in the presence of light from carbon dioxide and water by specialized structures in the cytoplasm of plant cells called chloroplasts. These chloroplasts contain not only two types of light-trapping green chlorophyll but also a vast array of protein substances called enzymes. In most plants, the water required by the photosynthesis process is absorbed from the soil by the roots and translocated through the xylem of the root and stem to the chlorophyll-laden leaves. Except for the usually small percentage used in respiration, the oxygen released in the process diffuses out of the leaf into the atmosphere through stomates. In simple terms, carbon dioxide is the fuel, and oxygen is the product of the chemical reaction. For each molecule of carbon dioxide

6. The word stored in paragraph 2 is closest in meaning to

Ⓐ retained
Ⓑ converted
Ⓒ discovered
Ⓓ specified

More Available

leaves. Except for the usually small percentage used in respiration, the oxygen released in the process diffuses out of the leaf into the atmosphere through stomates. In simple terms, carbon dioxide is the fuel, and oxygen is the product of the chemical reaction. For each molecule of carbon dioxide used, one molecule of oxygen is released. Here is a summary chemical equation for photosynthesis:

$$6CO_2 + 6H_2O \rightarrow C_6H_{12}O_6 + 6O_2$$

As a result of this process, radiant energy from the sun is stored as chemical energy. In turn, the chemical energy is used to decompose carbon dioxide and water. The products of their decomposition are recombined into a new compound, which successively builds up into the more and more complex substances that comprise the plant. These organic substances, that is, the sugars, starches, and cellulose, all belong to the class of organic molecules. In other words, the process of photosynthesis can be understood as an enzyme-induced chemical change from carbon dioxide and water into the simple sugar glucose. This carbohydrate, in turn, is utilized by the plant to generate other forms of

7. The word their in paragraph 2 refers to

Ⓐ radiant energy and chemical energy
Ⓑ carbon dioxide and water
Ⓒ products
Ⓓ complex substances

End

As a result of this process, radiant energy from the sun is stored as chemical energy. In turn, the chemical energy is used to decompose carbon dioxide and water. The products of their decomposition are recombined into a new compound, which successively builds up into the more and more complex substances that comprise the plant. These organic substances, that is, the sugars, starches, and cellulose, all belong to the class of organic molecules. In other words, the process of photosynthesis can be understood as an enzyme-induced chemical change from carbon dioxide and water into the simple sugar glucose. This carbohydrate, in turn, is utilized by the plant to generate other forms of energy, such as the long chains of plant cells or polymers that comprise the cellular structures of starches or cellulose. Many intermediate steps are involved in the production of a simple sugar or starch. At the same time, a balance of gases is preserved in the atmosphere by the process of photosynthesis.

8. The word successively in paragraph 2 is closest in meaning to

Ⓐ with effort
Ⓑ in a sequence
Ⓒ slowly
Ⓓ carefully

End

carbon dioxide and water. The products of their decomposition are recombined into a new compound, which successively builds up into the more and more complex substances that comprise the plant. These organic substances, that is, the sugars, starches, and cellulose, all belong to the class of organic molecules. In other words, the process of photosynthesis can be understood as an enzyme-induced chemical change from carbon dioxide and water into the simple sugar glucose. This carbohydrate, in turn, is utilized by the plant to generate other forms of energy, such as the long chains of plant cells or polymers that comprise the cellular structures of starches or cellulose. Many intermediate steps are involved in the production of a simple sugar or starch. At the same time, a balance of gases is preserved in the atmosphere by the process of photosynthesis.

9. Besides the manufacture of food for plants, what is another benefit of photosynthesis?

Ⓐ It produces solar energy.
Ⓑ It diffuses additional carbon dioxide into the air.
Ⓒ It maintains a balance of gases in the atmosphere.
Ⓓ It removes harmful gases from the air.

10. Which of the following is NOT true of the oxygen used in photosynthesis?

Ⓐ Oxygen is absorbed by the roots.
Ⓑ Oxygen is the product of photosynthesis.
Ⓒ Oxygen is used in respiration.
Ⓓ Oxygen is released into the atmosphere through the leaves.

Alfred Bernhard Nobel, a Swedish inventor and philanthropist, bequeathed most of his vast fortune to a trust that he designated as a fund from which annual prizes could be awarded to the individuals and organizations that had achieved through invention or discovery that which would have the greatest benefit to humanity in a particular year. According to the legend, Nobel's death had been erroneously reported in a newspaper, and the focus of the obituary was the fact that Nobel had invented dynamite. He rewrote his will in 1895, thereby establishing, with the original amount of nine million dollars, the Nobel Foundation as the legal owner and administering agent of the funds, and instituting the prizes that are named after him. Statutes to govern the awarding of the prizes were written, along with guidelines for operating procedures. Five years after Nobel's death, the first five prizes, worth about forty thousand dollars each, were to be awarded.

Originally the five classifications for outstanding contributions designated in Nobel's will included chemistry, physics, physiology or medicine, literature, and international peace. These prizes have been administered continually by the Nobel Foundation in Stockholm since they were first awarded in 1901. In 1969, a sixth prize, for accomplishments in the field of economics and endowed by the Central Bank of Sweden, was added. Candidates for the prizes must be nominated in writing by February 1 of each year by a qualified and recognized authority in each of the fields of competition. Recipients in physics, chemistry, and economics are selected by the Royal Swedish Academy, whereas recipients in peace are chosen by the Norwegian Nobel Committee appointed by Norway's parliament. With the King of Sweden officiating, the prizes are usually presented in Stockholm on December 10, the anniversary of Nobel's death. The value, fame, and prestige of the Nobel Prizes have continued to grow. Today the prize includes a medal, a diploma, and a cash award of about one million dollars.

11. What does this passage mainly discuss?

Ⓐ Alfred Bernhard Nobel
Ⓑ The Nobel Prizes
Ⓒ Great contributions to mankind
Ⓓ Swedish philanthropy

12. Why were the prizes named for Alfred Bernhard Nobel?

Ⓐ He left money in his will to establish a fund for the prizes.
Ⓑ He won the first Nobel Prize for his work in philanthropy.
Ⓒ He is now living in Sweden.
Ⓓ He serves as chairman of the committee to choose the recipients of the prizes.

13. The word will in paragraph 1 refers to

Ⓐ Nobel's wishes
Ⓑ a legal document
Ⓒ a future intention
Ⓓ a free choice

More Available

particular year. According to the legend, Nobel's death had been erroneously reported in a newspaper, and the focus of the obituary was the fact that Nobel had invented dynamite. He rewrote his will in 1895, thereby establishing, with the original amount of nine million dollars, the Nobel Foundation as the legal owner and administering agent of the funds, and instituting the prizes that are named after him. Statutes to govern the awarding of the prizes were written, along with guidelines for operating procedures. Five years after Nobel's death, the first five prizes, worth about forty thousand dollars each, were to be awarded.

Originally the five classifications for outstanding contributions designated in Nobel's will included chemistry, physics, physiology or medicine, literature, and international peace. These prizes have been administered continually by the Nobel Foundation in Stockholm since they were first awarded in 1901. In 1969, a sixth prize, for accomplishments in the field of economics and endowed by the Central Bank of Sweden, was added. Candidates for the prizes must be

14. How often are the Nobel Prizes awarded?

Ⓐ Five times a year
Ⓑ Once a year
Ⓒ Twice a year
Ⓓ Once every two years

15. The following sentence can be added to the passage.

When he read this objective summary of his life, the great chemist, it is said, decided that he wanted his name to be remembered for something more positive and humanitarian than inventing an explosive that was a potential weapon.

Where would it best fit in the passage?

Click on the square (■) to add the sentence to the passage.

Scroll the passage to see all of the choices.

More Available

particular year. According to the legend, Nobel's death had been erroneously reported in a newspaper, and the focus of the obituary was the fact that Nobel had invented dynamite. ■ He rewrote his will in 1895, thereby establishing, with the original amount of nine million dollars, the Nobel Foundation as the legal owner and administering agent of the funds, and instituting the prizes that are named after him. ■ Statutes to govern the awarding of the prizes were written, along with guidelines for operating procedures. ■ Five years after Nobel's death, the first five prizes, worth about forty thousand dollars each, were to be awarded. ■

Originally the five classifications for outstanding contributions designated in Nobel's will included chemistry, physics, physiology or medicine, literature, and international peace. These prizes have been administered continually by the Nobel Foundation in Stockholm since they were first awarded in 1901. In 1969, a sixth prize, for accomplishments in the field of economics and endowed by the Central Bank of Sweden, was added. Candidates for the prizes must be

16. The word outstanding in paragraph 2 could best be replaced by

Ⓐ recent
Ⓑ unusual
Ⓒ established
Ⓓ exceptional

More Available

awarding of the prizes were written, along with guidelines for operating procedures. Five years after Nobel's death, the first five prizes, worth about forty thousand dollars each, were to be awarded.

Originally the five classifications for outstanding contributions designated in Nobel's will included chemistry, physics, physiology or medicine, literature, and international peace. These prizes have been administered continually by the Nobel Foundation in Stockholm since they were first awarded in 1901. In 1969, a sixth prize, for accomplishments in the field of economics and endowed by the Central Bank of Sweden, was added. Candidates for the prizes must be nominated in writing by February 1 of each year by a qualified and recognized authority in each of the fields of competition. Recipients in physics, chemistry, and economics are selected by the Royal Swedish Academy, whereas recipients in peace are chosen by the Norwegian Nobel Committee appointed by Norway's parliament. With the King of Sweden officiating, the prizes are usually presented in Stockholm on December 10,

17. A Nobel Prize would NOT be given to

Ⓐ an author who wrote a novel
Ⓑ a doctor who discovered a vaccine
Ⓒ a composer who wrote a symphony
Ⓓ a diplomat who negotiated a peace settlement

18. What does the author mean by the statement These prizes have been administered continually by the Nobel Foundation in Stockholm since they were first awarded in 1901?

Ⓐ The Nobel Foundation oversees the management of the money and the distribution of the prizes.
Ⓑ The Nobel Foundation selects the recipients of the prizes.
Ⓒ The Nobel Foundation solicits applications and recommendations for the prizes.
Ⓓ The Nobel Foundation recommends new prize classifications.

End

Originally the five classifications for outstanding contributions designated in Nobel's will included chemistry, physics, physiology or medicine, literature, and international peace. These prizes have been administered continually by the Nobel Foundation in Stockholm since they were first awarded in 1901. In 1969, a sixth prize, for accomplishments in the field of economics and endowed by the Central Bank of Sweden, was added. Candidates for the prizes must be nominated in writing by February 1 of each year by a qualified and recognized authority in each of the fields of competition. Recipients in physics, chemistry, and economics are selected by the Royal Swedish Academy, whereas recipients in peace are chosen by the Norwegian Nobel Committee appointed by Norway's parliament. With the King of Sweden officiating, the prizes are usually presented in Stockholm on December 10, the anniversary of Nobel's death. The value, fame, and prestige of the Nobel Prizes have continued to grow. Today the prize includes a medal, a diploma, and a cash award of about one million dollars.

19. Why are the awards presented on December 10?

Ⓐ It is a tribute to the King of Sweden.
Ⓑ Alfred Bernhard Nobel died on that day.
Ⓒ That date was established in Alfred Nobel's will.
Ⓓ The Central Bank of Sweden administers the trust.

20. Look at the word prize in the passage. Click on the word or phrase in the **bold** text that is closest in meaning to prize.

End

by a qualified and recognized authority in each of the fields of competition. Recipients in physics, chemistry, and economics are selected by the Royal Swedish Academy, whereas recipients in peace are chosen by the Norwegian Nobel Committee appointed by Norway's parliament. **With the King of Sweden officiating, the prizes are usually presented in Stockholm on December 10, the anniversary of Nobel's death. The value, fame, and prestige of the Nobel Prizes have continued to grow. Today the prize includes a medal, a diploma, and a cash award of about one million dollars.**

Although stage plays have been set to music since the era of the ancient Greeks, when the dramas of Sophocles and Aeschylus were accompanied by lyres and flutes, the usually accepted date for the beginning of opera as we know it is 1600. As a part of the celebration of the marriage of King Henry IV of France to the Italian aristocrat Maria de Medici, the Florentine composer Jacopo Perí produced his famous *Euridice*, generally considered to be the first opera. Following his example, a group of Italian musicians, poets, and noblemen called the Camerata began to revive the style of musical story that had been used in Greek tragedy. The Camerata took most of the plots for their operas from Greek and Roman history and mythology, beginning the process of creating an opera by writing a libretto or drama that could be used to establish the framework for the music. They called their compositions *opera in musica* or musical works. It is from this phrase that the word "opera" was borrowed and abbreviated.

For several years, the center of opera was Florence in northern Italy, but gradually, during the baroque period, it spread throughout Italy. By the late 1600s, operas were being written and performed in many places throughout Europe, especially in England, France, and Germany. However, for many years, the Italian opera was considered the ideal, and many non-Italian composers continued to use Italian librettos. The European form deemphasized the dramatic aspect of the Italian model. New orchestral effects and even ballet were introduced under the guise of opera. Composers gave in to the demands of singers, writing many operas that were little more than a succession of brilliant tricks for the voice, designed to showcase the splendid voices of the singers who had requested them. It was thus that complicated arias, recitatives, and duets evolved. The aria, which is a long solo, may be compared to a song in which the characters express their thoughts and feelings. The recitative, which is also a solo of sorts, is a recitation set to music, the purpose of which is to continue the story line. The duet is a musical piece written for two voices, a musical device that may serve the function of either an aria or a recitative within the opera.

21. This passage is a summary of

Ⓐ opera in Italy
Ⓑ the Camerata
Ⓒ the development of opera
Ⓓ *Euridice*

22. Look at the word usually in the passage. Click on the word or phrase in the **bold** text that is closest in meaning to usually.

Beginning

Although stage plays have been set to music since the era of the ancient Greeks, when the dramas of Sophocles and Aeschylus were accompanied by lyres and flutes, the usually accepted date for the beginning of opera as we know it is 1600. As a part of the celebration of the marriage of King Henry IV of France to the Italian aristocrat Maria de Medici, the Florentine composer Jacopo Perí produced his famous *Euridice*, generally considered to be the first opera. Following his example, a group of Italian musicians, poets, and noblemen called the Camerata began to revive the style of musical story that had been used in Greek tragedy. The Camerata took most of the plots for their operas from Greek and Roman history and mythology, beginning the process of creating an opera by writing a libretto or drama that could be used to establish the framework for the music. They called their compositions *opera in musica* or musical works. It is from this phrase that the word "opera" was borrowed and abbreviated.

For several years, the center of opera was Florence in northern Italy, but gradually, during the

23. According to this passage, when did modern opera begin?

Ⓐ In the time of the ancient Greeks
Ⓑ In the fifteenth century
Ⓒ At the beginning of the sixteenth century
Ⓓ At the beginning of the seventeenth century

24. The word it in paragraph 1 refers to

Ⓐ opera
Ⓑ date
Ⓒ era
Ⓓ music

Beginning

Although stage plays have been set to music since the era of the ancient Greeks, when the dramas of Sophocles and Aeschylus were accompanied by lyres and flutes, the usually accepted date for the beginning of opera as we know it is 1600. As a part of the celebration of the marriage of King Henry IV of France to the Italian aristocrat Maria de Medici, the Florentine composer Jacopo Perí produced his famous *Euridice*, generally considered to be the first opera. Following his example, a group of Italian musicians, poets, and noblemen called the Camerata began to revive the style of musical story that had been used in Greek tragedy. The Camerata took most of the plots for their operas from Greek and Roman history and mythology, beginning the process of creating an opera by writing a libretto or drama that could be used to establish the framework for the music. They called their compositions *opera in musica* or musical works. It is from this phrase that the word "opera" was borrowed and abbreviated.

For several years, the center of opera was Florence in northern Italy, but gradually, during the

25. According to the author, what did Jacopo Perí write?

Ⓐ Greek tragedy
Ⓑ The first opera
Ⓒ The opera *Maria de Medici*
Ⓓ The opera *The Camerata*

26. The author suggests that *Euridice* was produced

Ⓐ in France
Ⓑ originally by Sophocles and Aeschylus
Ⓒ without much success
Ⓓ for the wedding of King Henry IV

27. What was the Camerata?

Ⓐ A group of Greek musicians
Ⓑ Musicians who developed a new musical drama based upon Greek drama
Ⓒ A style of music not known in Italy
Ⓓ The name given to the court of King Henry IV

28. The word revive in paragraph 1 could best be replaced by

Ⓐ appreciate
Ⓑ resume
Ⓒ modify
Ⓓ investigate

Beginning

Although stage plays have been set to music since the era of the ancient Greeks, when the dramas of Sophocles and Aeschylus were accompanied by lyres and flutes, the usually accepted date for the beginning of opera as we know it is 1600. As a part of the celebration of the marriage of King Henry IV of France to the Italian aristocrat Maria de Medici, the Florentine composer Jacopo Per produced his famous *Euridice*, generally considered to be the first opera. Following his example, a group of Italian musicians, poets, and noblemen called the Camerata began to revive the style of musical story that had been used in Greek tragedy. The Camerata took most of the plots for their operas from Greek and Roman history and mythology, beginning the process of creating an opera by writing a libretto or drama that could be used to establish the framework for the music. They called their compositions *opera in musica* or musical works. It is from this phrase that the word opera was borrowed and abbreviated.

For several years, the center of opera was Florence in northern Italy, but gradually, during the

29. The word plots in paragraph 1 is closest in meaning to

Ⓐ locations
Ⓑ instruments
Ⓒ stories
Ⓓ inspiration

More Available

know it is 1600. As a part of the celebration of the marriage of King Henry IV of France to the Italian aristocrat Maria de Medici, the Florentine composer Jacopo Perí produced his famous *Euridice*, generally considered to be the first opera. Following his example, a group of Italian musicians, poets, and noblemen called the Camerata began to revive the style of musical story that had been used in Greek tragedy. The Camerata took most of the plots for their operas from Greek and Roman history and mythology, beginning the process of creating an opera by writing a libretto or drama that could be used to establish the framework for the music. They called their compositions *opera in musica* or musical works. It is from this phrase that the word "opera" was borrowed and abbreviated.

For several years, the center of opera was Florence in northern Italy, but gradually, during the baroque period, it spread throughout Italy. By the late 1600s, operas were being written and performed in many places throughout Europe, especially in England, France, and Germany. However, for many years, the Italian opera was

30. From what did the term "opera" derive?

Ⓐ Greek and Roman history and mythology
Ⓑ Non-Italian composers
Ⓒ The Italian phrase that means "musical works"
Ⓓ The ideas of composer Jacopo Perí

31. Look at the word them in the passage. Click on the word or phrase in the **bold** text that them refers to.

End

However, for many years, the Italian opera was considered the ideal, and many non-Italian composers continued to use Italian librettos. The European form deemphasized the dramatic aspect of the Italian model. **New orchestral effects and even ballet were introduced under the guise of opera. Composers gave in to the demands of singers, writing many operas that were little more than a succession of brilliant tricks for the voice, designed to showcase the splendid voices of the singers who had requested them. It was thus that complicated arias, recitatives, and duets evolved.** The aria, which is a long solo, may be compared to a song in which the characters express their thoughts and feelings. The recitative, which is also a solo of sorts, is a recitation set to music, the purpose of which is to continue the story line. The duet is a musical piece written for two voices, a musical device that may serve the function of either an aria or a recitative within the opera.

32. Look at the word function in the passage. Click on the word or phrase in the **bold** text that is closest in meaning to function.

End

aspect of the Italian model. New orchestral effects and even ballet were introduced under the guise of opera. Composers gave in to the demands of singers, writing many operas that were little more than a succession of brilliant tricks for the voice, designed to showcase the splendid voices of the singers who had requested them. **It was thus that complicated arias, recitatives, and duets evolved. The aria, which is a long solo, may be compared to a song in which the characters express their thoughts and feelings. The recitative, which is also a solo of sorts, is a recitation set to music, the purpose of which is to continue the story line. The duet is a musical piece written for two voices, a musical device that may serve the function of either an aria or a recitative within the opera.**

According to the controversial sunspot theory, great storms or eruptions on the surface of the sun hurl streams of solar particles into space and eventually into the atmosphere of our planet, causing shifts in the weather on the Earth and interference with radio and television communications.

A typical sunspot consists of a dark central umbra, a word derived from the Latin word for shadow, which is surrounded by a lighter penumbra of light and dark threads extending out from the center like the spokes of a wheel. Actually, the sunspots are cooler than the rest of the photosphere, which may account for their apparently darker color. Typically, the temperature in a sunspot umbra is about 4000 K, whereas the temperature in a penumbra registers 5500 K, and the granules outside the spot are 6000 K.

Sunspots range in size from tiny granules to complex structures with areas stretching for billions of square miles. About 5 percent of all sunspots are large enough so that they can be seen from Earth without instruments; consequently, observations of sunspots have been recorded for thousands of years.

Sunspots have been observed in arrangements of one to more than one hundred spots, but they tend to occur in pairs. There is also a marked tendency for the two spots of a pair to have opposite magnetic polarities. Furthermore, the strength of the magnetic field associated with any given sunspot is closely related to the spot's size. Sunspots have also been observed to occur in cycles, over a period of eleven years. At the beginning of a cycle, the storms occur between 20 and 40 degrees north and south of the equator on the sun. As the cycle continues, some of the storms move closer to the equator. As the cycle diminishes, the number of sunspots decreases to a minimum and they cluster between 5 and 15 degrees north and south latitude.

Although there is no theory that completely explains the nature and function of sunspots, several models show scientists' attempts to relate the phenomenon to magnetic field lines along the lines of longitude from the north and south poles of the sun.

33. What is the author's main purpose in the passage?

Ⓐ To propose a theory to explain sunspots
Ⓑ To describe the nature of sunspots
Ⓒ To compare the umbra and the penumbra in sunspots
Ⓓ To argue for the existence of magnetic fields in sunspots

34. The word **controversial** in paragraph 1 is closest in meaning to

Ⓐ widely accepted
Ⓑ open to debate
Ⓒ just introduced
Ⓓ very complicated

Beginning

According to the **controversial** sunspot theory, great storms or eruptions on the surface of the sun hurl streams of solar particles into space and eventually into the atmosphere of our planet, causing shifts in the weather on the Earth and interference with radio and television communications.

A typical sunspot consists of a dark central umbra, a word derived from the Latin word for shadow, which is surrounded by a lighter penumbra of light and dark threads extending out from the center like the spokes of a wheel. Actually, the sunspots are cooler than the rest of the photosphere, which may account for their apparently darker color. Typically, the temperature in a sunspot umbra is about 4000 K, whereas the temperature in a penumbra registers 5500 K, and the granules outside the spot are 6000 K.

Sunspots range in size from tiny granules to complex structures with areas stretching for billions of square miles. About 5 percent of all sunspots are large enough so that they can be seen from Earth without instruments; consequently, observations of sunspots have been recorded for thousands of years.

35. Solar particles are hurled into space by

Ⓐ undetermined causes
Ⓑ disturbances of wind
Ⓒ small rivers on the surface of the sun
Ⓓ changes in the Earth's atmosphere

36. The word **particles** in paragraph 1 refers to

Ⓐ gas explosions in the atmosphere
Ⓑ light rays from the sun
Ⓒ liquid streams on the sun
Ⓓ small pieces of matter from the sun

Beginning

According to the controversial sunspot theory, great storms or eruptions on the surface of the sun hurl streams of solar **particles** into space and eventually into the atmosphere of our planet, causing shifts in the weather on the Earth and interference with radio and television communications.

A typical sunspot consists of a dark central umbra, a word derived from the Latin word for shadow, which is surrounded by a lighter penumbra of light and dark threads extending out from the center like the spokes of a wheel. Actually, the sunspots are cooler than the rest of the photosphere, which may account for their apparently darker color. Typically, the temperature in a sunspot umbra is about 4000 K, whereas the temperature in a penumbra registers 5500 K, and the granules outside the spot are 6000 K.

Sunspots range in size from tiny granules to complex structures with areas stretching for billions of square miles. About 5 percent of all sunspots are large enough so that they can be seen from Earth without instruments; consequently, observations of sunspots have been recorded for thousands of years.

37. How can we describe matter from the sun that enters the Earth's atmosphere?

Ⓐ Very small
Ⓑ Very hot
Ⓒ Very bright
Ⓓ Very hard

38. What does the author mean by the statement Actually, the sunspots are cooler than the rest of the photosphere, which may account for their apparently darker color?

Ⓐ Neither sunspots nor the photosphere is hot.
Ⓑ Sunspots in the photosphere do not have any color.
Ⓒ The color of sunspots could be affected by their temperature.
Ⓓ The size of a sunspot affects its temperature.

More Available

of light and dark threads extending out from the center like the spokes of a wheel. Actually, the sunspots are cooler than the rest of the photosphere, which may account for their apparently darker color. Typically, the temperature in a sunspot umbra is about 4000 K, whereas the temperature in a penumbra registers 5500 K, and the granules outside the spot are 6000 K.

Sunspots range in size from tiny granules to complex structures with areas stretching for billions of square miles. About 5 percent of all sunspots are large enough so that they can be seen from Earth without instruments; consequently, observations of sunspots have been recorded for thousands of years.

Sunspots have been observed in arrangements of one to more than one hundred spots, but they tend to occur in pairs. There is also a marked tendency for the two spots of a pair to have opposite magnetic polarities. Furthermore, the strength of the magnetic field associated with any given sunspot is closely related to the spot's size. Sunspots have also been observed to occur in cycles, over a period of eleven years. At the

39. Look at the word tiny in the passage. Click on the word or phrase in the **bold** text that is opposite in meaning to tiny.

More Available

color. Typically, the temperature in a sunspot umbra is about 4000 K, whereas the temperature in a penumbra registers 5500 K, and the granules outside the spot are 6000 K.

Sunspots range in size from tiny granules to complex structures with areas stretching for billions of square miles. About 5 percent of all sunspots are large enough so that they can be seen from Earth without instruments; consequently, observations of sunspots have been recorded for thousands of years.

Sunspots have been observed in arrangements of one to more than one hundred spots, but they tend to occur in pairs. There is also a marked tendency for the two spots of a pair to have opposite magnetic polarities. Furthermore, the strength of the magnetic field associated with any given sunspot is closely related to the spot's size. Sunspots have also been observed to occur in cycles, over a period of eleven years. At the beginning of a cycle, the storms occur between 20 and 40 degrees north and south of the equator on the sun. As the cycle continues, some of the storms move closer to the equator. As the cycle

40. The word they in paragraph 2 refers to

Ⓐ structures
Ⓑ spots
Ⓒ miles
Ⓓ granules

More Available

color. Typically, the temperature in a sunspot umbra is about 4000 K, whereas the temperature in a penumbra registers 5500 K, and the granules outside the spot are 6000 K.

Sunspots range in size from tiny granules to complex structures with areas stretching for billions of square miles. About 5 percent of all sunspots are large enough so that they can be seen from Earth without instruments; consequently, observations of sunspots have been recorded for thousands of years.

Sunspots have been observed in arrangements of one to more than one hundred spots, but they tend to occur in pairs. There is also a marked tendency for the two spots of a pair to have opposite magnetic polarities. Furthermore, the strength of the magnetic field associated with any given sunspot is closely related to the spot's size. Sunspots have also been observed to occur in cycles, over a period of eleven years. At the beginning of a cycle, the storms occur between 20 and 40 degrees north and south of the equator on the sun. As the cycle continues, some of the storms move closer to the equator. As the cycle

41. The word consequently in paragraph 2 could best be replaced by

Ⓐ as a result
Ⓑ nevertheless
Ⓒ without doubt
Ⓓ in this way

More Available

color. Typically, the temperature in a sunspot umbra is about 4000 K, whereas the temperature in a penumbra registers 5500 K, and the granules outside the spot are 6000 K.

Sunspots range in size from tiny granules to complex structures with areas stretching for billions of square miles. About 5 percent of all sunspots are large enough so that they can be seen from Earth without instruments; consequently, observations of sunspots have been recorded for thousands of years.

Sunspots have been observed in arrangements of one to more than one hundred spots, but they tend to occur in pairs. There is also a marked tendency for the two spots of a pair to have opposite magnetic polarities. Furthermore, the strength of the magnetic field associated with any given sunspot is closely related to the spot's size. Sunspots have also been observed to occur in cycles, over a period of eleven years. At the beginning of a cycle, the storms occur between 20 and 40 degrees north and south of the equator on the sun. As the cycle continues, some of the storms move closer to the equator. As the cycle

42. In which configuration do sunspots usually occur?

Ⓐ In one spot of varying size
Ⓑ In a configuration of two spots
Ⓒ In arrangements of one hundred or more spots
Ⓓ In groups of several thousand spots

43. How are sunspots explained?

Ⓐ Sunspots appear to be related to magnetic fields on the Earth.
Ⓑ Sunspots may be related to magnetic fields that follow longitudinal lines on the sun.
Ⓒ Sunspots are explained by storms that occur on the Earth.
Ⓓ Sunspots have no theory or model to explain them.

44. Click on the paragraph that discusses the visibility of sunspots.

Scroll the passage to see all of the paragraphs.

45. The sunspot theory is

Ⓐ not considered very important
Ⓑ widely accepted
Ⓒ subject to disagreement
Ⓓ relatively new

To check your answers for Model Test 1, refer to the Answer Key on page 545. For an explanation of the answers, refer to the Explanatory Answers for Model Test 1 on pages 553–560.

Writing Section Model Test 1

When you take a Model Test, you should use one sheet of paper, both sides. Time each Model Test carefully. After you have read the topic, you should spend 30 minutes writing. For results that would be closest to the actual testing situation, it is recommended that an English teacher score your test, using the guidelines on page 325 of this book.

Many people enjoy participating in sports for recreation; others enjoy participating in the arts. Give the benefits of each, take a position, and defend it.

Notes

Model Test 2
Computer-Assisted TOEFL

Section 1: Listening

The Listening section of the test measures the ability to understand conversations and talks in English. You will use headphones to listen to the conversations and talks. While you are listening, pictures of the speakers or other information will be presented on your computer screen. There are two parts to the Listening section, with special directions for each part.

On the day of the test, the amount of time you will have to answer all of the questions will appear on the computer screen. The time you spend listening to the test material will not be counted. The listening material and questions about it will be presented only one time. You will not be allowed to take notes or have any paper at your computer. You will both see and hear the questions before the answer choices appear. You can take as much time as you need to select an answer; however, it will be to your advantage to answer the questions as quickly as possible. You may change your answer as many times as you want before you confirm it. After you have confirmed an answer, you will not be able to return to the question.

Before you begin working on the Listening section, you will have an opportunity to adjust the volume of the sound. You will not be able to change the volume after you have started the test.

QUESTION DIRECTIONS — Part A

In Part A of the Listening section, you will hear short conversations between two people. In some of the conversations, each person speaks only once. In other conversations, one or both of the people speak more than once. Each conversation is followed by one question about it.

Each question in this part has four answer choices. You should click on the best answer to each question. Answer the questions on the basis of what is stated or implied by the speakers.

1. What had the man assumed?

Ⓐ The woman was not truthful.
Ⓑ Fewer students would attend.
Ⓒ There would be a large group.
Ⓓ Only foreign students would come.

2. What does the woman imply that the man should do?

Ⓐ Knock on the door.
Ⓑ Come back later.
Ⓒ See Dr. Smith.
Ⓓ Look at the sign.

3. What is the woman probably going to do?

Ⓐ Take a class from Professor Wilson.
Ⓑ Help the man with his class.
Ⓒ Take an extra class.
Ⓓ Do a project for her class.

4. What does the woman say about Paul?

Ⓐ That he wants something to eat.
Ⓑ That he will tell them if there is a problem.
Ⓒ That he is not hungry.
Ⓓ That he is angry.

5. What does the woman mean?

Ⓐ Good grades are not that important to her.
Ⓑ She did not get an A on the exam either.
Ⓒ Two students got higher grades than she did.
Ⓓ Besides hers, there were several other A grades.

6. What problem does the woman have?

Ⓐ There is no time to finish.
Ⓑ She cannot do it quickly.
Ⓒ She needs to study.
Ⓓ She doesn't know what time it is.

7. What does the woman mean?

Ⓐ She does not agree with the man.
Ⓑ She thinks that it is better to wait.
Ⓒ She thinks that it is better to drive at night.
Ⓓ She does not think that the man made a wise decision.

8. What is the man going to do?

Ⓐ Go to class.
Ⓑ See a movie.
Ⓒ Study at the library.
Ⓓ Make an appointment.

9. What does the man mean?

Ⓐ The message was not clear.
Ⓑ There was no message on the machine.
Ⓒ It was his intention to return the woman's call.
Ⓓ He did not hear the woman's message.

10. What does the woman mean?

Ⓐ They do not have as many people working as usual.
Ⓑ The machine is broken.
Ⓒ The man is next to be served.
Ⓓ There is usually a long line.

11. What does the woman suggest that the man do?

Ⓐ Get directions to the Math Department.
Ⓑ Speak with the secretary.
Ⓒ Go into Dr. Davis's office.
Ⓓ Take the elevator to the fourth floor.

12. What can be inferred about Tom?

Ⓐ He has finished the class.
Ⓑ He has been sick.
Ⓒ He does not have to take the final exam.
Ⓓ He is not very responsible.

13. What does the man mean?

Ⓐ He cannot find the woman's house.
Ⓑ He has to change their plans.
Ⓒ He will be happy to see the woman.
Ⓓ He wants to know whether they have a date.

14. What will the woman probably do?

Ⓐ Register for Dr. Collin's class.
Ⓑ Graduate at a later date.
Ⓒ Enroll in the section marked "staff."
Ⓓ Find out who is teaching the other section of the class.

15. What does the woman think that the man should do?

Ⓐ Wait for the results to be mailed.
Ⓑ Call about the score.
Ⓒ Take the test.
Ⓓ Show more concern.

16. What does the woman mean?

Ⓐ They have more time to travel.
Ⓑ They are taking advantage of travel opportunities.
Ⓒ They travel more than the man does.
Ⓓ They spend most of their time traveling.

17. What does the man mean?

Ⓐ The tickets are lost.
Ⓑ Judy was responsible for getting the tickets.
Ⓒ There were no ticket available.
Ⓓ He does not have the tickets yet.

QUESTION DIRECTIONS — Part B

In Part B of the Listening section, you will hear several longer conversations and talks. Each conversation or talk is followed by several questions. The conversations, talks, and questions will not be repeated.

The conversations and talks are about a variety of topics. You do not need special knowledge of the topics to answer the questions correctly. Rather, you should answer each question on the basis of what is stated or implied by the speakers in the conversations or talks.

For most of the questions, you will need to click on the best of four possible answers. Some questions will have special directions. The special directions will appear in a box on the computer screen.

18. What are the man and woman talking about?

Ⓐ A chapter in their textbook.
Ⓑ An experiment referred to in a group presentation.
Ⓒ A lecture in class.
Ⓓ A program on television.

19. Why is the moon an ideal environment for the experiment?

Ⓐ There is no air resistance on the moon.
Ⓑ There is no gravitational acceleration on the moon.
Ⓒ The gravity on the moon affects vertical motion.
Ⓓ There is no horizontal resistance for motions like pushing.

20. Why was it easier to lift the hammer on the moon?

Ⓐ The moon's gravitational acceleration was lower.
Ⓑ The hammer fell when it was released.
Ⓒ The surface of the moon encouraged motion.
Ⓓ The hammer was created for that environment.

21. How did the woman feel about the presentation?

Ⓐ She was surprised by it.
Ⓑ She was not interested in it.
Ⓒ She was impressed by it.
Ⓓ She was confused about it.

22. What was the video about?

Ⓐ The national health.
Ⓑ Stress.
Ⓒ Heart attacks.
Ⓓ Health care for women.

23. What did the students learn about women?

Ⓐ They are under more stress than men.
Ⓑ They have more heart attacks than men.
Ⓒ They do not get the same level of care as men.
Ⓓ They have less serious heart attacks than men.

24. How did the man feel about the video?

Ⓐ He did not see it.
Ⓑ He thought it was interesting.
Ⓒ He would not recommend it.
Ⓓ He was not surprised by it.

25. What will the woman probably do?

Ⓐ Discuss the video with the man.
Ⓑ Go to the library to see the video.
Ⓒ Check the video out of the library.
Ⓓ Get ready for class.

26. What is the main topic of this lecture?

Ⓐ Poet laureates.
Ⓑ The Victorian Period.
Ⓒ Love poems in the English language.
Ⓓ Elizabeth Barrett Browning.

27. According to the lecturer, what was one reason that Elizabeth Barrett was considered for the title of Poet Laureate?

Ⓐ Because her husband was a famous poet.
Ⓑ Because of her publication, *Sonnets from the Portuguese*.
Ⓒ Because the monarch was a woman.
Ⓓ Because of her friendship with William Wordsworth.

28. Where did Elizabeth and Robert Browning live after their elopement?

Ⓐ In Spain.
Ⓑ In Italy.
Ⓒ In Portugal.
Ⓓ In England.

29. When did Elizabeth Barrett Browning die?

Ⓐ In 1843.
Ⓑ In 1849.
Ⓒ In 1856.
Ⓓ In 1861.

30. What is the main topic of this lecture?

Ⓐ The history of medicine in Greece.
Ⓑ The contributions of biology to medicine.
Ⓒ The scientific method.
Ⓓ Medical advances in the twentieth century.

31. What was Hippocrates' greatest contribution to medicine?

Ⓐ The classification of plants on the basis of body structure.
Ⓑ The sterilization of surgical instruments.
Ⓒ The scientific recording of symptoms and treatments.
Ⓓ The theory that disease was caused by the gods.

32. Who is known as the father of biology?

Ⓐ Hippocrates.
Ⓑ Aristotle.
Ⓒ Dioscorides.
Ⓓ Edward Jenner.

33. What was the contribution made to medicine by William Harvey?

Ⓐ The theory of germs and bacteria.
Ⓑ The discovery of a vaccine against smallpox.
Ⓒ The discovery of a mechanism for the circulation of the blood.
Ⓓ The *Materia Medica*.

34. What was surprising about Thrasher's study?

Ⓐ The size of the study, which included 1300 gangs.
Ⓑ The excellent summary by the student who located the research.
Ⓒ The changes that were reported in the history of gangs in the United States.
Ⓓ The fact that gang activity has been prevalent for many years.

35. According to the study by Moore, what causes gang activity?

Ⓐ Cliques that form in high school.
Ⓑ Normal feelings of insecurity that teenagers experience.
Ⓒ Dangerous neighborhoods and schools.
Ⓓ Loyalty to friends and family.

36. In which two ways are gang members identified by law enforcement authorities?

Click on 2 answers.

[A] By their tattoos.
[B] By their clothing.
[C] By maps of their territories.
[D] By research studies.

37. What is the role of women in gangs?

Ⓐ Women are full members of the gangs.
Ⓑ Women are protected by the gangs.
Ⓒ Women are a support system for the gangs.
Ⓓ Women do not have any contact with the gangs.

38. What is Mary's problem?

Ⓐ She does not want to work for Dr. Brown.
Ⓑ She has a schedule conflict.
Ⓒ She has been late to work too often.
Ⓓ She needs to obtain a work-study position.

39. When is Mary's class next semester?

Ⓐ Every day in the afternoon.
Ⓑ Three hours a day, three times a week.
Ⓒ Ten-thirty on Monday.
Ⓓ Nine o'clock, three times a week.

40. How does Dr. Brown resolve the problem?

Ⓐ He changes her work hours.
Ⓑ He has her work fewer hours.
Ⓒ He finds a different job for her.
Ⓓ He gives her permission to arrive late.

41. What is a work-study employee?

Ⓐ A person who works on campus.
Ⓑ A new employee who is being trained.
Ⓒ A student who can study at work after the job is complete.
Ⓓ A part-time student with a full-time job.

42. What is the topic of this lecture?

Ⓐ Reinforced concrete in buildings.
Ⓑ Shear walls in earthquakes.
Ⓒ Earthquake-resistant buildings.
Ⓓ Understanding construction sites.

43. Which technique is used to reinforce walls?

Ⓐ Cross-bracing.
Ⓑ Shear cores.
Ⓒ Bolts.
Ⓓ Base isolators.

44. Which two materials are used in base isolators?

Click on 2 answers.

[A] Rubber.
[B] Steel.
[C] Concrete.
[D] Soil.

45. What happens to fill dirt during an earthquake?

Ⓐ It allows the building to sway.
Ⓑ It reduces earthquake damage.
Ⓒ It collapses.
Ⓓ It creates shock waves.

46. Which two types represent the most common vein patterns in leaves?

Click on 2 answers.

[A] Needle leaves.
[B] Parallel leaves.
[C] Palmate leaves.
[D] Pinnate leaves.

47. According to the lecturer, what is a midrib?

Ⓐ One of the major classifications of veins in plants.
Ⓑ The large vein that extends down the middle of a pinnate leaf.
Ⓒ The central vein in a parallel leaf.
Ⓓ The stem of a plant.

48. How does the lab assistant help students remember the palmate classification?

Ⓐ He shows them a visual.
Ⓑ He explains it carefully.
Ⓒ He compares it to his hand.
Ⓓ He refers them to their lab manual.

49. Match the leaves with their vein patterns.

Click on the leaf. Then click on the empty box in the correct row. Use each leaf only once.

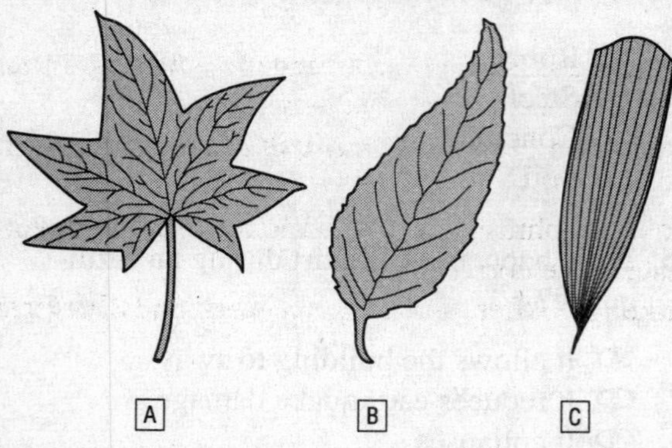

	Pinnate
	Palmate
	Parallel

50. What will the students probably do after the short lecture?

Ⓐ Classify leaves.
Ⓑ Take a lab quiz.
Ⓒ Read fifty-two pages in their manuals.
Ⓓ Discuss the lecture.

Section 2: Structure

This section measures the ability to recognize language that is appropriate for standard written English. There are two types of questions in this section.

In the first type of question, there are incomplete sentences. Beneath each sentence, there are four words or phrases. You will choose the one word or phrase that best completes the sentence.

Clicking on a choice darkens the oval. After you click on **Next** and **Confirm Answer**, the next question will be presented.

The second type of question has four underlined words or phrases. You will choose the one underlined word or phrase that must be changed for the sentence to be correct.

Clicking on an underlined word or phrase will darken it. After you click on **Next** and **Confirm Answer**, the next question will be presented.

1. One of the most effective vegetable protein substitutes is the soybean -------- used to manufacture imitation meat products.

   (A) which can be
   (B) it can be
   (C) who can be
   (D) can be

2. -------- 1000 species of finch have been identified.

   (A) As many as
   (B) As many
   (C) As much as
   (D) Much as

3. The first (A) electric lamp had two carbon rods from which (B) vapor serves (C) to conduct (D) the current across the gap.

4. A (A) thunderhead, dense clouds that rise (B) high (C) into the sky in huge columns, produce (D) hail, rain, or snow.

5. According to the economic laws, the greater the demand, -------- the price.

   (A) higher
   (B) high
   (C) the higher
   (D) the high

6. Although no country (A) has exactly the same folk music like (B) that (C) of any other, it is significant that similar songs exist among widely (D) separated people.

7. Despite of (A) the Taft-Hartley Act which forbids (B) unfair union practices, some unions such as (C) the air traffic controllers have voted to strike (D) even though this action might endanger the national security.

8. The Continental United States is -------- that there are four time zones.

   (A) much big
   (B) too big
   (C) so big
   (D) very big

9. Benjamin West contributed a great deal to American art: -------- .

   (A) painting, teaching, and lecturing
   (B) painting, as a teacher and lecturer
   (C) painting, teaching, and as a lecturer
   (D) painting, a teacher, and a lecturer

10. Operant conditioning involves rewarding or punishing certain behave (A) to reinforce (B) or extinguish (C) its occurrence (D).

11. There is (A) an unresolved controversy as to whom (B) is (C) the real author of the Elizabethan plays commonly (D) credited to William Shakespeare.

12. A catalytic agent such (A) platinum may be used so (B) that the chemical reaction advances (C) more rapidly (D).

13. Upon hatching, --------

(A) young ducks know how to swim
(B) swimming is known by young ducks
(C) the knowledge of swimming is in young ducks
(D) how to swim is known in young ducks

14. The observation deck at the World Trade Center -------- in New York.

(A) is highest than any other one
(B) is higher than any other one
(C) is highest that any other one
(D) is higher that any other one

15. When a patient's blood pressure is much (A) higher than it (B) should be (C), a doctor usually insists that he will not (D) smoke.

16. It (A) was (B) the invent (C) of the hand-held electronic calculator that provided the original technology for the present (D) generation of small but powerful computers.

17. -------- is necessary for the development of strong bones and teeth.

(A) It is calcium
(B) That calcium
(C) Calcium
(D) Although calcium

18. Located in (A) the cranial cavity in the skull, the brain (B) is the larger (C) mass of nerve tissue in the human body (D).

19. Alike (A) other forms of energy, natural gas may be used (B) to heat (C) homes, cook food, and even run (D) automobiles.

20. An organ is (A) a group of tissues (B) capable to perform (C) some special function, as, for example (D), the heart, the liver, or the lungs.

21. -------- withstands testing, we may not conclude that it is true, but we may retain it.

(A) If a hypothesis
(B) That a hypothesis
(C) A hypothesis
(D) Hypothesis

22. Insulin, it is (A) used to treat (B) diabetes and is (C) secured chiefly (D) from the pancreas of cattle and hogs.

23. Not until a monkey is several years old -------- to exhibit signs of independence from its mother.

(A) it begins
(B) does it begin
(C) and begin
(D) beginning

24. Since Elizabeth Barrett Browning's father never approved of -------- Robert Browning, the couple eloped to Italy, where they lived and wrote.

Ⓐ her to marry
Ⓑ her marrying
Ⓒ she marrying
Ⓓ she to marry

25. <u>In autumn</u>Ⓐ, brilliant yellow, orange, and red leaves are <u>commonly</u>Ⓑ <u>to</u>Ⓒ both the Sweet Gum tree <u>and</u>Ⓓ the Maple.

Section 3: Reading

This section measures the ability to read and understand short passages similar in topic and style to those that students are likely to encounter in North American universities and colleges. This section contains reading passages and questions about the passages. There are several different types of questions in this section.

In the Reading section, you will first have the opportunity to read the passage.

You will use the scroll bar to view the rest of the passage.

When you have finished reading the passage, you will use the mouse to click on **Proceed**. Then the questions about the passage will be presented. You are to choose the one best answer to each question. Answer all questions about the information in a passage on the basis of what is stated or implied in that passage.

Most of the questions will be multiple-choice questions. To answer these questions you will click on a choice below the question.

To answer some questions, you will click on a word or phrase.

To answer some questions, you will click on a sentence in the passage.

To answer some questions, you will click on a square to add a sentence to the passage.

Recent technological advances in manned and unmanned undersea vehicles, along with breakthroughs in satellite technology and computer equipment, have overcome some of the limitations of divers and diving equipment for scientists doing research on the great oceans of the world. Without a vehicle, divers often became sluggish, and their mental concentration was severely limited. Because undersea pressure affects their speech organs, communication among divers has always been difficult or impossible. But today, most oceanographers avoid the use of vulnerable human divers, preferring to reduce the risk to human life and make direct observations by means of instruments that are lowered into the ocean, from samples taken from the water, or from photographs made by orbiting satellites. Direct observations of the ocean floor can be made not only by divers but also by deep-diving submarines in the water and even by the technology of sophisticated aerial photography from vantage points above the surface of the water. Some submarines can dive to depths of more than seven miles and cruise at depths of fifteen thousand feet. In addition, radio-equipped buoys can be operated by remote control in order to transmit information back to land-based laboratories via satellite. Particularly important for ocean study are data about water temperature, currents, and weather. Satellite photographs can show the distribution of sea ice, oil slicks, and cloud formations over the ocean. Maps created from satellite pictures can represent the temperature and the color of the ocean's surface, enabling researchers to study the ocean currents from laboratories on dry land. Furthermore, computers help oceanographers to collect, organize, and analyze data from submarines and satellites. By creating a model of the ocean's movement and characteristics, scientists can predict the patterns and possible effects of the ocean on the environment.

Recently, many oceanographers have been relying more on satellites and computers than on research ships or even submarine vehicles because they can supply a greater range of information more quickly and more effectively. Some of humankind's most serious problems, especially those concerning energy and food, may be solved with the help of observations made possible by this new technology.

1. With what topic is the passage primarily concerned?

   Ⓐ Technological advances in oceanography
   Ⓑ Communication among divers
   Ⓒ Direct observation of the ocean floor
   Ⓓ Undersea vehicles

2. The word **sluggish** in paragraph 1 is closest in meaning to

   Ⓐ nervous
   Ⓑ confused
   Ⓒ slow moving
   Ⓓ very weak

Beginning

Recent technological advances in manned and unmanned undersea vehicles, along with breakthroughs in satellite technology and computer equipment, have overcome some of the limitations of divers and diving equipment for scientists doing research on the great oceans of the world. Without a vehicle, divers often became **sluggish**, and their mental concentration was severely limited. Because undersea pressure affects their speech organs, communication among divers has always been difficult or impossible. But today, most oceanographers avoid the use of vulnerable human divers, preferring to reduce the risk to human life and make direct observations by means of instruments that are lowered into the ocean, from samples taken from the water, or from photographs made by orbiting satellites. Direct observations of the ocean floor can be made not only by divers but also by deep-diving submarines in the water and even by the technology of sophisticated aerial photography from vantage points above the surface of the water. Some submarines can dive to depths of more than seven miles and cruise at

3. Divers have had problems in communicating underwater because

   Ⓐ the pressure affected their speech organs
   Ⓑ the vehicles they used have not been perfected
   Ⓒ they did not pronounce clearly
   Ⓓ the water destroyed their speech organs

4. This passage suggests that the successful exploration of the ocean depends upon

   Ⓐ vehicles as well as divers
   Ⓑ radios that divers use to communicate
   Ⓒ controlling currents and the weather
   Ⓓ the limitations of diving equipment

5. Undersea vehicles

Ⓐ are too small for a man to fit inside
Ⓑ are very slow to respond
Ⓒ have the same limitations that divers have
Ⓓ make direct observations of the ocean floor

6. The word cruise in paragraph 1 could best be replaced by

Ⓐ travel at a constant speed
Ⓑ function without problems
Ⓒ stay in communication
Ⓓ remain still

More Available

affects their speech organs, communication among divers has always been difficult or impossible. But today, most oceanographers avoid the use of vulnerable human divers, preferring to reduce the risk to human life and make direct observations by means of instruments that are lowered into the ocean, from samples taken from the water, or from photographs made by orbiting satellites. Direct observations of the ocean floor can be made not only by divers but also by deep-diving submarines in the water and even by the technology of sophisticated aerial photography from vantage points above the surface of the water. Some submarines can dive to depths of more than seven miles and cruise at depths of fifteen thousand feet. In addition, radio-equipped buoys can be operated by remote control in order to transmit information back to land-based laboratories via satellite. Particularly important for ocean study are data about water temperature, currents, and weather. Satellite photographs can show the distribution of sea ice, oil slicks, and cloud formations over the ocean. Maps created from satellite pictures can represent

7. How is a radio-equipped buoy operated?

Ⓐ By operators inside the vehicle in the part underwater
Ⓑ By operators outside the vehicle on a ship
Ⓒ By operators outside the vehicle on a diving platform
Ⓓ By operators outside the vehicle in a laboratory on shore

8. Look at the word information in the passage. Click on the word or phrase in the **bold** text that is closest in meaning to information.

End

important for ocean study are data about water temperature, currents, and weather. Satellite photographs can show the distribution of sea ice, oil slicks, and cloud formations over the ocean. Maps created from satellite pictures can represent the temperature and the color of the ocean's surface, enabling researchers to study the ocean currents from laboratories on dry land. **Furthermore, computers help oceanographers to collect, organize, and analyze data from submarines and satellites. By creating a model of the ocean's movement and characteristics, scientists can predict the patterns and possible effects of the ocean on the environment.**

Recently, many oceanographers have been relying more on satellites and computers than on research ships or even submarine vehicles because they can supply a greater range of information more quickly and more effectively. Some of humankind's most serious problems, especially those concerning energy and food, may be solved with the help of observations made possible by this new technology.

9. Which of the following are NOT shown in satellite photographs?

Ⓐ The temperature of the ocean's surface
Ⓑ Cloud formations over the ocean
Ⓒ A model of the ocean's movements
Ⓓ The location of sea ice

10. Look at the word those in the passage. Click on the word or phrase in the **bold** text that those refers to.

End

important for ocean study are data about water temperature, currents, and weather. Satellite photographs can show the distribution of sea ice, oil slicks, and cloud formations over the ocean. Maps created from satellite pictures can represent the temperature and the color of the ocean's surface, enabling researchers to study the ocean currents from laboratories on dry land. Furthermore, computers help oceanographers to collect, organize, and analyze data from submarines and satellites. By creating a model of the ocean's movement and characteristics, scientists can predict the patterns and possible effects of the ocean on the environment.

Recently, many oceanographers have been relying more on satellites and computers than on research ships or even submarine vehicles because they can supply a greater range of information more quickly and more effectively. Some of humankind's most serious problems, especially those concerning energy and food, may be solved with the help of observations made possible by this new technology.

11. Click on the paragraph in the passage that discusses problems that new technology might help eliminate.

Scroll the passage to see all of the paragraphs.

Although speech is generally accepted as the most advanced form of communication, there are many ways of communicating without using words. In every known culture, signals, signs, symbols, and gestures are commonly utilized as instruments of communication. There is a great deal of agreement among communication scientists as to what each of these methods is and how each differs from the others. For instance, the basic function of any signal is to impinge upon the environment in such a way that it attracts attention, as, for example, the dots and dashes that can be applied in a telegraph circuit. Coded to refer to speech, the potential for communication through these dots and dashes—short and long intervals as the circuit is broken—is very great. Less adaptable to the codification of words, signs also contain agreed upon meaning; that is, they convey information in and of themselves. Two examples are the hexagonal red sign that conveys the meaning of *stop*, and the red and white swirled pole outside a shop that communicates the meaning of *barber*.

Symbols are more difficult to describe than either signals or signs because of their intricate relationship with the receiver's cultural perceptions. In some cultures, applauding in a theater provides performers with an auditory symbol of approval. In other cultures, if done in unison, applauding can be a symbol of the audience's discontent with the performance. Gestures such as waving and handshaking also communicate certain cultural messages.

Although signals, signs, symbols, and gestures are very useful, they also have a major disadvantage in communication. They usually do not allow ideas to be shared without the sender being directly adjacent to the receiver. Without an exchange of ideas, interaction comes to a halt. As a result, means of communication intended to be used across long distances and extended periods must be based upon speech. To radio, television, and the telephone, one must add fax, paging systems, electronic mail, and the Internet, and no one doubts but that there are more means of communication on the horizon.

12. Which of the following would be the best title for the passage?

Ⓐ Signs and Signals
Ⓑ Gestures
Ⓒ Communication
Ⓓ Speech

13. What does the author say about speech?

Ⓐ It is the only true form of communication.
Ⓑ It is dependent upon the advances made by inventors.
Ⓒ It is necessary for communication to occur.
Ⓓ It is the most advanced form of communication.

14. Click on the sentence in paragraph 1 that defines the function of a signal.

Paragraph 1 is marked with an arrow (→).

Beginning

→ Although speech is generally accepted as the most advanced form of communication, there are many ways of communicating without using words. In every known culture, signals, signs, symbols, and gestures are commonly utilized as instruments of communication. There is a great deal of agreement among communication scientists as to what each of these methods is and how each differs from the others. For instance, the basic function of any signal is to impinge upon the environment in such a way that it attracts attention, as, for example, the dots and dashes that can be applied in a telegraph circuit. Coded to refer to speech, the potential for communication through these dots and dashes—short and long intervals as the circuit is broken—is very great. Less adaptable to the codification of words, signs also contain agreed upon meaning; that is, they convey information in and of themselves. Two examples are the hexagonal red sign that conveys the meaning of *stop*, and the red and white swirled pole outside a shop that communicates the meaning of *barber*.

Symbols are more difficult to describe than

15. The phrase **impinge upon** in paragraph 1 is closest in meaning to

Ⓐ intrude
Ⓑ improve
Ⓒ vary
Ⓓ prohibit

Beginning

Although speech is generally accepted as the most advanced form of communication, there are many ways of communicating without using words. In every known culture, signals, signs, symbols, and gestures are commonly utilized as instruments of communication. There is a great deal of agreement among communication scientists as to what each of these methods is and how each differs from the others. For instance, the basic function of any signal is to **impinge upon** the environment in such a way that it attracts attention, as, for example, the dots and dashes that can be applied in a telegraph circuit. Coded to refer to speech, the potential for communication through these dots and dashes—short and long intervals as the circuit is broken—is very great. Less adaptable to the codification of words, signs also contain agreed upon meaning; that is, they convey information in and of themselves. Two examples are the hexagonal red sign that conveys the meaning of *stop*, and the red and white swirled pole outside a shop that communicates the meaning of *barber*.

Symbols are more difficult to describe than

16. The word **it** in paragraph 1 refers to

Ⓐ function
Ⓑ signal
Ⓒ environment
Ⓓ way

Beginning

Although speech is generally accepted as the most advanced form of communication, there are many ways of communicating without using words. In every known culture, signals, signs, symbols, and gestures are commonly utilized as instruments of communication. There is a great deal of agreement among communication scientists as to what each of these methods is and how each differs from the others. For instance, the basic function of any signal is to impinge upon the environment in such a way that **it** attracts attention, as, for example, the dots and dashes that can be applied in a telegraph circuit. Coded to refer to speech, the potential for communication through these dots and dashes—short and long intervals as the circuit is broken—is very great. Less adaptable to the codification of words, signs also contain agreed upon meaning; that is, they convey information in and of themselves. Two examples are the hexagonal red sign that conveys the meaning of *stop*, and the red and white swirled pole outside a shop that communicates the meaning of *barber.*

Symbols are more difficult to describe than

17. The word **potential** in paragraph 1 could best be replaced by

Ⓐ range
Ⓑ advantage
Ⓒ organization
Ⓓ possibility

Beginning

Although speech is generally accepted as the most advanced form of communication, there are many ways of communicating without using words. In every known culture, signals, signs, symbols, and gestures are commonly utilized as instruments of communication. There is a great deal of agreement among communication scientists as to what each of these methods is and how each differs from the others. For instance, the basic function of any signal is to impinge upon the environment in such a way that it attracts attention, as, for example, the dots and dashes that can be applied in a telegraph circuit. Coded to refer to speech, the **potential** for communication through these dots and dashes—short and long intervals as the circuit is broken—is very great. Less adaptable to the codification of words, signs also contain agreed upon meaning; that is, they convey information in and of themselves. Two examples are the hexagonal red sign that conveys the meaning of *stop*, and the red and white swirled pole outside a shop that communicates the meaning of *barber.*

Symbols are more difficult to describe than

18. Look at the word themselves in the passage. Click on the word or phrase in the **bold** text that themselves refers to.

More Available

scientists as to what each of these methods is and how each differs from the others. For instance, the basic function of any signal is to impinge upon the environment in such a way that it attracts attention, as, for example, the dots and dashes that can be applied in a telegraph circuit. **Coded to refer to speech, the potential for communication through these dots and dashes—short and long intervals as the circuit is broken—is very great. Less adaptable to the codification of words, signs also contain agreed upon meaning; that is, they convey information in and of themselves. Two examples are the hexagonal red sign that conveys the meaning of *stop,* and the red and white swirled pole outside a shop that communicates the meaning of *barber.***

Symbols are more difficult to describe than either signals or signs because of their intricate relationship with the receiver's cultural perceptions. In some cultures, applauding in a theater provides performers with an auditory symbol of approval. In other cultures, if done in unison, applauding can be a symbol of the audience's discontent with the performance. Gestures such as waving and

19. The word intricate in paragraph 2 could best be replaced by which of the following?

Ⓐ inefficient
Ⓑ complicated
Ⓒ historical
Ⓓ uncertain

More Available

also contain agreed upon meaning; that is, they convey information in and of themselves. Two examples are the hexagonal red sign that conveys the meaning of *stop*, and the red and white swirled pole outside a shop that communicates the meaning of *barber.*

Symbols are more difficult to describe than either signals or signs because of their intricate relationship with the receiver's cultural perceptions. In some cultures, applauding in a theater provides performers with an auditory symbol of approval. In other cultures, if done in unison, applauding can be a symbol of the audience's discontent with the performance. Gestures such as waving and handshaking also communicate certain cultural messages.

Although signals, signs, symbols, and gestures are very useful, they also have a major disadvantage in communication. They usually do not allow ideas to be shared without the sender being directly adjacent to the receiver. Without an exchange of ideas, interaction comes to a halt. As a result, means of communication intended to be used across long distances and extended periods

20. Applauding was cited as an example of

Ⓐ a signal
Ⓑ a sign
Ⓒ a symbol
Ⓓ a gesture

21. The following sentence can be added to the passage.

A loud smacking of the lips after a meal can be either a kinesthetic and auditory symbol of approval and appreciation, or simply a rude noise.

Where would it best fit in the passage?

Click on the square (■) to add the sentence to the passage.

Scroll the passage to see all of the choices.

More Available

also contain agreed upon meaning; that is, they convey information in and of themselves. ■ Two examples are the hexagonal red sign that conveys the meaning of *stop*, and the red and white swirled pole outside a shop that communicates the meaning of *barber.*

■ Symbols are more difficult to describe than either signals or signs because of their intricate relationship with the receiver's cultural perceptions. In some cultures, applauding in a theater provides performers with an auditory symbol of approval. In other cultures, if done in unison, applauding can be a symbol of the audience's discontent with the performance. ■ Gestures such as waving and handshaking also communicate certain cultural messages.

Although signals, signs, symbols, and gestures are very useful, they also have a major disadvantage in communication. ■ They usually do not allow ideas to be shared without the sender being directly adjacent to the receiver. Without an exchange of ideas, interaction comes to a halt. As a result, means of communication intended to be used across long distances and extended periods

22. Why were the telephone, radio, and TV invented?

Ⓐ People were unable to understand signs, symbols, and signals.
Ⓑ People wanted to communicate across long distances.
Ⓒ People believed that signs, signals, and symbols were obsolete.
Ⓓ People wanted new forms of entertainment.

23. Look at the word communication in the passage. Click on the word or phrase in the **bold** text that is closest in meaning to communication.

End

In some cultures, applauding in a theater provides performers with an auditory symbol of approval. In other cultures, if done in unison, applauding can be a symbol of the audience's discontent with the performance. Gestures such as waving and handshaking also communicate certain cultural messages.

Although signals, signs, symbols, and gestures are very useful, they also have a major disadvantage in communication. They usually do not allow ideas to be shared without the sender being directly adjacent to the receiver. Without an exchange of ideas, interaction comes to a halt. As a result, means of communication intended to be used across long distances and extended periods must be based upon speech. To radio, television, and the telephone, one must add fax, paging systems, electronic mail, and the Internet, and no one doubts but that there are more means of communication on the horizon.

Fertilizer is any substance that can be added to the soil to provide chemical elements essential for plant nutrition so that the yield can be increased. Natural substances such as animal droppings, ashes from wood fires, and straw have been used as fertilizers in fields for thousands of years, and lime has been used since the Romans introduced it during the Empire. It was not until the nineteenth century, however, that chemical fertilizers became widely accepted as normal agricultural practice. Today, both natural and synthetic fertilizers are available in a variety of forms.

A complete fertilizer is usually marked with a formula consisting of three numbers, such as 4-8-2 or 6-6-4, which designate the percentage of content of nitrogen, phosphoric acid, and potash in the order stated. Synthetic fertilizers, produced by factories, are available in either solid or liquid form. Solids, in the shape of chemical granules, are in demand because they are not only easy to store but also easy to apply. Recently, liquids have shown an increase in popularity, accounting for about 20 percent of the nitrogen fertilizer used throughout the world. Formerly, powders were also used, but they were found to be less convenient than either solids or liquids.

Fertilizers have no harmful effects on the soil, the crop, or the consumer as long as they are used according to recommendations based on the results of local research. Occasionally, however, farmers may use more fertilizer than necessary, in which case the plants do not need, and therefore do not absorb, the total amount of fertilizer applied to the soil. The surplus of fertilizer thus can damage not only the crop but also the animals or human beings that eat the crop. Furthermore, fertilizer that is not used in the production of a healthy plant is leached into the water table. Accumulations of chemical fertilizer in the water supply accelerate the growth of algae and, consequently, may disturb the natural cycle of life, contributing to the death of fish. Too much fertilizer on grass can cause digestive disorders in cattle and in infants who drink cow's milk. Fertilizer must be used with great attention to responsible use or it can harm the environment.

24. With which of the following topics is the passage primarily concerned?

(A) Local research and harmful effects of fertilizer
(B) Advantages and disadvantages of liquid fertilizer
(C) A formula for the production of fertilizer
(D) Content, form, and effects of fertilizer

25. The word **essential** in paragraph 1 could best be replaced by which of the following?

(A) limited
(B) preferred
(C) anticipated
(D) required

Beginning

Fertilizer is any substance that can be added to the soil to provide chemical elements **essential** for plant nutrition so that the yield can be increased. Natural substances such as animal droppings, ashes from wood fires, and straw have been used as fertilizers in fields for thousands of years, and lime has been used since the Romans introduced it during the Empire. It was not until the nineteenth century, however, that chemical fertilizers became widely accepted as normal agricultural practice. Today, both natural and synthetic fertilizers are available in a variety of forms.

A complete fertilizer is usually marked with a formula consisting of three numbers, such as 4-8-2 or 6-6-4, which designate the percentage of content of nitrogen, phosphoric acid, and potash in the order stated. Synthetic fertilizers, produced by factories, are available in either solid or liquid form. Solids, in the shape of chemical granules, are in demand because they are not only easy to store but also easy to apply. Recently, liquids have shown an increase in popularity, accounting for about 20 percent of the nitrogen fertilizer used throughout the world. Formerly, powders were

26. Which of the following has the smallest percentage content in the formula 4-8-2?

(A) Nitrogen
(B) Phosphorus
(C) Acid
(D) Potash

27. What is the percentage of nitrogen in a 5-8-7 formula fertilizer?

(A) 3 percent
(B) 5 percent
(C) 7 percent
(D) 8 percent

28. The word **designate** in paragraph 2 could be replaced by

(A) modify
(B) specify
(C) limit
(D) increase

Beginning

Fertilizer is any substance that can be added to the soil to provide chemical elements essential for plant nutrition so that the yield can be increased. Natural substances such as animal droppings, ashes from wood fires, and straw have been used as fertilizers in fields for thousands of years, and lime has been used since the Romans introduced it during the Empire. It was not until the nineteenth century, however, that chemical fertilizers became widely accepted as normal agricultural practice. Today, both natural and synthetic fertilizers are available in a variety of forms.

A complete fertilizer is usually marked with a formula consisting of three numbers, such as 4-8-2 or 6-6-4, which **designate** the percentage of content of nitrogen, phosphoric acid, and potash in the order stated. Synthetic fertilizers, produced by factories, are available in either solid or liquid form. Solids, in the shape of chemical granules, are in demand because they are not only easy to store but also easy to apply. Recently, liquids have shown an increase in popularity, accounting for about 20 percent of the nitrogen fertilizer used throughout the world. Formerly, powders were

29. Which of the following statements about fertilizer is true?

(A) Powders are more popular than ever.
(B) Solids are difficult to store.
(C) Liquids are increasing in popularity.
(D) Chemical granules are difficult to apply.

30. The word **they** in paragraph 2 refers to

Ⓐ powders
Ⓑ solids
Ⓒ liquids
Ⓓ fertilizer

More Available

content of nitrogen, phosphoric acid, and potash in the order stated. Synthetic fertilizers, produced by factories, are available in either solid or liquid form. Solids, in the shape of chemical granules, are in demand because they are not only easy to store but also easy to apply. Recently, liquids have shown an increase in popularity, accounting for about 20 percent of the nitrogen fertilizer used throughout the world. Formerly, powders were also used, but **they** were found to be less convenient than either solids or liquids.

Fertilizers have no harmful effects on the soil, the crop, or the consumer as long as they are used according to recommendations based on the results of local research. Occasionally, however, farmers may use more fertilizer than necessary, in which case the plants do not need, and therefore do not absorb, the total amount of fertilizer applied to the soil. The surplus of fertilizer thus can damage not only the crop but also the animals or human beings that eat the crop. Furthermore, fertilizer that is not used in the production of a healthy plant is leached into the water table. Accumulations of chemical fertilizer in the water

31. The word **convenient** in paragraph 2 is closest in meaning to

Ⓐ effective
Ⓑ plentiful
Ⓒ easy to use
Ⓓ cheap to produce

More Available

content of nitrogen, phosphoric acid, and potash in the order stated. Synthetic fertilizers, produced by factories, are available in either solid or liquid form. Solids, in the shape of chemical granules, are in demand because they are not only easy to store but also easy to apply. Recently, liquids have shown an increase in popularity, accounting for about 20 percent of the nitrogen fertilizer used throughout the world. Formerly, powders were also used, but they were found to be less **convenient** than either solids or liquids.

Fertilizers have no harmful effects on the soil, the crop, or the consumer as long as they are used according to recommendations based on the results of local research. Occasionally, however, farmers may use more fertilizer than necessary, in which case the plants do not need, and therefore do not absorb, the total amount of fertilizer applied to the soil. The surplus of fertilizer thus can damage not only the crop but also the animals or human beings that eat the crop. Furthermore, fertilizer that is not used in the production of a healthy plant is leached into the water table. Accumulations of chemical fertilizer in the water

32. Click on the sentence in paragraph 3 that describes the effect of an accumulation of fertilizer in the water supply.

Paragraph 3 is marked with an arrow (→).

End

→ Fertilizers have no harmful effects on the soil, the crop, or the consumer as long as they are used according to recommendations based on the results of local research. Occasionally, however, farmers may use more fertilizer than necessary, in which case the plants do not need, and therefore do not absorb, the total amount of fertilizer applied to the soil. The surplus of fertilizer thus can damage not only the crop but also the animals or human beings that eat the crop. Furthermore, fertilizer that is not used in the production of a healthy plant is leached into the water table. Accumulations of chemical fertilizer in the water supply accelerate the growth of algae and, consequently, may disturb the natural cycle of life, contributing to the death of fish. Too much fertilizer on grass can cause digestive disorders in cattle and in infants who drink cow's milk. Fertilizer must be used with great attention to responsible use or it can harm the environment.

33. Look at the word harm in the passage. Click on the word or phrase in the **bold** text that is closest in meaning to harm.

End

Fertilizers have no harmful effects on the soil, the crop, or the consumer as long as they are used according to recommendations based on the results of local research. Occasionally, however, farmers may use more fertilizer than necessary, in which case the plants do not need, and therefore do not absorb, the total amount of fertilizer applied to the soil. **The surplus of fertilizer thus can damage not only the crop but also the animals or human beings that eat the crop. Furthermore, fertilizer that is not used in the production of a healthy plant is leached into the water table. Accumulations of chemical fertilizer in the water supply accelerate the growth of algae and, consequently, may disturb the natural cycle of life, contributing to the death of fish. Too much fertilizer on grass can cause digestive disorders in cattle and in infants who drink cow's milk. Fertilizer must be used with great attention to responsible use or it can harm the environment.**

34. The following sentence can be added to the passage.

One objection to powders was their propensity to become solid chunks if the bags got damp.

Where would it best fit in the passage?

Click on the square (■) to add the sentence to the passage.

Scroll the passage to see all of the choices.

More Available

content of nitrogen, phosphoric acid, and potash in the order stated. Synthetic fertilizers, produced by factories, are available in either solid or liquid form. Solids, in the shape of chemical granules, are in demand because they are not only easy to store but also easy to apply. ■ Recently, liquids have shown an increase in popularity, accounting for about 20 percent of the nitrogen fertilizer used throughout the world. ■ Formerly, powders were also used, but they were found to be less convenient than either solids or liquids. ■

Fertilizers have no harmful effects on the soil, the crop, or the consumer as long as they are used according to recommendations based on the results of local research. ■ Occasionally, however, farmers may use more fertilizer than necessary, in which case the plants do not need, and therefore do not absorb, the total amount of fertilizer applied to the soil. The surplus of fertilizer thus can damage not only the crop but also the animals or human beings that eat the crop. Furthermore, fertilizer that is not used in the production of a healthy plant is leached into the water table. Accumulations of chemical fertilizer in the water

The development of the horse has been recorded from the beginning through all of its evolutionary stages to the modern form. It is, in fact, one of the most complete and well-documented chapters of paleontological history. Fossil finds provide us not only with detailed information about the horse itself but also with valuable insights into the migration of herds, and even evidence for speculation about the climatic conditions that could have instigated such migratory behavior.

Geologists believe that the first horses appeared on Earth about sixty million years ago as compared with two million years ago for the appearance of human beings. There is evidence of early horses on both the American and European continents, but it has been documented that, almost twelve million years ago at the beginning of the Pliocene Age, a horse about midway through its evolutionary development crossed a land bridge where the Bering Strait is now located, from Alaska into the grasslands of Asia, and traveled all the way to Europe. This early horse was a hipparion, about the size of a modern-day pony with three toes and specialized cheek teeth for grazing. In Europe, the hipparion encountered another less advanced horse called the anchitheres, which had previously invaded Europe by the same route, probably during the Miocene Period. Less developed and smaller than the hipparion, the anchitheres was eventually completely replaced by it.

By the end of the Pleistocene Age both the anchitheres and the hipparion had become extinct in North America, where they had originated, as fossil evidence clearly indicates. In Europe, they evolved into the larger and stronger animal that is very similar to the horse as we know it today. For many years, the horse was probably hunted for food by early tribes of human beings. Then the qualities of the horse that would have made it a good servant were noted—mainly its strength and speed. It was time for the horse to be tamed, used as a draft animal at the dawning of agriculture, and then ridden as the need for transportation increased. It was the descendant of this domesticated horse that was brought back to the Americas by European colonists.

35. What is this passage mainly about?

(A) The evolution of the horse
(B) The migration of horses
(C) The modern-day pony
(D) The replacement of the anchitheres by the hipparion

36. According to the author, fossils are considered valuable for all of the following reasons EXCEPT

(A) they suggest how the climate may have been
(B) they provide information about migration
(C) they document the evolution of the horse
(D) they maintain a record of life prior to the Miocene Age

37. The word **instigated** in paragraph 1 could best be replaced by

(A) explained
(B) caused
(C) improved
(D) influenced

Beginning

The development of the horse has been recorded from the beginning through all of its evolutionary stages to the modern form. It is, in fact, one of the most complete and well-documented chapters of paleontological history. Fossil finds provide us not only with detailed information about the horse itself but also with valuable insights into the migration of herds, and even evidence for speculation about the climatic conditions that could have **instigated** such migratory behavior.

Geologists believe that the first horses appeared on Earth about sixty million years ago as compared with two million years ago for the appearance of human beings. There is evidence of early horses on both the American and European continents, but it has been documented that, almost twelve million years ago at the beginning of the Pliocene Age, a horse about midway through its evolutionary development crossed a land bridge where the Bering Strait is now located, from Alaska into the grasslands of Asia, and traveled all the way to Europe. This early horse was a hipparion, about the size of a modern-day pony with three toes and specialized

38. What does the author mean by the statement Geologists believe that the first horses appeared on Earth about sixty million years ago as compared with two million years ago for the appearance of human beings?

Ⓐ Horses appeared long before human beings according to the theories of geologists.
Ⓑ Both horses and human beings appeared several million years ago, if we believe geologists.
Ⓒ The geological records for the appearance of horses and human beings are not very accurate.
Ⓓ Horses and human beings cannot be compared by geologists because they appeared too long ago.

Beginning

The development of the horse has been recorded from the beginning through all of its evolutionary stages to the modern form. It is, in fact, one of the most complete and well-documented chapters of paleontological history. Fossil finds provide us not only with detailed information about the horse itself but also with valuable insights into the migration of herds, and even evidence for speculation about the climatic conditions that could have instigated such migratory behavior.

Geologists believe that the first horses appeared on Earth about sixty million years ago as compared with two million years ago for the appearance of human beings. There is evidence of early horses on both the American and European continents, but it has been documented that, almost twelve million years ago at the beginning of the Pliocene Age, a horse about midway through its evolutionary development crossed a land bridge where the Bering Strait is now located, from Alaska into the grasslands of Asia, and traveled all the way to Europe. This early horse was a hipparion, about the size of a modern-day pony with three toes and specialized

39. Which of the following conclusions may be made on the basis of information in the passage?

Ⓐ The hipparions migrated to Europe to feed in developing grasslands.
Ⓑ There are no fossil remains of either the anchitheres or the hipparion.
Ⓒ There were horses in North America when the first European colonists arrived.
Ⓓ Very little is known about the evolution of the horse.

40. According to this passage, the hipparions were

Ⓐ five-toed animals
Ⓑ not as highly developed as the anchitheres
Ⓒ larger than the anchitheres
Ⓓ about the size of a small dog

41. The word it in paragraph 2 refers to

Ⓐ anchitheres
Ⓑ hipparion
Ⓒ Miocene Period
Ⓓ route

More Available

appearance of human beings. There is evidence of early horses on both the American and European continents, but it has been documented that, almost twelve million years ago at the beginning of the Pliocene Age, a horse about midway through its evolutionary development crossed a land bridge where the Bering Strait is now located, from Alaska into the grasslands of Asia, and traveled all the way to Europe. This early horse was a hipparion, about the size of a modern-day pony with three toes and specialized cheek teeth for grazing. In Europe, the hipparion encountered another less advanced horse called the anchitheres, which had previously invaded Europe by the same route, probably during the Miocene Period. Less developed and smaller than the hipparion, the anchitheres was eventually completely replaced by it.

By the end of the Pleistocene Age both the anchitheres and the hipparion had become extinct in North America, where they had originated, as fossil evidence clearly indicates. In Europe, they evolved into the larger and stronger animal that is very similar to the horse as we know it today. For

42. The word extinct in paragraph 3 is closest in meaning to

Ⓐ familiar
Ⓑ widespread
Ⓒ nonexistent
Ⓓ tame

End

cheek teeth for grazing. In Europe, the hipparion encountered another less advanced horse called the anchitheres, which had previously invaded Europe by the same route, probably during the Miocene Period. Less developed and smaller than the hipparion, the anchitheres was eventually completely replaced by it.

By the end of the Pleistocene Age both the anchitheres and the hipparion had become extinct in North America, where they had originated, as fossil evidence clearly indicates. In Europe, they evolved into the larger and stronger animal that is very similar to the horse as we know it today. For many years, the horse was probably hunted for food by early tribes of human beings. Then the qualities of the horse that would have made it a good servant were noted—mainly its strength and speed. It was time for the horse to be tamed, used as a draft animal at the dawning of agriculture, and then ridden as the need for transportation increased. It was the descendant of this domesticated horse that was brought back to the Americas by European colonists.

43. Click on the paragraph that refers to the potential for conclusions from the evidence supplied by fossil remains.

Scroll the passage to see all of the paragraphs.

44. Look at the word domesticated in the passage. Click on the word or phrase in the **bold** text that is closest in meaning to domesticated.

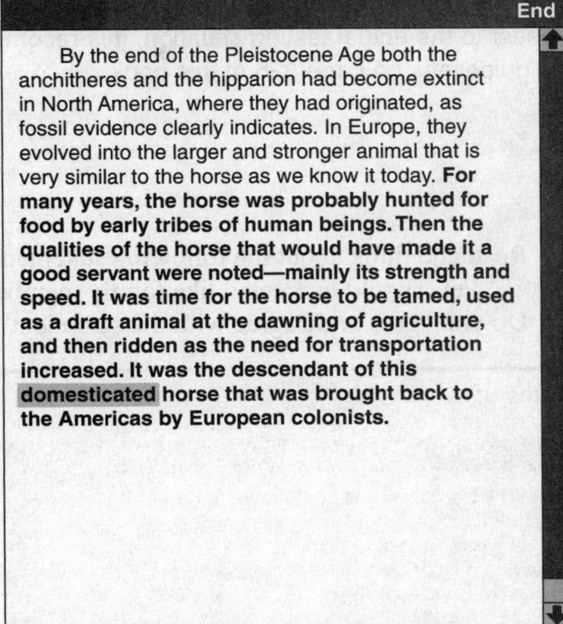
End

By the end of the Pleistocene Age both the anchitheres and the hipparion had become extinct in North America, where they had originated, as fossil evidence clearly indicates. In Europe, they evolved into the larger and stronger animal that is very similar to the horse as we know it today. **For many years, the horse was probably hunted for food by early tribes of human beings. Then the qualities of the horse that would have made it a good servant were noted—mainly its strength and speed. It was time for the horse to be tamed, used as a draft animal at the dawning of agriculture, and then ridden as the need for transportation increased. It was the descendant of this domesticated horse that was brought back to the Americas by European colonists.**

45. It can be concluded from this passage that the

Ⓐ Miocene Period was prior to the Pliocene
Ⓑ Pleistocene Period was prior to the Miocene
Ⓒ Pleistocene Period was prior to the Pliocene
Ⓓ Pliocene Period was prior to the Miocene

To check your answers for Model Test 2, refer to the Answer Key on page 545–546. For an explanation of the answers, refer to the Explanatory Answers for Model Test 2 on pages 561–568.

Writing Section Model Test 2

When you take a Model Test, you should use one sheet of paper, both sides. Time each Model Test carefully. After you have read the topic, you should spend 30 minutes writing. For results that would be closest to the actual testing situation, it is recommended that an English teacher score your test, using the guidelines on page 325 of this book.

Read and think about the following statement:

Pets should be treated like family members.

Do you agree or disagree with the statement? Give reasons to support your opinion.

Notes

Model Test 3
Computer-Assisted TOEFL

Section 1: Listening

The Listening section of the test measures the ability to understand conversations and talks in English. You will use headphones to listen to the conversations and talks. While you are listening, pictures of the speakers or other information will be presented on your computer screen. There are two parts to the Listening section, with special directions for each part.

On the day of the test, the amount of time you will have to answer all of the questions will appear on the computer screen. The time you spend listening to the test material will not be counted. The listening material and questions about it will be presented only one time. You will not be allowed to take notes or have any paper at your computer. You will both see and hear the questions before the answer choices appear. You can take as much time as you need to select an answer; however, it will be to your advantage to answer the questions as quickly as possible. You may change your answer as many times as you want before you confirm it. After you have confirmed an answer, you will not be able to return to the question.

Before you begin working on the Listening section, you will have an opportunity to adjust the volume of the sound. You will not be able to change the volume after you have started the test.

QUESTION DIRECTIONS — Part A

In Part A of the Listening section, you will hear short conversations between two people. In some of the conversations, each person speaks only once. In other conversations, one or both of the people speak more than once. Each conversation is followed by one question about it.

Each question in this part has four answer choices. You should click on the best answer to each question. Answer the questions on the basis of what is stated or implied by the speakers.

1. What does the woman mean?
   - (A) She will not go home for spring vacation.
   - (B) She has not taken a vacation for a long time.
   - (C) She does not plan to graduate.
   - (D) She does not want to go home after graduation in May.

2. What are the speakers talking about?
   - (A) The class.
   - (B) The weekend.
   - (C) Homework.
   - (D) Books.

3. What does the man mean?
   - (A) He should have prepared more.
   - (B) He is very worried.
   - (C) He has been studying a lot.
   - (D) He needs a few more days.

4. What will the man probably do?
   - (A) Buy a textbook.
   - (B) Come back later.
   - (C) Go to the bookstore.
   - (D) Drop his English class.

5. What does the woman mean?
   - (A) She does not like the class.
   - (B) Her classmates are really great.
   - (C) The professor is not very nice.
   - (D) The class is interesting.

6. What will the woman probably do?

Ⓐ Make an appointment with Dr. Peterson's T.A.
Ⓑ Cancel her appointment with the T.A.
Ⓒ Postpone her appointment with Dr. Peterson's T.A.
Ⓓ See the T.A. more often.

7. What does the man mean?

Ⓐ He would rather have American food.
Ⓑ He has always liked American food.
Ⓒ He is accustomed to eating American food.
Ⓓ He ate American food more in the past.

8. What does the man mean?

Ⓐ He should go to bed.
Ⓑ He did not know the time.
Ⓒ He is trying to bring his work up to date.
Ⓓ He is not sleepy yet.

9. What is the woman going to do?

Ⓐ Spend some time with the man.
Ⓑ Make a list of the names.
Ⓒ Pass out the names.
Ⓓ Let someone else call the names.

10. What does the man mean?

Ⓐ The woman has missed the deadline.
Ⓑ He will investigate the situation.
Ⓒ The deadline has been canceled.
Ⓓ An exception might be possible.

11. What does the man mean?

Ⓐ The book is confusing.
Ⓑ He is doing well in the class.
Ⓒ The teacher is not very clear.
Ⓓ The lectures are from the book.

12. What does the woman mean?

Ⓐ She wants to submit her paper early.
Ⓑ The answers on the paper are all correct.
Ⓒ The deadline has passed for the paper.
Ⓓ The paper is not quite finished.

13. What does the woman say about the class?

Ⓐ She does not like the class.
Ⓑ It is not a required class.
Ⓒ She has already taken the class.
Ⓓ The man will have to take the class.

14. What did the T.A. suggest the students do?

Ⓐ Study together.
Ⓑ Prepare for an oral final.
Ⓒ Review the quizzes.
Ⓓ Take the professor's advice.

15. What is the woman going to do?

Ⓐ Make an appointment.
Ⓑ Give the man a pen.
Ⓒ Sign the form for the man.
Ⓓ Wait for the man.

16. What is the woman going to do?

Ⓐ Revise her work.
Ⓑ Close the window.
Ⓒ Copy from the man.
Ⓓ Hand in the work.

17. What had the man assumed about the loan payment?

Ⓐ The computer made an error.
Ⓑ The payment is due on the fifth of every month.
Ⓒ The loan must be paid by the first of the month.
Ⓓ The loan had already been paid in full.

QUESTION DIRECTIONS — Part B

In Part B of the Listening section, you will hear several longer conversations and talks. Each conversation or talk is followed by several questions. The conversations, talks, and questions will not be repeated.

The conversations and talks are about a variety of topics. You do not need special knowledge of the topics to answer the questions correctly. Rather, you should answer each question on the basis of what is stated or implied by the speakers in the conversations or talks.

For most of the questions, you will need to click on the best of four possible answers. Some questions will have special directions. The special directions will appear in a box on the computer screen.

18. Why did Betty call Professor Hayes?

Ⓐ To enroll in a class.
Ⓑ To ask his opinion about a university.
Ⓒ To find out who is chair of the selection committee.
Ⓓ To get a letter for graduate school.

19. What does Professor Hayes think about Betty?

Ⓐ She might need to take his seminar.
Ⓑ She should do well in graduate school.
Ⓒ She had better go to another university.
Ⓓ She needs to apply before the end of April.

20. Who will decide whether Betty is accepted to the program?

Ⓐ The chair of the selection committee.
Ⓑ The entire selection committee.
Ⓒ Professor Hayes.
Ⓓ Dr. Warren.

21. When does Betty need to submit all her materials?

Ⓐ On May 1.
Ⓑ In three days.
Ⓒ Before the April 30th deadline.
Ⓓ Today.

22. Who is the speaker?

Ⓐ A professor of religion.
Ⓑ A professor of history.
Ⓒ A guest lecturer in a drama class.
Ⓓ A guest lecturer in a writing class.

23. According to the speaker, how did England control trade in the eighteenth century?

Ⓐ By threatening to go to war.
Ⓑ By competing with farmers.
Ⓒ By keeping manufacturing processes secret.
Ⓓ By stealing plans from the colonies.

24. What did Samuel Slater do?

Ⓐ He kept designs for English machinery from being used in the colonies.
Ⓑ He prevented Moses Brown from opening a mill.
Ⓒ He committed designs for English machinery to memory.
Ⓓ He smuggled drawings for English machines into the United States.

25. What happened as a result of the Slater-Brown partnership?

Ⓐ A change from agriculture to industry began to occur in the United States.
Ⓑ A rise in prices for English goods was evidenced.
Ⓒ Many small farmers began to send their products to England.
Ⓓ Americans had to keep their manufacturing processes secret.

26. What is the purpose of this conversation?

Ⓐ The man wants to reserve textbooks for the following semester.
Ⓑ The man is complaining about not having his books this semester.
Ⓒ The woman needs to order enough books for the class.
Ⓓ The woman is helping the man register for his courses.

27. What was the man's problem last semester?

Ⓐ The book store was closed for three weeks.
Ⓑ His books did not arrive before the semester began.
Ⓒ He did not have any books this semester.
Ⓓ He did not understand how to order his books.

28. How can the man order books?

Ⓐ The teacher will order books for the class.
Ⓑ He could fill out a form and pay for the books now.
Ⓒ He must wait until the semester begins.
Ⓓ He has to register for the classes, and the books will be ordered for him.

29. How will the man know that the books have arrived?

Ⓐ He will receive a form in the mail.
Ⓑ He will get a phone call.
Ⓒ He will stop by the bookstore at the beginning of the semester.
Ⓓ He will receive the books from his teacher in class.

30. What is the instructor defining?

Ⓐ The term "essay."
Ⓑ Prose writing.
Ⓒ Personal viewpoint.
Ⓓ Brainstorming.

31. What is the main point of the talk?

Ⓐ The work of Alexander Pope.
Ⓑ The difference between prose and poetry.
Ⓒ The general characteristics of essays.
Ⓓ The reason that the phrase "personal essay" is redundant.

32. According to the talk, which of the characteristics are NOT true of an essay?

Ⓐ It is usually short.
Ⓑ It can be either prose or poetry.
Ⓒ It expresses a personal point of view.
Ⓓ It discusses one topic.

33. What will the students probably do as an assignment?

Ⓐ They will prepare for a quiz.
Ⓑ They will write their first essay.
Ⓒ They will read works by Pope.
Ⓓ They will review their notes.

34. What is the main purpose of this talk?

Ⓐ To provide an overview of U.S. history from 1743 to 1826.
Ⓑ To discuss Jefferson's contribution to the American Revolution.
Ⓒ To analyze Jefferson's presidency.
Ⓓ To summarize Jefferson's life.

35. Jefferson was a member of which political group?

Ⓐ Monarchist.
Ⓑ Federalist.
Ⓒ Republican.
Ⓓ Democrat.

36 How did Jefferson become president?

Ⓐ He received the most votes.
Ⓑ Congress approved him.
Ⓒ Aaron Burr withdrew from the race.
Ⓓ As vice president, he automatically became president.

37. According to the lecturer, what was it that Jefferson was NOT?

Ⓐ An effective public speaker.
Ⓑ An architect.
Ⓒ A literary draftsman.
Ⓓ A diplomat.

38. What are the two most common places where fossils may be found?

Click on 2 answers.

[A] Ice.
[B] Mud.
[C] Sand.
[D] Water.

39. The professor briefly explains a process. Summarize the process by putting the events in order.

Click on a sentence. Then click on the space where it belongs. Use each sentence only once.

[A] A mold of the organism preserves the shape of the organism.
[B] Water soaks into the organism.
[C] Organisms are buried in mud or sand.
[D] Minerals in the water dissolve the original organism.

1 [ ]
2 [ ]
3 [ ]
4 [ ]

40. What is lost in the process of replacement?

Ⓐ The fine shapes of fragile structures.
Ⓑ The internal features of the plant or animal.
Ⓒ The minerals in the deposit.
Ⓓ The original fossil mold.

41. Why are the layers of sedimentary rock important to the fossil record?

Ⓐ The ages of the fossils may be determined by their location in the layers of rock.
Ⓑ The shapes of the fossils may be preserved in the layers of rock.
Ⓒ The rock protects the fossils from the mineral water that dissolves them.
Ⓓ Plants and animals that are formed at the same time are buried in different layers of rock.

42. Why didn't the man apply for graduation?

Ⓐ He wasn't sure that he had completed the requirements.
Ⓑ He did not have enough credit hours.
Ⓒ He did not have a program of study.
Ⓓ He did not understand that it was necessary.

43. How did the man select his courses?

Ⓐ By reading the catalog.
Ⓑ By consulting with the woman.
Ⓒ By referring to his signed program of study.
Ⓓ By making an appointment with his advisor.

44. What does the woman suggest?

Ⓐ The man should take the required courses for graduation.
Ⓑ The man should see an academic advisor to help him.
Ⓒ The man should read the requirements in the college catalog.
Ⓓ The man should bring her a copy of his transcript.

45. What is the man's problem?

Ⓐ He may not have enough credit hours to graduate.
Ⓑ He may not have taken the correct classes to graduate.
Ⓒ He may not be able to see an academic advisor before graduation.
Ⓓ He may not have time to take the rest of the required courses.

46. In which class would this discussion probably take place?

Ⓐ Sociology.
Ⓑ Education.
Ⓒ Linguistics.
Ⓓ Geography.

47. According to the discussion, what is the definition of a standard dialect?

Ⓐ The dialect that is selected by the government.
Ⓑ The dialect that is of a higher value than the others.
Ⓒ The dialect that is able to express everything necessary.
Ⓓ The dialect that is the model taught in schools.

48. What is the linguistic perspective put forward in the articles that were assigned?

Ⓐ Some accents are not permitted in schools.
Ⓑ There is only one standard accent in the United States.
Ⓒ There is one major dialect in the United States.
Ⓓ All dialects are of equal value.

49. Which two linguistic components are included in a dialect?

Click on 2 answers.

[A] Grammar.
[B] Pronunciation.
[C] Vocabulary.
[D] Spelling.

50. What do sociologists tell us about accents?

Ⓐ Some accents are more prestigious because they are spoken by the upper classes.
Ⓑ Because they are more comprehensible, some accents are inherently better than others.
Ⓒ One of the purposes of schools is to teach the accents that are considered most important.
Ⓓ In general, accents are not as important as dialects because there is no standard for them.

Section 2: Structure

This section measures the ability to recognize language that is appropriate for standard written English. There are two types of questions in this section.

In the first type of question, there are incomplete sentences. Beneath each sentence, there are four words or phrases. You will choose the one word or phrase that best completes the sentence.

Clicking on a choice darkens the oval. After you click on **Next** and **Confirm Answer**, the next question will be presented.

The second type of question has four underlined words or phrases. You will choose the one underlined word or phrase that must be changed for the sentence to be correct.

Clicking on an underlined word or phrase will darken it. After you click on **Next** and **Confirm Answer**, the next question will be presented.

1. In simple animals, --------- reflex movement or involuntary response to stimuli.

   (A) behavior mostly
   (B) most is behavior
   (C) most behavior is
   (D) the most behavior

2. Although the weather in Martha's Vineyard isn't ----------- to have a year-round tourist season, it has become a favorite summer resort.

   (A) goodly enough
   (B) good enough
   (C) good as enough
   (D) enough good

3. A swarm of locusts is responsible (A) the consumption of enough plant material (B) to feed (C) a million and a half (D) people.

4. Oyster farming (A) has been practice (B) in most (C) parts of the world for (D) many years.

5. It (A) was Shirley Temple Black which (B) represented (C) her country in the United Nations and later (D) became an ambassador.

6. According to the wave theory, --------- population of the Americas may have been the result of a number of separate migrations.

   (A) the
   (B) their
   (C) that
   (D) whose

7. It is presumed that rules governing the sharing of food influenced ----------- that the earliest cultures evolved.

   (A) that the way
   (B) is the way
   (C) the way
   (D) which way

8. The prices at (A) chain stores are (B) as reasonable, if not more (C) reasonable, as (D) those at discount stores.

9. Historically (A) there (B) has been (C) only (D) two major factions in the Republican Party—the liberals and the conservatives.

10. Whitman wrote *Leaves of Grass* as a tribute to the Civil War soldiers who had laid (A) on the battlefields and whom (B) he had seen (C) while serving (D) as an army nurse.

11. Calculus, ----------- elegant and economical symbolic system, can reduce complex problems to simple terms.

(A) it is an
(B) that an
(C) an
(D) is an

12. Canada does not require that U.S. citizens obtain passports to enter the country, and ----------- .

(A) Mexico does neither
(B) Mexico doesn't either
(C) neither Mexico does
(D) either does Mexico

13. The Chinese (A) were the first and large (B) ethnic group to work (C) on the construction of (D) the transcontinental railroad system.

14. The range of plant life on a mountainside is (A) a results (B) of differences (C) in temperature and precipitation at varying (D) altitudes.

15. The poet ----------- just beginning to be recognized as an important influence at the time of his death.

(A) being Walt Whitman
(B) who was Walt Whitman
(C) Walt Whitman
(D) Walt Whitman was

16. ----------- the formation of the sun, the planets, and other stars began with the condensation of an interstellar cloud.

(A) It accepted that
(B) Accepted that
(C) It is accepted that
(D) That is accepted

17. The more the relative humidity reading rises, (A) the worst (B) the heat affects (C) us. (D)

18. Because correlations are not causes, (A) statistical data which are (B) extremely easy (C) to misuse. (D)

19. As a general rule, the standard of living ----------- by the average output of each person in society.

(A) is fixed
(B) fixed
(C) has fixed
(D) fixes

20. Despite of (A) many (B) attempts to introduce (C) a universal language, notably Esperanto and Idiom Neutral, the effort has met with very little (D) success.

21. The *Consumer Price Index* lists ------- .

(A) how much costs every car
(B) how much does every car cost
(C) how much every car costs
(D) how much are every car cost

22. As (A) every other (B) nation, the United States used to define (C) its (D) unit of currency, the dollar, in terms of the gold standard.

23. The Ford Theater where Lincoln was shot ----------- .

(A) must restore
(B) must be restoring
(C) must have been restored
(D) must restored

24. John Dewey thought that children <u>will learn</u> (A) <u>better</u> (B) through participating in experiences <u>rather than</u> (C) through <u>listening to</u> (D) lectures.

25. <u>Some</u> (A) methods <u>to prevent</u> (B) soil erosion <u>are</u> (C) plowing parallel with the slopes of hills, <u>to plant</u> (D) trees on unproductive land, and rotating crops.

Section 3: Reading

This section measures the ability to read and understand short passages similar in topic and style to those that students are likely to encounter in North American universities and colleges. This section contains reading passages and questions about the passages. There are several different types of questions in this section.

In the Reading section, you will first have the opportunity to read the passage.

You will use the scroll bar to view the rest of the passage.

When you have finished reading the passage, you will use the mouse to click on **Proceed**. Then the questions about the passage will be presented. You are to choose the one best answer to each question. Answer all questions about the information in a passage on the basis of what is stated or implied in that passage.

Most of the questions will be multiple-choice questions. To answer these questions you will click on a choice below the question.

To answer some questions, you will click on a word or phrase.

To answer some questions, you will click on a sentence in the passage.

To answer some questions, you will click on a square to add a sentence to the passage.

Few men have influenced the development of American English to the extent that Noah Webster did. Born in West Hartford, Connecticut, in 1758, Webster graduated from Yale in 1778. He was admitted to the bar in 1781 and thereafter began to practice law in Hartford. Later, when he turned to teaching, he discovered how inadequate the available schoolbooks were for the children of a new and independent nation. In response to the need for truly American textbooks, Webster published *A Grammatical Institute of the English Language,* a three-volume work that consisted of a speller, a grammar, and a reader. The first volume, which was generally known as *The American Spelling Book,* was so popular that eventually it sold more than 80 million copies and provided him with a considerable income for the rest of his life. While teaching, Webster began work on the *Compendious Dictionary of the English Language,* which was published in 1806, and was also very successful.

In 1807, Noah Webster began his greatest work, *An American Dictionary of the English Language.* In preparing the manuscript, he devoted ten years to the study of English and its relationship to other languages, and seven more years to the writing itself. Published in two volumes in 1828, *An American Dictionary of the English Language* has become the recognized authority for usage in the United States. Webster's purpose in writing it was to demonstrate that the American language was developing distinct meanings, pronunciations, and spellings from those of British English. He is responsible for advancing simplified spelling forms: *develop* instead of *develope; plow* instead of *plough; jail* instead of *gaol; theater* and *center* instead of *theatre* and *centre; color* and *honor* instead of *colour* and *honour.*

Webster was the first author to gain copyright protection in the United States by being awarded a copyright for his *American Speller.* He continued, for the next fifty years, to lobby for improvements in the protection of intellectual properties, that is, authors' rights. In 1840 Webster brought out a second edition of his dictionary, which included 70,000 entries instead of the original 38,000. The name Webster has become synonymous with American dictionaries. This edition served as the basis for the many revisions that have been produced by others, ironically, under the uncopyrighted Webster name.

1. Which of the following would be the best title for the passage?

Ⓐ Webster's Work
Ⓑ Webster's Dictionaries
Ⓒ Webster's School
Ⓓ Webster's Life

2. The word inadequate in paragraph 1 could best be replaced by

Ⓐ unavailable
Ⓑ expensive
Ⓒ difficult
Ⓓ unsatisfactory

Beginning

Few men have influenced the development of American English to the extent that Noah Webster did. Born in West Hartford, Connecticut, in 1758, Webster graduated from Yale in 1778. He was admitted to the bar in 1781 and thereafter began to practice law in Hartford. Later, when he turned to teaching, he discovered how inadequate the available schoolbooks were for the children of a new and independent nation. In response to the need for truly American textbooks, Webster published *A Grammatical Institute of the English Language,* a three-volume work that consisted of a speller, a grammar, and a reader. The first volume, which was generally know as *The American Spelling Book,* was so popular that eventually it sold more than 80 million copies and provided him with a considerable income for the rest of his life. While teaching, Webster began work on the *Compendious Dictionary of the English Language,* which was published in 1806, and was also very successful.

In 1807, Noah Webster began his greatest work, *An American Dictionary of the English Language.* In preparing the manuscript, he devoted

3. Why did Webster write *A Grammatical Institute of the English Language*?

Ⓐ He wanted to supplement his income.
Ⓑ There were no books available after the Revolutionary War.
Ⓒ He felt that British books were not appropriate for American children.
Ⓓ The children did not know how to spell.

4. From which publication did Webster earn a lifetime income?

Ⓐ *Compendious Dictionary of the English Language*
Ⓑ *An American Dictionary of the English Language*
Ⓒ *An American Dictionary of the English Language: Second Edition*
Ⓓ *The American Spelling Book*

5. Look at the word popular in the passage. Click on the word or phrase in the **bold** text that is closest in meaning to popular.

Beginning

Few men have influenced the development of American English to the extent that Noah Webster did. Born in West Hartford, Connecticut, in 1758, Webster graduated from Yale in 1778. He was admitted to the bar in 1781 and thereafter began to practice law in Hartford. Later, when he turned to teaching, he discovered how inadequate the available schoolbooks were for the children of a new and independent nation. **In response to the need for truly American textbooks, Webster published *A Grammatical Institute of the English Language,* a three-volume work that consisted of a speller, a grammar, and a reader. The first volume, which was generally know as *The American Spelling Book*, was so popular that eventually it sold more than 80 million copies and provided him with a considerable income for the rest of his life. While teaching, Webster began work on the *Compendious Dictionary of the English Language,* which was published in 1806, and was also very successful.**

In 1807, Noah Webster began his greatest work, *An American Dictionary of the English Language*. In preparing the manuscript, he devoted

6. The word considerable in paragraph 1 most nearly means

Ⓐ large
Ⓑ prestigious
Ⓒ steady
Ⓓ unexpected

Beginning

Few men have influenced the development of American English to the extent that Noah Webster did. Born in West Hartford, Connecticut, in 1758, Webster graduated from Yale in 1778. He was admitted to the bar in 1781 and thereafter began to practice law in Hartford. Later, when he turned to teaching, he discovered how inadequate the available schoolbooks were for the children of a new and independent nation. In response to the need for truly American textbooks, Webster published *A Grammatical Institute of the English Language,* a three-volume work that consisted of a speller, a grammar, and a reader. The first volume, which was generally know as *The American Spelling Book*, was so popular that eventually it sold more than 80 million copies and provided him with a considerable income for the rest of his life. While teaching, Webster began work on the *Compendious Dictionary of the English Language*, which was published in 1806, and was also very successful.

In 1807, Noah Webster began his greatest work, *An American Dictionary of the English Language.* In preparing the manuscript, he devoted

7. When was *An American Dictionary of the English Language* published?

Ⓐ 1817
Ⓑ 1807
Ⓒ 1828
Ⓓ 1824

8. The word **it** in paragraph 2 refers to

Ⓐ language
Ⓑ usage
Ⓒ authority
Ⓓ dictionary

More Available

American Spelling Book, was so popular that eventually it sold more than 80 million copies and provided him with a considerable income for the rest of his life. While teaching, Webster began work on the *Compendious Dictionary of the English Language,* which was published in 1806, and was also very successful.

In 1807, Noah Webster began his greatest work, *An American Dictionary of the English Language.* In preparing the manuscript, he devoted ten years to the study of English and its relationship to other languages, and seven more years to the writing itself. Published in two volumes in 1828, *An American Dictionary of the English Language* has become the recognized authority for usage in the United States. Webster's purpose in writing **it** was to demonstrate that the American language was developing distinct meanings, pronunciations, and spellings from those of British English. He is responsible for advancing simplified spelling forms: *develop* instead of *develope; plow* instead of *plough; jail* instead of *gaol; theater* and *center* instead of *theatre* and *centre; color* and *honor* instead of *colour* and *honour.*

9. Click on the sentence in paragraph 2 that explains Webster's purpose for writing an American dictionary.

Paragraph 2 is marked with an arrow (→).

More Available

American Spelling Book, was so popular that eventually it sold more than 80 million copies and provided him with a considerable income for the rest of his life. While teaching, Webster began work on the *Compendious Dictionary of the English Language,* which was published in 1806, and was also very successful.

→ In 1807, Noah Webster began his greatest work, *An American Dictionary of the English Language.* In preparing the manuscript, he devoted ten years to the study of English and its relationship to other languages, and seven more years to the writing itself. Published in two volumes in 1828, *An American Dictionary of the English Language* has become the recognized authority for usage in the United States. Webster's purpose in writing it was to demonstrate that the American language was developing distinct meanings, pronunciations, and spellings from those of British English. He is responsible for advancing simplified spelling forms: *develop* instead of *develope; plow* instead of *plough; jail* instead of *gaol; theater* and *center* instead of *theatre* and *centre; color* and *honor* instead of *colour* and *honour.*

10. The word distinct in paragraph 2 is closest in meaning to

Ⓐ new
Ⓑ simple
Ⓒ different
Ⓓ exact

More Available

American Spelling Book, was so popular that eventually it sold more than 80 million copies and provided him with a considerable income for the rest of his life. While teaching, Webster began work on the *Compendious Dictionary of the English Language,* which was published in 1806, and was also very successful.

In 1807, Noah Webster began his greatest work, *An American Dictionary of the English Language.* In preparing the manuscript, he devoted ten years to the study of English and its relationship to other languages, and seven more years to the writing itself. Published in two volumes in 1828, *An American Dictionary of the English Language* has become the recognized authority for usage in the United States. Webster's purpose in writing it was to demonstrate that the American language was developing distinct meanings, pronunciations, and spellings from those of British English. He is responsible for advancing simplified spelling forms: *develop* instead of *develope; plow* instead of *plough; jail* instead of *gaol; theater* and *center* instead of *theatre* and *centre; color* and *honor* instead of *colour* and *honour.*

11. According to this passage, which one of the following spellings would Webster have approved in his dictionaries?

Ⓐ *Develope*
Ⓑ *Theatre*
Ⓒ *Color*
Ⓓ *Honour*

The San Andreas Fault line is a fracture at the congruence of two major plates of the Earth's crust, one of which supports most of the North American continent, and the other of which underlies the coast of California and part of the ocean floor of the Pacific Ocean. The fault originates about six hundred miles south of the Gulf of California, runs north in an irregular line along the western coast to San Francisco, and continues north for about two hundred more miles before angling off into the ocean. In places, the trace of the fault is marked by a trench, or, in geological terms, a rift, and small ponds called sag ponds dot the landscape. Its western side always moves north in relation to its eastern side. The total net slip along the San Andreas Fault and the length of time it has been active are matters of conjecture, but it has been estimated that, during the past fifteen million years, coastal California along the San Andreas Fault has moved about 190 miles in a northwesterly direction with respect to the North American plate. Although the movement along the fault averages only a few inches a year, it is intermittent and variable. Some segments of the fault do not move at all for long periods of time, building up tremendous pressure that must be released. For this reason, tremors are not unusual along the San Andreas Fault, some of which are classified as major earthquakes. Also for this reason, small tremors are interpreted as safe, since they are understood to be pressure that releases without causing much damage.

It is worth noting that the San Andreas Fault passes uncomfortably close to several major metropolitan areas, including Los Angeles and San Francisco. In addition, the San Andreas Fault has created smaller fault systems, many of which underlie the smaller towns and cities along the California coast. For this reason, Californians have long anticipated the recurrence of what they refer to as the "Big One," a chain reaction of destructive earthquakes that would measure near 8 on the Richter scale, similar in intensity to those that occurred in 1857 and 1906. Such a quake would wreak devastating effects on the life and property in the region. Unfortunately, as pressure continues to build along the fault, the likelihood of such an earthquake increases substantially.

12. What is the author's main purpose in the passage?

Ⓐ To describe the San Andreas Fault
Ⓑ To give a definition of a fault
Ⓒ To explain the reason for tremors and earthquakes
Ⓓ To classify different kinds of faults

13. How does the author define the San Andreas Fault?

Ⓐ A plate that underlies the North American continent
Ⓑ A crack in the Earth's crust between two plates
Ⓒ Occasional tremors and earthquakes
Ⓓ Intense pressure that builds up

14. The word **originates** in paragraph 1 could best be replaced by

Ⓐ gets wider
Ⓑ changes direction
Ⓒ begins
Ⓓ disappears

Beginning

The San Andreas Fault line is a fracture at the congruence of two major plates of the Earth's crust, one of which supports most of the North American continent, and the other of which underlies the coast of California and part of the ocean floor of the Pacific Ocean. The fault **originates** about six hundred miles south of the Gulf of California, runs north in an irregular line along the western coast to San Francisco, and continues north for about two hundred more miles before angling off into the ocean. In places, the trace of the fault is marked by a trench, or, in geological terms, a rift, and small ponds called sag ponds dot the landscape. Its western side always moves north in relation to its eastern side. The total net slip along the San Andreas Fault and the length of time it has been active are matters of conjecture, but it has been estimated that, during the past fifteen million years, coastal California along the San Andreas Fault has moved about 190 miles in a northwesterly direction with respect to the North American plate. Although the movement along the fault averages only a few inches a year, it is intermittent and variable. Some

15. In which direction does the western side of the fault move?

Ⓐ West
Ⓑ East
Ⓒ North
Ⓓ South

16. The word **it** in paragraph 1 refers to

Ⓐ San Francisco
Ⓑ ocean
Ⓒ coast
Ⓓ fault

Beginning

The San Andreas Fault line is a fracture at the congruence of two major plates of the Earth's crust, one of which supports most of the North American continent, and the other of which underlies the coast of California and part of the ocean floor of the Pacific Ocean. The fault originates about six hundred miles south of the Gulf of California, runs north in an irregular line along the western coast to San Francisco, and continues north for about two hundred more miles before angling off into the ocean. In places, the trace of the fault is marked by a trench, or, in geological terms, a rift, and small ponds called sag ponds dot the landscape. Its western side always moves north in relation to its eastern side. The total net slip along the San Andreas Fault and the length of time **it** has been active are matters of conjecture, but it has been estimated that, during the past fifteen million years, coastal California along the San Andreas Fault has moved about 190 miles in a northwesterly direction with respect to the North American plate. Although the movement along the fault averages only a few inches a year, it is intermittent and variable. Some

17. The word intermittent in paragraph 1 could best be replaced by which of the following?

Ⓐ dangerous
Ⓑ predictable
Ⓒ uncommon
Ⓓ occasional

Beginning

The San Andreas Fault line is a fracture at the congruence of two major plates of the Earth's crust, one of which supports most of the North American continent, and the other of which underlies the coast of California and part of the ocean floor of the Pacific Ocean. The fault originates about six hundred miles south of the Gulf of California, runs north in an irregular line along the western coast to San Francisco, and continues north for about two hundred more miles before angling off into the ocean. In places, the trace of the fault is marked by a trench, or, in geological terms, a rift, and small ponds called sag ponds dot the landscape. Its western side always moves north in relation to its eastern side. The total net slip along the San Andreas Fault and the length of time it has been active are matters of conjecture, but it has been estimated that, during the past fifteen million years, coastal California along the San Andreas Fault has moved about 190 miles in a northwesterly direction with respect to the North American plate. Although the movement along the fault averages only a few inches a year, it is intermittent and variable. Some

18. Along the San Andreas Fault, tremors are

Ⓐ small and insignificant
Ⓑ rare, but disastrous
Ⓒ frequent events
Ⓓ very unpredictable

19. The phrase "the Big One" refers to which of the following?

Ⓐ A serious earthquake
Ⓑ The San Andreas Fault
Ⓒ The Richter scale
Ⓓ California

20. Look at the word destructive in the passage. Click on the word or phrase in the **bold** text that is closest in meaning to destructive.

End

It is worth noting that the San Andreas Fault passes uncomfortably close to several major metropolitan areas, including Los Angeles and San Francisco. In addition, the San Andreas Fault has created smaller fault systems, many of which underlie the smaller towns and cities along the California coast. **For this reason, Californians have long anticipated the recurrence of what they refer to as the "Big One," a chain reaction of destructive earthquakes that would measure near 8 on the Richter scale, similar in intensity to those that occurred in 1857 and 1906. Such a quake would wreak devastating effects on the life and property in the region. Unfortunately, as pressure continues to build along the fault, the likelihood of such an earthquake increases substantially.**

21. Look at the word those in the passage. Click on the word or phrase in the **bold** text that those refers to.

End

It is worth noting that the San Andreas Fault passes uncomfortably close to several major metropolitan areas, including Los Angeles and San Francisco. In addition, the San Andreas Fault has created smaller fault systems, many of which underlie the smaller towns and cities along the California coast. For this reason, Californians have long anticipated the recurrence of what they refer to as the "Big One," a chain reaction of destructive earthquakes that would measure near 8 on the Richter scale, similar in intensity to those that occurred in 1857 and 1906. Such a quake would wreak devastating effects on the life and property in the region. Unfortunately, as pressure continues to build along the fault, the likelihood of such an earthquake increases substantially.

22. Which of the following words best describes the San Andreas Fault?

Ⓐ Straight
Ⓑ Deep
Ⓒ Wide
Ⓓ Rough

The body of an adult insect is subdivided into three sections, including a head, a three-segment thorax, and segmented abdomen. Ordinarily, the thorax bears three pairs of legs and a single or double pair of wings. The vision of most adult insects is specialized through two large compound eyes and multiple simple eyes.

Features of an insect's mouth parts are used in classifying insects into types. Biting mouth parts, called mandibles, such as the mouth parts found in grasshoppers and beetles, are common among insects. Behind the mandibles are located the maxillae, or lower jaw parts, which serve to direct food into the mouth between the jaws. A labrum above and one below are similar to another animal's upper and lower lips. In an insect with a sucking mouth function, the mandibles, maxillae, labrum, and labium are modified in such a way that they constitute a tube through which liquid such as water, blood, or flower nectar can be drawn. In a butterfly or moth, this coiled drinking tube is called the proboscis because of its resemblance, in miniature, to the trunk of an elephant or a very large nose. Composed chiefly of modified maxillae fitted together, the insect's proboscis can be flexed and extended to reach nectar deep in a flower. In mosquitoes or aphids, mandibles and maxillae are modified to sharp stylets with which the insect can drill through surfaces like human or vegetable skin membranes to reach juice. In a housefly, the expanding labium forms a spongelike mouth pad that it can use to stamp over the surface of food, sopping up food particles and juices.

Insects, the most numerous creatures on our planet, are also the most adaptable. They require little food because they are small. They easily find shelter and protection in small crevices in trees and surface geological formations. Species of insects can evolve quickly because of their rapid reproduction cycle; they live in every climate, some making their homes in the frozen Arctic regions and many others choosing the humid, warm, and nutrient-rich rain forest environment. An active part of the natural food cycle, insects provide nutrition for animals and devour waste products of other life forms.

23. What is the best title for this passage?

Ⓐ An Insect's Environment
Ⓑ The Structure of an Insect
Ⓒ Grasshoppers and Beetles
Ⓓ The Stages of Life of an Insect

24. Look at the word subdivided in the passage. Click on the word or phrase in the **bold** text that is closest in meaning to subdivided.

Beginning

The body of an adult insect is subdivided into three sections, including a head, a three-segment thorax, and segmented abdomen. Ordinarily, the thorax bears three pairs of legs and a single or double pair of wings. The vision of most adult insects is specialized through two large compound eyes and multiple simple eyes.

Features of an insect's mouth parts are used in classifying insects into types. Biting mouth parts, called mandibles, such as the mouth parts found in grasshoppers and beetles, are common among insects. Behind the mandibles are located the maxillae, or lower jaw parts, which serve to direct food into the mouth between the jaws. A labrum above and one below are similar to another animal's upper and lower lips. In an insect with a sucking mouth function, the mandibles, maxillae, labrum, and labium are modified in such a way that they constitute a tube through which liquid such as water, blood, or flower nectar can be drawn. In a butterfly or moth, this coiled drinking tube is called the proboscis because of its resemblance, in miniature, to the trunk of an elephant or a very large nose. Composed chiefly

25. How are insects classified?

Ⓐ By the environment in which they live
Ⓑ By the food they eat
Ⓒ By the structure of the mouth
Ⓓ By the number and type of wings

26. The word 0.14"co in paragraph 2 is closest in meaning to

Ⓐ normal
Ⓑ rare
Ⓒ important
Ⓓ necessary

Beginning

The body of an adult insect is subdivided into three sections, including a head, a three-segment thorax, and segmented abdomen. Ordinarily, the thorax bears three pairs of legs and a single or double pair of wings. The vision of most adult insects is specialized through two large compound eyes and multiple simple eyes.

Features of an insect's mouth parts are used in classifying insects into types. Biting mouth parts, called mandibles, such as the mouth parts found in grasshoppers and beetles, are common among insects. Behind the mandibles are located the maxillae, or lower jaw parts, which serve to direct food into the mouth between the jaws. A labrum above and one below are similar to another animal's upper and lower lips. In an insect with a sucking mouth function, the mandibles, maxillae, labrum, and labium are modified in such a way that they constitute a tube through which liquid such as water, blood, or flower nectar can be drawn. In a butterfly or moth, this coiled drinking tube is called the proboscis because of its resemblance, in miniature, to the trunk of an elephant or a very large nose. Composed chiefly

27. The author compares labrum and labium to

Ⓐ an upper and lower lip
Ⓑ mandibles
Ⓒ maxillae
Ⓓ jaws

28. What is the proboscis?

Ⓐ Nectar
Ⓑ A tube constructed of modified maxillae
Ⓒ A kind of butterfly
Ⓓ A kind of flower

29. Which of the following have mandibles and maxillae that have been modified to sharp stylets?

Ⓐ Grasshoppers
Ⓑ Butterflies
Ⓒ Mosquitoes
Ⓓ Houseflies

30. The phrase drill through in paragraph 2 could best be replaced by

Ⓐ penetrate
Ⓑ saturate
Ⓒ explore
Ⓓ distinguish

More Available

the maxillae, or lower jaw parts, which serve to direct food into the mouth between the jaws. A labrum above and one below are similar to another animal's upper and lower lips. In an insect with a sucking mouth function, the mandibles, maxillae, labrum, and labium are modified in such a way that they constitute a tube through which liquid such as water, blood, or flower nectar can be drawn. In a butterfly or moth, this coiled drinking tube is called the proboscis because of its resemblance, in miniature, to the trunk of an elephant or a very large nose. Composed chiefly of modified maxillae fitted together, the insect's proboscis can be flexed and extended to reach nectar deep in a flower. In mosquitoes or aphids, mandibles and maxillae are modified to sharp stylets with which the insect can drill through surfaces like human or vegetable skin membranes to reach juice. In a housefly, the expanding labium forms a spongelike mouth pad that it can use to stamp over the surface of food, sopping up food particles and juices.

Insects, the most numerous creatures on our planet, are also the most adaptable. They require

31. The word it in paragraph 2 refers to

Ⓐ pad
Ⓑ food
Ⓒ housefly
Ⓓ mouth

More Available

the maxillae, or lower jaw parts, which serve to direct food into the mouth between the jaws. A labrum above and one below are similar to another animal's upper and lower lips. In an insect with a sucking mouth function, the mandibles, maxillae, labrum, and labium are modified in such a way that they constitute a tube through which liquid such as water, blood, or flower nectar can be drawn. In a butterfly or moth, this coiled drinking tube is called the proboscis because of its resemblance, in miniature, to the trunk of an elephant or a very large nose. Composed chiefly of modified maxillae fitted together, the insect's proboscis can be flexed and extended to reach nectar deep in a flower. In mosquitoes or aphids, mandibles and maxillae are modified to sharp stylets with which the insect can drill through surfaces like human or vegetable skin membranes to reach juice. In a housefly, the expanding labium forms a spongelike mouth pad that it can use to stamp over the surface of food, sopping up food particles and juices.

Insects, the most numerous creatures on our planet, are also the most adaptable. They require

32. The following sentence can be added to the passage.

Although some insects, like the cockroach, have remained essentially unchanged for eons, most insects adapt readily to changing environmental conditions.

Where would it best fit in the passage?

Click on the square (■) to add the sentence to the passage.

Scroll the passage to see all of the choices.

End

proboscis can be flexed and extended to reach nectar deep in a flower. In mosquitoes or aphids, mandibles and maxillae are modified to sharp stylets with which the insect can drill through surfaces like human or vegetable skin membranes to reach juice. In a housefly, the expanding labium forms a spongelike mouth pad that it can use to stamp over the surface of food, sopping up food particles and juices.

■ Insects, the most numerous creatures on our planet, are also the most adaptable. They require little food because they are small. ■ They easily find shelter and protection in small crevices in trees and surface geological formations. ■ Species of insects can evolve quickly because of their rapid reproduction cycle; they live in every climate, some making their homes in the frozen Arctic regions and many others choosing the humid, warm, and nutrient-rich rain forest environment. An active part of the natural food cycle, insects provide nutrition for animals and devour waste products of other life forms. ■

33. What is the purpose of this passage?

Ⓐ To complain
Ⓑ To persuade
Ⓒ To entertain
Ⓓ To inform

The protozoans, minute aquatic creatures, each of which consists of a single cell of protoplasm, constitute a classification of the most primitive forms of animal life. The very name *protozoan* indicates the scientific understanding of the animals. *Proto-* means first or primitive, and *zoa* refers to animal. They are fantastically diverse, but three major groups may be identified on the basis of their motility. The Mastigophora have one or more long tails that they use to propel themselves forward. The Ciliata, which use the same basic means for locomotion as the Mastigophora, have a larger number of short tails. The Sarcodina, which include amoebae, float or row themselves about on their crusted bodies.

In addition to their form of movement, several other features discriminate among the three groups of protozoans. For example, at least two nuclei per cell have been identified in the Ciliata, usually a large nucleus that regulates growth but decomposes during reproduction, and a smaller one that contains the genetic code necessary to generate the large nucleus.

Chlorophyll, which is the green substance encountered in plants, is found in the bodies of some protozoans, enabling them to make some of their own food from water and carbon dioxide. Protozoans are not considered plants but animals, because unlike pigmented plants to which some protozoans are otherwise almost identical, they do not live on simple organic compounds. Their cell demonstrates all of the major characteristics of the cells of higher animals, such as eating, breathing, and reproducing.

Many species of protozoans collect into colonies, physically connected to one another and responding uniformly to outside stimulae. Current research into this phenomenon along with investigations carried out with advanced microscopes may necessitate a redefinition of what constitutes protozoans, even calling into question the basic premise that they have only one cell. Nevertheless, with the current data available, almost 40,000 species of protozoans have been identified. No doubt, as technology improves methods of observation, better models of classification of these simple single cells will be proposed.

34. With what topic is the passage primarily concerned?

Ⓐ Colonies of protozoans
Ⓑ Mastigophora
Ⓒ Motility in protozoans
Ⓓ Characteristics of protozoans

35. The word minute in paragraph 1 could best be replaced by

Ⓐ very common
Ⓑ very fast
Ⓒ very old
Ⓓ very small

Beginning

The protozoans, minute aquatic creatures, each of which consists of a single cell of protoplasm, constitute a classification of the most primitive forms of animal life. The very name *protozoan* indicates the scientific understanding of the animals. *Proto-* means first or primitive, and *zoa* refers to animal. They are fantastically diverse, but three major groups may be identified on the basis of their motility. The Mastigophora have one or more long tails that they use to propel themselves forward. The Ciliata, which use the same basic means for locomotion as the Mastigophora, have a larger number of short tails. The Sarcodina, which include amoebae, float or row themselves about on their crusted bodies.

In addition to their form of movement, several other features discriminate among the three groups of protozoans. For example, at least two nuclei per cell have been identified in the Ciliata, usually a large nucleus that regulates growth but decomposes during reproduction, and a smaller one that contains the genetic code necessary to generate the large nucleus.

Chlorophyll, which is the green substance

36. What is protoplasm?

Ⓐ A class of protozoan
Ⓑ The substance that forms the cell of a protozoan
Ⓒ A primitive animal similar to a protozoan
Ⓓ An animal that developed from a protozoan

37. Look at the word motility in the passage. Click on the word or phrase in the **bold** text that is closest in meaning to motility.

Beginning

The protozoans, minute aquatic creatures, each of which consists of a single cell of protoplasm, constitute a classification of the most primitive forms of animal life. The very name *protozoan* indicates the scientific understanding of the animals. *Proto-* means first or primitive, and *zoa* refers to animal. **They are fantastically diverse, but three major groups may be identified on the basis of their motility. The Mastigophora have one or more long tails that they use to propel themselves forward. The Ciliata, which use the same basic means for locomotion as the Mastigophora, have a larger number of short tails. The Sarcodina, which include amoebae, float or row themselves about on their crusted bodies.**

In addition to their form of movement, several other features discriminate among the three groups of protozoans. For example, at least two nuclei per cell have been identified in the Ciliata, usually a large nucleus that regulates growth but decomposes during reproduction, and a smaller one that contains the genetic code necessary to generate the large nucleus.

Chlorophyll, which is the green substance

38. What does the author mean by the statement They are fantastically diverse, but three major groups may be identified on the basis of their motility?

Ⓐ The three major groups are unique in that they all move in the same manner.
Ⓑ Everything we know about the protozoans is tied into their manner of movement.
Ⓒ The manner of movement is critical when classifying the three major groups of protozoa.
Ⓓ Mobility in the protozoans is insignificant.

Beginning

The protozoans, minute aquatic creatures, each of which consists of a single cell of protoplasm, constitute a classification of the most primitive forms of animal life. The very name *protozoan* indicates the scientific understanding of the animals. *Proto-* means first or primitive, and *zoa* refers to animal. They are fantastically diverse, but three major groups may be identified on the basis of their motility. The Mastigophora have one or more long tails that they use to propel themselves forward. The Ciliata, which use the same basic means for locomotion as the Mastigophora, have a larger number of short tails. The Sarcodina, which include amoebae, float or row themselves about on their crusted bodies.

In addition to their form of movement, several other features discriminate among the three groups of protozoans. For example, at least two nuclei per cell have been identified in the Ciliata, usually a large nucleus that regulates growth but decomposes during reproduction, and a smaller one that contains the genetic code necessary to generate the large nucleus.

Chlorophyll, which is the green substance

39. To which class of protozoans do the amoebae belong?

Ⓐ Mastigophora
Ⓑ Ciliata
Ⓒ Sarcodina
Ⓓ Motility

40. What is the purpose of the large nucleus in the Ciliata?

Ⓐ It generates the other nucleus.
Ⓑ It contains the genetic code for the small nucleus.
Ⓒ It regulates growth.
Ⓓ It reproduces itself.

41. Why are protozoans classified as animals?

Ⓐ They do not live on simple organic compounds.
Ⓑ They collect in colonies.
Ⓒ They respond uniformly to outside stimulae.
Ⓓ They may have more than one cell.

42. The word they in paragraph 3 refers to

Ⓐ protozoans
Ⓑ microscopes
Ⓒ investigations
Ⓓ colonies

More Available

In addition to their form of movement, several other features discriminate among the three groups of protozoans. For example, at least two nuclei per cell have been identified in the Ciliata, usually a large nucleus that regulates growth but decomposes during reproduction, and a smaller one that contains the genetic code necessary to generate the large nucleus.

Chlorophyll, which is the green substance encountered in plants, is found in the bodies of some protozoans, enabling them to make some of their own food from water and carbon dioxide. Protozoans are not considered plants but animals, because unlike pigmented plants to which some protozoans are otherwise almost identical, they do not live on simple organic compounds. Their cell demonstrates all of the major characteristics of the cells of higher animals, such as eating, breathing, and reproducing.

Many species of protozoans collect into colonies, physically connected to one another and responding uniformly to outside stimulae. Current research into this phenomenon along with investigations carried out with advanced

43. Click on the sentence in paragraph 4 that brings into question the current belief that protozoans are single celled.

Paragraph 4 is marked with an arrow (→).

End

some protozoans, enabling them to make some of their own food from water and carbon dioxide. Protozoans are not considered plants but animals, because unlike pigmented plants to which some protozoans are otherwise almost identical, they do not live on simple organic compounds. Their cell demonstrates all of the major characteristics of the cells of higher animals, such as eating, breathing, and reproducing.

→ Many species of protozoans collect into colonies, physically connected to one another and responding uniformly to outside stimulae. Current research into this phenomenon along with investigations carried out with advanced microscopes may necessitate a redefinition of what constitutes protozoans, even calling into question the basic premise that they have only one cell. Nevertheless, with the current data available, almost 40,000 species of protozoans have been identified. No doubt, as technology improves methods of observation, better models of classification of these simple single cells will be proposed.

44. The word **uniformly** in paragraph 4 is closest in meaning to

Ⓐ in the same way
Ⓑ once in a while
Ⓒ all of a sudden
Ⓓ in the long run

End

some protozoans, enabling them to make some of their own food from water and carbon dioxide. Protozoans are not considered plants but animals, because unlike pigmented plants to which some protozoans are otherwise almost identical, they do not live on simple organic compounds. Their cell demonstrates all of the major characteristics of the cells of higher animals, such as eating, breathing, and reproducing.

Many species of protozoans collect into colonies, physically connected to one another and responding **uniformly** to outside stimulae. Current research into this phenomenon along with investigations carried out with advanced microscopes may necessitate a redefinition of what constitutes protozoans, even calling into question the basic premise that they have only one cell. Nevertheless, with the current data available, almost 40,000 species of protozoans have been identified. No doubt, as technology improves methods of observation, better models of classification of these simple single cells will be proposed.

45. Which of the following statements is NOT true of protozoans?

Ⓐ There are approximately 40,000 species.
Ⓑ They are the most primitive forms of animal life.
Ⓒ They have a large cell and a smaller cell.
Ⓓ They are difficult to observe.

To check your answers for Model Test 3, refer to the Answer Key on page 546. For an explanation of the answers, refer to the Explanatory Answers for Model Test 3 on pages 569–576.

Writing Section Model Test 3

When you take a Model Test, you should use one sheet of paper, both sides. Time each Model Test carefully. After you have read the topic, you should spend 30 minutes writing. For results that would be closest to the actual testing situation, it is recommended that an English teacher score your test, using the guidelines on page 325 of this book.

Many people have learned a foreign language in their own country; others have learned a foreign language in the country in which it is spoken. Give the advantages of each and support your viewpoint.

Notes

Model Test 4
Computer-Assisted TOEFL

Section 1: Listening

The Listening section of the test measures the ability to understand conversations and talks in English. You will use headphones to listen to the conversations and talks. While you are listening, pictures of the speakers or other information will be presented on your computer screen. There are two parts to the Listening section, with special directions for each part.

On the day of the test, the amount of time you will have to answer all of the questions will appear on the computer screen. The time you spend listening to the test material will not be counted. The listening material and questions about it will be presented only one time. You will not be allowed to take notes or have any paper at your computer. You will both see and hear the questions before the answer choices appear. You can take as much time as you need to select an answer; however, it will be to your advantage to answer the questions as quickly as possible. You may change your answer as many times as you want before you confirm it. After you have confirmed an answer, you will not be able to return to the question.

Before you begin working on the Listening section, you will have an opportunity to adjust the volume of the sound. You will not be able to change the volume after you have started the test.

QUESTION DIRECTIONS — Part A

In Part A of the Listening section, you will hear short conversations between two people. In some of the conversations, each person speaks only once. In other conversations, one or both of the people speak more than once. Each conversation is followed by one question about it.

Each question in this part has four answer choices. You should click on the best answer to each question. Answer the questions on the basis of what is stated or implied by the speakers.

1. What will the woman probably do?

   Ⓐ Have a party.
   Ⓑ Attend the International Students' Association.
   Ⓒ Go to work.
   Ⓓ Get some rest.

2. What will the speakers probably do?

   Ⓐ Leave immediately.
   Ⓑ Watch the game on TV.
   Ⓒ Start to play.
   Ⓓ Eat a sandwich.

3. What did the man do after he lost his passport?

   Ⓐ He went to see the foreign student advisor.
   Ⓑ He went to Washington.
   Ⓒ He wrote to the Passport Office.
   Ⓓ He reported it to the Passport Office.

4. What does the woman suggest the man do?

   Ⓐ Ask Dr. Tyler to clarify the assignment.
   Ⓑ Show a preliminary version to Dr. Tyler.
   Ⓒ Let her see the first draft before Dr. Tyler sees it.
   Ⓓ Talk to some of the other students in Dr. Tyler's class.

5. What does the woman mean?

Ⓐ Dr. Clark is a good teacher.
Ⓑ Statistics is a boring class.
Ⓒ Two semesters of statistics are required.
Ⓓ The students do not like Dr. Clark.

6. What are the speakers discussing?

Ⓐ A teacher.
Ⓑ A textbook.
Ⓒ An assignment.
Ⓓ A movie.

7. What had the man assumed about the woman?

Ⓐ She was Sally Harrison's cousin.
Ⓑ She was Sally Harrison's sister.
Ⓒ She was Sally Harrison's friend.
Ⓓ She was Sally Harrison.

8. What is the woman's problem?

Ⓐ The desk drawer won't open.
Ⓑ The pen is out of ink.
Ⓒ She cannot find her pen.
Ⓓ She is angry with the man.

9. What does the man imply about John?

Ⓐ John is usually late.
Ⓑ John will be there at eight-thirty.
Ⓒ John will not show up.
Ⓓ John is usually on time.

10. What does the man mean?

Ⓐ The results of the tests are not available.
Ⓑ The experiment had unexpected results.
Ⓒ He has not completed the experiment yet.
Ⓓ It is taking a lot of time to do the experiment.

11. What does the man imply about Barbara?

Ⓐ She does not put much effort in her studies.
Ⓑ She is very likable.
Ⓒ She prefers talking to the woman.
Ⓓ She has a telephone.

12. What does the man suggest the woman do?

Ⓐ See the doctor.
Ⓑ Get another job.
Ⓒ Go to the counter.
Ⓓ Buy some medicine.

13. What does the woman mean?

Ⓐ She will try her best.
Ⓑ She has to save her money.
Ⓒ She is still undecided.
Ⓓ She needs an application.

14. What does the woman mean?

Ⓐ The man must stop working.
Ⓑ There is a little more time.
Ⓒ The test is important.
Ⓓ It is time for the test.

15. What does the man imply?

Ⓐ The woman's roommate took a different class.
Ⓑ The book is very expensive.
Ⓒ The textbook may have been changed.
Ⓓ The course is not offered this semester.

16. What does the woman imply?

Ⓐ Sally may get a bike for Christmas.
Ⓑ Sally already has a bike like that one.
Ⓒ Sally likes riding a bike.
Ⓓ Sally may prefer a different gift.

17. What does the woman suggest that the man do?

Ⓐ Take a break.
Ⓑ Go to work.
Ⓒ Do the other problems.
Ⓓ Keep trying.

QUESTION DIRECTIONS — Part B

In Part B of the Listening section, you will hear several longer conversations and talks. Each conversation or talk is followed by several questions. The conversations, talks, and questions will not be repeated.

The conversations and talks are about a variety of topics. You do not need special knowledge of the topics to answer the questions correctly. Rather, you should answer each question on the basis of what is stated or implied by the speakers in the conversations or talks.

For most of the questions, you will need to click on the best of four possible answers. Some questions will have special directions. The special directions will appear in a box on the computer screen.

18. What is the topic under discussion?

Ⓐ Whether to introduce the metric system in the United States.
Ⓑ How the metric system should be introduced in the United States.
Ⓒ Which system is better—the English system or the metric system.
Ⓓ How to convert measurements from the English system to the metric system.

19. What changes in measurement in the United States have the students observed?

Ⓐ Now the weather on radio and TV is reported exclusively in metrics.
Ⓑ Road signs have miles marked on them, but not kilometers.
Ⓒ Both the English system and the metric system are being used on signs, packages, and in weather reports.
Ⓓ Grocery stores use only metrics for their packaging.

20. What was Professor Baker's opinion?

Ⓐ He thought that a gradual adoption would be better for everyone.
Ⓑ He thought that only metrics should be used.
Ⓒ He thought that only the English system should be used.
Ⓓ He thought that adults should use both systems, but that children should be taught only the metric system.

21. Which word best describes Professor Baker's attitude toward his students?

Ⓐ Unfriendly.
Ⓑ Patronizing.
Ⓒ Uninterested.
Ⓓ Cooperative.

22. What is the talk mainly about?

Ⓐ Private industry.
Ⓑ Advances in medicine.
Ⓒ Space missions.
Ⓓ Technological developments.

23. Which of the advances listed are NOT mentioned as part of the technology developed for space missions?

Ⓐ Contact lenses.
Ⓑ Cordless tools.
Ⓒ Food packaging.
Ⓓ Ultrasound.

24. According to the speaker, why did NASA develop medical equipment?

Ⓐ To monitor the condition of astronauts in spacecraft.
Ⓑ To evaluate candidates who wanted to join the space program.
Ⓒ To check the health of astronauts when they returned from space.
Ⓓ To test spacecraft and equipment for imperfections.

25. Why does the speaker mention archeologic "stuff"?

Ⓐ Archaeologists and astronauts were compared.
Ⓑ Astronauts made photographs of the earth later used by archaeologists.
Ⓒ Archaeologists have used advances in medical technology developed for astronauts.
Ⓓ Space missions and underwater missions are very similar.

26. Why did the student want to see the professor?
    Ⓐ To give him a note from another student.
    Ⓑ To ask for an excused absence from class.
    Ⓒ To get notes from a class that she had missed.
    Ⓓ To make an appointment for help in a class.

27. What is the student's problem?
    Ⓐ She cannot see the slides and videos from her seat.
    Ⓑ Her friend's notes are difficult to read.
    Ⓒ She has been absent from class too often.
    Ⓓ Her family needs her help next week.

28. What does the professor offer to do?
    Ⓐ Ask another student to take notes for the woman.
    Ⓑ Meet with the woman to clarify the classes she will miss.
    Ⓒ Make an appointment for the woman with another professor.
    Ⓓ Repeat the lecture for the woman.

29. What is the professor's attitude in this conversation?
    Ⓐ Disinterested.
    Ⓑ Helpful.
    Ⓒ Appreciative.
    Ⓓ Confused.

30. What is the main purpose of this talk?
    Ⓐ Transportation on the Pacific Coast.
    Ⓑ History of California.
    Ⓒ Orientation to San Francisco.
    Ⓓ Specifications of the Golden Gate Bridge.

31. According to the speaker, what was the settlement called before it was renamed San Francisco?
    Ⓐ Golden Gate.
    Ⓑ San Francisco de Asis Mission.
    Ⓒ Military Post Seventy-six.
    Ⓓ Yerba Buena.

32. According to the speaker, what happened in 1848?
    Ⓐ Gold was discovered.
    Ⓑ The Transcontinental Railroad was completed.
    Ⓒ The Golden Gate Bridge was constructed.
    Ⓓ Telegraph communications were established with the East.

33. How long is the Golden Gate Bridge?
    Ⓐ Eighteen miles.
    Ⓑ 938 feet.
    Ⓒ One mile.
    Ⓓ Between five and six miles.

34. What does the lecturer mainly discuss?
    Ⓐ Transcendentalism.
    Ⓑ Puritanism.
    Ⓒ Ralph Waldo Emerson.
    Ⓓ Nature.

35. During which century did the literary movement develop?
    Ⓐ Seventeenth century.
    Ⓑ Eighteenth century.
    Ⓒ Nineteenth century.
    Ⓓ Twentieth century.

36. According to the speaker, what did the Puritans do?
    Ⓐ They stressed the importance of the individual.
    Ⓑ They supported the ideals of the Transcendental Club.
    Ⓒ They believed that society was more important than the individual.
    Ⓓ They established a commune at Brook Farm.

37. What is *Walden*?
    Ⓐ A book by Emerson.
    Ⓑ A history of Puritanism.
    Ⓒ A novel by Nathaniel Hawthorne.
    Ⓓ A book by Thoreau.

38. What is the purpose of this conversation?

Ⓐ The man is looking for help with his research.
Ⓑ The man is applying for a teaching position.
Ⓒ The man is being trained to give library orientation.
Ⓓ The man is interviewing for a job in the library.

39. Who is the man?

Ⓐ A teacher.
Ⓑ A librarian.
Ⓒ A graduate student.
Ⓓ A computer programmer.

40. What does the man need to do when he is not working?

Ⓐ Take a few days off.
Ⓑ Begin his own research.
Ⓒ Write his dissertation.
Ⓓ Take classes.

41. When would the man be available?

Ⓐ After he graduates.
Ⓑ When he completes his dissertation.
Ⓒ After work and on his days off.
Ⓓ Immediately.

42. Which two requirements are considered when mounting a solar collector on a roof?

Click on 2 answers.

[A] The angle of the collector.
[B] The thickness of the glass.
[C] The direction of the exposure.
[D] The temperature of the air.

43. Identify the fan in the solar heating system.

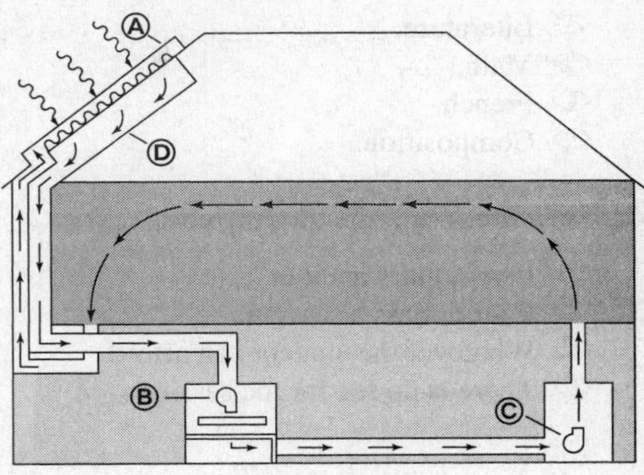

44. What problem does the professor point out?

Ⓐ Solar heating is very expensive.
Ⓑ The sun may not be available every day.
Ⓒ Solar storage systems are too small.
Ⓓ The sun does not supply enough energy without other power sources.

45. Why does the professor mention the project to place solar modules in orbit?

Ⓐ It has the potential to generate cheap power.
Ⓑ It is a research project that he is working on.
Ⓒ It is the same basic principles he has been explaining.
Ⓓ It is an example of a very complex model of a solar heating system.

46. What is the purpose of this conversation?

Ⓐ The man wants to apply for a tutoring position.
Ⓑ The man needs to arrange for tutoring.
Ⓒ The man is looking for a friend who works at the Tutoring Center.
Ⓓ The woman is tutoring the man.

47. For which course does the man want a tutor?

Ⓐ Literature.
Ⓑ Math.
Ⓒ French.
Ⓓ Composition.

48. How much will the tutoring cost?

Ⓐ Five dollars an hour.
Ⓑ Four dollars a session.
Ⓒ Whatever the student can afford.
Ⓓ There is no fee for the sessions.

49. When will the tutoring session begin?

Ⓐ Tuesday morning.
Ⓑ Thursday morning.
Ⓒ Tuesday afternoon.
Ⓓ Thursday afternoon.

50. What should the man bring to his tutoring session?

Ⓐ A check for five dollars.
Ⓑ Books and notes.
Ⓒ His class schedule.
Ⓓ A composition.

Section 2: Structure

This section measures the ability to recognize language that is appropriate for standard written English. There are two types of questions in this section.

In the first type of question, there are incomplete sentences. Beneath each sentence, there are four words or phrases. You will choose the one word or phrase that best completes the sentence.

Clicking on a choice darkens the oval. After you click on **Next** and **Confirm Answer**, the next question will be presented.

The second type of question has four underlined words or phrases. You will choose the one underlined word or phrase that must be changed for the sentence to be correct.

Clicking on an underlined word or phrase will darken it. After you click on **Next** and **Confirm Answer**, the next question will be presented.

1. Based on the premise that light was composed of color, the Impressionists came to the conclusion ---------- not really black.

   (A) which was that shadows
   (B) was shadows which
   (C) were shadows
   (D) that shadows were

2. ---------- a parliamentary system, the prime minister must be appointed on the basis of the distribution of power in the parliament.

   (A) The considered
   (B) To be considered
   (C) Considering
   (D) Considers

3. Interest <u>in</u> (A) automatic data processing has <u>grown</u> (B) <u>rapid</u> (C) <u>since</u> (D) the first large calculators were introduced in 1950.

4. Vaslav Nijinsky <u>achieved</u> (A) world recognition <u>as</u> (B) both <u>a dancer</u> (C) <u>as well as</u> (D) a choreographer.

5. ---------- of the play *Mourning Becomes Electra* introduces the cast of characters and hints at the plot.

   (A) The act first
   (B) Act one
   (C) Act first
   (D) First act

6. The plants that <u>they</u> (A) <u>belong to</u> (B) the family of ferns <u>are</u> (C) quite varied in <u>their</u> (D) size and structure.

7. As soon as -------- with an acid, salt, and sometimes water, is formed.

   (A) a base will react
   (B) a base reacts
   (C) a base is reacting
   (D) the reaction of a base

8. Columbus Day <u>is celebrated</u> (A) <u>on</u> (B) the <u>twelve</u> (C) of October <u>because</u> (D) on that day in 1492, Christopher Columbus first landed in the Americas.

9. One of <u>the most</u> (A) <u>influence</u> (B) newspapers in the U.S. <u>is</u> (C) *The New York Times,* which is <u>widely distributed</u> (D) throughout the world.

10. Weathering ---------- the action whereby surface rock is disintegrated or decomposed.

    (A) it is
    (B) is that
    (C) is
    (D) being

11. Coastal and inland waters are inhabited (A) not only (B) by fish but also by such (C) sea creature (D) as shrimps and clams.

12. Economists have tried to discourage (A) the use (B) of the phrase "underdeveloped nation" and encouraging (C) the more (D) accurate phrase "developing nation" in order to suggest an ongoing process.

13. A gas like (A) propane will combination (B) with water molecules in a saline solution to form (C) a solid called (D) a hydrate.

14. The people of Western Canada have been considering ---------- themselves from the rest of the provinces.

(A) to separate
(B) separated
(C) separate
(D) separating

15. Although it (A) cannot be proven, (B) presumable (C) the expansion of the universe will slow down as it approaches (D) a critical radius.

16. A City University professor reported that he discovers (A) a vaccine that (B) has been 80 percent effective in reducing (C) the instances of tooth decay among (D) small children.

17. When they have been (A) frightened, (B) as, for example, by (C) an electrical storm, dairy cows may refuse giving (D) milk.

18. Although Margaret Mead had several assistants during her long investigations of Samoa, the bulk of the research was done by ---------- alone.

(A) herself
(B) she
(C) her
(D) hers

19. Miami, Florida, is among (A) the few cities in the United States that (B) has been awarded (C) official status as (D) bilingual municipalities.

20. Fertilizers are used (A) primarily (B) to enrich soil (C) and increasing (D) yield.

21. ---------- war correspondent, Hemingway used his experiences for some of his most powerful novels.

(A) But a
(B) It is a
(C) While
(D) A

22. If the ozone gases of the atmosphere did not filter out (A) the ultraviolet rays of the sun, life as (B) we know it (C) would not have evolved on earth. (D)

23. Thirty-eight national sites are known as parks, another eighty-two as monuments, and ---------- .

(A) the another one hundred seventy-eight as historical sites
(B) the other one hundred seventy-eight as historical sites
(C) seventy-eight plus one hundred more as historical sites
(D) as historical sites one hundred seventy-eight

24. When he <u>was</u> (A) a little boy, Mark Twain <u>would walk</u> (B) along the piers, <u>watch</u> (C) the river boats, <u>swimming</u> (D) and fish in the Mississippi, much like his famous character, Tom Sawyer.

25. <u>Almost all</u> (A) books have a few errors in them <u>in spite of</u> (B) the care <u>taken</u> (C) to check <u>its</u> (D) proof pages before the final printing.

Section 3: Reading

This section measures the ability to read and understand short passages similar in topic and style to those that students are likely to encounter in North American universities and colleges. This section contains reading passages and questions about the passages. There are several different types of questions in this section.

In the Reading section, you will first have the opportunity to read the passage.

You will use the scroll bar to view the rest of the passage.

When you have finished reading the passage, you will use the mouse to click on **Proceed**. Then the questions about the passage will be presented. You are to choose the one best answer to each question. Answer all questions about the information in a passage on the basis of what is stated or implied in that passage.

Most of the questions will be multiple-choice questions. To answer these questions you will click on a choice below the question.

To answer some questions, you will click on a word or phrase.

To answer some questions, you will click on a sentence in the passage.

To answer some questions, you will click on a square to add a sentence to the passage.

Precipitation, commonly referred to as rainfall, is a measure of the quantity of atmospheric water in the form of rain, hail, or snow that reaches the ground. The average annual precipitation over the whole of the United States is thirty-six inches per year. It should be understood, however, that all precipitation is not measured equally. For example, a foot of snow does not equal a foot of precipitation. According to the general formula for computing the precipitation of snowfall, ten inches of snow equals one inch of precipitation. In upper New York State, for example, where there is typically a large amount of snowfall every winter, a hundred inches of snow in one year would be recorded as only ten inches of precipitation. On the other hand, rain is rain. Forty inches of rain would be recorded as forty inches of precipitation. The total annual precipitation for an area with forty inches of rain and one hundred inches of snow would be recorded as fifty inches of precipitation.

The amount of precipitation that an area receives is a combined result of several factors, including location, altitude, proximity to the sea, and the direction of prevailing winds. Most of the precipitation in the United States is brought originally by prevailing winds from the Pacific Ocean, the Gulf of Mexico, the Atlantic Ocean, and the Great Lakes. Because these prevailing winds generally come from the west, the Pacific Coast receives more annual precipitation than the Atlantic Coast. Along the Pacific Coast itself, however, altitude causes some diversity in rainfall. The mountain ranges of the United States, especially the Rocky Mountain Range and the Appalachian Mountain Range, influence the amount of precipitation in the areas to the windward and leeward sides of these ranges. East of the Rocky Mountains, the annual precipitation is substantially less than that west of the Rocky Mountains. The precipitation north of the Appalachian Mountains averages 40 percent less than that south of the Appalachian Mountains. As air currents from the oceans move over land, the air must rise to pass over the mountains. The air cools, and the water that is held in the clouds falls as rain or snow on the ascending side of the mountains. The air, therefore, is much drier on the other side of the mountains.

1. What does this passage mainly discuss?

Ⓐ Precipitation
Ⓑ Snowfall
Ⓒ New York State
Ⓓ A general formula

2. Which of the following is another word that is often used in place of precipitation?

Ⓐ Humidity
Ⓑ Wetness
Ⓒ Rainfall
Ⓓ Rain-snow

3. The term *precipitation* includes

Ⓐ only rainfall
Ⓑ rain, hail, and snow
Ⓒ rain, snow, and humidity
Ⓓ rain, hail, and humidity

4. What is the average annual rainfall in inches in the United States?

Ⓐ Thirty-six inches
Ⓑ Thirty-eight inches
Ⓒ Forty inches
Ⓓ Forty-two inches

5. If a state has 40 inches of snow in a year, by how much does this increase the annual precipitation?

Ⓐ By two feet
Ⓑ By four inches
Ⓒ By four feet
Ⓓ By 40 inches

6. The phrase **proximity to** in paragraph 2 is closest in meaning to

   (A) communication with
   (B) dependence on
   (C) nearness to
   (D) similarity to

More Available

The total annual precipitation for an area with forty inches of rain and one hundred inches of snow would be recorded as fifty inches of precipitation.

The amount of precipitation that an area receives is a combined result of several factors, including location, altitude, **proximity to** the sea, and the direction of prevailing winds. Most of the precipitation in the United States is brought originally by prevailing winds from the Pacific Ocean, the Gulf of Mexico, the Atlantic Ocean, and the Great Lakes. Because these prevailing winds generally come from the west, the Pacific Coast receives more annual precipitation than the Atlantic Coast. Along the Pacific Coast itself, however, altitude causes some diversity in rainfall. The mountain ranges of the United States, especially the Rocky Mountain Range and the Appalachian Mountain Range, influence the amount of precipitation in the areas to the windward and leeward sides of these ranges. East of the Rocky Mountains, the annual precipitation is substantially less than that west of the Rocky Mountains. The precipitation north of the Appalachian Mountains averages 40 percent less than that south of the

7. Click on the sentence in paragraph 2 that identifies the origins of most of the precipitation in the United States.

   Paragraph 2 is marked with an arrow (→).

More Available

The total annual precipitation for an area with forty inches of rain and one hundred inches of snow would be recorded as fifty inches of precipitation.

→ The amount of precipitation that an area receives is a combined result of several factors, including location, altitude, proximity to the sea, and the direction of prevailing winds. Most of the precipitation in the United States is brought originally by prevailing winds from the Pacific Ocean, the Gulf of Mexico, the Atlantic Ocean, and the Great Lakes. Because these prevailing winds generally come from the west, the Pacific Coast receives more annual precipitation than the Atlantic Coast. Along the Pacific Coast itself, however, altitude causes some diversity in rainfall. The mountain ranges of the United States, especially the Rocky Mountain Range and the Appalachian Mountain Range, influence the amount of precipitation in the areas to the windward and leeward sides of these ranges. East of the Rocky Mountains, the annual precipitation is substantially less than that west of the Rocky Mountains. The precipitation north of the Appalachian Mountains averages 40 percent less than that south of the

8. Where is the annual precipitation highest?

   (A) The Atlantic Coast
   (B) The Great Lakes
   (C) The Gulf of Mexico
   (D) The Pacific Coast

9. Which of the following was NOT mentioned as a factor in determining the amount of precipitation that an area will receive?

   (A) Mountains
   (B) Latitude
   (C) The sea
   (D) Wind

10. The word **substantially** in paragraph 2 could best be replaced by

   (A) fundamentally
   (B) slightly
   (C) completely
   (D) apparently

End

The mountain ranges of the United States, especially the Rocky Mountain Range and the Appalachian Mountain Range, influence the amount of precipitation in the areas to the windward and leeward sides of these ranges. East of the Rocky Mountains, the annual precipitation is **substantially** less than that west of the Rocky Mountains. The precipitation north of the Appalachian Mountains averages 40 percent less than that south of the Appalachian Mountains. As air currents from the oceans move over land, the air must rise to pass over the mountains. The air cools, and the water that is held in the clouds falls as rain or snow on the ascending side of the mountains. The air, therefore, is much drier on the other side of the mountains.

11. The word **that** in paragraph 2 refers to

Ⓐ decreases
Ⓑ precipitation
Ⓒ areas
Ⓓ mountain ranges

End

The mountain ranges of the United States, especially the Rocky Mountain Range and the Appalachian Mountain Range, influence the amount of precipitation in the areas to the windward and leeward sides of these ranges. East of the Rocky Mountains, the annual precipitation is substantially less than that west of the Rocky Mountains. The precipitation north of the Appalachian Mountains averages 40 percent less than **that** south of the Appalachian Mountains. As air currents from the oceans move over land, the air must rise to pass over the mountains. The air cools, and the water that is held in the clouds falls as rain or snow on the ascending side of the mountains. The air, therefore, is much drier on the other side of the mountains.

During the nineteenth century, women in the United States organized and participated in a large number of reform movements, including movements to reorganize the prison system, improve education, ban the sale of alcohol, grant rights to people who were denied them, and, most importantly, free slaves. Some women saw similarities in the social status of women and slaves. Women like Elizabeth Cady Stanton and Lucy Stone were not only feminists who fought for the rights of women but also fervent abolitionists who fought to do away with slavery. These brave people were social leaders who supported the rights of both women and blacks. They were fighting against a belief that voting should be tied to land ownership, and because land was owned by men, and in some cases by their widows, only those who held the greatest stake in government, that is the male landowners, were considered worthy of the vote. Women did not conform to the requirements.

A number of male abolitionists, including William Lloyd Garrison and Wendell Phillips, also supported the rights of women to speak and to participate equally with men in antislavery activities. Probably more than any other movement, abolitionism offered women a previously denied entry into politics. They became involved primarily in order to better their living conditions and improve the conditions of others. However, they gained the respect of those they convinced and also earned the right to be considered equal citizens.

When the civil war between the North and the South ended in 1865, the Fourteenth and Fifteenth Amendments to the Constitution adopted in 1868 and 1870 granted citizenship and suffrage to blacks but not to women. Discouraged but resolved, feminists worked tirelessly to influence more and more women to demand the right to vote. In 1869, the Wyoming Territory had yielded to demands by feminists, but the states on the East Coast resisted more stubbornly than before. A women's suffrage bill had been presented to every Congress since 1878, but it continually failed to pass until 1920, when the Nineteenth Amendment granted women the right to vote.

12. With what topic is the passage primarily concerned?

Ⓐ The Wyoming Territory
Ⓑ The Fourteenth and Fifteenth Amendments
Ⓒ Abolitionists
Ⓓ Women's suffrage

13. The word **ban** in paragraph 1 most nearly means to

Ⓐ encourage
Ⓑ publish
Ⓒ prohibit
Ⓓ limit

Beginning

During the nineteenth century, women in the United States organized and participated in a large number of reform movements, including movements to reorganize the prison system, improve education, **ban** the sale of alcohol, grant rights to people who were denied them, and, most importantly, free slaves. Some women saw similarities in the social status of women and slaves. Women like Elizabeth Cady Stanton and Lucy Stone were not only feminists who fought for the rights of women but also fervent abolitionists who fought to do away with slavery. These brave people were social leaders who supported the rights of both women and blacks. They were fighting against a belief that voting should be tied to land ownership, and because land was owned by men, and in some cases by their widows, only those who held the greatest stake in government, that is the male landowners, were considered worthy of the vote. Women did not conform to the requirements.

A number of male abolitionists, including William Lloyd Garrison and Wendell Phillips, also supported the rights of women to speak and to

14. Click on the sentence in paragraph 1 that explains the relationship between voting and property.

Paragraph 1 is marked with an arrow (→).

Beginning

→ During the nineteenth century, women in the United States organized and participated in a large number of reform movements, including movements to reorganize the prison system, improve education, ban the sale of alcohol, grant rights to people who were denied them, and, most importantly, free slaves. Some women saw similarities in the social status of women and slaves. Women like Elizabeth Cady Stanton and Lucy Stone were not only feminists who fought for the rights of women but also fervent abolitionists who fought to do away with slavery. These brave people were social leaders who supported the rights of both women and blacks. They were fighting against a belief that voting should be tied to land ownership, and because land was owned by men, and in some cases by their widows, only those who held the greatest stake in government, that is the male landowners, were considered worthy of the vote. Women did not conform to the requirements.

A number of male abolitionists, including William Lloyd Garrison and Wendell Phillips, also supported the rights of women to speak and to

15. The word **primarily** in paragraph 2 is closest in meaning to

Ⓐ above all
Ⓑ somewhat
Ⓒ finally
Ⓓ always

More Available

the rights of women but also fervent abolitionists who fought to do away with slavery. These brave people were social leaders who supported the rights of both women and blacks. They were fighting against a belief that voting should be tied to land ownership, and because land was owned by men, and in some cases by their widows, only those who held the greatest stake in government, that is the male landowners, were considered worthy of the vote. Women did not conform to the requirements.

A number of male abolitionists, including William Lloyd Garrison and Wendell Phillips, also supported the rights of women to speak and to participate equally with men in antislavery activities. Probably more than any other movement, abolitionism offered women a previously denied entry into politics. They became involved **primarily** in order to better their living conditions and improve the conditions of others. However, they gained the respect of those they convinced and also earned the right to be considered equal citizens.

When the civil war between the North and the

16. Look at the word improve in the passage. Click on the word or phrase in the **bold** text that is closest in meaning to improve.

More Available

rights of both women and blacks. They were fighting against a belief that voting should be tied to land ownership, and because land was owned by men, and in some cases by their widows, only those who held the greatest stake in government, that is the male landowners, were considered worthy of the vote. Women did not conform to the requirements.

A number of male abolitionists, including William Lloyd Garrison and Wendell Phillips, also supported the rights of women to speak and to participate equally with men in antislavery activities. **Probably more than any other movement, abolitionism offered women a previously denied entry into politics. They became involved primarily in order to better their living conditions and improve the conditions of others. However, they gained the respect of those they convinced and also earned the right to be considered equal citizens.**

When the civil war between the North and the South ended in 1865, the Fourteenth and Fifteenth Amendments to the Constitution adopted in 1868 and 1870 granted citizenship and suffrage to

17. What had occurred shortly after the Civil War?

Ⓐ The Wyoming Territory was admitted to the Union.
Ⓑ A women's suffrage bill was introduced in Congress.
Ⓒ The eastern states resisted the end of the war.
Ⓓ Black people were granted the right to vote.

18. The word suffrage in paragraph 3 could best be replaced by which of the following?

Ⓐ pain
Ⓑ citizenship
Ⓒ freedom from bondage
Ⓓ the right to vote

End

abolitionism offered women a previously denied entry into politics. They became involved primarily in order to better their living conditions and improve the conditions of others. However, they gained the respect of those they convinced and also earned the right to be considered equal citizens.

When the civil war between the North and the South ended in 1865, the Fourteenth and Fifteenth Amendments to the Constitution adopted in 1868 and 1870 granted citizenship and suffrage to blacks but not to women. Discouraged but resolved, feminists worked tirelessly to influence more and more women to demand the right to vote. In 1869, the Wyoming Territory had yielded to demands by feminists, but the states on the East Coast resisted more stubbornly than before. A women's suffrage bill had been presented to every Congress since 1878, but it continually failed to pass until 1920, when the Nineteenth Amendment granted women the right to vote.

19. The word it in paragraph 3 refers to

Ⓐ bill
Ⓑ Congress
Ⓒ Nineteenth Amendment
Ⓓ vote

End

abolitionism offered women a previously denied entry into politics. They became involved primarily in order to better their living conditions and improve the conditions of others. However, they gained the respect of those they convinced and also earned the right to be considered equal citizens.

When the civil war between the North and the South ended in 1865, the Fourteenth and Fifteenth Amendments to the Constitution adopted in 1868 and 1870 granted citizenship and suffrage to blacks but not to women. Discouraged but resolved, feminists worked tirelessly to influence more and more women to demand the right to vote. In 1869, the Wyoming Territory had yielded to demands by feminists, but the states on the East Coast resisted more stubbornly than before. A women's suffrage bill had been presented to every Congress since 1878, but it continually failed to pass until 1920, when the Nineteenth Amendment granted women the right to vote.

20. What does the Nineteenth Amendment guarantee?

Ⓐ Voting rights for blacks
Ⓑ Citizenship for blacks
Ⓒ Voting rights for women
Ⓓ Citizenship for women

21. When were women allowed to vote throughout the United States?

Ⓐ After 1866
Ⓑ After 1870
Ⓒ After 1878
Ⓓ After 1920

The *Acacia,* a genus of trees and shrubs of the *mimosa* family that originated in Australia, has long been used there in building simple mud and stick structures. The *acacia* is called a wattle in Australia, and the structures are said to be made of daub and wattle. The *acacia* is actually related to the family of plants known as *legumes* that includes peas, beans, lentils, peanuts, and pods with beanlike seeds. Some *acacias* actually produce edible crops. Other *Acacia* varieties are valued for the sticky resin, called gum arabic or gum acacia, used widely in medicines, foods, and perfumes, for the dark dense wood prized for making pianos, or for the bark, rich in tannin, a dark, acidic substance used to cure the hides of animals, transforming them into leather.

Nearly five hundred species of *Acacia* have been analyzed, identified, categorized, and proven capable of survival in hot and generally arid parts of the world; however, only a dozen of the three hundred Australian varieties thrive in the southern United States. Most *acacia* imports are low spreading trees, but of these, only three flower, including the *Bailey Acacia* with fernlike silver leaves and small, fragrant flowers arranged in rounded clusters, the *Silver Wattle,* similar to the *Bailey Acacia,* which grows twice as high, and the squat *Sydney Golden Wattle,* bushy with broad, flat leaves, showy bright yellow blossoms, and sharp spined twigs. Another variety, the *Black Acacia,* also called the *Blackwood,* has dark green foliage and unobtrusive blossoms. Besides being a popular ornamental tree, the *Black Acacia* is considered valuable for its dark wood, which is used in making furniture, as well as highly prized musical instruments.

The *Acacia's* unusual custom of blossoming in February has been commonly attributed to its Australian origins, as if the date and not the quality of light made the difference for a tree in its flowering cycle. In the Southern Hemisphere, the seasons are reversed, and February, which is wintertime in the United States, is summertime in Australia. Actually, however, the pale, yellow blossoms appear in August in Australia. Whether growing in the Northern or Southern Hemisphere, the lovely *acacia* blossoms in winter.

22. With which of the following topics is the passage primarily concerned?

Ⓐ The *Black Acacia*
Ⓑ Characteristics and varieties of the *Acacia*
Ⓒ Australian varieties of the *Acacia*
Ⓓ The use of *Acacia* wood in ornamental furniture

23. Look at the word prized in the passage. Click on the word or phrase in the **bold** text that is closest in meaning to prized.

More Available

includes peas, beans, lentils, peanuts, and pods with beanlike seeds. Some *acacias* actually produce edible crops. **Other *Acacia* varieties are valued for the sticky resin, called gum arabic or gum acacia, used widely in medicines, foods, and perfumes, for the dark dense wood prized for making pianos, or for the bark, rich in tannin, a dark, acidic substance used to cure the hides of animals, transforming them into leather.**

Nearly five hundred species of *Acacia* have been analyzed, identified, categorized, and proven capable of survival in hot and generally arid parts of the world; however, only a dozen of the three hundred Australian varieties thrive in the southern United States. Most *acacia* imports are low spreading trees, but of these, only three flower, including the *Bailey Acacia* with fernlike silver leaves and small, fragrant flowers arranged in rounded clusters, the *Silver Wattle*, similar to the *Bailey Acacia*, which grows twice as high, and the squat *Sydney Golden Wattle*, bushy with broad, flat leaves, showy bright yellow blossoms, and sharp spined twigs. Another variety, the *Black Acacia*, also called the *Blackwood*, has dark green

24. How many species of *Acacia* grow well in the southern United States?

Ⓐ Five hundred
Ⓑ Three hundred
Ⓒ Twelve
Ⓓ Three

25. The word thrive in paragraph 2 is closest in meaning to which of the following?

Ⓐ grow well
Ⓑ are found
Ⓒ were planted
Ⓓ can live

More Available

includes peas, beans, lentils, peanuts, and pods with beanlike seeds. Some *acacias* actually produce edible crops. Other *Acacia* varieties are valued for the sticky resin, called gum arabic or gum acacia, used widely in medicines, foods, and perfumes, for the dark dense wood prized for making pianos, or for the bark, rich in tannin, a dark, acidic substance used to cure the hides of animals, transforming them into leather.

Nearly five hundred species of *Acacia* have been analyzed, identified, categorized, and proven capable of survival in hot and generally arid parts of the world; however, only a dozen of the three hundred Australian varieties thrive in the southern United States. Most *acacia* imports are low spreading trees, but of these, only three flower, including the *Bailey Acacia* with fernlike silver leaves and small, fragrant flowers arranged in rounded clusters, the *Silver Wattle*, similar to the *Bailey Acacia*, which grows twice as high, and the squat *Sydney Golden Wattle*, bushy with broad, flat leaves, showy bright yellow blossoms, and sharp spined twigs. Another variety, the *Black Acacia*, also called the *Blackwood*, has dark green

26. The word these in paragraph 2 refers to

Ⓐ United States
Ⓑ varieties
Ⓒ species
Ⓓ trees and shrubs

More Available

includes peas, beans, lentils, peanuts, and pods with beanlike seeds. Some *acacias* actually produce edible crops. Other *Acacia* varieties are valued for the sticky resin, called gum arabic or gum acacia, used widely in medicines, foods, and perfumes, for the dark dense wood prized for making pianos, or for the bark, rich in tannin, a dark, acidic substance used to cure the hides of animals, transforming them into leather.

Nearly five hundred species of *Acacia* have been analyzed, identified, categorized, and proven capable of survival in hot and generally arid parts of the world; however, only a dozen of the three hundred Australian varieties thrive in the southern United States. Most *acacia* imports are low spreading trees, but of these, only three flower, including the *Bailey Acacia* with fernlike silver leaves and small, fragrant flowers arranged in rounded clusters, the *Silver Wattle*, similar to the *Bailey Acacia*, which grows twice as high, and the squat *Sydney Golden Wattle*, bushy with broad, flat leaves, showy bright yellow blossoms, and sharp spined twigs. Another variety, the *Black Acacia*, also called the *Blackwood*, has dark green

27. According to this passage, the *Silver Wattle*

Ⓐ is squat and bushy
Ⓑ has unobtrusive blossoms
Ⓒ is taller than the *Bailey Acacia*
Ⓓ is used for making furniture

28. In paragraph 2, the word flat most nearly means

Ⓐ smooth
Ⓑ pretty
Ⓒ pointed
Ⓓ short

More Available

includes peas, beans, lentils, peanuts, and pods with beanlike seeds. Some *acacias* actually produce edible crops. Other *Acacia* varieties are valued for the sticky resin, called gum arabic or gum acacia, used widely in medicines, foods, and perfumes, for the dark dense wood prized for making pianos, or for the bark, rich in tannin, a dark, acidic substance used to cure the hides of animals, transforming them into leather.

Nearly five hundred species of *Acacia* have been analyzed, identified, categorized, and proven capable of survival in hot and generally arid parts of the world; however, only a dozen of the three hundred Australian varieties thrive in the southern United States. Most *acacia* imports are low spreading trees, but of these, only three flower, including the *Bailey Acacia* with fernlike silver leaves and small, fragrant flowers arranged in rounded clusters, the *Silver Wattle*, similar to the *Bailey Acacia*, which grows twice as high, and the squat *Sydney Golden Wattle*, bushy with broad, flat leaves, showy bright yellow blossoms, and sharp spined twigs. Another variety, the *Black Acacia*, also called the *Blackwood*, has dark green

29. The word showy in paragraph 2 could best be replaced by

Ⓐ strange
Ⓑ elaborate
Ⓒ huge
Ⓓ fragile

More Available

includes peas, beans, lentils, peanuts, and pods with beanlike seeds. Some *acacias* actually produce edible crops. Other *Acacia* varieties are valued for the sticky resin, called gum arabic or gum acacia, used widely in medicines, foods, and perfumes, for the dark dense wood prized for making pianos, or for the bark, rich in tannin, a dark, acidic substance used to cure the hides of animals, transforming them into leather.

Nearly five hundred species of *Acacia* have been analyzed, identified, categorized, and proven capable of survival in hot and generally arid parts of the world; however, only a dozen of the three hundred Australian varieties thrive in the southern United States. Most *acacia* imports are low spreading trees, but of these, only three flower, including the *Bailey Acacia* with fernlike silver leaves and small, fragrant flowers arranged in rounded clusters, the *Silver Wattle*, similar to the *Bailey Acacia*, which grows twice as high, and the squat *Sydney Golden Wattle*, bushy with broad, flat leaves, showy bright yellow blossoms, and sharp spined twigs. Another variety, the *Black Acacia*, also called the *Blackwood*, has dark green

30. Which of the following *Acacias* has the least colorful blossoms?

Ⓐ *Bailey Acacia*
Ⓑ *Sydney Golden Wattle*
Ⓒ *Silver Wattle*
Ⓓ *Black Acacia*

31. Which of the following would most probably be made from a *Black Acacia* tree?

Ⓐ A flower arrangement
Ⓑ A table
Ⓒ A pie
Ⓓ Paper

32. When do *Acacia* trees bloom in Australia?

Ⓐ February
Ⓑ Summer
Ⓒ August
Ⓓ Spring

33. The following sentence can be added to the passage.

Some *acacias* are popular in landscaping because of their graceful shapes, lacey foliage, and fragrant blossoms.

Where would it best fit in the passage?

Click on the square (■) to add the sentence to the passage.

Scroll the passage to see all of the choices.

Beginning

The *Acacia*, a genus of trees and shrubs of the *mimosa* family that originated in Australia, has long been used there in building simple mud and stick structures. ■ The acacia is called a wattle in Australia, and the structures are said to be made of daub and wattle. ■ The acacia is actually related to the family of plants known as *legumes* that includes peas, beans, lentils, peanuts, and pods with beanlike seeds. Some *acacias* actually produce edible crops. ■ Other *Acacia* varieties are valued for the sticky resin, called gum arabic or gum acacia, used widely in medicines, foods, and perfumes, for the dark dense wood prized for making pianos, or for the bark, rich in tannin, a dark, acidic substance used to cure the hides of animals, transforming them into leather. ■

Nearly five hundred species of *Acacia* have been analyzed, identified, categorized, and proven capable of survival in hot and generally arid parts of the world; however, only a dozen of the three hundred Australian varieties thrive in the southern United States. Most *acacia* imports are low spreading trees, but of these, only three flower, including the *Bailey Acacia* with fernlike silver

In 1626, Peter Minuit, governor of the Dutch settlements in North America known as New Amsterdam, negotiated with Canarsee chiefs for the purchase of Manhattan Island for merchandise valued at sixty guilders or about $24.12. He purchased the island for the Dutch West India Company.

The next year, Fort Amsterdam was built by the company at the extreme southern tip of the island. Because attempts to encourage Dutch immigration were not immediately successful, offers, generous by the standards of the era, were extended throughout Europe. Consequently, the settlement became the most heterogeneous of the North American colonies. By 1637, the fort had expanded into the village of New Amsterdam, other small communities had grown up around it, including New Haarlem and Stuyvesant's Bouwery, and New Amsterdam began to prosper, developing characteristics of religious and linguistic tolerance unusual for the times. By 1643, it was reported that eighteen different languages could be heard in New Amsterdam alone.

Among the multilingual settlers was a large group of English colonists from Connecticut and Massachusetts who supported the English King's claim to all of New Netherlands set out in a charter that gave the territory to his brother James, Duke of York. In 1644, when the English sent a formidable fleet of warships into the New Amsterdam harbor, Dutch governor Peter Stuyvesant surrendered without resistance.

When the English acquired the island, the village of New Amsterdam was renamed New York in honor of the Duke. By the onset of the Revolution, New York City was already a bustling commercial center. After the war, it was selected as the first capital of the United States. Although the government was eventually moved, first to Philadelphia and then to Washington, D.C., New York maintained its status. It became a haven for pirates who conspired with leading merchants to exchange supplies for their ships in return for a share in the plunder. As a colony, New York exchanged many agricultural products for English manufactured goods. In addition, trade with the West Indies prospered. Three centuries after his initial trade with the Native Americans, Minuit's tiny investment was worth more than seven billion dollars.

34. Which of the following would be the best title for this passage?

Ⓐ A History of New York City
Ⓑ An Account of the Dutch Colonies
Ⓒ A Biography of Peter Minuit
Ⓓ The First Capital of the United States

35. What did the Native Americans receive in exchange for their island?

Ⓐ Sixty Dutch guilders
Ⓑ $24.12 U.S.
Ⓒ Goods and supplies
Ⓓ Land in New Amsterdam

36. Where was New Amsterdam located?

Ⓐ In Holland
Ⓑ In North America
Ⓒ On the island of Manhattan
Ⓓ In India

37. What does the author mean by the statement Because attempts to encourage Dutch immigration were not immediately successful, offers, generous by the standards of the era, were extended throughout Europe?

(A) Other Europeans were given opportunities to immigrate to the new world after a slow response by the Dutch.
(B) Since the Dutch immigration was so successful, opportunities were provided for the Europeans to immigrate to the new world also.
(C) The Dutch took advantage of opportunities to immigrate to Europe instead of to the new world.
(D) Immigration to the new world required that the Dutch and other Europeans wait until opportunities were available.

Beginning

In 1626, Peter Minuit, governor of the Dutch settlements in North America known as New Amsterdam, negotiated with Canarsee chiefs for the purchase of Manhattan Island for merchandise valued at sixty guilders or about $24.12. He purchased the island for the Dutch West India Company.

The next year, Fort Amsterdam was built by the company at the extreme southern tip of the island. Because attempts to encourage Dutch immigration were not immediately successful, offers, generous by the standards of the era, were extended throughout Europe. Consequently, the settlement became the most heterogeneous of the North American colonies. By 1637, the fort had expanded into the village of New Amsterdam, other small communities had grown up around it, including New Haarlem and Stuyvesant's Bouwery, and New Amsterdam began to prosper, developing characteristics of religious and linguistic tolerance unusual for the times. By 1643, it was reported that eighteen different languages could be heard in New Amsterdam alone.

Among the multilingual settlers was a large

38. The word heterogeneous in paragraph 2 could best be replaced by

(A) liberal
(B) renowned
(C) diverse
(D) prosperous

Beginning

In 1626, Peter Minuit, governor of the Dutch settlements in North America known as New Amsterdam, negotiated with Canarsee chiefs for the purchase of Manhattan Island for merchandise valued at sixty guilders or about $24.12. He purchased the island for the Dutch West India Company.

The next year, Fort Amsterdam was built by the company at the extreme southern tip of the island. Because attempts to encourage Dutch immigration were not immediately successful, offers, generous by the standards of the era, were extended throughout Europe. Consequently, the settlement became the most heterogeneous of the North American colonies. By 1637, the fort had expanded into the village of New Amsterdam, other small communities had grown up around it, including New Haarlem and Stuyvesant's Bouwery, and New Amsterdam began to prosper, developing characteristics of religious and linguistic tolerance unusual for the times. By 1643, it was reported that eighteen different languages could be heard in New Amsterdam alone.

Among the multilingual settlers was a large

39. Why were so many languages spoken in New Amsterdam?

Ⓐ The Dutch West India Company was owned by England.
Ⓑ The Dutch West India Company allowed freedom of speech.
Ⓒ The Dutch West India Company recruited settlers from many different countries in Europe.
Ⓓ The Indians who lived there before the Dutch West India Company purchase spoke many languages.

40. Look at the word his in the passage. Click on the word or phrase in the **bold** text that his refers to.

More Available

extended throughout Europe. Consequently, the settlement became the most heterogeneous of the North American colonies. By 1637, the fort had expanded into the village of New Amsterdam, other small communities had grown up around it, including New Haarlem and Stuyvesant's Bouwery, and New Amsterdam began to prosper, developing characteristics of religious and linguistic tolerance unusual for the times. By 1643, it was reported that eighteen different languages could be heard in New Amsterdam alone.

Among the multilingual settlers was a large group of English colonists from Connecticut and Massachusetts who supported the English King's claim to all of New Netherlands set out in a charter that gave the territory to his brother James, Duke of York. In 1644, when the English sent a formidable fleet of warships into the New Amsterdam harbor, Dutch governor Peter Stuyvesant surrendered without resistance.

When the English acquired the island, the village of New Amsterdam was renamed New York in honor of the Duke. By the onset of the Revolution, New York City was already a bustling

41. The word formidable in paragraph 3 is closest in meaning to

Ⓐ powerful
Ⓑ modern
Ⓒ expensive
Ⓓ unexpected

More Available

extended throughout Europe. Consequently, the settlement became the most heterogeneous of the North American colonies. By 1637, the fort had expanded into the village of New Amsterdam, other small communities had grown up around it, including New Haarlem and Stuyvesant's Bouwery, and New Amsterdam began to prosper, developing characteristics of religious and linguistic tolerance unusual for the times. By 1643, it was reported that eighteen different languages could be heard in New Amsterdam alone.

Among the multilingual settlers was a large group of English colonists from Connecticut and Massachusetts who supported the English King's claim to all of New Netherlands set out in a charter that gave the territory to his brother James, Duke of York. In 1644, when the English sent a formidable fleet of warships into the New Amsterdam harbor, Dutch governor Peter Stuyvesant surrendered without resistance.

When the English acquired the island, the village of New Amsterdam was renamed New York in honor of the Duke. By the onset of the Revolution, New York City was already a bustling

42. Click on the paragraph that explains the reason for renaming New Amsterdam.

Scroll the passage to see all of the paragraphs.

43. The word it in paragraph 4 refers to

Ⓐ Revolution
Ⓑ New York City
Ⓒ the island
Ⓓ the first capital

End

Massachusetts who supported the English King's claim to all of New Netherlands set out in a charter that gave the territory to his brother James, Duke of York. In 1644, when the English sent a formidable fleet of warships into the New Amsterdam harbor, Dutch governor Peter Stuyvesant surrendered without resistance.

When the English acquired the island, the village of New Amsterdam was renamed New York in honor of the Duke. By the onset of the Revolution, New York City was already a bustling commercial center. After the war, it was selected as the first capital of the United States. Although the government was eventually moved, first to Philadelphia and then to Washington, D.C., New York maintained its status. It became a haven for pirates who conspired with leading merchants to exchange supplies for their ships in return for a share in the plunder. As a colony, New York exchanged many agricultural products for English manufactured goods. In addition, trade with the West Indies prospered. Three centuries after his initial trade with the Indians, Minuit's tiny investment was worth more than seven billion dollars.

44. Which city was the first capital of the new United States?

Ⓐ New Amsterdam
Ⓑ New York
Ⓒ Philadelphia
Ⓓ Washington

45. On what date was Manhattan valued at $7 billion?

Ⓐ 1626
Ⓑ 1726
Ⓒ 1656
Ⓓ 1926

To check your answers for Model Test 4, refer to the Answer Key on page 547. For an explanation of the answers, refer to the Explanatory Answers for Model Test 4 on pages 577–584.

Writing Section Model Test 4

When you take a Model Test, you should use one sheet of paper, both sides. Time each Model Test carefully. After you have read the topic, you should spend 30 minutes writing. For results that would be closest to the actual testing situation, it is recommended that an English teacher score your test, using the guidelines on page 325 of this book.

In your opinion, what is the best way to choose a marriage partner? Use specific reasons and examples why you think this approach is best.

Notes

Model Test 5
Computer-Assisted TOEFL

Section 1: Listening

The Listening section of the test measures the ability to understand conversations and talks in English. You will use headphones to listen to the conversations and talks. While you are listening, pictures of the speakers or other information will be presented on your computer screen. There are two parts to the Listening section, with special directions for each part.

On the day of the test, the amount of time you will have to answer all of the questions will appear on the computer screen. The time you spend listening to the test material will not be counted. The listening material and questions about it will be presented only one time. You will not be allowed to take notes or have any paper at your computer. You will both see and hear the questions before the answer choices appear. You can take as much time as you need to select an answer; however, it will be to your advantage to answer the questions as quickly as possible. You may change your answer as many times as you want before you confirm it. After you have confirmed an answer, you will not be able to return to the question.

Before you begin working on the Listening section, you will have an opportunity to adjust the volume of the sound. You will not be able to change the volume after you have started the test.

QUESTION DIRECTIONS — Part A

In Part A of the Listening section, you will hear short conversations between two people. In some of the conversations, each person speaks only once. In other conversations, one or both of the people speak more than once. Each conversation is followed by one question about it.

Each question in this part has four answer choices. You should click on the best answer to each question. Answer the questions on the basis of what is stated or implied by the speakers.

1. What is the man going to do?

Ⓐ He will borrow some typing paper from the woman.
Ⓑ He will lend the woman some typing paper.
Ⓒ He will type the woman's paper.
Ⓓ He will buy some typing paper for the woman.

2. What can be inferred about the man?

Ⓐ He is a student at the university.
Ⓑ He is not driving a car.
Ⓒ He knows the woman.
Ⓓ He needs to go to the drug store.

3. What does the man imply?

Ⓐ He could not stay with his parents.
Ⓑ He did not want to change his plans.
Ⓒ He will not go to summer school.
Ⓓ He has completed all the courses.

4. What are the speakers discussing?

Ⓐ The telephone
Ⓑ An apartment
Ⓒ Utilities
Ⓓ Furniture

5. What does the woman imply?

Ⓐ She likes Dr. Taylor's class.
Ⓑ She is not sure how Dr. Taylor feels.
Ⓒ She did not get an A on the paper.
Ⓓ She is not doing very well in the class.

6. What does the man suggest that the woman do?

Ⓐ Pay ten dollars an hour
Ⓑ Be a subject in an experiment
Ⓒ Ask Sandy to participate
Ⓓ Go to a psychologist

7. What can be inferred about the study group meeting?

Ⓐ The speakers did not go to the study group meeting.
Ⓑ The woman went to the study group meeting, but the man did not.
Ⓒ The man went to the study group meeting, but the woman did not.
Ⓓ Both speakers went to the study group meeting.

8. What does the man mean?

Ⓐ The woman can borrow his pen.
Ⓑ A pen might be a good gift.
Ⓒ Her advisor would probably like a card.
Ⓓ A gift is not necessary.

9. What does the woman mean?

Ⓐ She does not want to leave.
Ⓑ She must stay.
Ⓒ She did not like the dorm.
Ⓓ She is undecided.

10. What does the woman imply?

Ⓐ The man may be taking on too much.
Ⓑ The job is more important than school.
Ⓒ The opportunity is very good.
Ⓓ The contract may not be valid.

11. What does the man suggest the woman do?

Ⓐ Call his family
Ⓑ Write a letter
Ⓒ Send postcards
Ⓓ Buy presents

12. What are the speakers discussing?

Ⓐ The length of time that it takes to get an answer from a university
Ⓑ Where the woman will go to school
Ⓒ States in the Midwest
Ⓓ The University of Minnesota

13. What will the woman probably do?

Ⓐ Buy a ticket
Ⓑ Go to room 27
Ⓒ Take a test in room 32
Ⓓ Show the man her ticket

14. What can be inferred about the woman?

Ⓐ She wasn't able to attend the reception.
Ⓑ She is an honors student.
Ⓒ She likes flowers very much.
Ⓓ She is a teacher.

15. What does the woman suggest that Terry do?

Ⓐ Try to be in class more often
Ⓑ Try to get the work done
Ⓒ Take the class twice
Ⓓ Take the class next term

16. What does the man mean?

Ⓐ He does not like English.
Ⓑ Graduate school is easier than teaching.
Ⓒ It is not surprising that the woman is doing well.
Ⓓ The course is very interesting.

17. What problem do the students have?

Ⓐ They are going to make a group presentation.
Ⓑ They don't want to have Jane in their group.
Ⓒ Carl does not want to be in their group.
Ⓓ They are not good presenters.

QUESTION DIRECTIONS — Part B

In Part B of the Listening section, you will hear several longer conversations and talks. Each conversation or talk is followed by several questions. The conversations, talks, and questions will not be repeated.

The conversations and talks are about a variety of topics. You do not need special knowledge of the topics to answer the questions correctly. Rather, you should answer each question on the basis of what is stated or implied by the speakers in the conversations or talks.

For most of the questions, you will need to click on the best of four possible answers. Some questions will have special directions. The special directions will appear in a box on the computer screen.

18. What problem do the speakers have?

Ⓐ They do not have a syllabus.
Ⓑ They do not understand the requirement for the research paper.
Ⓒ They do not have an appointment with the professor.
Ⓓ They do not know the professor's office hours.

19. How much does the research paper count toward the grade for the course?

Ⓐ It is not clear from the syllabus.
Ⓑ It is valued at half of the total points for the course.
Ⓒ It is worth ten points.
Ⓓ It will count thirty points.

20. What did the professor say last week?

Ⓐ She mentioned presentations.
Ⓑ She discussed the syllabus.
Ⓒ She answered questions.
Ⓓ She made appointments.

21. What will the students probably do?

Ⓐ Prepare a presentation of the research
Ⓑ Make an appointment to see the professor
Ⓒ Ask questions about the assignment in class
Ⓓ Go to see the professor during office hours

22. What is the main subject of this lecture?

Ⓐ Captain Cook's life
Ⓑ History of Hawaii
Ⓒ Captain Cook's exploration of Hawaii
Ⓓ Hawaiian culture

23. According to the lecturer, what were the two ships commanded by Captain Cook?

Click on 2 answers.

[A] *The Third Voyage*
[B] *The Resolution*
[C] *The Discovery*
[D] *The England*

24. Why does the professor mention the name *Launo?*

Ⓐ It was the original name for the Hawaiian Islands before Cook's arrival.
Ⓑ It was the name of the king of Hawaii at the time of Cook's exploration.
Ⓒ It was the name of the god that the islanders believed Cook embodied.
Ⓓ It was the name of the welcome ceremony that the islanders gave Cook.

25. The professor briefly explains a sequence of events in the history of Hawaii. Summarize the sequence by putting the events in order.

Click on a sentence. Then click on the space where it belongs.

Use each sentence only once.

[A] Captain Cook and four of his crew were killed.
[B] The islanders and the crew began to fight.
[C] The king was to be taken hostage.
[D] A small boat was stolen from the crew.

1 [ ]
2 [ ]
3 [ ]
4 [ ]

26. What is an alloy?

Ⓐ Impure metals that occur accidentally
Ⓑ Metals melted into liquid form
Ⓒ A planned combination of metals for a specific purpose
Ⓓ Industrial metals that do not have to be very pure

27. What does the speaker say about the properties of alloys?

Click on 2 answers.

[A] They are chosen for a particular purpose.
[B] They are combined in specific proportions.
[C] They are difficult to determine because there is more than one metal involved.
[D] They occur accidentally in nature.

28. Why does the speaker use the example of the aircraft industry?

Ⓐ To demonstrate how alloys can be used to solve industrial problems
Ⓑ To emphasize the importance of the aviation industry
Ⓒ To compare alloys and other mixtures
Ⓓ To illustrate how metals can be used without alloying them

29. What is the difference between combinations of metals in nature and alloys?

Ⓐ Mixtures of metals in nature are very pure.
Ⓑ Combinations of metals do not occur in nature.
Ⓒ Metals combined in nature are mixed in random proportion.
Ⓓ Alloys are mixtures, but metals that occur in nature are not.

30. What do the speakers mainly discuss?

Ⓐ British English pronunciation
Ⓑ Spelling patterns
Ⓒ British and American English
Ⓓ Movies

31. How are the words referred to in the discussion?

Click on a word. Then click on the empty box in the correct column.

Use each word only once.

[A] color [B] theater
[C] centre [D] honour

American English spelling		British English spelling	

32. What can be inferred about the word *flat* in British English?

Ⓐ It has a different spelling from that of American English.
Ⓑ It has a different meaning from that of American English.
Ⓒ The pronunciation is so different that it cannot be understood by Americans.
Ⓓ It is really about the same in American English.

33. On what did the class agree?

Ⓐ British English and American English are the same.
Ⓑ British English and American English are so different that Americans cannot understand the English when they speak.
Ⓒ British English and American English have different spelling and vocabulary but the same pronunciation.
Ⓓ British English and American English have slightly different spelling, vocabulary, and pronunciation, but Americans and the English still understand each other.

34. What is the presentation mainly about?

Ⓐ The National Department of Education
Ⓑ School boards
Ⓒ Public schools in the United States
Ⓓ Local control of schools

35. What surprised the presenter about her research?

Ⓐ Public schools are not the same throughout the United States.
Ⓑ The school board members are not professional educators.
Ⓒ The federal department is not the same as a department of education in many other countries.
Ⓓ The members of the school board serve without pay.

36. How does each of the persons identified contribute to the operation of schools in the United States?

Click on a word. Then click on the empty box in the correct row.

Use each word only once.

[A] superintendent
[B] school board member
[C] resident of the district

governs the local school district	
carries out the policies of the governing board	
elects the members of the governing board	

37. According to the speaker, what is the function of the department of education in the United States?

Click on 2 answers.

[A] To support research projects
[B] To organize a national curriculum
[C] To monitor national legislation for schools
[D] To appoint local school boards

38. What kind of meal plan does the man decide to buy?

Click on 2 answers.

[A] Breakfast
[B] Lunch
[C] Dinner
[D] Supper

39. How much does the plan cost?

Ⓐ Fourteen dollars a week
Ⓑ Thirty dollars a week
Ⓒ Thirty-six dollars a week
Ⓓ Forty-two dollars a week

40. Why do most residents order a pizza or go out to eat on Sundays?

Ⓐ Many of them live close enough to go home for the day.
Ⓑ They are tired of the food in the dormitory.
Ⓒ No meals are served on Sunday.
Ⓓ Some of them have dates on the weekend.

41. How will the man pay for the meals?

Ⓐ He will pay the woman in cash for the first quarter.
Ⓑ He will use his credit card to pay the woman.
Ⓒ He will wait to receive a bill from the dormitory.
Ⓓ He will write a check on a form provided by the woman.

42. What will the man probably do?

Ⓐ Pay the bill now
Ⓑ Give the woman his credit card
Ⓒ Fill out a form
Ⓓ Think about his options

43. What is hydroponics?

Ⓐ Growing plants without soil
Ⓑ Mixing nutrients in water
Ⓒ Finding the chemical composition of soil
Ⓓ Solving problems in the water system

44. Why does the professor suggest that the students refer to their lab workbook?

Ⓐ To see the diagram of the class experiment
Ⓑ To read an experiment on plant growth
Ⓒ To find a list of substances that plants need
Ⓓ To locate the instructions for building a hydroponics tank

45. According to the speaker, why are roots important to plants?

Click on 2 answers.

[A] To absorb water and nutrients
[B] To take in oxygen
[C] To suspend the plants directly in the solution
[D] To filter out toxins

46. Why was the pump attached to the tank in this experiment?

Ⓐ It was needed to mix the nutrients in the solution.
Ⓑ It was used to pump out harmful chemicals.
Ⓒ It was required to pump oxygen into the solution.
Ⓓ It was necessary to anchor the plants.

47. What does the professor want the students to do with the specimen of the nutrient solution?

Ⓐ Take a taste of it
Ⓑ Make a drawing of it
Ⓒ Observe it and draw conclusions
Ⓓ Put it in the tank

48. What are the speakers discussing?

Ⓐ A class that the woman missed
Ⓑ A book that they have both read
Ⓒ A TV show that the man saw
Ⓓ A video that they saw in class

49. Who was Harriet Tubman?

Ⓐ She was one of the first freed slaves to work on the railroad.
Ⓑ She was a slave who worked underground in the mines.
Ⓒ She was a former slave who lived in Canada.
Ⓓ She was a slave who escaped from her owners in Maryland during the Civil War.

50. What impressed the man about Harriet Tubman's story?

Ⓐ She used the North Star to guide her to a free state.
Ⓑ She returned to Maryland to help three hundred slaves escape.
Ⓒ She founded the underground railroad.
Ⓓ She was a slave for nineteen years.

Section 2: Structure

This section measures the ability to recognize language that is appropriate for standard written English. There are two types of questions in this section.

In the first type of question, there are incomplete sentences. Beneath each sentence, there are four words or phrases. You will choose the one word or phrase that best completes the sentence.

Clicking on a choice darkens the oval. After you click on **Next** and **Confirm Answer**, the next question will be presented.

The second type of question has four underlined words or phrases. You will choose the one underlined word or phrase that must be changed for the sentence to be correct.

Clicking on an underlined word or phrase will darken it. After you click on **Next** and **Confirm Answer**, the next question will be presented.

1. Gunpowder, in some ways (A) the most effective (B) of all (C) the explosive materials, were (D) a mixture of potassium nitrate, charcoal, and sulfur.

2. As the demand increases, manufacturers who previously (A) produced only a large, luxury car is (B) compelled to make (C) a smaller model (D) in order to compete in the market.

3. There are (A) twenty species of wild roses in North America, all of which have (B) prickly stems, pinnate leaves, and large flowers, which (C) usually smell sweetly (D).

4. Professional people expect ------- when it is necessary to cancel an appointment.
   - (A) you to call them
   - (B) that you would call them
   - (C) your calling them
   - (D) that you are calling them

5. In a new culture, many embarrassing situations occur ------- a misunderstanding.
   - (A) for
   - (B) of
   - (C) because of
   - (D) because

6. Factoring (A) is the process of finding (B) two or more expressions whose (C) product is equal as (D) the given expression.

7. Schizophrenia, a behavioral disorder typified by (A) a fundamental (B) break with reality, may be triggered (C) by genetic predisposition, stressful (D), drugs, or infections.

8. Sedimentary rocks are formed below the surface of the Earth -------- very high temperatures and pressures.
   - (A) where there are
   - (B) there are
   - (C) where are there
   - (D) there are where

9. If Grandma Moses having (A) been able to continue farming (B), she may never have begun (C) to paint (D).

10. A computer is usually chosen because of its simplicity of operation and ease of maintenance ------ its capacity to store information.

(A) the same as
(B) the same
(C) as well as
(D) as well

11. Although the Red Cross accepts (A) blood from most donors, the nurses will not leave (B) you give (C) blood if you have just had (D) a cold.

12. --------- that gold was discovered at Sutter's Mill and that the California Gold Rush began.

(A) Because in 1848
(B) That in 1848
(C) In 1848 that it was
(D) It was in 1848

13. Frost occurs in valleys and on low grounds --------- on adjacent hills.

(A) more frequently as
(B) as frequently than
(C) more frequently than
(D) frequently than

14. The native people of the Americas are called (A) Indians because (B) when Columbus landed in the Bahamas in 1492 (C), he thought that he has reached (D) the East Indies.

15. In the relatively (A) short history of industrial developing (B) in the United States (C), New York City has played (D) a vital role.

16. When a body enters the Earth's atmosphere, it travels ---------- .

(A) very rapidly
(B) in a rapid manner
(C) fastly
(D) with great speed

17. Employers often require that candidates have not only a degree ----------.

(A) but two years experience
(B) also two years experience
(C) but also two years experience
(D) but more two years experience

18. The salary of a bus driver is much higher ---------- .

(A) in comparison with the salary of a teacher
(B) than a teacher
(C) than that of a teacher
(D) to compare as a teacher

19. Farmers look forward to ----------- every summer.

(A) participating in the county fairs
(B) participate in the county fairs
(C) be participating in the county fairs
(D) have participated in the county fairs

20. A turtle differs from (A) all other (B) reptiles in that its body is encased in a protective shell of their (C) own (D).

21. Excavations in a mound or village
(A)
often reveal an ancient community that
(B)
had been laying under later reconstructions
(C) (D)
of the city.

22. One of the first and ultimately the most
(A)
important purposeful of a reservoir was
(B)
to control flooding.
(C) (D)

23. After seeing a movie based on a novel, ----------- .

(A) the book is read by many people
(B) the book made many people want to read it
(C) many people want to read the book
(D) the reading of the book interests many people

24. One of the world's best-selling authors,
(A)
Louis L'Amour said to have written 101
(B) (C)
books, mostly westerns.
(D)

25. No other quality is more important for a
(A) (B)
scientist to acquire as to observe carefully.
(C) (D)

Section 3:
Reading

This section measures the ability to read and understand short passages similar in topic and style to those that students are likely to encounter in North American universities and colleges. This section contains reading passages and questions about the passages. There are several different types of questions in this section.

In the Reading section, you will first have the opportunity to read the passage.

You will use the scroll bar to view the rest of the passage.

When you have finished reading the passage, you will use the mouse to click on **Proceed**. Then the questions about the passage will be presented. You are to choose the one best answer to each question. Answer all questions about the information in a passage on the basis of what is stated or implied in that passage.

Most of the questions will be multiple-choice questions. To answer these questions you will click on a choice below the question.

To answer some questions, you will click on a word or phrase.

To answer some questions, you will click on a sentence in the passage.

To answer some questions, you will click on a square to add a sentence to the passage.

Perhaps it was his own lack of adequate schooling that inspired Horace Mann to work so hard to accomplish the important reforms in education that he advocated. While he was still a boy, his father and older brother died, and he became responsible for supporting his family. Like most of the children in his town, he attended school only two or three months a year. Later, with the help of several teachers, he was able to study law and become a member of the Massachusetts bar, but he never forgot those early struggles.

While serving in the Massachusetts legislature, he signed an historic education bill that set up a state board of education. Without regret, he gave up his successful legal practice and political career to become the first secretary of the board. There he exercised an enormous influence during the critical period of reconstruction that brought into existence the American graded elementary school as a substitute for the older district school system. Under his leadership, the curriculum was restructured, the school year was increased to a minimum of six months, and mandatory schooling was extended to age sixteen. Other important reforms that came into existence under Mann's guidance included the establishment of state normal schools for teacher training, institutes for inservice teacher education, and lyceums for adult education. He was also instrumental in improving salaries for teachers and creating school libraries.

Mann's ideas about school reform were developed and distributed in the twelve annual reports to the state of Massachusetts that he wrote during his tenure as secretary of education. Considered quite radical at the time, the Massachusetts reforms later served as a model for the nation's educational system. Mann was formally recognized as the father of public education.

During his lifetime, Horace Mann worked tirelessly to extend educational opportunities to agrarian families and the children of poor laborers. In one of his last speeches he summed up his philosophy of education and life: "Be ashamed to die until you have won some victory for humanity." Surely, his own life was an example of that philosophy.

1. Which of the following titles would best express the main topic of the passage?

   (A) The Father of American Public Education
   (B) Philosophy of Education
   (C) The Massachusetts State Board of Education
   (D) Politics of Educational Institutions

2. Why does the author mention Horace Mann's early life?

   (A) As an example of the importance of an early education for success
   (B) To make the biography more complete
   (C) Because it served as the inspiration for his later work in education
   (D) In tribute to the teachers who helped him succeed

3. The word struggles in paragraph 1 could best be replaced by

   (A) valuable experiences
   (B) happy situations
   (C) influential people
   (D) difficult times

Beginning

Perhaps it was his own lack of adequate schooling that inspired Horace Mann to work so hard to accomplish the important reforms in education that he advocated. While he was still a boy, his father and older brother died, and he became responsible for supporting his family. Like most of the children in his town, he attended school only two or three months a year. Later, with the help of several teachers, he was able to study law and become a member of the Massachusetts bar, but he never forgot those early struggles.

While serving in the Massachusetts legislature, he signed an historic education bill that set up a state board of education. Without regret, he gave up his successful legal practice and political career to become the first secretary of the board. There he exercised an enormous influence during the critical period of reconstruction that brought into existence the American graded elementary school as a substitute for the older district school system. Under his leadership, the curriculum was restructured, the school year was increased to a minimum of six months, and mandatory schooling was extended to age

4. The word there refers to

Ⓐ the Massachusetts legislature
Ⓑ the state board of education
Ⓒ Mann's legal practice
Ⓓ his political career

Beginning

Perhaps it was his own lack of adequate schooling that inspired Horace Mann to work so hard to accomplish the important reforms in education that he advocated. While he was still a boy, his father and older brother died, and he became responsible for supporting his family. Like most of the children in his town, he attended school only two or three months a year. Later, with the help of several teachers, he was able to study law and become a member of the Massachusetts bar, but he never forgot those early struggles.

While serving in the Massachusetts legislature, he signed an historic education bill that set up a state board of education. Without regret, he gave up his successful legal practice and political career to become the first secretary of the board. There he exercised an enormous influence during the critical period of reconstruction that brought into existence the American graded elementary school as a substitute for the older district school system. Under his leadership, the curriculum was restructured, the school year was increased to a minimum of six months, and mandatory schooling was extended to age

5. The word mandatory in paragraph 2 is closest in meaning to

Ⓐ required
Ⓑ equal
Ⓒ excellent
Ⓓ basic

Beginning

Perhaps it was his own lack of adequate schooling that inspired Horace Mann to work so hard to accomplish the important reforms in education that he advocated. While he was still a boy, his father and older brother died, and he became responsible for supporting his family. Like most of the children in his town, he attended school only two or three months a year. Later, with the help of several teachers, he was able to study law and become a member of the Massachusetts bar, but he never forgot those early struggles.

While serving in the Massachusetts legislature, he signed an historic education bill that set up a state board of education. Without regret, he gave up his successful legal practice and political career to become the first secretary of the board. There he exercised an enormous influence during the critical period of reconstruction that brought into existence the American graded elementary school as a substitute for the older district school system. Under his leadership, the curriculum was restructured, the school year was increased to a minimum of six months, and mandatory schooling was extended to age

6. Look at the word extended in the passage. Click on another word or phrase in the **bold** text that is closest in meaning to extended.

More available

law and become a member of the Massachusetts bar, but he never forgot those early struggles.

While serving in the Massachusetts legislature, he signed an historic education bill that set up a state board of education. Without regret, he gave up his successful legal practice and political career to become the first secretary of the board. There he exercised an enormous influence during the critical period of reconstruction that brought into existence the American graded elementary school as a substitute for the older district school system. Under his leadership, the curriculum was restructured, the school year was increased to a minimum of six months, and mandatory schooling was extended to age sixteen. Other important reforms that came into existence under Mann s guidance included the establishment of state normal schools for teacher training, institutes for inservice teacher education, and lyceums for adult education. He was also instrumental in improving salaries for teachers and creating school libraries.

Mann s ideas about school reform were developed and distributed in the twelve annual

7. Click on the paragraph that explains how the educational reforms were distributed.

Scroll the passage to see all of the paragraphs.

8. With which of the following statements would the author most probably agree?

   Ⓐ Horace Mann's influence on American education was very great.
   Ⓑ A small but important influence on American education was exerted by Horace Mann.
   Ⓒ Few educators fully understood Horace Mann's influence on American education.
   Ⓓ The influence on American education by Horace Mann was not accepted or appreciated.

9. Horace Mann advocated all of the following EXCEPT

   Ⓐ a state board of education
   Ⓑ a district school system
   Ⓒ classes for adults
   Ⓓ graded elementary schools

10. The reforms that Horace Mann achieved

   Ⓐ were not very radical for the time
   Ⓑ were used only by the state of Massachusetts
   Ⓒ were later adopted by the nation as a model
   Ⓓ were enforced by the Massachusetts bar

11. With which of the following statements would Horace Mann most probably agree?

   Ⓐ Think in new ways.
   Ⓑ Help others.
   Ⓒ Study as much as possible.
   Ⓓ Work hard.

Organic architecture—that is, natural architecture—may vary in concept and form, but it is always faithful to natural principles. The architect dedicated to the promulgation of organic architecture rejects outright all rules imposed by individual preference or mere aesthetics in order to remain true to the nature of the site, the materials, the purpose of the structure, and the people who will ultimately use it. If these natural principles are upheld, then a bank cannot be built to look like a Greek temple. Form does not follow function; rather, form and function are inseparably two aspects of the same phenomenon. In other words, a building should be inspired by nature's forms and constructed with materials that retain and respect the natural characteristics of the setting to create harmony between the structure and its natural environment. It should maximize people's contact with and utilization of the outdoors. Furthermore, the rule of functionalism is upheld; that is, the principle of excluding everything that serves no practical purpose.

Natural principles, then, are principles of design, not style, expressed by means and modes of construction that reflect unity, balance, proportion, rhythm, and scale. Like a sculptor, the organic architect views the site and materials as an innate form that develops organically from within. Truth in architecture results in a natural, spontaneous structure in total harmony with the setting. For the most part, these structures find their geometric shapes in the contours of the land and their colors in the surrounding palette of nature.

From the outside, an organic structure is so much a part of nature that it is often obscured by it. In other words, it may not be easy, or maybe not even possible, for the human eye to separate the artificial structure from the natural terrain. Natural light, air, and view permeate the whole structure, providing a sense of communication with the outdoors. From the inside, living spaces open into one another. The number of walls for separate rooms is reduced to a minimum, allowing the functional spaces to flow together. Moreover, the interiors are sparse. Organic architecture incorporates built-in architectural features such as benches and storage areas to take the place of furniture.

12. According to the passage, what is another name for organic architecture?

Ⓐ Natural architecture
Ⓑ Aesthetic architecture
Ⓒ Principle architecture
Ⓓ Varied architecture

13. Look at the word it in the passage. Click on the word or phrase in the **bold** text that it refers to.

Beginning

Organic architecture—that is, natural architecture—may vary in concept and form, but it is always faithful to natural principles. The architect dedicated to the promulgation of organic architecture rejects outright all rules imposed by individual preference or mere aesthetics in order to remain true to the nature of the site, the materials, the purpose of the structure, and the people who will ultimately use it. If these natural principles are upheld, then a bank cannot be built to look like a Greek temple. Form does not follow function; rather, form and function are inseparably two aspects of the same phenomenon. In other words, a building should be inspired by nature's forms and constructed with materials that retain and respect the natural characteristics of the setting to create harmony between the structure and its natural environment. It should maximize people's contact with and utilization of the outdoors. Furthermore, the rule of functionalism is upheld; that is, the principle of excluding everything that serves no practical purpose.

Natural principles, then, are principles of design, not style, expressed by means and modes

14. The word ultimately in paragraph 1 could best be replaced by

Ⓐ fortunately
Ⓑ eventually
Ⓒ supposedly
Ⓓ obviously

Beginning

Organic architecture—that is, natural architecture—may vary in concept and form, but it is always faithful to natural principles. The architect dedicated to the promulgation of organic architecture rejects outright all rules imposed by individual preference or mere aesthetics in order to remain true to the nature of the site, the materials, the purpose of the structure, and the people who will ultimately use it. If these natural principles are upheld, then a bank cannot be built to look like a Greek temple. Form does not follow function; rather, form and function are inseparably two aspects of the same phenomenon. In other words, a building should be inspired by nature's forms and constructed with materials that retain and respect the natural characteristics of the setting to create harmony between the structure and its natural environment. It should maximize people's contact with and utilization of the outdoors. Furthermore, the rule of functionalism is upheld; that is, the principle of excluding everything that serves no practical purpose.

Natural principles, then, are principles of design, not style, expressed by means and modes

15. The word upheld in paragraph 1 is closest in meaning to

Ⓐ invalidated
Ⓑ disputed
Ⓒ promoted
Ⓓ perceived

Beginning

Organic architecture—that is, natural architecture—may vary in concept and form, but it is always faithful to natural principles. The architect dedicated to the promulgation of organic architecture rejects outright all rules imposed by individual preference or mere aesthetics in order to remain true to the nature of the site, the materials, the purpose of the structure, and the people who will ultimately use it. If these natural principles are upheld, then a bank cannot be built to look like a Greek temple. Form does not follow function; rather, form and function are inseparably two aspects of the same phenomenon. In other words, a building should be inspired by nature's forms and constructed with materials that retain and respect the natural characteristics of the setting to create harmony between the structure and its natural environment. It should maximize people's contact with and utilization of the outdoors. Furthermore, the rule of functionalism is upheld; that is, the principle of excluding everything that serves no practical purpose.

Natural principles, then, are principles of design, not style, expressed by means and modes

16. The following examples are all representative of natural architecture EXCEPT

Ⓐ a bank that is built to look like a Greek temple
Ⓑ a bank built so that the location is important to the structure
Ⓒ a bank that is built to conform to the colors of the natural surroundings
Ⓓ a bank that is built to be functional rather than beautiful

17. Why does the author compare an organic architect to a sculptor?

Ⓐ To emphasize aesthetics
Ⓑ To give an example of natural principles
Ⓒ To make a point about the development of geometry
Ⓓ To demonstrate the importance of style

18. The word obscured in paragraph 3 is closest in meaning to

Ⓐ difficult to see
Ⓑ in high demand
Ⓒ not very attractive
Ⓓ mutually beneficial

End

structure in total harmony with the setting. For the most part, these structures find their geometric shapes in the contours of the land and their colors in the surrounding palette of nature.

From the outside, an organic structure is so much a part of nature that it is often obscured by it. In other words, it may not be easy, or maybe not even possible, for the human eye to separate the artificial structure from the natural terrain. Natural light, air, and view permeate the whole structure, providing a sense of communication with the outdoors. From the inside, living spaces open into one another. The number of walls for separate rooms is reduced to a minimum, allowing the functional spaces to flow together. Moreover, the interiors are sparse. Organic architecture incorporates built-in architectural features such as benches and storage areas to take the place of furniture.

19. Look at the word contours in the passage. Click on another word or phrase in the **bold** text that is closest in meaning to contours.

End

architect views the site and materials as an innate form that develops organically from within. Truth in architecture results in a natural, spontaneous structure in total harmony with the setting. **For the most part, these structures find their geometric shapes in the contours of the land and their colors in the surrounding palette of nature.**

From the outside, an organic structure is so much a part of nature that it is often obscured by it. In other words, it may not be easy, or maybe not even possible, for the human eye to separate the artificial structure from the natural terrain. Natural light, air, and view permeate the whole structure, providing a sense of communication with the outdoors. From the inside, living spaces open into one another. The number of walls for separate rooms is reduced to a minimum, allowing the functional spaces to flow together. Moreover, the interiors are sparse. Organic architecture incorporates built-in architectural features such as benches and storage areas to take the place of furniture.

20. Click on the sentence in paragraph 3 that describes the furnishings appropriate for natural architecture.

Paragraph 3 is marked with an arrow (→).

End

architect views the site and materials as an innate form that develops organically from within. Truth in architecture results in a natural, spontaneous structure in total harmony with the setting. For the most part, these structures find their geometric shapes in the contours of the land and their colors in the surrounding palette of nature.

→ From the outside, an organic structure is so much a part of nature that it is often obscured by it. In other words, it may not be easy, or maybe not even possible, for the human eye to separate the artificial structure from the natural terrain. Natural light, air, and view permeate the whole structure, providing a sense of communication with the outdoors. From the inside, living spaces open into one another. The number of walls for separate rooms is reduced to a minimum, allowing the functional spaces to flow together. Moreover, the interiors are sparse. Organic architecture incorporates built-in architectural features such as benches and storage areas to take the place of furniture.

21. With which of the following statements would the author most probably agree?

Ⓐ Form follows function.
Ⓑ Function follows form.
Ⓒ Function is not important to form.
Ⓓ Form and function are one.

22. Which of the following statements best describes the architect's view of nature?

Ⓐ Nature should be conquered.
Ⓑ Nature should not be considered.
Ⓒ Nature should be respected.
Ⓓ Nature should be improved.

Although its purpose and techniques were often magical, alchemy was, in many ways, the predecessor of the modern science of chemistry. The fundamental premise of alchemy derived from the best philosophical dogma and scientific practice of the time, and the majority of educated persons between 1400 and 1600 believed that alchemy had great merit.

The earliest authentic works on European alchemy are those of the English monk Roger Bacon and the German philosopher St. Albertus Magnus. In their treatises they maintained that gold was the perfect metal and that inferior metals such as lead and mercury were removed by various degrees of imperfection from gold. They further asserted that these base metals could be transmuted to gold by blending them with a substance more perfect than gold. This elusive substance was referred to as the "philosopher's stone." The process was called transmutation.

Most of the early alchemists were artisans who were accustomed to keeping trade secrets and often resorted to cryptic terminology to record the progress of their work. The term *sun* was used for gold, *moon* for silver, and the five known planets for base metals. This convention of substituting symbolic language attracted some mystical philosophers who compared the search for the perfect metal with the struggle of humankind for the perfection of the soul. The philosophers began to use the artisan's terms in the mystical literature that they produced. Thus, by the fourteenth century, alchemy had developed two distinct groups of practitioners—the laboratory alchemist and the literary alchemist. Both groups of alchemists continued to work throughout the history of alchemy, but, of course, it was the literary alchemist who was more likely to produce a written record; therefore, much of what is known about the science of alchemy is derived from philosophers rather than from the alchemists who labored in laboratories.

Despite centuries of experimentation, laboratory alchemists failed to produce gold from other materials. However, they gained wide knowledge of chemical substances, discovered chemical properties, and invented many of the tools and techniques that are used by chemists today. Many laboratory alchemists earnestly devoted themselves to the scientific discovery of new compounds and reactions and, therefore, must be considered the legitimate forefathers of modern chemistry. They continued to call themselves alchemists, but they were becoming true chemists.

23. Which of the following is the main point of the passage?

(A) There were both laboratory and literary alchemists.
(B) Base metals can be transmuted to gold by blending them with a substance more perfect than gold.
(C) Roger Bacon and St. Albertus Magnus wrote about alchemy.
(D) Alchemy was the predecessor of modern chemistry.

24. The word authentic in paragraph 2 could best be replaced by

(A) valuable
(B) genuine
(C) complete
(D) comprehensible

Beginning

Although its purpose and techniques were often magical, alchemy was, in many ways, the predecessor of the modern science of chemistry. The fundamental premise of alchemy derived from the best philosophical dogma and scientific practice of the time, and the majority of educated persons between 1400 and 1600 believed that alchemy had great merit.

The earliest authentic works on European alchemy are those of the English monk Roger Bacon and the German philosopher St. Albertus Magnus. In their treatises they maintained that gold was the perfect metal and that inferior metals such as lead and mercury were removed by various degrees of imperfection from gold. They further asserted that these base metals could be transmuted to gold by blending them with a substance more perfect than gold. This elusive substance was referred to as the "philosopher's stone." The process was called transmutation.

Most of the early alchemists were artisans who were accustomed to keeping trade secrets and often resorted to cryptic terminology to record the progress of their work. The term *sun* was used for

25. Look at the word those in the passage. Click on the word or phrase in the **bold** text that those refers to.

Beginning

Although its purpose and techniques were often magical, alchemy was, in many ways, the predecessor of the modern science of chemistry. The fundamental premise of alchemy derived from the best philosophical dogma and scientific practice of the time, and the majority of educated persons between 1400 and 1600 believed that alchemy had great merit.

The earliest authentic works on European alchemy are those of the English monk Roger Bacon and the German philosopher St. Albertus Magnus. In their treatises they maintained that gold was the perfect metal and that inferior metals such as lead and mercury were removed by various degrees of imperfection from gold. They further asserted that these base metals could be transmuted to gold by blending them with a substance more perfect than gold. This elusive substance was referred to as the "philosopher's stone." The process was called transmutation.

Most of the early alchemists were artisans who were accustomed to keeping trade secrets and often resorted to cryptic terminology to record the progress of their work. The term *sun* was used for

26. According to the alchemists, what is the difference between base metals and gold?

Ⓐ Perfection
Ⓑ Chemical content
Ⓒ Temperature
Ⓓ Weight

27. Look at the word asserted in the passage. Click on the word or phrase in the **bold** text that is closest in meaning to asserted.

Beginning

Although its purpose and techniques were often magical, alchemy was, in many ways, the predecessor of the modern science of chemistry. The fundamental premise of alchemy derived from the best philosophical dogma and scientific practice of the time, and the majority of educated persons between 1400 and 1600 believed that alchemy had great merit.

The earliest authentic works on European alchemy are those of the English monk Roger Bacon and the German philosopher St. Albertus Magnus. **In their treatises they maintained that gold was the perfect metal and that inferior metals such as lead and mercury were removed by various degrees of imperfection from gold. They further asserted that these base metals could be transmuted to gold by blending them with a substance more perfect than gold.** This elusive substance was referred to as the "philosopher's stone." The process was called transmutation.

Most of the early alchemists were artisans who were accustomed to keeping trade secrets and often resorted to cryptic terminology to record the progress of their work. The term *sun* was used for

28. According to the passage, what is the "philosopher's stone"?

Ⓐ Lead that was mixed with gold
Ⓑ An element that was never found
Ⓒ Another name for alchemy
Ⓓ A base metal

29. The word **cryptic** in paragraph 3 could be replaced by which of the following?

Ⓐ scholarly
Ⓑ secret
Ⓒ foreign
Ⓓ precise

More Available

further asserted that these base metals could be transmuted to gold by blending them with a substance more perfect than gold. This elusive substance was referred to as the "philosopher's stone." The process was called transmutation.

Most of the early alchemists were artisans who were accustomed to keeping trade secrets and often resorted to **cryptic** terminology to record the progress of their work. The term *sun* was used for gold, *moon* for silver, and the five known planets for base metals. This convention of substituting symbolic language attracted some mystical philosophers who compared the search for the perfect metal with the struggle of humankind for the perfection of the soul. The philosophers began to use the artisan's terms in the mystical literature that they produced. Thus, by the fourteenth century, alchemy had developed two distinct groups of practitioners—the laboratory alchemist and the literary alchemist. Both groups of alchemists continued to work throughout the history of alchemy, but, of course, it was the literary alchemist who was more likely to produce a written record; therefore, much of what is known about the science

30. Why did the early alchemists use the terms *sun* and *moon*?

Ⓐ To keep the work secret
Ⓑ To make the work more literary
Ⓒ To attract philosophers
Ⓓ To produce a written record

31. Who were the first alchemists?

Ⓐ Chemists
Ⓑ Writers
Ⓒ Artisans
Ⓓ Linguists

32. In paragraph 3, the author suggests that we know about the history of alchemy because

Ⓐ the laboratory alchemists kept secret notes
Ⓑ the literary alchemists recorded it in writing
Ⓒ the mystical philosophers were not able to hide the secrets of alchemy
Ⓓ the historians were able to interpret the secret writings of the alchemists

Paragraph 3 is marked with an arrow (→).

More Available

further asserted that these base metals could be transmuted to gold by blending them with a substance more perfect than gold. This elusive substance was referred to as the "philosopher's stone." The process was called transmutation.

→ Most of the early alchemists were artisans who were accustomed to keeping trade secrets and often resorted to cryptic terminology to record the progress of their work. The term *sun* was used for gold, *moon* for silver, and the five known planets for base metals. This convention of substituting symbolic language attracted some mystical philosophers who compared the search for the perfect metal with the struggle of humankind for the perfection of the soul. The philosophers began to use the artisan's terms in the mystical literature that they produced. Thus, by the fourteenth century, alchemy had developed two distinct groups of practitioners—the laboratory alchemist and the literary alchemist. Both groups of alchemists continued to work throughout the history of alchemy, but, of course, it was the literary alchemist who was more likely to produce a written record; therefore, much of what is known about the science

33. With which of the following statements would the author most probably agree?

Ⓐ Alchemy must be considered a complete failure.
Ⓑ Some very important scientific discoveries were made by alchemists.
Ⓒ Most educated people dismissed alchemy during the time that it was practiced.
Ⓓ The literary alchemists were more important than the laboratory alchemists.

Human memory, formerly believed to be rather inefficient, is really much more sophisticated than that of a computer. Researchers approaching the problem from a variety of points of view have all concluded that there is a great deal more stored in our minds than has been generally supposed. Dr. Wilder Penfield, a Canadian neurosurgeon, proved that by stimulating their brains electrically, he could elicit the total recall of complex events in his subjects' lives. Even dreams and other minor events supposedly forgotten for many years suddenly emerged in detail.

The memory trace is the term for whatever forms the internal representation of the specific information about the event stored in the memory. Assumed to have been made by structural changes in the brain, the memory trace is not subject to direct observation but is rather a theoretical construct that is used to speculate about how information presented at a particular time can cause performance at a later time. Most theories include the strength of the memory trace as a variable in the degree of learning, retention, and retrieval possible for a memory. One theory is that the fantastic capacity for storage in the brain is the result of an almost unlimited combination of interconnections between brain cells, stimulated by patterns of activity. Repeated references to the same information support recall. Or, to say that another way, improved performance is the result of strengthening the chemical bonds in the memory.

Psychologists generally divide memory into at least two types, short-term and long-term memory, which combine to form working memory. Short-term memory contains what we are actively focusing on at any particular time, but items are not retained longer than twenty or thirty seconds without verbal rehearsal. We use short-term memory when we look up a telephone number and repeat it to ourselves until we can place the call. On the other hand, long-term memory can store facts, concepts, and experiences after we stop thinking about them. All conscious processing of information, as in problem solving for example, involves both short-term and long-term memory. As we repeat, rehearse, and recycle information, the memory trace is strengthened, allowing that information to move from short-term memory to long-term memory.

34. Which of the following is the main topic of the passage?

(A) Wilder Penfield
(B) Neurosurgery
(C) Human memory
(D) Chemical reactions

35. The word **formerly** in paragraph 1 could best be replaced by

(A) in the past
(B) from time to time
(C) in general
(D) by chance

Beginning

Human memory, **formerly** believed to be rather inefficient, is really much more sophisticated than that of a computer. Researchers approaching the problem from a variety of points of view have all concluded that there is a great deal more stored in our minds than has been generally supposed. Dr. Wilder Penfield, a Canadian neurosurgeon, proved that by stimulating their brains electrically, he could elicit the total recall of complex events in his subjects' lives. Even dreams and other minor events supposedly forgotten for many years suddenly emerged in detail.

The memory trace is the term for whatever forms the internal representation of the specific information about the event stored in the memory. Assumed to have been made by structural changes in the brain, the memory trace is not subject to direct observation but is rather a theoretical construct that is used to speculate about how information presented at a particular time can cause performance at a later time. Most theories include the strength of the memory trace as a variable in the degree of learning, retention, and retrieval possible for a memory. One theory is

36. Compared with a computer, human memory is

(A) more complex
(B) more limited
(C) less dependable
(D) less durable

37. Look at the word sophisticated in the passage. Click on the word in the **bold** text that is closest in meaning to sophisticated.

Beginning

Human memory, formerly believed to be rather inefficient, is really much more sophisticated than that of a computer. **Researchers approaching the problem from a variety of points of view have all concluded that there is a great deal more stored in our minds than has been generally supposed. Dr. Wilder Penfield, a Canadian neurosurgeon, proved that by stimulating their brains electrically, he could elicit the total recall of complex events in his subjects' lives.** Even dreams and other minor events supposedly forgotten for many years suddenly emerged in detail.

The memory trace is the term for whatever forms the internal representation of the specific information about the event stored in the memory. Assumed to have been made by structural changes in the brain, the memory trace is not subject to direct observation but is rather a theoretical construct that is used to speculate about how information presented at a particular time can cause performance at a later time. Most theories include the strength of the memory trace as a variable in the degree of learning, retention, and retrieval possible for a memory. One theory is

38. Look at the word that in the passage. Click on the word or phrase in the **bold** text that that refers to.

Beginning

Human memory, formerly believed to be rather inefficient, is really much more sophisticated than that of a computer. Researchers approaching the problem from a variety of points of view have all concluded that there is a great deal more stored in our minds than has been generally supposed. Dr. Wilder Penfield, a Canadian neurosurgeon, proved that by stimulating their brains electrically, he could elicit the total recall of complex events in his subjects' lives. Even dreams and other minor events supposedly forgotten for many years suddenly emerged in detail.

The memory trace is the term for whatever forms the internal representation of the specific information about the event stored in the memory. Assumed to have been made by structural changes in the brain, the memory trace is not subject to direct observation but is rather a theoretical construct that is used to speculate about how information presented at a particular time can cause performance at a later time. Most theories include the strength of the memory trace as a variable in the degree of learning, retention, and retrieval possible for a memory. One theory is

39. How did Penfield stimulate dreams and other minor events from the past?

Ⓐ By surgery
Ⓑ By electrical stimulation
Ⓒ By repetition
Ⓓ By chemical stimulation

40. According to the passage, the capacity for storage in the brain

Ⓐ can be understood by examining the physiology of the brain
Ⓑ is stimulated by patterns of activity
Ⓒ has a limited combination of relationships
Ⓓ is not influenced by repetition

41. The word bonds in paragraph 2 means

Ⓐ promises
Ⓑ agreements
Ⓒ connections
Ⓓ responsibilities

More Available

forms the internal representation of the specific information about the event stored in the memory. Assumed to have been made by structural changes in the brain, the memory trace is not subject to direct observation but is rather a theoretical construct that is used to speculate about how information presented at a particular time can cause performance at a later time. Most theories include the strength of the memory trace as a variable in the degree of learning, retention, and retrieval possible for a memory. One theory is that the fantastic capacity for storage in the brain is the result of an almost unlimited combination of interconnections between brain cells, stimulated by patterns of activity. Repeated references to the same information support recall. Or, to say that another way, improved performance is the result of strengthening the chemical bonds in the memory.

Psychologists generally divide memory into at least two types, short-term and long-term memory, which combine to form working memory. Short-term memory contains what we are actively focusing on at any particular time, but items are not retained longer than twenty or thirty seconds

42. Click on the sentence in paragraph 3 that defines working memory.

Paragraph 3 is marked with an arrow (→).

End

interconnections between brain cells, stimulated by patterns of activity. Repeated references to the same information support recall. Or, to say that another way, improved performance is the result of strengthening the chemical bonds in the memory.

→ Psychologists generally divide memory into at least two types, short-term and long-term memory, which combine to form working memory. Short-term memory contains what we are actively focusing on at any particular time, but items are not retained longer than twenty or thirty seconds without verbal rehearsal. We use short-term memory when we look up a telephone number and repeat it to ourselves until we can place the call. On the other hand, long-term memory can store facts, concepts, and experiences after we stop thinking about them. All conscious processing of information, as in problem solving for example, involves both short-term and long-term memory. As we repeat, rehearse, and recycle information, the memory trace is strengthened, allowing that information to move from short-term memory to long-term memory.

43 Why does the author mention looking up a telephone number?

- Ⓐ It is an example of short-term memory.
- Ⓑ It is an example of a weak memory trace.
- Ⓒ It is an example of an experiment.
- Ⓓ It is an example of how we move short-term memory to long-term memory.

44. All of the following are true of a memory trace EXCEPT that

- Ⓐ it is probably made by structural changes in the brain
- Ⓑ it is able to be observed directly by investigators
- Ⓒ it is a theoretical construct that we use to form hypotheses
- Ⓓ it is related to the degree of recall supported by repetition

45. With which of the following statements would the author most likely agree?

- Ⓐ The mind has a much greater capacity for memory than was previously believed.
- Ⓑ The physical basis for memory is clear.
- Ⓒ Different points of view are valuable.
- Ⓓ Human memory is inefficient.

To check your answers for Model Test 5, refer to the Answer Key on page 547–548. For an explanation of the answers, refer to the Explanatory Answers for Model Test 5 on pages 585–592.

Writing Section Model Test 5

When you take a Model Test, you should use one sheet of paper, both sides. Time each Model Test carefully. After you have read the topic, you should spend 30 minutes writing. For results that would be closest to the actual testing situation, it is recommended that an English teacher score your test, using the guidelines on page 325 of this book.

Some people believe that it is very important to make large amounts of money, while others are satisfied to earn a comfortable living. Analyze each viewpoint and take a stand.

Notes

Model Test 6
Computer-Assisted TOEFL

Section 1: Listening

The Listening section of the test measures the ability to understand conversations and talks in English. You will use headphones to listen to the conversations and talks. While you are listening, pictures of the speakers or other information will be presented on your computer screen. There are two parts to the Listening section, with special directions for each part.

On the day of the test, the amount of time you will have to answer all of the questions will appear on the computer screen. The time you spend listening to the test material will not be counted. The listening material and questions about it will be presented only one time. You will not be allowed to take notes or have any paper at your computer. You will both see and hear the questions before the answer choices appear. You can take as much time as you need to select an answer; however, it will be to your advantage to answer the questions as quickly as possible. You may change your answer as many times as you want before you confirm it. After you have confirmed an answer, you will not be able to return to the question.

Before you begin working on the Listening section, you will have an opportunity to adjust the volume of the sound. You will not be able to change the volume after you have started the test.

QUESTION DIRECTIONS — Part A

In Part A of the Listening section, you will hear short conversations between two people. In some of the conversations, each person speaks only once. In other conversations, one or both of the people speak more than once. Each conversation is followed by one question about it.

Each question in this part has four answer choices. You should click on the best answer to each question. Answer the questions on the basis of what is stated or implied by the speakers.

1. What does the woman mean?

Ⓐ She does not know how to play tennis.
Ⓑ She has to study.
Ⓒ She does not like the man.
Ⓓ She does not qualify to play.

2. What does the woman mean?

Ⓐ She has no attendance policy.
Ⓑ The attendance policy is not the same for undergraduates and graduate students.
Ⓒ The grade will be affected by absences.
Ⓓ This class is not for graduate students.

3. What does the woman say about Ali?

Ⓐ He is studying only at the American Language Institute.
Ⓑ He is taking three classes at the university.
Ⓒ He is a part-time student.
Ⓓ He is surprised.

4. What does the woman mean?

Ⓐ She will help the man.
Ⓑ She is not Miss Evans.
Ⓒ Dr. Warren has already gone.
Ⓓ The man should wait for Dr. Warren to answer the call.

5. What will the woman probably do?

(A) Return home
(B) Ask someone else about the shuttle
(C) Make a telephone call
(D) Board the bus

6. What does the woman mean?

(A) She will go to the bookstore.
(B) The books were too expensive.
(C) There weren't any math and English books left.
(D) She does not need any books.

7. What does the woman suggest the man do?

(A) Take a different route
(B) Leave earlier than planned
(C) Wait until seven to leave
(D) Stay at home

8. What does the woman mean?

(A) The class with the graduate assistant is very enjoyable.
(B) The students make a log of errors in the class.
(C) The graduate assistant ridicules his students.
(D) She is sorry that she took the class with the graduate assistant.

9. What does the man mean?

(A) He did not mean to insult the woman.
(B) What he said to Susan was true.
(C) The woman does not have an accent.
(D) Susan did not report the conversation accurately.

10. What does the woman agree to do for the man?

(A) Tell him the time
(B) Take care of his bag
(C) Help him find his books
(D) Go with him

11. What does the man mean?

(A) He has heard the woman talk about this often.
(B) He understands the woman's point of view.
(C) He is too tired to talk about it.
(D) He can hear the woman very well.

12. What does the woman imply?

(A) Mike does not have a car.
(B) Mike's brother is taking a break.
(C) Mike is in Florida.
(D) Mike is visiting his brother.

13. What does the woman advise the man to do?

(A) Get a job
(B) Finish the assignment
(C) Begin his project
(D) Pay his bills

14. What does the woman mean?

(A) She is not sure about going.
(B) She does not want to go to the show.
(C) She wants to know why the man asked her.
(D) She would like to go with the man.

15. What had the woman assumed about Bill and Carol?

(A) They would not get married.
(B) They were still away on their honeymoon.
(C) They didn't go on a honeymoon.
(D) They had not planned a large wedding.

16. What does the woman mean?

(A) She has already reviewed for the test.
(B) The test is important to her.
(C) The review session will not be helpful.
(D) The man does not understand her.

17. What will the man probably do?

(A) Telephone his sponsor
(B) Collect his check
(C) Help the woman to look for his check
(D) Ask the woman to look again

QUESTION DIRECTIONS — Part B

In Part B of the Listening section, you will hear several longer conversations and talks. Each conversation or talk is followed by several questions. The conversations, talks, and questions will not be repeated.

The conversations and talks are about a variety of topics. You do not need special knowledge of the topics to answer the questions correctly. Rather, you should answer each question on the basis of what is stated or implied by the speakers in the conversations or talks.

For most of the questions, you will need to click on the best of four possible answers. Some questions will have special directions. The special directions will appear in a box on the computer screen.

18. What is Gary's problem?

Ⓐ He is sick with the flu.
Ⓑ He is in the hospital.
Ⓒ He has missed some quizzes.
Ⓓ He is behind in lab.

19. What does Gary want Margaret to do?

Ⓐ Go to lab for him
Ⓑ Let him copy her notes
Ⓒ Help him study
Ⓓ Be his lab partner

20. What does Margaret offer to do?

Ⓐ Meet with him to clarify her notes
Ⓑ Make a copy of the quizzes for him
Ⓒ Read his notes before the next lab
Ⓓ Show him how to do the lab experiments

21. What is Margaret's attitude in this conversation?

Click on 2 answers.

[A] Helpful
[B] Worried
[C] Apologetic
[D] Friendly

22. What is the main topic of this lecture?

Ⓐ Novelists of this century
Ⓑ F. Scott Fitzgerald's work
Ⓒ First novels by young authors
Ⓓ Film versions of F. Scott Fitzgerald's novels

23. Why wasn't Fitzgerald more successful in his later life?

Click on 2 answers.

[A] He had little natural talent.
[B] He was a compulsive drinker.
[C] The film versions of his books were not successful.
[D] He did not adjust to a changing world.

24. According to the lecturer, what do we know about the novels written by F. Scott Fitzgerald?

Ⓐ They described the Jazz Age.
Ⓑ They described the Deep South.
Ⓒ They were based upon war experiences.
Ⓓ They were written in stream-of-consciousness style.

25. What does the professor want the class to do after the lecture?

Ⓐ Write a book report
Ⓑ Read one of Fitzgerald's books
Ⓒ Watch and discuss a video
Ⓓ Research Fitzgerald's life

26. What is the main purpose of the talk?

Ⓐ To explain chamber music
Ⓑ To give examples of composers
Ⓒ To congratulate the University Quartet
Ⓓ To introduce madrigal singing

27. What is the origin of the term *chamber music*?

Ⓐ A medieval musical instrument
Ⓑ An old word that means small group
Ⓒ A place where the music was played
Ⓓ A name of one of the musicians who created it

28. According to the speaker, which instruments are the most popular for chamber music?

Click on 2 answers.

[A] Piano
[B] Brass
[C] Strings
[D] Percussion

29. Why does the speaker mention Johann Sebastian Bach?

(A) He was a famous composer.
(B) He composed the pieces that will be performed.
(C) He wrote vocal chamber music.
(D) He wrote trio sonatas.

30. What will the listeners hear next?

(A) A discussion of music from the eighteenth century
(B) A concert by the University Quartet
(C) An introduction to religious music
(D) A history of music from the Elizabethan Period

31. Why did the man go to the Chemical Engineering Department?

(A) To make an appointment
(B) To cancel his appointment
(C) To change his appointment time
(D) To rearrange his schedule so that he could keep his appointment

32. What does the woman say about Dr. Benjamin?

(A) He is busy on Wednesday.
(B) He will not be in on Wednesday.
(C) He does not schedule appointments on Wednesday.
(D) He will be moving his Wednesday appointment to Thursday this week.

33. What did the secretary offer to do?

(A) Give him an appointment at three o'clock on Wednesday
(B) Give him an appointment at either four-thirty on Wednesday or ten o'clock on Thursday
(C) Give him an appointment at lunch time
(D) Give him a new appointment earlier on the same day as his original appointment

34. What did the man decide to do?

(A) Make a new appointment later
(B) Cancel his regular appointment
(C) Rearrange his schedule to keep his original appointment
(D) Call back later when Dr. Benjamin is in

35. What is the main topic of this lecture?

(A) Health food
(B) The processing of bread
(C) Organic gardens
(D) Poisons

36. Which term is used to identify foods that have not been processed or canned?

(A) Refined foods
(B) Natural foods
(C) Organic foods
(D) Unprocessed foods

37. What happens to food when it is processed?

Click on 2 answers.

[A] Some toxic chemicals may be added.
[B] The food is cooked.
[C] Vitamins are added to the food.
[D] The vitamin content is reduced.

38. Which word best describes the speaker's attitude toward health foods?

(A) Uninformed
(B) Convinced
(C) Uncertain
(D) Humorous

39. How did the professor define the Stone Age?
    Ⓐ The time when the first agricultural communities were established
    Ⓑ The time when the glaciers from the last Ice Age receded
    Ⓒ The time when prehistoric humans began to make tools
    Ⓓ The time when metals were introduced as material for tools and weapons

40. According to the lecturer, which two occupations describe the Neanderthals?
    Ⓐ Farmers
    Ⓑ Hunters
    Ⓒ Gatherers
    Ⓓ Artisans

41. Identify the three time periods associated with the Stone Age.

    Click on a phrase. Then click on the empty box in the correct row.

    Use each phrase only once.

    [A] **appearance of *Homo sapiens***
    [B] **establishment of agricultural villages**
    [C] **use of tools**

Old Stone Age	
Middle Stone Age	
Late Stone Age	

42. Why did tools change during the Late Stone Age?
    Ⓐ They began to be used for domestic purposes.
    Ⓑ They were not strong enough for the cold weather.
    Ⓒ They were adapted as farm tools.
    Ⓓ They were more complex as humans became more creative.

43. What marked the end of the Stone Age?
    Ⓐ The introduction of farming
    Ⓑ The preference for metal tools
    Ⓒ The decline of Neanderthals
    Ⓓ The onset of the Ice Age

44. What is a trap?
    Ⓐ A man-made storage area for oil
    Ⓑ Gas and water that collect near oil deposits
    Ⓒ An underground formation that stops the flow of oil
    Ⓓ Cracks and holes that allow the oil to move

45. Select the diagram of the anticline trap that was described in the lecture.

    Click on a diagram.

[A]

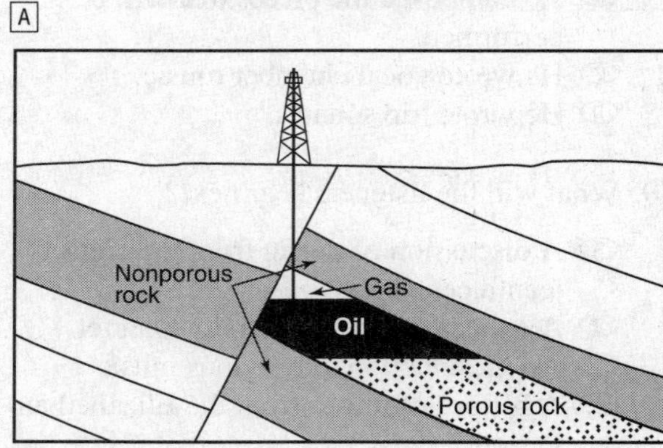

[B]

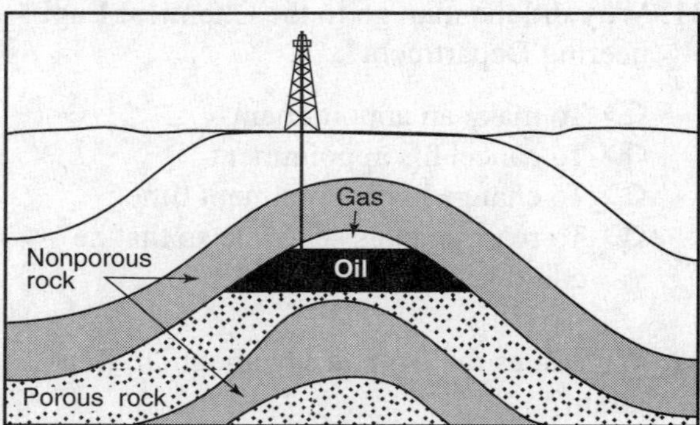

[C]

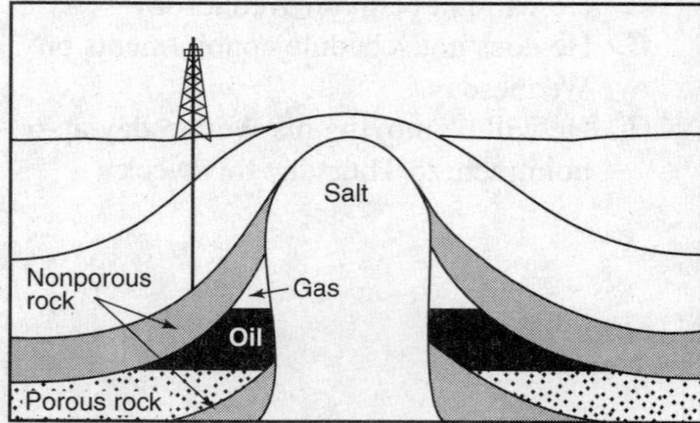

46. Identify the nonporous rock in the diagram.

Click on the letter.

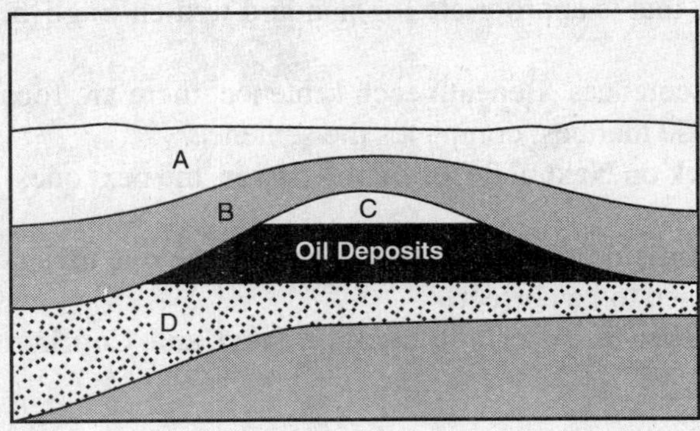

47. According to the speaker, how can geologists locate salt domes?

(A) They look for a bulge in an otherwise flat area.
(B) They look for an underground rock formation shaped like an arch.
(C) They look for salt on the surface of the area.
(D) They look for a large crack in the Earth.

48. What is the woman's problem?

(A) She does not want to take the course.
(B) She does not know which professor to choose.
(C) She does not understand the course requirements.
(D) She does not want to take the man's advice.

49. What do Dr. Perkins and Dr. Robinson have in common?

(A) They teach two different sections of the same class.
(B) They both use traditional teaching methods.
(C) They have been teaching for a long time.
(D) They are not considered very good teachers.

50. Why did the woman decide to take the class with Dr. Robinson?

Click on 2 answers.

[A] She has already taken classes with Dr. Robinson.
[B] She prefers to take lecture classes.
[C] She wants to take the class with the man.
[D] She likes a more traditional approach to teaching.

Section 2: Structure

This section measures the ability to recognize language that is appropriate for standard written English. There are two types of questions in this section.

In the first type of question, there are incomplete sentences. Beneath each sentence, there are four words or phrases. You will choose the one word or phrase that best completes the sentence.

Clicking on a choice darkens the oval. After you click on **Next** and **Confirm Answer**, the next question will be presented.

The second type of question has four underlined words or phrases. You will choose the one underlined word or phrase that must be changed for the sentence to be correct.

Clicking on an underlined word or phrase will darken it. After you click on **Next** and **Confirm Answer**, the next question will be presented.

1. When friends insist on ------ expensive gifts, it makes most Americans uncomfortable.

   (A) them to accept
   (B) their accepting
   (C) they accepting
   (D) they accept

2. Gilbert Stuart is considered by most art critics ------ greatest portrait painter in the North American colonies.

   (A) that he was
   (B) as he was
   (C) who was the
   (D) the

3. The extent to which (A) an individual is a product of either heredity or environment cannot proved (B), but several theories (C) have been (D) proposed.

4. A child in the first grade tends to be --------- all of the other children in the class.

   (A) the same old to
   (B) the same age than
   (C) as old like
   (D) the same age as

5. The bird's egg is such an efficient structure for protecting the embryo inside ------ difficult for the hatchling to break.

   (A) that is
   (B) that
   (C) and is
   (D) that it is

6. Jane Addams had already (A) established Hull House in Chicago (B) and began (C) her work in the Women's Suffrage Movement when she was awarded (D) the Nobel Prize for peace.

7. The flag of the original first (A) colonies may or may not have been made (B) by Betsy Ross (C) during the Revolution (D).

8. As a safety measure, the detonator for a nuclear device may be made of ------, each of which is controlled by a different employee.

   (A) two equipments
   (B) two pieces of equipments
   (C) two pieces of equipment
   (D) two equipment pieces

9. -------- that the English settled in Jamestown.

Ⓐ In 1607 that it was
Ⓑ That in 1607
Ⓒ Because in 1607
Ⓓ It was in 1607

10. The most common (A) form of (B) treatment it (C) is mass inoculation and chlorination of water sources. (D)

11. An equilateral triangle is a triangle ------ and three angles of equal size.

Ⓐ that have three sides of equal length
Ⓑ it has three sides equally long
Ⓒ that has three sides of equal length
Ⓓ having three equal length sides in it

12. ------ are found on the surface of the moon.

Ⓐ Craters and waterless seas that
Ⓑ When craters and waterless seas
Ⓒ Craters and waterless seas
Ⓓ Since craters and waterless seas

13. Without alphabetical order, dictionaries (A) would be (B) impossibility (C) to use. (D)

14. ------ two waves pass a given point simultaneously, they will have no effect on each other's subsequent motion.

Ⓐ So that
Ⓑ They are
Ⓒ That
Ⓓ If

15. The (A) Pickerel Frog, native to southern Canada and the eastern United States, should be avoided (B) because their (C) skin secretions are lethal to small animals and irritating (D) to humans.

16. Staying in a hotel costs ------ renting a room in a dormitory for a week.

Ⓐ twice more than
Ⓑ twice as much as
Ⓒ as much twice as
Ⓓ as much as twice

17. Unlike most Europeans, many Americans ------ a bowl of cereal for breakfast every day.

Ⓐ used to eating
Ⓑ are used to eat
Ⓒ are used to eating
Ⓓ use to eat

18. Scientists had previously (A) estimated that the Grand Canyon in Arizona is (B) ten million years old, but now, by using (C) a more modern dating method, they agree that the age is closer to six million years. (D)

19. Although jogging (A) is a good way to lose weight and improve one's physical condition, most (B) doctors recommend that the potential jogger begin in a correct manner (C) by getting (D) a complete checkup.

20. Some (A) conifers, that is, (B) tree (C) that have cones, are (D) able to thrive on poor, thin soil.

21. Fast-food restaurants have become popular because many working people want -------- .

Ⓐ to eat quickly and cheaply
Ⓑ eating quickly and cheaply
Ⓒ eat quickly and cheaply
Ⓓ the eat quickly and cheaply

22. Airports must be located (A) near to (B) major population centers for the advantage of air transportation (C) to be retained (D).

23. On an untimed test, to answer accurately is more important than ------.

(A) a quick finish
(B) to finish quickly
(C) finishing quickly
(D) you finish quickly

24. It is (A) imperative that a graduate student maintains (B) a grade point average of (C) "B" in his (D) major field.

25. Dairying is (A) concerned not only with (B) the production of milk, but (C) with the manufacture of milk products such as (D) butter and cheese.

Section 3: Reading

This section measures the ability to read and understand short passages similar in topic and style to those that students are likely to encounter in North American universities and colleges. This section contains reading passages and questions about the passages. There are several different types of questions in this section.

In the Reading section, you will first have the opportunity to read the passage.

You will use the scroll bar to view the rest of the passage.

When you have finished reading the passage, you will use the mouse to click on **Proceed**. Then the questions about the passage will be presented. You are to choose the one best answer to each question. Answer all questions about the information in a passage on the basis of what is stated or implied in that passage.

Most of the questions will be multiple-choice questions. To answer these questions you will click on a choice below the question.

To answer some questions, you will click on a word or phrase.

To answer some questions, you will click on a sentence in the passage.

To answer some questions, you will click on a square to add a sentence to the passage.

A geyser is the result of underground water under the combined conditions of high temperatures and increased pressure beneath the surface of the Earth. Since temperature rises about 1°F for every sixty feet under the Earth's surface, and pressure increases with depth, water that seeps down in cracks and fissures until it reaches very hot rocks in the Earth's interior becomes heated to a temperature of approximately 290°F.

Water under pressure can remain liquid at temperatures above its normal boiling point, but in a geyser, the weight of the water nearer the surface exerts so much pressure on the deeper water that the water at the bottom of the geyser reaches much higher temperatures than does the water at the top of the geyser. As the deep water becomes hotter, and consequently lighter, it suddenly rises to the surface and shoots out of the surface in the form of steam and hot water. In turn, the explosion agitates all the water in the geyser reservoir, creating further explosions. Immediately afterward, the water again flows into the underground reservoir, heating begins, and the process repeats itself.

In order to function, then, a geyser must have a source of heat, a reservoir where water can be stored until the temperature rises to an unstable point, an opening through which the hot water and steam can escape, and underground channels for resupplying water after an eruption.

Favorable conditions for geysers exist in regions of geologically recent volcanic activity, especially in areas of more than average precipitation. For the most part, geysers are located in three regions of the world: New Zealand, Iceland, and the Yellowstone National Park area of the United States. The most famous geyser in the world is Old Faithful in Yellowstone Park. Old Faithful erupts every hour, rising to a height of 125 to 170 feet and expelling more than ten thousand gallons during each eruption. Old Faithful earned its name because, unlike most geysers, it has never failed to erupt on schedule even once in eighty years of observation.

1. Which of the following is the main topic of the passage?

Ⓐ The Old Faithful geyser in Yellowstone National Park
Ⓑ The nature of geysers
Ⓒ The ratio of temperature to pressure in underground water
Ⓓ Regions of geologically recent volcanic activity

2. In order for a geyser to erupt

Ⓐ hot rocks must rise to the surface of the Earth
Ⓑ water must flow underground
Ⓒ it must be a warm day
Ⓓ the earth must not be rugged or broken

3. Look at the word approximately in the passage. Click on another word or phrase in the **bold** text that is closest in meaning to approximately.

Beginning

A geyser is the result of underground water under the combined conditions of high temperatures and increased pressure beneath the surface of the Earth. **Since temperature rises about 1°F for every sixty feet under the Earth's surface, and pressure increases with depth, water that seeps down in cracks and fissures until it reaches very hot rocks in the Earth's interior becomes heated to a temperature of approximately 290°F.**

Water under pressure can remain liquid at temperatures above its normal boiling point, but in a geyser, the weight of the water nearer the surface exerts so much pressure on the deeper water that the water at the bottom of the geyser reaches much higher temperatures than does the water at the top of the geyser. As the deep water becomes hotter, and consequently lighter, it suddenly rises to the surface and shoots out of the surface in the form of steam and hot water. In turn, the explosion agitates all the water in the geyser reservoir, creating further explosions. Immediately afterward, the water again flows into the underground reservoir, heating begins, and the process repeats itself.

4. The word **it** in paragraph 1 refers to

Ⓐ water
Ⓑ depth
Ⓒ pressure
Ⓓ surface

Beginning

A geyser is the result of underground water under the combined conditions of high temperatures and increased pressure beneath the surface of the Earth. **Since temperature rises about 1°F for every sixty feet under the Earth's surface, and pressure increases with depth, water that seeps down in cracks and fissures until it reaches very hot rocks in the Earth's interior becomes heated to a temperature of approximately 290°F.**

Water under pressure can remain liquid at temperatures above its normal boiling point, but in a geyser, the weight of the water nearer the surface exerts so much pressure on the deeper water that the water at the bottom of the geyser reaches much higher temperatures than does the water at the top of the geyser. As the deep water becomes hotter, and consequently lighter, it suddenly rises to the surface and shoots out of the surface in the form of steam and hot water. In turn, the explosion agitates all the water in the geyser reservoir, creating further explosions. Immediately afterward, the water again flows into the underground reservoir, heating begins, and the process repeats itself.

5. Click on the paragraph that explains the role of water pressure in an active geyser.

Scroll the passage to see all of the paragraphs.

6. As depth increases

Ⓐ pressure increases but temperature does not
Ⓑ temperature increases but pressure does not
Ⓒ both pressure and temperature increase
Ⓓ neither pressure nor temperature increases

7. Why does the author mention **New Zealand** and **Iceland** in paragraph 4?

Ⓐ To compare areas of high volcanic activity
Ⓑ To describe the Yellowstone National Park
Ⓒ To provide examples of areas where geysers are located
Ⓓ To name the two regions where all geysers are found

Paragraph 4 is marked with an arrow (→).

End

Immediately afterward, the water again flows into the underground reservoir, heating begins, and the process repeats itself.

In order to function, then, a geyser must have a source of heat, a reservoir where water can be stored until the temperature rises to an unstable point, an opening through which the hot water and steam can escape, and underground channels for resupplying water after an eruption.

→ Favorable conditions for geysers exist in regions of geologically recent volcanic activity, especially in areas of more than average precipitation. For the most part, geysers are located in three regions of the world: New Zealand, Iceland, and the Yellowstone National Park area of the United States. The most famous geyser in the world is Old Faithful in Yellowstone Park. Old Faithful erupts every hour, rising to a height of 125 to 170 feet and expelling more than ten thousand gallons during each eruption. Old Faithful earned its name because, unlike most geysers, it has never failed to erupt on schedule even once in eighty years of observation.

8. How often does Old Faithful erupt?

Ⓐ Every 10 minutes
Ⓑ Every 60 minutes
Ⓒ Every 125 minutes
Ⓓ Every 170 minutes

9. The word expelling in paragraph 4 is closest in meaning to

Ⓐ heating
Ⓑ discharging
Ⓒ supplying
Ⓓ wasting

End

Immediately afterward, the water again flows into the underground reservoir, heating begins, and the process repeats itself.

In order to function, then, a geyser must have a source of heat, a reservoir where water can be stored until the temperature rises to an unstable point, an opening through which the hot water and steam can escape, and underground channels for resupplying water after an eruption.

Favorable conditions for geysers exist in regions of geologically recent volcanic activity, especially in areas of more than average precipitation. For the most part, geysers are located in three regions of the world: New Zealand, Iceland, and the Yellowstone National Park area of the United States. The most famous geyser in the world is Old Faithful in Yellowstone Park. Old Faithful erupts every hour, rising to a height of 125 to 170 feet and expelling more than ten thousand gallons during each eruption. Old Faithful earned its name because, unlike most geysers, it has never failed to erupt on schedule even once in eighty years of observation.

10. What does the author mean by the statement Old Faithful earned its name because, unlike most geysers, it has never failed to erupt on schedule even once in eighty years of observation?

Ⓐ Old Faithful always erupts on schedule.
Ⓑ Old Faithful is usually predictable.
Ⓒ Old Faithful erupts predictably like other geysers.
Ⓓ Old Faithful received its name because it has been observed for many years.

11. According to the passage, what is required for a geyser to function?

Ⓐ A source of heat, a place for water to collect, an opening, and underground channels
Ⓑ An active volcano nearby and a water reservoir
Ⓒ Channels in the Earth and heavy rainfall
Ⓓ Volcanic activity, underground channels, and steam

This question has often been posed: Why were the Wright brothers able to succeed in an effort at which so many others had failed? Many explanations have been mentioned, but three reasons are most often cited. First, they were a team. Both men worked congenially and cooperatively, read the same books, located and shared information, talked incessantly about the possibility of manned flight, and served as a consistent source of inspiration and encouragement to each other. Quite simply, two geniuses are better than one.

Both were glider pilots. Unlike some other engineers who experimented with the theories of flight, Orville and Wilbur Wright experienced the practical aspects of aerodynamics by building and flying in kites and gliders. Each craft they built was slightly superior to the last, as they incorporated knowledge that they had gained from previous failures. They had realized from their experiments that the most serious challenge in manned flight would be stabilizing and maneuvering the aircraft once it was airborne. While others concentrated their efforts on the problem of achieving lift for take-off, the Wright brothers were focusing on developing a three-axis control for guiding their aircraft. By the time that the brothers started to build an airplane, they were already among the world's best glider pilots; they knew the problems of riding the air first hand.

In addition, the Wright brothers had designed more effective wings for the airplane than had been previously engineered. Using a wind tunnel, they tested more than two hundred different wing designs, recording the effects of slight variations in shape on the pressure of air on the wings. The data from these experiments allowed the Wright brothers to construct a superior wing for their aircraft.

In spite of these advantages, however, the Wright brothers might not have succeeded had they not been born at precisely the opportune moment in history. Attempts to achieve manned flight in the early nineteenth century were doomed because the steam engines that powered the aircrafts were too heavy in proportion to the power that they produced. But by the end of the nineteenth century, when the brothers were experimenting with engineering options, a relatively light internal combustion engine had already been invented, and they were able to bring the ratio of weight to power within acceptable limits for flight.

12. Which of the following is the main topic of the passage?

Ⓐ The reasons why the Wright brothers succeeded in manned flight
Ⓑ The advantage of the internal combustion engine in the Wright brothers' experiments
Ⓒ The Wright brothers' experience as pilots
Ⓓ The importance of gliders to the development of airplanes

13. The word cited in paragraph 1 is closest in meaning to which of the following?

Ⓐ disregarded
Ⓑ mentioned
Ⓒ considered
Ⓓ proven

Beginning

This question has often been posed: Why were the Wright brothers able to succeed in an effort at which so many others had failed? Many explanations have been mentioned, but three reasons are most often cited. First, they were a team. Both men worked congenially and cooperatively, read the same books, located and shared information, talked incessantly about the possibility of manned flight, and served as a consistent source of inspiration and encouragement to each other. Quite simply, two geniuses are better than one.

Both were glider pilots. Unlike some other engineers who experimented with the theories of flight, Orville and Wilbur Wright experienced the practical aspects of aerodynamics by building and flying in kites and gliders. Each craft they built was slightly superior to the last, as they incorporated knowledge that they had gained from previous failures. They had realized from their experiments that the most serious challenge in manned flight would be stabilizing and maneuvering the aircraft once it was airborne. While others concentrated their efforts on the problem of achieving lift for

14. The word incessantly in paragraph 1 could best be replaced by which of the following?

Ⓐ confidently
Ⓑ intelligently
Ⓒ constantly
Ⓓ optimistically

Beginning

This question has often been posed: Why were the Wright brothers able to succeed in an effort at which so many others had failed? Many explanations have been mentioned, but three reasons are most often cited. First, they were a team. Both men worked congenially and cooperatively, read the same books, located and shared information, talked incessantly about the possibility of manned flight, and served as a consistent source of inspiration and encouragement to each other. Quite simply, two geniuses are better than one.

Both were glider pilots. Unlike some other engineers who experimented with the theories of flight, Orville and Wilbur Wright experienced the practical aspects of aerodynamics by building and flying in kites and gliders. Each craft they built was slightly superior to the last, as they incorporated knowledge that they had gained from previous failures. They had realized from their experiments that the most serious challenge in manned flight would be stabilizing and maneuvering the aircraft once it was airborne. While others concentrated their efforts on the problem of achieving lift for

15. What kind of experience did the Wright brothers have that distinguished them from their competitors?

Ⓐ They were geniuses.
Ⓑ They were glider pilots.
Ⓒ They were engineers.
Ⓓ They were inventors.

16. Click on the sentence in paragraph 2 that explains the most serious problem that the Wright brothers anticipated in constructing a manned aircraft.

Paragraph 2 is marked with an arrow (→).

More Available

consistent source of inspiration and encouragement to each other. Quite simply, two geniuses are better than one.

→ Both were glider pilots. Unlike some other engineers who experimented with the theories of flight, Orville and Wilbur Wright experienced the practical aspects of aerodynamics by building and flying in kites and gliders. Each craft they built was slightly superior to the last, as they incorporated knowledge that they had gained from previous failures. They had realized from their experiments that the most serious challenge in manned flight would be stabilizing and maneuvering the aircraft once it was airborne. While others concentrated their efforts on the problem of achieving lift for take-off, the Wright brothers were focusing on developing a three-axis control for guiding their aircraft. By the time that the brothers started to build an airplane, they were already among the world's best glider pilots; they knew the problems of riding the air first hand.

In addition, the Wright brothers had designed more effective wings for the airplane than had been previously engineered. Using a wind tunnel,

17. Look at the word maneuvering in the passage. Click on the word or phrase in the **bold** text that is closest in meaning to maneuvering.

More Available

Both were glider pilots. Unlike some other engineers who experimented with the theories of flight, Orville and Wilbur Wright experienced the practical aspects of aerodynamics by building and flying in kites and gliders. Each craft they built was slightly superior to the last, as they incorporated knowledge that they had gained from previous failures. **They had realized from their experiments that the most serious challenge in manned flight would be stabilizing and maneuvering the aircraft once it was airborne. While others concentrated their efforts on the problem of achieving lift for take-off, the Wright brothers were focusing on developing a three-axis control for guiding their aircraft.** By the time that the brothers started to build an airplane, they were already among the world's best glider pilots; they knew the problems of riding the air first hand.

In addition, the Wright brothers had designed more effective wings for the airplane than had been previously engineered. Using a wind tunnel, they tested more than two hundred different wing designs, recording the effects of slight variations in shape on the pressure of air on the wings. The

18. Why does the author suggest that the experiments with the wind tunnel were important?

Ⓐ Because they allowed the Wright brothers to decrease the weight of their airplane to acceptable limits
Ⓑ Because they resulted in a three-axis control for their airplane
Ⓒ Because they were important in the refinement of the wings for their airplane
Ⓓ Because they used the data to improve the engine for their airplane

19. The word **they** in paragraph 3 refers to

Ⓐ the Wright brothers
Ⓑ aircraft
Ⓒ engines
Ⓓ attempts

End

more effective wings for the airplane than had been previously engineered. Using a wind tunnel, they tested more than two hundred different wing designs, recording the effects of slight variations in shape on the pressure of air on the wings. The data from these experiments allowed the Wright brothers to construct a superior wing for their aircraft.

In spite of these advantages, however, the Wright brothers might not have succeeded had they not been born at precisely the opportune moment in history. Attempts to achieve manned flight in the early nineteenth century were doomed because the steam engines that powered the aircrafts were too heavy in proportion to the power that **they** produced. But by the end of the nineteenth century, when the brothers were experimenting with engineering options, a relatively light internal combustion engine had already been invented, and they were able to bring the ratio of weight to power within acceptable limits for flight.

20. The word **doomed** in paragraph 4 is closest in meaning to

Ⓐ destined to fail
Ⓑ difficult to achieve
Ⓒ taking a risk
Ⓓ not well planned

End

more effective wings for the airplane than had been previously engineered. Using a wind tunnel, they tested more than two hundred different wing designs, recording the effects of slight variations in shape on the pressure of air on the wings. The data from these experiments allowed the Wright brothers to construct a superior wing for their aircraft.

In spite of these advantages, however, the Wright brothers might not have succeeded had they not been born at precisely the opportune moment in history. Attempts to achieve manned flight in the early nineteenth century were **doomed** because the steam engines that powered the aircrafts were too heavy in proportion to the power that they produced. But by the end of the nineteenth century, when the brothers were experimenting with engineering options, a relatively light internal combustion engine had already been invented, and they were able to bring the ratio of weight to power within acceptable limits for flight.

21. In paragraph 4, the author suggests that the steam engines used in earlier aircraft had failed because

Ⓐ They were too small to power a large plane.
Ⓑ They were too light to generate enough power.
Ⓒ They did not have internal combustion power.
Ⓓ They did not have enough power to lift their own weight.

Paragraph 4 is marked with an arrow (→).

End

more effective wings for the airplane than had been previously engineered. Using a wind tunnel, they tested more than two hundred different wing designs, recording the effects of slight variations in shape on the pressure of air on the wings. The data from these experiments allowed the Wright brothers to construct a superior wing for their aircraft.

→ In spite of these advantages, however, the Wright brothers might not have succeeded had they not been born at precisely the opportune moment in history. Attempts to achieve manned flight in the early nineteenth century were doomed because the steam engines that powered the aircrafts were too heavy in proportion to the power that they produced. But by the end of the nineteenth century, when the brothers were experimenting with engineering options, a relatively light internal combustion engine had already been invented, and they were able to bring the ratio of weight to power within acceptable limits for flight.

22. The passage discusses all of the following reasons that the Wright brothers succeeded EXCEPT

Ⓐ They worked very well together.
Ⓑ They both had practical experience building other aircraft.
Ⓒ They made extensive tests before they completed the design.
Ⓓ They were well funded.

The influenza virus is a single molecule composed of millions of individual atoms. Although bacteria can be considered a type of plant, secreting poisonous substances into the body of the organism they attack, viruses, like the influenza virus, are living organisms themselves. We may consider them regular chemical molecules since they have strictly defined atomic structure; but on the other hand, we must also consider them as being alive since they are able to multiply in unlimited quantities.

An attack brought on by the presence of the influenza virus in the body produces a temporary immunity, but, unfortunately, the protection is against only the type of virus that caused the influenza. Because the disease can be produced by any one of three types, referred to as A, B, or C, and many varieties within each type, immunity to one virus will not prevent infection by other types or strains. Protection from the influenza virus is also complicated by the fact that immunity to a specific virus persists for less than a year. Finally, because a virus may periodically change characteristics, the problem of mutation makes it difficult to carry out a successful immunization program. Vaccines are often ineffective against newly evolving strains.

Approximately every ten years, worldwide epidemics of influenza called pandemics occur. Thought to be caused by new strains of type-A virus, these pandemic viruses have spread rapidly, infecting millions of people.

Vaccines have been developed that have been found to be 70 to 90 percent effective for at least six months against either A or B types of the influenza virus, and a genetically engineered live-virus vaccine is under development. Currently, the United States Public Health Service recommends annual vaccination only for those at greatest risk of complications from influenza, including pregnant women and the elderly. Nevertheless, many other members of the general population request and receive flu shots every year, and even more are immunized during epidemic or pandemic cycles.

23. Which of the following is the main topic of the passage?

Ⓐ The influenza virus
Ⓑ Immunity to disease
Ⓒ Bacteria
Ⓓ Chemical molecules

24. According to this passage, bacteria are

Ⓐ poisons
Ⓑ very small
Ⓒ larger than viruses
Ⓓ plants

25. Look at the word themselves in the passage. Click on the word or phrase in the **bold** text that themselves refers to.

Beginning

The influenza virus is a single molecule composed of millions of individual atoms. **Although bacteria can be considered a type of plant, secreting poisonous substances into the body of the organism they attack, viruses, like the influenza virus, are living organisms themselves. We may consider them regular chemical molecules since they have strictly defined atomic structure;** but on the other hand, we must also consider them as being alive since they are able to multiply in unlimited quantities.

An attack brought on by the presence of the influenza virus in the body produces a temporary immunity, but, unfortunately, the protection is against only the type of virus that caused the influenza. Because the disease can be produced by any one of three types, referred to as A, B, or C, and many varieties within each type, immunity to one virus will not prevent infection by other types or strains. Protection from the influenza virus is also complicated by the fact that immunity to a specific virus persists for less than a year. Finally, because a virus may periodically change characteristics, the problem of mutation makes it difficult to carry out a successful immunization program. Vaccines are often ineffective

26. The word strictly in paragraph 1 could best be replaced by

Ⓐ unusually
Ⓑ completely
Ⓒ broadly
Ⓓ exactly

Beginning

The influenza virus is a single molecule composed of millions of individual atoms. Although bacteria can be considered a type of plant, secreting poisonous substances into the body of the organism they attack, viruses, like the influenza virus, are living organisms themselves. We may consider them regular chemical molecules since they have strictly defined atomic structure; but on the other hand, we must also consider them as being alive since they are able to multiply in unlimited quantities.

An attack brought on by the presence of the influenza virus in the body produces a temporary immunity, but, unfortunately, the protection is against only the type of virus that caused the influenza. Because the disease can be produced by any one of three types, referred to as A, B, or C, and many varieties within each type, immunity to one virus will not prevent infection by other types or strains. Protection from the influenza virus is also complicated by the fact that immunity to a specific virus persists for less than a year. Finally, because a virus may periodically change characteristics, the problem of mutation makes it difficult to carry out a successful immunization program. Vaccines are often ineffective

27. The atomic structure of viruses

Ⓐ is variable
Ⓑ is strictly defined
Ⓒ cannot be analyzed chemically
Ⓓ is more complex than that of bacteria

28. Why does the author say that viruses are alive?

Ⓐ They have a complex atomic structure.
Ⓑ They move.
Ⓒ They multiply.
Ⓓ They need warmth and light.

29. The word unlimited in paragraph 1 could best be replaced by which of the following?

Ⓐ very small
Ⓑ very large
Ⓒ very similar
Ⓓ very different

More Available

poisonous substances into the body of the organism they attack, viruses, like the influenza virus, are living organisms themselves. We may consider them regular chemical molecules since they have strictly defined atomic structure; but on the other hand, we must also consider them as being alive since they are able to multiply in unlimited quantities.

An attack brought on by the presence of the influenza virus in the body produces a temporary immunity, but, unfortunately, the protection is against only the type of virus that caused the influenza. Because the disease can be produced by any one of three types, referred to as A, B, or C, and many varieties within each type, immunity to one virus will not prevent infection by other types or strains. Protection from the influenza virus is also complicated by the fact that immunity to a specific virus persists for less than a year. Finally, because a virus may periodically change characteristics, the problem of mutation makes it difficult to carry out a successful immunization program. Vaccines are often ineffective against newly evolving strains.

Approximately every ten years, worldwide epidemics of influenza called pandemics occur.

30. Look at the word strains in the passage. Click on another word or phrase in the **bold** text that is closest in meaning to strains.

More Available

only the type of virus that caused the influenza. Because the disease can be produced by any one of three types, referred to as A, B, or C, and many varieties within each type, **immunity to one virus will not prevent infection by other types or strains. Protection from the influenza virus is also complicated by the fact that immunity to a specific virus persists for less than a year. Finally, because a virus may periodically change characteristics, the problem of mutation makes it difficult to carry out a successful immunization program.** Vaccines are often ineffective against newly evolving strains.

Approximately every ten years, worldwide epidemics of influenza called pandemics occur. Thought to be caused by new strains of type-A virus, these pandemic viruses have spread rapidly, infecting millions of people.

Vaccines have been developed that have been found to be 70 to 90 percent effective for at least six months against either A or B types of the influenza virus, and a genetically engineered live-virus vaccine is under development. Currently, the United States Public Health Service recommends annual vaccination only for those at greatest risk of complications from

31. The following sentence can be added to the passage.

Epidemics or regional outbreaks have appeared on the average every two or three years for type-A virus, and every four or five years for type-B virus.

Where would it best fit into the passage?

Click on the square (■) to add the sentence to the passage.

Scroll the passage to see all of the choices.

End

mutation makes it difficult to carry out a successful immunization program. Vaccines are often ineffective against newly evolving strains.

■ Approximately every ten years, worldwide epidemics of influenza called pandemics occur. Thought to be caused by new strains of type-A virus, these pandemic viruses have spread rapidly, infecting millions of people.

Vaccines have been developed that have been found to be 70 to 90 percent effective for at least six months against either A or B types of the influenza virus, and a genetically engineered live-virus vaccine is under development. ■Currently, the United States Public Health Service recommends annual vaccination only for those at greatest risk of complications from influenza, including pregnant women and the elderly. ■Nevertheless, many other members of the general population request and receive flu shots every year, and even more are immunized during epidemic or pandemic cycles.■

32. According to the passage, how does the body react to the influenza virus?

Ⓐ It prevents further infection to other types and strains of the virus.
Ⓑ It produces immunity to the type and strain of virus that invaded it.
Ⓒ It becomes immune to types A, B, and C viruses, but not to various strains within the types.
Ⓓ After a temporary immunity, it becomes even more susceptible to the type and strain that caused the influenza.

33. The passage discusses all of the following as characteristics of pandemics EXCEPT

Ⓐ they spread very quickly
Ⓑ they are caused by type-A virus
Ⓒ they are regional outbreaks
Ⓓ they occur once every ten years

The Federal Reserve System, as an independent agency of the United States government, is charged with overseeing the national banking system. Since 1913 the Federal Reserve System, commonly called the Fed, has served as the central bank for the United States. The system consists of twelve District Reserve Banks and their branch offices, along with several committees and councils. All national commercial banks are required by law to be members of the Fed, and all deposit-taking institutions like credit unions are subject to regulation by the Fed regarding the amount of deposited funds that must be held in reserve and that by definition, therefore, are not available for loans. The most powerful body is the seven-member Board of Governors in Washington, appointed by the President and confirmed by the Senate.

The System's primary function is to control monetary policy by influencing the cost and availability of money and credit through the purchase and sale of government securities. If the Federal Reserve provides too little money, interest rates tend to be high, borrowing is expensive, business activity slows down, unemployment goes up, and danger of recession is augmented. If there is too much money, interest rates decline, and borrowing can lead to excess demand, pushing up prices and fueling inflation.

The Fed has several responsibilities in addition to controlling the money supply. In collaboration with the U.S. Department of the Treasury, the Fed puts new coins and paper currency into circulation by issuing them to banks. It also supervises the activities of member banks abroad, and regulates certain aspects of international finance.

It has been said that the Federal Reserve is actually a fourth branch of the United States government because it is composed of national policy makers. However, in practice, the Federal Reserve does not stray from the financial policies established by the executive branch of the government. Although it is true that the Fed does not depend on Congress for budget allocations, and therefore is free from the partisan politics that influence most of the other governmental bodies, it is still responsible for frequent reports to the Congress on the conduct of monetary policies.

34. Which of the following is the most appropriate title for the passage?

(A) Banking
(B) The Federal Reserve System
(C) The Board of Governors
(D) Monetary Policies

35. The word **overseeing** in paragraph 1 is closest in meaning to

(A) supervising
(B) maintaining
(C) financing
(D) stimulating

Beginning

The Federal Reserve System, as an independent agency of the United States government, is charged with **overseeing** the national banking system. Since 1913 the Federal Reserve System, commonly called the Fed, has served as the central bank for the United States. The system consists of twelve District Reserve Banks and their branch offices, along with several committees and councils. All national commercial banks are required by law to be members of the Fed, and all deposit-taking institutions like credit unions are subject to regulation by the Fed regarding the amount of deposited funds that must be held in reserve and that by definition, therefore, are not available for loans. The most powerful body is the seven-member Board of Governors in Washington, appointed by the President and confirmed by the Senate.

The System's primary function is to control monetary policy by influencing the cost and availability of money and credit through the purchase and sale of government securities. If the Federal Reserve provides too little money, interest rates tend to be high, borrowing is expensive,

36. The word **confirmed** in paragraph 1 could best be replaced by

(A) modified
(B) considered
(C) examined
(D) approved

Beginning

The Federal Reserve System, as an independent agency of the United States government, is charged with overseeing the national banking system. Since 1913 the Federal Reserve System, commonly called the Fed, has served as the central bank for the United States. The system consists of twelve District Reserve Banks and their branch offices, along with several committees and councils. All national commercial banks are required by law to be members of the Fed, and all deposit-taking institutions like credit unions are subject to regulation by the Fed regarding the amount of deposited funds that must be held in reserve and that by definition, therefore, are not available for loans. The most powerful body is the seven-member Board of Governors in Washington, appointed by the President and **confirmed** by the Senate.

The System's primary function is to control monetary policy by influencing the cost and availability of money and credit through the purchase and sale of government securities. If the Federal Reserve provides too little money, interest rates tend to be high, borrowing is expensive,

37. According to the passage, the principal responsibility of the Federal Reserve System is

(A) to borrow money
(B) to regulate monetary policies
(C) to print government securities
(D) to appoint the Board of Governors

38. The word securities in paragraph 2 is intended to mean

Ⓐ debts
Ⓑ bonds
Ⓒ protection
Ⓓ confidence

More Available

Fed, and all deposit-taking institutions like credit unions are subject to regulation by the Fed regarding the amount of deposited funds that must be held in reserve and that by definition, therefore, are not available for loans. The most powerful body is the seven-member Board of Governors in Washington, appointed by the President and confirmed by the Senate.

The System's primary function is to control monetary policy by influencing the cost and availability of money and credit through the purchase and sale of government securities. If the Federal Reserve provides too little money, interest rates tend to be high, borrowing is expensive, business activity slows down, unemployment goes up, and danger of recession is augmented. If there is too much money, interest rates decline, and borrowing can lead to excess demand, pushing up prices and fueling inflation.

The Fed has several responsibilities in addition to controlling the money supply. In collaboration with the U.S. Department of the Treasury, the Fed puts new coins and paper currency into circulation by issuing them to banks. It also supervises the

39. What happens when the Federal Reserve provides too little money?

Ⓐ Demand for loans increases.
Ⓑ Unemployment slows down.
Ⓒ Interest rates go up.
Ⓓ Businesses expand.

40. In paragraph 2, the author suggests that inflation is caused by

Ⓐ high unemployment rates
Ⓑ too much money in the economy
Ⓒ very high fuel prices
Ⓓ a limited supply of goods

Paragraph 2 is marked with an arrow (→).

More Available

Fed, and all deposit-taking institutions like credit unions are subject to regulation by the Fed regarding the amount of deposited funds that must be held in reserve and that by definition, therefore, are not available for loans. The most powerful body is the seven-member Board of Governors in Washington, appointed by the President and confirmed by the Senate.

→ The System's primary function is to control monetary policy by influencing the cost and availability of money and credit through the purchase and sale of government securities. If the Federal Reserve provides too little money, interest rates tend to be high, borrowing is expensive, business activity slows down, unemployment goes up, and danger of recession is augmented. If there is too much money, interest rates decline, and borrowing can lead to excess demand, pushing up prices and fueling inflation.

The Fed has several responsibilities in addition to controlling the money supply. In collaboration with the U.S. Department of the Treasury, the Fed puts new coins and paper currency into circulation by issuing them to banks. It also supervises the

41. Look at the word them in the passage. Click on the word or phrase in the **bold** text that them refers to.

End

The Fed has several responsibilities in addition to controlling the money supply. In collaboration with the U.S. Department of the Treasury, the Fed puts new coins and paper currency into circulation by issuing them to banks. It also supervises the activities of member banks abroad, and regulates certain aspects of international finance.

It has been said that the Federal Reserve is actually a fourth branch of the United States government because it is composed of national policy makers. However, in practice, the Federal Reserve does not stray from the financial policies established by the executive branch of the government. Although it is true that the Fed does not depend on Congress for budget allocations, and therefore is free from the partisan politics that influence most of the other governmental bodies, it is still responsible for frequent reports to the Congress on the conduct of monetary policies.

42. Click on the paragraph that outlines the responsibilities of the Fed to banks overseas.

Scroll the passage to see all of the paragraphs.

43. What does the author mean by the statement However, in practice, the Federal Reserve does not stray from the financial policies established by the executive branch of the government?

Ⓐ The Fed is more powerful than the executive branch of the government.
Ⓑ The policies of the Fed and those of the executive branch of the government are not the same.
Ⓒ The Fed tends to follow the policies of the executive branch of the government.
Ⓓ The Fed reports to the executive branch of the government.

44. All of the following statements could be included in a summary of the passage EXCEPT:

Ⓐ The Federal Reserve is an independent agency of the United States government.
Ⓑ The Federal Reserve controls the flow of money and credit by buying and selling government securities.
Ⓒ The Federal Reserve issues new coins and currency to banks.
Ⓓ The Federal Reserve receives its yearly budget from Congress.

45. The following sentence can be added to the passage.

In fact, the Fed is not confined by the usual checks and balances that apply to the three official branches of government—the executive, the legislative, and the judicial.

Where would it best fit in the passage?

Click on the square (■) to add the sentence to the passage.

Scroll the passage to see all of the choices.

End

The Fed has several responsibilities in addition to controlling the money supply. In collaboration with the U.S. Department of the Treasury, the Fed puts new coins and paper currency into circulation by issuing them to banks. It also supervises the activities of member banks abroad, and regulates certain aspects of international finance.

■ It has been said that the Federal Reserve is actually a fourth branch of the United States government because it is composed of national policy makers. ■ However, in practice, the Federal Reserve does not stray from the financial policies established by the executive branch of the government. ■ Although it is true that the Fed does not depend on Congress for budget allocations, and therefore is free from the partisan politics that influence most of the other governmental bodies, it is still responsible for frequent reports to the Congress on the conduct of monetary policies. ■

To check your answers for Model Test 6, refer to the Answer Key on pages 548 and 549. For an explanation of the answers, refer to the Explanatory Answers for Model Test 6 on pages 593–600.

Writing Section Model Test 6

When you take a Model Test, you should use one sheet of paper, both sides. Time each Model Test carefully. After you have read the topic, you should spend 30 minutes writing. For results that would be closest to the actual testing situation, it is recommended that an English teacher score your test, using the guidelines on page 325 of this book.

Advances in transportation and communication like the airplane and the telephone have changed the way that nations interact with each other in a global society. Choose another technological innovation that you think is important. Give specific reasons for your choice.

Notes

Model Test 7
Computer-Assisted TOEFL

Section 1: Listening

The Listening section of the test measures the ability to understand conversations and talks in English. You will use headphones to listen to the conversations and talks. While you are listening, pictures of the speakers or other information will be presented on your computer screen. There are two parts to the Listening section, with special directions for each part.

On the day of the test, the amount of time you will have to answer all of the questions will appear on the computer screen. The time you spend listening to the test material will not be counted. The listening material and questions about it will be presented only one time. You will not be allowed to take notes or have any paper at your computer. You will both see and hear the questions before the answer choices appear. You can take as much time as you need to select an answer; however, it will be to your advantage to answer the questions as quickly as possible. You may change your answer as many times as you want before you confirm it. After you have confirmed an answer, you will not be able to return to the question.

Before you begin working on the Listening section, you will have an opportunity to adjust the volume of the sound. You will not be able to change the volume after you have started the test.

QUESTION DIRECTIONS — Part A

In Part A of the Listening section, you will hear short conversations between two people. In some of the conversations, each person speaks only once. In other conversations, one or both of the people speak more than once. Each conversation is followed by one question about it.

Each question in this part has four answer choices. You should click on the best answer to each question. Answer the questions on the basis of what is stated or implied by the speakers.

1. What does the woman mean?

Ⓐ The man should leave the dorm.
Ⓑ The apartment would be noisy, too.
Ⓒ The man should not find an apartment.
Ⓓ The man is working too hard.

2. What can we assume from this conversation?

Ⓐ The man and woman are eating lunch now.
Ⓑ The man will call the woman to arrange for lunch.
Ⓒ The man and woman have lunch at the same time.
Ⓓ The woman does not want to have lunch with the man.

3. What will the woman probably do?

Ⓐ Send two transcripts to San Diego State
Ⓑ Prepare two transcripts
Ⓒ Give two transcripts to the man, and send one to San Diego State
Ⓓ Give the man three transcripts

4. What does the woman suggest the man do?

Ⓐ Leave a note for the professor
Ⓑ Give a note to the professor
Ⓒ Wait to speak with the professor
Ⓓ Go to the professor's class

5. What can be inferred about Susan?

Ⓐ She will have two major fields of study.
Ⓑ She prefers teaching.
Ⓒ She does not talk with the woman very often.
Ⓓ She cannot make up her mind.

6. What are the speakers talking about?

Ⓐ The mail
Ⓑ Grades for a class
Ⓒ The newspaper
Ⓓ The time of day

7. What had the woman assumed?

Ⓐ The graduation list has an error on it.
Ⓑ The man had already graduated.
Ⓒ The man's name is the same as that of another student.
Ⓓ The graduation will not be until next spring.

8. What does the woman mean?

Ⓐ She did not apply yet.
Ⓑ She is still not sure.
Ⓒ She has decided to compete.
Ⓓ She already has a scholarship.

9. What does the man imply?

Ⓐ He does not like the woman.
Ⓑ He does not usually study at the library.
Ⓒ He has received a letter.
Ⓓ He will not go to the library.

10. What are the speakers talking about?

Ⓐ Toronto
Ⓑ Plane fares
Ⓒ Little towns
Ⓓ The woman's vacation

11. How does the woman feel about the presentation?

Ⓐ She wants to go to the bookstore.
Ⓑ She prefers to do the presentation alone.
Ⓒ She does not want a book.
Ⓓ She is not interested in the presentation.

12. What do we learn about the two students in this conversation?

Ⓐ Neither the man nor the woman was in class on Friday.
Ⓑ The woman was at the airport while the man was in class.
Ⓒ The man was with his mother while the woman was in class.
Ⓓ The man and the woman were in New York together.

13. What does the man mean?

Ⓐ Returning home is not very expensive.
Ⓑ There hasn't been any time to think about the trip.
Ⓒ The time has passed quickly.
Ⓓ He expected to be more enthusiastic.

14. What does the woman mean?

Ⓐ She always eats in the snack bar.
Ⓑ She used to eat in the snack bar.
Ⓒ She occasionally eats in the snack bar.
Ⓓ She has never eaten in the snack bar.

15. What does the woman mean?

Ⓐ The man should rest.
Ⓑ The man's health has improved.
Ⓒ The man worries too much.
Ⓓ The man is very ill.

16. What does the man mean?

Ⓐ He does not have an economics class.
Ⓑ He likes to study economics.
Ⓒ He used to take economics.
Ⓓ He does not enjoy their economics class.

17. What does the man imply?

Ⓐ He does not have a topic for his project yet.
Ⓑ He needs more than thirty-five participants.
Ⓒ He is discouraged about the research.
Ⓓ He lost some data for his research project.

QUESTION DIRECTIONS — Part B

In Part B of the Listening section, you will hear several longer conversations and talks. Each conversation or talk is followed by several questions. The conversations, talks, and questions will not be repeated.

The conversations and talks are about a variety of topics. You do not need special knowledge of the topics to answer the questions correctly. Rather, you should answer each question on the basis of what is stated or implied by the speakers in the conversations or talks.

For most of the questions, you will need to click on the best of four possible answers. Some questions will have special directions. The special directions will appear in a box on the computer screen.

18. What prompted this conversation?

Ⓐ The student's final grade in a course
Ⓑ The professor's error
Ⓒ The student's midterm exam
Ⓓ The professor's book

19. Where is this conversation taking place?

Ⓐ In a doctor's office
Ⓑ In a college professor's office
Ⓒ In Rick's office
Ⓓ At a driver's license center

20. What is the grade that Rick received for the course?

Ⓐ B–
Ⓑ C+
Ⓒ D
Ⓓ F

21. Why did Rick receive a lower grade?

Ⓐ He did not do well on the midterm exam.
Ⓑ He failed the final exam.
Ⓒ He was often absent.
Ⓓ The system was not fair.

22. Why does the professor call on Diane?

Ⓐ She is a good student.
Ⓑ She asks a lot of questions.
Ⓒ She has young children.
Ⓓ She is majoring in linguistics.

23. What are two characteristics of the language of toddlers?

Click on 2 answers.

[A] They use a large number of commands.
[B] They repeat nouns and noun phrases.
[C] They delete the endings of verbs.
[D] They create one-word sentences.

24. What can be concluded about the phrase "We runned"?

Ⓐ The child is probably about two years old.
Ⓑ The child is learning regular verb endings now.
Ⓒ The child is correcting previous errors.
Ⓓ The child needs to be corrected.

25. By which age have most children learned the basic structures of language?

Ⓐ Three years old
Ⓑ Four years old
Ⓒ Five years old
Ⓓ Ten years old

26. What does the professor say about languages other than English?

Ⓐ Basically, the stages for language acquisition are the same for all languages.
Ⓑ The stages of learning a language discussed in this lecture are unique to English.
Ⓒ The basic stages of language acquisition cannot be generalized across language groups.
Ⓓ There is no evidence for the stages that children learn languages to compare language groups.

27. What suggestion does the professor make about the reading assignments?

Ⓐ Read them before class
Ⓑ Read them after the discussion
Ⓒ Read them following the lecture
Ⓓ Read them before the midterm

28. How are the points distributed for the course requirements?

Click on the number of points. Then click on the empty box in the correct row. Use each number only once.

[A] 20 points [B] 30 points [C] 50 points

Final Examination	
Midterm Examination	
Final Project	

29. What are the choices for a project?

Click on 2 answers.

[A] A book report to the class
[B] A thirty-minute presentation
[C] Readings on an assigned topic
[D] A paper on a topic to be chosen by the writer

30. According to the professor, what should students do if they must be absent?

Ⓐ Call or send an e-mail to the professor
Ⓑ Let the secretary know
Ⓒ Do extra assignments
Ⓓ Come in during office hours to make up the class

31. What is the main purpose of this lecture?

Ⓐ To compare Earth with other planets
Ⓑ To explain a theory of the formation of diamonds
Ⓒ To introduce a group of astronomers from the University of Arizona
Ⓓ To criticize Marvin Ross

32. Which planets are being discussed?

Click on 2 answers.

[A] Earth
[B] Uranus
[C] Neptune
[D] Pluto

33. The professor briefly explains a process. Summarize the process by putting the events in order.

Click on a sentence. Then click on the space where it belongs. Use each sentence only once.

[A] Methane separates into hydrogen and carbon.
[B] Diamonds are formed on the surface of the planet.
[C] High pressure squeezes the carbon atoms.
[D] Methane clouds cover the planet.

1 [ ]
2 [ ]
3 [ ]
4 [ ]

34. How does the speaker feel about the theory?

Ⓐ He is studying it at the university.
Ⓑ He agrees with it.
Ⓒ He is interested in it.
Ⓓ He thinks it is a joke.

35. What is the electoral college?

Ⓐ A representative group of citizens
Ⓑ The men who wrote the Constitution
Ⓒ An organization of all the political parties
Ⓓ All the candidates on the ballot

36. Why does the speaker mention Aaron Burr and Thomas Jefferson?

Ⓐ To give an example of an election before the electoral college was formed
Ⓑ To explain how candidates are nominated
Ⓒ To illustrate why there is a separate vote for vice-president
Ⓓ To demonstrate how well the system works

37. How are the people nominated for the electoral college?

Ⓐ Each political party nominates electors.
Ⓑ Congress chooses electors.
Ⓒ Candidates select their party's electors.
Ⓓ The people present names to the electoral college.

38. What is the popular vote?

Ⓐ The people vote directly for the candidates.
Ⓑ The electors vote for their party's candidate.
Ⓒ The registered voters choose the electors.
Ⓓ The Congress holds elections.

39. What is the man's problem?

Ⓐ He did not attend class.
Ⓑ He did not take notes.
Ⓒ He did not understand the lecture.
Ⓓ He did not read the book.

40. Which type of meteorite is the most common?

Ⓐ The stone meteorite
Ⓑ The iron meteorite
Ⓒ The iron-metal meteorite
Ⓓ The stony iron meteorite

41. How were most meteorites formed?

Click on 2 answers.

[A] They were fragments of the Earth that escaped into space during the formation of the planet.
[B] They were fragments of large asteroids or comets that have broken loose.
[C] They were pieces of the moon or Mars that broke off during impact from an asteroid.
[D] They were small moons from planets that no longer exist in space.

42. What helped the woman follow the lecture?

Ⓐ She took excellent notes during the lecture.
Ⓑ She read the chapters in the book before class.
Ⓒ She re-read the chapters in the book after class.
Ⓓ She compared notes with the man after class.

43. What is the purpose of this talk?

Ⓐ To summarize the history of the whaling industry
Ⓑ To explain a folk art tradition
Ⓒ To describe the life of sailors in the 1800s
Ⓓ To discuss where scrimshaw may have gotten its name

44. Why does the lecturer mention the American Revolution and the Civil War?

Ⓐ The dates of the war provide a time frame for the lecture.
Ⓑ The lecturer is discussing art produced by soldiers during the wars.
Ⓒ The history of military art is the topic of the lecture.
Ⓓ In general, the designs on scrimshaw are battle scenes.

45. Identify the two techniques used to create scrimshaw.

Click on 2 answers.

[A] Draw designs with ink on wood, stone, and bone.
[B] Carve bone into figures.
[C] Cut designs on bone and fill them with ink.
[D] Carve designs from wood and stone.

46. Select the object that is the best example of scrimshaw.

Click on a picture.

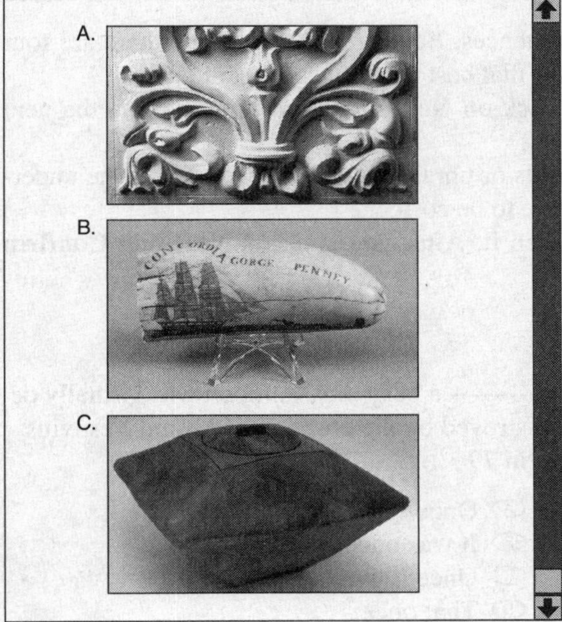

47. Why has scrimshaw become so valuable?

Ⓐ There are fewer artists who know the techniques.
Ⓑ The art is very difficult and time consuming to produce.
Ⓒ Many practical objects made in the 1800s have not survived.
Ⓓ Few modern collectors are interested in purchasing it.

48. What is the man trying to decide?

Ⓐ He may keep a zero balance on his credit card.
Ⓑ He may apply for a new credit card.
Ⓒ He may close his current credit card account.
Ⓓ He may pay the balance on his credit card.

49. Why is the man interested in the credit card?

Click on 2 answers.

[A] The card does not require a credit check.
[B] The card has lower interest rates.
[C] The card has no annual fee.
[D] The card allows a $200 balance without interest.

50. Why does the man decide not to get the card?

Ⓐ He already has a credit card and does not need another one.
Ⓑ He is suspicious because everyone on campus received a letter.
Ⓒ His roommate advises him not to send in the application.
Ⓓ The card holder must maintain charges of at least $200 every month.

Section 2: Structure

This section measures the ability to recognize language that is appropriate for standard written English. There are two types of questions in this section.

In the first type of question, there are incomplete sentences. Beneath each sentence, there are four words or phrases. You will choose the one word or phrase that best completes the sentence.

Clicking on a choice darkens the oval. After you click on **Next** and **Confirm Answer**, the next question will be presented.

The second type of question has four underlined words or phrases. You will choose the one underlined word or phrase that must be changed for the sentence to be correct.

Clicking on an underlined word or phrase will darken it. After you click on **Next** and **Confirm Answer**, the next question will be presented.

1. Besides rain, ------ is seldom pure.

   (A) water naturally
   (B) natural water
   (C) water of nature
   (D) the nature's water

2. Anyone reproducing (A) copyrighted works without the permission of the holders of the copyrights are (B) breaking (C) the law (D).

3. Nitrogen must be combine (A) with another element (B) such as (C) hydrogen or oxygen to be useful (D) in agriculture or industry.

4. In the sixteenth century (A), François Vieta, a French mathematician, used (B) the vowels *a, e, i, o, u* to represent (C) a (D) unknown number.

5. Burrowing animals provide paths for water in soil, and so do the roots of plants --------- .

   (A) decaying and they dying
   (B) when they die and decay
   (C) they die and decay
   (D) when they will die and decay

6. -------- a busy city, Pompeii was virtually destroyed by the eruption of Mount Vesuvius in 79 A.D.

   (A) Once
   (B) It was once
   (C) Once it was
   (D) That once

7. The FDA was set up in 1940 --------- that maintain standards for the sale of food and drugs.

   (A) to enforce the laws
   (B) to enforcing laws
   (C) enforcing laws
   (D) enforced the laws

8. Vasco da Gama, accompanied by a large crew (A) and a fleet of twenty ships, were (B) trying to establish (C) Portuguese domination in Africa and India (D) during the sixteenth century.

9. The bridge at Niagara Falls (A) spans the longer (B) unguarded border in the history of the world, symbolizing the peace and goodwill that exist (C) between (D) Canada and the United States.

10. In ancient times and throughout the Middle Ages, <u>many people</u> (A) <u>believed</u> (B) that <u>the Earth</u> (C) <u>is</u> (D) motionless.

11. Doublestars orbit --------- .

(A) each to the other
(B) each other
(C) each other one
(D) other each one

12. With <u>his</u> (A) father's guidance, Mozart <u>begun</u> (B) <u>playing</u> (C) the clavier at the age of three and <u>composing</u> (D) at the age of five.

13. Programs <u>such as</u> (A) Head Start <u>were developed</u> (B) <u>to prepare</u> (C) children from deprived situations to enter school <u>without to experience</u> (D) unusual difficulties.

14. <u>Almost</u> (A) poetry <u>is</u> (B) <u>more enjoyable</u> (C) when <u>it is</u> (D) read aloud.

15. All the cereal grains -------- grow on the prairies and plains of the United States.

(A) but rice
(B) except the rice
(C) but for rice
(D) excepting rice

16. Supersonic transport <u>such</u> (A) the Concorde was never <u>widely accepted</u> (B) in part <u>because</u> (C) <u>of</u> (D) the problems of noise and atmospheric pollution.

17. Oscillatona, one of the few plants that can move about, ------ a wavy, gliding motion.

(A) having
(B) has
(C) being
(D) with

18. -------- a teacher in New England, Webster wrote the *Dictionary of the American Language.*

(A) It was while
(B) When
(C) When was
(D) While

19. A vine climbs from one tree to another, continuing <u>to grow</u> (A) and support <u>itself</u> (B) even when the original <u>supporting</u> (C) tree is <u>not longer</u> (D) alive.

20. <u>Sometime</u> (A) ants keep <u>smaller insects</u> (B) that give off honeydew, milking them <u>regularly</u> (C) and even building barns <u>to shelter</u> (D) them.

21. If a ruby is heated it -------- temporarily lose its color.

(A) would
(B) will
(C) does
(D) has

22. The neutron bomb provided the <u>capable</u> (A) of a <u>limited</u> (B) nuclear war <u>in which</u> (C) buildings <u>would be preserved</u> (D), but people would be destroyed.

23. <u>In</u> (A) 1776 to 1800, <u>the population</u> (B) of the U.S. continued <u>to rise</u> (C), <u>reaching</u> (D) five million citizens by the turn of the century.

24. Not until a student has mastered algebra -------- the principles of geometry, trigonometry, and physics.

(A) he can begin to understand
(B) can he begin to understand
(C) he begins to understand
(D) begins to understand

25. <u>From space,</u> (A) astronauts are <u>able</u> (B) <u>to clearly see</u> (C) the outline <u>of</u> (D) the whole Earth.

Section 3: Reading

This section measures the ability to read and understand short passages similar in topic and style to those that students are likely to encounter in North American universities and colleges. This section contains reading passages and questions about the passages. There are several different types of questions in this section.

In the Reading section, you will first have the opportunity to read the passage.

You will use the scroll bar to view the rest of the passage.

When you have finished reading the passage, you will use the mouse to click on **Proceed**. Then the questions about the passage will be presented. You are to choose the one best answer to each question. Answer all questions about the information in a passage on the basis of what is stated or implied in that passage.

Most of the questions will be multiple-choice questions. To answer these questions you will click on a choice below the question.

To answer some questions, you will click on a word or phrase.

To answer some questions, you will click on a sentence in the passage.

To answer some questions, you will click on a square to add a sentence to the passage.

Smallpox was the first widespread disease ever to be eliminated by human intervention. A highly contagious viral disease, it was endemic in Europe, causing the deaths of millions of people until the development of the vaccination by Edward Jenner around 1800. In many non-European nations, it remained a dreaded, often fatal illness until very recently. Its victims suffered high fever, vomiting, and painful, itchy pustules, pus-filled skin eruptions that left pits or pockmark scars. In villages and cities all over the world, scarred people showed that they had survived smallpox.

In May 1966, the World Health Organization (WHO), an agency of the United Nations, was authorized to initiate a global campaign to eradicate smallpox. The goal was to eliminate the disease in one decade. At the time, the disease posed a serious threat to people in thirty nations. More than 700 physicians, nurses, scientists, and other personnel from WHO joined about 200,000 health workers in the infected nations to battle the disease. Because similar projects for malaria and yellow fever had failed, few believed that a disease as widespread as smallpox could actually be eradicated, but eleven years after the initial organization of the anti-smallpox campaign, no cases were reported in the field.

The strategy that developed was to combat the disease at several levels. There was an education campaign, of course, so that the people in the threatened countries could be taught more about how the disease spread and become active participants in the fight against smallpox. Other strategies included not only providing mass vaccinations but also isolating patients with active smallpox in order to contain the spread of the disease, thus breaking the chain of human transmission. Monetary rewards for reporting smallpox assisted in motivating the public to aid health workers. One by one, each smallpox victim was sought out, removed from contact with others, and treated. At the same time, the entire village where the victim had lived was vaccinated.

By April of 1978, WHO officials announced that they had isolated the last known case of the disease, but health workers continued to search for new cases for two additional years to be completely sure. In May 1980, a formal statement was made to the global community. Today smallpox is no longer a threat to humanity. Routine vaccinations have been stopped worldwide.

1. Which of the following is the best title for the passage?

   Ⓐ The World Health Organization
   Ⓑ The Eradication of Smallpox
   Ⓒ Smallpox Vaccinations
   Ⓓ Infectious Diseases

2. Look at the word eradicate in the passage. Click on the word in the **bold** text that is closest in meaning to eradicate.

More Available

eruptions that left pits or pockmark scars. In villages and cities all over the world, scarred people showed that they had survived smallpox.

In May 1966, the World Health Organization (WHO), an agency of the United Nations, was authorized to initiate a global campaign to eradicate smallpox. The goal was to eliminate the disease in one decade. At the time, the disease posed a serious threat to people in thirty nations. More than 700 physicians, nurses, scientists, and other personnel from WHO joined about 200,000 health workers in the infected nations to battle the disease. Because similar projects for malaria and yellow fever had failed, few believed that a disease as widespread as smallpox could actually be eradicated, but eleven years after the initial organization of the anti-smallpox campaign, no cases were reported in the field.

The strategy that developed was to combat the disease at several levels. There was an education campaign, of course, so that the people in the threatened countries could be taught more about how the disease spread and become active participants in the fight against smallpox. Other

3. The word threat in paragraph 2 could best be replaced by

Ⓐ debate
Ⓑ humiliation
Ⓒ risk
Ⓓ bother

More Available

eruptions that left pits or pockmark scars. In villages and cities all over the world, scarred people showed that they had survived smallpox.

In May 1966, the World Health Organization (WHO), an agency of the United Nations, was authorized to initiate a global campaign to eradicate smallpox. The goal was to eliminate the disease in one decade. At the time, the disease posed a serious threat to people in thirty nations. More than 700 physicians, nurses, scientists, and other personnel from WHO joined about 200,000 health workers in the infected nations to battle the disease. Because similar projects for malaria and yellow fever had failed, few believed that a disease as widespread as smallpox could actually be eradicated, but eleven years after the initial organization of the anti-smallpox campaign, no cases were reported in the field.

The strategy that developed was to combat the disease at several levels. There was an education campaign, of course, so that the people in the threatened countries could be taught more about how the disease spread and become active participants in the fight against smallpox. Other

4. Click on the paragraph that explains the goal of the campaign against smallpox.

Scroll the passage to see all of the paragraphs.

5. According to the passage, what was the strategy used to eliminate the spread of smallpox?

Ⓐ Vaccinations of entire villages
Ⓑ Treatment of individual victims
Ⓒ Isolation of victims and mass vaccinations
Ⓓ Extensive reporting of outbreaks

6. The word they in paragraph 4 refers to

Ⓐ health workers
Ⓑ officials
Ⓒ victims
Ⓓ cases

End

education campaign, of course, so that the people in the threatened countries could be taught more about how the disease spread and become active participants in the fight against smallpox. Other strategies included not only providing mass vaccinations but also isolating patients with active smallpox in order to contain the spread of the disease, thus breaking the chain of human transmission. Monetary rewards for reporting smallpox assisted in motivating the public to aid health workers. One by one, each smallpox victim was sought out, removed from contact with others, and treated. At the same time, the entire village where the victim had lived was vaccinated.

By April of 1978, WHO officials announced that they had isolated the last known case of the disease, but health workers continued to search for new cases for two additional years to be completely sure. In May 1980, a formal statement was made to the global community. Today smallpox is no longer a threat to humanity. Routine vaccinations have been stopped worldwide.

7. The word isolated in paragraph 4 is closest in meaning to

Ⓐ restored
Ⓑ separated
Ⓒ attended
Ⓓ located

End

education campaign, of course, so that the people in the threatened countries could be taught more about how the disease spread and become active participants in the fight against smallpox. Other strategies included not only providing mass vaccinations but also isolating patients with active smallpox in order to contain the spread of the disease, thus breaking the chain of human transmission. Monetary rewards for reporting smallpox assisted in motivating the public to aid health workers. One by one, each smallpox victim was sought out, removed from contact with others, and treated. At the same time, the entire village where the victim had lived was vaccinated.

By April of 1978, WHO officials announced that they had isolated the last known case of the disease, but health workers continued to search for new cases for two additional years to be completely sure. In May 1980, a formal statement was made to the global community. Today smallpox is no longer a threat to humanity. Routine vaccinations have been stopped worldwide.

8. How was the public motivated to help the health workers?

Ⓐ By educating them
Ⓑ By rewarding them for reporting cases
Ⓒ By isolating them from others
Ⓓ By giving them vaccinations

9. Which one of the statements does NOT refer to smallpox?

Ⓐ Previous projects had failed.
Ⓑ People are no longer vaccinated for it.
Ⓒ The World Health Organization mounted a worldwide campaign to eradicate the disease.
Ⓓ It was a serious threat.

10. It can be inferred from the passage that

Ⓐ no new cases of smallpox have been reported this year
Ⓑ malaria and yellow fever have been reported this year
Ⓒ smallpox victims no longer die when they contract the disease
Ⓓ smallpox is not transmitted from one person to another

11. The following sentence can be added to the passage.

The number of smallpox-infected countries gradually decreased.

Where would it best fit in the passage?

Click on the square (■) to add the sentence to the passage.

Scroll the passage to see all of the choices.

End

education campaign, of course, so that the people in the threatened countries could be taught more about how the disease spread and become active participants in the fight against smallpox. Other strategies included not only providing mass vaccinations but also isolating patients with active smallpox in order to contain the spread of the disease, thus breaking the chain of human transmission. Monetary rewards for reporting smallpox assisted in motivating the public to aid health workers. One by one, each smallpox victim was sought out, removed from contact with others, and treated. At the same time, the entire village where the victim had lived was vaccinated. ■

By April of 1978, WHO officials announced that they had isolated the last known case of the disease, but health workers continued to search for new cases for two additional years to be completely sure. ■ In May 1980, a formal statement was made to the global community. ■ Today smallpox is no longer a threat to humanity. ■ Routine vaccinations have been stopped worldwide.

The nuclear family, consisting of a mother, father, and their children, may be more an American ideal than an American reality. Of course, the so-called traditional American family was always more varied than we had been led to believe, reflecting the very different racial, ethnic, class, and religious customs among different American groups, but today diversity is even more obvious.

The most recent government census statistics reveal that only about one third of all current American families fits the traditional mold of two parents and their children, and another third consists of married couples who either have no children or have none still living at home. An analysis of the remaining one third of the population reveals that about 20 percent of the total number of American households are single people, the most common descriptor being women over sixty-five years of age. A small percentage, about 3 percent of the total, consists of unmarried people who choose to live together; and the rest, about 7 percent, are single parents, with at least one child.

There are several easily identifiable reasons for the growing number of single-parent households. First, the sociological phenomenon of single-parent households reflects changes in cultural attitudes toward divorce and also toward unmarried mothers. A substantial number of adults become single parents as a result of divorce. In addition, the number of children born to unmarried women who choose to keep their children and rear them by themselves has increased dramatically. Finally, there is a small percentage of single-parent families that have resulted from untimely death. Today, these varied family types are typical and, therefore, normal.

In addition, because many families live far from relatives, close friends have become a more important part of family life than ever before. The vast majority of Americans claim that they have people in their lives whom they regard as family although they are not related. A view of family that only accepts the traditional nuclear arrangement not only ignores the reality of modern American family life, but also undervalues the familial bonds created in alternative family arrangements. Apparently, many Americans are achieving supportive relationships in family forms other than the traditional one.

12. Which of the following is the main topic of the passage?

Ⓐ The traditional American family
Ⓑ The nuclear family
Ⓒ The current American family
Ⓓ The ideal family

13. Look at the word reality in the passage. Click on the word or phrase in the **bold** text that is opposite in meaning to reality.

Beginning

The nuclear family, consisting of a mother, father, and their children, may be more an American ideal than an American reality. Of course, the so-called traditional American family was always more varied than we had been led to believe, reflecting the very different racial, ethnic, class, and religious customs among different American groups, but today diversity is even more obvious.

The most recent government census statistics reveal that only about one third of all current American families fits the traditional mold of two parents and their children, and another third consists of married couples who either have no children or have none still living at home. An analysis of the remaining one third of the population reveals that about 20 percent of the total number of American households are single people, the most common descriptor being women over sixty-five years of age. A small percentage, about 3 percent of the total, consists of unmarried people who choose to live together; and the rest, about 7 percent, are single parents, with at least one child.

There are several easily identifiable reasons

14. The word current in paragraph 2 could best be replaced by which of the following?

Ⓐ typical
Ⓑ present
Ⓒ perfect
Ⓓ traditional

Beginning

The nuclear family, consisting of a mother, father, and their children, may be more an American ideal than an American reality. Of course, the so-called traditional American family was always more varied than we had been led to believe, reflecting the very different racial, ethnic, class, and religious customs among different American groups, but today diversity is even more obvious.

The most recent government census statistics reveal that only about one third of all current American families fits the traditional mold of two parents and their children, and another third consists of married couples who either have no children or have none still living at home. An analysis of the remaining one third of the population reveals that about 20 percent of the total number of American households are single people, the most common descriptor being women over sixty-five years of age. A small percentage, about 3 percent of the total, consists of unmarried people who choose to live together; and the rest, about 7 percent, are single parents, with at least one child.

There are several easily identifiable reasons

15. The word none in paragraph 2 refers to

Ⓐ parents
Ⓑ children
Ⓒ couples
Ⓓ families

Beginning

The nuclear family, consisting of a mother, father, and their children, may be more an American ideal than an American reality. Of course, the so-called traditional American family was always more varied than we had been led to believe, reflecting the very different racial, ethnic, class, and religious customs among different American groups, but today diversity is even more obvious.

The most recent government census statistics reveal that only about one third of all current American families fits the traditional mold of two parents and their children, and another third consists of married couples who either have no children or have none still living at home. An analysis of the remaining one third of the population reveals that about 20 percent of the total number of American households are single people, the most common descriptor being women over sixty-five years of age. A small percentage, about 3 percent of the total, consists of unmarried people who choose to live together; and the rest, about 7 percent, are single parents, with at least one child.

There are several easily identifiable reasons

16. How many single people were identified in the survey?

Ⓐ One third of the total surveyed
Ⓑ One fourth of the total surveyed
Ⓒ One fifth of the total surveyed
Ⓓ Less than one tenth of the total surveyed

17. Who generally constitutes a one-person household?

Ⓐ A single man in his twenties
Ⓑ An elderly man
Ⓒ A single woman in her late sixties
Ⓓ A divorced woman

18. Look at the phrase the rest in the passage. Click on the word or phrase in the **bold** text that the rest refers to.

More Available

The most recent government census statistics reveal that only about one third of all current American families fits the traditional mold of two parents and their children, and another third consists of married couples who either have no children or have none still living at home. **An analysis of the remaining one third of the population reveals that about 20 percent of the total number of American households are single people, the most common descriptor being women over sixty-five years of age. A small percentage, about 3 percent of the total, consists of unmarried people who choose to live together; and the rest, about 7 percent, are single parents, with at least one child.**

There are several easily identifiable reasons for the growing number of single-parent households. First, the sociological phenomenon of single-parent households reflects changes in cultural attitudes toward divorce and also toward unmarried mothers. A substantial number of adults become single parents as a result of divorce. In addition, the number of children born to unmarried women who choose to keep their

19. Click on the sentence in paragraph 4 that refers to the way that most Americans feel about close friends.

Paragraph 4 is marked with an arrow (→).

End

unmarried women who choose to keep their children and rear them by themselves has increased dramatically. Finally, there is a small percentage of single-parent families that have resulted from untimely death. Today, these varied family types are typical and, therefore, normal.

→ In addition, because many families live far from relatives, close friends have become a more important part of family life than ever before. The vast majority of Americans claim that they have people in their lives whom they regard as family although they are not related. A view of family that only accepts the traditional nuclear arrangement not only ignores the reality of modern American family life, but also undervalues the familial bonds created in alternative family arrangements. Apparently, many Americans are achieving supportive relationships in family forms other than the traditional one.

20. The word undervalues in paragraph 4 is closest in meaning to

Ⓐ does not appreciate
Ⓑ does not know about
Ⓒ does not include
Ⓓ does not understand

End

unmarried women who choose to keep their children and rear them by themselves has increased dramatically. Finally, there is a small percentage of single-parent families that have resulted from untimely death. Today, these varied family types are typical and, therefore, normal.

In addition, because many families live far from relatives, close friends have become a more important part of family life than ever before. The vast majority of Americans claim that they have people in their lives whom they regard as family although they are not related. A view of family that only accepts the traditional nuclear arrangement not only ignores the reality of modern American family life, but also undervalues the familial bonds created in alternative family arrangements. Apparently, many Americans are achieving supportive relationships in family forms other than the traditional one.

21. The passage discusses all of the following reasons for an increase in single-parent households EXCEPT

Ⓐ a rising divorce rate
Ⓑ death of one of the parents
Ⓒ increased interest in parenting by fathers
Ⓓ babies born to single women

22. With which of the following statements would the author most probably agree?

Ⓐ There have always been a wide variety of family arrangements in the United States.
Ⓑ Racial, ethnic, and religious groups have preserved the traditional family structure.
Ⓒ The ideal American family is the best structure.
Ⓓ Fewer married couples are having children.

Although noise, commonly defined as unwanted sound, is a widely recognized form of pollution, it is very difficult to measure because the discomfort experienced by different individuals is highly subjective and, therefore, variable. Exposure to lower levels of noise may be slightly irritating, whereas exposure to higher levels may actually cause hearing loss. Particularly in congested urban areas, the noise produced as a byproduct of our advancing technology causes physical and psychological harm but it also detracts from the quality of life for those exposed to it.

Unlike the eyes, which can be covered by the eyelids against strong light, the ear has no lid, and is, therefore, always open and vulnerable; noise penetrates without protection.

Noise causes effects that the hearer cannot control and to which the body never becomes accustomed. Loud noises instinctively signal danger to any organism with a hearing mechanism, including human beings. In response, heartbeat and respiration accelerate, blood vessels constrict, the skin pales, and muscles tense. In fact, there is a general increase in functioning brought about by the flow of adrenaline released in response to fear, and some of these responses persist even longer than the noise, occasionally as long as thirty minutes after the sound has ceased.

Because noise is unavoidable in a complex, industrial society, we are constantly responding in the same ways that we would respond to danger. Recently, researchers have concluded that noise and our response may be much more than an annoyance. It may be a serious threat to physical and psychological health and well-being, causing damage not only to the ear and brain but also to the heart and stomach. We have long known that hearing loss is America's number one nonfatal health problem, but now we are learning that some of us with heart disease and ulcers may be victims of noise as well. Fetuses exposed to noise tend to be overactive, they cry easily, and they are more sensitive to gastrointestinal problems after birth. In addition, the psychological effect of noise is very important. Nervousness, irritability, tension, and anxiety increase, affecting the quality of rest during sleep, and the efficiency of activities during waking hours, as well as the way that we interact with one another.

23. Which of the following is the author's main point?

Ⓐ Noise may pose a serious threat to our physical and psychological health.
Ⓑ Loud noises signal danger.
Ⓒ Hearing loss is America's number one nonfatal health problem.
Ⓓ The ear is not like the eye.

24. According to the passage, what is noise?

Ⓐ Unwanted sound
Ⓑ A byproduct of technology
Ⓒ Physical and psychological harm
Ⓓ Congestion

25. Why is noise difficult to measure?

Ⓐ It causes hearing loss.
Ⓑ All people do not respond to it in the same way.
Ⓒ It is unwanted.
Ⓓ People become accustomed to it.

26. The word congested in paragraph 1 could best be replaced by

Ⓐ hazardous
Ⓑ polluted
Ⓒ crowded
Ⓓ rushed

Beginning

Although noise, commonly defined as unwanted sound, is a widely recognized form of pollution, it is very difficult to measure because the discomfort experienced by different individuals is highly subjective and, therefore, variable. Exposure to lower levels of noise may be slightly irritating, whereas exposure to higher levels may actually cause hearing loss. Particularly in congested urban areas, the noise produced as a byproduct of our advancing technology causes physical and psychological harm but it also detracts from the quality of life for those exposed to it.

Unlike the eyes, which can be covered by the eyelids against strong light, the ear has no lid, and is, therefore, always open and vulnerable; noise penetrates without protection.

Noise causes effects that the hearer cannot control and to which the body never becomes accustomed. Loud noises instinctively signal danger to any organism with a hearing mechanism, including human beings. In response, heartbeat and respiration accelerate, blood vessels constrict, the skin pales, and muscles tense. In fact, there is a general increase in functioning brought about by

27. According to the passage, people respond to loud noises in the same way that they respond to

Ⓐ annoyance
Ⓑ danger
Ⓒ damage
Ⓓ disease

28. Look at the word accelerate in the passage. Click on the word or phrase in the **bold** text that is closest in meaning to accelerate.

More Available

eyelids against strong light, the ear has no lid, and is, therefore, always open and vulnerable; noise penetrates without protection.

Noise causes effects that the hearer cannot control and to which the body never becomes accustomed. Loud noises instinctively signal danger to any organism with a hearing mechanism, including human beings. In response, heartbeat and respiration accelerate, blood vessels constrict, the skin pales, and muscles tense. **In fact, there is a general increase in functioning brought about by the flow of adrenaline released in response to fear, and some of these responses persist even longer than the noise, occasionally as long as thirty minutes after the sound has ceased.**

Because noise is unavoidable in a complex, industrial society, we are constantly responding in the same ways that we would respond to danger. Recently, researchers have concluded that noise and our response may be much more than an annoyance. It may be a serious threat to physical and psychological health and well-being, causing damage not only to the ear and brain but also to the heart and stomach. We have long known that

29. Look at the word it in the passage. Click on the word or phrase in the **bold** text that it refers to.

Beginning

Although noise, commonly defined as unwanted sound, is a widely recognized form of pollution, it is very difficult to measure because the discomfort experienced by different individuals is highly subjective and, therefore, variable. Exposure to lower levels of noise may be slightly irritating, whereas exposure to higher levels may actually cause hearing loss. **Particularly in congested urban areas, the noise produced as a byproduct of our advancing technology causes physical and psychological harm but it also detracts from the quality of life for those exposed to it.**

Unlike the eyes, which can be covered by the eyelids against strong light, the ear has no lid, and is, therefore, always open and vulnerable; noise penetrates without protection.

Noise causes effects that the hearer cannot control and to which the body never becomes accustomed. Loud noises instinctively signal danger to any organism with a hearing mechanism, including human beings. In response, heartbeat and respiration accelerate, blood vessels constrict, the skin pales, and muscles tense. In fact, there is a general increase in functioning brought about by

30. The phrase as well in paragraph 4 is closest in meaning to which of the following?

Ⓐ after all
Ⓑ also
Ⓒ instead
Ⓓ regardless

End

Because noise is unavoidable in a complex, industrial society, we are constantly responding in the same ways that we would respond to danger. Recently, researchers have concluded that noise and our response may be much more than an annoyance. It may be a serious threat to physical and psychological health and well-being, causing damage not only to the ear and brain but also to the heart and stomach. We have long known that hearing loss is America's number one nonfatal health problem, but now we are learning that some of us with heart disease and ulcers may be victims of noise as well. Fetuses exposed to noise tend to be overactive, they cry easily, and they are more sensitive to gastrointestinal problems after birth. In addition, the psychological effect of noise is very important. Nervousness, irritability, tension, and anxiety increase, affecting the quality of rest during sleep, and the efficiency of activities during waking hours, as well as the way that we interact with one another.

31. It can be inferred from this passage that the eye

Ⓐ responds to fear
Ⓑ enjoys greater protection than the ear
Ⓒ increases functions
Ⓓ is damaged by noise

32. With which of the following statements would the author most probably agree?

Ⓐ Noise is not a serious problem today.
Ⓑ Noise is America's number-one problem.
Ⓒ Noise is an unavoidable problem in an industrial society.
Ⓓ Noise is a complex problem.

33. The following sentence can be added to the passage.

Investigations on human subjects have demonstrated that babies are affected by noise even before they are born.

Where would it best fit in the passage?

Click on the square (■) to add the sentence to the passage.

Scroll the passage to see all of the choices.

End

Because noise is unavoidable in a complex, industrial society, we are constantly responding in the same ways that we would respond to danger. Recently, researchers have concluded that noise and our response may be much more than an annoyance. ■ It may be a serious threat to physical and psychological health and well-being, causing damage not only to the ear and brain but also to the heart and stomach. ■ We have long known that hearing loss is America's number one nonfatal health problem, but now we are learning that some of us with heart disease and ulcers may be victims of noise as well. ■ Fetuses exposed to noise tend to be overactive, they cry easily, and they are more sensitive to gastrointestinal problems after birth. ■ In addition, the psychological effect of noise is very important. Nervousness, irritability, tension, and anxiety increase, affecting the quality of rest during sleep, and the efficiency of activities during waking hours, as well as the way that we interact with one another.

Very few people in the modern world obtain their food supply by hunting and gathering in the natural environment surrounding their homes. This method of harvesting from nature's provision, however, is not only the oldest known subsistence strategy, but also the one that has been practiced continuously in some parts of the world for at least the last two million years. It was, indeed, the only way to obtain food until rudimentary farming and very crude methods for the domestication of animals were introduced about 10,000 years ago.

Because hunter-gatherers have fared poorly in comparison with their agricultural cousins, their numbers have dwindled, and they have been forced to live in the marginal wastelands. In higher latitudes, the shorter growing season has restricted the availability of plant life. Such conditions have caused a greater dependence on hunting and, along the coasts and waterways, on fishing. The abundance of vegetation in the lower latitudes of the tropics, on the other hand, has provided a greater opportunity for gathering a variety of plants. In short, the environmental differences have restricted the diet and have limited possibilities for the development of subsistence societies.

Contemporary hunter-gatherers may help us understand our prehistoric ancestors. We know from observation of modern hunter-gatherers in both Africa and Alaska that a society based on hunting and gathering must be very mobile. Following the food supply can be a way of life. If a particular kind of wild herding animal is the basis of the food for a group of people, those people must move to stay within reach of those animals. For many of the native people of the great central plains of North America, following the buffalo, who were in turn following the growth of grazing foods, determined their way of life.

For gathering societies, seasonal changes mean a great deal. While the entire community camps in a central location, a smaller party harvests the food within a reasonable distance from the camp. When the food in the area is exhausted, the community moves on to exploit another site. We also notice a seasonal migration pattern evolving for most hunter-gatherers, along with a strict division of labor between the sexes. These patterns of behavior may be similar to those practiced by humankind during the Paleolithic Period.

34. Which of the following is the main topic of the passage?

Ⓐ The Paleolithic Period
Ⓑ Subsistence farming
Ⓒ Hunter-gatherers
Ⓓ Marginal environments

35. Which is the oldest subsistence strategy?

Ⓐ Migrating
Ⓑ Domesticating animals
Ⓒ Farming
Ⓓ Hunting and gathering

36. When was hunting and gathering introduced?

Ⓐ Ten million years ago
Ⓑ Two million years ago
Ⓒ Ten thousand years ago
Ⓓ Two thousand years ago

37. Look at the word rudimentary in the passage. Click on the word or phrase in the **bold** text that is closest in meaning to rudimentary.

Beginning

Very few people in the modern world obtain their food supply by hunting and gathering in the natural environment surrounding their homes. **This method of harvesting from nature's provision, however, is not only the oldest known subsistence strategy, but also the one that has been practiced continuously in some parts of the world for at least the last two million years. It was, indeed, the only way to obtain food until rudimentary farming and very crude methods for the domestication of animals were introduced about 10,000 years ago.**

Because hunter-gatherers have fared poorly in comparison with their agricultural cousins, their numbers have dwindled, and they have been forced to live in the marginal wastelands. In higher latitudes, the shorter growing season has restricted the availability of plant life. Such conditions have caused a greater dependence on hunting and, along the coasts and waterways, on fishing. The abundance of vegetation in the lower latitudes of the tropics, on the other hand, has provided a greater opportunity for gathering a variety of plants. In short, the environmental differences have restricted the diet and have limited possibilities for

38. The word dwindled in paragraph 2 is closest in meaning to

Ⓐ disagreed
Ⓑ decreased
Ⓒ disappeared
Ⓓ died

More Available

way to obtain food until rudimentary farming and very crude methods for the domestication of animals were introduced about 10,000 years ago.

Because hunter-gatherers have fared poorly in comparison with their agricultural cousins, their numbers have dwindled, and they have been forced to live in the marginal wastelands. In higher latitudes, the shorter growing season has restricted the availability of plant life. Such conditions have caused a greater dependence on hunting and, along the coasts and waterways, on fishing. The abundance of vegetation in the lower latitudes of the tropics, on the other hand, has provided a greater opportunity for gathering a variety of plants. In short, the environmental differences have restricted the diet and have limited possibilities for the development of subsistence societies.

Contemporary hunter-gatherers may help us understand our prehistoric ancestors. We know from observation of modern hunter-gatherers in both Africa and Alaska that a society based on hunting and gathering must be very mobile. Following the food supply can be a way of life. If a particular kind of wild herding animal is the basis

39. Look at the phrase such conditions in the passage. Click on the word or phrase in the **bold** text that such conditions refers to.

More Available

way to obtain food until rudimentary farming and very crude methods for the domestication of animals were introduced about 10,000 years ago.

Because hunter-gatherers have fared poorly in comparison with their agricultural cousins, their numbers have dwindled, and they have been forced to live in the marginal wastelands. **In higher latitudes, the shorter growing season has restricted the availability of plant life. Such conditions have caused a greater dependence on hunting and, along the coasts and waterways, on fishing. The abundance of vegetation in the lower latitudes of the tropics, on the other hand, has provided a greater opportunity for gathering a variety of plants.** In short, the environmental differences have restricted the diet and have limited possibilities for the development of subsistence societies.

Contemporary hunter-gatherers may help us understand our prehistoric ancestors. We know from observation of modern hunter-gatherers in both Africa and Alaska that a society based on hunting and gathering must be very mobile. **Following the food supply can be a way of life. If a particular kind of wild herding animal is the basis**

40. In paragraph 2, the author explains that hunters and gatherers in lower latitudes found

Ⓐ more animals to hunt
Ⓑ more coasts and waterways for fishing
Ⓒ a shorter growing season
Ⓓ a large variety of plant life

Paragraph 2 is marked with an arrow (→).

More Available

continuously in some parts of the world for at least the last two million years. It was, indeed, the only way to obtain food until rudimentary farming and very crude methods for the domestication of animals were introduced about 10,000 years ago.

→ Because hunter-gatherers have fared poorly in comparison with their agricultural cousins, their numbers have dwindled, and they have been forced to live in the marginal wastelands. In higher latitudes, the shorter growing season has restricted the availability of plant life. Such conditions have caused a greater dependence on hunting and, along the coasts and waterways, on fishing. The abundance of vegetation in the lower latitudes of the tropics, on the other hand, has provided a greater opportunity for gathering a variety of plants. In short, the environmental differences have restricted the diet and have limited possibilities for the development of subsistence societies.

Contemporary hunter-gatherers may help us understand our prehistoric ancestors. We know from observation of modern hunter-gatherers in both Africa and Alaska that a society based on hunting and gathering must be very mobile.

41. Why does the author mention contemporary hunter-gatherers in paragraph 3?

(A) Their seasonal migration patterns are important.
(B) Studying them gives us insights into the lifestyle of prehistoric people.
(C) There are very few examples of modern hunter-gatherer societies.
(D) Their societies are quite different from those of their ancestors.

Paragraph 3 is marked with an arrow (→).

More Available

the tropics, on the other hand, has provided a greater opportunity for gathering a variety of plants. In short, the environmental differences have restricted the diet and have limited possibilities for the development of subsistence societies.

→ Contemporary hunter-gatherers may help us understand our prehistoric ancestors. We know from observation of modern hunter-gatherers in both Africa and Alaska that a society based on hunting and gathering must be very mobile. Following the food supply can be a way of life. If a particular kind of wild herding animal is the basis of the food for a group of people, those people must move to stay within reach of those animals. For many of the native people of the great central plains of North America, following the buffalo, who were in turn following the growth of grazing foods, determined their way of life.

For gathering societies, seasonal changes mean a great deal. While the entire community camps in a central location, a smaller party harvests the food within a reasonable distance from the camp. When the food in the area is exhausted, the community moves on to exploit

42. The word **exploit** in paragraph 4 is closest in meaning to

(A) use
(B) find
(C) take
(D) prepare

End

particular kind of wild herding animal is the basis of the food for a group of people, those people must move to stay within reach of those animals. For many of the native people of the great central plains of North America, following the buffalo, who were in turn following the growth of grazing foods, determined their way of life.

For gathering societies, seasonal changes mean a great deal. While the entire community camps in a central location, a smaller party harvests the food within a reasonable distance from the camp. When the food in the area is exhausted, the community moves on to **exploit** another site. We also notice a seasonal migration pattern evolving for most hunter-gatherers, along with a strict division of labor between the sexes. These patterns of behavior may be similar to those practiced by humankind during the Paleolithic Period.

43. What does the author mean by the statement **While the entire community camps in a central location, a smaller party harvests the food within a reasonable distance from the camp**?

(A) Everyone is involved in hunting and gathering the food for the community.
(B) When the food has been harvested, the community has a celebration.
(C) A small group hunts and gathers food near the camp.
(D) The reason that the community harvests the food is that it is near the camp.

44. All of the patterns of behavior for hunter-gatherers are mentioned in the passage EXCEPT

Ⓐ a small group plants food near the camp.
Ⓑ the group moves when the food supply is low.
Ⓒ men and women each have specific roles.
Ⓓ the seasons dictate the movement of the group.

45. Which of the following sentences should NOT be included in a summary of the passage?

Ⓐ Hunter-gatherers are mobile, tending to migrate seasonally.
Ⓑ Hunter-gatherers share different responsibilities between the sexes.
Ⓒ Hunter-gatherers camp in a central location.
Ⓓ Hunter-gatherers have many social celebrations.

To check your answers for Model Test 7, refer to the Answer Key on page 549. For an explanation of the answers, refer to the Explanatory Answers for Model Test 7 on pages 601–608.

Writing Section Model Test 7

When you take a Model Test, you should use one sheet of paper, both sides. Time each Model Test carefully. After you have read the topic, you should spend 30 minutes writing. For results that would be closest to the actual testing situation, it is recommended that an English teacher score your test, using the guidelines on page 325 of this book.

Leaders like John F. Kennedy and Martin Luther King have made important contributions to humanity. Name another world leader you think is important. Give specific reasons for your choice.

Notes

Model Test 8
Computer-Assisted TOEFL

Section 1: Listening

The Listening section of the test measures the ability to understand conversations and talks in English. You will use headphones to listen to the conversations and talks. While you are listening, pictures of the speakers or other information will be presented on your computer screen. There are two parts to the Listening section, with special directions for each part.

On the day of the test, the amount of time you will have to answer all of the questions will appear on the computer screen. The time you spend listening to the test material will not be counted. The listening material and questions about it will be presented only one time. You will not be allowed to take notes or have any paper at your computer. You will both see and hear the questions before the answer choices appear. You can take as much time as you need to select an answer; however, it will be to your advantage to answer the questions as quickly as possible. You may change your answer as many times as you want before you confirm it. After you have confirmed an answer, you will not be able to return to the question.

Before you begin working on the Listening section, you will have an opportunity to adjust the volume of the sound. You will not be able to change the volume after you have started the test.

QUESTION DIRECTIONS — Part A

In Part A of the Listening section, you will hear short conversations between two people. In some of the conversations, each person speaks only once. In other conversations, one or both of the people speak more than once. Each conversation is followed by one question about it.

Each question in this part has four answer choices. You should click on the best answer to each question. Answer the questions on the basis of what is stated or implied by the speakers.

1. What can be inferred about the woman?

   Ⓐ She is not his advisor.
   Ⓑ She is not polite.
   Ⓒ She does not have a course request form.
   Ⓓ She will help the man.

2. What does the man mean?

   Ⓐ He is lost.
   Ⓑ He needs a different course.
   Ⓒ He will not withdraw from the class.
   Ⓓ He doesn't know what he will do.

3. What can be inferred about the man?

   Ⓐ He did not go to Dr. Peterson's class today.
   Ⓑ The man is a student in the class that the woman teaches.
   Ⓒ The man works in the same office as the woman.
   Ⓓ The man is a teaching assistant for Dr. Peterson.

4. What will the man and woman probably do?

   Ⓐ Get the man some glasses
   Ⓑ Sit together
   Ⓒ Move to the front of the room
   Ⓓ Have an argument

5. How did the man feel about Montreal?

Ⓐ He liked Montreal in the winter.
Ⓑ He liked Montreal spring, summer, and fall.
Ⓒ He liked Montreal all year round.
Ⓓ He did not like Montreal.

6. What does the man mean?

Ⓐ He will place a wager.
Ⓑ He will pay later for his purchases.
Ⓒ He will do more than the required assignments.
Ⓓ He will go to his job.

7. What did the woman suggest?

Ⓐ Use will power
Ⓑ Chew gum
Ⓒ Wear a nicotine patch
Ⓓ Join a support group

8. What does the man mean?

Ⓐ The class is too long.
Ⓑ The class is too small.
Ⓒ He does not like the subject.
Ⓓ He does not want to say.

9. What does the man mean?

Ⓐ He is asking where to go.
Ⓑ He is telling the woman to leave.
Ⓒ He is calling the woman a liar.
Ⓓ He is congratulating the woman.

10. What does the woman mean?

Ⓐ Her roommate got the assistantship.
Ⓑ She is not going to take a full load.
Ⓒ Teaching is more difficult than studying.
Ⓓ The man is correct.

11. What is the woman's problem?

Ⓐ Her back pack is too heavy.
Ⓑ She is not a very good student.
Ⓒ She cannot find her notebook.
Ⓓ She needs a ride home from class.

12. What does the woman mean?

Ⓐ She already has an ID card.
Ⓑ She does not need her picture taken.
Ⓒ She is ready to leave.
Ⓓ She does not know where to go.

13. What does the woman suggest?

Ⓐ The man should invite his friends to dinner.
Ⓑ The man's friends should come to his house.
Ⓒ The man could take a plant to his friends.
Ⓓ The man likes candy.

14. What will the woman probably do?

Ⓐ Go with the man
Ⓑ Look on the other side of the hall
Ⓒ Get a different room
Ⓓ Return to the front desk

15. What does the woman imply?

Ⓐ The application was lost.
Ⓑ The process takes about three weeks.
Ⓒ The response is probably in the mail.
Ⓓ The man should be patient.

16. What does the woman mean?

Ⓐ She wants to use her passport for ID.
Ⓑ She does not have a driver's license.
Ⓒ She prefers to pay with a credit card.
Ⓓ She does not have any checks.

17. What does the man mean?

Ⓐ He was polite to the committee.
Ⓑ The meeting went very well.
Ⓒ Additional members are needed for the committee.
Ⓓ The committee did not meet.

QUESTION DIRECTIONS — Part B

In Part B of the Listening section, you will hear several longer conversations and talks. Each conversation or talk is followed by several questions. The conversations, talks, and questions will not be repeated.

The conversations and talks are about a variety of topics. You do not need special knowledge of the topics to answer the questions correctly. Rather, you should answer each question on the basis of what is stated or implied by the speakers in the conversations or talks.

For most of the questions, you will need to click on the best of four possible answers. Some questions will have special directions. The special directions will appear in a box on the computer screen.

18. Why is the student in the dean's office?

Ⓐ Because he failed a class
Ⓑ Because he needs some advice
Ⓒ Because he was caught plagiarizing
Ⓓ Because he stole a book

19. What is the student's excuse?

Ⓐ He says he didn't understand.
Ⓑ He says someone else did it.
Ⓒ He says he is sorry.
Ⓓ He says he needs a tutor.

20. How does the dean punish the student?

Ⓐ By expelling him
Ⓑ By giving him a failing grade in the course
Ⓒ By warning him
Ⓓ By sending him to the Learning Resources Center

21. What advice does the dean give the student?

Ⓐ To come back to her office
Ⓑ To get a tutor to help him
Ⓒ To use his own ideas next time
Ⓓ To go to another university

22. What is the woman trying to decide?

Ⓐ Whether to go to graduate school
Ⓑ If she wants to transfer or not
Ⓒ Which job to accept
Ⓓ What to do about her grades

23. What does she like about the college she is attending?

Ⓐ The prestige of a large school
Ⓑ The friends she has made
Ⓒ The attitude of the teachers
Ⓓ The opportunities for employment

24. How does the man respond to her problem?

Ⓐ He is not interested.
Ⓑ He gives her advice.
Ⓒ He shares his plans.
Ⓓ He just listens without comment.

25. What does the man plan to do?

Ⓐ Go to a large graduate institution
Ⓑ Continue his friendship with the woman
Ⓒ Finish his degree at another school
Ⓓ Schedule job interviews

26. What is the topic of this lecture?

Ⓐ The role of fine arts in civilization
Ⓑ A definition of culture in anthropology
Ⓒ Customs of American society
Ⓓ The study of complex societies

27. According to the speaker, what do most people mean when they use the word *culture* in ordinary conversation?

Ⓐ Customs for a particular society
Ⓑ Ethnic groups that share common experiences
Ⓒ Values that are characteristic of society
Ⓓ Familiarity with the arts

28. According to the speaker, what do anthropologists mean when they say a thought or activity is to be included as part of culture?

Ⓐ It must be considered appropriate by small groups within society.
Ⓑ It must be acquired by visiting museums, galleries, and theaters.
Ⓒ It must be commonly shared by a group.
Ⓓ It must be comprised of many diverse ethnic groups.

29. How does the professor explain American culture?

- Ⓐ Practices that are common to all Americans of diverse ethnicity
- Ⓑ The combination of diverse ethnic practices by different groups in America
- Ⓒ Diverse ethnic practices that are recognized but not practiced by all Americans
- Ⓓ Practices that the majority of Americans participate in

30. According to the speaker, what is a subculture?

- Ⓐ A museum or a gallery
- Ⓑ An informal culture
- Ⓒ A smaller group within the entire society
- Ⓓ The behaviors, beliefs, attitudes, and values of the majority society

31. How does the World Health Organization estimate compare with actual trends?

- Ⓐ The estimate is very accurate compared with the actual numbers.
- Ⓑ The estimate appears to be lower than the actual numbers.
- Ⓒ The estimate was much too high compared with the actual numbers.
- Ⓓ The estimate accounted for about two-thirds of the actual numbers.

32. The guest speaker briefly discusses a trend. Summarize the trend by putting the events in order.

Click on a sentence. Then click on the space where it belongs.
Use each sentence only once.

- [A] Heterosexual contact accounted for most new infections.
- [B] Many children were born with HIV.
- [C] Rates of exposure and infection of women rose.
- [D] The majority of AIDS victims were homosexual men.

1 ______
2 ______
3 ______
4 ______

33. Why are women so susceptible to the AIDS virus?

Click on 2 answers.

- [A] More women today tend to have multiple partners than they did in the past.
- [B] Some cultures do not encourage the use of protection.
- [C] Women are biologically more at risk for all sexually transmitted diseases.
- [D] Traditionally, women have not been the partner responsible for protection.

34. Which segments of the population will probably constitute the majority of AIDS cases in the twenty-first century?

Click on 2 answers.

- [A] Children
- [B] Teens
- [C] Women
- [D] Men

35. What causes jet lag?

- Ⓐ Adjustment to a longer or shorter day
- Ⓑ Air travel from west to east
- Ⓒ Different foods and drinks while traveling
- Ⓓ Lack of sleep during air travel

36. Who would suffer most from jet lag?

- Ⓐ A young person
- Ⓑ A person traveling west
- Ⓒ A person who has a regular routine
- Ⓓ A person who does not travel often

37. How can jet lag be minimized?

Click on 2 answers.

- [A] Eat a large meal on the plane
- [B] Drink lots of water on the plane
- [C] Arrive at your destination early in the evening
- [D] Try not to sleep very much during the flight

38. How long does it take to adjust to a new time zone?

Ⓐ One half day for every time zone
Ⓑ Twenty-four hours after arrival
Ⓒ One day for every time zone
Ⓓ Three days after arrival

39. What is Elderhostel?

Ⓐ A college program taught by retired professors
Ⓑ A summer program for senior citizens
Ⓒ An educational program for older adult students
Ⓓ A travel program that includes inexpensive dormitory accommodations

40. Which of the statements is true of Elderhostel?

Click on 2 answers.

[A] The courses are offered for credit.
[B] There are no final exams.
[C] Anyone may participate.
[D] College faculty teach the classes.

41. Which of the people in the picture would most probably be enrolled in an Elderhostel program?

A

B

C

D

42. What should you do if you are interested in finding out more about Elderhostel?

Ⓐ Write the national office
Ⓑ Call your local college
Ⓒ Listen to the radio station
Ⓓ Attend an Elderhostel meeting

43. What problem does the lecturer point out?

Ⓐ Pyrite looks like gold and is often mistaken for it.
Ⓑ Pyrite is very flammable and can easily burst into flames.
Ⓒ Pyrite is difficult to find in most parts of the world.
Ⓓ Pyrite does not have an easily identifiable crystal formation.

44. What will the professor do with the specimen he has brought to class?

Ⓐ He will return it to the museum.
Ⓑ He will keep it in his office.
Ⓒ He will use it for an experiment.
Ⓓ He will put it in the mineral lab.

45. Select the specimen that is most similar to the one that the professor showed in class.

Click on a picture.

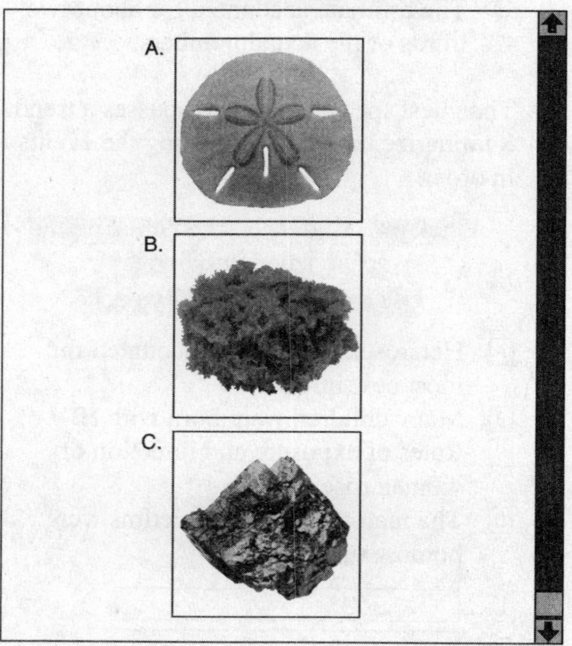

46. Identify the properties of pyrite.

Click on 2 answers.

[A] It is soft.
[B] It is brittle.
[C] It is flammable.
[D] It is rare.

47. What is an easy way to identify pyrite?

(A) Heat the specimen
(B) Put acid on the sample
(C) Look for green and brown streaks
(D) Smell the mineral

48. What prompted this conversation?

(A) The man is studying for a test.
(B) The man is looking for the Student Union.
(C) The man has lost a book.
(D) The man wants to meet the woman.

49. Where does the man think he left his book?

(A) In class
(B) At the Student Union
(C) In the cafeteria
(D) At the library

50. What does the woman suggest that the man do?

Click on 2 answers.

[A] Go to the Student Union immediately
[B] Study for his test
[C] Come back to see her tomorrow
[D] Check the lost and found tomorrow

Section 2: Structure

This section measures the ability to recognize language that is appropriate for standard written English. There are two types of questions in this section.

In the first type of question, there are incomplete sentences. Beneath each sentence, there are four words or phrases. You will choose the one word or phrase that best completes the sentence.

Clicking on a choice darkens the oval. After you click on **Next** and **Confirm Answer**, the next question will be presented.

The second type of question has four underlined words or phrases. You will choose the one underlined word or phrase that must be changed for the sentence to be correct.

Clicking on an underlined word or phrase will darken it. After you click on **Next** and **Confirm Answer**, the next question will be presented.

1. The consistency of protoplasm and that of glue ------ .

   (A) they are alike
   (B) are similar to
   (C) are similar
   (D) the same

2. The decomposition of microscopic animals (A) at the bottom of the sea results (B) in an accumulation (C) of the oil (D).

3. Nerve impulses ------ to the brain at a speed of about one hundred yards per second.

   (A) sending sensations
   (B) to send sensations
   (C) send sensations
   (D) sensations

4. A calorie (A) is (B) the quantity of heat required (C) to rise (D) one gallon of water one degree centrigrade at one atmospheric pressure.

5. The Supreme Court does not hear a case unless -------- , except those involving foreign ambassadors.

   (A) a trial
   (B) already tried
   (C) it already trying
   (D) it has already been tried

6. The yearly path of the sun around the heavens ------ .

   (A) is known as the ecliptic
   (B) known as the ecliptic
   (C) it is known to be ecliptic
   (D) knowing as the ecliptic

7. Before Alexander Fleming discovered penicillin, many people died ------ .

   (A) infected with simple bacteria
   (B) from simple bacterial infections
   (C) infections were simple bacteria
   (D) infecting of simple bacteria

8. Wholly (A) the plow is being displaced (B) by new techniques (C) that protect the land and promise (D) more abundant crops.

9. Although exact statistics vary because of political changes, -------- separate nation states are included in the official lists at any one time.

   (A) more than two hundred
   (B) as much as two hundred
   (C) many as two hundred
   (D) most that two hundred

10. Studies of job satisfaction are unreliable because there is (A) so many (B) variables and because (C) the admission of dissatisfaction may be viewed (D) as a personal failure.

11. ------ owe much of their success as a group to their unusual powers of migration.

(A) That birds
(B) A bird
(C) The bird
(D) Birds

12. ------ unknown quantities is the task of algebra.

(A) To found
(B) Find
(C) The find
(D) Finding

13. New synthetic materials have (A) improved the construction (B) of artificial body parts (C) by provide (D) both the power and the range of action for a natural limb.

14. If (A) England had not imposed (B) a tax on tea over two hundred and twenty years ago, (C) will (D) the United States have remained part of the British Commonwealth?

15. Research in the work place reveals that people work for many reasons ------ .

(A) money beside
(B) money besides
(C) beside money
(D) besides money

16. Both liquids and gases flow freely from a container because they have ------ .

(A) not definite shape
(B) none definite shape
(C) nothing definite shape
(D) no definite shape

17. A dolphin ------ a porpoise in that it has a longer nose.

(A) different
(B) differs
(C) different than
(D) differs from

18. Scientific fish farming, known as (A) aquaculture, has existed for more than (B) 4000 years, but scientists who make (C) research in this field are only recently providing the kind of information that growers need to increase (D) production.

19. That most natural time units are not simple multiples of each other ------ in constructing a calendar.

(A) it is a primary problem
(B) is a primary problem
(C) a primary problem is
(D) a primary problem

20. The native people in the Americas were referred to (A) as Indians because, according to (B) the believe (C) at the time, Christopher Columbus had reached (D) the the East Indies.

21. Only after food has been dried or canned -------- .

    (A) that it should be stored for later consumption
    (B) should be stored for later consumption
    (C) should it be stored for later consumption
    (D) it should be stored for later consumption

22. Aging (A) in most animals (B) can be readily modified when they (C) will limit (D) caloric intake.

23. Although we are concerned about (A) the problem of energy sources, we must not (B) fail recognizing (C) the need for (D) environmental protection.

24. --------, Carl Sandburg is also well known for his multivolume biography of Lincoln.

    (A) An eminent American poet
    (B) He is an eminent American poet
    (C) An eminent American poet who is
    (D) Despite an eminent American poet

25. The CBT will test (A) your ability to understand spoken (B) English, to read nontechnical language, and writing (C) correctly (D).

Section 3: Reading

This section measures the ability to read and understand short passages similar in topic and style to those that students are likely to encounter in North American universities and colleges. This section contains reading passages and questions about the passages. There are several different types of questions in this section.

In the Reading section, you will first have the opportunity to read the passage.

You will use the scroll bar to view the rest of the passage.

When you have finished reading the passage, you will use the mouse to click on **Proceed**. Then the questions about the passage will be presented. You are to choose the one best answer to each question. Answer all questions about the information in a passage on the basis of what is stated or implied in that passage.

Most of the questions will be multiple-choice questions. To answer these questions you will click on a choice below the question.

To answer some questions, you will click on a word or phrase.

To answer some questions, you will click on a sentence in the passage.

To answer some questions, you will click on a square to add a sentence to the passage.

Seismologists have devised two scales of measurement to enable them to describe and record information about earthquakes in quantitative terms. The most widely known measurement is the Richter scale, a numerical logarithmic scale developed and introduced by American seismologist Charles R. Richter in 1935. The purpose of the scale is to measure the amplitude of the largest trace recorded by a standard seismograph one hundred kilometers from the epicenter of an earthquake. Tables have been formulated to demonstrate the magnitude of any earthquake from any seismograph. For example, a one-unit increase in magnitude translates into an increase of times thirty in released energy. To put that another way, each number on the Richter scale represents an earthquake ten times as strong as one of the next lower magnitude. Specifically, an earthquake of magnitude 6 is ten times as strong as an earthquake of magnitude 5.

On the Richter scale, earthquakes of 6.75 are considered great and 7.0 to 7.75 are considered major. An earthquake that reads 4 to 5.5 would be expected to have caused localized damage, and those of magnitude 2 may be felt.

The other earthquake-assessment scale, introduced by the Italian seismologist Giuseppe Mercalli, measures the intensity of shaking, using gradations from 1 to 12. Because the effects of such shaking dissipate with distance from the epicenter of the earthquake, the Mercalli rating depends on the site of the measurement. Earthquakes of Mercalli 2 or 3 are basically the same as those of Richter 3 or 4; measurements of 11 or 12 on the Mercalli scale can be roughly correlated with magnitudes of 8 or 9 on the Richter scale. In either case, the relative power or energy released by the earthquake can be understood, and the population waits to hear how bad the earthquake that just passed really was.

It is estimated that almost one million earthquakes occur each year, but most of them are so minor that they pass undetected. In fact, more than one thousand earthquakes of a magnitude of 2 or lower on the Richter scale occur every day.

1. Which of the following is the main topic of the passage?

   Ⓐ Earthquakes
   Ⓑ The Richter scale
   Ⓒ Charles F. Richter
   Ⓓ Seismography

2. According to information in the passage, what does the Richter scale record?

   Ⓐ The distance from the epicenter
   Ⓑ The amplitude of the largest trace
   Ⓒ The degree of damage
   Ⓓ The location of the epicenter

3. The word standard in paragraph 1 could be replaced by

   Ⓐ reliable
   Ⓑ complex
   Ⓒ conventional
   Ⓓ abandoned

Beginning

Seismologists have devised two scales of measurement to enable them to describe and record information about earthquakes in quantitative terms. The most widely known measurement is the Richter scale, a numerical logarithmic scale developed and introduced by American seismologist Charles R. Richter in 1935. The purpose of the scale is to measure the amplitude of the largest trace recorded by a standard seismograph one hundred kilometers from the epicenter of an earthquake. Tables have been formulated to demonstrate the magnitude of any earthquake from any seismograph. For example, a one-unit increase in magnitude translates into an increase of times thirty in released energy. To put that another way, each number on the Richter scale represents an earthquake ten times as strong as one of the next lower magnitude. Specifically, an earthquake of magnitude 6 is ten times as strong as an earthquake of magnitude 5.

On the Richter scale, earthquakes of 6.75 are considered great and 7.0 to 7.75 are considered major. An earthquake that reads 4 to 5.5 would be

4. What is the value of the tables?

   Ⓐ They allow us to interpret the magnitude of earthquakes.
   Ⓑ They help us to calculate our distance from earthquakes.
   Ⓒ They record all earthquakes.
   Ⓓ They release the energy of earthquakes.

5. How does each number on the Richter scale compare?

Ⓐ Each number is one hundred times as strong as the previous number.
Ⓑ Each magnitude is ten times stronger than the previous magnitude.
Ⓒ The strength of each magnitude is one less than the previous magnitude.
Ⓓ The scale decreases by five or six for each number.

6. Look at the word those in the passage. Click on the word or phrase in the **bold** text that those refers to.

More Available

released energy. To put that another way, each number on the Richter scale represents an earthquake ten times as strong as one of the next lower magnitude. Specifically, an earthquake of magnitude 6 is ten times as strong as an earthquake of magnitude 5.

On the Richter scale, earthquakes of 6.75 are considered great and 7.0 to 7.75 are considered major. An earthquake that reads 4 to 5.5 would be expected to have caused localized damage, and those of magnitude 2 may be felt.

The other earthquake-assessment scale, introduced by the Italian seismologist Giuseppe Mercalli, measures the intensity of shaking, using gradations from 1 to 12. Because the effects of such shaking dissipate with distance from the epicenter of the earthquake, the Mercalli rating depends on the site of the measurement. Earthquakes of Mercalli 2 or 3 are basically the same as those of Richter 3 or 4; measurements of 11 or 12 on the Mercalli scale can be roughly correlated with magnitudes of 8 or 9 on the Richter scale. In either case, the relative power or energy released by the earthquake can be

7. What does the author mean by the statement Because the effects of such shaking dissipate with distance from the epicenter of the earthquake, the Mercalli rating depends on the site of the measurement ?

Ⓐ The Mercalli rating will vary depending on the location of the measurement.
Ⓑ The results of the Mercalli rating are less accurate at greater distances from the epicenter.
Ⓒ The stronger shaking of the earthquake at the center is not detected by the Mercalli rating.
Ⓓ The Mercalli rating is useful because it is taken farther away from the center of the earthquake.

8. Look at the word roughly in the passage. Click on the word or phrase in the **bold** text that is closest in meaning to the word roughly.

End

major. An earthquake that reads 4 to 5.5 would be expected to have caused localized damage, and those of magnitude 2 may be felt.

The other earthquake-assessment scale, introduced by the Italian seismologist Giuseppe Mercalli, measures the intensity of shaking, using gradations from 1 to 12. Because the effects of such shaking dissipate with distance from the epicenter of the earthquake, the Mercalli rating depends on the site of the measurement. **Earthquakes of Mercalli 2 or 3 are basically the same as those of Richter 3 or 4; measurements of 11 or 12 on the Mercalli scale can be roughly correlated with magnitudes of 8 or 9 on the Richter scale.** In either case, the relative power or energy released by the earthquake can be understood, and the population waits to hear how bad the earthquake that just passed really was.

It is estimated that almost one million earthquakes occur each year, but most of them are so minor that they pass undetected. In fact, more than one thousand earthquakes of a magnitude of 2 or lower on the Richter scale occur every day.

9. The word undetected in paragraph 4 is closest in meaning to

Ⓐ with no damage
Ⓑ with no notice
Ⓒ with no name
Ⓓ with no problem

End

major. An earthquake that reads 4 to 5.5 would be expected to have caused localized damage, and those of magnitude 2 may be felt.

The other earthquake-assessment scale, introduced by the Italian seismologist Giuseppe Mercalli, measures the intensity of shaking, using gradations from 1 to 12. Because the effects of such shaking dissipate with distance from the epicenter of the earthquake, the Mercalli rating depends on the site of the measurement. Earthquakes of Mercalli 2 or 3 are basically the same as those of Richter 3 or 4; measurements of 11 or 12 on the Mercalli scale can be roughly correlated with magnitudes of 8 or 9 on the Richter scale. In either case, the relative power or energy released by the earthquake can be understood, and the population waits to hear how bad the earthquake that just passed really was.

It is estimated that almost one million earthquakes occur each year, but most of them are so minor that they pass undetected. In fact, more than one thousand earthquakes of a magnitude of 2 or lower on the Richter scale occur every day.

10. With which of the following statements would the author most probably agree?

Ⓐ Only the Richter scale describes earthquakes in quantitative terms.
Ⓑ Both the Richter scale and the Mercalli Scale measure earthquakes in the same way.
Ⓒ Most earthquakes are measurable on either the Richter or the Mercalli scale.
Ⓓ The Mercalli and the Richter scales are different but they can be compared.

11. The passage discusses all of the following in the explanation of the Richter scale EXCEPT

Ⓐ It was introduced in 1935.
Ⓑ It was developed by an American seismologist.
Ⓒ It has a scale of 1 to 12.
Ⓓ It measures the magnitude of earthquakes.

Charles Ives, who is nowadays acclaimed as the first great American composer of the twentieth century, had to wait many years for the public recognition he deserved. Born to music as the son of a bandmaster, Ives played drums in his father's community band, and organ at the local church. He entered Yale University at twenty to study musical composition with Horatio Parker, but after graduation, he chose not to pursue a career in music. He suspected correctly that the public would not accept the music he wrote, for Ives did not follow the musical fashion of his times. While his contemporaries wrote lyrical songs, Ives transfigured music and musical form. He quoted, combined, insinuated, and distorted familiar hymns, marches, and battle songs, while experimenting with the effects of polytonality, or the simultaneous use of two or more keys, and dissonance, or the clash of keys with conflicting rhythms and time. Even when he could convince some musicians to show some interest in his compositions, after assessing them, conductors and performers said that they were essentially unplayable.

Instead, he became a successful insurance executive, building his company into the largest agency in the country in only two decades. Although he occasionally hired musicians to play one of his works privately for him, he usually heard his music only in his imagination.

After he recovered from a serious heart attack, he became reconciled to the fact that his ideas, especially the use of dissonance and special effects, were just too different for the musical mainstream to accept. Determined to share his music with the few people who might appreciate it, he published his work privately and distributed it free.

In 1939, when Ives was sixty-five, American pianist John Kirkpatrick played *Concord Sonata* in Town Hall. The reviews were laudatory. One reviewer proclaimed it "the greatest music composed by an American." By 1947, Ives was famous. His *Second Symphony* was presented to the public in a performance by the New York Philharmonic, fifty years after it had been written. The same year, Ives received the Pulitzer Prize. He was seventy-three.

12. Which of the following is the main topic of the passage?

Ⓐ Modern musical composition
Ⓑ Charles Ives' life
Ⓒ The Pulitzer Prize
Ⓓ Career choices

13. Why didn't the public appreciate Ives' music?

Ⓐ It was not performed for a long time.
Ⓑ It was very different from the music of the time.
Ⓒ The performers did not play it well.
Ⓓ He did not write it down.

14. Look at the word dissonance in the passage. Click on the word in the **bold** text that is closest in meaning to dissonance.

More Available

marches, and battle songs, **while experimenting with the effects of polytonality, or the simultaneous use of two or more keys, and dissonance, or the clash of keys with conflicting rhythms and time.** Even when he could convince some musicians to show some interest in his compositions, after assessing them, conductors and performers said that they were essentially unplayable.

Instead, he became a successful insurance executive, building his company into the largest agency in the country in only two decades. Although he occasionally hired musicians to play one of his works privately for him, he usually heard his music only in his imagination.

After he recovered from a serious heart attack, he became reconciled to the fact that his ideas, especially the use of dissonance and special effects, were just too different for the musical mainstream to accept. Determined to share his music with the few people who might appreciate it, he published his work privately and distributed it free.

In 1939, when Ives was sixty-five, American pianist John Kirkpatrick played *Concord Sonata* in

15. The word they in paragraph 1 refers to

Ⓐ conductors
Ⓑ performers
Ⓒ interest
Ⓓ compositions

More Available

marches, and battle songs, while experimenting with the effects of polytonality, or the simultaneous use of two or more keys, and dissonance, or the clash of keys with conflicting rhythms and time. Even when he could convince some musicians to show some interest in his compositions, after assessing them, conductors and performers said that they were essentially unplayable.

Instead, he became a successful insurance executive, building his company into the largest agency in the country in only two decades. Although he occasionally hired musicians to play one of his works privately for him, he usually heard his music only in his imagination.

After he recovered from a serious heart attack, he became reconciled to the fact that his ideas, especially the use of dissonance and special effects, were just too different for the musical mainstream to accept. Determined to share his music with the few people who might appreciate it, he published his work privately and distributed it free.

In 1939, when Ives was sixty-five, American pianist John Kirkpatrick played *Concord Sonata* in

16. How did Ives make a living for most of his life?

Ⓐ He conducted a band.
Ⓑ He taught musical composition.
Ⓒ He owned an insurance company.
Ⓓ He published music.

17. The phrase became reconciled to in paragraph 3 is closest in meaning to

Ⓐ accepted
Ⓑ repeated
Ⓒ disputed
Ⓓ neglected

More Available

marches, and battle songs, while experimenting with the effects of polytonality, or the simultaneous use of two or more keys, and dissonance, or the clash of keys with conflicting rhythms and time. Even when he could convince some musicians to show some interest in his compositions, after assessing them, conductors and performers said that they were essentially unplayable.

Instead, he became a successful insurance executive, building his company into the largest agency in the country in only two decades. Although he occasionally hired musicians to play one of his works privately for him, he usually heard his music only in his imagination.

After he recovered from a serious heart attack, he became reconciled to the fact that his ideas, especially the use of dissonance and special effects, were just too different for the musical mainstream to accept. Determined to share his music with the few people who might appreciate it, he published his work privately and distributed it free.

In 1939, when Ives was sixty-five, American pianist John Kirkpatrick played *Concord Sonata* in

18. According to the passage, Ives shared his music

Ⓐ by publishing free copies
Ⓑ by playing it himself
Ⓒ by hiring musicians to perform
Ⓓ by teaching at Yale

19. Which of the following characteristics is NOT true of the music of Charles Ives?

Ⓐ It included pieces of familiar songs.
Ⓑ It was very experimental.
Ⓒ It was difficult to play.
Ⓓ It was never appreciated.

20. How was the performance of *Concord Sonata* received?

Ⓐ There were no reviews.
Ⓑ The musicians felt it was unplayable.
Ⓒ The public would not accept it.
Ⓓ It established Ives as an important composer.

21. Look at the word it in the passage. Click on the word or phrase in the **bold** text that it refers to.

End

executive, building his company into the largest agency in the country in only two decades. Although he occasionally hired musicians to play one of his works privately for him, he usually heard his music only in his imagination.

After he recovered from a serious heart attack, he became reconciled to the fact that his ideas, especially the use of dissonance and special effects, were just too different for the musical mainstream to accept. Determined to share his music with the few people who might appreciate it, he published his work privately and distributed it free.

In 1939, when Ives was sixty-five, American pianist John Kirkpatrick played *Concord Sonata* in Town Hall. The reviews were laudatory. One reviewer proclaimed it "the greatest music composed by an American." By 1947, Ives was famous. His *Second Symphony* was presented to the public in a performance by the New York Philharmonic, fifty years after it had been written. The same year, Ives received the Pulitzer Prize. He was seventy-three.

22. The following sentence can be added to the passage.

Even during such a busy time in his career, he still dedicated himself to composing music in the evenings, on weekends, and during vacations.

Where would it best fit in the passage?

Click on the square (■) to add the sentence to the passage.

Scroll the passage to see all of the choices.

More Available

marches, and battle songs, while experimenting with the effects of polytonality, or the simultaneous use of two or more keys, and dissonance, or the clash of keys with conflicting rhythms and time. Even when he could convince some musicians to show some interest in his compositions, after assessing them, conductors and performers said that they were essentially unplayable. ■

Instead, he became a successful insurance executive, building his company into the largest agency in the country in only two decades. ■ Although he occasionally hired musicians to play one of his works privately for him, he usually heard his music only in his imagination. ■

After he recovered from a serious heart attack, he became reconciled to the fact that his ideas, especially the use of dissonance and special effects, were just too different for the musical mainstream to accept. ■ Determined to share his music with the few people who might appreciate it, he published his work privately and distributed it free.

In 1939, when Ives was sixty-five, American pianist John Kirkpatrick played *Concord Sonata* in

Bats are not dirty, bloodthirsty monsters as portrayed in vampire films. These winged mammals groom themselves carefully like cats and only rarely carry rabies. Of the hundreds of species of bats, only three rely on blood meals. In fact, the majority eat fruit, insects, spiders, or small animals; some species gather nectar and pollen from flowers. The environmental benefits of bats are myriad. They consume an enormous number of pests, pollinate many varieties of plant life, and help reforest huge tracts of barren land by excreting millions of undigested seeds.

Bats also have served as models for sophisticated navigation systems in naval and airplane technology. Living models for radar and sonar, almost all bats use echolocation to navigate, especially at night. As they fly, they emit a series of high-pitched squeaks at the rate of about fifty per minute. As these signals bounce off objects in their path, an echo is detected by the bats' sensitive ears that informs them of the direction, distance, and nature of obstacles so that they can undertake corrective or evasive action. Echoes are used by bats but not because of physical limitations or impairments, for bats are not blind as widely assumed. In fact, all species of bats can see, probably about as well as human beings. Another myth, about bats being aggressive, intentionally entangling themselves in the hair of human beings, is also totally unfounded. It has been shown in studies not only that bats are timid, but also that they will assiduously avoid contact with larger creatures than themselves if possible.

Aggregation during the day may vary from small groups consisting of a single male and a dozen or more females to huge colonies of many thousands or even millions of individuals, hanging upside down in caves or in hollow trees, buildings, or other protected shelters. Within their social systems, bats assume specialized roles. Some guard the entrance to their caves, others scout for food, and still others warn the colony of approaching danger. An adult female bat usually gives birth to only one pup per year, tenderly caring for it, and a nursery colony within a larger colony may provide mother bats with a safe, supportive environment in which to rear their young.

23. With which of the following statements would the author most probably agree?

Ⓐ Bats are dirty and they carry rabies.
Ⓑ Bats are like the monsters in vampire films.
Ⓒ Bats are clean, helpful members of the animal world.
Ⓓ Bats are not very important in the animal world.

24. According to the passage, what do most bats eat?

Ⓐ Blood meals
Ⓑ Fruit and insects
Ⓒ Leaves and trees
Ⓓ Large animals

25. Look at the word enormous in the passage. Click on the word in the **bold** text that is closest in meaning to enormous.

Beginning

Bats are not dirty, bloodthirsty monsters as portrayed in vampire films. These winged mammals groom themselves carefully like cats and only rarely carry rabies. Of the hundreds of species of bats, only three rely on blood meals. In fact, the majority eat fruit, insects, spiders, or small animals; some species gather nectar and pollen from flowers. The environmental benefits of bats are myriad. **They consume an enormous number of pests, pollinate many varieties of plant life, and help reforest huge tracts of barren land by excreting millions of undigested seeds.**

Bats also have served as models for sophisticated navigation systems in naval and airplane technology. Living models for radar and sonar, almost all bats use echolocation to navigate, especially at night. As they fly, they emit a series of high-pitched squeaks at the rate of about fifty per minute. As these signals bounce off objects in their path, an echo is detected by the bats' sensitive ears that informs them of the direction, distance, and nature of obstacles so that they can undertake corrective or evasive action. Echoes are used by bats but not because of

26. How do bats help reforest the land?

Ⓐ By eating pests
Ⓑ By hanging upside down in trees at night
Ⓒ By excreting seeds
Ⓓ By taking evasive action

27. Which of the following is NOT characteristic of most bats?

Ⓐ They pollinate plants.
Ⓑ They have specialized roles in their colony.
Ⓒ They use echolocation.
Ⓓ They eat blood.

28. The word emit in paragraph 2 is closest in meaning to

Ⓐ send
Ⓑ continue
Ⓒ find
Ⓓ stop

Beginning

Bats are not dirty, bloodthirsty monsters as portrayed in vampire films. These winged mammals groom themselves carefully like cats and only rarely carry rabies. Of the hundreds of species of bats, only three rely on blood meals. In fact, the majority eat fruit, insects, spiders, or small animals; some species gather nectar and pollen from flowers. The environmental benefits of bats are myriad. They consume an enormous number of pests, pollinate many varieties of plant life, and help reforest huge tracts of barren land by excreting millions of undigested seeds.

Bats also have served as models for sophisticated navigation systems in naval and airplane technology. Living models for radar and sonar, almost all bats use echolocation to navigate, especially at night. As they fly, they emit a series of high-pitched squeaks at the rate of about fifty per minute. As these signals bounce off objects in their path, an echo is detected by the bats' sensitive ears that informs them of the direction, distance, and nature of obstacles so that they can undertake corrective or evasive action. Echoes are used by bats but not because of

29. According to the passage, how do bats navigate?

Ⓐ By responding to the echoes of their signals bouncing off objects
Ⓑ By warning the colony of approaching danger with high squeaks
Ⓒ By beating their wings fifty times per minute
Ⓓ By using their sensitive ears to hear the noises in their environment

30. The word them in paragraph 2 refers to

Ⓐ signals
Ⓑ objects
Ⓒ bats
Ⓓ squeaks

Beginning

Bats are not dirty, bloodthirsty monsters as portrayed in vampire films. These winged mammals groom themselves carefully like cats and only rarely carry rabies. Of the hundreds of species of bats, only three rely on blood meals. In fact, the majority eat fruit, insects, spiders, or small animals; some species gather nectar and pollen from flowers. The environmental benefits of bats are myriad. They consume an enormous number of pests, pollinate many varieties of plant life, and help reforest huge tracts of barren land by excreting millions of undigested seeds.

Bats also have served as models for sophisticated navigation systems in naval and airplane technology. Living models for radar and sonar, almost all bats use echolocation to navigate, especially at night. As they fly, they emit a series of high-pitched squeaks at the rate of about fifty per minute. As these signals bounce off objects in their path, an echo is detected by the bats' sensitive ears that informs them of the direction, distance, and nature of obstacles so that they can undertake corrective or evasive action. Echoes are used by bats but not because of

31. Click on the sentence in paragraph 2 that refers to the visual range of bats.

Paragraph 2 is marked with an arrow (→).

More Available

→ Bats also have served as models for sophisticated navigation systems in naval and airplane technology. Living models for radar and sonar, almost all bats use echolocation to navigate, especially at night. As they fly, they emit a series of high-pitched squeaks at the rate of about fifty per minute. As these signals bounce off objects in their path, an echo is detected by the bats' sensitive ears that informs them of the direction, distance, and nature of obstacles so that they can undertake corrective or evasive action. Echoes are used by bats but not because of physical limitations or impairments, for bats are not blind as widely assumed. In fact, all species of bats can see, probably about as well as human beings. Another myth, about bats being aggressive, intentionally entangling themselves in the hair of human beings, is also totally unfounded. It has been shown in studies not only that bats are timid, but also that they will assiduously avoid contact with larger creatures than themselves if possible.

Aggregation during the day may vary from small groups consisting of a single male and a dozen or more females to huge colonies of many

32. Look at the word Some in the passage. Click on the word or phrase in the **bold** text that Some refers to.

End

intentionally entangling themselves in the hair of human beings, is also totally unfounded. It has been shown in studies not only that bats are timid, but also that they will assiduously avoid contact with larger creatures than themselves if possible.

Aggregation during the day may vary from small groups consisting of a single male and a dozen or more females to huge colonies of many thousands or even millions of individuals, hanging upside down in caves or in hollow trees, buildings, or other protected shelters. **Within their social systems, bats assume specialized roles. Some guard the entrance to their caves, others scout for food, and still others warn the colony of approaching danger.** An adult female bat usually gives birth to only one pup per year, tenderly caring for it, and a nursery colony within a larger colony may provide mother bats with a safe, supportive environment in which to rear their young.

33. The following sentence can be added to the passage.

It is a little known fact that bats are highly social creatures.

Where would it best fit in the passage?

Click on the square (■) to add the sentence to the passage.

Scroll the passage to see all of the choices.

End

intentionally entangling themselves in the hair of human beings, is also totally unfounded. It has been shown in studies not only that bats are timid, but also that they will assiduously avoid contact with larger creatures than themselves if possible.

■ Aggregation during the day may vary from small groups consisting of a single male and a dozen or more females to huge colonies of many thousands or even millions of individuals, hanging upside down in caves or in hollow trees, buildings, or other protected shelters. ■ Within their social systems, bats assume specialized roles. ■ Some guard the entrance to their caves, others scout for food, and still others warn the colony of approaching danger. ■ An adult female bat usually gives birth to only one pup per year, tenderly caring for it, and a nursery colony within a larger colony may provide mother bats with a safe, supportive environment in which to rear their young.

The fact that most Americans live in urban areas does not mean that they reside in the center of large cities. In fact, more Americans live in the suburbs of large metropolitan areas than in the cities themselves.

The Bureau of the Census regards any area with more than 2500 people as an urban area, and does not consider boundaries of cities and suburbs. According to the Bureau, the political boundaries are less significant than the social and economic relationships and the transportation and communication systems that integrate a locale. The term used by the Bureau for an integrated metropolis is an MSA, which stands for Metropolitan Statistical Area. In general, an MSA is any area that contains a city and its surrounding suburbs and has a total population of 50,000 or more.

At the present time, the Bureau reports more than 280 MSAs, which together account for 75 percent of the US population. In addition, the Bureau recognizes eighteen megapolises, that is, continuous adjacent metropolitan areas. One of the most obvious megapolises includes a chain of hundreds of cities and suburbs across ten states on the East Coast from Massachusetts to Virginia, including Boston, New York, and Washington, D.C. In the Eastern Corridor, as it is called, a population of 45 million inhabitants is concentrated. Another megapolis that is growing rapidly is the California coast from San Francisco through Los Angeles to San Diego.

34. Which of the following is the best title for the passage?

Ⓐ Metropolitan Statistical Areas
Ⓑ Types of Population Centers
Ⓒ The Bureau of the Census
Ⓓ Megapolises

35. According to the passage, where do most Americans live?

Ⓐ In the center of cities
Ⓑ In the suburbs surrounding large cities
Ⓒ In rural areas
Ⓓ In small towns

36. Look at the word reside in the passage. Click on the word in the **bold** text that is closest in meaning to reside.

Beginning

The fact that most Americans live in urban areas does not mean that they reside in the center of large cities. In fact, more Americans live in the suburbs of large metropolitan areas than in the cities themselves.

The Bureau of the Census regards any area with more than 2500 people as an urban area, and does not consider boundaries of cities and suburbs. According to the Bureau, the political boundaries are less significant than the social and economic relationships and the transportation and communication systems that integrate a locale. The term used by the Bureau for an integrated metropolis is an MSA, which stands for Metropolitan Statistical Area. In general, an MSA is any area that contains a city and its surrounding suburbs and has a total population of 50,000 or more.

At the present time, the Bureau reports more than 280 MSAs, which together account for 75 percent of the US population. In addition, the Bureau recognizes eighteen megapolises, that is, continuous adjacent metropolitan areas. One of the most obvious megapolises includes a chain of hundreds of cities and suburbs across ten states on the East Coast from Massachusetts to Virginia, including Boston, New

37. According to the Bureau of the Census, what is an urban area?

Ⓐ An area with 2500 people or more
Ⓑ An area with at least 50,000 people
Ⓒ The eighteen largest cities
Ⓓ A chain of adjacent cities

38. Which of the following are NOT considered important in defining an urban area?

Ⓐ Political boundaries
Ⓑ Transportation networks
Ⓒ Social relationships
Ⓓ Economic systems

39. The word integrate in paragraph 2 is closest in meaning to

Ⓐ benefit
Ⓑ define
Ⓒ unite
Ⓓ restrict

Beginning

The fact that most Americans live in urban areas does not mean that they reside in the center of large cities. In fact, more Americans live in the suburbs of large metropolitan areas than in the cities themselves.

The Bureau of the Census regards any area with more than 2500 people as an urban area, and does not consider boundaries of cities and suburbs. According to the Bureau, the political boundaries are less significant than the social and economic relationships and the transportation and communication systems that integrate a locale. The term used by the Bureau for an integrated metropolis is an MSA, which stands for Metropolitan Statistical Area. In general, an MSA is any area that contains a city and its surrounding suburbs and has a total population of 50,000 or more.

At the present time, the Bureau reports more than 280 MSAs, which together account for 75 percent of the US population. In addition, the Bureau recognizes eighteen megapolises, that is, continuous adjacent metropolitan areas. One of the most obvious megapolises includes a chain of hundreds of cities and suburbs across ten states on the East Coast from Massachusetts to Virginia, including Boston, New

40. Look at the word locale in the passage. Click on the word in the **bold** text that is closest in meaning to locale.

End

According to the Bureau, the political boundaries are less significant than the social and economic relationships and the transportation and communication systems that integrate a locale. **The term used by the Bureau for an integrated metropolis is an MSA, which stands for Metropolitan Statistical Area. In general, an MSA is any area that contains a city and its surrounding suburbs and has a total population of 50,000 or more.**

At the present time, the Bureau reports more than 280 MSAs, which together account for 75 percent of the US population. In addition, the Bureau recognizes eighteen megapolises, that is, continuous adjacent metropolitan areas. One of the most obvious megapolises includes a chain of hundreds of cities and suburbs across ten states on the East Coast from Massachusetts to Virginia, including Boston, New York, and Washington, D.C. In the Eastern Corridor, as it is called, a population of 45 million inhabitants is concentrated. Another megapolis that is growing rapidly is the California coast from San Francisco through Los Angeles to San Diego.

41. The word its in paragraph 2 refers to

Ⓐ the MSA's
Ⓑ the area's
Ⓒ the city's
Ⓓ the population's

End

According to the Bureau, the political boundaries are less significant than the social and economic relationships and the transportation and communication systems that integrate a locale. The term used by the Bureau for an integrated metropolis is an MSA, which stands for Metropolitan Statistical Area. In general, an MSA is any area that contains a city and its surrounding suburbs and has a total population of 50,000 or more.

At the present time, the Bureau reports more than 280 MSAs, which together account for 75 percent of the US population. In addition, the Bureau recognizes eighteen megapolises, that is, continuous adjacent metropolitan areas. One of the most obvious megapolises includes a chain of hundreds of cities and suburbs across ten states on the East Coast from Massachusetts to Virginia, including Boston, New York, and Washington, D.C. In the Eastern Corridor, as it is called, a population of 45 million inhabitants is concentrated. Another megapolis that is growing rapidly is the California coast from San Francisco through Los Angeles to San Diego.

42. Click on the paragraph that identifies the U.S. population now living in MSAs.

Scroll the passage to see all of the paragraphs.

43. The word adjacent in paragraph 3 is closest in meaning to

Ⓐ beside each other
Ⓑ growing very fast
Ⓒ the same size
Ⓓ densely populated

End

Area. In general, an MSA is any area that contains a city and its surrounding suburbs and has a total population of 50,000 or more.

At the present time, the Bureau reports more than 280 MSAs, which together account for 75 percent of the US population. In addition, the Bureau recognizes eighteen megapolises, that is, continuous adjacent metropolitan areas. One of the most obvious megapolises includes a chain of hundreds of cities and suburbs across ten states on the East Coast from Massachusetts to Virginia, including Boston, New York, and Washington, D.C. In the Eastern Corridor, as it is called, a population of 45 million inhabitants is concentrated. Another megapolis that is growing rapidly is the California coast from San Francisco through Los Angeles to San Diego.

44. According to the passage, what is a megapolis?

Ⓐ One of the ten largest cities in the United States
Ⓑ One of the eighteen largest cities in the United States
Ⓒ One of the one hundred cities between Boston and Washington
Ⓓ Any number of continuous adjacent cities and suburbs

45. Why does the author mention the Eastern Corridor and the California coast in paragraph 3?

Ⓐ As examples of megapolises
Ⓑ Because 75 percent of the population lives there
Ⓒ To conclude the passage
Ⓓ The Bureau of the Census is located there

Paragraph 3 is marked with an arrow (→).

End

Area. In general, an MSA is any area that contains a city and its surrounding suburbs and has a total population of 50,000 or more.

→ At the present time, the Bureau reports more than 280 MSAs, which together account for 75 percent of the US population. In addition, the Bureau recognizes eighteen megapolises, that is, continuous adjacent metropolitan areas. One of the most obvious megapolises includes a chain of hundreds of cities and suburbs across ten states on the East Coast from Massachusetts to Virginia, including Boston, New York, and Washington, D.C. In the Eastern Corridor, as it is called, a population of 45 million inhabitants is concentrated. Another megapolis that is growing rapidly is the California coast from San Francisco through Los Angeles to San Diego.

To check your answers for Model Test 8, refer to the Answer Key on page 550. For an explanation of the answers, refer to the Explanatory Answers for Model Test 8 on pages 609–616.

Writing Section Model Test 8

When you take a Model Test, you should use one sheet of paper, both sides. Time each Model Test carefully. After you have read the topic, you should spend 30 minutes writing. For results that would be closest to the actual testing situation, it is recommended that an English teacher score your test, using the guidelines on page 325 of this book.

Read and think about the following statement: The college years are the best time in a person's life. Do you agree or disagree with the statement? Give reasons to support your opinion.

Notes

ANSWER KEYS FOR THE TOEFL REVIEW EXERCISES AND MODEL TESTS

ANSWER KEY—EXERCISES FOR STRUCTURE

Patterns

Problems 1–15

Problem		*Part A*	*Part B*
Problem	1	**(A)**	**(A)** have
Problem	2	**(C)**	**(A)** to evolve
Problem	3	**(D)**	**(B)** smoking
Problem	4	**(D)**	**(B)** permitting
Problem	5	**(C)**	**(A)** saw
Problem	6	**(D)**	**(B)** fly
Problem	7	**(A)**	**(C)** must have originated
Problem	8	**(C)**	**(A)** reproducing
Problem	9	**(A)**	**(B)** must mate
Problem	10	**(A)**	**(B)** knew how
Problem	11	**(B)**	**(C)** used to moving
Problem	12	**(A)**	**(B)** advertise
Problem	13	**(D)**	**(A)** use
Problem	14	**(D)**	**(D)** changed
Problem	15	**(B)**	**(A)** don't park

Review Exercise: Problems 1–15

1 **(A)**
2 **(A)**
3 **(B)**
4 **(C)** to have
5 **(C)** recover
6 **(B)** used to roam
7 **(B)** to resemble
8 **(C)** have served
9 **(D)** must be producing
10 **(A)** ran

Problems 16–26

Problem		*Part A*	*Part B*
Problem	16	**(A)**	**(C)** turn
Problem	17	**(A)**	**(D)** appraised
Problem	18	**(A)**	**(A)** printed
Problem	19	**(A)**	**(A)** continue
Problem	20	**(B)**	**(D)** (to) nourish
Problem	21	**(A)**	**(B)** turns *or* will turn
Problem	22	**(A)**	**(C)** will have to pay *or* may have to pay
Problem	23	**(D)**	**(D)** would occur
Problem	24	**(C)**	**(A)** had
Problem	25	**(A)**	**(B)** would be
Problem	26	**(A)**	**(C)** unless they complete

Review Exercise: Problems 16–26

1 **(D)**
2 **(B)**
3 **(C)**
4 **(C)** pasteurize
5 **(C)** found
6 **(B)** follow
7 **(D)** delivered
8 **(A)** drive
9 **(A)** Unless there are complications
10 **(A)** were

Problems 27–41

Problem		*Part A*	*Part B*
Problem	27	**(D)**	**(B)** be used
Problem	28	**(D)**	**(B)** appear
Problem	29	**(B)**	**(A)** be
Problem	30	**(B)**	**(B)** for making *or* to make
Problem	31	**(C)**	**(C)** measured
Problem	32	**(A)**	**(C)** by high frequency radiation
Problem	33	**(C)**	**(B)** to be constructed
Problem	34	**(D)**	**(D)** repairing *or* to be repaired
Problem	35	**(A)**	**(A)** It is believed
Problem	36	**(C)**	**(D)** have buried
Problem	37	**(C)**	**(A)** preserved
Problem	38	**(D)**	**(C)** will have succeeded
Problem	39	**(C)**	**(A)** would be
Problem	40	**(B)**	**(B)** is losing
Problem	41	**(B)**	**(D)** should be discontinued

Review Exercise: Problems 27–41

1 **(C)**
2 **(C)**
3 **(D)**
4 **(B)** register
5 **(D)** is known as
6 **(B)** to maintain
7 **(C)** will have been
8 **(A)** to practice
9 **(B)** are born
10 **(A)** he would be able

Problems 42–140

Problem		*Part A*	*Part B*
Problem	42	(A)	(B) he
Problem	43	(B)	(A) she
Problem	44	(C)	(C) him
Problem	45	(A)	(D) for them
Problem	46	(D)	(C) his
Problem	47	(D)	(A) his hands and feet
Problem	48	(A)	(A) which
Problem	49	(B)	(A) who
Problem	50	(B)	(D) himself
Problem	51	(D)	(D) each other
Problem	52	(C)	(C) eight or ten computers
Problem	53	(C)	(A) Religion
Problem	54	(B)	(A) Space
Problem	55	(B)	(A) people
Problem	56	(C)	(A) Progress
Problem	57	(B)	(C) pieces of equipment
Problem	58	(B)	(A) kind of tool
Problem	59	(C)	(A) Spelling *or* To spell
Problem	60	(A)	(A) The writing of
Problem	61	(B)	(A) It is
Problem	62	(A)	(C) an
Problem	63	(A)	(A) The philosophy
Problem	64	(C)	(A) Soil
Problem	65	(D)	(B) no
Problem	66	(C)	(A) causes
Problem	67	(C)	(D) little news
Problem	68	(A)	(A) Much
Problem	69	(C)	(B) a little
Problem	70	(A)	(A) Only a few early scientists
Problem	71	(C)	(A) The number
Problem	72	(C)	(A) Most of *or* Almost all of
Problem	73	(A)	(B) enough earnings
Problem	74	(C)	(B) secure enough
Problem	75	(D)	(D) another *or* the other
Problem	76	(C)	(B) the rest *or* the rest of them
Problem	77	(A)	(C) the first
Problem	78	(C)	(A) Sex education
Problem	79	(A)	(B) four-stage
Problem	80	(C)	(A) surprising
Problem	81	(A)	(B) so expensive
Problem	82	(A)	(A) such a brilliant scientist *or* so brilliant a scientist
Problem	83	(B)	(C) too
Problem	84	(A)	(D) very long
Problem	85	(B)	(B) good
Problem	86	(B)	(B) the same
Problem	87	(A)	(C) similar
Problem	88	(C)	(D) like
Problem	89	(C)	(C) the same temperature as
Problem	90	(B)	(D) as deep as
Problem	91	(B)	(D) different from
Problem	92	(A)	(B) differ from *or* are different from
Problem	93	(C)	(A) as much as
Problem	94	(A)	(A) more than
Problem	95	(C)	(C) as many as
Problem	96	(B)	(C) more efficient
Problem	97	(C)	(B) most
Problem	98	(C)	(B) worse
Problem	99	(B)	(A) efficiently
Problem	100	(C)	(A) the more intense
Problem	101	(A)	(B) like that of England
Problem	102	(B)	(D) than those of Eastern ladies
Problem	103	(D)	(D) among
Problem	104	(A)	(D) on
Problem	105	(A)	(B) in April
Problem	106	(B)	(B) besides
Problem	107	(A)	(D) but *or* except
Problem	108	(A)	(D) instead of
Problem	109	(B)	(D) such as
Problem	110	(A)	(A) In spite of *or* Despite
Problem	111	(C)	(C) because
Problem	112	(C)	(D) from eating
Problem	113	(C)	(D) for studying *or* to study
Problem	114	(C)	(C) taxing
Problem	115	(A)	(D) to 1852
Problem	116	(A)	(A) and
Problem	117	(A)	(C) as well as
Problem	118	(D)	(D) also easy to install
Problem	119	(B)	(C) but
Problem	120	(C)	(D) too
Problem	121	(B)	(D) should
Problem	122	(B)	(B) so that
Problem	123	(B)	(D) complete
Problem	124	(D)	(C) the plane is
Problem	125	(A)	(A) Whenever
Problem	126	(C)	(B) widely

Problem		Part A	Part B
Problem	127	(D)	(B) fast
Problem	128	(C)	(A) Sometimes
Problem	129	(B)	(B) does the same major league baseball team win
Problem	130	(D)	(A) Once
Problem	131	(A)	(A) While
Problem	132	(D)	(B) no longer
Problem	133	(C)	(A) since 1930
Problem	134	(D)	(A) the fourth of July *or* July fourth
Problem	135	(B)	(C) as high as
Problem	136	(C)	(B) as a whole
Problem	137	(B)	(B) that
Problem	138	(B)	(A) which are
Problem	139	(B)	(C) use
Problem	140	(B)	(D) use

Style

Problems 1–30

Problem		Part A	Part B
Problem	1	(C)	(C) were
Problem	2	(A)	(A) was
Problem	3	(C)	(B) gave
Problem	4	(A)	(B) was
Problem	5	(B)	(B) enables
Problem	6	(C)	(C) makes
Problem	7	(C)	(A) is
Problem	8	(B)	(A) There are
Problem	9	(B)	(C) is
Problem	10	(A)	(C) needs
Problem	11	(D)	(D) its
Problem	12	(B)	(C) their
Problem	13	(D)	(C) one's *or* his
Problem	14	(C)	(B) its native habitat
Problem	15	(B)	(A) Having designed
Problem	16	(D)	(C) find
Problem	17	(C)	(B) to develop
Problem	18	(B)	(D) to use as currency
Problem	19	(B)	(B) rapidly
Problem	20	(B)	(A) an old one *or* an ancient one
Problem	21	(C)	(A) ~~it~~
Problem	22	(B)	(A) raised
Problem	23	(C)	(A) lies
Problem	24	(B)	(B) sits
Problem	25	(A)	(D) telling
Problem	26	(C)	(C) let
Problem	27	(A)	(B) lend
Problem	28	(B)	(C) do
Problem	29	(A)	(B) depends on
Problem	30	(B)	(B) differ

Cumulative Review Exercises for Structure

Cumulative Review Exercise for Verbs

1. In the entire history of the solar system, thirty billion planets may ~~has~~ have been lost or destroyed.
2. A victim of the influenza virus usually ~~with~~ has headache, fever, chills, and body ache.
3. Rubber is a good insulator of electricity, and so ~~does~~ is glass.
4. Light rays can make the desert ~~appears~~ appear to be a lake.

5. It is essential that nitrogen is present in the soil for plants to grow.

6. A great many athletes have managed to overcome serious physical handicaps.

7. If the eucalyptus tree was to become extinct, the koala bear would also die.

8. Various species must begin their development in similar ways, since the embryos of a fish and a cat appear to be very similar during the early stages of life.

9. Some teachers argue that students who used to using a calculator may forget how to do mental calculations.

10. Last year Americans spended six times as much money for pet food as they did for baby food.

11. Secretaries are usually eligible for higher salaries when they know how shorthand.

12. A new automobile needs to tuned up after the first five thousand miles.

13. Financial planners usually recommend that an individual save two to six months' income for emergencies.

14. If a baby is held up so that the sole of the foot touches a flat surface, well-coordinated walking movements will be triggered.

15. Generally, the use of one building material in preference to another indicates that it found in large quantities in the construction area and does an adequate job of protecting the inhabitants from the weather.

Cumulative Review Exercise for Pronouns

1. College students like to entertain themselves by playing Frisbee, a game of catch played with a plastic disk instead of a ball.

2. The final member of the Bach family, Dr. Otto Bach died in 1893, taking with he the musical genius that had entertained Germany for two centuries.

3. When recessive genes combine with each the other one, a child with blue eyes can be born to parents both of whom have brown eyes.

4. Almost all of the people who ultimately commit suicide have made a previous unsuccessful attempt to kill themselves or have threatened to do so.

5. Officials at a college or university must see a student's transcripts and financial guarantees prior to them issuing him or her a form I-20.

6. Through elected officials, a representative democracy includes citizens like you and I in the decision-making process.

7. It was her, Anne Sullivan, who stayed with Helen Keller for fifty years, teaching and encouraging her student.

8. To appreciate what the hybrid corn breeder does, it is necessary to understand how corn reproduces its.

9. Most foreign students realize that it is important for they to buy health insurance while they are living in the United States, because hospital costs are very high.

10. Top management in a firm is usually interpreted to mean the president and the vice-presidents that report to him or her.

11. The barnacle produces glue and attaches itself to ship bottoms and other places.

12. Peers are people of the same general age and educational level with whom an individual associates.

13. When an acid and a base neutralize one the other, the hydrogen from the acid and the oxygen from the base join to form water.

14. About two thirds of the world is inhabited by people which are severely undernourished.

15. In order for a caller to charge a call from another location to his home telephone number, the operator insists on him using a credit card or waiting until someone at the home number can verify that charges will be paid.

Cumulative Review Exercise for Nouns

1. Tuition at state universities has risen by one hundred fifty-dollar.

2. Although polyester was very popular and is still used in making clothing, cloths made of natural fibers is more fashionable today.

3. The peace in the world is the goal of the United Nations.

4. Dam is a wall constructed across a valley to enclose an area in which water is stored.

5. The light travels in a straight line.

6. To hitchhike in the United States is very dangerous.

7. The ptarmigan, like a large number of Arctic animal, is white in winter and brown in summer.

8. Even children in elementary school are assigned homeworks.

9. Spirituals were influenced by a music from the African coast.

10. The stare at a computer screen for long periods of time can cause severe eyestrain.

11. There are two kind of major joints in the body of a vertebrate, including the hinge joint and the ball and socket joint.

12. That an earthquake of magnitude eight on the Richter scale occurs once every five or ten years.

13. ~~Art~~ The art of colonial America was very functional, consisting mainly of useful objects such as furniture and household utensils.

14. To ~~producing~~ produce one ton of coal it may be necessary to strip as much as thirty tons of rock.

15. A [piece of] mail that is postmarked on Monday before noon and sent express can be delivered the next day anywhere in the United States.

Cumulative Review Exercise for Adjectives and Adjective-Related Structures

1. Today's modern TV cameras require only a ~~few~~ little light as compared with earlier models.

✓ 2. Diamonds that are not good enough to be made into gems are used in industry for cutting and drilling.

3. Cane sugar contains ~~not~~ no vitamins.

4. Humorist Will Rogers was brought up on a cattle ranch in the Oklahoma Indian territory, but the life of a cowboy was not ~~excited~~ exciting enough for him.

✓ 5. One of the most distinctive features of Islamic architecture is the arch.

6. It is impossible to view Picasso's *Guernica* without feeling ~~badly~~ bad about the fate of the people portrayed.

✓ 7. The Erie was so large a canal that more than eighty locks and twenty aqueducts were required.

8. ~~An~~ A usual treatment for the flu is to drink plenty of liquids.

9. The United States did not issue any stamps until 1847 when one was printed for use east of the Mississippi and ~~one~~ another for use west of the Mississippi.

10. Red corpuscles are so numerous that a thimbleful of ~~human's~~ human blood would contain almost ten thousand million of them.

11. The Malay Archipelago is the world's largest group of islands, forming a ten-thousand-~~islands~~ island chain.

12. Some ~~property~~ properties of lead are its softness and its resistance.

13. Aristotle is considered the father of ~~the~~ logic.

14. Metals such as iron and magnesium are quite common, but are mostly found in silicates, making them ~~so~~ too expensive to extract.

15. ~~History~~ The history of the war in Vietnam is just being written.

Cumulative Review Exercise for Comparatives

1. One object will not be the same weight than another object because the gravitational attraction differs from place to place on the Earth's surface.

2. An identical twin is always the same sex as his or her twin because they develop from the same zygote.

3. As many 100 billion stars are in the Milky Way.

4. Compared with numbers fifty years ago, there are twice more students in college today.

5. The valuablest information we currently have on the ocean floors is that which was obtained by oceanographic satellites such as *Seasat.*

6. The oxygen concentration in the lungs is higher than the blood.

7. Since the Earth is spherical, the larger the area, the worser the distortion on a flat map.

8. The eyes of an octopus are remarkably similar to those of a human being.

9. The terms used in one textbook may be different another text.

10. During very cold winters, residential utility bills are as high sixteen hundred dollars a month in New England.

11. When the ratio of gear teeth is five:one, the small gear rotates five times as fast as the large gear.

12. Although lacking in calcium and vitamin A, grains have most carbohydrates than any other food.

13. The more narrow the lens diameter, the more great the depth of field.

14. No fingerprint is exactly alike another.

15. There is disagreement among industrialists as to whether the products of this decade are inferior to the past.

Cumulative Review Exercise for Prepositions

1. It is possible to find the weight of anything that floats for weighing the water that it displaces.

2. Metals such copper, silver, iron, and aluminum are good conductors of electricity.

3. The Mother Goose nursery rhymes have been traced back to a collection that appeared in England on 1760.

4. In making a distinction between butterflies and moths, it is best to examine the antennae.

5. None of the states but for Hawaii is an island.

6. ~~Beside~~ *Besides* copper, which is the principal metal produced, gold, silver, lead, zinc, iron, and uranium are mined in Utah.

7. This year, ~~beside~~ *besides* figuring standard income tax, taxpayers might also have to compute alternative minimum tax.

8. Jet engines are used instead *of* piston engines for almost all but the smallest aircraft.

9. Trained athletes have slower heart rates because ~~of~~ their hearts can pump more blood with every beat.

10. Tools ~~as such~~ *such as* axes, hammerstones, sickles, and awls were made by Paleolithic man using a method called pressure flaking.

11. Despite ~~of~~ *OR In spite of* some opposition, many city authorities still fluoridate water to prevent tooth decay.

12. The White House is ~~on~~ *at* 1700 Pennsylvania Avenue.
The White House is on Pennsylvania Avenue.

✓13. Ice skating surfaces can be made of interlocking plastic squares instead of ice.

14. In supply-side economics, a balanced budget results from ~~to reduce~~ *reducing* government spending.

✓15. All of the Native Americans but the Sioux were defeated by the European settlers.

Cumulative Review Exercise for Conjunctions

✓ 1. Foreign students who are making a decision about which school to attend may not know exactly where the choices are located.

2. Now, classes taught by television are equipped with boom microphones in the classrooms so *that* students can stop the action, ask their questions, and receive immediate answers.

✓ 3. The Colosseum received its name not for its size but for a colossally large statue of Nero near it.

4. A wind instrument is really just a pipe arranged so *that* air can be blown into it at one end.

5. It is very difficult to compute how much ~~does an item cost~~ *an item costs* in dollars when one is accustomed to calculating in another monetary system.

6. Adolescence, or the transitional period between childhood and adulthood, is not only a biological concept but *also* a social concept.

7. Light is diffused when it ~~will strike~~ *strikes* a rough surface.

✓ 8. The koala bear is not a bear at all, but a marsupial.

✓ 9. Ferns will grow wherever the soil is moist and the air is humid.

10. Although most rocks contain several minerals, limestone contains only one, and marble ~~is~~ *does* too.

11. Learners use both visual and auditory ~~as well that~~ *as well as* analytical means to understand a new language.

12. In a recent study, many high school students did not know where were important geographical entities on the map of the United States.

13. It is not only lava but poisonous gases that cause destruction and death during the eruption of a volcano.

14. Until recently West Point did not admit women and neither Annapolis.

15. The Federal Trade Commission may intervene whenever unfair business practices, particularly monopolies, are suspected.

Cumulative Review Exercise for Adverbs and Adverb-Related Structures

1. Not once Lincoln has been painted smiling.

2. The first *Skylab* crew was launched on twenty-fifth May, 1973.

3. Wholly, artificial insemination has contributed to the quality of maintaining dairy herds.

4. Thor Heyerdahl worked diligent to prove his theory of cultural diffusion.

5. The Navajos have lived in Arizona for almost one thousand years.

6. That once a serious problem, measles can now be prevented by a vaccine.

7. Because the British fleet arrived lately off the Yorktown Peninsula, the French were able to control the seas, thereby aiding the United States during the Revolution.

8. When the chemicals inside a cell not longer produce ions, the cell stops functioning.

9. The common goldfish may live as long twenty-five years.

10. When a mechanic working at odd jobs, Elisha Otis invented the elevator.

11. Sometimes students fail to score well on examinations because they are too nervous to concentrate.

12. Alligators are no longer on the endangered species list.

13. The standard for atomic weight has been provided by the carbon isotope C12 since 1961.

14. That it was once a busy mining settlement, Virginia City is now a small town with a population of one thousand people.

15. Not until the late Middle Ages glass did become a major construction material.

Cumulative Review Exercise for Sentences and Clauses

1. Since 1927, ~~that~~ the Academy Awards have been given for outstanding contributions to the film industry.

✓ 2. The Guggenheim Museum is cast in concrete with a smooth finish and curving walls that offer a unique backdrop for the art exhibited there.

✓ 3. Solar panels that convert sunlight into electricity are still not being exploited fully.

4. During a total eclipse of the sun, ~~that~~ the Earth ~~moving~~ moves into the shadow of the moon.

5. Founded by John Smith, ~~that~~ Jamestown became the first successful English colony in America.

✓ 6. A chameleon is a tree lizard that can change colors in order to conceal itself in the vegetation.

7. Many of the names of cities in California ~~that~~ are adapted from the Spanish language because of the influence of early missionaries and settlers from Spain.

✓ 8. The oceans, which cover two thirds of the Earth's surface, are the object of study for oceanographers.

9. Sports heros in the United States earn salaries that ~~they~~ are extraordinarily high in comparison with those of most other occupations.

10. The atoms of elements ~~that joining~~ join together to form compounds or molecules.

✓11. Rafts made from the trunks of trees may have been the earliest vehicles.

12. The idea of a set ~~which~~ is the most fundamental concept in mathematics.

✓13. Water that has had the minerals removed is called "soft" water.

14. A feeling of superiority based on pride in cultural achievements and characteristics ~~that calling~~ is called ethnocentrism.

✓15. Skeletal muscles are voluntary muscles which are controlled directly by the nervous system.

Cumulative Review Exercise for Point of View

1. Until she died at the age of forty, Marilyn Monroe ~~is~~ was the most glamorous star in Hollywood.

2. American colleges ~~do~~ did not have very many foreign students learning English full time before 1970.

✓ 3. Ted Kennedy told the American people that he could not run for president for personal reasons.

4. George Washington Carver was one of the first educators who ~~try~~ tried to establish schools of higher education for blacks.

5. Before the 1920s, no women ~~will have~~ had voted in national elections in the United States.

6. Styles that ~~have been~~ were popular in the 1940s have recently reappeared in high-fashion boutiques.

7. Since his murder, John Lennon has become a legend among those who had been his fans.

8. When Lyndon Johnson became president in 1963, he had already served in politics for thirty-two years.

9. Early TV programs like the "Arthur Godfrey Show" are beginning as radio programs.

10. Dr. Howard Evans of Colorado State University reported that insects solve the food shortage if we could adjust to eating them.

11. The year that James Smithson died, he was leaving a half million dollars to the United States government to found the Smithsonian Institute.

12. Mary Decker said that she ran every day to train for the Olympics.

13. A liquid crystal is among the few unstable molecular arrangements that are on the borderline between solids and liquids and whose molecules were easily changed from one to the other.

14. The chestnut tree used to be an important species in the Eastern forests of the United States until a blight kills a large number of trees.

15. The Cincinnati Reds win the championship several years ago.

Cumulative Review Exercise for Agreement

1. Thirty-five thousand dollars are the average income for a four-person family living in a medium-sized community in the United States.

2. Mary Ovington, along with a number of journalists and social workers, were instrumental in establishing the Negro National Committee, now called the NAACP.

3. Fossils show that early people was only four feet six inches tall on the average.

4. Each of the Medic Alert bracelets worn by millions of Americans who suffer from diabetes and drug allergic reactions is individually engraved with the wearer's name.

5. The Yon Ho, which is still in use today and is recognized as one of the world's great canals, date from the sixth century.

6. Since the Federal Deposit Insurance Corporation started guaranteeing bank accounts of $100,000 or less, there is no reason for small investors to fear losing their savings.

7. One hundred eighty-six thousand miles per second are the speed of light.

8. It is believed that dodo birds forgot how to fly and eventually became extinct because there was no natural enemies on the island of Mauritius, where they lived.

9. Several arid areas in Arizona has been irrigated and reclaimed for cultivation.

10. The nucleus of a human cell, except those of eggs and sperm, contain forty-six thread-like structures called chromosomes.

11. In spite of its fragile appearance, a newborn infant is extremely sturdy.

12. The ozone layer, eight to thirty miles above the Earth, protect us from too many ultraviolet rays.

13. Although amendments have been added, not once has the American Constitution been changed.

14. Michael Jackson, with members of his band, travel to key cities to give concerts and make public appearances.

15. Over 90 percent of the world's population now uses the metric system.

Cumulative Review Exercise for Introductory Verbal Modifiers

1. Having ruled since the sixth century, the present emperor of Japan has a long and noble tradition.

2. Built on 230 acres, the palace of Versailles is one of the showplaces of France.

3. Believing that true emeralds could not be broken, Spanish soldiers in Pizarro's expedition to Peru tested the jewels they found by pounding them with hammers.

4. Adopted as the laws of the former British colonies after the Revolutionary War, Canada was invited to become a member of the Confederation under the Articles of Confederation.

5. After surrendering in 1886 and being imprisoned in Florida and Alabama, the Apache chief Geronimo became a farmer and lived out his life on a military reservation in Oklahoma.

6. While hibernating, the respiration of animals decreases.

7. To improve the study of chemical reactions, the introduction of effective quantitative methods by Lavoisier.

8. Migrating in a wedge formation, a goose conserves energy by flying in the air currents created by the goose ahead of it.

9. Invented in China about 105 A.D., paper was manufactured in Baghdad and later in Spain four hundred years before the first English paper mill was founded.

10. After lasting for six centuries, it has never been explained why the Mayan culture collapsed.

11. Wounded by an assassin's bullet while he was watching a play at the Ford Theater, death came to Lincoln a few hours after being shot.

12. While viewing objects under a microscope, Robert Hooke discovered that all living things were made up of cells.

13. Located in San Francisco Bay and nicknamed the "Rock," dangerous criminals were once incarcerated in Alcatraz.

14. Having calculated the length of time for the first voyages to the moon, Kepler wrote that passengers would have to be drugged.

15. To prepare the fields for planting and irrigation, farmers use laser beams.

Cumulative Review Exercise for Parallel Structure

1. We are indebted to the Arabs not only for reviving Greek works but also they introduced useful ideas from India.

2. A century ago in America, all postal rates were determined not by weighing the mail but measuring the distance that the mail had to travel.

3. The four basic elements that make up all but 1 percent of terrestrial matter include carbon, hydrogen, nitrogen, and oxygen is also.

4. The three thousand stars visible to the naked eye can be seen because they are either extremely bright or they are relatively close to the earth.

5. George Kaufman distinguished himself as a newspaperman, a dramatic critic, and he was a successful playwright.

6. To apply for a passport, fill out the application form, attach two recent photographs, and taking it to your local passport office.

7. Shakespeare was both a writer and he acted.

8. To save on heating and finding cheaper labor are two of the most common reasons that companies give for moving from the Midwest to the South.

9. Both plants and animals have digestive systems, respiratory systems, and reproduce.

10. Pollution control involves identifying the sources of contamination, development improved or alternative technologies and sources of raw material, and persuading industries and citizens to adopt them either voluntarily or legally.

11. Tobacco was considered a sacred plant, and it was used to indicate friendship and concluded peace negotiations between Native Americans and whites.

12. The kidneys both eliminate water and salt.

13. A person who purchases a gun for protection is six times more likely to kill a friend or relative than killing an intruder.

14. The Brooklyn Bridge was remarkable not only for the early use of the pneumatic caisson but also for the introduction of steel wire.

15. Microwaves are used for cooking, for telecommunications, and also medical diagnosis is made from them.

Cumulative Review Exercise for Redundancy

1. Many dentists now say that plaque can cause damage ~~of a more serious nature and degree~~ to teeth than cavities.

2. The most common name in the world ~~it~~ is Mohammad.

3. The idea for the Monroe Doctrine was originally ~~first~~ proposed not by Monroe but by the British Secretary for Foreign Affairs, George Canning.

4. That comets' tails are caused by solar wind ~~it~~ is generally accepted.

5. One hundred thousand earthquakes are felt every year, one thousand of which cause severe ~~serious~~ damage.

6. Irving Berlin, America's most prolific songwriter, ~~he~~ never learned to read or write music.

7. The corporation, which is by far the most influential form of business ownership, is a comparatively new ~~innovation~~.

8. That the Earth and the moon formed simultaneously ~~at the same time~~ is a theory that accounts for the heat of the early atmosphere surrounding the Earth.

9. The longest mountain range, the Mid-Atlantic Range, is ~~not~~ hardly visible because most of it lies under the ocean.

10. The Navajo language was used ~~in a successful manner~~ as a code by the United States in World War II.

11. One of the magnificent Seven Wonders of the Ancient World was the enormous ~~large~~ statue known as the Colossus of Rhodes.

12. ~~It is the~~ first digit that appears on any zip code ~~that it~~ refers to one of ten geographical areas in the United States.

13. Limestone formations growing downward from the roofs of caves ~~that they~~ are stalactites.

14. All matter is composed of molecules or atoms that are in motion ~~in a constant way.~~

15. ~~The fact~~ that the earth rotates wasn't known until ~~the years of~~ the 1850s.

Cumulative Review Exercise for Word Choice

1. The ~~manage~~ of a small business requires either education or experience in sales and accounting.

2. Because of the traffic in ancient Rome, Julius Caesar would not let anyone use a wheeled vehicle on the streets during the day.

3. Occasionally dolphins need to ~~raise~~ to the surface of the water to take in oxygen.

4. Thomas Jefferson's home, which he designed and built, ~~sets~~ on a hill overlooking the Virginia countryside.

5. Once, the gold reserve of the United States Treasury was saved when J.P. Morgan, then the richest man in America, borrowed more than fifty million dollars' worth of gold to the federal government.

6. Dreams may be the expression of fears and desires that we are not conscious of during our waking hours.

7. Ice has the same hard as concrete.

8. We might never have heard about Daniel Boone had he not told a schoolmaster his stories about the frontier.

9. Terrorists are capable to hijacking planes and taking hostages in spite of security at international airports.

10. It is not the TOEFL but the academic preparation of students that is the best indicator of their successfully.

11. Some business analysts argue that the U.S. automobile industry is suffering because Congress will not impose heavier import duties, but others say that the cars themselves are inferior with the foreign competition.

12. Lotteries are used to rise money for the states that sponsor them.

13. When a human being gets hurt, the brain excretes a chemical called enkaphalin to numb the painful.

14. Benjamin Franklin told that the turkey should be our national bird.

15. The prime rate is the rate of interest that a bank will charge when it lends money to its best clients.

ANSWER KEY—EXERCISES FOR READING

Problem 1. Previewing

A black hole is a region of space created by the total gravitational collapse of matter. It is so intense that nothing, not even light or radiation, can escape. In other words, it is a one-way surface through which matter can fall inward but cannot emerge.

Some astronomers believe that a black hole may be formed when a large star collapses inward from its own weight. So long as they are emitting heat and light into space, stars support themselves against their own gravitational pull with the outward thermal pressure generated by heat from nuclear reactions deep in their interiors. But if a star eventually exhausts its nuclear fuel, then its unbalanced gravitational attraction could cause it to contract and collapse. Furthermore, it could begin to pull in surrounding matter, including nearby comets and planets, creating a black hole.

The topic is black holes.

Problem 2. Reading for Main Ideas

For more than a century, despite attacks by a few opposing scientists, Charles Darwin's theory of evolution by natural selection has stood firm. Now, however, some respected biologists are beginning to question whether the theory accounts for major developments such as the shift from water to land habitation. Clearly, evolution has not proceeded steadily but has progressed by radical advances. Recent research in molecular biology, particularly in the study of DNA, provides us with a new possibility. Not only environmental changes but also genetic codes in the underlying structure of DNA could govern evolution.

The main idea is that biologists are beginning to question Darwin's theory.
A good title would be "Questions about Darwin's Theory."

Problem 3. Using Contexts for Vocabulary

1. *To auction* means to sell.
2. *Proprietor* means an owner.
3. *Formerly* means in the past.
4. *To sample* means to try or to taste.
5. *Royalty* means payment.

Problem 4. Scanning for Details

To prepare for a career in engineering, a student must begin planning in high school. Mathematics and science should form the core curriculum. For example, in a school where sixteen credit hours are required for high school graduation, four should be in mathematics, one each in chemistry, biology, and physics. The remaining credits should include four in English and at least three in the humanities and social sciences. The average entering freshman in engineering should have achieved at least a 2.5 grade point average on a 4.0 scale in his or her high school. Although deficiencies can be corrected during the first year, the student who needs additional work should expect to spend five instead of four years to complete a degree.

1. What is the average grade point for an entering freshman in engineering?

   2.5

2. When should a student begin planning for a career in engineering?

   in high school

3. How can a student correct deficiencies in preparation?

   by spending five years

4. How many credits should a student have in English?

   four

5. How many credits are required for a high school diploma?

   sixteen

Problem 5. Making Inferences

When an acid is dissolved in water, the acid molecule divides into two parts, a hydrogen ion and another ion. An ion is an atom or a group of atoms which has an electrical charge. The charge can be either positive or negative. If hydrochloric acid is mixed with water, for example, it divides into hydrogen ions and chlorine ions.

A strong acid ionizes to a great extent, but a weak acid does not ionize so much. The strength of an acid, therefore, depends on how much it ionizes, not on how many hydrogen ions are produced. It is interesting that nitric acid and sulfuric acid become greatly ionized whereas boric acid and carbonic acid do not.

1. What kind of acid is sulfuric acid?

   A strong acid ionizes to a great extent, and sulfuric acid becomes greatly ionized.
   Conclusion: Sulfuric acid is a strong acid.

2. What kind of acid is boric acid?

   A weak acid does not ionize so much and boric acid does not ionize greatly.
   Conclusion: Boric acid is a weak acid.

Problem 6. Identifying Exceptions

All music consists of two elements—expression and design. Expression is inexact and subjective, and may be enjoyed in a personal or instinctive way. Design, on the other hand is exact and must be analyzed objectively in order to be understood and appreciated. The folk song, for example, has a definite musical design which relies on simple repetition with a definite beginning and ending. A folk song generally consists of one stanza of music repeated for each stanza of verse.

Because of their communal, and usually uncertain origin, folk songs are often popular verse set to music. They are not always recorded, and tend to be passed on in a kind of musical version of oral history. Each singer revises and perfects the song. In part as a consequence of this continuous revision process, most folk songs are almost perfect in their construction and design. A particular singer's interpretation of the folk song may provide an interesting expression, but the simple design that underlies the song itself is stable and enduring.

1. All of the following are true of a folk song EXCEPT

✓ There is a clear start and finish.
✓ The origin is often not known.
The design may change in the interpretation.
✓ Simple repetition is characteristic of its design.

Problem 7. Locating References

The National Road, also known as the Cumberland Road, was constructed in the early 1800s to provide transportation between the established commercial areas of the East and Northwest Territory. By 1818, the road had reached Wheeling, West Virginia, 130 miles from its point of origin in Cumberland, Maryland. The cost was a monumental thirteen thousand dollars per mile.

Upon reaching the Ohio River, the National Road became one of the major trade routes to the western states and territories, providing Baltimore with a trade advantage over neighboring cities. In order to compete, New York state authorized the construction of the Erie Canal, and Philadelphia initiated a transportation plan to link it with Pittsburgh. Towns along the rivers, canals, and the new National Road became important trade centers.

1. The word "its" in line 4 refers to the road.

2. The word "it" in line 9 refers to the canal.

Problem 8. Referring to the Passage

In September of 1929, traders experienced a lack of confidence in the stock market's ability to continue its phenomenal rise. Prices fell. For many inexperienced investors, the drop produced a panic. They had all their money tied up in the market, and they were pressed to sell before the prices fell even lower. Sell orders were coming in so fast that the ticker tape at the New York Stock Exchange could not accommodate all the transactions.

To try to reestablish confidence in the market, a powerful group of New York bankers agreed to pool their funds and purchase stock above current market values. Although the buy orders were minimal, they were counting on their reputations to restore confidence on the part of the smaller investors, thereby affecting the number of sell orders. On Thursday, October 24, Richard Whitney, the Vice President of the New York Stock Exchange and a broker for the J.P. Morgan Company, made the effort on their behalf. Initially, it appeared to have been successful, then, on the following Tuesday, the crash began again and accelerated. By 1932, stocks were worth only twenty percent of their value at the 1929 high. The results of the crash had extended into every aspect of the economy, causing a long and painful depression, referred to in American history as the Great Depression.

1. Where in the passage does the author refer to the reason for the stock market crash? Lines 1-3.

2. Where in the passage does the author suggest that there was a temporary recovery in the stock market? Lines 11-12.

ANSWER KEY—MODEL TESTS

Model Test 1—Computer-Assisted TOEFL

Section 1: Listening

1. **(C)**	6. **(B)**	11. **(B)**	16. **(C)**	21. **(B)**	26. **(C)**	31. **(C)**	36. **(C)**	41. **(B)**	46. **(A)**
2. **(A)**	7. **(D)**	12. **(A)**	17. **(C)**	22. **(C)**	27. **(D)**	32. **(A)**	37. **(B)**	42. **(A)**	47. **(B)**
3. **(C)**	8. **(C)**	13. **(C)**	18. **(D)**	23. **(B)**	28. **(B)**	33. **(C)**	38. **(B)**	43. **(A)(C)**	48. **(C)**
4. **(A)**	9. **(D)**	14. **(B)**	19. **(C)**	24. **(D)**	29. **(A)**	34. **(A)**	39. **(A)**	44. **(B)**	49. **(B)**
5. **(A)**	10. **(C)**	15. **(C)**	20. **(B)**	25. **(C)**	30. **(A)**	35. **(C)**	40. **(C)(D)**	45. **(C)**	50. **(B)**

Section 2: Structure

1. **(B)**	5. **(C)**	9. **(A)**	13. **(D)**	17. **(A)**	21. **(D)**	25. **(A)**
2. **(C)**	6. **(B)**	10. **(B)**	14. **(C)**	18. **(A)**	22. **(D)**	
3. **(A)**	7. **(B)**	11. **(C)**	15. **(C)**	19. **(A)**	23. **(B)**	
4. **(D)**	8. **(A)**	12. **(A)**	16. **(D)**	20. **(B)**	24. **(D)**	

Section 3: Reading

1. **(B)**	10. **(A)**	17. **(C)**	27. **(B)**	37. **(A)**
2. **(B)**	11. **(B)**	18. **(A)**	28. **(B)**	38. **(C)**
3. **(D)**	12. **(A)**	19. **(B)**	29. **(C)**	39. **large**
4. **(A)**	13. **(B)**	20. **award**	30. **(C)**	40. **(B)**
5. **sentence 6, paragraph 1**	14. **(B)**	21. **(C)**	31. **brilliant tricks**	41. **(A)**
6. **(A)**	15. **"...invented dynamite. When he read..."**	22. **generally**	32. **purpose**	42. **(B)**
7. **(B)**	16. **(D)**	23. **(D)**	33. **(B)**	43. **(B)**
8. **(B)**		24. **(A)**	34. **(B)**	44. **sentence 2, paragraph 3**
9. **(C)**		25. **(B)**	35. **(B)**	45. **(C)**
		26. **(D)**	36. **(D)**	

Model Test 2—Computer-Assisted TOEFL

Section 1: Listening

1. **(B)**	7. **(B)**	13. **(D)**	19. **(A)**	25. **(B)**	31. **(C)**	37. **(C)**	43. **(A)**	49. **(B)(A)(C)**
2. **(D)**	8. **(A)**	14. **(C)**	20. **(A)**	26. **(D)**	32. **(B)**	38. **(B)**	44. **(A)(B)**	50. **(A)**
3. **(D)**	9. **(C)**	15. **(A)**	21. **(C)**	27. **(C)**	33. **(C)**	39. **(D)**	45. **(C)**	
4. **(B)**	10. **(A)**	16. **(B)**	22. **(B)**	28. **(B)**	34. **(D)**	40. **(A)**	46. **(C)(D)**	
5. **(D)**	11. **(B)**	17. **(B)**	23. **(C)**	29. **(D)**	35. **(B)**	41. **(C)**	47. **(B)**	
6. **(A)**	12. **(D)**	18. **(B)**	24. **(B)**	30. **(B)**	36. **(A)(B)**	42. **(C)**	48. **(C)**	

Section 2: Structure

1. **(A)**	5. **(C)**	9. **(A)**	13. **(A)**	17. **(C)**	21. **(A)**	25. **(B)**
2. **(A)**	6. **(B)**	10. **(A)**	14. **(B)**	18. **(C)**	22. **(A)**	
3. **(C)**	7. **(A)**	11. **(B)**	15. **(D)**	19. **(A)**	23. **(B)**	
4. **(D)**	8. **(C)**	12. **(A)**	16. **(C)**	20. **(C)**	24. **(B)**	

Section 3: Reading

1. (A)
2. (C)
3. (A)
4. (A)
5. (D)
6. (A)
7. (D)
8. data
9. (C)
10. problems
11. sentence 2, paragraph 2
12. (C)
13. (D)
14. sentence 4, paragraph 1
15. (A)
16. (B)
17. (D)
18. signs
19. (B)
20. (C)
21. "…a rude noise. Gestures such as…"
22. (B)
23. interaction
24. (D)
25. (D)
26. (D)
27. (B)
28. (B)
29. (C)
30. (A)
31. (C)
32. sentence 4, paragraph 3
33. damage
34. "…solids or liquids. One objection…"
35. (A)
36. (D)
37. (B)
38. (A)
39. (A)
40. (C)
41. (B)
42. (C)
43. sentence 3, paragraph 1
44. tamed
45. (A)

Model Test 3—Computer-Assisted TOEFL

Section 1: Listening

1. (A)
2. (C)
3. (C)
4. (A)
5. (A)
6. (A)
7. (C)
8. (C)
9. (D)
10. (B)
11. (A)
12. (A)
13. (D)
14. (A)
15. (C)
16. (A)
17. (B)
18. (D)
19. (B)
20. (B)
21. (C)
22. (B)
23. (C)
24. (C)
25. (A)
26. (A)
27. (B)
28. (B)
29. (B)
30. (A)
31. (C)
32. (B)
33. (B)
34. (D)
35. (C)
36. (B)
37. (A)
38. (B)(C)
39. (C)(B)(D)(A)
40. (B)
41. (A)
42. (D)
43. (A)
44. (B)
45. (B)
46. (C)
47. (D)
48. (D)
49. (A)(C)
50. (A)

Section 2: Structure

1. (C)
2. (B)
3. (A)
4. (B)
5. (B)
6. (A)
7. (C)
8. (D)
9. (C)
10. (A)
11. (C)
12. (B)
13. (B)
14. (B)
15. (D)
16. (C)
17. (B)
18. (B)
19. (A)
20. (A)
21. (C)
22. (A)
23. (C)
24. (A)
25. (D)

Section 3: Reading

1. (A)
2. (D)
3. (C)
4. (D)
5. very successful
6. (A)
7. (C)
8. (D)
9. sentence 4, paragraph 2
10. (C)
11. (C)
12. (A)
13. (B)
14. (C)
15. (C)
16. (D)
17. (D)
18. (C)
19. (A)
20. devastating
21. earthquakes
22. (D)
23. (B)
24. segmented
25. (C)
26. (A)
27. (A)
28. (B)
29. (C)
30. (A)
31. (C)
32. "…other life forms. Although some insects…"
33. (D)
34. (D)
35. (D)
36. (B)
37. locomotion
38. (C)
39. (C)
40. (C)
41. (A)
42. (A)
43. sentence 4, paragraph 1
44. (A)
45. (C)

Model Test 4—Computer-Assisted TOEFL

Section 1: Listening

1. (C)	6. (C)	11. (A)	16. (D)	21. (D)	26. (B)	31. (D)	36. (C)	41. (D)	46. (B)
2. (A)	7. (B)	12. (D)	17. (A)	22. (D)	27. (D)	32. (A)	37. (D)	42. (A)(C)	47. (D)
3. (A)	8. (C)	13. (A)	18. (B)	23. (A)	28. (B)	33. (C)	38. (D)	43. (B)	48. (D)
4. (B)	9. (A)	14. (A)	19. (C)	24. (D)	29. (B)	34. (A)	39. (C)	44. (B)	49. (C)
5. (D)	10. (B)	15. (C)	20. (D)	25. (B)	30. (C)	35. (C)	40. (C)	45. (C)	50. (B)

Section 2: Structure

1. (D)	5. (B)	9. (B)	13. (B)	17. (D)	21. (D)	25. (D)
2. (B)	6. (A)	10. (C)	14. (D)	18. (C)	22. (A)	
3. (C)	7. (B)	11. (D)	15. (C)	19. (C)	23. (B)	
4. (D)	8. (C)	12. (C)	16. (A)	20. (D)	24. (D)	

Section 3: Reading

1. (A)	11. (B)	21. (D)	32. (C)	40. the English King's
2. (C)	12. (D)	22. (B)	33. "…fragrant blossoms. Other *Acacia…*"	41. (A)
3. (B)	13. (C)	23. valued	34. (A)	42. sentence 1, paragraph 4
4. (A)	14. sentence 5, paragraph 1	24. (C)	35. (C)	43. (B)
5. (B)	15. (A)	25. (A)	36. (B)	44. (B)
6. (C)	16. better	26. (B)	37. (A)	45. (D)
7. sentence 2, paragraph 2	17. (D)	27. (C)	38. (C)	
8. (D)	18. (D)	28. (A)	39. (C)	
9. (B)	19. (A)	29. (B)		
10. (A)	20. (C)	30. (D)		
		31. (B)		

Model Test 5—Computer-Assisted TOEFL

Section 1: Listening

1. (D)	11. (C)	21. (C)	31. (A)(B)(C)(D)	41. (C)
2. (B)	12. (B)	22. (C)	32. (B)	42. (C)
3. (C)	13. (B)	23. (B)(C)	33. (D)	43. (A)
4. (B)	14. (B)	24. (C)	34. (D)	44. (C)
5. (B)	15. (D)	25. (D)(C)(B)(A)	35. (A)	45. (A)(B)
6. (C)	16. (C)	26. (C)	36. (B)(A)(C)	46. (C)
7. (A)	17. (A)	27. (A)(B)	37. (A)(C)	47. (C)
8. (B)	18. (B)	28. (A)	38. (B)(C)	48. (C)
9. (D)	19. (D)	29. (C)	39. (C)	49. (D)
10. (A)	20. (A)	30. (C)	40. (C)	50. (B)

Section 2: Structure

1. (D)
2. (B)
3. (D)
4. (A)
5. (C)
6. (D)
7. (D)
8. (A)
9. (A)
10. (C)
11. (B)
12. (D)
13. (C)
14. (D)
15. (B)
16. (A)
17. (C)
18. (C)
19. (A)
20. (C)
21. (C)
22. (B)
23. (C)
24. (B)
25. (C)

Section 3: Reading

1. (A)
2. (C)
3. (D)
4. (B)
5. (A)
6. increased
7. sentence 1, paragraph 3
8. (A)
9. (B)
10. (C)
11. (B)
12. (A)
13. architecture
14. (B)
15. (C)
16. (A)
17. (B)
18. (A)
19. shapes
20. sentence 7, paragraph 3
21. (D)
22. (C)
23. (D)
24. (B)
25. works
26. (A)
27. maintained
28. (B)
29. (B)
30. (A)
31. (C)
32. (B)
33. (B)
34. (C)
35. (A)
36. (A)
37. complex
38. the memory
39. (B)
40. (B)
41. (C)
42. sentence 1, paragraph 3
43. (A)
44. (B)
45. (A)

Model Test 6—Computer-Assisted TOEFL

Section 1: Listening

1. (B)
2. (B)
3. (C)
4. (C)
5. (C)
6. (C)
7. (B)
8. (C)
9. (A)
10. (B)
11. (B)
12. (C)
13. (C)
14. (D)
15. (A)
16. (C)
17. (A)
18. (D)
19. (B)
20. (A)
21. (A)(D)
22. (B)
23. (B)(D)
24. (A)
25. (C)
26. (A)
27. (C)
28. (A)(C)
29. (B)
30. (B)
31. (C)
32. (A)
33. (B)
34. (C)
35. (A)
36. (B)
37. (A)(D)
38. (B)
39. (C)
40. (B)(C)
41. (C)(A)(B)
42. (C)
43. (B)
44. (C)
45. (B)
46. (B)
47. (A)
48. (B)
49. (A)
50. (B)(D)

Section 2: Structure

1. (B)
2. (D)
3. (B)
4. (D)
5. (D)
6. (C)
7. (A)
8. (C)
9. (D)
10. (C)
11. (C)
12. (C)
13. (C)
14. (D)
15. (C)
16. (B)
17. (C)
18. (B)
19. (C)
20. (C)
21. (A)
22. (B)
23. (B)
24. (B)
25. (C)

Section 3: Reading

1. (B)
2. (B)
3. about
4. (A)
5. sentence 1, paragraph 2
6. (C)
7. (C)
8. (B)
9. (B)
10. (A)
11. (A)
12. (A)
13. (B)
14. (C)
15. (B)
16. sentence 4, paragraph 2
17. guiding
18. (C)
19. (C)
20. (A)
21. (D)
22. (D)
23. (A)
24. (D)
25. the viruses
26. (D)
27. (B)
28. (C)
29. (B)
30. types
31. "...for type-B virus. Approximately every..."
32. (B)
33. (C)
34. (B)
35. (A)
36. (D)
37. (B)
38. (B)
39. (C)
40. (B)
41. coins and paper currency
42. sentence 3, paragraph 3
43. (C)
44. (D)
45. "...policy makers. In fact, the Fed..."

Model Test 7—Computer-Assisted TOEFL

Section 1: Listening

1. (A)
2. (B)
3. (C)
4. (A)
5. (B)
6. (B)
7. (B)
8. (C)
9. (D)
10. (D)
11. (D)
12. (A)
13. (D)
14. (C)
15. (A)
16. (D)
17. (B)
18. (A)
19. (B)
20. (C)
21. (C)
22. (C)
23. (A)(C)
24. (B)
25. (C)
26. (A)
27. (A)
28. (C)(B)(A)
29. (B)(D)
30. (A)
31. (B)
32. (B)(C)
33. (D)(A)(C)(B)
34. (C)
35. (A)
36. (C)
37. (A)
38. (C)
39. (C)
40. (A)
41. (B)(C)
42. (B)
43. (B)
44. (A)
45. (B)(C)
46. (B)
47. (A)
48. (B)
49. (B)(C)
50. (D)

Section 2: Structure

1. (B)
2. (B)
3. (A)
4. (D)
5. (B)
6. (A)
7. (A)
8. (B)
9. (B)
10. (D)
11. (B)
12. (B)
13. (D)
14. (A)
15. (A)
16. (A)
17. (B)
18. (D)
19. (D)
20. (A)
21. (B)
22. (A)
23. (A)
24. (B)
25. (C)

Section 3: Reading

1. (B)
2. eliminate
3. (C)
4. sentence 2, paragraph 2
5. (C)
6. (B)
7. (B)
8. (B)
9. (A)
10. (A)
11. "...was vaccinated. The number of..."
12. (C)
13. ideal
14. (B)
15. (B)
16. (C)
17. (C)
18. of the single people
19. sentence 2, paragraph 4
20. (A)
21. (C)
22. (A)
23. (A)
24. (A)
25. (B)
26. (C)
27. (B)
28. increase
29. the noise
30. (B)
31. (B)
32. (C)
33. "...before they are born. Fetuses exposed..."
34. (C)
35. (D)
36. (B)
37. crude
38. (B)
39. the shorter growing season
40. (D)
41. (B)
42. (A)
43. (C)
44. (A)
45. (D)

Model Test 8—Computer-Assisted TOEFL

Section 1: Listening

1. (A)
2. (C)
3. (A)
4. (C)
5. (B)
6. (C)
7. (C)
8. (C)
9. (D)
10. (A)
11. (C)
12. (C)
13. (C)
14. (B)
15. (D)
16. (A)
17. (B)
18. (C)
19. (A)
20. (C)
21. (B)
22. (B)
23. (C)
24. (C)
25. (A)
26. (B)
27. (D)
28. (C)
29. (A)
30. (C)
31. (B)
32. (D)(A)(C)(B)
33. (C)(D)
34. (A)(C)
35. (A)
36. (C)
37. (B)(C)
38. (A)
39. (C)
40. (B)(D)
41. (C)
42. (B)
43. (A)
44. (D)
45. (C)
46. (B)(C)
47. (A)
48. (C)
49. (C)
50. (A)(D)

Section 2: Structure

1. (C)
2. (D)
3. (C)
4. (D)
5. (D)
6. (A)
7. (B)
8. (A)
9. (A)
10. (A)
11. (D)
12. (D)
13. (D)
14. (D)
15. (D)
16. (D)
17. (D)
18. (C)
19. (B)
20. (C)
21. (C)
22. (D)
23. (C)
24. (A)
25. (C)

Section 3: Reading

1. (D)
2. (B)
3. (C)
4. (A)
5. (B)
6. earthquakes
7. (A)
8. basically
9. (B)
10. (D)
11. (C)
12. (B)
13. (B)
14. clash of keys...
15. (D)
16. (C)
17. (A)
18. (A)
19. (D)
20. (D)
21. *Concord Sonata*
22. "...in only two decades. Even during such..."
23. (C)
24. (B)
25. huge
26. (C)
27. (D)
28. (A)
29. (A)
30. (C)
31. sentence 5, paragraph 2
32. bats
33. "...highly social creatures. Aggregation during..."
34. (B)
35. (B)
36. live
37. (A)
38. (A)
39. (C)
40. area
41. (C)
42. sentence 1, paragraph 3
43. (A)
44. (D)
45. (A)

9

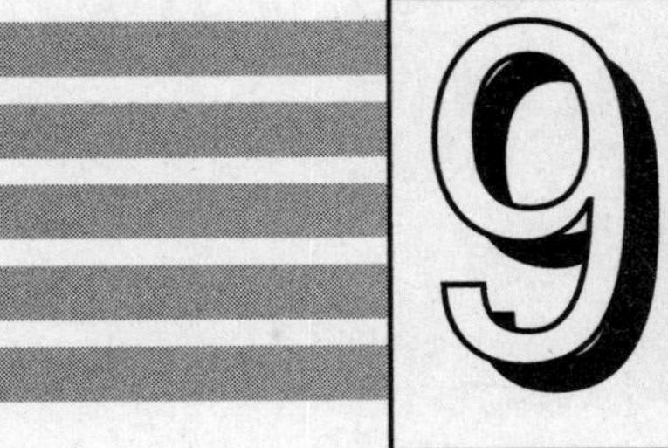

EXPLANATORY ANSWERS FOR THE TOEFL MODEL TESTS

Model Test 1—Computer Assisted TOEFL

Section 1: Listening

1. **(C)** Since the man says that there aren't any seats left, it must be concluded that he has to stand when he takes the bus to school. Choice (B) refers to the woman's suggestion, not to the man's response. Choices (A) and (D) are not mentioned and may not be concluded from information in the conversation.
2. **(A)** *Who cares* means that it isn't important (that her advisor might be offended). Choices (B), (C), and (D) are not mentioned and may not be concluded from information in the conversation.
3. **(C)** Because the woman says that the invitation sounds "great," and she thanks the man for asking her, it must be concluded that she would go out with the man on another occasion. Choice (A) contradicts the fact that she responds so positively while refusing the invitation. Choices (B) and (D) contradict the fact that she has plans to attend a lecture.
4. **(A)** *In good shape* is an idiomatic expression that means the item is in good condition. Choice (B) contradicts the fact that the man thinks the bike is new, and that the woman says it is in good shape. Choice (C) contradicts the fact that the speakers are talking about a bike that is able to be seen. Choice (D) contradicts the fact that the woman got the bike almost five years ago.
5. **(A)** The man says that he would rather have something cold. Choices (B), (C), and (D) refer to what the man likes, not to what he wants. (Refer to Patterns, Problem 8 in the Review of Structure section of Chapter 4.)
6. **(B)** "...it isn't too far to walk [to the shopping center]." Choice (A) contradicts the fact that he is already giving the woman information about the shopping center. Choices (C) and (D) are alternative possibilities that the man mentions before making his suggestion.
7. **(D)** Since the man says that he is just checking the schedule now, it must be concluded that he has not registered yet. Choice (A) contradicts the fact that he is checking the schedule for a class. Choices (B) and (C) are not mentioned and may not be concluded from information in the conversation.
8. **(C)** To *not mind* is an idiomatic expression that means the speaker will not be bothered by an activity or situation. Choices (A), (B), and (D) are not paraphrases of the expression.
9. **(D)** "She'd better see someone at the Counseling Center." Choices (A), (B), and (C) are not mentioned and may not be concluded from information in the conversation.
10. **(C)** *Please go on* is an idiomatic expression that means the speaker wants the other person to continue. Choices (A), (B), and (D) are not paraphrases of the expression.
11. **(B)** Since the man apologizes for going ahead of the woman in line, he will most probably allow her to go ahead of him. Choice (A) contradicts the fact that it is the man, not the woman, who apologizes. Choice (C) contradicts the fact that he has already apologized. Choice (D) is not mentioned and may not be concluded from information in the conversation.
12. **(A)** *Not again* is an idiomatic expression that means the speaker is impatient with some kind of repeated behavior or activity. Choice (C) contradicts the fact that she does not know about the party until the man informs her. Choices (B) and (D) are not mentioned and may not be concluded from information in the conversation.
13. **(C)** *That's too bad* is an idiomatic expression that means the speaker is sorry about the news. Choice (D) contradicts the fact that the woman thought the professor would give the man an extension. Choices (A) and (B) are not mentioned and may not be concluded from information in the conversation.
14. **(B)** Since the man says that they should have left already, it must be concluded that they are late. Choice (A) is not likely because of the woman's suggestion that they make a call. Choices (C) and (D) are not mentioned and may not be concluded from information in the conversation.
15. **(C)** Since the woman says that she has her rent paid until the 15th, she will probably stay where she is living until the 15th. The reference to half a month in Choice (A) refers to the fact that the woman already has

her rent paid until the 15th, not to what she will do. Choice (B) contradicts the fact that the woman, not the man, is planning to move. Choice (D) contradicts the fact that the woman mentions having her rent paid.

16. **(C)** Since the man expresses surprise, it must be concluded that he thought she had not taken the placement test. Choice (A) contradicts the fact that the man was surprised. Choices (B) and (D) are not mentioned and may not be concluded from information in the conversation.
17. **(C)** To *catch cold* is an idiomatic expression that means to get sick. Choices (A), (B), and (D) are not paraphrases of the expression, and may not be concluded from information in the conversation.
18. **(D)** "I need your technical writing class.... In that case, I'll sign an override for you." Choice (A) contradicts the fact that he went early to registration. Choice (B) contradicts the fact that his advisor signed his course request. Choice (C) contradicts the fact that the course will not be taught until fall semester.
19. **(C)** "...I'll sign an override.... Take this form back to the registration area and they'll get you in." Choice (D) refers to something that the professor tells Mike to do, not to something that Mike wants the professor to do. Choices (A) and (B) are not mentioned and may not be concluded from information in the conversation.
20. **(B)** "...I can't graduate without your class." Choice (A) contradicts the fact that he plans to graduate in the spring. Choices (C) and (D) are not mentioned and may not be concluded from information in the conversation.
21. **(B)** "...I'll sign an override for you." Choice (A) refers to the suggestion that the professor makes at the beginning of the conversation, not to what he actually decides to do. Choices (C) and (D) are not mentioned and may not be concluded from information in the conversation.
22. **(C)** "...background music, more commonly known as MUZAK." Choice (A) is one kind of MUZAK, but it contradicts the fact that MUZAK can be upbeat songs, too. Choice (B) is one place where MUZAK is played, but it contradicts the fact that MUZAK can be played in the workplace and the supermarket, too. Choice (D) contradicts the fact that MUZAK is more than a pleasant addition to the environment.
23. **(B)** "In one survey, overall productivity increased by thirty percent, although five to ten percent is the average." Choice (D) refers to one survey, not to the average. Choices (A) and (C) are not mentioned and may not be concluded from information in the talk.
24. **(D)** "...stimulus progression...starts with a slow, soft song...and builds up...to an upbeat song...programmed...when people are generally starting to tire." Choice (A) refers to the first stage of stimulus progression, not to the total progression. Choices (B) and (C) refer to varieties of MUZAK, not to stimulus progression.
25. **(C)** "In supermarkets, slow music can influence shoppers to walk slower and buy more." Choice (D) contradicts the fact that it can influence shoppers to buy more. Choices (A) and (B) are not mentioned and may not be concluded from information in the talk.
26. **(C)** "...Community College offers a series of video telecourses to meet the needs of students who prefer to complete coursework in their homes." Choices (A) and (B) are secondary themes used to develop the main theme of the talk. Choice (D) is not mentioned and may not be concluded from information in the conversation.
27. **(D)** "Some telecourses will also be broadcast on KCC-TV's 'Sun-Up Semester.'" Choice (A) contradicts the fact that students should call the Community College Distance Learning Program to register. Choice (C) contradicts the fact that a listing of courses is printed in the television guide. Choice (B) is not mentioned and may not be concluded from information in the conversation.
28. **(B)** "To register for a telecourse, phone the Community College...." Choice (A) contradicts the fact that the program is designed to meet the needs of students who are not able to come to campus. Choices (C) and (D) are not mentioned and may not be concluded from information in the conversation.
29. **(A)** "...you can use either an 800 telephone number or an e-mail address to contact your instructor." Choices (B), (C), and (D) are not mentioned and may not be concluded from information in the conversation.

30. **(A)** "I thought I had a cold, but it was mono....It's a virus...." The word *joke* in Choice (C) refers to the phrase *no joke* which means something that isn't funny. Choice (D) is mentioned but is not the main topic of the conversation. Choice (B) is not mentioned and may not be concluded from information in the conversation.
31. **(C)** "I had to drop out last semester." Choices (A) and (B) are probably true, but they caused her problem; they were not the problem. Choice (D) contradicts the fact that she had to withdraw last semester, not this semester.
32. **(A)** "A lot of college students get it [mono]." The word *joke* in Choice (C) refers to the phrase *no joke* which means something that isn't funny. Choices (B) and (D) are not mentioned and may not be concluded from information in the conversation.
33. **(C)** "...if you get sick...you'll end up with an extra semester....so you might as well slow down." The woman warns the man that he will have to drop out of school if he gets sick, but she does not advise him to drop out as in Choice (A). Choices (B) and (D) contradict the fact that the woman suggests that the man slow down.
34. **(A)** "I would like to outline the development of the Sapir-Whorf Hypothesis concerning the relationship between language and culture." Choices (B), (C), and (D) are secondary themes that are used to develop the main theme of the lecture.
35. **(C)** "In 1936, he [Whorf] wrote 'An American Indian Model of the Universe,' which explored the implications of the Hopi verb system ...." Choice (A) refers to historical linguistics, not to the languages that Whorf used in his research. Choices (B) and (D) are not mentioned and may not be concluded from information in the talk.
36. **(C)** "...'linguistic relativity' which states, at least as a hypothesis, that the grammar of a man's language influences the manner in which he understands reality and behaves with respect to it." Choice (D) contradicts the fact that grammar influences cultural behavior. Choices (A) and (B) are not mentioned and may not be concluded from information in the talk.
37. **(B)** "...it [linguistic relativity] came to be called the Sapir-Whorf Hypothesis." Choice (A) is incomplete because it does not include the name of Whorf. Choice (C) includes the name of Boas, who contributed to the hypothesis but was not named in it. Choice (D) refers to a paper written by Whorf regarding the Hopi verb system, not to linguistic relativity.
38. **(B)** "Let's begin our discussion today by defining acid rain." Choices (A), (C), and (D) are all secondary points of discussion that are used to develop the main topic of the discussion.
39. **(A)** "...Acid rain is...sulfur dioxide and nitrogen oxide [that] combine with water vapor and form sulfuric acid and nitric acid." Choice (C) refers to the result of acid rain, not to a definition of it. Choice (D) contradicts the fact that it is sulfur dioxide and nitrogen oxide, not just sulfur, that combines with water vapor. Choice (B) is not mentioned and may not be concluded from information in the discussion.
40. **(C) (D)** "Acidity...has all but eliminated ...fish populations...in the Great Lakes.... [and] rain has caused a chemical change in the soil....Plants don't get the nutrients they need...." Choices (A) and (B) are not mentioned and may not be concluded from information in the discussion.
41. **(B)** "...Air Quality Accord...to establish limits for the amount of acidic deposits that may flow across international boundaries." Choice (A) refers to the result of the legislation, not to the conditions of it. Choice (C) contradicts the fact that the problem of automobile emissions is a larger challenge to governments and their agencies. Choice (D) contradicts the fact that the fuels are lower in sulfur, but some sulfur still remains in the fuels.
42. **(A)** "There are three main types of bacteria...." Choices (B), (C), and (D) are all secondary points of discussion that are used to develop the main topic of discussion.
43. **(A) (C)** "Bacteria is the common name for a very large group of one-celled microscopic organisms....bacteria reproduce very rapidly...." Choice (B) contradicts the fact that, for the most part, bacteria live harmlessly on the skin, in the mouth, and in the intestines. Choice (D) is not mentioned and may not be

concluded from information in the lecture.

44. **(B)** Visual B is the slide for the cocci bacteria. Visual A is the slide for the bacilli bacteria. Visual C is the slide for the spirilla bacteria.
45. **(C)** "Bacterial cells resemble the cells of other life forms...." Choice (A) contradicts the fact that bacteria cells resemble the cells of other life forms. Choices (B) and (D) are true, but they are not the reasons that bacteria are being used in research studies.
46. **(A)** "It [the class] was supposed to be offered at three o'clock...the time has been changed...." Choice (B) contradicts the fact that the man has a job in the morning that conflicts with his class schedule. Choice (C) contradicts the fact that the man has a student loan. Choice (D) contradicts the fact that the man is already a sociology major.
47. **(B)** "I have to be a full-time student in order to qualify for my student loan." Choice (D) contradicts the fact that the courses are electives. Choices (A) and (C) are not mentioned and may not be concluded from information in the lecture.
48. **(C)** "Dr. Brown teaches Soc 560....I've been trying to take a class with her...." Choice (A) contradicts the fact that it is an elective, not a required course. Choice (B) contradicts the fact that it has been changed to nine in the morning. Choice (D) contradicts the fact that both courses are sociology classes.
49. **(B)** "...when I scheduled that class, it was supposed to be offered at three o'clock... but...the time has been changed...." Choice (A) contradicts the fact that the man is trying to register for classes. Choice (C) contradicts the fact that the man already has a student loan. Choice (D) contradicts the fact that the man is a sociology major, and he is trying to add a sociology class.
50. **(B)** "...tell Dr. Brown what happened when you see her in class." Choices (A), (C), and (D) contradict the fact that he will tell Dr. Brown what happened when he goes to her class.

Section 2: Structure

1. **(B)** A cardinal number is used after a noun. *The* is used with an ordinal number before a noun. Choice (A) is incomplete because there is no verb after *who*. Choices (C) and (D) are redundant. (Refer to Patterns, Problem 77, page 173.)
2. **(C)** *But also* is used in correlation with the inclusive *not only*. Choice (B) would be used in correlation with *both*. Choices (A) and (D) are not used in correlation with another inclusive. (Refer to Patterns, Problem 118, page 223.)
3. **(A)** A past form in the condition requires either *would* or *could* and a verb word in the result. Because the past form *planted* is used in the condition, *will* should be *would* in the result. (Refer to Patterns, Problem 23, page 100.)
4. **(D)** In order to refer to an *increase* in the rate of inflation, *rises* should be used. *To raise* means to move to a higher place. *To rise* means to increase. (Refer to Style, Problem 22, page 278.)
5. **(C)** A form of *have* with someone such as *General Lee* and a verb word expresses a causative. Choice (A) is an infinitive, not a verb word. Choice (B) is a participle. Choice (D) is an *-ing* form. (Refer to Patterns, Problem 18, page 94.)
6. **(B)** Ideas after exclusives should be expressed by parallel structures. *To hunt* should be *in hunting* to provide for parallelism with the phrase *in planting*. (Refer to Style, Problem 18, page 272.)
7. **(B)** *Effect on* is a prepositional idiom. *In* should be *on*. (Refer to Style, Problem 29, page 286.)
8. **(A)** *Because* is used before a subject and verb to introduce cause. Choices (B), (C), and (D) are not accepted for statements of cause. (Refer to Patterns, Problem 111, page 214.)
9. **(A)** The word order for a passive sentence is a form of BE followed by a participle. *Call* should be *called*. (Refer to Patterns, Problem 31, page 112.)
10. **(B)** *Form* should be *formation*. Although both are nouns derived from verbs, the *-ation* ending is needed here. *Form* means the structure. *Formation* means the process of forming over time. (Refer to Style, Problem 30, page 288.)
11. **(C)** For scientific results, a present form in the condition requires a present or future form in the result. Choices (A), (B), and (D)

are not conditional statements. (Refer to Patterns, Problem 21, page 98.)

12. **(A)** Ideas in a series should be expressed by parallel structures. Only *to sell* in Choice (A) provides for parallelism with the infinitive *to increase.* Choices (B), (C), and (D) are not parallel. (Refer to Style, Problem 17, page 271.)
13. **(D)** Because it is a prepositional phrase, *as grass* should be *like grass. As* functions as a conjunction. *Like* functions as a preposition. (Refer to Patterns, Problem 88, page 187.)
14. **(C)** Ideas in a series should be expressed by parallel structures. *It is* should be deleted to provide for parallelism with the adjectives *interesting, informative,* and *easy.* (Refer to Style, Problem 17, page 271.)
15. **(C)** Activities of the dead logically establish a point of view in the past. *Lives* should be *lived* in order to maintain the point of view. (Refer to Style, Problem 4, page 255.)
16. **(D)** In contrary-to-fact clauses, *were* is the only accepted form of the verb BE. Choices (A), (B), and (C) are forms of the verb BE, but they are not accepted in contrary-to-fact clauses. (Refer to Patterns, Problem 25, page 103.)
17. **(A)** The anticipatory clause *it is generally believed that* introduces a subject and verb, *Java Man...is.* In Choices (B) and (C) the verb *is* is repeated. Choice (D) may be used as a subject clause preceding a main verb, not preceding a subject and verb. "That it is generally believed that Java Man, who lived before the first Ice Age, is the first manlike animal *is* the result of entries in textbooks" would also be correct. (Refer to Patterns, Problem 35, page 117.)
18. **(A)** A verb word must be used in a clause after an impersonal expression. *Is not* should be *not be* after the impersonal expression *it is essential.* (Refer to Patterns, Problem 29, page 109.)
19. **(A)** *Who* should be *whom* because it is the complement of the clause *many people consider. Who* functions as a subject. *Whom* functions as a complement. (Refer to Patterns, Problem 49, page 134.)
20. **(B)** Only Choice (B) may be used with a noncount noun such as *money.* Choices (A), (C), and (D) may be used with count nouns. (Refer to Patterns, Problem 67, page 160.)
21. **(D)** *By* expresses means before an *-ing* form. *Refine* should be *refining* after the preposition *by.* (Refer to Patterns, Problem 114, page 217.)
22. **(D)** There must be agreement between pronoun and antecedent. *Their* should be *its* to agree with the singular antecedent *atmosphere.* (Refer to Style, Problem 11, page 263.)
23. **(B)** Most adverbs of manner are formed by adding *-ly* to adjectives. *Broad* should be *broadly* to qualify the manner in which the speaking was done. (Refer to Patterns, Problem 126, page 233.)
24. **(D)** An adjective clause modifies a noun in the main clause. *That provides food* modifies *the one.* Choice (A) is a subject and verb without the clause marker *that.* Choice (B) is a clause marker *that* with an *-ing* form, not a verb. Choice (C) is a verb without a clause marker. (Refer to Patterns, Problem 140, page 250.)
25. **(A)** Plural count nouns are used after a number or a reference to a number of items. *Term* should be *terms.* (Refer to Patterns, Problem 52, page 139.)

Section 3: Reading

1. **(B)** "The Process of Photosynthesis" is the best title because it states the main idea of the passage. The other choices are secondary ideas which are used to develop the main idea. Choice (A) describes the process in the form of an equation. In Choice (C), the parts of plants are named because of their roles in the process. Choice (D) is one of the products of the process.
2. **(B)** "...the green parts of plants use carbon dioxide from the atmosphere and release oxygen to it. Oxygen is the product of the reaction." The water referred to in Choice (A) and the carbon referred to in Choice (C) are used in photosynthesis, but neither one is mentioned as occurring in excess as a result of the process. Choice (D) refers to the natural substance in the chloroplasts of plants, not to a chemical combination of carbon dioxide and water.
3. **(D)** "These exchanges are the opposite of those that occur in respiration." Choices (A), (B), and (C) refer to processes which occur in photosynthesis, not to processes which are the opposite.

4. **(A)** "...radiant energy from the sun is stored as chemical energy." In Choice (B), it is water, not energy from the sun, which is conducted from the xylem to the leaves. Choice (C) contradicts the fact that energy from the sun is the source of the chemical energy used in decomposing carbon dioxide and water. Choice (D) is incorrect because it is oxygen, not energy, that is released one to one for each molecule of carbon dioxide used.
5. "Except for the usually small percentage used in respiration, the oxygen released in the process diffuses out of the leaf into the atmosphere through stomates." Quotation from sentence 6, paragraph 1.
6. **(A)** In the context of this passage, stored is closest in meaning to retained. Choices (B), (C), and (D) are not accepted definitions of the word.
7. **(B)** "The products of their decomposition [carbon dioxide and water] are recombined into a new compound, which is successively built up into more and more complex substances." Choices (A), (C), and (D) would change the meaning of the sentence.
8. **(B)** In the context of this passage, successively is closest in meaning to in a sequence. Choices (A), (C), and (D) are not accepted definitions of the word.
9. **(C)** "At the same time, a balance of gases is preserved in the atmosphere." Energy from the sun, referred to in Choice (A), and carbon dioxide, referred to in Choice (B), are used in the process of photosynthesis, not produced as a result of it. Choice (D) is not mentioned and may not be concluded from information in the passage.
10. **(A)** Choices (B), (C), and (D) are mentioned in sentences 6 and 7, paragraph 1. Water, not oxygen, is absorbed by the roots.
11. **(B)** The other choices are secondary ideas that are used to develop the main idea, "the Nobel Prizes." Choices (A), (C), and (D) are historically significant to the discussion.
12. **(A)** "The Nobel Prizes...were made available by a fund bequeathed for that purpose...by Alfred Bernhard Nobel." Because of the reference to *bequeath*, it must be concluded that Nobel left money in a will. In Choice (B), Nobel was the founder of the prizes, not a recipient. Choice (C) refers to the place where Nobel was born, not to where he is living now. Since Nobel has bequeathed funds, it must be concluded that he is dead and could not serve as chairman of a committee as in Choice (D).
13. **(B)** In the context of this passage, will refers to a legal document Choices (A), (C), and (D) are not accepted definitions of the word in this context.
14. **(B)** "The Nobel Prizes, awarded annually ..." Because of the reference to *annually*, it must be concluded that the prizes are awarded once a year. Choices (A), (C), and (D) are not mentioned and may not be concluded from information in the passage.
15. "According to the legend, Nobel's death had been erroneously reported in a newspaper, and the focus of the obituary was the fact that Nobel had invented dynamite. When he read this objective summary of his life [the obituary], the great chemist, it is said, decided that he wanted his name to be remembered for something more positive and humanitarian than inventing an explosive that was a potential weapon." The connection between these two sentences is the reference to "the obituary."
16. **(D)** In the context of this passage, outstanding could best be replaced by exceptional. Choices (A), (B), and (C) are not accepted definitions of the word.
17. **(C)** "The Nobel Prizes [are] awarded annually for distinguished work in chemistry, physics, physiology or medicine, literature, and international peace." Since there is no prize for music, a composer, in Choice (C) would not be eligible for an award. Choice (A) could be awarded a prize for literature. Choice (B) would be awarded a prize for medicine. Choice (D) could be awarded a prize for peace.
18. **(A)** Choice (A) is a restatement of the sentence referred to in the passage. To *administer* means to oversee or to manage. Choices (B), (C), and (D) would change the meaning of the original sentence.
19. **(B)** "The awards are ... presented ... on December 10 ... on the anniversary of his [Alfred Nobel's] death." Choice (A) is incorrect because it is a tribute to Nobel, not to the King of Sweden. Choice (D) contradicts the fact that the Nobel Foundation, not the Central Bank of Sweden, administers the trust.

Choice (C) is not mentioned and may not be concluded from information in the passage.

20. In the context of this passage, the word award is closest in meaning to prize. No other words or phrases in the **bold** text are close to the meaning of the word prize.
21. **(C)** The other choices are secondary ideas that are used to develop the main idea, "the development of opera." Choices (A), (B), and (D) are historically significant to the discussion.
22. In the context of this passage, the word generally is closest in meaning to usually. No other words or phrases in the **bold** text are close to the meaning of the word usually.
23. **(D)** "The usually accepted date for the beginning of opera as we know it is 1600." Choice (A) refers to Greek tragedy, the inspiration for modern opera. Choices (B) and (C) are not mentioned and may not be concluded from information in the passage.
24. **(A)** "Although stage plays have been set to music since the era of the ancient Greeks, when the dramas of Sophocles and Aeschylus were accompanied by lyres and flutes, the usually accepted date for the beginning of opera as we know it [the opera] is 1600." Choices (B), (C), and (D) would change the meaning of the sentence.
25. **(B)** "...composer Jacopo Perí produced his famous *Euridice*, generally considered to be the first opera." Choice (A) refers to the form of musical story that inspired Perí, not to the opera that he wrote. Choice (C) refers to the wife of Henry IV for whose marriage the opera was written, not to the title of the opera. Choice (D) refers to the group of musicians who introduced the opera form, not to the title of an opera written by them.
26. **(D)** "As part of the celebration of the marriage of King Henry IV...Jacopo Perí produced his famous *Euridice*." Choice (A) contradicts the fact that *Euridice* was produced in Florence, the native city of King Henry's wife and the place where the wedding was celebrated. Choice (B) refers to Greek tragedy, not to modern opera. Choice (C) is improbable because *Euridice* has become so famous.
27. **(B)** "...a group of Italian musicians called the Camerata began to revive the style of musical story that had been used in Greek tragedy." In Choice (A), musicians in the Camerata were Italian, not Greek. Choice (C) contradicts the fact that the center of the Camerata was Florence, Italy. King Henry IV referred to in Choice (D) was a patron of opera, but the name given to his court was not mentioned and may not be concluded from information in the passage.
28. **(B)** In the context of this passage, revive could best be replaced by resume. Choices (A), (C), and (D) are not accepted definitions of the word.
29. **(C)** In the context of this passage, plots is closest in meaning to stories. Choices (A), (B), and (D) are not accepted definitions of the word.
30. **(C)** "They called their compositions *opera in musica* or musical works. It is from this phrase that the word 'opera' is borrowed." Choice (A) refers to the origin of the plots for opera, not to the term. Choice (B) contradicts the fact that the Camerata was a group of Italian musicians. Choice (D) refers to the composer of the first opera.
31. "Composers gave in to the demands of singers, writing many operas that were little more than a succession of brilliant tricks for the voice, designed to showcase the splendid voices of the singers who had requested them [brilliant tricks]." Other choices would change the meaning of the sentence.
32. In the context of this passage, the word purpose is closest in meaning to function. No other words or phrases in the **bold** text are close to the meaning of the word function.
33. **(B)** The author's main purpose is to describe the nature of sunspots. Choice (A) contradicts the fact that there is no theory that completely explains sunspots. Choices (C) and (D) are important to the discussion, and provide details that support the main idea.
34. **(B)** In the context of this passage, controversial is closest in meaning to open to debate. Choices (A), (C), and (D) are not accepted definitions of the word.
35. **(B)** "...great storms on the surface of the sun hurl streams of solar particles into the atmosphere." *Storms* refer to disturbances of wind. Choice (A) contradicts the fact that great storms have been identified as the cause of particles being hurled into space. In Choice

(C), there are storms, not rivers on the surface of the sun. Choice (D) refers to what happens as a result of the particles being hurled into space.

36. **(D)** In the context of this passage, particles refers to small pieces of matter. Choices (A), (B), and (C) are not accepted definitions of the word.
37. **(A)** "...streams of solar particles [are hurled] into the atmosphere." Because of the reference to *particles*, it must be concluded that the matter is very small. Choices (B), (C), and (D) are not mentioned and may not be concluded from information in the passage.
38. **(C)** Choice (C) is a restatement of the sentence referred to in the passage. The fact that the cooler sunspots may account for their color means that the color could be affected by the cooler temperature.
39. In the context of this passage, the word large is most opposite in meaning to tiny. No other words or phrases in the **bold** text are opposite in meaning to the word tiny.
40. **(B)** "About five percent of the spots are large enough so that they [the spots] can be seen without instruments; consequently, observations of sunspots have been recorded for several thousand years." Choices (A), (C), and (D) would change the meaning of the sentence.
41. **(A)** In the context of this passage, consequently could best be replaced by as a result. Choices (B), (C), and (D) are not accepted definitions of the word.
42. **(B)** "Sunspots...tend to occur in pairs." Choices (A) and (C) refer to possibilities for arrangements, but not to the configuration in which sunspots usually occur. Choice (D) is not mentioned in the range of numbers for sunspots, from one to more than one hundred. The number *one thousand* refers to the number of years sunspots have been recorded, not to the number in a configuration.
43. **(B)** "...several models attempt to relate the phenomenon [of sunspots] to magnetic fields along the lines of longitude from the north and south poles of the sun." Choice (A) is incorrect because the magnetic fields are on the sun, not the Earth. Choice (C) is incorrect because the storms are on the sun, not on the Earth. Choice (D) contradicts the fact that several models attempt to relate sunspots to magnetic fields.
44. "About 5 percent of all sunspots are large enough so that they can be seen from Earth without instruments; consequently, observations of sunspots have been recorded for thousands of years." Quotation from sentence 2, paragraph 3.
45. **(C)** "...the controversial sunspot theory." Because the theory is controversial, it must be concluded that it is subject to disagreement. Choice (B) contradicts the fact that the theory is controversial. Choices (A) and (D) are not mentioned and may not be concluded from information in the passage.

Model Test 2—Computer-Assisted TOEFL

Section 1: Listening

1. **(B)** *You don't mean it* is an idiomatic expression that means the speaker is surprised. Choice (C) contradicts the fact that the man is surprised by the large turn out. Choices (A) and (D) are not mentioned and may not be concluded from information in the conversation.
2. **(D)** Since the woman points out the sign on the door, she implies that the man should look at it. Choices (A), (B), and (C) are not mentioned and may not be concluded from information in the conversation.
3. **(D)** Since the woman expressed interest in and enthusiasm for the opportunity to do a project for extra credit, it must be concluded that she intends to do one. Choice (A) contradicts the fact that the woman is already taking a class from Professor Wilson. Choice (C) contradicts the fact that the reference to "extra" is to extra credit, not to an extra class. Choice (B) is not mentioned and may not be concluded from information in the conversation.
4. **(B)** Listen carefully for the distinction between the words *angry* and *hungry*. Because the woman says that Paul would tell them if he were angry, it must be concluded that Paul would tell them if there were a problem. In choices (A) and (C), the word *angry* is confused with the word *hungry*. Choice (B) refers to what the woman, not the man, thinks about Paul.
5. **(D)** Since the woman says that there were a couple of As, it must be concluded that several other students received A grades. Choice (B) contradicts the fact that she refers to other As, implying that she received one. Choices (A) and (C) are not mentioned and may not be concluded from information in the conversation.
6. **(A)** Since the man says that the clock is fast, it must be concluded that the woman still has time to study. Choice (B) contradicts the fact that there is only a half hour left. Choice (D) contradicts the fact that the man knows the clock is fast. Choice (C) is not mentioned and may not be concluded from information in the conversation.
7. **(B)** *To not agree more* means to agree very much. Choices (A) and (D) misinterpret the phrase *couldn't agree more* as a negative. Choice (C) is not mentioned and may not be concluded from information in the conversation.
8. **(A)** The man says that he has to go to class. Choice (B) refers to what the woman, not the man, is going to do. Choices (C) and (D) are not mentioned and may not be concluded from information in the conversation.
9. **(C)** *Meaning to* is an idiomatic expression that means intention on the part of the speaker. To "get back with" someone means to return a call or otherwise communicate. Choice (B) contradicts the fact that a message was left on the machine. Choice (D) contradicts the fact that the man acknowledges the message. Choice (A) is not mentioned and may not be concluded from information in the conversation.
10. **(A)** To be *out* is an idiomatic expression that means to be absent. Choices (B), (C), and (D) are not paraphrases of the expression, and may not be concluded from information in the conversation.
11. **(B)** "Check with the secretary before going in…" Choice (A) contradicts the fact that the woman has already given him directions to the Math Department. Choice (C) contradicts the fact that the woman tells him to check with the secretary first. Choice (D) is not mentioned and may not be concluded from information in the conversation.
12. **(D)** Since Tom is often absent, and there is doubt that he will be present for the final exam, it must be concluded that Tom is not very responsible. Choices (A), (B), and (C) are not mentioned and may not be concluded from information in the conversation.
13. **(D)** *Are we still on* is an idiomatic expression that is used to confirm a date. Choice (C) refers to the woman's feelings, not to the man's feelings. Choices (A) and (B) are not mentioned and may not be concluded from information in the conversation.

14. **(C)** Since the woman must have the course to graduate and Dr. Collin's section is closed, she will probably enroll in the section marked "staff." Choice (A) contradicts the fact that Dr. Collin's section is closed. Choice (B) contradicts the fact that the woman is distressed because she is planning to graduate soon. Choice (D) contradicts the fact that she needs the course to graduate and is more interested in the course than in the instructor.
15. **(A)** Since the woman says that it takes six weeks to receive the score, she implies that the man should wait for the results to be mailed. Choice (B) refers to the man's plan, not to the woman's suggestion. Choice (C) contradicts the fact that the man has already taken the test and is waiting for the score. Choice (D) contradicts the fact that the woman tells him not to worry.
16. **(B)** To *make the most of* something is an idiomatic expression that means to take advantage of an opportunity. Choices (A), (C), and (D) are not paraphrases of the expression and may not be concluded from information in the conversation.
17. **(B)** To *take care of something* is an idiomatic expression that means to be responsible for it. Choices (A), (C), and (D) are not paraphrases of the expression and may not be concluded from information in the conversation.
18. **(B)** "Did you understand that experiment that Bill mentioned in the group presentation?" Choices (A), (C), and (D) are not mentioned and may not be concluded from information in the discussion.
19. **(A)** "...since there is no air resistance on the moon, it is the ideal environment for the experiment." Choice (B) refers to the fact that the moon has a lower gravitational acceleration, not that there is no gravitational acceleration. Choices (C) and (D) are true, but they are not the reason the moon is an ideal environment.
20. **(A)** "...much easier...to lift the hammer on the moon...because of the moon's lower rate of gravitational acceleration." Choice (B) is true, but it is not the reason it is easier to lift the hammer on the moon. Choices (C) and (D) are not mentioned and may not be concluded from information in the discussion.
21. **(C)** "I really liked the presentation." Choice (A) refers to information about the hammer, not to the entire presentation. Choice (B) contradicts the fact that she liked the presentation. Choice (D) is not mentioned and may not be concluded from information in the discussion.
22. **(B)** "It [the video] was about stress." Choices (A), (C), and (D) are secondary themes used to develop the main theme of the video.
23. **(C)** "They said that women usually don't get the same level of care that men do...." Choice (D) contradicts the fact that the heart attacks suffered by women are likely to be more serious. Choices (A) and (B) are not mentioned and may not be concluded from information in the conversation.
24. **(B)** "Really it was [good]." Choice (A) contradicts the fact that he explains the video to the woman. Choice (C) contradicts the fact that he encourages the woman to view it. Choice (D) contradicts the fact that he was surprised by the report on the number of women who have heart attacks.
25. **(B)** "It's on reserve in the library...." Choice (A) refers to the fact that the man and woman have already discussed the video tape, not to what the woman will do. Choice (C) contradicts the fact that tapes on reserve cannot be checked out. Choice (D) refers to what the woman will do after she sees the video.
26. **(D)** Elizabeth Barrett Browning is the main topic of this lecture. Choices (A), (B), and (C) are secondary topics that are used to develop the main topic of the lecture.
27. **(C)** "In part because the sovereign was a woman, there was great support for a movement to break with the tradition of a male Poet Laureate." Choice (A) contradicts the fact that Elizabeth Barrett was not married at the time that she was considered for the title of Poet Laureate. Choice (B) contradicts the fact that *Sonnets from the Portuguese* was not published at the time that she was considered for the title. Choice (D) is not mentioned and may not be concluded from information in the talk.
28. **(B)** "...she married Robert Browning, himself a gifted poet, and they fled to Florence, Italy." The place in Choice (C) refers to the title of one of Elizabeth's most famous works, *Sonnets from the Portuguese*, not to a

place where she lived. The place in Choice (D) refers to the country where she lived before, not after her marriage. Choice (A) is not mentioned and may not be concluded from information in the talk.

29. **(D)** "*Aurora Leigh*, her longest work, appeared in 1856, only five years before her death in 1861." Choice (A) refers to the date when Elizabeth Barrett was suggested to replace the Poet Laureate, not to the date of her death. Choice (B) refers to the date when her son was born, one year before she published her collected works in 1850. Choice (C) refers to the date when *Aurora Leigh* was published, five years before her death.

30. **(B)** The contributions of biology to medicine are the main topic of this lecture. Choices (A), (C), and (D) are secondary topics that are used to develop the main topic of the lecture.

31. **(C)** "Hippocrates…began…to apply scientific method to the problems of diagnosis and the treatment of diseases…. he kept careful records of symptoms and treatments." Choice (A) refers to the work of Aristotle, not Hippocrates. Choice (B) refers to the work of Sir Joseph Lister. Choice (D) refers to a theory that Hippocrates discarded in favor of the scientific method, not to his work.

32. **(B)** "Because of his great contribution to the field, Aristotle has been called the father of biology." Choice (A) refers to the father of modern medicine, not to the father of biology. Choice (C) refers to the author of *Materia Medica*. Choice (D) refers to the physician who established the science of immunization.

33. **(C)** "…the English physician and anatomist William Harvey discovered a mechanism for the circulation of the blood in the body." Choice (A) refers to a contribution by Louis Pasteur, not by William Harvey. Choice (B) refers to a contribution by Edward Jenner. Choice (D) refers to a reference book that was a contribution by Dioscorides.

34. **(D)** "…gangs have been prevalent for much longer than I had assumed. I was so surprised." The number in Choice (A) is true, but it was not what surprised the student. Choice (C) contradicts the fact that not much has changed over the years. Choice (B) is not mentioned and may not be concluded from information in the discussion.

35. **(B)** "…Joan Moore, indicated that gang behavior is probably caused by normal adolescent insecurities…." Choice (A) refers to a similar form of behavior, but not to the cause of gang activity. Choice (C) refers to the neighborhoods where gang activity takes place, but it is not the cause of gang activity. Choice (D) is not mentioned and may not be concluded from information in the discussion.

36. **(A) (B)** "…a gang member will be recognizable because of gang-related tattoos, clothing…." The phrase *research studies* in Choice (D) refers to the research reported in the discussion, not to ways that gang members are identified. Choice (C) is not mentioned and may not be concluded from information in the discussion.

37. **(C)** "They [women] are viewed as more of a support system…." Choice (A) contradicts the fact that women are not considered members of gangs. Choice (D) contradicts the fact that women are part of the extended social group of a gang. Choice (B) is not mentioned and may not be concluded from information in the discussion.

38. **(B)** "I have a problem with my schedule." Choice (A) contradicts the fact that Mary really likes her job. Choice (D) contradicts the fact that she is a work-study employee. Choice (C) is not mentioned and may not be concluded from information in the conversation.

39. **(D)** "I have a required class at nine o'clock on Monday, Wednesday, and Friday." The phrase *every day* in Choice (A) refers to her work schedule, not to her class schedule. The phrase *ten-thirty on Monday* in Choice (C) refers to the time she will report to work, not to the time for her class. Choice (B) is not mentioned and may not be concluded from information in the conversation.

40. **(A)** "…you could come in at ten-thirty and work until two-thirty…." Choice (B) contradicts the fact that she will continue to work four hours a day. Choice (D) contradicts the fact that he changes her work schedule. Choice (C) is not mentioned and may not be concluded from information in the conversation.

41. **(C)** "You're a work-study employee, and that means...you can study on the job as long as the work is done first." Choice (A) is true, but it is not a complete definition of a work-study employee. Choices (B) and (D) are not mentioned and may not be concluded from information in the conversation.
42. **(C)** "...we have developed several techniques for building more earthquake-resistant structures." Choices (A), (B), and (D) are all mentioned in the lecture, but they are secondary ideas used to develop the main topic of the lecture.
43. **(A)** "Walls can also be reinforced, using cross-bracing." Choice (B) refers to a structure in the center of a building. Choice (D) refers to a device positioned below the building. Choice (C) is not mentioned and may not be concluded from information in the lecture.
44. **(A) (B)** "Most...base isolators...are made of...layers of steel and synthetic rubber." Choice (C) refers to construction material, but not to material used in base isolators. Choice (D) refers to fill dirt.
45. **(C)** "...fill dirt can lose its bearing strength...and the buildings constructed on it can...disappear into the Earth." Choice (A) refers to the characteristics of a moat, not to those of fill dirt. Choice (B) refers to the techniques for building earthquake-resistant structures. The phrase *shock waves* in Choice (D) refers to the advantage of rubber, not to a characteristic of fill dirt.
46. **(C) (D)** "The most common [vein patterns] are the pinnate and the palmate." Choices (A) and (B) refer to vein patterns, but they are not the most common vein patterns.
47. **(B)** "...a pinnate leaf has one large central vein called the midrib...that extends the full length of the leaf." Choice (A) contradicts the fact that the pinnate leaf, not the midrib, is one of the major classifications. Choice (C) contradicts the fact that the midrib is a central vein in the pinnate, not the parallel leaf. Choice (D) is not mentioned and may not be concluded from information in the lecture.
48. **(C)** "A good way to remember this classification [palmate] is to think of the palm of your hand." Choices (A) and (B) are both true, but he did not use the visual or the explanation as a memory aid. The phrase *lab manual* in Choice (D) refers to a reference for the lab activity, not to a way to remember the classification.
49. **(B)** Pinnate **(A)** Palmate **(C)** Parallel
50. **(A)** "...work with your lab partner to classify the veining of each leaf." The word *fifty-two* in Choice (C) refers to the page number in the lab manual, not to the number of pages to read. Choices (B) and (D) are not mentioned and may not be concluded from information in the lecture.

Section 2: Structure

1. **(A)** In some dependent clauses, the clause marker is the subject of the dependent clause. *Which* refers to *the soybeans* and is the subject of the verb *can be used.* Choices (B) and (D) do not have clause markers. Choice (C) is a clause marker that refers to a person, not to *soybeans.* (Refer to Patterns, Problem 138, page 248.)
2. **(A)** Only Choice (A) may be used with a count noun like *species* and a number. Choices (C) and (D) may be used with non-count nouns. Choice (B) may be used with count nouns without a number. "As many species of finch have been identified" would also be correct. (Refer to Patterns, Problem 95, page 195.)
3. **(C)** The verb *had* establishes a point of view in the past. *Serves* should be *served* in order to maintain the point of view. (Refer to Style, Problem 1, page 252.)
4. **(D)** There must be agreement between subject and verb. *Produce* should be *produces* to agree with the singular subject *a thunderhead.* (Refer to Style, Problem 7, page 259.)
5. **(C)** When the degree of one quality, *the price*, is dependent upon the degree of another quality, *the demand*, two comparatives are required, each of which must be preceded by *the.* Choice (A) is a comparative, but it is not preceded by *the.* Choices (B) and (D) are not accepted comparative forms. (Refer to Patterns, Problem 100, page 200.)
6. **(B)** *The same like* is a combination of *the same as* and *like. Like* should be *as* in the phrase with *the same.* (Refer to Patterns, Problem 86, page 184.)
7. **(A)** *Despite of* is a combination of *despite*

and *in spite of*. Either *despite* or *in spite of* should be used. (Refer to Patterns, Problem 110, page 213.)

8. **(C)** *So* is used with an adjective to express cause. Choice (A) may be used before a noun, not before an adjective such as *big*. Choices (B) and (D) may not be used to express cause before a clause of result such as *that there are four time zones*. "The United States is very big" would be correct without the clause of result. (Refer to Patterns, Problem 81, page 178.)
9. **(A)** Ideas in a series should be expressed by parallel structures. Only Choice (A) has three parallel *-ing* forms. Choices (B), (C), and (D) are not parallel. (Refer to Style, Problem 17, page 271.)
10. **(A)** *Behave* should be *behavior*. *Behave* is a verb. *Behavior* is a noun. (Refer to Style, Problem 30, page 288.)
11. **(B)** *Whom* should be *who* because it is the subject of the verb *is*. *Whom* functions as a complement. *Who* functions as a subject. (Refer to Patterns, Problem 49, page 134.)
12. **(A)** *Such as* is commonly used to introduce an example. (Refer to Patterns, Problem 109, page 212.)
13. **(A)** An introductory verbal phrase should immediately precede the noun that it modifies. Only Choice (A) provides a noun that could be logically modified by the introductory verbal phrase *upon hatching*. *Swimming, the knowledge,* and *how to swim* could not logically *hatch* as would be implied by Choices (B), (C), and (D). (Refer to Style, Problem 15, page 268.)
14. **(B)** Comparative forms are usually followed by *than*. *Highest* in Choices (A) and (C) may be used to compare more than two decks. Choice (D) correctly compares *this deck* with *any other one*, but *that*, not *than*, follows the comparative. (Refer to Patterns, Problem 96, page 196.)
15. **(D)** A verb word must be used in a clause after the verb *to insist*. *Will not smoke* should be *not smoke*. (Refer to Patterns, Problem 27, page 107.)
16. **(C)** *Invent* should be *invention*. *Invent* is a verb. *Invention* is a noun. (Refer to Style, Problem 30, page 288.)
17. **(C)** *Calcium* is the subject of the verb *is*. Choice (A) may be used with the word *that*. Choice (B) may be used as a subject clause preceding a main verb. Choice (D) may be used preceding a subject and verb. "It is calcium *that* is necessary for the development of strong bones and teeth." "That calcium is necessary for the development of strong bones and teeth *is* known," and "Although calcium is necessary for strong bones and teeth, *other minerals are* also important" would also be correct. (Refer to Style, Problem 19, page 274.)
18. **(C)** *Larger* should be *largest*. Because there are more than two masses of nerve tissue in the human body, a superlative form must be used. (Refer to Patterns, Problem 97, page 197.)
19. **(A)** *Like* is a preposition. *Alike* should be *like*. (Refer to Patterns, Problem 88, page 187.)
20. **(C)** *Capable of* is a prepositional idiom. *To perform* should be *of performing*. (Refer to Style, Problem 29, page 286.)
21. **(A)** For scientific results, a present form in the condition requires a present or future form in the result. Only Choice (A) introduces a conditional. (Refer to Patterns, Problem 21, page 98.)
22. **(A)** Repetition of the subject by a subject pronoun is redundant. *It* should be deleted. (Refer to Style, Problem 21, page 276.)
23. **(B)** A negative phrase introduces inverted order. *Not until* requires an auxiliary verb, subject, and main verb. In Choice (A) there is no auxiliary. In Choices (C) and (D), there is no subject and no auxiliary. (Refer to Patterns, Problem 129, page 237.)
24. **(B)** The verb phrase *to approve of* requires an *-ing* form in the complement. *-Ing* forms are modified by possessive pronouns. Choices (A) and (D) are infinitives, not *-ing* forms. Choice (C) is an *-ing* form, but it is modified by a subject, not a possessive pronoun. (Refer to Patterns, Problem 4, page 76.)
25. **(B)** *Commonly* should be *common*. *Commonly* is an adverb. *Common* is an adjective. (Refer to Style, Problem 30, page 288.)

Section 3: Reading

1. **(A)** The other choices are secondary ideas that are used to develop the main idea, "Technological Advances in Oceanography." Choices (B), (C), and (D) are impor-

tant to the discussion, and provide details that support the main idea.

2. **(C)** In the context of this passage, sluggish is closest in meaning to slow moving. Choices (A), (B), and (D) are not accepted definitions of the word.
3. **(A)** "Because of undersea pressure that affected their speech organs, communication among divers was difficult or impossible." Choices (B), (C), and (D) are not mentioned and may not be concluded from information in the passage.
4. **(A)** "Direct observations of the ocean floor are made not only by divers but also by deep-diving submarines." Choices (B), (C), and (D) contradict the fact that observations are made by deep-diving submarines as well as by divers.
5. **(D)** "Direct observations of the ocean floor are made ... by deep-diving submarines." Choice (A) contradicts the fact that some of the vehicles are manned. Choice (B) refers to the divers, not to the undersea vehicles. Choice (C) contradicts the fact that undersea vehicles have overcome some of the limitations of divers.
6. **(A)** In the context of this passage, cruise could best be replaced by travel at a constant speed. Choices (B), (C), and (D) are not accepted definitions of the word.
7. **(D)** "Radio-equipped buoys can be operated by remote control in order to transmit information back to the land-based laboratories." Choices (A), (B), and (C) are not mentioned and may not be concluded from information in the passage.
8. In the context of this passage, the word data is closest in meaning to information. No other words or phrases in the **bold** text are close to the meaning of the word information.
9. **(C)** Choices (A), (B) and (D) are mentioned in sentences 8 and 9, paragraph 1. (C) refers to computers, not to satellites.
10. "Some of humankind's most serious problems, especially those [problems] concerning energy and food, may be solved with the help of observations made possible by this new technology." Other choices would change the meaning of the sentence.
11. "Some of humankind's most serious problems, especially those concerning energy and food, may be solved with the help of observations made possible by this new technology." Quotation from sentence 2, paragraph 2.
12. **(C)** "Communication" is the best title because it states the main idea of the passage. The other choices are all examples of communication that provide details in support of the main idea.
13. **(D)** "Whereas speech is the most advanced form of communication...." Choice (A) contradicts the fact that there are many ways to communicate without speech including signals, signs, symbols, and gestures. Choice (B) is incorrect because the advances are dependent upon speech; speech is not dependent upon the advances. Choice (C) is not mentioned and may not be concluded from information in the passage.
14. "For instance, the function of any signal is to impinge upon the environment in such a way that it attracts attention, as for example, the dots and dashes that can be applied in a telegraph circuit." Quotation from sentence 4, paragraph 1.
15. **(A)** In the context of this passage, impinge upon is closest in meaning to intrude. Choices (B), (C), and (D) are not accepted definitions of the word.
16. **(B)** "The basic function of a signal is to impinge upon the environment in such a way that it [the signal] attracts attention, as, for example, the dots and dashes of a telegraph circuit." Choices (A), (C), and (D) would change the meaning of the sentence.
17. **(D)** In the context of this passage, potential could best be replaced by possibility. Choices (A), (B), and (C) are not accepted definitions of the word.
18. "Less adaptable to the codification of words, signs also contain agreed upon meaning; that is, they [signs] convey information in and of themselves [the signs]." Other choices would change the meaning of the sentence.
19. **(B)** In the context of this passage, intricate could best be replaced by complicated. Choices (A), (C), and (D) are not accepted definitions of the word.
20. **(C)** "...applauding in a theater provides performers with an auditory symbol." A telegraph circuit was cited as an example of

Choice (A). A stop sign and a barber pole were cited as examples of Choice (B). Waving and handshaking were cited as examples of Choice (D).

21. "A loud smacking of the lips after a meal can be either a kinesthetic and auditory symbol of approval and appreciation, or simply a rude noise. Gestures such as waving and handshaking also communicate certain cultural messages." The connection between the two sentences is the reference to cultural symbols and cultural messages. The second sentence with the word *also* must be mentioned after the first sentence.

22. **(B)** "...means of communication intended to be used for long distances and extended periods are based upon speech. Radio, television, and telephone are only a few." Choices (A), (C), and (D) are not mentioned and may not be concluded from information in the passage.

23. In the context of this passage, the word interaction is closest in meaning to communication. No other words or phrases in the **bold** text are close to the meaning of the word communication.

24. **(D)** Choices (A), (B), and (C) are important to the discussion and provide details that support the primary topic, "the content, form, and effects of fertilizer."

25. **(D)** In the context of this passage, essential could best be replaced by required. Choices (A), (B), and (C) are not accepted definitions of the word.

26. **(D)** Since the last number in the formula represents the percentage content of potash, and since the last number is the smallest, it must be concluded that potash has the smallest percentage content. Choice (A) refers to the number 4 in the formula. Choices (B) and (C) are the substances found in phosphoric acid which refers to the number 8 in the formula.

27. **(B)** Since the content of nitrogen is represented by the first number in the formula, it must be concluded that there is 5 percent nitrogen in the fertilizer. The number in Choice (A) refers to the quantity of numbers in the formula. The percentage in Choice (C) refers to potash. The percentage in Choice (D) refers to phosphoric acid.

28. **(B)** In the context of this passage, designate could best be replaced by specify. Choices (A), (C), and (D) are not accepted definitions of the word.

29. **(C)** "Recently, liquids have shown an increase in popularity...." Choice (A) refers to a form of fertilizers that used to be used, but was found to be less convenient, not to a form that is more popular than ever. Choices (B) and (D) contradict the fact that solids in the shape of chemical granules are easy to store and apply.

30. **(A)** "Formerly, powders were also used, but these [powders] were found to be less convenient than either solids or liquids." Choices (B), (C), and (D) would change the meaning of the sentence.

31. **(C)** In the context of this passage, convenient is closest in meaning to easy to use. Choices (A), (B), and (D) are not accepted definitions of the word.

32. "Accumulations of chemical fertilizer in the water supply accelerate the growth of algae and, consequently, may disturb the natural cycle of life, contributing to the death of fish." Quotation from sentence 4, paragraph 3.

33. In the context of this passage, the word damage is closest in meaning to harm. No other words or phrases in the **bold** text are close to the meaning of the word harm.

34. "Formerly, powders were also used, but these were found to be less convenient than either solids or liquids. One objection to powders was their propensity to become solid chunks if the bags got damp." The connection between the two sentences is the reference to "powders." The first sentence is a general sentence, and the second sentence is an example.

35. **(A)** The other choices are secondary ideas that are used to develop the main idea, "the evolution of the horse." Choices (B), (C), and (D) are significant steps in the evolution.

36. **(D)** Choices (A), (B), and (C) are mentioned in sentence 3, paragraph 1. The Miocene Age is the earliest historical period mentioned in the passage.

37. **(B)** In the context of this passage, instigated could best be replaced by caused. Choices (A), (C), and (D) are not accepted definitions of the word.

38. **(A)** Choice (A) is a restatement of the sentence referred to in the passage. Since horses appeared 60 million years ago and humans appeared two million years ago, it must be concluded that horses appeared long before human beings.
39. **(A)** "...a horse crossed...from Alaska into the grasslands of Europe." Because of the reference to *grasslands*, it must be concluded that the hipparions migrated to Europe to feed in developing grasslands. Choice (B) contradicts the fact that the European colonists brought horses to North America where the species had become extinct. Choice (D) contradicts the fact that the evolution of the horse has been recorded from its beginnings through all of its evolutionary stages.
40. **(C)** "...smaller than the hipparion, the anchitheres was completely replaced by it." Choice (A) refers to the very early form of the horse, not to the hipparion. Choice (B) contradicts the fact that the hipparion was a more highly evolved form than the anchitheres. Choice (D) contradicts the fact that the hipparion was about the size of a small pony.
41. **(B)** "Less developed and smaller than the hipparion, the anchitheres was completely replaced by it [the hipparion]." Choices (A), (C), and (D) would change the meaning of the sentence.
42. **(C)** In the context of this passage, extinct is closest in meaning to nonexistent. Choices (A), (B), and (D) are not accepted definitions of the word.
43. "Fossil finds provide us not only with detailed information about the horse itself, but also with valuable insights into the migration of herds, and even evidence for speculation about the climatic conditions that could have instigated such migratory behavior." Quotation from sentence 3, paragraph 1.
44. In the context of this passage, tamed is closest in meaning to domesticated. No other words or phrases in the **bold** text are close to the meaning of the word domesticated.
45. **(A)** "At the beginning of the Pliocene Age, a horse...crossed...into the grasslands of Europe. The horse was the hipparion....The hipparion encountered...the anchitheres, which had previously invaded Europe... probably during the Miocene Period." Because the anchitheres invaded Europe during the Miocene and was already there when the hipparion arrived in the Pliocene, it must be concluded that the Miocene Period was prior to the Pliocene Period. By the Pleistocene referred to in Choices (B) and (C), the anchitheres and the hipparion had become extinct. Therefore, the Pleistocene Period must have been after both the Miocene and the Pliocene.

Model Test 3—Computer-Assisted TOEFL

Section 1: Listening

1. **(A)** Since the woman agrees with the man, it must be concluded that she will not go home for spring vacation. Choice (C) contradicts the fact that she will be graduating in May. Choices (B) and (D) are not mentioned and may not be concluded from information in the conversation.
2. **(C)** From the reference to *the assignment for Monday*, it must be concluded that the speakers are talking about homework. Choices (A), (B), and (D) are all mentioned in the conversation in reference to the assignment.
3. **(C)** *Cramming* is an idiomatic expression that means studying a lot, especially just before a test. Choices (A), (B), and (D) contradict the fact that the man is confident about being ready for the test.
4. **(A)** Since the man says that he needs a book for an English course, it must be concluded that he will buy the textbook. Choice (C) contradicts the fact that he is already in the bookstore. Choice (D) contradicts the fact that he needs a book for the course. Choice (B) is not mentioned and may not be concluded from information in the conversation.
5. **(A)** To *turn someone off* is an idiomatic expression that means the speaker does not like something or someone. Choice (D) contradicts the fact that the woman does not like the class. Choice (C) contradicts the fact that the woman thinks Professor Collins is a great person. Choice (B) is not mentioned and may not be concluded from information in the conversation.
6. **(A)** To *not put off* is an idiomatic expression that means to stop postponing. Choices (B) and (C) contradict the fact that the woman has not made an appointment yet. Choice (D) is not mentioned and may not be concluded from information in the conversation.
7. **(C)** To be *used to something* is an idiomatic expression that means to be accustomed to something. Choices (A), (B), and (D) are not paraphrases of the expression and may not be concluded from information in the conversation.
8. **(C)** To *get caught up* is an idiomatic expression that means to bring work or assignments up to date. Choice (B) contradicts the fact that the man says he knows what time it is. Choices (A) and (D) are not mentioned and may not be concluded from information in the conversation.
9. **(D)** To *pass* is an idiomatic expression that means to lose a turn. Choices (A), (B), and (C) are not paraphrases of the expression and may not be concluded from information in the conversation.
10. **(B)** To *look into something* is an idiomatic expression that means to investigate. Choice (A) refers to the woman's conclusion, not to the man's intention. Choices (C) and (D) are not mentioned and may not be concluded from information in the conversation.
11. **(A)** To *get mixed up* is an idiomatic expression that means to become confused. Choice (C) contradicts the fact that the man understands the lectures. Choices (B) and (D) are not mentioned and may not be concluded from information in the conversation.
12. **(A)** To *turn in* is an idiomatic expression that means to submit. "Ahead of time" means early. Choice (C) contradicts the fact that she wants to turn in the paper before it is due. Choice (D) contradicts the fact that she is ready to turn the paper in. Choice (B) is not mentioned and may not be concluded from information in the conversation.
13. **(D)** "You have to take it [the class] in order to graduate." Choice (A) refers to the man's attitude, not to the woman's opinion. Choice (B) contradicts the fact that the class is required for graduation. Choice (C) is not mentioned and may not be concluded from information in the conversation.
14. **(A)** "...the T.A. said to get into a study group and quiz each other." Choice (B) refers to the type of exam that they will be given, not to the T.A.'s suggestion. Choice (C) refers to quizzes, but the T.A. suggests that they "quiz each other," which means to ask each other questions. Choice (D) contradicts the fact that the professor recommends studying alone, not in a group.

15. **(C)** Since the woman goes to get a pen, it must be concluded that she will sign the form. Choice (A) contradicts the fact that the woman says he doesn't need an appointment. Choice (B) refers to the pen that the woman, not the man, will use. Choice (D) contradicts the fact that the man is asked to wait for the woman.
16. **(A)** "I'd better make one more draft." A "draft" is a revision of written work. Choice (D) refers to the man's suggestion, not to what the woman is going to do. Choices (B) and (C) are not mentioned and may not be concluded from information in the conversation.
17. **(B)** "That's what I thought [that the computer...scheduled for the fifth]." Choice (C) refers to the woman's original statement, not to her final conclusion. Choice (D) contradicts the fact that payments are still due. Choice (A) refers to an error made by the woman, not the computer.
18. **(D)** "...I need three letters of recommendation. Would you be willing to write me one?" Choice (A) contradicts the fact that Betty is already in the professor's seminar class. Choice (C) refers to additional information that the professor gives to Betty, not to the purpose of her call. Choice (B) is not mentioned and may not be concluded from information in the conversation.
19. **(B)** "I think you are an excellent candidate for graduate school." Choice (A) contradicts the fact that Betty is already taking the seminar. Choice (D) contradicts the fact that the professor does not recall the deadline for applications. Choice (C) is not mentioned and may not be concluded from information in the conversation.
20. **(B)** "The committee meets on April 30." Choices (A) and (D) refer to the person who will receive the letter, not to who will make the decision. Choice (C) refers to the person who will make a recommendation.
21. **(C)** "The committee meets on April 30, so all the materials must be submitted before then." Choice (A) contradicts the fact that the materials must be submitted before April 30. Choices (B) and (D) are not mentioned and may not be concluded from information in the conversation.
22. **(B)** Because the speaker is introduced as a professor of history and discusses trade during the eighteenth century, it must be concluded that he is a professor of history. It is not as probable that the lecturers mentioned in Choices (A), (C), and (D) would discuss this topic.
23. **(C)** "To maintain this favorable balance of trade, England went to fantastic lengths to keep secret the advanced manufacturing processes..." Choice (D) contradicts the fact that it was the colony (America), not England, that stole the plans. Choices (A) and (B) are not mentioned and may not be concluded from information in the talk.
24. **(C)** "Determined to take nothing in writing, Slater memorized the intricate designs for all the machines in an English textile mill...." Choices (A) and (B) contradict the fact that Slater, in partnership with Brown, opened a mill in the United States in the state of Rhode Island. Choice (D) contradicts the fact that he took nothing in writing.
25. **(A)** "...in part as a result of Slater and Brown, America had changed from a country of small farmers and craftsmen to an industrial nation...." Choices (B), (C), and (D) are not mentioned and may not be concluded from information in the talk.
26. **(A)** "I understand that I can reserve textbooks for next semester." Choice (B) is true, but it is a comment, not the purpose of the conversation. Choice (C) contradicts the fact that the faculty member, not the woman, orders books for the whole class. Choice (D) is not mentioned and may not be concluded from information in the conversation.
27. **(B)** "This semester I couldn't get two of my books until three weeks into the semester...." Choice (C) contradicts the fact that he received his books three weeks after the semester started. Choice (D) refers to this semester, not last semester. Choice (A) is not mentioned and may not be concluded from information in the conversation.
28. **(B)** "Just fill out one of these forms.... Then pay for your books...and we'll place the order." Choice (A) is true but refers to ordering books for the whole class. Choices (C) and (D) are not mentioned and may not be concluded from information in the conversation.
29. **(B)** "We'll call you as soon as they [the

books] come in." Choice (C) refers to the student's question about receiving his books, but is not how he will know when the books arrive. The word *form* in Choice (A) refers to the system for ordering books, not to the way to know that books have arrived. Choice (D) is not mentioned and may not be concluded from information in the conversation.

30. **(A)** "So many different kinds of writing have been called essays, it is difficult to define exactly what an essay is." Choices (B), (C), and (D) are secondary themes used to develop a definition of the essay.
31. **(C)** "...four characteristics that are true of most essays." Choices (A), (B), and (D) are secondary themes used to develop the main theme of the talk.
32. **(B)** "...an essay [is] a short, prose composition with a personal viewpoint that discusses one topic." Choice (B) contradicts the fact that an essay is written in prose, not poetry. Choices (A), (C), and (D) are all included in the definition.
33. **(B)** "...let's brainstorm some topics for your first essay assignment." Choices (A), (C), and (D) are not mentioned and may not be concluded from information in the conversation.
34. **(D)** The main purpose of this talk is to summarize Jefferson's life. Choices (A), (B), and (C) are secondary themes in the life of Jefferson.
35. **(C)** "Although Jefferson was a Republican, he at first tried to cooperate with Alexander Hamilton, a Federalist...." Choice (A) refers to Jefferson's opinion of Hamilton's political affiliation. Choice (B) refers to Hamilton, not Jefferson. Choice (D) is not mentioned and may not be concluded from information in the talk.
36. **(B)** "He [Jefferson] and Federalist Aaron Burr received an identical vote, but the Republican Congress elected to approve Jefferson as president." Choice (A) contradicts the fact that Jefferson and Burr received an identical vote. Choices (C) and (D) are not mentioned and may not be concluded from information in the conversation.
37. **(A)** "Thomas Jefferson was a statesman, a diplomat, an author, and an architect.... Not a gifted public speaker, he was most talented as a literary draftsman." Choices (B), (C), and (D) are all mentioned as attributes of Jefferson.
38. **(B) (C)** "They [fossils] are occasionally preserved in ice, but most have been buried in mud or sand...at the bottom...of water...." Choice (A) refers to a place where fossils are occasionally preserved, not the most usual place. Choice (D) refers to the location of the mud and sand, under water.
39. **(C) (B) (D) (A)** "...animals and plants must be buried quickly...mineral-rich water soaks into the...plant or animal...minerals in the water dissolve the original organism, leaving a fossil mold."
40. **(B)** "...the internal features of the organism are not preserved...." Choice (A) contradicts the fact that the shapes of fragile feathers and fur are preserved. The word *minerals* in Choice (C) refers to a part of the process, not to what is lost in the process. Choice (D) contradicts the fact that the mold is left.
41. **(A)** "The location of fossils in layers of...sedimentary rock shows...the order in which they were buried, that is, their relative ages." Choice (B) is true, but it is not the reason that the layers are important to the fossil record. Choice (C) contradicts the fact that the mineral water dissolves the organisms. Choice (D) contradicts the fact that plants and animals buried in the same layers of rock lived at approximately the same time.
42. **(D)** "...I thought I would [graduate] automatically." Choice (A) contradicts the fact that the student believes he has completed all of the course work for graduation. Choice (B) contradicts the fact that he has enough hours to graduate. Choice (C) is true, but does not explain why the man did not apply for graduation.
43. **(A)** "The requirements are...in the catalog..." Choice (B) contradicts the fact that the man has to explain how he selected his courses. Choice (C) contradicts the fact that the man did not have a program of study. Choice (D) contradicts the fact that the man did not have an advisor.
44. **(B)** "The first thing we need to do is to assign you an advisor..." Choice (A) contradicts the fact that the man may have taken the required courses. Choice (C) contradicts the fact that the man referred to the requirements in the catalog. Choice (D) contradicts the fact that the man has his latest transcript with him.

45. **(B)** "...if you...failed to take a critical course, then you may not be eligible for graduation." Choice (A) contradicts the fact that the man is told that he has enough hours to graduate. Choice (C) contradicts the fact that the woman will try to get the man in to see someone that day. Choice (D) is not mentioned and may not be concluded from information in the conversation.
46. **(C)** Since this is a linguistics class, "the articles were written by linguists...." Choices (A), (B), and (D) are subjects that are referred to in the discussion, but they are not the class in which the discussion takes place.
47. **(D)** "A standard dialect is the dialect that is selected as the educational model." Choice (B) contradicts the fact that all dialects of a language are of equal value. Choice (C) is true of all dialects, but it is not the definition of a standard dialect. Choice (A) is not mentioned and may not be concluded from information in the discussion.
48. **(D)** "...from a linguistic point of view, all dialects of a language are of equal value." Choice (A) contradicts the fact that the accents taught with standard grammar may be regional accents. Choice (B) contradicts the fact that the school may teach a standard dialect with a regional accent. Choice (C) contradicts the fact that several major dialect regions have been identified.
49. **(A) (C)** "Standard English has a common grammar and vocabulary. These [grammar and vocabulary] are the basic building blocks of a dialect." Choice (B) refers to accent, not dialect. Choice (D) is not mentioned and may not be concluded from information in the discussion.
50. **(A)** "Some accents are associated with a higher socioeconomic class, and therefore tend to be the preferred standard accent in schools." Choice (B) contradicts the fact that the prestige of a social group makes a dialect more desirable. Choice (D) refers to the linguistic perspective of accents, not the sociological perspective. Choice (C) is not mentioned and may not be concluded from information in the discussion.

Section 2: Structure

1. **(C)** *Most* is used before a noncount noun to express a quantity that is larger than half the amount. A singular verb follows the noncount noun. Choice (A) does not have a verb. In Choice (B), the verb is before, not after the noun. In Choice (D), *the* is used before *most*. (Refer to Patterns, Problem 72, page 166.)
2. **(B)** An adjective is used before *enough* to express sufficiency. In Choice (A), *goodly* is ungrammatical. The adverbial form of the adjective *good* is *well*. In Choice (C), *as* is unnecessary and incorrect. In Choice (D), the adjective is used after, not before *enough*. (Refer to Patterns, Problem 74, page 169.)
3. **(A)** *Responsible for* is a prepositional idiom. *Responsible the* should be *responsible for the*. (Refer to Style, Problem 29, page 286.)
4. **(B)** A form of BE is used with the participle in passive sentences. *Practice* should be *practiced.* (Refer to Patterns, Problem 31, page 112.)
5. **(B)** There must be agreement between pronoun and antecedent. *Which* should be *who* to refer to the antecedent *Shirley Temple Black. Which* refers to things. *Who* refers to persons. (Refer to Patterns, Problem 48, page 133.)
6. **(A)** *The* can be used before a noncount noun that is followed by a qualifying phrase. *Population* should be *the population* before the qualifying phrase *of the Americas*. (Refer to Patterns, Problem 63, page 156.)
7. **(C)** An adjective clause modifies a noun in the main clause. *That the earliest cultures evolved* modifies *the way*. Choice (A) is a clause marker *that* and a noun. Choice (B) is a verb and a noun. Choice (D) is a clause marker *which* and a noun. (Refer to Patterns, Problem 140, page 250.)
8. **(D)** Comparative forms are usually followed by *than.* After the comparative *more reasonable, as* should be *than.* (Refer to Patterns, Problem 96, page 196.)
9. **(C)** *There* introduces inverted order, but there must still be agreement between subject and verb. *Has been* should be *have been* to agree with the plural subject *two major factions*. (Refer to Style, Problem 8, page 260.)
10. **(A)** In order to refer to occupying a place on the battlefields, *lain* should be used. *To lay* means to put in a place, and the participle is *laid. To lie* means to occupy a place, and the participle is *lain.* (Refer to Style, Problem 23, page 279.)

11. **(C)** A sentence has a subject and a verb. Choice (A) is redundant because the subject pronoun *it* is used consecutively with the subject *calculus*. Choice (B) has the marker *that* to introduce a main clause. Choice (D) is redundant because it has a verb that replaces the main verb *can reduce*. (Refer to Patterns, Problem 137 and Style, Problem 21, pages 247 and 276.)
12. **(B)** Subject-verb order and a negative verb with *either* expresses negative agreement. Negative agreement with *neither* requires verb-subject order and an affirmative verb. In Choice (A), verb-subject order is reversed. In Choice (C), verb-subject order is reversed, and *neither* is used at the beginning, not at the end of the clause. In Choice (D) *either*, not *neither*, is used with verb-subject order and an affirmative verb. "Neither does Mexico" would also be correct. (Refer to Patterns, Problem 121, page 226.)
13. **(B)** *Large* should be *largest.* Because there were more than two ethnic groups, a superlative form must be used. (Refer to Patterns, Problem 97, page 197.)
14. **(B)** The determiner *a* is used before a singular count noun. *Results* should be *result.* (Refer to Patterns, Problem 62, page 154.)
15. **(D)** A sentence has a subject and a verb. Choice (A) does not have a verb. Choices (B) and (C) introduce a main clause subject and verb. (Refer to Patterns, Problem 137, page 247.)
16. **(C)** The anticipatory clause *it is accepted that* introduces a subject and verb, *the formation...began.* Choices (A), (B), and (D) are incomplete and ungrammatical. (Refer to Patterns, Problem 35, page 117.)
17. **(B)** When the degree of one quality, *the heat,* is dependent upon the degree of another quality, *the humidity,* two comparatives are used, each preceded by *the. The worst* should be *the worse* because it is a comparative. (Refer to Patterns, Problem 100, page 200.)
18. **(B)** A dependent clause modifies an independent clause. *Which are* should be *are* to provide a verb for the subject *statistical data,* of the independent clause. (Refer to Patterns, Problem 138, page 248.)
19. **(A)** The word order for a passive sentence is a form of BE followed by a participle. Only Choice (A) has the correct word order. Choice (B) does not have a BE form. Choice (C) has a HAVE, not a BE form. Choice (D) is a present tense verb, not BE followed by a participle. (Refer to Patterns, Problem 31, page 112.)
20. **(A)** *Despite of* is a combination of *despite* and *in spite of.* Either *despite* or *in spite of* should be used. (Refer to Patterns, Problem 110, page 213.)
21. **(C)** Subject-verb order is used in the clause after a question word connector such as *how much.* In Choice (A), subject-verb order is reversed. In Choice (B), the auxiliary *does* is unnecessary and incorrect. In Choice (D), the verb *are* is repetitive. "The Consumer Price Index lists how much every car *is*" would also be correct. (Refer to Patterns, Problem 124, page 230.)
22. **(A)** Because it is a prepositional phrase, in a comparison *as every nation* should be *like every nation. As* functions as a conjunction. *Like* functions as a preposition. (Refer to Patterns, Problem 88, page 187.)
23. **(C)** A logical conclusion about the past is expressed by *must have* and a participle. Choices (A), (B), and (D) are not logical because they imply that the theater will act to restore itself. (Refer to Patterns, Problem 7, page 80.)
24. **(A)** The verb *thought* establishes a point of view in the past. *Will* should be *would* in order to maintain the point of view. (Refer to Style, Problem 2, page 253.)
25. **(D)** Ideas in a series should be expressed by parallel structures. *To plant* should be *planting* to provide for parallelism with the *-ing* forms *plowing* and *rotating.* (Refer to Style, Problem 17, page 271.)

Section 3: Reading

1. **(A)** "Webster's Work" is the best title because it states the main idea of the passage. Choice (B) is incorrect because Webster's dictionaries represent only part of the work referred to in the passage. Choices (C) and (D) are mentioned briefly in the discussion, but are not the most important topics.
2. **(D)** In the context of this passage, inadequate could best be replaced by unsatisfactory Choices (A), (B), and (C) are not accepted definitions of the word.

3. **(C)** "…he discovered how inadequate the available schoolbooks were for the children of a new and independent nation…. In response to the need for truly American textbooks, Webster published *A Grammatical Institute of the English Language*." Choice (A) is a result of having written *A Grammatical Institute*, not a reason for writing it. Choice (B) contradicts the fact that British books were available, but not appropriate. Choice (D) is not mentioned and may not be concluded from information in the passage.
4. **(D)** "…*The American Spelling Book*…provided him with a considerable income for the rest of his life." Choices (A), (B), and (C) are all publications by Webster, but the income afforded by each is not mentioned and may not be concluded from information in the passage.
5. In the context of this passage, popular is closest in meaning to the phrase very successful. No other words or phrases in the **bold** text are close to the meaning of the word popular.
6. **(A)** In the context of this passage, considerable is closest in meaning to large. Choices (B), (C), and (D) are not accepted definitions of the word.
7. **(C)** "Published…in 1828, *An American Dictionary of the English Language* has become the recognized authority for usage…." Choice (A) refers to the date that Webster finished his study of English and began writing the dictionary. Choice (B) refers to the date that Webster began work on the dictionary. Choice (D) refers to the date that Webster finished writing the dictionary, not to the date that it was published.
8. **(D)** "Webster's purpose in writing it [the dictionary] was to demonstrate that the American language was developing distinct meanings, pronunciations, and spellings from those of British English." Choices (A), (B), and (C) would change the meaning of the sentence.
9. "Webster's purpose in writing it [an American dictionary] was to demonstrate that the American language was developing distinct meanings, pronunciations, and spellings from those of British English." Quotation from sentence 4, paragraph 2.
10. **(C)** In the context of this passage, distinct is closest in meaning to different. Choices (A), (B), and (D) are not accepted definitions.
11. **(C)** "He [Webster] is responsible for advancing the form color…instead of colour." Choices (A), (B), and (D) are British English spellings.
12. **(A)** Choice (A) is the author's main purpose because the passage refers to the San Andreas Fault specifically. The general information referred to in Choices (B), (C), and (D) is not mentioned and may not be concluded from information in the passage.
13. **(B)** "The San Andreas Fault is a fracture at the congruence of two major plates of the Earth's crust." Choice (A) refers to the plates, not to the fracture. Choices (C) and (D) refer to the results of the movement along the fracture, not to the fault.
14. **(C)** In the context of this passage, originates could best be replaced by begins. Choices (A), (B), and (D) are not accepted definitions of the word.
15. **(C)** "Its western side always moves north in relation to its eastern side." Choices (A), (B), and (D) contradict the fact that the western side always moves north, not in any other direction.
16. **(D)** "Its western side always moves north in relation to its [the fault's] eastern side." Choices (A), (B), and (C) would change the meaning of the sentence.
17. **(D)** intermittent means occasional. Choices (A), (B), and (C) are not accepted definitions of the word.
18. **(C)** "Tremors are not unusual along the San Andreas Fault…." Choice (B) contradicts the fact that tremors are not unusual. Choices (A) and (D) are not mentioned and may not be concluded from information in the passage.
19. **(A)** "Californians have long anticipated the recurrence of what they refer to as the 'Big One,' a chain reaction of destructive earthquakes…." Choices (B), (C), or (D) would change the meaning of the sentence.
20. In the context of this passage, devastating is closest in meaning to destructive. No other words or phrases in the **bold** text are close to the meaning of the word destructive.
21. "Californians have long anticipated the recurrence of what they refer to as the 'Big One,' a chain reaction of destructive earth-

quakes that would measure near 8 on the Richter scale, similar in intensity to those [earthquakes] that occurred in 1857 and 1906." Other choices would change the meaning of the sentence.

22. **(D)** "...the San Andreas Fault...runs north in an irregular line...." The word *uneven* in Choice (D) means irregular. Choice (A) contradicts the fact that the line is irregular. Choices (B) and (C) are not mentioned and may not be concluded from information in the passage.
23. **(B)** "The Structure of an Insect" is the best title because it states the main idea of the passage. Choice (C) is a secondary idea that is used to develop the main idea. Choices (A) and (D) are not mentioned and may not be concluded from information in the passage.
24. In the context of this passage, the word segmented is closest in meaning to subdivided. No other words or phrases in the **bold** text are close to the meaning of the word subdivided.
25. **(C)** "Features of the mouth parts are very helpful in classifying the many kinds of insects." Choices (A), (B), and (D) are discussed, but not as a basis for classification.
26. **(A)** In the context of this passage, the word normal is closest in meaning to common. Choices (B), (C), and (D) are not accepted definitions of the word.
27. **(A)** "A labrum above and a labium below are similar to an upper and lower lip." Choice (B) is compared to Choice (D). Choice (C) is discussed, but not compared to anything.
28. **(B)** "...the coiled drinking tube...called the proboscis...[is] composed...of modified maxillae." Choice (A) refers to food, not to the proboscis that is used in reaching it. Choices (C) and (D) are not mentioned and may not be concluded from information in the passage.
29. **(C)** "In a mosquito or an aphid, mandibles and maxillae are modified to sharp stylets." The insect referred to in choice (A) has mandibles similar to jaws, not sharp stylets. The insect referred to in Choice (B) has a proboscis. The insect referred to in Choice (D) has a spongelike mouth pad.
30. **(A)** In the context of this passage, drill through could best be replaced by penetrate. Choices (B), (C), and (D) are not accepted definitions of the phrase.
31. **(C)** "In a housefly, the expanding labium forms a spongelike mouth pad that it [the housefly] can use to stamp over the surface of food." Choices (A), (B), and (D) would change the meaning of the sentence.
32. "An active part of the natural food cycle, insects provide nutrition for animals and devour waste products of other life forms. Although some insects, like the cockroach, have remained essentially unchanged for eons, most insects adapt readily to changing environmental conditions." The connection between the two sentences occurs on the paragraph level. The first sentence in the paragraph introduces the idea that insects are adaptable, and the four sentences that follow provide examples. The inserted sentence is a conclusion that reinforces the first sentence.
33. **(D)** Because the passage is a statement of scientific facts written from an objective point of view, it must be concluded that the purpose is to inform. Choices (A) and (B) are improbable because the passage is not written from a subjective point of view. Choice (C) is improbable because of the scientific content.
34. **(D)** The primary topic is the characteristics of protozoans. Choices (A), (B), and (C) are important to the discussion and provide details that support the primary topic.
35. **(D)** In the context of this passage, minute could best be replaced by very small. Choices (A), (B), and (C) are not accepted definitions of the word.
36. **(B)** "The protozoans...[consist] of a single cell of protoplasm...." Choices (A), (C), and (D) contradict the fact that the cell of a protozoan is composed of protoplasm.
37. In the context of this passage, locomotion is closest in meaning to motility. No other words or phrases in the **bold** text are close to the meaning of the word motility.
38. **(C)** Choice (C) is a restatement of the sentence referred to in the passage. *Motility* means the manner of movement. Choices (A), (B), and (D) would change the meaning of the original sentence.
39. **(C)** "The Sarcodina, which include amoebae...." Choices (A) and (B) refer to two other groups of protozoans that do not include amoebae. Choice (D) refers to the basis of classification for the three major groups of protozoans.

40. **(C)** "...a large nucleus that regulates growth but decomposes during reproduction..." Choice (A) refers to the small, not the large, nucleus. Choice (B) contradicts the fact that the small nucleus contains the genetic code for the large nucleus. Choice (D) contradicts the fact that the large nucleus decomposes during reproduction.
41. **(A)** "Protozoans are considered animals because...they do not live on simple organic compounds." Choices (B) and (C) refer to characteristics of some protozoans, not to a reason why they are considered animals. Choice (D) contradicts the fact that they have only one cell, although current research is calling that into question.
42. **(A)** "Current research into this phenomenon along with investigations carried out with advanced microscopes may necessitate a redefinition of what constitutes a protozoan, even calling into question the basic premise that they [protozoans] have only one cell." Choices (B), (C), and (D) would change the meaning of the sentence.
43. "They are fantastically diverse, but three major groups may be identified on the basis of their motility." Quotation from sentence 4, paragraph 1.
44. **(A)** In the context of this passage, uniformly is closest in meaning to in the same way. Choices (B), (C), and (D) are not accepted definitions of the word.
45. **(C)** Choice (A) is mentioned in sentence 3, paragraph 4. Choice (B) is mentioned in sentence 1, paragraph 1. Choice (D) is mentioned in sentence 4, paragraph 4. Protozoans consist of a single cell, although in the case of Ciliata, the cell may have a larger nucleus and a smaller nucleus.

Model Test 4—Computer-Assisted TOEFL

Section 1: Listening

1. **(C)** *I wish I could* is an idiomatic expression that means the speaker would like to but is not able to do something. Choice (A) refers to a party that the Association, not the woman, will have. Choice (B) refers to what the woman would like to do, not to what she will probably do. Choice (D) is not mentioned and may not be concluded from information in the conversation.
2. **(A)** Since they have just enough time to get there, it must be concluded that they will leave immediately. Choices (B), (C), and (D) are not mentioned and may not be concluded from information in the conversation.
3. **(A)** The man said that he went to see the foreign student advisor. Choice (D) refers to what the advisor did, not to what the man did himself. The Passport Office is in Washington, D.C., but Choices (B) and (C) are not mentioned and may not be concluded from information in the conversation.
4. **(B)** "I'd write a rough draft and ask Dr. Tyler to look at it." A "rough draft" is a preliminary version. Choice (C) contradicts the fact that the woman says to show the draft to Dr. Tyler, not to her. Choices (A) and (D) are not mentioned and may not be concluded from information in the conversation.
5. **(D)** To *put up with* is an idiomatic expression that means to tolerate. It must be concluded that the students do not like Dr. Clark. Choices (A), (B), and (C) are not paraphrases of the expression, and may not be concluded from information in the conversation.
6. **(C)** The references to a *textbook* and a *movie* in Choices (B) and (D) relate to the assignment for the class. Choice (A) is not mentioned and may not be concluded from information in the conversation.
7. **(B)** Since the man asks whether the woman is Sally Harrison's sister, it must be concluded that he assumed the women were sisters. Choice (A) refers to who the woman is, not to the man's assumption. Choices (C) and (D) contradict the fact that the woman is Sally Harrison's cousin.
8. **(C)** Since the woman says that she can't find her pen, it must be concluded that finding her pen is the problem. Choices (A), (B), and (D) are not mentioned and may not be concluded from information in the conversation.
9. **(A)** Because John agreed to arrive at eight-thirty but the man estimates that he won't arrive until nine o'clock, or one half-hour later, it must be concluded that John is usually late. Choice (B) refers to the time when John agreed to arrive, not to a conclusion that the man wants us to make. Choice (C) contradicts both the fact that John had agreed to come and the fact that the man estimates John's arrival at nine o'clock. Choice (D) contradicts the fact that the man estimates John's arrival one half-hour after he has agreed to arrive.
10. **(B)** "…it didn't turn out quite like I thought it would." Choice (A) contradicts the fact that the man knows how it turned out. Choice (C) contradicts the fact that the man says the experiment is finished. Choice (D) is not mentioned and may not be concluded from information in the conversation.
11. **(A)** Since the man expresses exasperation about the woman's attention to her classes, he implies that she does not put much effort in her studies. Choice (D) is true, but it is not what the man implies by his comment. Choices (B) and (C) are not mentioned and may not be concluded from information in the conversation.
12. **(D)** "…I'd try some over-the-counter medication…." Choice (A) refers to the woman's plan, not to the man's suggestion. Choice (B) refers to the idiom "do the job" which means to cure. Choice (C) refers to the place to buy nonprescription medicine [over the counter], not to the man's suggestion.
13. **(A)** To *give it all you've got* is an idiomatic expression that means to try your best. Choices (B), (C), and (D) are not paraphrases of the expression and may not be concluded from information in the conversation.
14. **(A)** Since the woman denies the man's

request for a few more minutes, it must be concluded that the man must stop working on the test. Choice (B) contradicts the fact that the man cannot have a few more minutes to finish. Choice (D) contradicts the fact that the test is in progress, not about to start. Choice (C) is not mentioned and may not be concluded from information in the conversation.

15. **(C)** Since the man thinks they are using a different book this semester, he implies that the textbook may have been changed. Choice (D) contradicts the fact that they are discussing plans for this semester. Choices (A) and (B) are not mentioned and may not be concluded from information in the conversation.
16. **(D)** Since the woman questions whether Sally would like a bike, she implies that Sally may prefer a different gift. Choice (A) refers to the man's idea, not to the woman's comment. Choices (B) and (C) are not mentioned and may not be concluded from information in the conversation.
17. **(A)** "...get some rest and try it again later." Choices (B) and (D) contradict the fact that the woman recommends rest. Choice (C) is not mentioned and may not be concluded from information in the conversation.
18. **(B)** "...the question is not whether the metric system should be introduced in the United States, but rather, how it should be introduced." Choice (A) contradicts the fact that the question is not whether the metric system should be introduced. Choices (C) and (D) are not mentioned and may not be concluded from information in the discussion.
19. **(C)** "They [cans and packages] are marked in both ounces and grams.... And the weather reporters on radio and TV give the temperature readings in both degrees Fahrenheit and degrees Celsius now.... Some road signs have the distances marked in both miles and kilometers...." Choice (A) contradicts the fact that the temperature readings are in both degrees Fahrenheit and degrees Celsius. Choice (B) contradicts the fact that the road signs have distances marked in both miles and kilometers. Choice (D) contradicts the fact that cans and packages are marked in both ounces and grams.
20. **(D)** "I [Professor Baker] agree that a gradual adoption is better for those of us who have already been exposed to the English system of measurement. But I would favor teaching only metrics in the elementary schools." Choice (A) refers to the woman's suggestion, not to Professor Baker's opinion. The opinions expressed in Choices (B) and (C) are not mentioned and may not be concluded from information in the discussion.
21. **(D)** Because Professor Baker invites a free exchange of ideas and does not criticize his students, it must be concluded that he is cooperative. The words in Choices (A), (B), and (C) do not describe Professor Baker's manner in the conversation.
22. **(D)** "...an extensive research effort, which, in cooperation with private industry, has transferred technology to the international marketplace." Choices (A), (B), and (C) are secondary themes used to develop the main theme of the talk.
23. **(A)** "Hundreds of everyday products can be traced back to the space mission, including cordless electric tools, airtight food packaging.... ultrasound...." Choice (A) is not mentioned and may not be concluded from information in the talk.
24. **(D)** "First used to detect flaws in spacecraft, ultrasound is now standard equipment in almost every hospital...." Choice (A) refers to implants and pacemakers, not to ultrasound. Choices (B) and (C) are not mentioned and may not be concluded from information in the conversation.
25. **(B)** "...archaeologists have been able to explore the earth...cities...have been located ...and the sea floor has been mapped using photographs from outer space." Choices (A), (C), and (D) are not mentioned and may not be concluded from information in the conversation.
26. **(B)** "Is there any way you could give me an excused absence...." The word *note* in Choice (A) refers to the notes that Beverly plans to borrow from her friend Gloria, not to a note she has for the professor. Choice (C) contradicts the fact that she never misses class. Choice (D) is not mentioned and may not be concluded from information in the conversation.
27. **(D)** "I have a family emergency, and I am needed at home for at least a week." Choice (A) contradicts the fact that Beverly sits in

front to see better. Choice (B) refers to the professor's concern, not to the student's problem. Choice (C) contradicts the fact that the professor says she never misses class.

28. **(B)** "If you need some clarification, I can meet with you for a few minutes before class on Monday." Choice (A) contradicts the fact that the woman has already arranged to borrow notes from her friend, Gloria. Choices (C) and (D) are not mentioned and may not be concluded from information in the conversation.
29. **(B)** "You're very welcome. And I hope that everything goes well for you at home." Choice (A) contradicts the fact that the professor spends so much time talking with Beverly. Choice (C) describes the woman's attitude, not that of the professor. The word *confused* in Choice (D) refers to the professor's comment about how difficult it can be to understand someone else's notes, not to his attitude.
30. **(C)** The speaker discusses the history, economy, and landmarks of San Francisco. Choices (A), (B), and (D) are secondary themes used to support the main purpose of the talk, an orientation to the City of San Francisco.
31. **(D)** "...the name was changed from Yerba Buena to San Francisco." Choice (A) refers to the name of the bridge, not a settlement. Choice (B) refers to a mission established before Yerba Buena was settled. Choice (C) refers to a military post established before the settlement of Yerba Buena.
32. **(A)** "...in 1848, with the discovery of gold, the population grew to ten thousand." Choice (B) refers to what happened in 1869, not 1848. Choice (C) refers to what happened in 1937. Choice (D) refers to what happened in 1862.
33. **(C)** "The bridge, which is more than one mile long, spans the harbor from San Francisco to Marin County...." Choice (A) refers to the length of the Port of San Francisco, not to the length of the Golden Gate Bridge. Choice (B) refers to the altitude of the city. The number in Choice (D) refers to the number of tons of cargo handled at the Port of San Francisco every year.
34. **(A)** "Today we will discuss Transcendentalism...." Choices (B), (C), and (D) are secondary themes that are used to develop the main theme of the lecture.
35. **(C)** "Today we will discuss Transcendentalism, which is a philosophical and literary movement that developed in New England in the early nineteenth century." Choices (A), (B), and (D) are not mentioned and may not be concluded from information in the talk.
36. **(C)** "This group [the Transcendental Club] was the advance guard of a reaction against the rigid Puritanism of the period, especially insofar as it emphasized society at the expense of the individual." Choices (A) and (D) refer to the Transcendental Club, not to the Puritans. Choice (B) contradicts the fact that the Transcendental Club reacted against the Puritans.
37. **(D)** "Thoreau built a small cabin along the shores of Walden Pond...he published an account of his experiences in *Walden*...." Choices (A), (B), and (C) are not mentioned and may not be concluded from information in the talk.
38. **(D)** "Do you have any experience working in a library?" Choice (A) contradicts the fact that the man does his own research in the library and knows how to use most of the search equipment. The phrase *teaching position* in Choice (B) refers to a job that the man had before he came back to school, not to a position that he is applying for now. The phrase *library orientation* in Choice (C) refers to one of the responsibilities of the position that the man is applying for, not to training that he is receiving now.
39. **(C)** "I am working toward my doctorate at the University...." Choice (A) contradicts the fact that he was a teacher before he came back to school, not now. Choice (B) contradicts the fact that he has never been an employee in a library. The word *computer* in Choice (D) refers to the type of library searches that the students need to do for their term papers, not to the man's background.
40. **(C)** "I'm writing my dissertation....I plan to do that [write my dissertation] after work and on my days off." Choice (B) contradicts the fact that he has most of his own research finished. Choice (D) contradicts the fact that he is not taking any classes now. Choice (A) is not mentioned and may not be concluded from information in the conversation.

41. **(D)** "...when could you start? Right away!" Choices (A) and (B) contradict the fact that he will complete his dissertation after work and on his days off, and he will graduate after the dissertation is complete. Choice (C) refers to when he will write his dissertation, not to when he will be available for work.
42. **(A) (C)** "...a solar collector is mounted...at a...steep angle...with a southern exposure." Choices (B) and (D) are not mentioned and may not be concluded from information in the lecture.
43. **(B)** Choice (A) is a solar collector. Choice (C) is a backup heater. Choice (D) is the space under the collector.
44. **(B)** "...one of the problems with solar heat is the intermittent nature of solar radiation as an energy source. Especially in climates where the sun does not shine regularly...." Choices (A), (C), and (D) are not mentioned as problems and may not be concluded from information in the lecture.
45. **(C)** "The principle [of the solar orbit system] would be basically the same as that of the much simpler model that I showed you." Choice (A) contradicts the fact that the system is costly. Choice (B) contradicts the fact that he identifies scientists as those involved in working on the project and does not include himself. Choice (D) is true, but it is not the reason that the professor mentioned the project.
46. **(B)** "...is this where I request a tutor?" Choice (A) contradicts the fact that the man asks for a tutor, not for a position. Choice (D) contradicts the fact that the woman is helping the man to arrange for tutoring. Choice (C) is not mentioned and may not be concluded from information in the conversation.
47. **(D)** "Which course do you need help in? English...Composition...." The word *literature* in Choice (A) refers to a question that the woman asked, not to the course that the man needs help in. Choice (B) refers to the course that Janine was tutored for, not to the course for which the man needs a tutor. Choice (C) refers to the other course that Janine tutors in, not to the course that the man will receive tutoring in.
48. **(D)** "This is a free service...." Choices (A), (B), and (C) contradict the fact that the tutoring is a free service.
49. **(C)** "...should I just come back on Tuesday at four? Yes." Choices (A) and (B) refer to the times for the man's classes. Choice (D) refers to one of the times for which the man scheduled tutoring, but not the first session.
50. **(B)** "...bring your books...a syllabus, your class notes...." Choice (A) contradicts the fact that the service is free. The word *composition* in Choice (D) refers to the course in which the man will receive tutoring, not to an essay that he should bring to his tutoring session. Choice (C) is not mentioned and may not be concluded from information in the conversation.

Section 2: Structure

1. **(D)** A dependent clause modifies an independent clause. Choice (A) has two clause markers, *which* and *that*. Choice (B) is a verb followed by a noun and a clause marker. Choice (C) does not have a clause marker. (Refer to Patterns, Problem 138, page 248.)
2. **(B)** A passive infinitive is used to express purpose. Choice (A) is a noun. Choice (C) is an *-ing* form. Choice (D) is a present verb. (Refer to Patterns, Problem 33, page 114.)
3. **(C)** Most adverbs of manner are formed by adding *-ly* to adjectives. *Rapid* should be *rapidly* to qualify the manner in which automatic data processing has grown. (Refer to Patterns, Problem 126, page 233.)
4. **(D)** *As well as* should be *and*, which is used in correlation with *both*. (Refer to Patterns, Problem 116, page 220.)
5. **(B)** A cardinal number is used after a noun. *The* is used with an ordinal number before a noun. In Choices (A) and (C) an ordinal number is used after, not before a noun. Choice (D) is incomplete because it does not include *the* before the ordinal number. (Refer to Patterns, Problem 77, page 173.)
6. **(A)** Repetition of the subject by a subject pronoun is redundant. *They* should be deleted. (Refer to Style, Problem 21, page 276.)
7. **(B)** *As soon as* is an idiom that introduces a limit of time. The phrase *as soon as* is followed by a noun and a simple present verb. Choice (A) is a modal and a verb word, not a simple present verb. Choice (D) is a noun. Choice (C) uses a present but not a simple pre-

sent form. (Refer to Patterns, Problem 135, page 244.)

8. **(C)** Because dates require ordinal numbers, *twelve* should be *twelfth*. (Refer to Patterns, Problem 134, page 242.)
9. **(B)** *Influence* should be *influential*. *Influence* is a noun. *Influential* is an adjective. (Refer to Style, Problem 30, page 288.)
10. **(C)** *Weathering* is the subject of the verb *is*. Choices (A) and (B) are redundant and indirect. Choice (D) is an *-ing* form, not a verb. (Refer to Style, Problem 19, page 274.)
11. **(D)** *Such as* introduces the example *shrimps and clams,* which must refer to a plural antecedent. *Sea creature* should be *sea creatures*. (Refer to Patterns, Problem 109, page 212.)
12. **(C)** Ideas in a series should be expressed by parallel structures. *Encouraging* should be *to encourage* to provide for parallelism with the infinitive *to discourage*. (Refer to Style, Problem 17, page 271.)
13. **(B)** *Combination* should be *combine*. *Combination* is a noun. *Combine* is a verb. (Refer to Style, Problem 30, page 288.)
14. **(D)** The verb *to consider* requires an *-ing* form in the complement. Choice (A) is an infinitive, not an *-ing* form. Choice (B) is a participle. Choice (C) is a verb word. (Refer to Patterns, Problem 3, page 74.)
15. **(C)** *Presumable* should be *presumably*. *Presumable* is an adjective. *Presumably* is an adverb. (Refer to Style, Problem 30, page 288.)
16. **(A)** The verb *reported* establishes a point of view in the past. *Discovers* should be *discovered* in order to maintain the point of view. (Refer to Style, Problem 2, page 253.)
17. **(D)** Because the verb *refuse* requires an infinitive in the complement, *giving* should be *to give*. (Refer to Patterns, Problem 2, page 73.)
18. **(C)** Object pronouns are used after prepositions such as *by*. Choice (A) is a reflexive pronoun, not an object pronoun. Choices (B) and (D) are possessive pronouns. "The work was done *by herself*" without the repetitive word *alone* would also be correct. (Refer to Patterns, Problem 45, page 130.)
19. **(C)** There must be agreement between subject and verb. *Has* should be *have* to agree with the plural subject *the few cities*. (Refer to Style, Problem 9, page 261.)
20. **(D)** Ideas in a series should be expressed by parallel structures. *Increasing* should be *to increase* to provide for parallelism with the infinitive *to enrich*. (Refer to Style, Problem 17, page 271.)
21. **(D)** An appositive does not require connectors or an additional subject. Choices (A) and (C) include connecting conjunctions. Choice (B) is an anticipatory *it* clause, not an appositive. (Refer to Style, Problem 7, page 259.)
22. **(A)** *Would have* and a participle in the result requires *had* and a participle in the condition. Because *would not have evolved* is used in the result, *did not filter out* should be *had not filtered out* in the condition. (Refer to Patterns, Problem 24, page 102.)
23. **(B)** Consecutive order must be maintained, along with parallel structure. (Refer to Patterns, Problem 75 and Style, Problem 17, pages 170 and 271.)
24. **(D)** Ideas in a series should be expressed by parallel structures. *Swimming* should be *swim* to provide for parallelism with the verb words *walk, watch,* and *fish*. (Refer to Style, Problem 17, page 271.)
25. **(D)** There must be agreement between pronoun and antecedent. *Its* should be *their* to agree with the plural antecedent *books*. (Refer to Style, Problem 11, page 263.)

Section 3: Reading

1. **(A)** The other choices are secondary ideas that are used to develop the main idea, "precipitation." Choices (B), (C), and (D) provide details and examples.
2. **(C)** "Precipitation [is] commonly referred to as rainfall." Choices (A), (B), and (D) are not mentioned and may not be concluded from information in the passage.
3. **(B)** "Precipitation, commonly referred to as rainfall, is a measure of the quantity of water in the form of either rain, hail, or snow." Choice (A) is incomplete because it does not include hail and snow. Humidity referred to in Choices (C) and (D) is not mentioned and may not be concluded from information in the passage.
4. **(A)** "The average annual precipitation over the whole of the United States is thirty-six inches." Choice (B) refers to the formula for

computing precipitation, not to the annual rainfall over the United States. Choice (C) refers to the amount of rain recorded in New York State, not in the United States. Choice (D) refers to the total annual precipitation recorded in New York State.

5. **(B)** "A general formula for computing the precipitation of snowfall is that ten inches of snow is equal to one inch of precipitation." Forty inches of snow divided by 10 inches per one inch of precipitation is four inches, or one-third foot. Choices (A), (C), and (D) may not be computed on the basis of the formula in the passage.
6. **(C)** In the context of this passage, proximity to is closest in meaning to nearness to. Choices (A), (B), and (D) are not accepted definitions of the phrase.
7. "Most of the precipitation in the United States is brought originally by prevailing winds from the Pacific Ocean, the Gulf of Mexico, the Atlantic Ocean, and the Great Lakes." Quotation from sentence 2, paragraph 2.
8. **(D)** "...the Pacific Coast receives more annual precipitation than the Atlantic Coast." Choices (A), (B), and (C) refer to the prevailing winds, not to the highest annual precipitation.
9. **(B)** Choice (A) is mentioned in sentence 5, paragraph 1. Choices (C) and (D) are mentioned in sentence 1, paragraph 2. Choice (B) is not mentioned and may not be concluded from information in the passage.
10. **(A)** In the context of this passage, substantially could best be replaced by fundamentally. Choices (B), (C), and (D) are not accepted definitions of the word.
11. **(B)** "East of the Rocky Mountains, the annual precipitation decreases substantially from that [precipitation] west of the Rocky Mountains." Choices (A), (C), and (D) would change the meaning of the sentence.
12. **(D)** Choices (A), (B), and (C) are important to the discussion, and provide details that support the main topic, "women's suffrage."
13. **(C)** In the context of this passage, ban most nearly means to prohibit. Choices (A), (B), and (D) are not accepted definitions of the word.
14. "They were fighting against a belief that voting should be tied to land ownership, and because land was owned by men, and in some cases by their widows, only those who held the greatest stake in government, that is the male landowners, were considered worthy of the vote." Quotation from sentence 5, paragraph 1.
15. **(A)** In the context of this passage, primarily is closest in meaning to above all. Choices (B), (C), and (D) are not accepted definitions of the word.
16. In the context of this passage, better is closest in meaning to improve. No other words or phrases in the **bold** text are close to the meaning of the word improve.
17. **(D)** "When the Civil War ended...the Fifteenth Amendment...granted...suffrage to blacks...." *Suffrage* means the right to vote. Choice (B) contradicts the fact that the bill was presented to Congress in 1878, not immediately after the Civil War. Choice (C) refers to the fact that the eastern states resisted the women's suffrage bill, not the end of the Civil War. Choice (A) is not mentioned and may not be concluded from information in the passage.
18. **(D)** *Suffrage* means the right to vote; the exercise of such a right. Choice (A) is a definition of the word *suffering*, not *suffrage*. Choices (B) and (C) are related to the word *suffrage*, but they are not accepted definitions of it.
19. **(A)** "A women's suffrage bill had been presented to every Congress since 1878 but it [the bill] continually failed to pass until 1920, when the Nineteenth Amendment granted women the right to vote." Choices (B), (C), and (D) would change the meaning of the sentence.
20. **(C)** "...the Nineteenth Amendment granted women the right to vote." Choice (A) refers to the Fifteenth, not the Nineteenth Amendment. Choice (B) refers to the Fourteenth Amendment. Choice (D) is not mentioned and may not be concluded from information in the passage.
21. **(D)** "...1920 when the Nineteenth Amendment granted women the right to vote." Choice (A) refers to the date when the Civil War ended. Choice (B) refers to the date when the Fifteenth Amendment was adopted granting blacks, not women, the right to vote. Choice (C) refers to the date when the

bill to grant women the right to vote was presented to Congress, not to the date that it was passed and became law.

22. **(B)** The other choices are secondary topics that are used to develop the primary topic, "characteristics and varieties of the *Acacia*." Choices (A), (C), and (D) are important details and examples.

23. In the context of this passage, valued is closest in meaning to prized. No other words or phrases in the **bold** text are close to the meaning of the word prized.

24. **(C)** "Only about a dozen of the three hundred Australian varieties grow well in the southern United States." Choice (A) refers to the number of species identified, not to the number that grow well in the United States. Choice (B) refers to the number of species that grow well in Australia, not in the southern United States. Choice (D) refers to the number of species that have flowers, not to the total number of species that grow well in the southern United States.

25. **(A)** In the context of this passage, thrive is closest in meaning to the phrase grow well. Choices (B), (C), and (D) are not accepted definitions of the word.

26. **(B)** "Although nearly five hundred species of *Acacia* have been identified, only about a dozen of the three hundred Australian varieties grow well in the southern United States, and of these [varieties], only three are flowering." Choices (A), (C), and (D) would change the meaning of the sentence.

27. **(C)** "The *Silver Wattle*, although very similar to the *Bailey Acacia*, grows twice as high." Choice (A) refers to the *Sydney Golden Wattle*, not to the *Silver Wattle*. Choices (B) and (D) refer to the *Black Acacia*.

28. **(A)** In the context of this passage, flat most nearly means smooth. Choices (B), (C), and (D) are not accepted definitions of the word.

29. **(B)** In the context of this passage, showy could best be replaced by elaborate. Choices (A), (C), and (D) are not accepted definitions of the word.

30. **(D)** "...the *Black Acacia* or *Blackwood*, has dark green leaves and unobtrusive blossoms." The species referred to in Choices (A), (B), and (C) have fragrant clusters of yellow flowers.

31. **(B)** "...the *Black Acacia* is valuable for its dark wood which is used in making cabinets and furniture." Choices (A), (C), and (D) are not mentioned and may not be concluded from information in the passage.

32. **(C)** "...the pale yellow blossoms appear in August in Australia." Choice (A) refers to the month that the *Acacia* blooms in the United States, not in Australia. Choices (B) and (D) refer to the reversal of seasons in the northern and southern hemispheres, but not to the blossoming of the *Acacia*.

33. "Some acacias are popular in landscaping because of their graceful shapes, lacey foliage, and fragrant blossoms. Other *Acacia* varieties are valued for the sticky resin, called gum Arabic or gum acacia, used widely in medicines, foods, and perfumes, for the dark dense wood prized for making pianos, or for the bark, rich in tannin, a dark, acidic substance used to cure the hides of animals, transforming them into leather." The connection between the two sentences occurs in the first words—*Some* and *Other*, which determine consecutive order.

34. **(A)** "A History of New York City" is the best title because it states the main idea of the passage. Choices (C) and (D) are details used to develop the main idea. Choice (B) is not specific enough.

35. **(C)** "Peter Minuit...negotiated with Indian chiefs for the purchase of Manhattan Island for merchandise...." Choices (A) and (B) refer to the value of the merchandise, not to what the Native Americans received. Choice (D) refers to where the Dutch settlements were located.

36. **(B)** "...Dutch settlements in North America known as New Amsterdam...." Choice (C) refers to the location of the land that was purchased from the Native Americans. Choices (A) and (D) are not mentioned and may not be concluded from information in the passage.

37. **(A)** Choice (A) is a restatement of the sentence in the passage. Since offers were extended throughout Europe, it must be assumed that other Europeans were given opportunities to immigrate.

38. **(C)** In the context of this passage, heterogeneous could best be replaced by diverse. Choices (A), (B), and (D) are not accepted

definitions of the word.

39. **(C)** "...offers, generous by the standards of the era, were extended throughout Europe. Consequently, the settlement became the most heterogeneous of the North American colonies." Choice (A) contradicts the fact that it was New Amsterdam, not the Dutch West India Company, that the English acquired. Choices (B) and (D) are not mentioned and may not be concluded from information in the passage.

40. "Among the multilingual settlers was a large group of English colonists from Connecticut and Massachusetts who supported the English King's claim to all of New Netherlands set out in a charter that gave the territory to his [the English King's] brother James, Duke of York." Other choices would change the meaning of the sentence.

41. **(A)** In the context of this passage, formidable is closest in meaning to powerful. Choices (B), (C), and (D) are not accepted definitions of the word.

42. "When the English acquired the island, the village of New Amsterdam was renamed New York in honor of the Duke." Quotation from sentence 1, paragraph 4.

43. **(B)** "After the war, it [New York] was selected as the first capital of the United States." Choices (A), (C), and (D) would change the meaning of the sentence.

44. **(B)** "After the war, it [New York] was selected as the first capital of the United States." Choice (A) refers to the former name for New York, which had already been changed when it became the first capital. Choices (C) and (D) refer to cities that became the capital after New York.

45. **(D)** "Three centuries after his initial trade...Minuit's tiny investment was worth more than seven billion dollars." Choice (A) refers to the date that the Dutch purchased Manhattan Island from the Native Americans. Choice (B) refers to the date one century after the purchase. Choice (C) refers to the date three decades after the purchase.

Model Test 5—Computer-Assisted TOEFL

Section 1: Listening

1. (**D**) The man offers to get some paper at the bookstore. Choice (A) is incorrect because it is the woman, not the man, who wants to borrow some typing paper. Choice (B) contradicts the fact that the man doesn't have any paper either. Choice (C) is not mentioned and may not be concluded from information in the conversation.
2. (**B**) "...walk three more blocks ..." Since the woman gives directions for walking, it must be concluded that the man is not driving a car. Choice (C) contradicts the fact that the man calls the woman *Miss*. Choices (A) and (D) are not mentioned and may not be concluded from information in the conversation.
3. (**C**) To *fall through* is an idiomatic expression that means not to happen as planned. Choice (D) contradicts the fact that he planned to go to summer school. Choices (A) and (B) are not mentioned and may not be concluded from information in the conversation.
4. (**B**) Choices (A), (C), and (D) are mentioned in reference to the main topic of discussion in the apartment.
5. (**B**) Since the woman mentions that Dr. Taylor does not interact with her in class despite her good grades, she implies that she is not sure how Dr. Taylor feels. Choices (C) and (D) contradict the fact that she was the only one who received an A on her paper. Choice (A) is not mentioned and may not be concluded from information in the conversation.
6. (**C**) Since the man inquires whether she has asked Sandy, he implies that she should ask her. Choice (A) refers to the payment for participation, not to the man's suggestion. Choice (B) refers to the woman's request, not to the man's suggestion. Choice (D) refers to the experiment in psychology, not to a person that the woman should see.
7. (**A**) Because *either* means that the speaker is including herself in her statement, it must be concluded that the woman did not go to the meeting. The man said that he did not go because of a headache. Choice (B) contradicts the use of the word *either* in the woman's question. Choice (C) contradicts the man's negative response to the question of whether he went to the meeting. Choice (D) contradicts both the use of the word *either* and the man's negative response.
8. (**B**) "How about [buying] a nice pen?" Choice (C) refers to the card that the woman has already purchased, not to the man's idea. Choice (D) contradicts the fact that the man offers a suggestion for a gift. Choice (A) is not mentioned and may not be concluded from information in the conversation.
9. (**D**) To *not make up one's mind* is an idiomatic expression that means to be undecided. Choices (A) and (C) contradict the fact that she is still considering both alternatives. Choice (B) contradicts the fact that she has a choice.
10. (**A**) Since the woman asks whether the man can work and go to school, she implies that he may be taking on too much. Choices (B), (C), and (D) are not mentioned and may not be concluded from information in the conversation.
11. (**C**) Since the man suggests that the woman buy postcards, it must be concluded that she should send postcards to her family. Choice (B) contradicts the fact that she does not have time to write a letter. Choice (A) refers to the man's family, not to the woman's family. Choice (D) is not mentioned and may not be concluded from information in the conversation.
12. (**B**) Choices (A), (C), and (D) are all mentioned as they relate to the main topic of the conversation, "where the woman will go to school."
13. (**B**) Since the man says that ticket number 32 is in room 27, the woman will probably go to room 27. Choice (A) contradicts the fact that the woman already has a ticket. Choice (C) refers to the number of the ticket, not to the number of the room. Choice (D) contradicts the fact that the man has already seen her ticket.
14. (**B**) Since the teachers gave flowers to all of the honors students, and the woman has a flower, it must be concluded that she is an

honors student. Choice (A) contradicts the fact that she has a flower that was presented at the reception. Choice (D) contradicts the fact that she received a flower for students. Choice (C) is not mentioned and may not be concluded from information in the conversation.

15. **(D)** "...Take it over next term." Choices (B) and (C) contradict the fact that the woman says to drop the class. Choice (A) is not mentioned and may not be concluded from information in the conversation.
16. **(C)** Since the woman used to teach English, the man is not surprised that she likes the course. *No wonder* is an idiomatic expression that means the information is logical. Choice (D) refers to the woman's interest, not to the course. Choices (A) and (B) are not mentioned and may not be concluded from information in the conversation.
17. **(A)** Since they are discussing potential group members and their value to a presentation, it must be concluded that they are planning to make a presentation. Choice (B) contradicts the fact that the second woman says they should ask Jane. Choices (C) and (D) are not mentioned and may not be concluded from information in the conversation.
18. **(B)** "I really don't know what Dr. Brown wants us to do.... The assignment was pretty vague." Choice (A) contradicts the fact that they looked in the syllabus. Choice (C) refers to the fact that the man was thinking of making an appointment with Dr. Brown to resolve the problem. Choice (D) contradicts the fact that the man was considering stopping by Dr. Brown's office during her office hours.
19. **(D)** "...it says under the course requirements...'Research paper, thirty points.' " Choice (A) contradicts the fact that it says thirty points in the syllabus. Choice (B) contradicts the fact that thirty points is one-third, not one-half of the total grade. Choice (C) contradicts the fact that it is thirty, not ten points.
20. **(A)** "...then she started talking about presentations." Choice (C) refers to the fact that the students are planning to ask questions in the next class, not to questions that were asked last week. Choices (B) and (D) are not mentioned and may not be concluded from information in the conversation.
21. **(C)** "...maybe we should ask about it in class tomorrow." Since the man agrees that she has a good idea, it must be concluded that they will ask questions about the assignment in class. Choices (B) and (D) were discussed earlier in the conversation before they decided to ask in class. Choice (A) contradicts the fact that they do not understand the assignment.
22. **(C)** "On his third exploratory voyage, as captain of two ships...Captain James Cook came upon...the Hawaiian Islands." Choices (A), (B), and (D) are secondary themes used to develop the main theme of the talk.
23. **(B) (C)** "...as captain in charge of two ships, the *Resolution* and the *Discovery*, he came upon a group of uncharted islands...." Choice (A) refers to the fact that this was Cook's third voyage to explore the Pacific Ocean, not to the name of his ship. *England* in Choice (D) refers to the country that commissioned Cook, not to the name of his ship.
24. **(C)** "Some historians contend that the islanders welcomed Cook, believing that he was the god Launo, protector of peace and agriculture." Choices (A), (B), and (D) are not mentioned and may not be concluded from information in the lecture.
25. **(D) (C) (B) (A)** "...Cook demanded that the king be taken as a hostage until the boat was returned.... In the fighting that followed, Cook and four other crewmen were killed."
26. **(C)** "Alloys are mixtures that have been deliberately combined in specific proportion for a definite purpose." Choice (A) refers to natural combinations of metals, not to alloys. Choice (B) is true, but incomplete because it does not mention the specific purposes. Choice (D) is not mentioned and may not be concluded from information in the conversation.
27. **(A) (B)** "...alloys are mixtures that have been deliberately combined in specific proportion for a definite purpose." Choice (D) refers to impure metals, not to alloys. Choice (C) is not mentioned and may not be concluded from information in the conversation.
28. **(A)** "In the aircraft industry, there is a need for metals that are both strong and light." Choice (D) contradicts the fact that the metals referred to are alloys. Choices (B) and

(C) are not mentioned and may not be concluded from information in the conversation.

29. **(C)** "Both [alloys and combinations in nature] are mixtures, but alloys are mixtures that have been deliberately combined in specific proportion for a definite purpose." Choice (A) contradicts the fact that metals that occur accidentally in nature are impure. Choice (B) contradicts the fact that combinations of metals occur accidentally in nature. Choice (D) contradicts the fact that both alloys and combinations of metals that occur in nature are mixtures.
30. **(C)** "We all agree that British English and American English are different. Right?...But not so different that it prevents us from understanding each other." Choices (A), (B), and (D) are secondary points of discussion that are used to develop the main topic of the discussion.
31. **(A) (B) (C) (D)** "Words like *theater* and *center* end in *re* in England instead of *er* the way that we [Americans] spell them.... many words that end in *or* in American English are spelled *our* in British English, like *color* and *honor*."
32. **(B)** "I remember seeing an English movie where the actors kept calling their apartment a *flat*. Half of the movie was over before I realized what they were talking about." Choice (D) contradicts the fact that the man did not understand the word. Choices (A) and (C) are not mentioned and may not be concluded from information in the discussion.
33. **(D)** "We all agree that British English and American English are different.... But not so different that it prevents us from understanding each other." Choice (A) refers to the man's opinion at the beginning of the discussion, not to the opinion of the class at the conclusion of the discussion. The opinions expressed in Choices (B) and (C) are not mentioned and may not be concluded from information in the discussion.
34. **(D)** "My report is on local control of schools." Choices (A), (B), and (C) are secondary themes used to develop the main theme of the report.
35. **(A)** "...I was surprised to learn that public schools in the United States are not the same in every state or even from community to community...." Choices (B), (C), and (D) are all true, but they are not what surprised the presenter about her research.
36. **(B) (A) (C)** "...a governing board, called the school board, that makes the decisions ... a superintendent...to carry out policies.... In most communities, the board is elected by the residents in their local school district."
37. **(A) (C)** "The function of the national department is...supporting research and projects, and supervising the compliance of schools with national legislation." Choice (B) contradicts the fact that the school board makes decisions about the curriculum in the local district. Choice (D) contradicts the fact that local school boards are elected by the people or appointed by the mayor.
38. **(B) (C)** "The two-meal plan includes lunch and dinner." Choice (A) contradicts the fact that there is no breakfast included. Choice (D) is not mentioned and may not be concluded from information in the conversation.
39. **(C)** "It's thirty-six dollars a week, which works out to about three dollars a meal." The number in Choice (A) refers to the number of meals that the man uses to calculate, not the cost. Choice (D) refers to the cost of two meals per day for seven days, not to the cost of a six-day plan. Choice (B) is not mentioned and may not be concluded from information in the conversation.
40. **(C)** "...we don't serve meals on Sunday." Choice (A) refers to the situation that some students have, but not to the reason that they eat out. Choices (B) and (D) are not mentioned and may not be concluded from information in the conversation.
41. **(C)** "Just fill out this form, and we'll bill you." Choice (B) refers to the man's question about credit cards, not to the way that he will pay. Choices (A) and (D) contradict the fact that the man will be billed.
42. **(C)** "Just fill out this form, and we'll bill you." Choice (A) contradicts the fact that the man does not have to pay now. Choice (B) refers to the man's offer, not to what he will probably do. Choice (D) is not mentioned and may not be concluded from information in the conversation.
43. **(A)** "...hydroponics is the science of growing plants without soil...." Choice (B) refers to the nutrients that are used in the solution in order to grow the plants, not to a definition

of hydroponics. Choices (C) and (D) are not mentioned and may not be concluded from information in the lecture.

44. **(C)** "You can refer to your lab workbook for the list of substances and the proportions needed for proper plant growth." Choice (A) contradicts the fact that the professor shows the diagram. Choice (D) contradicts the fact that the hydroponics tank is already built and displayed in class. Choice (B) is not mentioned and may not be concluded from information in the lecture.
45. **(A) (B)** "...for plants grown in soil, the roots not only absorb water and nutrients but also serve to anchor the plant.... oxygen is also taken in by the roots...." Choice (C) contradicts the fact that hydroponic plants are not placed directly in the water and nutrient solution. Choice (D) is not mentioned and may not be concluded from information in the lecture.
46. **(C)** "Because oxygen is also taken in by the roots, we had to attach an air pump to mix oxygen into the solution." Choice (D) contradicts the fact that the wood chips and wire mesh anchored the plants. Choices (A) and (B) are not mentioned and may not be concluded from information in the lecture.
47. **(C)** "I'd also like you to take a closer look at this specimen of nutrient solution. What conclusions can you draw?" Choice (B) confuses the word *draw* with the idiom *to draw conclusions*. Choices (A) and (D) are not mentioned and may not be concluded from information in the lecture.
48. **(C)** "Did you watch *American Biography* last night?" Choice (A) contradicts the fact that the woman had a class. Choice (B) contradicts the fact that the man watched the show. Choice (D) contradicts the fact that program was scheduled last night, and may be rerun.
49. **(D)** "...she escaped from her owners in Maryland...." Tubman was a member of the underground railroad, but it was not mentioned whether she worked on the regular railroad or underground in a mine as in Choices (A) and (B). Choice (C) refers to the destination of many slaves who were helped by the underground railroad, not to Tubman's home.
50. **(B)** "What really impressed me though was the fact that after she escaped, she went back to Maryland nineteen times...[and] freed more than three hundred slaves." Choice (A) is true, but it is not what impressed the man. The number nineteen in Choice (D) refers to the number of times that she returned to Maryland to help others, not to the number of years she spent in slavery. Choice (C) is not mentioned and may not be concluded from information in the conversation.

Section 2: Structure

1. **(D)** There must be agreement between subject and verb, not between the verb and words in the appositive after the subject. *Were* should be *was* to agree with the singular subject *gunpowder*. (Refer to Style, Problem 7, page 259.)
2. **(B)** There must be agreement between subject and verb. *Is* should be *are* to agree with the plural subject *manufacturers*. (Refer to Style, Problem 5, page 257.)
3. **(D)** Because adjectives are used after verbs of the senses, *sweetly* should be *sweet* after the verb *smell*. *Sweetly* is an adverb. *Sweet* is an adjective. (Refer to Patterns, Problem 85, page 182.)
4. **(A)** The verb *to expect* requires an infinitive in the complement. Choices (B), (C), and (D) are not infinitives. (Refer to Patterns, Problem 3, page 74.)
5. **(C)** *Because of* is used before nouns such as *a misunderstanding* to express cause. Choices (A) and (B) are not accepted for statements of cause. Choice (D) is used before a subject and verb, not a noun, to express cause. (Refer to Patterns, Problem 111, page 214.)
6. **(D)** *Equal to* is a prepositional idiom. *As* should be *to*. (Refer to Style, Problem 29, page 286.)
7. **(D)** Ideas in a series should be expressed by parallel structures. *Stressful* should be *stress* to provide for parallelism with the nouns *predisposition, drugs,* or *infection.* (Refer to Style, Problem 17, page 271.)
8. **(A)** Subject-verb order is used in the clause after a question word connector such as *where.* In Choice (B), there is no question word connector. In Choice (C), the subject-verb order is reversed. In Choice (D), the question word connector is used after, not

before, the subject and verb. (Refer to Patterns, Problem 124, page 230.)

9. (**A**) *May* and a verb word in the result require a past form in the condition. Because *may have* is used in the result, *having* should be *had* in the condition. (Refer to Patterns, Problem 23, page 100.)
10. (**C**) *As well as* is used in correlation with the inclusive *and.* Choices (A) and (B) would be used in clauses of comparison, not correlation. Choice (D) is incomplete because it does not include the final word *as*. (Refer to Patterns, Problem 117, page 221.)
11. (**B**) In order to refer to nurses not allowing you to give blood, *let* should be used. *To leave* means to go. *To let* means to allow. (Refer to Style, Problem 26, page 283.)
12. (**D**) The anticipatory clause *it was in 1848 that* introduces a subject and verb, *gold was discovered.* Choice (A) may be used preceding a subject and verb without *that*. Choice (B) may be used as a subject clause preceding a main verb. Choice (C) is redundant and indirect. "Because in 1848 gold was discovered at Sutter's Mill, the California Gold Rush began," and "That in 1848 gold was discovered at Sutter's Mill was the cause of the California Gold Rush" would also be correct. (Refer to Patterns, Problem 35, page 117.)
13. (**C**) Comparative forms for three-syllable adverbs are usually preceded by *more* and followed by *than.* Choice (A) is followed by *as.* Choice (B) is preceded by *as.* Choice (D) is not preceded by *more.* (Refer to Patterns, Problem 96, page 196.)
14. (**D**) The verb *thought* establishes a point of view in the past. *Has* should be *had* in order to maintain the point of view. (Refer to Style, Problem 2, page 253.)
15. (**B**) *Developing* should be *development.* Although both are nouns derived from verbs, the *-ment* ending is preferred. *Developing* means progressing. *Development* means the act of developing or the result of developing. (Refer to Style, Problem 30, page 288.)
16. (**A**) Most adverbs of manner are formed by adding *-ly* to adjectives. Choices (B) and (D) are redundant and indirect. Choice (C) is ungrammatical because the adverb *fast* does not have an *-ly* ending. (Refer to Patterns, Problem 126, page 233.)
17. (**C**) *But also* is used in correlation with the inclusive *not only.* Choice (A) would be used in correlation with *not*, not in correlation with *not only.* Choices (B) and (D) are not used in correlation with another inclusive. (Refer to Patterns, Problem 118, page 223.)
18. (**C**) Comparisons must be made with logically comparable nouns. Choices (A) and (D) are redundant and indirect. Choice (B) makes an illogical comparison of *a salary* with *a teacher.* Only Choice (C) compares two salaries. (Refer to Patterns, Problem 102, page 203.)
19. (**A**) The verb phrase *to look forward to* requires an *-ing* form in the complement. Choices (B) and (D) are not *-ing* forms. Choice (C) is BE and an *-ing* form. (Refer to Patterns, Problem 4, page 76.)
20. (**C**) There must be agreement between pronoun and antecedent. *Their* should be *its* to agree with the singular antecedent *a turtle.* (Refer to Style, Problem 11, page 263.)
21. (**C**) In order to refer to a city which has been *occupying a place, lying* should be used. *To lay* means to put in a place. *To lie* means to occupy a place. (Refer to Style, Problem 23, page 279.)
22. (**B**) *Purposeful* should be *purposes. Purposeful* is an adjective. *Purposes* is a noun. (Refer to Style, Problem 30, page 288.)
23. (**C**) An introductory verbal phrase should immediately precede the noun that it modifies. Only Choice (C) provides a noun which could be logically modified by the introductory verbal phrase, *after seeing the movie.* Neither *the book* nor *the reading* could logically *see a movie* as would be implied by Choices (A), (B), and (D). (Refer to Style, Problem 15, page 268.)
24. (**B**) A form of BE is used with the participle in passive sentences. *Said* should be *is said.* (Refer to Patterns, Problem 41, page 123.)
25. (**C**) Comparative forms are usually followed by *than.* After the comparative *more important, as* should be *than.* (Refer to Patterns, Problem 96, page 196.)

Section 3: Reading

1. (**A**) "The Father of American Public Education" is the best title because it states the main idea of the passage. Choice (C) is a detail used to develop the main idea. Choices

(B) and (D) are not specific enough.

2. **(C)** "Perhaps it was his own lack of adequate schooling that inspired Horace Mann to work so hard for the important reforms in education that he accomplished." Choice (A) contradicts the fact that Mann did not have benefit of an early education. Choice (B) contradicts the fact that the biography is limited to Horace Mann's work as an educator. Choice (D) contradicts the fact that the teachers are mentioned only briefly.
3. **(D)** In the context of this passage, struggles could best be replaced by difficult times. Choices (A), (C), and (B) are not accepted definitions of the word.
4. **(B)** "...to become first secretary of the board [of education]. There [at the board of education] he exercised an enormous influence...." Choices (A), (C), and (D) would change the meaning of the sentence.
5. **(A)** In the context of this passage, mandatory is closest in meaning to required. Choices (B), (C), and (D) are not accepted definitions of the word.
6. In the context of this passage, the word extended could best be replaced by increased. No other words or phrases in the **bold** text are close to the meaning of the word extended.
7. "Mann's ideas about school reform were developed and distributed in twelve annual reports to the state of Massachusetts...." Quotation from sentence 1, paragraph 3.
8. **(A)** "Mann was recognized as the father of public education." Choice (B) contradicts the fact that Horace Mann exercised an enormous influence. Choices (C) and (D) are unlikely since his influence resulted in a change in the school system.
9. **(B)** "There he exercised an enormous influence during the critical period of reconstruction that brought into existence the American graded elementary school as a substitute for the older district school system." Choice (A) refers to "the historic education bill that set up a state board of education" and to the fact that Mann served as first secretary of the board. Choice (C) refers to "the lyceums for adult education," which he founded. Choice (D) refers to the new system that was brought into existence under Mann's influence.
10. **(C)** "...the Massachusetts reforms later served as a model for the nation." Choice (A) contradicts the fact that the reforms were considered quite radical at the time. Choice (B) contradicts the fact that they served as a model for the nation. Choice (D) is not mentioned and may not be concluded from information in the passage.
11. **(B)** "Be ashamed to die until you have won some victory for humanity." Choices (A), (C), and (D) are not mentioned specifically as part of Mann's philosophy.
12. **(A)** "Organic architecture, that is, natural architecture...." Choice (B) refers to the rule rejected by organic architecture, not to another name for it. Choices (C) and (D) refer to the fact that organic architecture may be varied but always remains true to natural principles. Neither principle architecture nor varied architecture was cited as another name for organic architecture, however.
13. "Organic architecture—that is, natural architecture—may be varied in concept and form, but it [the architecture] is always faithful to natural principles." Other choices would change the meaning of the sentence.
14. **(B)** In the context of this passage, ultimately could best be replaced by eventually. Choices (A), (C), and (D) are not accepted definitions of the word.
15. **(C)** In the context of this passage, upheld is closest in meaning to promoted. Choices (A), (B), and (D) are not accepted definitions of the word.
16. **(A)** "If these natural principles are upheld, then a bank cannot be built to look like a Greek temple." Choice (B) refers to the fact that natural principles require "total harmony with the setting." Choice (C) refers to the fact that the colors are taken from "the surrounding palette of nature." Choice (D) refers to the fact that "the rule of functionalism is upheld."
17. **(B)** "Natural principles then, are principles of design, not style.... Like a sculptor, the organic architect views the site and materials as an innate form that develops organically from within." Choice (C) refers to the geometric themes mentioned later in the passage. Choice (D) contradicts the fact that the author emphasizes design, not style. Choice (A) is not mentioned and may not be concluded from information in the passage.
18. **(A)** In the context of this passage, obscured is

closest in meaning to difficult to see. Choices (B), (C), and (D) are not accepted definitions of the word.

19. In the context of this passage, the word shapes is closest in meaning to contours. No other words or phrases in the **bold** text are close to the meaning of the word contours.
20. "Organic architecture incorporates built-in architectural features such as benches and storage areas to take the place of furniture." Quotation from sentence 7, paragraph 3.
21. (**D**) "Form does not follow function; form is inseparable from function." Choice (A) contradicts the fact that form does not follow function. Choices (B) and (C) contradict the fact that form is inseparable from function.
22. (**C**) "...a building should...respect the natural characteristics of the setting to create harmony with its natural environment." Choices (A), (B), and (D) contradict the fact that nature should be respected.
23. (**D**) Choices (A), (B), and (C) are important to the discussion and provide details that support the main point that alchemy was the predecessor of modern chemistry.
24. (**B**) In the context of the passage, authentic could best be replaced by genuine. Choices (A), (C), and (D) are not accepted definitions of the word.
25. "The earliest authentic works on European alchemy are those [works] of the English monk Roger Bacon and the German philosopher St. Albertus Magnus." Other choices would change the meaning of the sentence.
26. (**A**) "...inferior metals such as lead and mercury were removed by various degrees of imperfection from gold." Choices (B), (C), and (D) are not mentioned and may not be concluded from information in the passage.
27. In the context of this passage, the word maintained is closest in meaning to asserted. No other words or phrases in the **bold** text are close to the meaning of the word asserted.
28. (**B**) "...base metals could be transmuted to gold by blending them with a substance even more perfect than gold. This elusive substance was referred to as the 'philosopher's stone.' " Choices (A) and (D) contradict the fact that the "philosopher's stone" was more perfect than gold. Choice (C) contradicts the fact that the "philosopher's stone" was an element that alchemists were searching for, not another name for their art.
29. (**B**) In the context of this passage, cryptic could be replaced by secret. Choices (A), (C), and (D) are not accepted definitions of the word.
30. (**A**) Because the early alchemists were "artisans who were accustomed to keeping trade secrets," it must be concluded that early alchemists used cryptic terms like *sun* and *moon* to keep the work secret. Choices (B) and (C) refer to the fact that philosophers were attracted to alchemy and began to use the symbolic language in their literature, but they are not reasons why the alchemists used the terms. Choice (D) refers to the record of the progress of the work that was produced by alchemists, not to the reason for cryptic language.
31. (**C**) "Most of the early alchemists were artisans...." Choice (B) refers to the second group, not the first group, of alchemists. Choices (A) and (D) are not mentioned and may not be concluded from information in the passage.
32. (**B**) "...it was the literary alchemist who was most likely to produce a written record; therefore, much of what is known about the science of alchemy is derived from philosophers rather than from the alchemists who labored in laboratories." Choice (A) is true, but it is not the reason that we know about the history of alchemy. Choices (C) and (D) are not mentioned and may not be concluded from information in the passage.
33. (**B**) "...they [laboratory alchemists] did gain a wide knowledge of chemical substances, discovered chemical properties, and invented many of the tools and techniques that are still used by chemists today." Choice (A) contradicts the fact that the alchemists made scientific discoveries and were considered the legitimate forefathers of modern chemistry. Choice (C) contradicts the fact that the majority of educated persons in the period from 1400 to 1600 believed that alchemy had great merit. Although the author mentions the work of both laboratory and literary alchemists, Choice (D) is not mentioned and may not be concluded from information in the passage.

34. (**C**) The other choices are secondary ideas that are used to develop the main idea, "human memory." Choices (A), (B), and (D) are important to the discussion, but are not the main topic.
35. (**A**) In the context of this passage, formerly could best be replaced by in the past. Choices (B), (C), and (D) are not accepted definitions of the word.
36. (**A**) "Human memory…is really more sophisticated than that of a computer." Choice (B) contradicts the statement that human memory is more sophisticated. Choices (C) and (D) are not mentioned and may not be concluded from information in the passage.
37. In the context of this passage, the word complex is closest in meaning to sophisticated. No other words or phrases in the **bold** text are close to the meaning of the word sophisticated.
38. "Human memory, formerly believed to be rather inefficient, is really more sophisticated than that [the memory] of a computer." Other choices would change the meaning of the sentence.
39. (**B**) "…by stimulating their brains electrically, he could elicit the total recall of complex events." Choice (A) refers to the fact that Penfield was a neurosurgeon, but he did not rely on surgery to elicit dreams. Choice (C) refers to the procedure for supporting recall. Choice (D) refers to the way that performance is improved in memory, not to the procedure for eliciting dreams.
40. (**B**) "…the…capacity for storage in the brain is the result of an almost unlimited combination of interconnections…stimulated by patterns of activity." Choice (A) contradicts the fact that the physical basis for memory is not yet understood. Choice (C) contradicts the statement that storage in the brain is the result of an almost unlimited combination of interconnections. Choice (D) contradicts the fact that repeated references to the same information supports recall.
41. (**C**) Although Choices (A), (B), and (D) are definitions of the word bonds, the meaning in the context of the sentence is connections.
42. "Psychologists generally divide memory into at least two types, short-term and long-term, which combine to form working memory." Quotation from sentence 1, paragraph 3.
43. (**A**) "We use short-term memory when we look up a telephone number and repeat it to ourselves until we can place the call." Choices (B), (C), and (D) are not mentioned and may not be concluded from information in the passage.
44. (**B**) "The memory trace is…made by structural changes in the brain…is not subject to direct observation…is rather a theoretical construct…. Repeated references to the same information supports recall." Choices (A), (C), and (D) are all mentioned in the passage. Choice (B) contradicts the fact that the memory trace is not subject to direct observation.
45. (**A**) "…there is a great deal more stored in our minds than has been generally supposed." Choice (B) contradicts the statement that the physical basis for memory is not yet understood. Choice (C) refers to the fact that researchers have approached the problem from a variety of points of view, but it may not be concluded that different points of view are valuable. Choice (D) contradicts the statement that memory was formerly believed to be inefficient, but is really sophisticated.

Model Test 6—Computer-Assisted TOEFL

Section 1: Listening

1. (**B**) According to the woman, she has to study for her qualifying examinations. Choices (A) and (C) contradict the fact that the woman says she is tempted to go. Choice (D) is incorrect because the woman is taking a qualifying examination [for a degree]. She is not trying to qualify in order to play tennis.
2. (**B**) "I have an attendance requirement for undergraduates, but not for graduate students." Choice (A) contradicts the fact that she has a policy for undergraduates. Choice (C) contradicts the fact that the woman says "no" when she is asked whether attendance will count toward the grade. Choice (D) contradicts the fact that the woman has an attendance requirement for undergraduates, but not for this class, which implies that it is a graduate course.
3. (**C**) The woman says that Ali is a part-time student this term. Choice (A) is incomplete because Ali is studying at the university and the American Language Institute. The number in Choice (B) refers to the number of classes that Ali is taking at the Institute, not at the university. Choice (D) is incorrect because it is the man in the conversation, not Ali, who is surprised. The woman says that Ali's situation is not surprising.
4. (**C**) To *just miss* someone is an idiomatic expression that means that the person has already left. Choices (A), (B), and (D) are not paraphrases of the expression and may not be concluded from information in the conversation.
5. (**C**) Since the woman asks where she can find a telephone, she will probably make a phone call. Choice (D) contradicts the fact that the shuttle has already departed. Choices (A) and (B) are not mentioned and may not be concluded from information in the conversation.
6. (**C**) *Sold out* is an idiomatic expression that means there are none left. Choice (A) contradicts the fact that she has already tried to buy her books at the bookstore. Choice (D) contradicts the fact that she tried to buy the books. Choice (B) is not mentioned and may not be concluded from information in the conversation.
7. (**B**) "You'd better leave a few minutes early." Choice (C) refers to the time the man has to be there, not to the time he should leave. Choices (A) and (D) are not mentioned and may not be concluded from information in the conversation.
8. (**C**) To *make fun of* is an idiomatic expression that means to ridicule. Choices (A), (B), and (D) are not paraphrases of the expression and may not be concluded from information in the conversation.
9. (**A**) A *put down* is an idiomatic expression that means an insult. Choices (B), (C), and (D) are not paraphrases of the expression and may not be concluded from information in the conversation.
10. (**B**) "Can you watch my book bag?" Choice (D) contradicts the fact that the man wants the woman to stay with his book bag. Choices (A) and (C) are not mentioned and may not be concluded from information in the conversation.
11. (**B**) *I hear you* is an idiomatic expression that means the speaker understands the other person's point of view. Choices (A), (C), and (D) are not paraphrases of the expression, and may not be concluded from information in the conversation.
12. (**C**) Since Mike's brother is using the car while Mike is away, it must be concluded that Mike is in Florida as planned. Choice (A) contradicts the fact that Mike's brother is using his car. Choice (B) refers to Mike, not to his brother. Choice (D) contradicts the fact that Mike's brother is here and Mike is in Florida.
13. (**C**) "You'd better start working on that project." Choice (B) contradicts the fact that the man has not started yet. Choices (A) and (D) are not mentioned and may not be concluded from information in the conversation.
14. (**D**) *Why not?* is an idiomatic expression that means the speaker agrees with the other person's plan. Choices (A), (B), and (C) are not

paraphrases of the expression and may not be concluded from information in the conversation.

15. (**A**) Since the woman registers surprise, it must be concluded that she thought the couple would not get married. Choices (B) and (C) contradict the fact that the woman made her comment about the wedding, not the honeymoon. The size of the wedding in Choice (D) is not mentioned and may not be concluded from information in the conversation.
16. (**C**) *What's the point?* is an idiomatic expression that means the speaker does not believe that the suggestion will be helpful. Choices (A), (B), and (D) are not paraphrases of the expression, and may not be concluded from information in the conversation.
17. (**A**) Since the woman says "I suggest that you call your sponsor," the man will probably do it. Choice (B) contradicts the fact that the check isn't here. Choices (C) and (D) are not mentioned and may not be concluded from information in the conversation.
18. (**D**) "I've been sick....Now I'm worried about getting caught up." Choice (A) refers to the fact that the man has been sick, but he is not sick now. Choice (B) contradicts the fact that he stayed out of the hospital. Choice (C) contradicts the fact that he has not missed any quizzes.
19. (**B**) "I was hoping you'd let me make a copy of your notes." Choice (C) refers to the offer that she makes, not to what Gary asks Margaret to do. Choices (A) and (D) are not mentioned and may not be concluded from information in the conversation.
20. (**A**) "...why don't we get together...so that I can explain [my notes] to you." Choice (B) contradicts the fact that he hasn't missed any quizzes. Choices (C) and (D) are not mentioned and may not be concluded from information in the conversation.
21. (**A**) (**D**) Since Margaret agrees to let Gary borrow her notes, it must be concluded that she is helpful. Her attitude is positive and friendly. Choices (B) and (C) cannot be concluded from information in the conversation.
22. (**B**) The main topic of this talk is F. Scott Fitzgerald's work. The other topics are secondary themes used to develop the main topic.
23. (**B**) (**D**) "Fitzgerald had a great natural talent, but he became a compulsive drinker. He never made the adjustments necessary to a maturing writer in a changing world." Choice (A) contradicts the fact that Fitzgerald had a great natural talent. Choice (C) contradicts the fact that his reputation is greater since the film version of his novel *The Great Gatsby* was released.
24. (**A**) "He wrote novels that describe the post-war American society...caught up in the rhythms of jazz." Choice (C) contradicts the fact that his novels describe post-war society, not war experiences. Choices (B) and (D) are not mentioned and may not be concluded from information in the talk.
25. (**C**) "...I am going to run the video version of *The Great Gatsby*, and then we'll divide up into groups to talk about it." Choices (A), (B), and (D) are not mentioned and may not be concluded from information in the talk.
26. (**A**) "...let me tell you a little bit about chamber music." Choice (B) is a detail used to develop the main purpose of the talk. Choices (C) and (D) are not mentioned and may not be concluded from information in the talk.
27. (**C**) "So when they were not performing at religious functions, they were playing in the chambers of stately homes. And they came to be known as chamber players." The musical instrument in Choice (A) might be a recorder, harpsichord, or viola, not chamber music. The musicians in Choice (D) refer to Handel and Bach. Choice (B) is not mentioned and may not be concluded from information in the lecture.
28. (**A**) (**C**) "...any combination of instruments can be used for chamber music. The most popular are the piano, strings, and woodwinds...." Choices (B) and (D) are not mentioned and may not be concluded from information in the talk.
29. (**B**) "This evening the University Quartet will perform two of the later pieces by Bach." Choices (A) and (D) are true, but they are not the reason that the speaker mentions Bach. Choice (C) contradicts the fact that Bach wrote music after vocal chamber music was popular.
30. (**B**) "Ladies and Gentlemen, the University Quartet." Choices (A), (C), and (D) are mentioned earlier in the talk.

31. (**C**) "...I was wondering whether he has an earlier appointment available on the same day [as my regular appointment]." Choice (A) contradicts the fact that he has an appointment at three o'clock on Wednesday. Choice (B) contradicts the fact that he asked for an early appointment. Choice (D) refers to what the man ultimately decided to do, not to the purpose of his call.
32. (**A**) "...Dr. Benjamin is tied up in a meeting until noon, and he has two appointments scheduled before yours...." Choices (B), (C), and (D) contradict the fact that Dr. Benjamin has a meeting and appointments on Wednesday.
33. (**B**) "There is a later appointment time open ...at four-thirty...or...Thursday morning at ten." Choice (A) refers to the man's regular appointment time, not to the new appointment that the secretary offered to make. Choice (D) refers to what the man wanted to do, not to what the secretary offered to do. Choice (C) was not mentioned and may not be concluded from information in the conversation.
34. (**C**) "I think I'll just rearrange my own schedule so I can keep my regular appointment." Choices (A), (B), and (D) are not mentioned and may not be concluded from information in the conversation.
35. (**A**) "Health food is a general term applied to all kinds of foods that are considered more healthful than the types of food widely sold in supermarkets." Although Choices (B), (C), and (D) are all mentioned in the talk, they are secondary ideas used to develop the main idea.
36. (**B**) "A narrower classification of health food is natural food. This term [natural food] is used to distinguish between types of the same food. Fresh fruit is a natural food, but canned fruit, with sugars and other additives, is not." Choice (A) refers to foods like refined sugar, but is not mentioned as a term to distinguish between types of the same food. Choice (C) refers to food grown on a particular kind of farm. Choice (D) refers to organic foods that are not refined after harvest.
37. (**A**) (**D**) "...the allegations that processed foods contain chemicals, some of which are ...toxic, and that vitamin content is greatly reduced in processed foods." Choice (C) contradicts the fact that vitamin content is reduced. Choice (B) is not mentioned and may not be concluded from information in the talk.
38. (**B**) "Eat health foods, preferably the organic variety." Choice (A) contradicts the fact that the speaker has provided detailed information in the talk. Choice (C) contradicts the fact that the speaker recommends eating health foods. Choice (D) may not be concluded from the manner in which the talk was delivered.
39. (**C**) "...the Stone Age is the time...when prehistoric people started to make tools and weapons." Choice (A) refers to an event in the Late Stone Age, not to a defining feature of the Stone Age. Choice (D) contradicts the fact that the introduction of metals marked the end of the Stone Age. Choice (B) is not mentioned and may not be concluded from information in the discussion.
40. (**B**) (**C**) "They were Neanderthals, and they were nomads. And they survived by hunting and gathering." Choice (A) contradicts the fact that farming did not appear until the Middle Stone Age, after the decline of the Neanderthals. Choice (D) is not mentioned and may not be concluded from information in the lecture.
41. (**C**) (**A**) (**B**) "...the use of flint for tools... was the beginning of the Old Stone Age... Homo Sapiens emerged...[which] marks... the beginning of the Middle Stone Age...it was during the...Late Stone Age [that agricultural] villages started to develop...."
42. (**C**) "Some of the tools previously used for hunting were adapted for rudimentary farming...." Choice (A) contradicts the fact that tools for domestic purposes were being used during the Old Stone Age. Choices (B) and (D) are not mentioned and may not be concluded from information in the discussion.
43. (**B**) "...the introduction of metals was usually considered the defining event that brought an end to the Stone Age." Choice (A) refers to Chuck's idea, not to the event that marked the end of the Stone Age. Choices (C) and (D) occurred much earlier.
44. (**C**) "...oil moves up...until it reaches a nonporous rock deposit which will not allow it to continue moving. The oil becomes trapped under the nonporous rock deposit."

Choice (A) contradicts the fact that traps are underground formations that occur in nature. Choice (B) is true, but it is not the definition of a trap. Choice (D) contradicts the fact that the trap stops the flow of oil through the cracks and holes.

45. (**B**) Choice (A) is a diagram of a fault trap, not an anticline trap. Choice (C) is a diagram of a salt dome trap.
46. (**B**) "…in all traps, the oil is collected in the porous rock and trapped underground by the nonporous rock." Choice (B) is the nonporous rock where the oil collects. Choice (A) is above ground. Choice (C) is a water and gas deposit. Choice (D) is porous rock.
47. (**A**) "…a bulge in a flat surface may signal the presence of a salt dome." Choice (B) refers to an anticline trap, not a salt dome. Choices (C) and (D) are not mentioned and may not be concluded from information in the lecture.
48. (**B**) "…I have a choice between Dr. Perkins and Dr. Robinson." Choice (D) contradicts the fact that she asks for the man's advice and tells him that it was helpful. Choices (A) and (C) are not mentioned and may not be concluded from information in the conversation.
49. (**A**) Since the woman has a choice between Dr. Perkins and Dr. Robinson, it must be concluded that they teach two different sections of the same class. Choice (B) refers to Dr. Robinson, not to Dr. Perkins. Choice (D) contradicts the fact that the man says they are both good in their own way. Choice (C) is not mentioned and may not be concluded from information in the conversation.
50. (**B**) (**D**) "I'd call [Robinson] traditional…. If you like to listen to lectures and take notes…I'd say Robinson." Since the woman decides to take the class with Dr. Robinson, it must be concluded that she prefers lectures and a more traditional approach to teaching. Choice (A) contradicts the fact that she does not know about either of the professors. Choice (C) contradicts the fact that the man is recalling information about the professor, which implies that he has already taken the class that the woman is going to take.

Section 2: Structure

1. (**B**) The verb phrase *to insist on* requires an *-ing* form in the complement. *-Ing* forms are modified by possessive pronouns. Choice (A) is an infinitive modified by an object pronoun. Choice (C) is an *-ing* form, but it is modified by a subject, not a possessive pronoun. Choice (D) is a verb word. (Refer to Patterns, Problem 3 and Patterns, Problem 46, pages 74 and 131.)
2. (**D**) *The* must be used with a superlative. Choices (A), (B), and (C) are wordy and ungrammatical. (Refer to Patterns, Problem 97, page 197.)
3. (**B**) A form of BE is used with the participle in passive sentences. *Cannot proved* should be *cannot be proved*. (Refer to Patterns, Problem 41, page 123.)
4. (**D**) *The same* is used with a quality noun such as *age*, and *as* in comparisons. *As* is used with a quality adjective such as *old*, and *as*. Choice (A) is a quality adjective, not a noun, with *to*. In Choice (B), *the same* is used with *than*, not *as*. "As old as" would also be correct. (Refer to Patterns, Problem 89, page 188.)
5. (**D**) *Such* is used with a noun phrase to express cause before *that* and a subject and verb that expresses result. Choice (A) does not have a subject. Choice (B) does not have a subject or verb. Choice (C) is not a *that* clause. (Refer to Patterns, Problem 82, page 179.)
6. (**C**) *Began* should be *begun* because the auxiliary *had* requires a participle. *Began* is a past form. *Begun* is a participle. (Refer to Patterns, Problem 36, page 118.)
7. (**A**) Using words with the same meaning consecutively is repetitive. *First* should be deleted because *original* means *first*. (Refer to Style, Problem 20, page 275.)
8. (**C**) Singular and plural expressions of noncount nouns such as *equipment* occur in idiomatic phrases, often *piece* or *pieces of*. Choices (A), (B), and (D) are not idiomatic. (Refer to Patterns, Problem 57, page 148.)
9. (**D**) The anticipatory clause *it was in 1607 that* introduces a subject and verb, *the English settled*. Choice (A) is wordy and indirect. Choice (B) may be used as part of a subject clause preceding a main verb. Choice

(C) may be used without *that* preceding a subject and verb. "That in 1607 the English settled in Jamestown *has changed* the history of the Americas," and "Because in 1607 the English settled in Jamestown, *the history* of the Americas *has changed*" would also be correct. (Refer to Patterns, Problem 35, page 116.)

10. **(C)** Repetition of the subject by a subject pronoun is redundant. *It* should be deleted. (Refer to Style, Problem 21, page 276.)
11. **(C)** There must be agreement between subject and verb. *Have* should be *has* to agree with the singular subject *triangle*. (Refer to Style, Problem 5, page 257.)
12. **(C)** A sentence has a subject and a verb. Choice (A) is the subject, but there is no main clause verb. Choices (B) and (D) introduce a main clause subject and verb. (Refer to Patterns, Problem 137, page 247.)
13. **(C)** *Impossibility* should be *impossible. Impossibility* is a noun. *Impossible* is an adjective. (Refer to Style, Problem 30, page 288.)
14. **(D)** For scientific results, a present form in the condition requires a present or future form in the result. Only Choice (D) introduces a conditional. (Refer to Patterns, Problem 21, page 98.)
15. **(C)** There must be agreement between pronoun and antecedent. *Their* should be *its* to refer to the singular antecedent *Pickerel Frog*. (Refer to Style, Problem 11, page 263.)
16. **(B)** Multiple comparatives like *twice* are expressed by the multiple followed by the phrase *as much as*. Choice (A) is a multiple number followed by the phrase *more than*. Choices (C) and (D) reverse the order of the multiple number and the phrase. (Refer to Patterns, Problem 93, page 193.)
17. **(C)** *Used to* requires a verb word. When preceded by a form of BE, *used to* requires an *-ing* form. In Choice (A), *used to* requires a verb word, not an *-ing* form. In Choice (B), *used to* preceded by a form of BE may be used with an *-ing* form, not an infinitive. Choice (D) uses the incorrect form, *use to*. (Refer to Patterns, Problem 11, page 84.)
18. **(B)** The adverb *previously* establishes a point of view in the past. *Is* should be *was* in order to maintain the point of view. (Refer to Style, Problem 3, page 254.)
19. **(C)** Redundant, indirect phrases should be avoided. *In a correct manner* is a redundant pattern. The adverb *correctly* is simple and more direct. (Refer to Style, Problem 19, page 274.)
20. **(C)** The noun in the appositive must agree with the antecedent. *Tree* should be *trees* to agree with the antecedent *conifers*. (Refer to Style, Problem 14, page 266.)
21. **(A)** The verb *to want* requires an infinitive complement. Choice (B) is an *-ing* form, not an infinitive. Choice (C) is a verb word. Choice (D) is ungrammatical. (Refer to Patterns, Problem 2, page 73.)
22. **(B)** *Near* does not require a preposition. *Near to* should be *near*. *Nearby* would also be correct. (Refer to Style, Problem 29, page 286.)
23. **(B)** Ideas in a series should be expressed by parallel structures. Only *to finish* in Choice (B) provides for parallelism with the infinitive *to answer*. Choices (A), (C), and (D) are not parallel. (Refer to Style, Problem 17, page 271.)
24. **(B)** A verb word must be used in a clause after an impersonal expression. *Maintains* should be *maintain* after the impersonal expression *it is imperative*. (Refer to Patterns, Problem 29, page 109.)
25. **(C)** *But* should be *but also*, which is used in correlation with the inclusive *not only*. (Refer to Patterns, Problem 118, page 223.)

Section 3: Reading

1. **(B)** The other choices are secondary ideas used to develop the main idea, "the nature of geysers." Choices (A), (C), and (D) are subtopics that provide details and examples.
2. **(B)** "A geyser is the result of underground water under the combined conditions of high temperatures and increased pressure beneath the surface of the Earth." Choice (A) contradicts the fact that water, not hot rocks, rises to the surface. Choice (C) contradicts the fact that the hot rocks are in the Earth's interior, not on the surface. Choice (D) contradicts the fact that the water seeps down in cracks and fissures in the Earth.
3. In the context of this passage, approximately could best be replaced by about. No other words or phrases in the **bold** text are close to the meaning of the

word approximately.

4. (**A**) "Since temperature rises about 1° F for every sixty feet under the Earth's surface, and pressure increases with depth, water that seeps down in cracks and fissures until it [water] reaches very hot rocks in the Earth's interior becomes heated to a temperature of approximately 290° F." Choices (B), (C), and (D) would change the meaning of the sentence.
5. "Water under pressure ..." Quotation from sentence 1, paragraph 2.
6. (**C**) "Since temperature rises...and pressure increases with depth ..." Choices (A), (B), and (D) contradict the fact that both temperature and pressure increase with depth.
7. (**C**) "For the most part, geysers are located in three regions of the world: New Zealand, Iceland, and the Yellowstone National Park area of the United States." Choice (A) contradicts the fact that no comparisons are made among the areas. Choice (B) contradicts the fact that Yellowstone National Park is in the United States, not in New Zealand or Iceland. Choice (D) contradicts the fact that geysers are also found in a third region, the Yellowstone National Park area of the United States.
8. (**B**) "Old Faithful erupts almost every hour." The number in Choice (A) refers to the number of thousand gallons of water that is expelled during an eruption, not to the number of minutes between eruptions. The numbers in Choices (C) and (D) refer to the number of feet to which the geyser rises during an eruption.
9. (**B**) In the context of this passage, expelling is closest in meaning to discharging. Choices (A), (C), and (D) are not accepted definitions of the word.
10. (**A**) Choice (A) is a restatement of the sentence referred to in the passage. *Never failed* means always. Choices (B), (C), and (D) would change the meaning of the original sentence.
11. (**A**) "...a geyser must have a source of heat, a reservoir where water can be stored...an opening through which the hot water and steam can escape, and underground channels.... Favorable conditions for geysers exist in regions of geologically recent volcanic activity...in areas of more than average precipitation." Choice (C) includes some of, but not all, the necessary conditions. Choices (B) and (D) contradict the fact that the volcanic activity should be recent, but not active.
12. (**A**) Choice (A) is the author's main point because the reasons for success are referred to throughout the passage. Choices (B), (C), and (D) are each specific reasons for success.
13. (**B**) In the context of this passage, cited is closest in meaning to mentioned. Choices (A), (C), and (D) are not accepted definitions of the word.
14. (**C**) Incessantly means constantly. Choices (A), (B), and (D) are not accepted definitions of the word.
15. (**B**) "They were also both glider pilots. Unlike some other engineers who experimented with the theories of flight, [they] experienced the practical side...." Choices (A), (C), and (D) were all true of the Wright brothers, but these experiences were not different from those of their competitors.
16. "They had realized from their experiments that the most serious problems in manned flight would be stabilizing and maneuvering the aircraft once it was airborne." Quotation from sentence 4, paragraph 2.
17. In the context of this passage, the word guiding is closest in meaning to maneuvering. No other words or phrases in the **bold** text are close to the meaning of the word maneuvering.
18. (**C**) "The data from these experiments [using the wind tunnel] allowed the Wright brothers to construct a superior wing for their craft." Choice (A) contradicts the fact that the light internal combustion engine had already been invented by someone else. Choice (B) contradicts the fact that they developed a three-axis control while experimenting with gliders, not with the wind tunnel. Choice (D) contradicts the fact that they used the data to improve the wings, not the engine for their airplane.
19. (**C**) "Attempts to achieve manned flight in the early nineteenth century were doomed because the steam engines that powered the aircraft were too heavy in proportion to the power that they [the engines] produced." Choices (A), (B), and (D) would change the meaning of the sentence.

20. (**A**) In the context of this passage, doomed is closest in meaning to destined to fail. Choices (B), (C), and (D) are not accepted definitions of the word.
21. (**D**) "...they were able to bring the ratio of weight to power within acceptable limits for flight." From the reference to the ratio of weight to power and *acceptable limits*, it must be concluded that previous engines did not have acceptable limits of weight to power and, thus, did not have enough power to lift their own weight. Choice (B) contradicts the fact that the engines were relatively heavy. Choice (C) contradicts the fact that they were experimenting with internal combustion engines. The size in Choice (A) is not mentioned and may not be concluded from information in the passage.
22. (**D**) Choice (A) refers to the fact that the Wright brothers were "a team." Choice (B) refers to the fact that they were "among the best glider pilots in the world." Choice (C) refers to the "experiments [that] allowed the Wright brothers to construct a superior wing for their craft." Choice (D) is not mentioned and may not be concluded from information in the passage.
23. (**A**) The other choices are secondary ideas used to develop the main idea, "the influenza virus." Choices (B), (C), and (D) are subtopics that provide details and examples.
24. (**D**) "...bacteria can be considered a type of plant...." Choice (A) refers to the secretions of bacteria, not to the bacteria themselves. Although it may be true that bacteria are very small, as in Choice (B), or larger than viruses, as in Choice (C), this information is not mentioned and may not be concluded from reading the passage.
25. "...viruses, like the influenza virus, are living organisms [the viruses] themselves." Other choices would change the meaning of the sentence.
26. (**D**) In the context of this passage, strictly could best be replaced by exactly. Choices (A), (B), and (C) are not accepted definitions of the word.
27. (**B**) "...they [viruses] have strictly defined atomic structure...." Choice (A) contradicts the fact that viruses have a strictly defined atomic structure. Choice (C) contradicts the fact that we may consider them as regular chemical molecules. Although Choice (D) is implied, it may not be concluded from information in the passage.
28. (**C**) "...we must also consider them [viruses] as being alive since they are able to multiply in unlimited quantities." Choice (A) is the reason that we must consider them as regular chemical molecules, not the reason that we must consider them as being alive. Choices (B) and (D) are not mentioned and may not be concluded from information in the passage.
29. (**B**) Unlimited means without limits; very large. Choices (A), (C), and (D) are not accepted definitions of the word.
30. In the context of this passage, the word types is closest in meaning to strains. No other words or phrases in the **bold** text are close to the meaning of the word strains.
31. "Epidemics or regional outbreaks have appeared on the average every two or three years for type-A virus, and every four or five years for type-B virus. Approximately every ten years, worldwide epidemics of influenza called pandemics also occur." The connection between the two sentences is the reference to "epidemics" and the transition word "also." The second sentence with the word "also" must be mentioned after the first sentence.
32. (**B**) "...the protection is against only the type of virus that caused the influenza." Choices (A) and (C) contradict the fact that the protection is against only the one type of virus. Choice (D) is not mentioned and may not be concluded from information in the passage.
33. (**C**) "...every ten years...pandemics occur. Thought to be caused by new strains of type-A virus, these pandemics spread rapidly." Choices (A), (B), and (D) are all mentioned in the passage. Choice (C) refers to epidemics, not to pandemics.
34. (**B**) The other choices are secondary ideas that are used to develop the main idea, "The Federal Reserve System." Choices (A), (C), and (D) are important to the discussion as they relate to the Federal Reserve System.
35. (**A**) In the context of this passage, oversee is closest in meaning to supervise. Choices (B), (C), and (D) are not accepted definitions of the word.

36. **(D)** In the context of this passage, confirmed could best be replaced by approved. Choices (A), (B), and (C) are not accepted definitions of the word.
37. **(B)** "The System's primary function is to control monetary policy by influencing the cost and availability of money and credit through the purchase and sale of government securities." Choice (A) refers to the effect of regulation on the public, not to the System's responsibility. Choice (D) contradicts the statement that the Board of Governors is appointed by the President. Choice (C) is not mentioned and may not be concluded from information in the passage.
38. **(B)** Although Choices (A), (C), and (D) are definitions of the word securities, the meaning in the context of the sentence is bonds.
39. **(C)** "If the Federal Reserve provides too little money, interest rates tend to be high, borrowing is expensive, business activity slows down, unemployment goes up...." Choice (A) contradicts the fact that interest rates are high and borrowing is expensive. Choice (B) contradicts the fact that unemployment goes up. Choice (D) contradicts the fact that business activity slows down.
40. **(B)** "If there is too much money, interest rates decline, and borrowing can lead to excess demand, pushing up prices and fueling inflation." Choice (A) contradicts the statement that during times of too little money, unemployment goes up. Choice (C) misinterprets the word *fuel* to mean *oil*. Choice (D) is not mentioned and may not be concluded from information in the passage.
41. "In collaboration with the U.S. Department of the Treasury, the Fed puts new coins and paper currency into circulation by issuing them [coins and paper currency] to banks." Other choices would change the meaning of the sentence.
42. "It [the Fed] also supervises the activities of member banks abroad, and regulates certain aspects of international finance." Quotation from sentence 3, paragraph 3.
43. **(C)** Choice (C) is a restatement of the sentence referred to in the passage. *Not stray* means *follow*. Choices (A), (B), and (D) would change the meaning of the original sentence.
44. **(D)** Choice (A) refers to the fact that the "Federal Reserve System is an independent agency of the United States government that helps oversee the national banking system." Choice (B) refers to the fact that the Federal Reserve's "...primary function is to control monetary policy...through the purchase and sale of government securities." Choice (C) refers to the fact that "the Fed puts new coins and paper currency into circulation by issuing them to banks." Choice (D) contradicts the fact that "the Fed does not depend on Congress for budget allocations" although it does send "frequent reports to the Congress."
45. "It has been said that the Federal Reserve is actually an informal branch of the United States government because it is composed of national policy makers. In fact, the Fed is not confined by the usual checks and balances that apply to the three official branches of government—the executive, the legislative, and the judicial." The connection between the two sentences is the reference to an "informal branch" in the first sentence and a reference to "the three official branches of government" in the second sentence.

Model Test 7—Computer-Assisted TOEFL

Section 1: Listening

1. (**A**) *Why not* means you should. Choice (C) contradicts the fact that the woman says to move into an apartment. Choices (B) and (D) are not mentioned and may not be concluded from information in the conversation.
2. (**B**) Because the man suggests that they have lunch, and the woman responds that the idea sounds good, inviting him to call her, it must be concluded that the man will call the woman to arrange for lunch. Choice (A) contradicts the fact that the invitation is for the future. Choice (D) contradicts the fact that the woman invites the man to give her a call. Choice (C) is not mentioned and may not be concluded from information in the conversation.
3. (**C**) Since the man needs one transcript for San Diego State and two for himself, the woman will probably send one to San Diego State and give two to him. Choice (A) contradicts the fact that he only needs one for San Diego State. Choice (B) contradicts the fact that he needs a total of three transcripts. Choice (D) refers to the total number of transcripts that the man requested, not to how many he wants to take himself.
4. (**A**) "You can just leave a note." Choice (C) refers to the man's plan, not to the woman's suggestion. Choices (B) and (D) are not mentioned and may not be concluded from information in the conversation.
5. (**B**) Since Susan chose education for her major, it must be concluded that she prefers teaching. Choice (D) contradicts the fact that she declared her major. Choices (A) and (C) are not mentioned and may not be concluded from information in the conversation.
6. (**B**) From the reference to the *grades* being *posted* it must be concluded that they are talking about grades. The verb *posted* does not refer to mail as in Choice (A), and the *papers* are assignments, not newspapers as in Choice (C). Choice (D) is not mentioned and may not be concluded from the information in the conversation.
7. (**B**) Since the woman saw the man's name on the graduation list, she had assumed that he had already graduated. Choice (C) refers to the man's explanation, not to the woman's assumption. Choice (D) refers to the man's plan for graduation. Choice (A) is not mentioned and may not be concluded from information in the conversation.
8. (**C**) To *go for it* is an idiomatic expression that means to compete. Choices (A) and (D) contradict the fact that she is competing now. Choice (B) contradicts the fact that she has decided.
9. (**D**) Since the man says he is waiting for the mail to come, he implies that he will not go to the library with the woman. Choice (C) contradicts the fact that he is waiting for the mail, which has not yet arrived. Choices (A) and (B) are not mentioned and may not be concluded from information in the conversation.
10. (**D**) "How was your vacation?" Choices (A), (B), and (C) are all mentioned as they relate to the main topic of the conversation, the woman's vacation.
11. (**D**) *I couldn't care less* is an idiomatic expression that means the speaker is not interested. Choices (A), (B), and (C) are not paraphrases of the expression and may not be concluded from information in the conversation.
12. (**A**) Since the man asks whether or not the woman was in class on Friday and uses the word *either*, it must be concluded that he was not in class on that day. Choice (B) contradicts the fact that the man was not in class. Choice (C) contradicts the fact that the woman was not in class. Choice (D) contradicts the fact that the woman's mother, not the man and the woman, was in New York.
13. (**D**) Since the man says that he is not as excited as he thought he would be, it must be concluded that he expected to be more enthusiastic. Choices (A), (B), and (C) are not mentioned and may not be concluded from information in the conversation.
14. (**C**) *Now and then* is an idiomatic expression that means occasionally. Choices (A), (B),

and (D) contradict the fact that the woman eats in the snack bar occasionally.

15. (**A**) To *take it easy* is an idiomatic expression that means to rest. Choice (B) refers to the man's comment, not to the woman's observation. Choice (C) contradicts the fact that the man warns the woman not to worry. Choice (D) refers to the fact that the man was sick in the past, not that he is sick now.
16. (**D**) Since the man says "neither do I" when the woman comments about not liking the class, it must be concluded that he does not enjoy the economics class either. Choice (A) contradicts the fact that neither the man nor the woman enjoys the class. Choices (B) and (C) are not mentioned and may not be concluded from information in the conversation.
17. (**B**) Since the man has thirty-five subjects and that is not enough, it must be concluded that he needs more than thirty-five participants. Choice (A) contradicts the fact that he has started working on the project. Choice (C) contradicts the fact that he feels he has a good start. Choice (D) is not mentioned and may not be concluded from information in the conversation.
18. (**A**) "I want to talk to you about my final grade." Choice (C) is mentioned as an argument for changing the grade. Choice (D) refers to the professor's grade book, not to what prompted the conversation. Choice (B) is not mentioned and may not be concluded from information in the conversation.
19. (**B**) From the reference to a *grade*, a *grade book*, a *test*, *exams*, a *course*, and *class*, it must be concluded that the conversation is taking place in a college professor's office. Choice (C) contradicts the fact that Rick brought his test with him to the meeting. Choices (A) and (D) are not mentioned and may not be concluded from information in the conversation.
20. (**C**) "Well, I was surprised to get a D...." Choices (A) and (B) refer to the grades that Rick claims he should have gotten, not to the grade that he received. Choice (D) refers to the grade that Rick received in class participation, not to the grade that he received for the course.
21. (**C**) "You received an F in class participation because you missed too many days, and that brought your grade down." Choice (A) contradicts the fact that Rick got a B on the midterm exam. Choice (B) contradicts the fact that Rick passed the final with a C. Choice (D) contradicts the fact that Dr. Wilson gave Rick a syllabus on the first day of class and the grading system was outlined in it.
22. (**C**) "Diane, you have young children at home, so you will be able to help us with a lot of examples." Choice (B) contradicts the fact that Diane does not ask any questions during the discussion. Choices (A) and (D) are not mentioned and may not be concluded from information in the discussion.
23. (**A**) (**C**) "...toddlers are beginning to use commands....one of the most interesting features of this stage [toddlers] is the omission of small words such as 'is' and 'the' as well as word endings like 'I-N-G' on verbs." Choices (B) and (D) refer to the pre-toddler stage, not to the toddler stage.
24. (**B**) "What is actually happening there [when Diane's child is saying 'runned'] is that he is learning the regular verb endings...." Choice (A) contradicts the fact that the child is three, not two, years old. Choice (C) refers to language acquisition by a child four years old, not to the phrase "We runned." Choice (D) is not mentioned and may not be concluded from information in the discussion.
25. (**C**) "By age five...there is evidence that children have learned the basic structures of their language...." Choice (A) refers to the age when children are learning verb endings, not to the age when they have learned the basic structures of their language. Choice (B) refers to the age when children are correcting previous errors. Choice (D) refers to the age when children are still acquiring several grammatical structures.
26. (**A**) "There is evidence that the basic stages [of language acquisition] are the same for all languages." Choices (B), (C), and (D) contradict the professor's statement.
27. (**A**) "...it is better to read the assigned pages before you come to class so that you will be prepared to participate in the discussion that follows the lecture." Choices (B) and (C) contradict the fact that the reading should be done before the lecture and discussion. Choice (D) is not mentioned and may not be concluded from information in the talk.

28. **(C) (B) (A)** "The midterm is worth 30 points and the final is worth 50 points. That leaves 20 points for the project...."
29. **(B) (D)** "You can either write a paper or make a half-hour presentation on a topic of your choice." Choices (A) and (C) are not mentioned and may not be concluded from information in the talk.
30. **(A)** "If you must miss class for whatever reason, please get in touch with me." Choices (B), (C), and (D) are not mentioned and may not be concluded from information in the talk.
31. **(B)** The main purpose of this lecture is to explain a theory of the formation of diamonds on Neptune and Uranus. Choices (A), (C), and (D) are mentioned during the explanation, but are not central to the theory.
32. **(B) (C)** "...the seventh and eighth planets from our sun, Uranus and Neptune...." Choice (A) refers to the planet that is compared with Uranus and Neptune, not to one of the planets discussed in the lecture. Choice (D) is not mentioned and may not be concluded from information in the lecture.
33. **(D) (A) (C) (B)** "...Neptune [has]...methane ice clouds...[and] Uranus [has]...2 percent methane....[The] methane could have separated into the carbon and hydrogen atoms... [which] at high pressures...squeezed into a layer of diamonds...."
34. **(C)** "Today I'm going to share a rather interesting theory with you." Choice (D) contradicts the fact that he believes that the theory is interesting. Choices (A) and (B) are not mentioned and may not be concluded from information in the talk.
35. **(A)** "...a system whereby a representative group of citizens called the electoral college would be responsible for making the choice." Choices (B), (C), and (D) are mentioned in the lecture but are not a definition of the electoral college.
36. **(C)** "...when Aaron Burr and Thomas Jefferson received an equal number of votes, the system had to be changed to provide for separate voting for president and vice-president." Choice (A) contradicts the fact that the electoral college voted for Burr and Jefferson. Choice (D) contradicts the fact that the system had to be changed. Choice (B) is not mentioned and may not be concluded from information in the talk.
37. **(A)** "...the [political] parties nominated candidates and then chose electors...." Choices (B), (C), and (D) contradict the fact that the parties make the nominations.
38. **(C)** "...vote by the people for electors is called the popular vote ..." Choice (A) refers to direct vote, not popular vote. Choice (B) occurs after the popular vote. Choice (D) is not mentioned and may not be concluded from information in the talk.
39. **(C)** Since the man asks whether the woman understood the last lecture, and he tells her that he can't understand his notes, it must be concluded that he did not understand the lecture. Choices (A) and (B) contradict the fact that the man can't understand the notes that he took during the lecture. Choice (D) refers to the fact that the man reads the book after the lecture, not before the lecture, but reading the book is not the man's problem.
40. **(A)** "The stone meteorite is the most common.... Stone meteorites account for almost 90 percent." Choice (B) refers to the meterorite that accounts for 9 percent. Choice (D) refers to the meteorite that accounts for only about 1 percent of the total. Choice (C) is not mentioned and may not be concluded from information in the discussion.
41. **(B) (C)** "...most meteorites are...fragments of either asteroids or comets, but...some stone meteorites may have dislodged themselves from the moon or from Mars during the impact from a large asteroid." Choices (A) and (D) are not mentioned and may not be concluded from information in the discussion.
42. **(B)** "...I read the chapter [in the book] before class so that made it a little easier to follow [the lecture]." Choice (A) contradicts the fact that the woman says her notes aren't great either. Choice (D) is true, but it is not what helped the woman. Choice (C) is not mentioned and may not be concluded from information in the discussion.
43. **(B)** The purpose of this talk is to discuss scrimshaw, which is a folk art tradition. Choices (A), (C), and (D) are mentioned during the discussion, but are secondary themes used to develop the main theme of the talk.

44. **(A)** "In the period between the American Revolution and the Civil War...the hunting of whales was a major industry...whale bones became valuable for...carvings...." Choice (B) contradicts the fact that sailors, not soldiers, produced the art. Choice (C) contradicts the fact that scrimshaw, not military art, is the topic of the lecture. Choice (D) contradicts the fact that the examples are not battle scenes.
45. **(B)** **(C)** "There are two techniques for scrimshaw. One is to carve the bone into figures....The other is to cut designs on the bone, and then fill them with ink...." Choices (A) and (D) are not mentioned as techniques for scrimshaw.
46. **(B)** Choice (B) is the only example of scrimshaw. The other two pictures are examples of other kinds of folk art.
47. **(A)** "...because of the decline in whaling, there has also been a decline in the number of folk artists who produce scrimshaw." Choices (B), (C), and (D) are not mentioned and may not be concluded from information in the lecture.
48. **(B)** "I'm thinking about applying for a [credit] card." The phrase "zero balance" in Choices (A) and (D) refers to the options that the woman mentions, not to the man's decision. Choice (C) is not mentioned and may not be concluded from information in the conversation.
49. **(B)** **(C)** "...this [credit card] doesn't have an annual fee, and the interest charges are lower." Choice (D) contradicts the fact that you have to carry a $200 balance, which automatically accrues interest. Choice (A) is not mentioned and may not be concluded from information in the conversation.
50. **(D)** "...you have to carry a $200 balance ...so you can't pay it off every month." Choice (A) contradicts the fact that the man says he has a credit card while he is still considering the new card. It is the woman, not the man, who thinks one credit card is enough. Choice (C) refers to the woman's not the man's roommate. Choice (B) is not mentioned and may not be concluded from information in the conversation.

Section 2: Structure

1. **(B)** When two nouns are used consecutively, the first often functions as an adjective. Choices (A), (C), and (D) are redundant and unidiomatic. (Refer to Patterns, Problem 78, page 175.)
2. **(B)** There must be agreement between subject and verb. *Are* should be *is* to agree with the singular subject *anyone*. (Refer to Style, Problem 9, page 261.)
3. **(A)** A form of BE is used with a participle in passive sentences. *Combine* should be *combined.* (Refer to Patterns, Problem 31, page 112.)
4. **(D)** *A* should be *an* before the vowel sound *u* in *unknown*. *A* is used before consonant sounds. *An* is used before vowel sounds. (Refer to Patterns, Problem 62, page 154.)
5. **(B)** A present tense verb is used after *when* to express future. (Refer to Patterns, Problem 123, page 229.)
6. **(A)** *Once* means at one time in the past. *Once* is used in an introductory phrase with *a busy city* to modify the noun *Pompeii.* (Refer to Patterns, Problem 130, page 238.)
7. **(A)** An infinitive is used to express purpose. (Refer to Patterns, Problem 30, page 111.)
8. **(B)** There must be agreement between subject and verb. *Were* should be *was* to agree with the singular subject *Vasco da Gama*. The phrase of accompaniment, *accompanied by a large crew and a fleet of twenty ships*, is not the subject. (Refer to Style, Problem 6, page 258.)
9. **(B)** *The longer* should be *the longest*. Because there are more than two unguarded borders in the history of the world, a superlative form must be used. (Refer to Patterns, Problem 97, page 197.)
10. **(D)** The clause *many people believed* establishes a point of view in the past. *Is* should be *was* to maintain the point of view. (Refer to Style, Problem 1, page 252.)
11. **(B)** *Each other* is used to express mutual acts. Choices (A), (C), and (D) are not idiomatic. "One another" would also be correct. (Refer to Patterns, Problem 51, page 136.)
12. **(B)** *Begun* should be *began* because a past form is required to refer to Mozart's childhood. *Begun* is a participle. *Began* is a past

form. (Refer to Patterns, Problem 5, page 77.)

13. **(D)** *To experience* should be *experiencing* after the preposition *without*. *-Ing* nouns and noun forms are used after prepositions. (Refer to Patterns, Problems with Prepositions, pages 205–219.)
14. **(A)** *Almost* should be *most*. "Almost all of the poetry" would also be correct. (Refer to Patterns, Problem 72, page 166.)
15. **(A)** *But* means except. "All of the cereal grains except rice" would also be correct. (Refer to Patterns, Problem 107, page 209.)
16. **(A)** *Such* should be *such as*, which introduces the example *the Concorde*. (Refer to Patterns, Problem 109, page 212.)
17. **(B)** Every sentence must have a main verb. Choices (A), (C), and (D) are not main verbs. (Refer to Patterns, Problem 1, page 72.)
18. **(D)** *While* means at the same time. *While* is used in an introductory phrase with *a* to modify the noun *Webster*. (Refer to Patterns, Problem 131, page 239.)
19. **(D)** *No longer* is an idiom that means *not any more*. *Not* should be *no* before *longer*. (Refer to Patterns, Problem 132, page 240.)
20. **(A)** In order to refer to *occasionally, sometimes* should be used. *Sometimes* means occasionally. *Sometime* means at some time in the future. (Refer to Patterns, Problem 128, page 235.)
21. **(B)** In scientific results, a present form in the condition requires a present or future form in the result. Choice (A) is a past, not future form. Choices (C) and (D) are present forms but they are auxiliary verbs. (Refer to Patterns, Problem 21, page 98.)
22. **(A)** *Capable* should be *capability. Capable* is an adjective. *Capability* is a noun. (Refer to Style, Problem 30, page 288.)
23. **(A)** *From* is used with *to* to express a time limit. *In* should be *From*. (Refer to Patterns, Problem 115, page 218.)
24. **(B)** A negative phrase introduces inverted order. *Not until* requires an auxiliary verb, subject, and main verb. In Choice (A), the subject precedes the auxiliary. In Choice (C), there is no auxiliary. In Choice (D), there is no auxiliary and no subject. (Refer to Patterns, Problem 129, page 237.)
25. **(C)** The two words in an infinitive should not be divided by an adverb of manner. *Clearly* should be placed at the end of the sentence. (Refer to Patterns, Problem 126, page 233.)

Section 3: Reading

1. **(B)** "The Eradication of Smallpox" is the best title because it states the main idea of the passage. The other choices are secondary ideas that are used to develop the main idea. Choice (A) refers to the organization that initiated the campaign to eradicate smallpox. Choice (C) refers to one of the methods used to contain the spread of the disease. Choice (D) refers to the kind of disease that smallpox is.

2 In the context of this passage, the word eliminate is closest in meaning to eradicate. No other words or phrases in the **bold** text are close to the meaning of the word eradicate.

3. **(C)** In the context of this passage, threat could best be replaced by risk. Choices (A), (B), and (D) are not accepted definitions of the word.
4. "The goal was to eliminate the disease in one decade." Quotation from sentence 2, paragraph 2.
5. **(C)** "The strategy was not only to provide mass vaccinations but also to isolate patients...." Choice (A) refers to only one part of the strategy. It contradicts the fact that individual victims were treated. Choice (B) refers to only one part of the strategy. It contradicts the fact that entire villages were vaccinated. Choice (D) refers to a method to locate both villages and individuals for treatment.
6. **(B)** "By April of 1978, WHO officials announced that they [the officials] had isolated the last known case of the disease, but health workers continued to search for new cases for two additional years to be completely sure." Choices (A), (C), and (D) would change the meaning of the sentence.
7. **(B)** In the context of this passage, isolated is closest in meaning to separated. Choices (A), (C), and (D) are not accepted definitions of the word.
8. **(B)** "Rewards for reporting smallpox assisted in motivating the public." Choices (A), (C), and (D) refer to procedures for eliminating

the spread of the disease, not to ways to motivate the public to help health workers.

9. **(A)** "...the World Health Organization...was authorized to initiate a global campaign to eradicate smallpox.... Today smallpox is no longer a threat [as it was in the past].... Routine vaccinations have been stopped...." Choices (B), (C), and (D) refer to smallpox. Choice (A) refers to malaria and yellow fever.
10. **(A)** "...eleven years after the initial organization of the campaign, no cases [of smallpox] were reported in the field." Choice (B) contradicts the fact that similar projects for malaria and yellow fever had failed. Choice (C) contradicts the fact that no cases are being reported. Choice (D) contradicts the fact that patients had to be isolated to contain the spread of the disease.
11. "At the same time, the entire village where the victim had lived was vaccinated. The number of smallpox-infected countries gradually decreased." The connection between the two sentences is cause and result. The first sentence explains the strategy that caused the decrease referred to in the second sentence.
12. **(C)** The other choices are secondary ideas that are used to develop the main idea, "the current American family." Choices (A), (B), and (D) are classifications of families among those included in the current American family.
13. In the context of this passage, the word ideal is most opposite in meaning to reality. No other words or phrases in the **bold** text are opposite in meaning to the word reality.
14. **(B)** Current means present. Choices (A), (C), and (D) are not accepted definitions of the word.
15. **(B)** "The most recent government statistics reveal that only about one third of all current American families fit the traditional mold of two parents and their children, and another third consists of married couples who either have no children or have none [no children] still living at home." Choices (A), (C), and (D) would change the meaning of the sentence.
16. **(C)** "Of the final one third, about 20 percent of the total number of American households are single people...." Choice (A) refers to the final one third, not to the 20 percent who are single. Choices (B) and (D) contradict the fact that 20 percent equals one fifth.
17. **(C)** "...about 20 percent...are single people, usually women over sixty-five years of age." Choice (D) refers to 7 percent, not to the majority of one-person households. Choices (A) and (B) are not mentioned and may not be concluded from information in the passage.
18. "...about 20 percent of the total number of American households are single people, usually women over sixty-five years of age. A small percentage [of the single people]...consists of unmarried people who choose to live together; and the rest [of the single people]...are single parents, with at least one child." Other choices would change the meaning of the sentence.
19. "The vast majority of Americans claim that they have people in their lives whom they regard as family although they are not related." Quotation from sentence 2, paragraph 4.
20. **(A)** In the context of this passage, undervalues is closest in meaning to does not appreciate. Choices (B), (C), and (D) are not accepted definitions of the word.
21. **(C)** "...the number of births to unmarried women...divorce...deaths result in single-parent families." Choices (A), (B), and (D) are all mentioned in the reference to single-parent families. Choice (C) is not mentioned and may not be concluded from information in the passage.
22. **(A)** "...the so-called traditional American family was always more varied than we had been led to believe, reflecting the very different racial, ethnic, class, and religious customs among different American groups." Choice (B) contradicts the fact that customs are different among these groups. Choices (C) and (D) are not mentioned and may not be concluded from information in the passage.
23. **(A)** The other choices are secondary ideas that are used to develop the main idea that "noise may pose a serious threat to our physical and psychological health." Choices (B), (C), and (D) are all true, but they are details, not the main idea.
24. **(A)** "Noise, commonly defined as unwanted sound ..." Choices (B) and (D) refer to the origins of noise, not to definitions of it.

Choice (C) refers to the effects of noise.

25. (**B**) "...it [noise] is very difficult to measure because the discomfort experienced by different individuals is highly subjective and, therefore, variable." Choices (A), (C), and (D) are all mentioned in reference to noise, but are not the reason that noise is difficult to measure.
26. (**C**) In the context of this passage, congested could best be replaced by crowded. Choices (A), (B), and (D) are not accepted definitions of the word.
27. (**B**) "Loud noises instinctively signal danger...we are constantly responding [to noise] in the same ways that we would respond to danger." Choice (A) contradicts the fact that noise and our response to it may be more than an annoyance. Choices (C) and (D) refer to the results of our response to noise, not to the source of our response.
28. In the context of this passage, the word increase is closest in meaning to accelerate. No other words or phrases in the **bold** text are close to the meaning of the word accelerate.
29. "...the noise produced as a byproduct of our advancing technology causes physical and psychological harm, and detracts from the quality of life for those who are exposed to it [the noise]." Other choices would change the meaning of the sentence.
30. (**B**) In the context of this passage, as well is closest in meaning to also. Choices (A), (C), and (D) are not accepted definitions of the phrase.
31. (**B**) "Unlike the eyes [which have lids], the ear has no lid...therefore,...noise penetrates without protection." Choices (A), (C), and (D) are not mentioned and may not be concluded from information in the passage.
32. (**C**) "...noise is unavoidable in a complex industrial society...." Choice (A) contradicts the fact that it [noise] is a serious threat to physical and psychological well-being. Choice (B) refers to hearing loss, which is America's number one nonfatal health problem, not to noise. Choice (D) refers to an industrial society, not to noise.
33. "Investigations on human subjects have demonstrated that babies are affected by noise even before they are born. Fetuses exposed to noise tend to be overactive, they cry easily, and they are more sensitive to gastrointestinal problems after birth." The connection between the two sentences is the reference to "babies...before they are born" and "fetuses." The first sentence is a general statement followed by examples in the second sentence.
34. (**C**) Choices (A), (B), and (D) are important to the discussion and provide details that support the main topic, "hunter-gatherers."
35. (**D**) "This method of harvesting from nature's provision [hunting and gathering] is the oldest known subsistence strategy." Choice (A) refers to a practice engaged in by hunter-gatherers in order to locate new sources of food, not to the subsistence strategy. Choices (B) and (C) refer to later strategies for subsistence.
36. (**B**) "This method [hunting and gathering] has been practiced for at least the last 2 million years." Choice (C) refers to the date when farming and the domestication of animals, not hunting and gathering, were introduced. Choices (A) and (D) are not mentioned and may not be concluded from information in the passage.
37. In the context of this passage, the word crude is closest in meaning to rudimentary. No other words or phrases in the **bold** text are close to the meaning of the word rudimentary.
38. (**B**) In the context of this passage, dwindled is closest in meaning to decreased. Choices (A), (C), and (D) are not accepted definitions of the word.
39. "In higher latitudes, the shorter growing season has restricted the availability of plant life. Such conditions [the shorter growing season] have caused a greater dependence on hunting...." Other choices would change the meaning of the sentence.
40. (**D**) "The abundance of vegetation in the lower latitudes...has provided a greater opportunity for gathering a variety of plants." Choices (A), (B), and (C) refer to the higher latitudes, not to the lower latitudes.
41. (**B**) "Contemporary hunter-gatherers may help us understand our prehistoric ancestors." Choices (A) and (C) may be true, but they are not mentioned as a reason to study contemporary hunter-gatherer societies. Choice (D) contradicts the fact that the

author believes the patterns of behavior of contemporary hunter-gatherers may be similar to those practiced by mankind during the Paleolithic Period.

42. (**A**) In the context of this passage, exploit is closest in meaning to use. Choices (B), (C), and (D) are not accepted definitions of the word.

43. (**C**) Choice (C) is a restatement of the sentence referred to in the passage. *Within a reasonable distance* means near. Choices (A), (B), and (D) would change the meaning of the original sentence.

44. (**A**) "It [hunting-gathering] was…the only way to obtain food until rudimentary farming and very crude methods for the domestication of animals were introduced…." Choice (A) refers to farming, not to patterns of behavior for hunter-gatherers. The small group harvests the food by gathering it, not by planting it. Choices (B), (C), and (D) are all mentioned in paragraph 3.

45. (**D**) Choice (A) refers to the fact that a society based on hunting and gathering must be very mobile. Choice (B) refers to the fact that there is a strict division of labor between the sexes. Choice (C) refers to the fact that the camp is located near the food supply. Only Choice (D) is not mentioned and may not be concluded from information in the passage.

Model Test 8—Computer-Assisted TOEFL

Section 1: Listening

1. **(A)** Because the woman refuses to sign and tells the man that he has to get his advisor's signature, we must conclude that she is not the man's advisor. In Choice (B), although she says she is sorry, that is not the reason she cannot sign the form. Choice (C) contradicts the fact that the man asks her to sign a course request form. In Choice (D), it is true that he needs his advisor's signature, but that is not the reason the woman cannot sign the form.
2. **(C)** *No way* is an idiomatic expression that means it is not going to happen. Choice (A) misinterprets the phrase *no way* to mean directions. Choice (B) contradicts the fact that he will not withdraw from the course he is in. Choice (D) contradicts the fact that he gives the woman a definitive answer to her question.
3. **(A)** Since the man is asking what happened in Dr. Peterson's class, it must be concluded that the man did not go to class. Choice (B) contradicts the fact that the woman is in Dr. Peterson's class. Choices (C) and (D) are not mentioned and may not be concluded from information in the conversation.
4. **(C)** Since the man suggests that they sit closer to the front and the woman agrees, they will probably move to the front of the room. Choice (B) contradicts the fact that they are already sitting together. Choice (D) contradicts the fact that the woman agrees with the man. Choice (A) is not mentioned and may not be concluded from information in the conversation.
5. **(B)** Because the man objected to the cold winter but said he liked Montreal the rest of the year, it must be concluded that he liked Montreal in the spring, summer, and fall. Choice (A) contradicts the fact that the man objected to the cold winter. Choice (C) contradicts the fact that the man liked Montreal most of the time. Choice (D) contradicts the fact that the man said "yes" when he was asked if he liked living in Montreal.
6. **(C)** *You bet* means certainly. Choice (A) misinterprets the word *bet* to mean a wager. Choices (B) and (D) are not mentioned and may not be concluded from information in the conversation.
7. **(C)** The woman says she got a nicotine patch. Choices (A), (B), and (D) refer to the methods that the man has used to quit smoking in the past.
8. **(C)** To *not be too big on* something means to not like it very much. Choice (D) contradicts the fact that he responds to the woman's question. Choices (A) and (B) are not mentioned and may not be concluded from information in the conversation.
9. **(D)** *Way to go* means congratulations. Choices (A), (B), and (C) misinterpret the meaning of the phrase *way to go*.
10. **(A)** "You must be thinking of my roommate [who got an assistantship]." Choice (B) contradicts the fact that she will be studying full time. Choice (D) contradicts the fact that the man has confused the woman with her roommate. Choice (C) is not mentioned and may not be concluded from information in the conversation.
11. **(C)** *I wish I knew* is an idiomatic expression that means one does not know. Choices (A), (B), and (D) are not paraphrases of the expression and may not be concluded from information in the conversation.
12. **(C)** To be *on one's way* is an idiomatic expression that means to be ready to leave. Choices (A), (B), and (D) are not paraphrases of the expression and may not be concluded from information in the conversation.
13. **(C)** "…you could get a plant." Choice (D) refers to the fact that the man considered taking candy to his friends, not to the woman's suggestion. Choices (A) and (B) are not mentioned and may not be concluded from information in the conversation.
14. **(B)** Since the woman's room number is 119, and the man points out that the odd numbers are on the other side, the woman will probably look on the other side of the hall. Choices

(A), (C), and (D) are not mentioned and may not be concluded from information in the conversation.

15. (**D**) Since the woman assures the man that it takes a long time to process the application, she implies that he should be patient. Choice (B) contradicts the fact that it takes six weeks, not three weeks, to process. Choices (A) and (C) are not mentioned and may not be concluded from information in the conversation.
16. (**A**) Since the woman offers her passport, it must be concluded that she wants to use it for ID. Choice (C) refers to the method of payment, not to the identification required. Choice (D) contradicts the fact that she is paying with a traveler's check. Choice (B) is not mentioned and may not be concluded from information in the conversation.
17. (**B**) *I couldn't have been more pleased* is an idiomatic expression that means the speaker was very pleased. Choice (D) contradicts the fact that the man was pleased with the meeting. Choices (A) and (C) were not mentioned and may not be concluded from information in the conversation.
18. (**C**) "You are here because you are accused of plagiarism." Choice (A) refers to the fact that the professor gave him a failing grade, not to the reason why the student is in the dean's office. The dean gives the student some advice, but Choice (B) is not mentioned as a reason for his being in the dean's office. Choice (D) is incorrect because the dean refers to the fact that plagiarism is intellectual theft, not to the theft of a book.
19. (**A**) "That [using ideas with a citation] is what I don't understand." Choice (D) refers to the dean's suggestion that the student get a tutor, not to the student's excuse. Choices (B) and (C) are not mentioned and may not be concluded from information in the conversation.
20. (**C**) "I'm going to give you a warning this time." Choice (A) refers to the dean's decision to expel the student if she ever sees him in her office for a similar offense. Choice (B) refers to the professor's, not the dean's, punishment of the student. Choice (D) refers to the advice, not the punishment, that the dean gave the student.
21. (**B**) "I suggest that you go over to the Learning Resources Center for some tutoring." Choices (A), (C), and (D) are not mentioned and may not be concluded from information in the conversation.
22. (**B**) "I'm trying to decide whether to stay here or to transfer to a larger school." Choices (A), (C), and (D) are not mentioned and may not be concluded from information in the conversation.
23. (**C**) "...your teachers know you, and they really seem to care about you." Choices (A) and (D) refer to the advantages of a larger school, not to what she likes about the college she is attending. Choice (B) is not mentioned and may not be concluded from information in the conversation.
24. (**C**) "...I'm planning to go to graduate school, so my plan is to get really good grades here and try to get into a well-known university for my master's degree." Choice (A) contradicts the fact that he listens to the woman. Choice (D) contradicts the fact that he tries to understand her point of view, and shares his plans. Choice (B) is not mentioned and may not be concluded from information in the conversation.
25. (**A**) "...try to get into a well-known university for my master's degree." Choice (C) contradicts the fact that his plan is to get good grades in the undergraduate program at his current school. Choices (B) and (D) are not mentioned and may not be concluded from information in the conversation.
26. (**B**) "In anthropology, however, *culture* is defined in a very different way. To an anthropologist, culture refers to...." Choices (A), (C), and (D) are secondary themes used to support the main theme of the lecture, culture in anthropology.
27. (**D**) "In informal conversation, the word *culture* refers to a desirable personal attribute ...and that's what most people think of when they hear the word culture." Choices (A), (B), and (C) refer to the definition of *culture* in anthropology, not in informal conversation.
28. (**C**) "For a thought or activity to be included as part of a culture, it must be commonly shared by or considered appropriate for the group." Choice (A) refers to a subculture, not a culture. Choice (B) refers to the word *culture* as it is understood in informal

conversation. Choice (D) refers to the United States and societies like it.

29. (**A**) "...in...the United States, which comprises many diverse ethnic groups, there are practices common to all Americans, and these practices constitute American culture." Choice (B) refers to a subculture, not to the culture of the United States. Choice (C) contradicts the fact that the practices are common to all Americans. Choice (D) contradicts the fact that the practices are common to all, not just the majority, of Americans.

30. (**C**) "...the smaller groups within the larger society have shared customs that are specific to their group...a subculture." Choices (A) and (B) refer to an informal definition of culture, not to subcultures. Choice (D) refers to a definition of culture by an anthropologist, not to a definition of a subculture.

31. (**B**) "If the current trends continue, however, that estimate will fall far short of actual numbers...." Choices (A) and (C) contradict the fact that the estimate is lower than the actual numbers, not the same or higher. The fraction in Choice (D) refers to the AIDS cases accounted for by homosexual men in the 1980s, not to the actual numbers compared with the estimate.

32. (**D**) (**A**) (**C**) (**B**) "In the 1980s, homosexual men...accounted for...two thirds of all AIDS cases.... today almost ninety percent of new adult infections result from heterosexual contact.... the rates of exposure and infection are rising for women, with an accompanying rise in the number of children...with HIV...."

33. (**C**) (**D**) "...women are biologically more susceptible to all sexually transmitted diseases...and the traditional role of the man as the partner in control of the sexual activity inhibits women in many cultures...." The multiple partners in Choice (A) refer to those of older men, not women. The cultures in Choice (B) refer to restrictions for women using protection, not to restrictions on the use of protection.

34. (**A**) (**C**) "By the twenty-first century, it is now expected that the majority of AIDS victims will be heterosexual women and their young children." Choices (B) and (D) are not mentioned in the estimate and may not be concluded from information in the talk.

35. (**A**) "...most travelers are not able to adjust to the shorter or longer day." Choice (B) refers to a situation that affects the severity of jet lag, not to the cause. Choices (C) and (D) are not mentioned and may not be concluded from information in the discussion.

36. (**C**) "...people over thirty who tend to have a more established routine are likely to suffer the most from jet lag." Choice (A) contradicts the fact that people over thirty, not younger people, suffer the most. Choice (B) contradicts the fact that an adjustment from air travel east to west is a little easier. Choice (D) is not mentioned and may not be concluded from information in the discussion.

37. (**B**) (**C**) "...to minimize the effects of jet lag...[try] scheduling an early evening arrival...drink lots of water." Choice (A) contradicts the fact that a full stomach increases the symptoms of jet lag. Choice (D) is not mentioned and may not be concluded from information in the discussion.

38. (**A**) "...studies show that we require half a day for each time zone crossed." Choices (B), (C), and (D) contradict the research results.

39. (**C**) "One of the most successful educational programs for adults is the Elderhostel...." Choice (A) contradicts the fact that the classes are taught by highly qualified faculty at the host college, not by retired professors. Although Elderhostel was originally a summer program, Choice (B) contradicts the fact that it is now offered year round. Choice (D) contradicts the fact that Elderhostel is an educational program with travel included, not a travel program.

40. (**B**) (**D**) "Although courses are not offered for credit, and no exams are required, the classes are taught by highly qualified faculty at the host college." Choice (A) contradicts the fact that the courses are not offered for credit. Choice (C) contradicts the fact that Elderhostel is for people over the age of sixty.

41. (**C**) "Elderhostel [is] designed for students over the age of sixty." Choice (C) is a person sixty years or older. The other people in the picture, Choices (A), (B), and (D), are too young to enroll in Elderhostel.

42. **(B)** "...call your local college." Choices (A), (C), and (D) are not mentioned and may not be concluded from information in the talk.
43. **(A)** "...the resemblance of pyrite to gold causes prospectors worldwide to mistake fool's gold [pyrite] for real gold." Choice (C) contradicts the fact that it is a very common mineral. Choice (D) contradicts the fact that the specimen [of pyrite] shows well-defined crystal formations. Choice (B) is true, but it is referred to as an advantageous characteristic, not a problem.
44. **(D)** "I will be putting another specimen in the mineral lab for you after today's lecture." Choices (A), (B), and (C) are not mentioned and may not be concluded from information in the lecture.
45. **(C)** Choice (C) is the most similar to the specimen that the professor showed in class. Choices (A) and (B) are not minerals.
46. **(B) (C)** "...pyrite is much more brittle than gold.... and when pyrite is struck with a hammer, it will create sparks." Choice (A) refers to a property of gold, not to that of pyrite. Choice (D) contradicts the fact that pyrite is found in all kinds of geological environments and is considered a very common mineral.
47. **(A)** "...all you have to do [to tell the difference between pyrite and gold] is heat your sample." Choices (B) and (D) refer to the smell of sulfuric acid that pyrite produces when heated, but using acid or smelling the sample are not mentioned as tests for pyrite. Choice (C) refers to the description of the pyrite specimen that the professor has brought to class, but the fact that so many prospectors worldwide mistake pyrite for gold implies that it cannot be identified by looking at it.
48. **(C)** Since the man begins the conversation by asking whether anyone has turned in a lost book, it must be concluded that the lost book is the reason for the conversation. Choice (A) is true, but it is not the reason for the conversation. Choice (B) contradicts the fact that the man knows where the Student Union is. Choice (D) is not mentioned and may not be concluded from information in the conversation.
49. **(C)** "...I think I left it [my book] under the table...when I was in here [the cafeteria]." Choice (B) refers to the location of the lost-and-found, not to where the man left his book. Choice (D) refers to where the man noticed that his book was missing. Choice (A) is not mentioned and may not be concluded from information in the conversation.
50. **(A) (D)** "There's a lost-and-found in the Student Union.... If you don't find it there today, you should probably check again tomorrow." Choices (B) and (C) are not mentioned and may not be concluded from information in the conversation.

Section 2: Structure

1. **(C)** *Similar* is used after the two nouns *protoplasm* and *glue* to compare them. Choice (A) is redundant because the pronoun *they* is used consecutively after the nouns to which it refers. Choice (B) has the same meaning as the correct answer, but *similar to* is used before, not after, the second noun compared. Choice (D) does not have a verb. (Refer to Patterns, Problem 87, page 185.)
2. **(D)** *Oil* is a noncount noun because it is a liquid that can change shape, depending on the shape of the container. (Refer to Patterns, Problem 53, page 140.)
3. **(C)** Every sentence must have a main verb. Choices (A), (B), and (D) are not main verbs. (Refer to Patterns, Problem 1, page 72.)
4. **(D)** In order to refer to a gallon of water being *moved to a higher place, raise* not *rise* should be used. To *raise* means to move to a higher place. To *rise* means to go up without assistance; to increase. (Refer to Style, Problem 22, page 278.)
5. **(D)** *Unless* introduces a subject and verb that express a change in conditions. Choices (A), (B), and (C) do not have a subject and verb. (Refer to Patterns, Problem 26, page 105.)
6. **(A)** The word order for a passive sentence is BE followed by a participle. Choice (B) is a participle, but the form of BE is missing. Choice (C) is redundant because the pronoun *it* is used consecutively after the subject *path.* Choice (D) is an *-ing* form, not a passive. (Refer to Patterns, Problem 31, page 112.)
7. **(B)** *From* introduces cause. Choices (A),

(C), and (D) are not idiomatic. (Refer to Patterns, Problem 112, page 215.)

8. **(A)** *Wholly* should be *As a whole. As a whole* means *generally. Wholly* means *completely.* (Refer to Patterns, Problem 136, page 245.)
9. **(A)** *More than* is used before a specific number to express an estimate. "As many as two hundred" would also be correct. (Refer to Patterns, Problem 94, page 194.)
10. **(A)** *There* introduces inverted order, but there must still be agreement between subject and verb. *Is* should be *are* to agree with the plural subject, *so many variables.* (Refer to Style, Problem 8, page 260.)
11. **(D)** No article before a noncount noun or a plural count noun means *all*. Choice (A) would be an incomplete sentence because it is missing a main verb. Choices (B) and (C) contain articles and would change the meaning of the sentence. (Refer to Patterns, Problem 64, page 157.)
12. **(D)** Either an *-ing* form or an infinitive may be used as the subject of a sentence. Choice (A) is an infinitive that means *to establish*, not *to identify*. Choice (B) is a verb word. Choice (C) is a noun. "To find" would also be correct. (Refer to Patterns, Problem 59, page 150.)
13. **(D)** *By* expresses means before an *-ing* form. *Provide* should be *providing.* (Refer to Patterns, Problem 114, page 217.)
14. **(D)** *Had* and a participle in the condition requires *would have* and a participle in the result. *Will* should be *would.* (Refer to Patterns, Problem 24, page 102.)
15. **(D)** *Besides* is used before a noun or an adjective. It means *in addition to.* Choices (A) and (C) include the word *beside*, which means *near*, not *besides.* In Choice (B), the word *besides* is used after, not before, the noun. (Refer to Patterns, Problem 106, page 208.)
16. **(D)** *No* is used before a noun phrase like *definite shape*. *Not* in Choice (A) should be used before a verb. *None* in Choice (B) and *nothing* in Choice (C) are pronouns that are used instead of the noun phrase. (Refer to Patterns, Problem 65, page 158.)
17. **(D)** To *differ from* is a verb that expresses difference. Because Choices (A) and (C) are not verbs, the sentence would not have a main verb in it. Choice (B) is a verb, but the preposition *from* is missing. "A dolphin is different from a porpoise" would also be correct. (Refer to Patterns, Problem 92, page 192.)
18. **(C)** *Do* is usually used before complements that describe work and chores. *Make* should be *do* before the complement *research.* (Refer to Style, Problem 28, page 285.)
19. **(B)** *That most natural time units are not simple multiples of each other* functions as the noun phrase subject of the main verb *is.* Choice (A) is redundant because the pronoun *it* is used consecutively after the noun phrase subject. In Choice (C), the usual subject-verb-object order of English sentences is reversed. Choice (D) does not include a main verb. (Refer to Patterns, Problem 61, page 152.)
20. **(C)** *Believe* should be *belief. Believe* is a verb. *Belief* is a noun. (Refer to Style, Problem 30, page 288.)
21. **(C)** A negative phrase introduces inverted order. *Only after* requires an auxiliary verb, subject, and main verb. In Choices (A) and (D) the subject precedes the auxiliary. In Choice (B) there is no subject. (Refer to Patterns, Problem 129, page 237.)
22. **(D)** A present tense verb is used after *when* to express future. *Will limit* should be *limit.* (Refer to Patterns, Problem 123, page 229.)
23. **(C)** Because the verb *to fail* requires an infinitive in the complement, *recognizing* should be *to recognize.* (Refer to Patterns, Problem 2, page 73.)
24. **(A)** An introductory phrase should immediately precede the subject noun that it modifies. It does not have a main verb. Choices (B) and (C) contain both subjects and verbs. Choice (D) does not modify the subject noun, *Carl Sandburg*. (Refer to Patterns, Problem 131, page 239.)
25. **(C)** Ideas in a series should be expressed by parallel structures. *Writing* should be *to write* to provide for parallelism with the infinitives *to understand* and *to read.* (Refer to Style, Problem 17, page 271.)

Section 3: Reading

1. **(D)** The other choices are secondary ideas that are used to develop the main idea,

"Seismography." Choices (A), (B), and (C) are important to the discussion as they relate to the Richter scale.

2. (**B**) The Richter scale was developed "to measure the amplitude of the largest trace...." Choices (A) and (D) refer to the placement of the seismograph in order to record the amplitude. Choice (C) refers to the numerical reference that estimates the degree of damage.
3. (**C**) In the context of this passage, standard could best be replaced by conventional. Choices (A), (B), and (D) are not accepted definitions of the word.
4. (**A**) The "tables have been formulated to demonstrate the magnitude of any earthquake...." Choice (D) refers to the release of energy, one of the factors that is considered in formulating the magnitude. Choices (B) and (C) are not mentioned in reference to the value of the tables.
5. (**B**) "...each number on the Richter scale represents an earthquake ten times as strong as one of the next lower magnitude." Choices (A), (C), and (D) contradict the fact that each magnitude is ten times stronger than the previous one.
6. "An earthquake that reads 4 to 5.5 would be expected to cause localized damage, and those [earthquakes] of magnitude 2 on the Richter scale may be felt." Other choices would change the meaning of the sentence.
7. (**A**) Choice (A) is a restatement of the sentence referred to in the passage. *Site* means location. Choices (B), (C), and (D) would change the meaning of the original sentence.
8. In the context of this passage, the word basically is closest in meaning to roughly. No other words or phrases in the **bold** text are close to the meaning of the word roughly.
9. (**B**) In the context of this passage, undetected is closest in meaning to with no notice. Choices (A), (C), and (D) are not accepted definitions of the word.
10. (**D**) Because the author states that "Earthquakes of Mercalli 2 or 3 are basically the same as those of Richter 3 or 4" and "measurements of 11 or 12 on the Mercalli scale can be roughly correlated with magnitudes of 8 or 9 on the Richter scale," it must be concluded that the two scales are different but can be compared. Choice (A) contradicts the fact that two scales of measurement describe earthquakes in quantitative terms. Choice (B) contradicts the fact that the Richter scale measures the amplitude of the largest trace, and the Mercalli scale measures the intensity of the shaking. Choice (C) contradicts the fact that most earthquakes are so minor that they pass undetected.
11. (**C**) "...the Richter scale,...developed and introduced by American seismologist Charles R. Richter in 1935." Choices (A) and (B) are both mentioned in the reference to the Richter scale. Choice (D) refers to the purpose of the scale, which is "to measure the amplitude of the largest trace...." Choice (C) refers to the Mercalli scale, not to the Richter scale.
12. (**B**) The passage mainly discusses Charles Ives' life, including references to the details referred to in Choices (A), (C), and (D).
13. (**B**) "...the use of dissonance and special effects was just too different for the musical mainstream." Choice (A) is true but is not a reason that the public did not appreciate his music. Choice (D) contradicts the fact that he wrote music. In Choice (C), although the performers felt his music was unplayable, there is no reference to the fact that they did not play it well.
14. In the context of this passage, the phrase clash of keys with conflicting rhythms is closest in meaning to the word dissonance. No other words or phrases in the **bold** text are close to the meaning of the word dissonance.
15. (**D**) "Even the few conductors and performers he tried to interest in his compositions felt that they [the compositions] were unplayable." Choices (A), (B), and (C) would change the meaning of the sentence.
16. (**C**) "...he became a successful insurance executive...." Choice (A) refers to his father's profession. Choice (B) refers to Horatio Parker's profession. Although it is true that Ives published his own music as in Choice (D), he did not make a living from it.
17. (**A**) In the context of this passage, became reconciled to is closest in meaning to accepted. Choices (B), (C), and (D) are not

accepted definitions of the word.

18. (**A**) "...he published his work privately and distributed it free." Choice (C) refers to the fact that he occasionally hired musicians to play his works, but they were private, not public performances. Choices (B) and (D) are not mentioned and may not be concluded from information in the passage.
19. (**D**) Choice (A) refers to the fact that Ives "...quoted, combined, insinuated, and distorted familiar hymns, marches, and battle songs...." Choice (B) refers to the fact that Ives was "...experimenting with polytonality...and dissonance...." Choice (C) refers to the fact that "the few conductors and performers he tried to interest in his compositions felt that they were unplayable." Choice (D) contradicts the fact that Ives became "famous" near the end of his life and "received the Pulitzer Prize."
20. (**D**) "...the greatest music composed by an American." Choice (A) contradicts the fact that the reviews were laudatory. Choices (B) and (C) refer to Ives' music prior to the *Concord Sonata* performance.
21. "John Kirkpatrick played *Concord Sonata* in Town Hall.... One reviewer proclaimed it [*Concord Sonata*] 'the greatest music composed by an American.' " Other choices would change the meaning of the sentence.
22. "Instead, he became a successful insurance executive, building his company into the largest agency in the country in only two decades. Even during such a busy time in his career, he still dedicated himself to composing music in the evenings, on weekends, and during vacations." The connection between the two sentences is the reference to "building his company into the largest agency" and "such a busy time in his career." Chronological order requires the second sentence to follow the first.
23. (**C**) Because the author states that bats are "not...dirty...groom themselves carefully...and help reforest barren land," it must be concluded that the author views bats as clean, helpful members of the animal world. Choice (A) contradicts the author's statements that bats are not dirty and only rarely carry rabies. Choice (B) contradicts the author's statement that bats are not the monsters that they are portrayed in vampire films. Choice (D) contradicts the author's statement that bats consume pests, pollinate plants, and reforest land, all of which are important contributions to the animal world.
24. (**B**) "...the majority [of bats] eat fruit, insects, spiders or other small animals." Choice (A) contradicts the fact that only three species rely on blood meals. Choice (D) contradicts the fact that bats eat small, not large, animals. Choice (C) is not mentioned and may not be concluded from information in the passage.
25. In the context of this passage, the word huge is closest in meaning to enormous. No other words or phrases in the **bold** text are close to the meaning of the word enormous.
26. (**C**) "They...help reforest...barren land by excreting millions of undigested seeds." Choices (A), (B), and (D) all refer to the activities of bats, but not to how they reforest the land.
27. (**D**) "Of the hundreds of species of bats, only three rely on blood meals." Choice (A) contradicts the fact that bats pollinate many varieties of plant life. Choice (B) contradicts the fact that bats assume specialized roles within their social system. Choice (C) contradicts the fact that almost all bats use echolocation.
28. (**A**) In the context of this passage, emit is closest in meaning to send. Choices (B), (C), and (D) are not accepted definitions of the word.
29. (**A**) "As these signals bounce off objects in their path, an echo is detected by the bats' sensitive ears...[and] they...undertake corrective or evasive action." Choice (B) refers to one of the roles of bats within their social system, not to their navigational skills. Choice (C) is incorrect because the number fifty refers to the number of high-pitched squeaks per minute, not to the number of times bats beat their wings. Choice (D) is true, but the specific noises they hear are the echoes referred to in Choice (A).
30. (**C**) "As these signals bounce off objects in their path, an echo is detected by the bats' sensitive ears that informs them [the bats] of the direction, distance, and nature of obstacles..." Other choices would change the meaning of the sentence.
31. "In fact, all species of bats can see, probably

about as well as human beings." Quotation from sentence 5, paragraph 2.

32. "Within their social systems, bats assume specialized roles. Some [bats] may guard the entrance to their caves, others may scout for food, and still others may warn the colony of approaching danger." Other choices would change the meaning of the sentence.
33. "It is a little known fact that bats are highly social creatures. Aggregation during the day may vary from small groups consisting of a single male and a dozen or more females to huge colonies of many thousands or even millions of individuals, hanging upside down in caves or in hollow trees, buildings, and other protected shelters." The connection between the two sentences is the social nature of bats. The first sentence is a general statement followed by examples in the second sentence.
34. (**B**) The passage includes descriptions of various kinds of population centers. Choices (A) and (D) are two kinds of population centers described in the passage. Choice (C) refers to the source of the information about population centers, not to the topic of the passage.
35. (**B**) "...more Americans live in the suburbs of large metropolitan areas than in the cities themselves." Choice (A) contradicts the statement that more Americans live in the suburbs. Choices (C) and (D) are not mentioned and may not be concluded from information in the passage.
36. In the context of this passage, the word live is closest in meaning to reside. No other words or phrases in the **bold** text are close to the meaning of the word reside.
37. (**A**) "The Bureau of the Census regards any area with more than 2500 people as an urban area...." Choice (B) refers to an MSA, not to an urban area. The number in Choice (C) refers to megapolises, not to urban areas. Choice (D) refers to the definition of a megapolis.
38. (**A**) "...the political boundaries are less significant than the social and economic relationships and the transportation and communication systems...." Because the political boundaries are less significant, it must be concluded that the factors in Choices (B), (C), and (D) are more significant.
39. (**C**) In the context of this passage, integrate is closest in meaning to unite. Choices (A), (B), and (D) are not accepted definitions of the word.
40. In the context of this passage, the word area is closest in meaning to locale. No other words or phrases in the **bold** text are close to the meaning of the word locale.
41. (**C**) "...an MSA is any area that contains a city and its [the city's] surrounding suburbs and has a total population of 50,000...." Other choices would change the meaning of the sentence.
42. "...the Bureau reports more than 280 MSAs, which together account for 75 percent of the US population." Quotation from sentence 1, paragraph 3. Paragraph 2 defines an MSA by the number of people living in it but does not contain any references to the total population living in all MSAs.
43. (**A**) In the context of this passage, the phrase beside each other is closest in meaning to the word adjacent. Choices (B), (C), and (D) describe megapolises, but they are not close in meaning to the word adjacent.
44. (**D**) "...the Bureau recognizes eighteen megapolises, that is, continuous adjacent metropolitan areas." Choices (A), (B), and (C) contradict the fact that a megapolis includes more than one adjacent city.
45. (**A**) "One of the most obvious megapolises [is]...the Eastern Corridor.... Another megapolis that is growing rapidly is the California coast...." Choice (B) refers to the population of all the MSAs, not to the population of the Eastern Corridor and the California coast. Choice (C) is true, but it is not the reason that the Eastern Corridor and the California coast are mentioned. Choice (D) is not mentioned and may not be concluded from information in the passage.

SCORE ESTIMATES

Important Background Information

It is not possible for you to determine the exact score that you will receive on the TOEFL. There are three reasons why this is true. First, the testing conditions on the day of your official TOEFL will affect your score If you are in an uncomfortable room, if there are noisy distractions, if you are upset because you almost arrived late for the test, or if you are very nervous, then these factors can affect your score. The administration of a Model Test is more controlled. You will probably not be as stressed when you take one of the tests in this book. Second, the Model Tests in the book are designed to help you practice the most frequently tested item types on the official TOEFL. Because they are constructed to teach as well as to test, there is more repetition in Model Tests than there is on official TOEFL tests. Tests that are not constructed for exactly the same purposes are not exactly comparable. Third, the TOEFL scores received by the same student will vary from one official Computer-Based TOEFL examination to another official Computer-Based TOEFL examination by as many as 20 points, even when the examinations are taken on the same day. In testing and assessment, this is called a standard error of measurement. Therefore, a TOEFL score cannot be predicted precisely even when two official tests are used.

But, of course, you would like to know how close you are to your goal. To do that, you can use the following procedure to estimate your TOEFL score. An estimate is an approximation. In this case, it is a range of scores.

Score Correspondence Procedure

1. Use the charts on the following pages to determine your percentage scores for each section of the TOEFL.

2. Determine the total percentage score for the TOEFL.
   Listening Section = one third the total
   Structure Section = one sixth the total
   Reading Section = one third the total
   Writing Section = one sixth the total

3. Use the Score Correspondence Table to estimate an official TOEFL score.

Listening Section

Number Correct	Percentage Score
50	100
49	98
48	96
47	94
46	92
45	90
44	88
43	86
42	84
41	82
40	80
39	78
38	76
37	74
36	72
35	70
34	68
33	66
32	64
31	62
30	60
29	58
28	56
27	54
26	52
25	50
24	48
23	46
22	44
21	42
20	40
19	38
18	36
17	34
16	32
15	30
14	28
13	26
12	24
11	22
10	20
9	18
8	16
7	14
6	12
5	10
4	8
3	6
2	4
1	2
0	0

Structure Section

Number Correct	Percentage Score
25	100
24	96
23	94
22	88
21	84
20	80
19	76
18	72
17	68
16	64
15	60
14	56
13	52
12	48
11	44
10	40
9	36
8	32
7	28
6	24
5	20
4	16
3	12
2	8
1	4
0	0

Reading Section

Number Correct	Percentage Score
45	100
44	98
43	96
42	93
41	91
40	89
39	87
38	84
37	82
36	80
35	78
34	76
33	73
32	71
31	69
30	67
29	64
28	62
27	60
26	58
25	56
24	53
23	51
22	49
21	47
20	44
19	42
18	40
17	38
16	36
15	33
14	31
13	29
12	27
11	24
10	22
9	20
8	18
7	16
6	13
5	11
4	9
3	7
2	4
1	2
0	0

Writing Section

Scaled Score	Percentage Score
6.0	100
5.5	92
5.0	84
4.5	76
4.0	68
3.5	60
3.0	52
2.5	44
2.0	36
1.5	28
1.0	20
0	0

Score Correspondence Table

Model Test Percentage Scores	Computer-Based TOEFL Score Ranges	Paper-Based TOEFL Score Ranges
100	287–300	660–677
95	273–283	640–657
90	260–270	620–637
85	250–260	600–617
80	237–247	580–597
75	220–233	560–577
70	207–220	540–557
65	190–203	520–537
60	173–187	500–517
55	157–170	480–497
50	140–153	460–477
45	123–137	440–457
40	110–123	420–437
35	97–107	400–417
30	83–93	380–397
25	70–80	360–377
20	60–70	340–357
15	47–57	320–337
10	40–47	310–317
5		
0		

Progress Chart

Percentage Scores

	Listening ⅓	Structure ⅙	Reading ⅓	Writing ⅙	=	Total	=	Score Ranges
One								
Two								
Three								
Four								
Five								
Six								
Seven								
Eight								

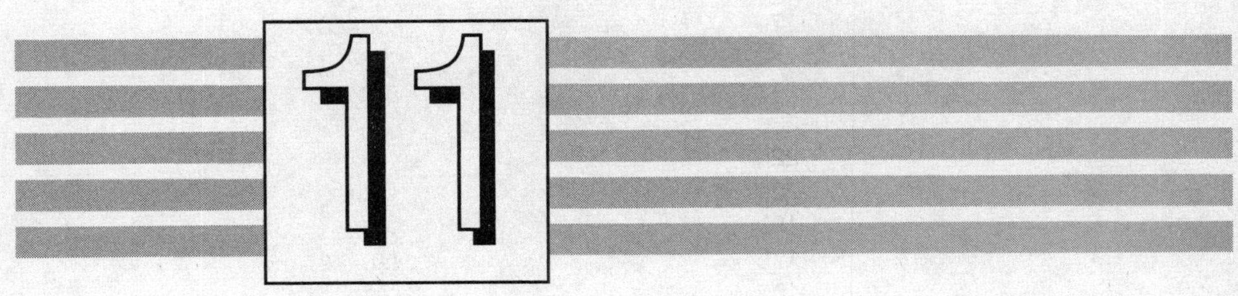

TRANSCRIPT FOR THE LISTENING SECTIONS OF THE TOEFL MODEL TESTS

The following is the transcript for the Listening sections for the TOEFL Model Tests included in this book. Note that the Listening sections always appear as Section 1 of the examinations.

When you take the Model Tests in this book as a preliminary step in your preparation for the actual examination, you should use either the CD-ROM, the compact disks, or the cassette tapes that supplement this book. If you use a CD-ROM, you will see visuals on your computer screen. If you use compact disks, you will hear the audio, but you will not see the visuals.

If you have someone read the TOEFL transcript to you, be sure that he or she understands the timing sequences. The reader should work with a stopwatch or with a regular watch with a second hand in order to keep careful track of the timed pauses between questions. The total amount of time for each section is noted both on the transcript and on the Model Tests. In addition, the time for the pauses between questions is also given on the transcript. Be sure that the reader speaks clearly and at a moderately paced rate. For results that would be closest to the actual testing situation, it is recommended that three persons be asked to read, since some of the Listening Sections include dialogues.

Model Test 1
Computer-Assisted TOEFL

Section 1: Listening

The Listening section of the test measures the ability to understand conversations and talks in English. On the actual TOEFL exam, you will use headphones to listen to the conversations and talks. While you are listening, pictures of the speakers or other information will be presented on your computer screen. There are two parts to the Listening section, with special directions for each part.

On the day of the test, the amount of time you will have to answer all of the questions will appear on the computer screen. The time you spend listening to the test material will not be counted. The listening material and questions about it will be presented only one time. You will not be allowed to take notes or have any paper at your computer. You will both see and hear the questions before the answer choices appear. You can take as much time as you need to select an answer; however, it will be to your advantage to answer the questions as quickly as possible. You may change your answer as many times as you want before you confirm it. After you have confirmed an answer, you will not be able to return to the question.

Before you begin working on the Listening section, you will have an opportunity to adjust the volume of the sound. You will not be able to change the volume after you have started the test.

QUESTION DIRECTIONS—Part A

In Part A of the Listening section, you will hear short conversations between two people. In some of the conversations, each person speaks only once. In other conversations, one or both of the people speak more than once. Each conversation is followed by one question about it.

Each question in this part has four answer choices. You should click on the best answer to each question. Answer the questions on the basis of what is stated or implied by the speakers.

1. Woman: If I were you I'd take the bus to school. Driving in that rush-hour traffic is terrible.
   Man: But by the time the bus gets to my stop, there aren't any seats left.
   Narrator: What is the man's problem?

2. Woman: I'd like to take Dr. Sullivan's section of Physics 100, but my advisor is teaching it too, and I don't want her to be offended.
Man: Who cares?
Woman: Well, I don't want to get on her bad side.
Man: I wouldn't worry about it.
Narrator: What does the man mean?

3. Man: Let's go to the dance at the Student Center on Friday.
Woman: Sounds great, but I'm going to a lecture. Thanks for asking me though.
Narrator: What does the woman imply?

4. Man: That's a nice bike.
Woman: I got it almost five years ago.
Man: You did? It looks new.
Woman : Yes, it's still in really good shape.
Narrator: What does the woman mean?

5. Woman: Would you like some hot coffee or tea?
Man: I like them both, but I'd rather have something cold.
Narrator: What does the man want to drink?

6. Woman: How can I get to the shopping center from here? Not the one on campus. The one downtown.
Man: You can take a bus or a taxi, but it isn't too far to walk.
Narrator: What does the man suggest the woman do?

7. Man: Have you found a class yet?
Woman: I'm just checking the schedule now.
Narrator: What can be inferred about the man?

8. Woman: Do you mind if I turn on the radio for a while?
Man: No, I don't mind.
Narrator: What does the man mean?

9. Man: I'm worried about Anna. She's really been depressed lately. All she does is stay in her room all day.
Woman: That sounds serious. She'd better see someone at the Counseling Center.
Narrator: What does the woman suggest Anna do?

10. Woman: If you have a few minutes, I'd like to talk with you about my project.
Man : Please go on.
Narrator: What does the man mean?

11. Woman: Excuse me. I was in line here first.
Man: Oh, I'm sorry. I didn't realize that you were waiting.
Narrator: What will the man probably do?

12. Man: The neighbors are going to have another party.
Woman: Not again!
Narrator: What does the woman imply?

13. Man: You mean Dr. Franklin said you couldn't have an extension?
Woman: He said it was not his policy.
Man: Really?
Woman: Yes, so now I have to work over the holiday weekend.
Narrator: What had the man assumed?

14. Man: We really should have left already.
Woman: Maybe we ought to call and let them know.
Narrator: What problem do the man and woman have?

15. Man: Have you moved out of your apartment yet?
Woman: No. I'm paid up until the 15th.
Narrator: What is the woman probably going to do?

16. Woman: Mary Anne took the math placement test.
Man: So, she *finally* did it!
Narrator: What had the man assumed about Mary Anne?

17. Woman: Where have you been? I haven't seen you in class all week.
Man: I caught cold, so I stayed in.
Narrator: What does the man mean?

QUESTION DIRECTIONS—Part B

In Part B of the Listening section, you will hear several longer conversations and talks. Each conversation or talk is followed by several questions. The conversations, talks, and questions will not be repeated.

The conversations and talks are about a variety of topics. You do not need special knowledge of the topics to answer the questions correctly. Rather, you should answer each question on the basis of what is stated or implied by the speakers in the conversations or talks.

For most of the questions, you will need to click on the best of four possible answers. Some questions will have special directions. The special directions will appear in a box on the computer screen.

Narrator: Listen to a conversation with a professor.

Man: Professor Day, may I see you for a minute?
Woman: Sure. Come on in, Mike. What's the matter?
Man: I've got a problem.
Woman: Okay.
Man: I need your technical writing class. And, I knew I had to have it so I went early to registration, but by the time I got to the front of the line, it was closed. See, my advisor signed my course request and everything. I was just too far back in the line.
Woman: That's a big class already, Mike. If it's closed, that means I have fifty students in it.
Man: I'm not surprised. It's supposed to be a really good class.
Woman: Can't you take it next year? We offer it every fall.
Man: Well, that's the problem. I'm supposed to be graduating this spring. But, of course, I can't graduate without your class.
Woman: I see. In that case, I'll sign an override for you. It looks like there will be fifty-one. Take this form back to the registration area and they'll get you in.
Man: Thanks, Professor Day. I really appreciate this!

Now get ready to answer the questions

Narrator: 18. What is Mike's problem?

19. What does Mike want Professor Day to do?

20. What does Mike say about graduation?

21. What does Professor Day decide to do?

Narrator: Listen to a talk by a business instructor.

Today's lecture is about the effects of background music on employee performance and retail sales. As you know, every day millions of people in offices and factories around the world do their work to the accompaniment of background music, more commonly known as MUZAK. But did you know that MUZAK is more than a pleasant addition to the environment? Studies show that this seemingly innocent background music can be engineered to control behavior. In fact, MUZAK can improve employee performance by reducing stress, boredom, and fatigue. In one survey, overall productivity increased by thirty percent, although five to ten percent is the average.

The key to MUZAK's success is something called stimulus progression, which means quite simply that the background music starts with a slow, soft song that is low in stimulus value and builds up gradually to an upbeat song that is high in stimulus value. The fastest, loudest sounds are programmed for about ten-thirty in the morning and two-thirty in the afternoon when people are generally starting to tire.

Besides employee performance, MUZAK can increase sales. In supermarkets, slow music can influence shoppers to walk slower and buy more. In restaurants, fast music can cause customers to eat quickly so that the same number of tables may be used to serve more people during peak times such as the lunch hour.

Now get ready to answer the questions

Narrator: 22. What is MUZAK?

23. What is the average increase in productivity when MUZAK is introduced?

24. What is stimulus progression?

25. How does MUZAK influence sales in supermarkets?

Narrator: Listen to a public service announcement.

Community College understands that everyone who wants to attend college will not be able to come to campus. So, as part of the Distance Learning Program, Community College offers a series of video telecourses to meet the needs of students who prefer to complete coursework in their homes, at their convenience.

These telecourses are regular college credit classes taught on videocassette tapes by a Community College professor. To use the materials for the course, you will need your own VHS-type VCR player. Some telecourses will also be broadcast on KCC7-TV's "Sun-Up Semester." This program airs from six o'clock in the morning to seven-thirty, Monday through Friday, and a complete listing of courses is printed in your regular television guide.

To register for a telecourse, phone the Community College Distance Learning Program at 782-6394. The course syllabus, books, and videotapes will be available at the Community College bookstore. During the first week of classes, your instructor will contact you to discuss the course and answer any questions you might have about the course requirements. Then, throughout the rest of the semester, you can use either an 800 telephone number or an e-mail address to contact your instructor.

Now get ready to answer the questions

Narrator: 26. What is this announcement mainly about?

27. Why does the speaker mention the "Sun-Up Semester"?

28. How can students register for a course?

29. How can students contact the instructor?

Narrator: Listen to part of a conversation between two friends on campus.

Donna: Hi, Bill.
Bill: Hi, Donna. Where have you been? I haven't seen you for weeks.
Donna: I know. I had to drop out last semester. I thought I had a cold, but it was mono.
Bill: I'm sorry to hear that. What is mono anyway?
Donna: It's a virus, actually, that attacks your immune system. You really become susceptible to it when you stay up late, stress out, and get run down. It was my own fault. I just kept going, studying late. I didn't get enough rest. You know the story.
Bill: Wow! All too well. I'm surprised that we all don't have it.
Donna: A lot of college students do get it. In fact, it is jokingly called the "college disease." I can tell you though, it's no joke.
Bill: So how are you now?
Donna: I'm still tired. But I learned my lesson though. This semester I'm taking twelve hours, and I'm not pushing myself so hard.
Bill: Good for you. I'm taking twenty-one hours. Sometimes I just don't know why I put so much pressure on myself. If I took one more semester to finish my program, then I wouldn't be so overloaded.
Donna: Listen, if you get sick like I did, you'll have to drop out and you'll end up with an extra semester anyway. So you might as well slow down.
Bill: True. Well, it's something to think about. Take care of yourself, Donna.
Donna: I will. You, too.

Now get ready to answer the questions

Narrator: 30. What is the main topic of this conversation?

31. What was the woman's problem?

32. Why is mono called the "college disease"?

33. What advice does the woman give the man?

Narrator: Listen to a talk by a college professor.

When Edward Sapir was teaching at Yale, Benjamin Lee Whorf enrolled in his class. Whorf was recognized for his investigations of the Hopi language, including his authorship of a grammar book and a dictionary. Even in his early publications, it is clear that he was developing the theory that the very different grammar of Hopi might indicate a different manner of conceiving and perceiving the world on the part of the native speaker of Hopi.

In 1936, he wrote "An American Indian Model of the Universe," which explored the implications of the Hopi verb system with regard to the Hopi conception of space and time.

Whorf is probably best known for his article "The Relation of Habitual Thought and Behavior to Language" and for the three articles that appeared in 1941 in the *Technology Review.*

In these articles, he proposed what he called the principle of "linguistic relativity," which states, at least as a hypothesis, that the grammar of a language influences the manner in which the speaker understands reality and behaves with respect to it.

Since the theory did not emerge until after Whorf had begun to study with Sapir, and since Sapir had most certainly shared in the development of the idea, it came to be called the Sapir-Whorf Hypothesis.

Now get ready to answer the questions

Narrator: 34. What central theme does the lecture examine?

35. Which languages did Whorf use in his research?

36. According to the lecturer, what is linguistic relativity?

37. What is another name for linguistic relativity?

Narrator: Listen to part of a class discussion in an environmental science class.

Dr. Green: Let's begin our discussion today by defining acid rain. Joanne?
Joanne: Acid rain is, uh, pollution that results when sulfur dioxide and nitrogen oxide mix with the water vapor in the atmosphere.
Dr. Green: Good. But why do we call it acid rain, then?
Joanne: Oh, well, sulfur dioxide and nitrogen oxide combine with water vapor and form sulfuric acid and nitric acid.
Dr. Green: And the acid corrodes the environment?
Joanne: It does. According to the book, acid reaches the Earth as rain, sleet, snow, fog, or even mist, but we call all of these various forms of pollution acid rain.
Dr. Green: Exactly right. Now, who can explain how the sulfur dioxide and nitrogen oxide are introduced into the atmosphere in the first place? Ted?
Ted: Fossil fuels, mostly. Right?
Dr. Green: Right. Could you elaborate on that a little?
Ted: Sure. The fossil fuels can be the result of natural events such as volcanic eruptions or forest fires, but most of the time, they are introduced into the atmosphere by industrial processes like the smelting of metals or the burning of oil, coal, and gas.
Dr. Green: Anything else we should add to that? Yes, Joanne?
Joanne: Dr. Green, I think it's important to mention the extent of the damage to areas like the Great Lakes.
Dr. Green: Good point, Joanne. Acidity in the water and on the shorelines has all but eliminated some of the fish populations once found in the Great Lakes region along the United States-Canadian border. Any other damaging effects?

Ted: I'm an agriculture major, Dr. Green, so I am more familiar with the large concentrations of acids that have been deposited in the soil around the Great Lakes.

Dr. Green: And what has happened to the vegetation in that region?

Ted: Well, the rain has caused a chemical change in the soil, which is absorbed by the roots of plants. The plants don't get the nutrients they need, and as a consequence, they die, and uh…

Dr. Green: Yes?

Ted: And it just occurred to me that acid rain is having an adverse effect not only on the environment but also on the economy, especially forestry and agriculture.

Dr. Green: Excellent deduction. Now, let me give you the good news. In the Great Lakes region that was mentioned in our book, an Air Quality Accord was signed by Canada and the United States about ten years ago to establish limits for the amount of acidic deposits that may flow across international boundaries. Since then, many companies on both sides of the border have installed equipment that limits sulfur dioxide emissions, and some have even changed to fuels that are lower in sulfur content.

Ted: Excuse me. Isn't it automobile emission that accounts for a high percentage of the nitrogen oxide?

Dr. Green: Yes, it is, Ted. And that problem presents a somewhat larger challenge to the governments and their agencies.

Now get ready to answer the questions

Narrator: 38. What is the topic of this discussion?

39. What is acid rain?

40. In which two ways has the environment been damaged along the Great Lakes?

41. What are the conditions of the Air Quality Accord?

Narrator: Listen to part of a lecture in a microbiology class.

Bacteria is the common name for a very large group of one-celled microscopic organisms that, we believe, may be the smallest, simplest, and perhaps even the very first form of cellular life that evolved on Earth. Because they are so small, bacteria must be measured in microns, with one micron measuring about 0.00004 inches long. Most bacteria range from about 0.1 microns to 4 microns wide and 0.2 microns to 50 microns long. So you can understand that they are observable only under a microscope.

There are three main types of bacteria, which are classified according to their shape. The slides that I am going to show you are photographic enlargements of bacteria that I observed under the microscope in the lab earlier today. This slide is an example of bacilli.

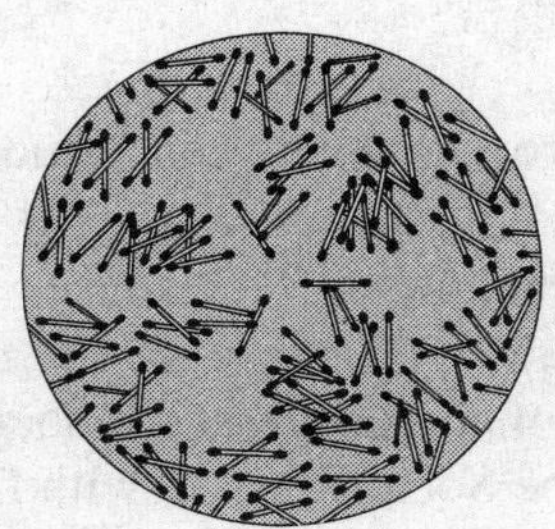

The bacilli are a group of bacteria that occur in the soil and air. As you can see, they are shaped like rods, and if you were to see them in motion, they would be rolling or tumbling under the microscope. These bacilli are largely responsible for food spoilage.

The next slide is a very different shape of bacteria.

It is referred to as the cocci group, and it tends to grow in chains. This example is of the common streptococci that causes strep throat.

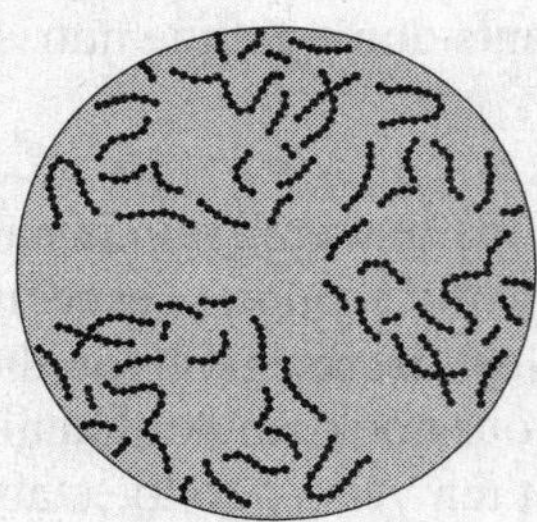

Finally, let's look at the spiral-shaped bacteria called the spirilla. They look a little like corkscrews, and they are responsible for a number of diseases in humans.

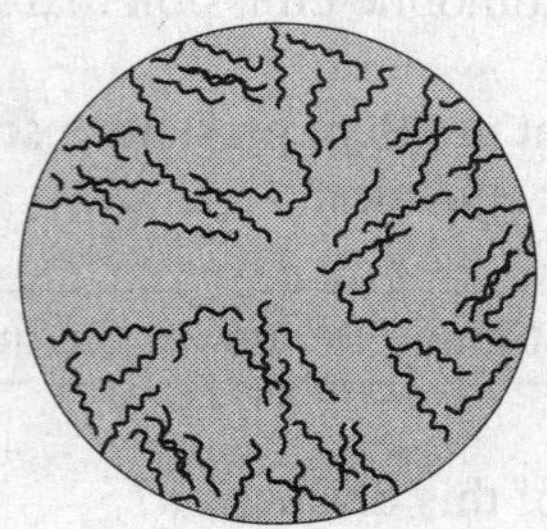

Some species of bacteria do cause diseases, but for the most part, bacteria live harmlessly on the skin, in the mouth, and in the intestines. In fact, bacteria are very helpful to researchers. Bacterial cells resemble the cells of other life forms in many ways, and may be studied to give us insights. For example, we have a major research project in genetics in progress here at the University. Since bacteria reproduce very rapidly, we are using them to determine how certain characteristics are inherited.

Now get ready to answer the questions

Narrator: 42. What is the topic of this lecture?

43. Which two characteristics are common in bacteria?

44. Which of the following slides contain cocci bacteria?

45. Why are bacteria being used in the research study at the University?

Narrator: Listen to part of a conversation between a student and an academic advisor on campus.

Man: Dr. Kelly, do you have a minute?
Dr. Kelly: Sure. Come in.
Man: Thanks. I need to talk with you about my sociology class.
Dr. Kelly: Let's see, that would be Sociology 530 with Dr. Brown.
Man: Right. The problem is that when I scheduled that class, it was supposed to be offered at three o'clock in the afternoon, Tuesdays and Thursdays, but for some reason the time has been changed to nine in the morning. Since I work mornings, I can't take it at that time.

Dr. Kelly: I see. Well, would you like to drop the class?

Man: Yes, but I also need to pick up another class. I have to be a full-time student in order to qualify for my student loan.

Dr. Kelly: So you need at least twelve hours. And you need afternoon classes.

Man: That's right. Or evening classes.

Dr. Kelly: Did you have anything in mind?

Man: Yes. I was considering Sociology 560 or 570. I thought I'd get your opinion.

Dr. Kelly: Either one will fit into your program since you are a Soc major, and they are both electives. Too bad you can't get a required course.

Man: I know, but they all seem to be offered in the morning.

Dr. Kelly: Okay, then. Which one is the most interesting to you?

Man: I'm interested in both of them, but I was thinking since Dr. Brown teaches Soc 560, I might prefer that one. I've been trying to take a class with her because I hear that she is an excellent professor.

Dr. Kelly: Good. The class is open, and I'll just sign that drop-add form for you to drop 530 and add 560. You can just tell Dr. Brown what happened when you see her in class.

Man: Okay. Thanks a lot, Dr. Kelly. I really appreciate it.

Dr. Kelly: Don't mention it.

Now get ready to answer the questions

Narrator: 46. What is the purpose of this conversation?

47. Why does the man need to take at least twelve hours?

48. Why does the man prefer Sociology 560?

49. What will Dr. Kelly do?

50. What will the man probably do after the conversation?

Model Test 2
Computer-Assisted TOEFL

Section 1: Listening

The Listening section of the test measures the ability to understand conversations and talks in English. On the actual TOEFL exam, you will use headphones to listen to the conversations and talks. While you are listening, pictures of the speakers or other information will be presented on your computer screen. There are two parts to the Listening section, with special directions for each part.

On the day of the test, the amount of time you will have to answer all of the questions will appear on the computer screen. The time you spend listening to the test material will not be counted. The listening material and questions about it will be presented only one time. You will not be allowed to take notes or have any paper at your computer. You will both see and hear the questions before the answer choices appear. You can take as much time as you need to select an answer; however, it will be to your advantage to answer the questions as quickly as possible. You may change your answer as many times as you want before you confirm it. After you have confirmed an answer, you will not be able to return to the question.

Before you begin working on the Listening section, you will have an opportunity to adjust the volume of the sound. You will not be able to change the volume after you have started the test.

QUESTION DIRECTIONS—Part A

In Part A of the Listening section, you will hear short conversations between two people. In some of the conversations, each person speaks only once. In other conversations, one or both of the people speak more than once. Each conversation is followed by one question about it.

Each question in this part has four answer choices. You should click on the best answer to each question. Answer the questions on the basis of what is stated or implied by the speakers.

1. Man: How many did you have for the orientation?
Woman: Well, let me see. Fifty had registered, but everyone didn't show up. I believe that we had twenty-five from the Middle East and at least fifteen from Latin America.
Man: You don't mean it!
Narrator: What had the man assumed?

2. Man: Excuse me. Could you tell me when Dr. Smith has office hours?
Woman: Not really, but there's a sign on the door I think.
Narrator: What does the woman imply that the man should do?

3. Man: I heard that Professor Wilson will let you do a project for extra credit.
Woman: That's great! I could use some.
Narrator: What is the woman probably going to do?

4. Man: Is Paul angry?
Woman: If he were, he'd tell us.
Narrator: What does the woman say about Paul?

5. Man: I heard you got an A on the final exam. I think you're the only one who did!
Woman: Not really. There were a couple of other As.
Narrator: What does the woman mean?

6. Woman: Oh, no. It's five o'clock already and I haven't finished studying for the quiz in Dr. Taylor's class.
Man: Don't worry. That clock is half an hour fast.
Narrator: What problem does the woman have?

7. Man: It's much better to wait until tomorrow to go. Don't you agree?
Woman: Yes. I couldn't agree more.
Narrator: What does the woman mean?

8. Man: I have to go to class because I have a test, but if I could, I'd go with you to the movie.
Woman: That's too bad. I wish that you could come along.
Narrator: What is the man going to do?

9. Woman: I left a message on your answering machine a couple of days ago.
Man: Yes. I've been meaning to get back with you.
Narrator: What does the man mean?

10. Man: I think it's my turn.
Woman: Sorry you had to wait so long. One of the other secretaries is out today.
Narrator: What does the woman mean?

11. Man: Could you please tell me what room Dr. Robert Davis is in?
Woman: Yes, he's in the Math Department on the fourth floor. Check with the secretary before going in, though.
Narrator: What does the woman suggest that the man do?

12. Man: Tom wasn't in class again today!
Woman: I know. I wonder whether he'll show up for the final exam.
Narrator: What can be inferred about Tom?

13. Man: Hey, Kathy.
Woman: Hi Ted. How are you doing?
Man: Fine. Are we still on for tonight?
Woman: I'm looking forward to it.
Narrator: What does the man mean?

14. Woman: So the course *is* closed. This is terrible! I have to have it to graduate.
Man: You're okay. Just Dr. Collin's section is closed. There's another section that's still open, but nobody knows who's teaching it. It's marked "staff."
Narrator: What will the woman probably do?

15. Woman: What's wrong?
Man: I still haven't received my score on the GMAT test. Maybe I should call to check on it.
Woman: Don't worry so much. It takes at least six weeks to receive your score.
Narrator: What does the woman think that the man should do?

16. Man: You've been doing a lot of traveling, haven't you?
Woman: Yes. We want to make the most of our time here.
Narrator: What does the woman mean?

17. Woman: Did you get your tickets?
Man: I talked to Judy about it, and she took care of it for me.
Narrator: What does the man mean?

QUESTION DIRECTIONS—Part B

In Part B of the Listening section, you will hear several longer conversations and talks. Each conversation or talk is followed by several questions. The conversations, talks, and questions will not be repeated.

The conversations and talks are about a variety of topics. You do not need special knowledge of the topics to answer the questions correctly. Rather, you should answer each question on the basis of what is stated or implied by the speakers in the conversations or talks.

For most of the questions, you will need to click on the best of four possible answers. Some questions will have special directions. The special directions will appear in a box on the computer screen.

Narrator: Listen to part of a conversation between two classmates on a college campus.

Man: Did you understand that experiment that Bill mentioned in the group presentation?
Woman: The one about free fall?
Man: Right. The one that was conducted on the moon.
Woman: Sure. The astronaut held a hammer in one hand and a feather in the other. Then he dropped them at the same time…
Man: …and both of them hit the ground at the same time.
Woman: Yes. So that proves Galileo's theory that all objects fall at the same rate in the absence of air resistance.
Man: Okay. That was the part that was missing for me. The part about air resistance.
Woman: Oh. Well, since there is no air resistance on the moon, it is the ideal environment for the experiment.
Man: That makes sense.
Woman: Actually, the part that surprised me was how much easier it is to lift the hammer on the moon than it is on Earth because of the moon's lower rate of gravitational acceleration.
Man: But didn't they say that it was just as difficult to push the hammer along the surface when it fell?
Woman: Right again. Because gravity only governs vertical motion like lifting, but not horizontal motion like pushing.
Man: Thanks for going over this with me.
Woman: You're welcome. I really liked the presentation. I think the group did a good job.

Now get ready to answer the questions

Narrator: 18. What are the man and woman talking about?

19. Why is the moon an ideal environment for the experiment?

20. Why was it easier to lift the hammer on the moon?

21. How did the woman feel about the presentation?

Narrator: Listen to a conversation between two college students.

Man: What did you think about the video we were supposed to watch for Professor Stephen's class?
Woman: I didn't see it. Was it good?
Man: Really it was. It was about stress.
Woman: How to relieve stress?
Man: Not really. More the effects of stress on the national health.
Woman: Oh.
Man: But it was interesting, though.
Woman: Really?
Man: Yes. I think they said that one out of nine women age forty-five through sixty-five will have a heart attack.
Woman: I'm surprised at that.
Man: I was, too. Oh, another thing. They said that women usually don't get the same level of care that men do, so the heart attack is likely to be more serious.

Woman: Why is that?

Man: Because many members of the medical profession still think of a heart attack as a male problem, so they don't recognize the symptoms in their women patients.

Woman: Well, it does sound like an interesting video. I'm going to try to see it before class next time so I'll be ready for the discussion.

Man: It's on reserve in the library, so you can't check it out, but you can use one of the viewing rooms. It's only an hour long.

Now get ready to answer the questions

Narrator: 22. What was the video about?

23. What did the students learn about women?

24. How did the man feel about the video?

25. What will the woman probably do?

Narrator: Listen to a lecture by an English intructor.

The romance and marriage of Elizabeth Barrett to Robert Browning inspired some of the greatest love poems written in the English language. Elizabeth, without a doubt the greatest woman poet of the Victorian period, was born in Durham County, England, in 1806. Her first important publication was *The Seraphim and Other Poems,* which appeared in 1838.

By 1843, she was so widely recognized that her name was suggested to replace the late Poet Laureate as the official national poet of England. In part because the sovereign was a woman, there was great support for a movement to break with the tradition of a male Poet Laureate. Nevertheless, she lost the competition to William Wordsworth.

A short time later, she married Robert Browning, himself a gifted poet, and they fled to Florence, Italy. A play, *The Barretts of Wimpole Street*, recounts their confrontation with Elizabeth's father and their eventual elopement against his wishes.

While living in Florence, their only son was born. A year later, in 1850, Elizabeth published her collected works, along with a volume of new poems entitled *Sonnets from the Portuguese*, so named because her husband often called her his "Portuguese." *Aurora Leigh*, her longest work, appeared in 1856, only five years before her death in Italy in 1861.

Now get ready to answer the questions

Narrator: 26. What is the main topic of this lecture?

27. According to the lecturer, what was one reason that Elizabeth Barrett was considered for the title of Poet Laureate?

28. Where did Elizabeth and Robert Browning live after their elopement?

29. When did Elizabeth Barrett Browning die?

Narrator: Listen to a lecture by a biology instructor.

Today's lecture will include the most outstanding achievements in biology as it relates to the medical sciences.

Early in Greek history, Hippocrates began to study the human body and to apply scientific method to the problems of diagnosis and the treatment of diseases. Unlike other physicians of his time, he discarded the theory that disease was caused by the gods. Instead, he kept careful records of symptoms and treatments, indicating the success or failure of the patient's cure. He has been recognized as the father of modern medicine.

About a century later, Aristotle began a scientific study of plants and animals, classifying more than five hundred types on the basis of body structure. Because of his great contribution to the field, Aristotle has been called the father of biology.

By the first century A.D., Dioscorides had collected a vast amount of information on plants, which he recorded in the now famous *Materia Medica,* a book that remained an authoritative reference among physicians for fifteen hundred years.

During the Middle Ages, scientific method was scorned in favor of alchemy. Thus, medicine and biology had advanced very little from the time of the ancients until the seventeenth century when the English physician and anatomist William Harvey discovered a mechanism for the circulation of the blood in the body.

Now get ready to answer the questions

Narrator: 30. What is the main topic of this lecture?

31. What was Hippocrates' greatest contribution to medicine?

32. Who is known as the father of biology?

33. What was the contribution made to medicine by William Harvey?

Narrator: Listen to part of a class discussion in a sociology class.

Dr. Jackson: Last class, I asked you to locate some articles about gang activity. Let's just go around the table and share what we found. Tracy, will you begin please?

Tracy: Okay. Actually, I did a search of sociological studies on gang activity, and I found that gangs have been prevalent for much longer than I had assumed. I was so surprised. For some reason, I thought that gang activity was a fairly recent phenomenon, but actually, one of the largest studies was carried out by Thrasher in 1936.

Dr. Jackson: Good. Good. I'm pleased that you did that. Thrasher's study is a classic research investigation. Can you summarize the findings?

Tracy: Sure. First, I should say that the study included more than 1300 gangs with more than 25,000 members. According to Thrasher, a gang is a group that may form spontaneously, but after that, will integrate through conflict and violence. Over time, a spirit of solidarity and an attachment to a local territory form. What is most interesting, besides the long history of gangs in the United States, is the fact that not much has changed over the years. And, oh yes, gang behavior seems pretty similar even across cultures.

Dr. Jackson: That is interesting.

Bill: Dr. Jackson, may I go next? I have just a brief comment that seems to fit in here.

Dr. Jackson: Please.

Bill: Well, another classic study, much later, about 1987 or 8, I think, by Joan Moore, indicated that gang behavior is probably caused by normal adolescent insecurities—the desire for peer approval, respect, support, acceptance, and, in some cases, protection, if the neighborhood is perceived as dangerous. It seems that gangs take the place of the more childish and acceptable cliques that develop in high schools.

Sandy: Is it my turn? Well, I looked up the definitions of gang members by police departments and law enforcement agencies. According to the California Youth Gang Task Force, for example, a gang member will be recognizable because of gang-related tattoos, clothing, and paraphernalia like scarves and hats that identify a particular gang, and allow others to confirm that the wearer has a right to be on the gang's turf. And, to follow up on Tracy's comments about the history of gangs, these criteria have been in place for a long time.

Dr. Jackson: Good job. So far, what I am hearing, though, refers to male gang membership. What about females? Did anyone find any research on their role in gang activity?

Bill: I did. Although there are a few girl gangs, females are generally not considered members of the male-dominated gang. They are viewed as more of a support system, and an extended social group—friends and girlfriends to party with.

Sandy: That's what I found, too.

Now get ready to answer the questions

Narrator: 34. What was surprising about Thrasher's study?

35. According to the study by Moore, what causes gang activity?

36. In which two ways are gang members identified by law enforcement authorities?

37. What is the role of women in gangs?

Narrator: Listen to part of a conversation between a student and a professor in the professor's office.

Mary: Dr. Brown, could I speak with you for a minute?

Dr. Brown: Sure, Mary. Come in.

Mary: I'm afraid I have a problem.

Dr. Brown: Oh?

Mary: You see, I really like my job here.

Dr. Brown: That's good. Because we really like having you here.

Mary: Thank you. But the problem is I won't be able to work here next semester. You see, I have a problem with my schedule at school.

Dr. Brown: Well, what exactly is the problem?

Mary: I have a required class at nine o'clock on Monday, Wednesday, and Friday.

Dr. Brown: Oh. Okay. Remind me what your hours are here.

Mary: I work from nine to one every day. Which has been great, because I have been able to schedule all my classes in the afternoon, until now.

Dr. Brown: I see. When does the class end?

Mary: It's a three-hour class, so it meets for an hour three times a week.

Dr. Brown: So you're finished at ten.

Mary: Yes. And it would take me half an hour to get here after class, so you see, I would be an hour and a half late on those days.

Dr. Brown: Well, we need someone four hours a day. But, how about this—you could come in at ten-thirty on Monday, Wednesday, and Friday, and work until two-thirty on those days. That would give you a fairly late lunch, but if that's not a problem for you, then we can do it.

Mary: That would be great. So I'd just keep my regular hours on Tuesday and Thursday then.

Dr. Brown: Right. Listen, Mary. You're a work-study employee, and that means that you have two responsibilities—to work and to study. We know that. As long as you put in the hours to get the job done, we expect to fit your work hours around your school schedule. And don't forget, you can study on the job as long as the work is done first.

Now get ready to answer the questions

Narrator: 38. What is Mary's problem?

39. When is Mary's class next semester?

40. How does Dr. Brown resolve the problem?

41. What is a work-study employee?

Narrator: Listen to part of a lecture in an engineering class.

In recent years, we have developed several techniques for building more earthquake-resistant structures. For relatively small buildings, all we have to do is bolt the buildings to their foundations and provide some support walls.

These walls are referred to as shear walls in your textbook. They are made of reinforced concrete, and by that I mean concrete with steel rods embedded in it. This not only strengthens the structure but also diminishes the forces that tend to shake a building during a quake. In addition to the shear walls that surround a building, shear walls can be situated in the center of a building around an elevator shaft or a stairwell. This is really an excellent reinforcement. It is commonly known as a shear core, and it, too, contains reinforced concrete.

Walls can also be reinforced, using a technique called cross-bracing. Imagine steel beams that cross diagonally from the ceiling to the floor of each story in a building. Before the walls are finished, you can see a vertical row of steel x's on the structure.

Besides steel reinforcements, engineers have also devised base isolators, which are positioned below the building to absorb the shock of the sideways shaking that can undermine a building and cause it to collapse. Most of the base isolators that are currently being used are made of alternating layers of steel and synthetic rubber. The steel is for strength, but the rubber absorbs shock waves. In higher buildings, a moat of flexible materials allows the building to sway during seismic activity.

The combination of a reinforced structure and flexible materials has been proven to reduce earthquake damage. But even these engineering techniques are insufficient if the building has been constructed on filled ground. Soil used in fill dirt can lose its bearing strength when subjected to the shock waves of an earthquake, and the buildings constructed on it can literally disappear into the Earth.

In areas where earthquakes are known to occur, understanding the terrain and using the techniques we have discussed today can greatly reduce property damage, and can save lives as well.

Now get ready to answer the questions

Narrator: 42. What is the topic of this lecture?

43. Which technique is used to reinforce walls?

44. Which two materials are used in base isolators?

45. What happens to fill dirt during an earthquake?

Narrator: Listen to part of a lecture in a botany lab. The lab assistant is talking about leaves.

Food and water are carried throughout leaves by their veins. Today we will be looking at some examples of the main types of vein patterns in leaves. The most common are the pinnate and the palmate. This is a pinnate leaf, which is characteristic of trees like the beech and birch that you see outside this building on campus.

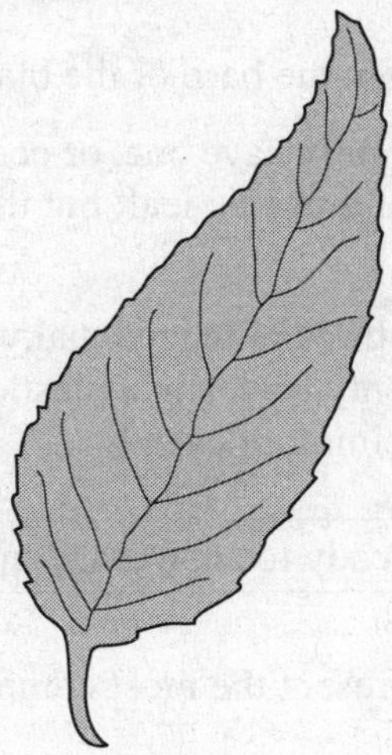

Remember that a pinnate leaf has one large central vein called the midrib, with large veins branching off on each side of it. The midrib extends the full length of the leaf.

Notice how different this leaf is. This is an example of a palmate leaf from a maple tree. A good way to remember this classification is to think of the palm of your hand. In a palmate leaf, there are several main veins of about equal size that originate at the base of the leaf and extend out to the edge of the leaf like fingers.

A few very narrow leaves are neither pinnate nor palmate. This leaf of grass for example has a parallel pattern.

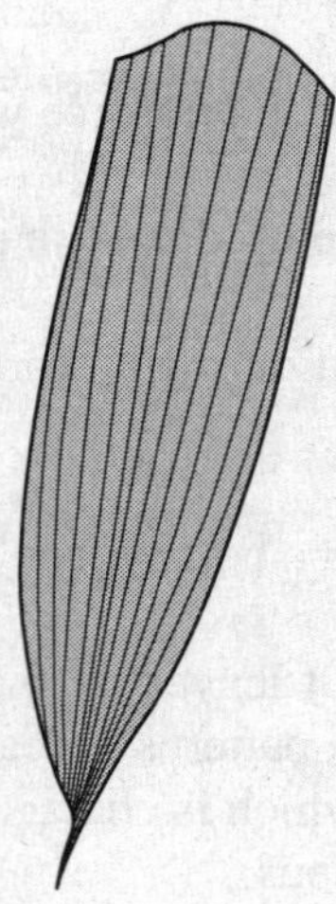

Several veins extend themselves from the base of the blade to the tip, as you can see here.

Needle leaves are so small that they only have one, or occasionally two, veins in the center of the needle. I don't have a good slide of a needle leaf, but there is a drawing in your lab manual for you to refer to.

Now, I'd like you to turn to chapter three in the manual, and use page fifty-two as a reference for your lab activity. You will find twenty leaves in a plastic bag on your lab table. Please work with your lab partner to classify the veining of each leaf.

Now get ready to answer the questions

Narrator: 46. Which two types represent the most common vein patterns in leaves?

47. According to the lecturer, what is a midrib?

48. How does the lab assistant help students remember the palmate classification?

49. Match the leaves with their vein patterns.

50. What will the students probably do after the short lecture?

Model Test 3
Computer-Assisted TOEFL

Section 1: Listening

The Listening section of the test measures the ability to understand conversations and talks in English. On the actual TOEFL exam, you will use headphones to listen to the conversations and talks. While you are listening, pictures of the speakers or other information will be presented on your computer screen. There are two parts to the Listening section, with special directions for each part.

On the day of the test, the amount of time you will have to answer all of the questions will appear on the computer screen. The time you spend listening to the test material will not be counted. The listening material and questions about it will be presented only one time. You will not be allowed to take notes or have any paper at your computer. You will both see and hear the questions before the answer choices appear. You can take as much time as you need to select an answer; however, it will be to your advantage to answer the questions as quickly as possible. You may change your answer as many times as you want before you confirm it. After you have confirmed an answer, you will not be able to return to the question.

Before you begin working on the Listening section, you will have an opportunity to adjust the volume of the sound. You will not be able to change the volume after you have started the test.

QUESTION DIRECTIONS—Part A

In Part A of the Listening section, you will hear short conversations between two people. In some of the conversations, each person speaks only once. In other conversations, one or both of the people speak more than once. Each conversation is followed by one question about it.

Each question in this part has four answer choices. You should click on the best answer to each question. Answer the questions on the basis of what is stated or implied by the speakers.

1. Man: It doesn't make any sense for us to go home for spring vacation now.
   Woman: Especially since we'll be graduating in May.
   Narrator: What does the woman mean?

2. Man: Could you please explain the assignment for Monday, Miss Smith?
   Woman: Certainly. Read the next chapter in your textbook and come to class prepared to discuss what you've read.
   Narrator: What are the speakers talking about?

3. Woman: Are you ready for this?
   Man: I should be. I've been cramming for the past three days.
   Narrator: What does the man mean?

4. Man: I need a book for English two-twenty-one.
   Woman: All of the textbooks are on the shelves in the back of the store.
   Narrator: What will the man probably do?

5. Man: You're in my economics class, aren't you?
   Woman: Yes. I'm not an economics major, though.
   Man: So, what do you think of Professor Collins?
   Woman: I think he's a great person, but the class just turns me off.
   Narrator: What does the woman mean?

6. Man: Have you made an appointment with Dr. Peterson's T.A. yet?
Woman: No. And I really can't put it off anymore.
Narrator: What will the woman probably do?

7. Woman: How do you like American food?
Man: I'm used to it now.
Narrator: What does the man mean?

8. Woman: Are you still studying? It's two o'clock in the morning.
Man: I know. I just can't seem to get caught up.
Narrator: What does the man mean?

9. Man: It's your turn to call the names on the list if you want to.
Woman: I think I'll pass this time.
Narrator: What is the woman going to do?

10. Woman: I'm pretty sure that the deadline for applications has passed.
Man: Why don't you let me look into it for you?
Narrator: What does the man mean?

11. Man: This is the first time I've had to get a tutor.
Woman: What seems to be the problem?
Man: Well, I understand the lectures but I get mixed up when I try to read the book.
Narrator: What does the man mean?

12. Man: The paper isn't due until next week.
Woman: Yes, I know. But I wanted to turn it in ahead of time if that's all right.
Narrator: What does the woman mean?

13. Man: I can't stand this class!
Woman: Well, you might as well get used to it. You have to take it in order to graduate.
Narrator: What does the woman say about the class?

14. Woman: How are you going to get ready for an oral final?
Man: The professor said we should study alone, but the T.A. said to get into a study group and quiz each other.
Narrator: What did the T.A. suggest the students do?

15. Man: I need an advisor's signature on my course request form. Could I make an appointment, please?
Woman: Oh, well, you don't need to make an appointment. Just wait here. I'll get a pen.
Narrator: What is the woman going to do?

16. Woman: Thanks for reading my paper.
Man: Sure. This copy looks good. Why don't you just hand it in?
Woman: No, I'd better make one more draft.
Narrator: What is the woman going to do?

17. Woman: Your loan payment is due on the first. Oh, sorry, the computer has you scheduled for the fifth.
Man: That's good. That's what I thought.
Narrator: What had the man assumed about the loan payment?

QUESTION DIRECTIONS—Part B

In Part B of the Listening section, you will hear several longer conversations and talks. Each conversation or talk is followed by several questions. The conversations, talks, and questions will not be repeated.

The conversations and talks are about a variety of topics. You do not need special knowledge of the topics to answer the questions correctly. Rather, you should answer each question on the basis of what is stated or implied by the speakers in the conversations or talks.

For most of the questions, you will need to click on the best of four possible answers. Some questions will have special directions. The special directions will appear in a box on the computer screen.

Narrator: Listen to a conversation between a student and a professor.

Woman: Hello, Professor Hayes. I'm Betty Peterson. I'm in your senior seminar this semester.
Man: Oh, yes, Betty. How are you?
Woman: Just fine, thanks. I'm here because I'm applying for graduate school, and I need three letters of recommendation. Would you be willing to write me one?
Man: Why yes, Betty. I'd be happy to. I think you are an excellent candidate for graduate school. Are you applying here or to another university?
Woman: Here. That's why I think your letter is so important. Everyone on the selection committee knows and respects you.
Man: Let's see, Dr. Warren is the chair of that committee, isn't she?
Woman: Yes. So, if you would just write the letter to her, that would be great.
Man: Okay. And when do you need this? I don't recall the deadline for applications.
Woman: The committee meets on April 30, so all the materials must be submitted before then.
Man: All right. I'll send it directly to her office.
Woman: Thank you. I really appreciate it.
Man: You're welcome. Glad to do it.

Now get ready to answer the questions

Narrator: 18. Why did Betty see Professor Hayes?

19. What does Professor Hayes think about Betty?

20. Who will decide whether Betty is accepted to the program?

21. When does Betty need to submit all her materials?

Narrator: Listen to a lecture by a history professor.

I know that this is probably a digression from the topic of today's lecture, but it is worth noting that although England no longer ruled her former colonies after the eighteenth century, she controlled trade with them by selling products so cheaply that it was not possible for the new countries to manufacture and compete with English prices. To maintain this favorable balance of trade, England went to fantastic lengths to keep secret the advanced manufacturing processes upon which such a monopoly depended.

Enterprising Americans made all kinds of ingenious attempts to smuggle drawings for the most modern machines out of England, but it was an Englishman, Samuel Slater, who finally succeeded.

Although textile workers were forbidden to emigrate, Slater traveled to the United States in secret. Determined to take nothing in writing, he memorized the intricate designs for all the machines in an English textile mill, and in partnership with Moses Brown, a Quaker merchant, recreated the mill in Rhode Island.

Forty-five years later, in part as a result of the initial model by Slater and Brown, America had changed from a country of small farmers and craftsmen to an industrial nation in competition with England.

Now get ready to answer the questions

Narrator: 22. Who is the speaker?

23. According to the speaker, how did England control trade in the eighteenth century?

24. What did Samuel Slater do?

25. What happened as a result of the Slater-Brown partnership?

Narrator: Listen to part of a conversation between a student and an employee in the bookstore on campus.

Man: Hi. I understand that I can reserve textbooks for next semester.
Woman: That's right. If you know what courses you will be taking, we can have your order waiting for you the week before classes start.
Man: Great! This semester I couldn't get two of my books until three weeks into the semester because you ran out of them before I made it to the book store.
Woman: That has been a problem for a lot of students, and that's why we are trying this system. If we know that you want them, we can order books right away instead of waiting until faculty members place their orders for the whole class.
Man: What do I have to do?
Woman: Just fill out one of these forms. Be sure that you include both the course number and the section number for each course because different instructors may not be using the same books. Then pay for your books at the register, and we'll place the order.
Man: Then do I just stop by the bookstore at the beginning of the semester?
Woman: There's a space for your phone number on the form. We'll call you as soon as they come in. Sometimes we get them before the end of the current semester.
Man: That would be great. Then I could take them home with me over the break to get a head start on the reading.
Woman: Quite a few students do that now.

Now get ready to answer the questions

Narrator: 26. What is the purpose of this conversation?

27. What was the man's problem last semester?

28. How can the man order books?

29. How will the man know that the books have arrived?

Narrator: Listen to a talk by a college instructor in an English class.

So many different kinds of writing have been called essays, it is difficult to define exactly what an essay is. Perhaps the best way is to point out four characteristics that are true of most essays. First, an essay is about one topic. It does not start with one subject and digress to another and another. Second, although a few essays are long enough to be considered a small book, most essays are short. Five hundred words is the most common length for an essay. Third, an essay is written in prose, not poetry. True, Alexander Pope did call two of his poems essays, but that word is part of a title, and after all, the "Essay on Man" and the "Essay on Criticism" really are not essays at all. They are long poems. Fourth, and probably most important, an essay is personal. It is the work of one person whose purpose is to share a thought, idea, or point of view. Let me also state here that since an essay is always personal, the term "personal essay" is redundant. Now, taking into consideration all of these characteristics, perhaps we can now define an essay as a short, prose composition that has a personal viewpoint that discusses one topic. With that in mind, let's brainstorm some topics for your first essay assignment.

Now get ready to answer the questions

Narrator: 30. What is the instructor defining?

31. What is the main point of the talk?

32. According to the talk, which of the characteristics are NOT true of an essay?

33. What will the students probably do as an assignment?

Narrator: Listen to a talk by a guest speaker in a history class.

Not a gifted public speaker, Thomas Jefferson was most talented as a literary draftsman. Sent to Congress by the Virginia Convention in 1775, he was elected to the committee to draft a declaration of independence from England. Although John Adams and Benjamin Franklin also served on the committee, the composition of the Declaration of Independence belongs indisputably to Jefferson. In 1779, Jefferson was elected governor of the state of Virginia, an office he held until Congress appointed him to succeed Franklin as U.S. minister to France. Upon returning to Washington, he accepted the position of secretary of state.

Although Jefferson was a Republican, he at first tried to cooperate with Alexander Hamilton, a Federalist who was first among President Washington's advisors. When he concluded that Hamilton was really in favor of a monarchy, hostility between the two men sharpened.

Having served as vice-president in John Adams' administration, Jefferson ran for president in the election of 1800. He and Federalist Aaron Burr received an identical vote, but the Republican Congress elected to approve Jefferson as president. The most outstanding accomplishment of his administration was the purchase of the Louisiana Territory from France in 1803. He was easily re-elected in 1804. When he left office four years later, he returned here to Monticello, where he promoted the formation of a liberal university for Virginia.

Now get ready to answer the questions

Narrator: 34. What is the main purpose of this talk?

35. Jefferson was a member of which political group?

36. How did Jefferson become president?

37. According to the lecturer, what was it that Jefferson was NOT?

Narrator: Listen to part of a lecture on geology.

Fossils are the remains of organisms that have been preserved. Some of the most common fossils are shells, skeletons, leaves, and insects. They are occasionally preserved in ice, but most have been buried in mud or sand that collects at the bottom of bodies of water, especially lakes, swamps, and oceans. In order for fossils to form, the animals and plants must be buried quickly; otherwise, the organisms will disintegrate. If they are buried in loose sediment, the soft tissues will begin to decay. But the harder structures such as bones and shells will remain intact for much longer. After years of pressure from the layers of sediment above them, the lower layers of sediment turn into rock, encapsulating the organisms.

There are several different mineral processes that continue the fossilization of organisms in the sedimentary rocks. A few plants and animals become fossilized after mineral-rich water soaks into the pores and openings in the hard tissues of the plant or animal. In these fossils, the original body of the organism is strengthened by the infusion of mineral deposits, and every detail of the organism is preserved. But in most fossils, the minerals in the water dissolve the original organism, leaving a fossil mold. Minerals continue to be deposited in the mold at the same time, a process that results in the replacement of the living organism by a mineral deposit of exactly the same shape. In the casts of these molds, the internal features of the organism are not preserved, but the outer structure is accurate in every detail. Sometimes the fine shapes of even very fragile feathers and fur are preserved by mineral replacement.

Although the fossil record is incomplete, the composite of fossil findings chronicles the forms of life that existed at various periods in the past. In a sense the fossil record is a history of life. The location of fossils in layers of undisturbed sedimentary rock shows not only which groups of organisms lived at approximately the same time but also indicates the order in which they were buried, that is, their relative ages. Plants and animals on the lower layers are presumed to be older than those buried after them in the layers above.

Now get ready to answer the questions

Narrator: 38. What are the two most common places where fossils may be found?

39. The professor briefly explains a process. Summarize the process by putting the events in order.

40. What is lost in the process of replacement?

41. Why are the layers of sedimentary rock important to the fossil record?

Narrator: Listen to part of a conversation between a student and a secretary on campus.

Woman: Let me see if I understand this. You have completed all of your course work for graduation.

Man: Right.

Woman: But you didn't apply to graduate.

Man: Right.
Woman: But you want to graduate this semester.
Man: Yes, and I thought I would, automatically. I mean, I didn't understand that I had to do anything.
Woman: Who is your advisor?
Man: I'm not sure. I have been sort of advising myself.
Woman: You have?
Man: It's not that hard. The requirements are all spelled out in the catalog, and I have just been taking the required courses, and keeping track of all my grades. Here's my latest transcript, and as you can see, I've got all the credits I need.
Woman: So you don't even have a signed program of study.
Man: Not signed, no. But I have a program of study. I used the program in the catalog.
Woman: I know. But I am talking about a form that is filed by your advisor.
Man: No, I don't have that.
Woman: Okay. The first thing we need to do is to assign you an advisor to go over all your transcripts and help you create a program of study.
Man: How long will that take?
Woman: We'll try to get you in to see someone today. If you really have been able to take all the requirements, then there shouldn't be anything missing from the program and your advisor can sign it and also help you apply for graduation. But if you have misread the catalog or failed to take a critical course, then you may not be eligible for graduation. All I can tell you right now is that you have enough hours to graduate, but only an academic advisor can verify that you have completed the correct course work.
Man: Oh no. You mean I might not graduate?
Woman: I don't know. Let's make that appointment and go from there.

Now get ready to answer the questions

Narrator: 42. Why didn't the man apply for graduation?

43. How did the man select his courses?

44. What does the woman suggest?

45. What is the man's problem?

Narrator: Listen to part of a class discussion about American English.

Dr. Wilson: Because the United States is so large, and has such a diverse population, several major dialect regions have been identified. The question is whether there is one universally acceptable standard of American English. Any thoughts?
Laura: Dr. Wilson? I know that the two articles we read both argued that no dialect is inherently better than any other. Isn't that right?
Dr. Wilson: Yes, I would say so. Since this is a linguistics class, the articles were written by linguists, and from a linguistic point of view, all dialects of a language are of equal value.
Laura: Okay. And that is because all dialects can express everything that is necessary for a language community to communicate.
Dr. Wilson: Precisely. But, I think you are going somewhere with this argument.

Laura: I am. All dialects are linguistically equal, but are they equal socially? In other words, aren't some dialects more well-respected than others?

Dr. Wilson: Interesting observation. In fact, your comment anticipates our assignment for the next class period when we will discuss standard dialects. For now, let me just say that, although there are several definitions of a standard dialect, the definition that we will use for our class is this: A standard dialect is the dialect that is selected as the educational model.

Laura: Does that mean that the dialect of the schools is the standard?

Dr. Wilson: Exactly.

Vicki: Now I have a question.

Dr. Wilson: Okay.

Vicki: In different regions of the country, the pronunciation is very different, so the schools in each of these regions would have a different standard dialect. Isn't there a standard for the whole country?

Dr. Wilson: Indeed, there is. Standard English has a common grammar and vocabulary. These are the basic building blocks of a dialect. The pronunciation is an accent, not a dialect. So the accent may be regional, but as long as the grammar and vocabulary are standard, the school is teaching the standard American English dialect with, let's say, a Southern accent or a New York accent.

Vicki: So an accent is different from a dialect?

Dr. Wilson: Technically, yes. However, certain accents tend to attach themselves to particular dialects.

Laura: Oh, I see. So there is a standard accent, too, then.

Dr. Wilson: Some linguists would say no, there isn't. But a number of sociologists would answer your question in a different way. Some accents are associated with a higher socioeconomic class and, therefore, tend to be the preferred standard accent in schools.

Laura: I think I understand. There isn't anything inherently better about any dialect or accent, but the prestige of the social group that uses it makes some more desirable than others, so they are chosen for the language of the schools, and become the standard.

Dr. Wilson: Well said.

Now get ready to answer the questions

Narrator: 46. In which class would this discussion probably take place?

47. According to the discussion, what is the definition of a standard dialect?

48. What is the linguistic perspective put forward in the articles that were assigned?

49. Which two linguistic components are included in a dialect?

50. What do sociologists tell us about accents?

Model Test 4
Computer-Assisted TOEFL

Section 1: Listening

The Listening section of the test measures the ability to understand conversations and talks in English. On the actual TOEFL exam, you will use headphones to listen to the conversations and talks. While you are listening, pictures of the speakers or other information will be presented on your computer screen. There are two parts to the Listening section, with special directions for each part.

On the day of the test, the amount of time you will have to answer all of the questions will appear on the computer screen. The time you spend listening to the test material will not be counted. The listening material and questions about it will be presented only one time. You will not be allowed to take notes or have any paper at your computer. You will both see and hear the questions before the answer choices appear. You can take as much time as you need to select an answer; however, it will be to your advantage to answer the questions as quickly as possible. You may change your answer as many times as you want before you confirm it. After you have confirmed an answer, you will not be able to return to the question.

Before you begin working on the Listening section, you will have an opportunity to adjust the volume of the sound. You will not be able to change the volume after you have started the test.

QUESTION DIRECTIONS—Part A

In Part A of the Listening section, you will hear short conversations between two people. In some of the conversations, each person speaks only once. In other conversations, one or both of the people speak more than once. Each conversation is followed by one question about it.

Each question in this part has four answer choices. You should click on the best answer to each question. Answer the questions on the basis of what is stated or implied by the speakers.

1. Man: The International Students' Association is having a party Saturday night. Can you come or do you have to work at the hospital?
   Woman: I wish I could.
   Narrator: What will the woman probably do?

2. Woman: I think that the game starts at eight.
   Man: Good. We have just enough time to get there.
   Narrator: What will the speakers probably do?

3. Woman: What did you do after you lost your passport?
   Man: I went to see the foreign student advisor, and he reported it to the Passport Office in Washington.
   Narrator: What did the man do after he lost his passport?

4. Man: I'm not sure what Dr. Tyler wants us to do.
   Woman: If I were you, I'd write a rough draft and ask Dr. Tyler to look at it.
   Narrator: What does the woman suggest the man do?

5. Man: Dr. Clark is the only one teaching statistics this term.
   Woman: You mean we have to put up with her for another semester?
   Narrator: What does the woman mean?

6. Woman: Did we have an assignment for Monday? I don't have anything written down.
   Man: Nothing to read in the textbook, but we have to see a movie and write a paragraph about it.
   Narrator: What are the speakers discussing?

7. Man: Excuse me. Are you Sally Harrison's sister?
   Woman: No, I'm not. I'm her cousin.
   Narrator: What had the man assumed about the woman?

8. Woman: I can't find my pen. It was right here on the desk yesterday and now it's gone. Have you seen it?
   Man: Yes. I put it in the desk drawer.
   Narrator: What is the woman's problem?

9. Woman: When is John coming?
   Man: Well, he said he'd be here at eight-thirty, but if I know him, it will be at least nine o'clock.
   Narrator: What does the man imply about John?

10. Woman: How is your experiment coming along?
    Man: It's finished, but it didn't turn out quite like I thought it would.
    Narrator: What does the man mean?

11. Woman: Barbara sure likes to talk on the phone.
    Man: If only she liked her classes as well!
    Narrator: What does the man imply about Barbara?

12. Man: What's the matter?
    Woman: My allergies are really bothering me. I guess I'll have to go to the doctor.
    Man: If I were you, I'd try some over-the-counter medications first. They usually do the job.
    Narrator: What does the man suggest the woman do?

13. Man: What did you decide about the scholarship? Did you fill out the application?
    Woman: I'm going to give it all I've got.
    Narrator: What does the woman mean?

14. Woman: Please pass your papers in.
    Man: Could I have a few more minutes to finish?
    Woman: I'm afraid not. It's a timed test.
    Narrator: What does the woman mean?

15. Man: Dr. Taylor's class is supposed to be really good.
    Woman: The best part is I can use my roommate's book.
    Man: I'm not so sure about that. I think they're using a different book this semester.
    Narrator: What does the man imply?

16. Man: I'm going to get Sally a bike for Christmas.
    Woman: Are you sure she'd like one?
    Narrator: What does the woman imply?

17. Man: I just can't get the answer to this problem! I've been working on it for three hours.
Woman: Maybe you should get some rest and try it again later.
Narrator: What does the woman suggest that the man do?

QUESTION DIRECTIONS—Part B

In Part B of the Listening section, you will hear several longer conversations and talks. Each conversation or talk is followed by several questions. The conversations, talks, and questions will not be repeated.

The conversations and talks are about a variety of topics. You do not need special knowledge of the topics to answer the questions correctly. Rather, you should answer each question on the basis of what is stated or implied by the speakers in the conversations or talks.

For most of the questions, you will need to click on the best of four possible answers. Some questions will have special directions. The special directions will appear in a box on the computer screen.

Narrator: Listen to a class discussion.

Baker: It seems to me that the question is not whether the metric system should be introduced in the United States, but rather, how it should be introduced.

Woman: I think that it should be done gradually to give everyone enough time to adjust.

Man: Yes. Perhaps we could even have two systems for a while. I mean, we could keep the English system and use metrics as an optional system.

Woman: That's what they seem to be doing. When you go to the grocery store, look at the labels on the cans and packages. They are marked in both ounces and grams.

Man: Right. I've noticed that too. And the weather reporters on radio and TV give the temperature readings in both degrees Fahrenheit and degrees Celsius now.

Woman: Some road signs have the distances marked in both miles and kilometers, especially on the interstate highways. What do you think, Professor Baker?

Baker: Well, I agree that a gradual adoption is better for those of us who have already been exposed to the English system of measurement. But I would favor teaching only metrics in the elementary schools.

Man: I see your point. It might be confusing to introduce two systems at the same time.

Now get ready to answer the questions

Narrator: 18. What is the topic under discussion?

19. What changes in measurement in the United States have the students observed?

20. What was Professor Baker's opinion?

21. Which word best describes Professor Baker's attitude toward his students?

Narrator: Listen to part of a lecture in a science class.

Since the National Aeronautics and Space Administration was established in 1961, NASA has been engaged in an extensive research effort, which, in cooperation with private industry, has transferred technology to the international marketplace. Hundreds of everyday products can be traced back to the space mission, including cordless electrical tools, airtight food packaging, water purification systems, and even scratch coating for eyeglasses.

In addition, many advances in medical technology can be traced back to NASA laboratories. First used to detect flaws in spacecraft, ultrasound is now standard equipment in almost every hospital for diagnosis and assessment of injuries and disease; equipment first used by NASA to transmit images from space to Earth is used to assist in cardiac imaging, and lasers first used to test satellites are now used in surgical procedures. Under-the-skin implants for the continuous infusion of drugs, and small pacemakers to regulate the heart were originally designed to monitor the physical condition of astronauts in space.

Finally, with the help of images that were obtained during space missions, and NASA technology, archaeologists have been able to explore the earth. Cities lost under desert sands have been located and rediscovered, and the sea floor has been mapped using photographs from outer space.

Now get ready to answer the questions

Narrator: 22. What is the talk mainly about?

23. Which of the advances listed are NOT mentioned as part of the technology developed for space missions?

24. According to the speaker, why did NASA develop medical equipment?

25. Why does the speaker mention archaeology?

Narrator: Listen to part of a conversation between a student and a professor in the professor's office.

Beverly: Oh, Dr. Williams. I expected to leave you a note since this is not one of your office hours. But I would really appreciate a few minutes of your time. I'm Beverly Jackson, and I'm in your two o'clock political science class.

Dr. Williams: Yes, Beverly. I remember you. You always sit in the front.

Beverly: I do. I really like the class, and I want to be able to see all the slides and videos.

Dr. Williams: Good, so what can I do for you?

Beverly: I'm hoping you can help me. I have a family emergency, and I am needed at home for at least a week. That means I'll have to miss your Wednesday and Friday class, but I'm sure that I can be back by class on Monday.

Dr. Williams: Oh.

Beverly: I know that attendance is part of the evaluation, and I want to get a good grade in the class. Is there any way you could give me an excused absence or something so it won't bring my grade down? I would be happy to do extra work to make up the time.

Dr. Williams: Oh, don't worry about that, Beverly. You never miss class, and I'm sure you have a very good reason to be absent this time. I'll be glad to give you an excused absence for Wednesday and Friday. Is there anything else I can do?

Beverly: Not really. I have already arranged to get the notes from Gloria Hayes. She and I always study together.

Dr. Williams: Fine. Well, when you get back, and you read Gloria's notes, let me know if there is anything you don't understand. Sometimes it's hard to understand someone else's notes. If you need some clarification, I can meet with you for a few minutes before class on Monday.

Beverly: That's very nice of you, Dr. Williams. I'll call to set up an appointment, if I need to. But I think I'll be okay with the notes. Thanks for the excused absence.

Dr. Williams: You're very welcome. And I hope that everything goes well for you at home.
Beverly: Thank you, Dr. Williams. I really appreciate it.

Now get ready to answer the questions

Narrator: 26. Why did the student want to see the professor?

27. What is the student's problem?

28. What does the professor offer to do?

29. What is the professor's attitude in this conversation?

Narrator: Listen to part of a talk in a history class.

The first permanent settlement was made in San Francisco in 1776, when a Spanish military post was established on the end of that peninsula. During the same year, some Franciscan Fathers founded the Mission San Francisco de Asis on a hill above the post. A trail was cleared from the military post to the mission, and about halfway between the two, a station was established for travelers called *Yerba Buena*, which means "good herbs."

For thirteen years the village had fewer than one hundred inhabitants. But in 1848, with the discovery of gold, the population grew to ten thousand. That same year, the name was changed from Yerba Buena to San Francisco.

By 1862 telegraph communications linked San Francisco with eastern cities, and by 1869, the first transcontinental railroad connected the Pacific coast with the Atlantic seaboard. Today San Francisco has a population of almost three million. It is the financial center of the West, and serves as the terminus for trans-Pacific steamship lines and air traffic. The port of San Francisco, which is almost eighteen miles long, handles between five and six million tons of cargo annually.

If you travel to San Francisco, you will see the most identifiable landmark, the Golden Gate Bridge. The bridge, which is more than one mile long, spans the harbor from San Francisco to Marin County and the Redwood Highway. It was completed in 1937 at a cost of thirty-two million dollars and is still one of the largest suspension bridges in the world.

Now get ready to answer the questions

Narrator: 30. What is the main purpose of this talk?

31. According to the speaker, what was the settlement called before it was renamed San Francisco?

32. According to the speaker, what happened in 1848?

33. How long is the Golden Gate Bridge?

Narrator: Listen to a talk by an English professor.

Transcendentalism began with the formation in 1836 of the Transcendental Club in Boston, Massachusetts, by a group of artists and writers. This group advanced a reaction against the rigid Puritanism of the period, especially insofar as it emphasized society at the expense of the individual.

One of the most distinguished members of the club was Ralph Waldo Emerson, who served as editor of the literary magazine *Dial.* His writing stressed the importance of the individual. In one of his best-known essays, "Self-Reliance," he appealed to intuition as a source of ethics, asserting that people should be the judge of their own actions, without the rigid restrictions of society.

From 1841 to 1843, Emerson entertained in his home the naturalist and author Henry David Thoreau, who also became a member of the Transcendental Club. Probably more than any other member, he demonstrated by his lifestyle the ideas that the group advanced. He preferred to go to jail rather than to pay taxes to the federal government for a war of which he did not approve.

Upon leaving Emerson's home, Thoreau built a small cabin along the shores of Walden Pond near Concord, Massachusetts, where he lived alone for two years. Devoting himself to the study of nature and to writing, he published an account of his experiences in *Walden*, a book that is generally acknowledged as the most original and sincere contribution to literature by the Transcendentalists.

Now get ready to answer the questions

Narrator: 34. What does the lecturer mainly discuss?

35. During which century did this literary movement develop?

36. According to the lecturer, what did the Puritans do?

37. What is *Walden?*

Narrator: Listen to part of a conversation between a student and a librarian.

Woman: Do you have any experience working in a library?

Man: No, not as an employee. But I am working toward my doctorate at the University, and I have spent a great deal of time doing my own research in the library. I'm finishing my dissertation now.

Woman: So you are familiar with the electronic search equipment?

Man: Yes, I am. I used several databases for my review of the literature in my dissertation, and I know how to use most of the search equipment that you have here, because this is where I am doing most of my own research.

Woman: Good. Can you think of anything else that would qualify you for the job?

Man: Yes. I like helping students. My undergraduate degree was in education, and I was a high school teacher for twelve years before I came back to school. The ad says that you want someone to show new students how to do computer searches for their term papers, and I think that my teaching experience would be very useful.

Woman: Good, good. But what about the hours? If you are working on your dissertation, will you be able to work? This job requires twenty hours of your time per week, and the hours are not regular. You see, in addition to helping students one-on-one, we make appointments for faculty to bring their classes to the library for orientation before they make their first term paper assignments.

Man: That sounds very interesting. I feel that I can handle a job now. I have most of my own research finished, and I'm writing my dissertation. I plan to do that after work and on my days off.

Woman: So you aren't taking any classes now?

Man: No. That's another advantage I have. I can schedule my time around the appointments.

Woman: And if you are the successful candidate, when could you start?
Man: Right away!

Now get ready to answer the questions

Narrator: 38. What is the purpose of this conversation?

39. Who is the man?

40. What does the man need to do when he is not working?

41. When would the man be available?

Narrator: Listen to part of a lecture on solar heating.

In general, solar heating requires a solar collector, a water or air distribution system, and a storage system. Most of the time, a solar collector is mounted on the roof of a building at a somewhat steep angle, positioned with a southern exposure. In the hot water system that I am going to show you, the collector is a glass plate with another plate under it, and an air space between the two, through which water can be pumped. I think it will make more sense when you see the model, so let's look at it now.

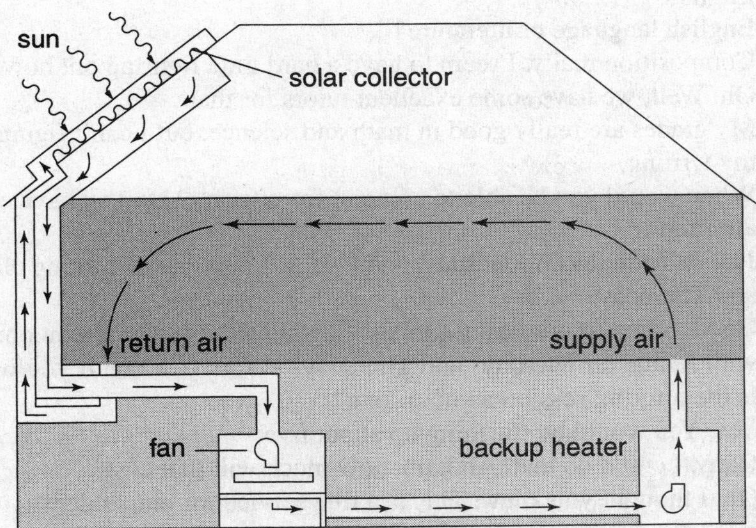

Notice that water that has been heated by the sun is pumped in closely positioned tubes through the space between the plates. The hot water is then pumped to a storage tank, and warmed air is circulated to the other side of the building with a fan. You will also see a backup heater in this system, usually a conventional furnace, because only about 20 to 30 percent of the solar energy can actually be used in this design. The supply air moves across the space to be heated, and enters the return air exchanger where it rises and, with exposure to the sun, begins heating again to raise the temperature of the water in the tubes below. So, the process begins again.

Of course, one of the problems with solar heat is the intermittent nature of solar radiation as an energy source. Especially in climates where the sun does not shine regularly, it just isn't a feasible option without large, and often complex, storage systems. However, scientists are now working on a project to place solar modules in orbit around the Earth, where energy generated by the sun could be converted to microwaves and beamed to antennas for conversion to electric power. It is estimated that such a system, although costly and somewhat cumbersome, could potentially generate as much power as five large nuclear power plants. The principle would be basically the same as that of the much simpler model that I showed you. A solar collector, an air distribution center, and a storage system would be required. So if you understand the model here, you can understand even the most complex solar heating unit.

Now get ready to answer the questions

Narrator: 42. Which two requirements are considered when mounting a solar collector on a roof?

43. Identify the fan in the solar heating system.

44. What problem does the professor point out?

45. Why does the professor mention the project to place solar modules in orbit?

Narrator: Listen to part of a conversation between a student and a secretary in the Tutoring Center.

Man: Excuse me, is this where I request a tutor?
Woman: Yes, it is. Which course do you need help in?
Man: English.
Woman: English language or literature?
Man: Composition really. I seem to have a hard time figuring out how to write my essays.
Woman: Oh. Well, we have some excellent tutors for that.
Man: My grades are really good in math and science, but I can't figure out how to organize my writing.
Woman: When would you be able to come in for tutoring? Do you have classes in the afternoon?
Man: Just on Monday, Wednesday, and Friday. I only have morning classes on Tuesday and Thursday.
Woman: Good. Some of our best tutors for English work in the afternoon. I could set you up with Janine on Tuesdays and Thursdays at four o' clock if you want.
Man: Is the tutoring session an hour long?
Woman: Yes. You would be finishing up about five.
Man: Okay. I could do that. And, uh, how much will that cost?
Woman: Oh, I thought you knew. This is a free service for our students.
Man: It is? No, I wasn't aware of that.
Woman: Actually, a lot of students who receive tutoring come back and serve as tutors once they get squared away themselves.
Man: That's really a great system.
Woman: Janine needed some tutoring in math a few years ago, as I recall, and now she helps us in English composition and French.
Man: So, should I just come back on Tuesday at four?
Woman: Yes. I have your name down. Just check in with me when you get here, and I'll take you over to Janine's table. And, bring your books for the class that you need help in, along with a syllabus, your class notes, and anything that might help your tutor to understand the course requirements.
Man: Thank you so much. I'll see you Tuesday, then.

Now get ready to answer the questions

Narrator: 46. What is the purpose of this conversation?

47. For which course does the man want a tutor?

48. How much will the tutoring cost?

49. When will the tutoring session begin?

50. What should the man bring to his tutoring session?

Model Test 5
Computer-Assisted TOEFL

Section 1: Listening

The Listening section of the test measures the ability to understand conversations and talks in English. On the actual TOEFL exam, you will use headphones to listen to the conversations and talks. While you are listening, pictures of the speakers or other information will be presented on your computer screen. There are two parts to the Listening section, with special directions for each part.

On the day of the test, the amount of time you will have to answer all of the questions will appear on the computer screen. The time you spend listening to the test material will not be counted. The listening material and questions about it will be presented only one time. You will not be allowed to take notes or have any paper at your computer. You will both see and hear the questions before the answer choices appear. You can take as much time as you need to select an answer; however, it will be to your advantage to answer the questions as quickly as possible. You may change your answer as many times as you want before you confirm it. After you have confirmed an answer, you will not be able to return to the question.

Before you begin working on the Listening section, you will have an opportunity to adjust the volume of the sound. You will not be able to change the volume after you have started the test.

QUESTION DIRECTIONS—Part A

In Part A of the Listening section, you will hear short conversations between two people. In some of the conversations, each person speaks only once. In other conversations, one or both of the people speak more than once. Each conversation is followed by one question about it.

Each question in this part has four answer choices. You should click on the best answer to each question. Answer the questions on the basis of what is stated or implied by the speakers.

1. Woman: I'm out of typing paper. Will you lend me some?
Man: I don't have any either, but I'll be glad to get you some when I go to the bookstore.
Narrator: What is the man going to do?

2. Man: Excuse me, Miss. Could you please tell me how to get to the University City Bank?
Woman: Sure. Go straight for two blocks, then turn left and walk three more blocks until you get to the drugstore. It's right across the street.
Narrator: What can be inferred about the man?

3. Woman: Are you still going to summer school at the university near your parent's house?
Man: That plan kind of fell through because there weren't enough courses.
Narrator: What does the man imply?

4. Man: How much is the rent for the apartment?
Woman: It's six hundred and fifty dollars a month unfurnished or eight hundred dollars a month furnished. Utilities are seventy-five dollars extra, not including the telephone. It's expensive, but it's worth it because it's within walking distance from the university.
Narrator: What are the speakers discussing?

5. Man: Dr. Taylor must have really liked your paper. You were about the only one who got an A.
Woman: I know.
Man: So why are you so down?
Woman: He never seems to call on me in class.
Narrator: What does the woman imply?

6. Woman: Do you know anyone who would like to participate in a psychology experiment? It pays ten dollars an hour.
Man: Have you asked Sandy?
Woman: No. Do you think she would do it?
Man: I think she would.
Narrator: What does the man suggest that the woman do?

7. Woman: Didn't you go to the study group meeting last night either?
Man: No. I had a slight headache.
Narrator: What can be inferred about the study group meeting?

8. Woman: I have a card, but now I need a farewell gift for my advisor.
Man: How about a nice pen?
Narrator: What does the man mean?

9. Man: Are you going to move out of the dorm next semester?
Woman: I just can't seem to make up my mind.
Narrator: What does the woman mean?

10. Man: I signed the contract.
Woman: Do you really think you can work and go to school full time?
Narrator: What does the woman imply?

11. Woman: I owe everyone in my family a letter, but I really don't have time to sit down and write them and it's too expensive to call.
Man: Why don't you just buy some postcards?
Narrator: What does the man suggest the woman do?

12. Man: Are you going to stay here for graduate school?
Woman: I don't think so.
Man: Have you heard from any schools yet?
Woman: Yes, I was accepted at Kansas State, the University of Oklahoma, and the University of Nebraska, but I'm going to wait until I hear one way or another from the University of Minnesota.
Narrator: What are the speakers discussing?

13. Woman: I thought I was supposed to take the test in Room 32.
Man: No. Ticket number 32 is in Room 27.
Narrator: What will the woman probably do?

14. Man: Where did you get the flower?
Woman: At the Honors Reception. The teachers gave them to all of the honors students.
Narrator: What can be inferred about the woman?

15. Man: Terry is really having trouble in Dr. Wise's class. She's missed too much to catch up.
Woman: If I were Terry, I'd drop the course, and take it over next semester.
Narrator: What does the woman suggest that Terry do?

16. Woman: I used to teach English before I came back to graduate school.
Man: No wonder you like this course!
Narrator: What does the man mean?

17. Man: We should ask Carl to be in our group.
Woman: We probably ought to ask Jane, too. She's really good at making presentations.
Narrator: What problem do the students have?

QUESTION DIRECTIONS—Part B

In Part B of the Listening section, you will hear several longer conversations and talks. Each conversation or talk is followed by several questions. The conversations, talks, and questions will not be repeated.

The conversations and talks are about a variety of topics. You do not need special knowledge of the topics to answer the questions correctly. Rather, you should answer each question on the basis of what is stated or implied by the speakers in the conversations or talks.

For most of the questions, you will need to click on the best of four possible answers. Some questions will have special directions. The special directions will appear in a box on the computer screen.

Narrator: Listen to part of a conversation between two students on campus.

Man: To tell the truth, I really don't know what Dr. Brown wants us to do. The assignment was pretty vague.

Woman: I know. I've already looked in the syllabus, but all it says under the course requirements is "Research paper, thirty points."

Man: Thirty points? I hadn't realized that it counted so much. That's almost one-third of the grade for the course.

Woman: That's why I'm so worried about it. At first I thought she wanted us to do library research, and write it up; then she started talking about presentations. Last week she said there would be time during the next to the last class for us to present.

Man: I was thinking about making an appointment to see her, or just stopping by during her office hours.

Woman: You could do that. But since so many of us are confused, maybe we should ask about it in class tomorrow. I bet we won't be the only ones with questions either.

Man: That's a good idea.

Now get ready to answer the questions

Narrator: 18. What problem do the speakers have?

19. How much does the research paper count toward the grade for the course?

20. What did the professor say last week?

21. What will the students probably do?

Narrator: Listen to part of a lecture in a world history class. Today the professor will talk about exploration and discovery. She will focus on the Hawaiian Islands.

On his third exploratory voyage, as captain of two ships, the *Resolution* and the *Discovery*, Captain James Cook came upon a group of uncharted islands that he named the Sandwich Islands as a tribute to his friend, the Earl of Sandwich. Today the islands are known as the Hawaiian Islands.

Some historians contend that the islanders welcomed Cook, believing that he was the god Launo, protector of peace and agriculture. I have that name written on the board for you. Of course, it didn't take long for them to realize that Launo had not returned.

These islanders were short, strong people, with a well-organized social system. The men fished and raised crops, including taro, coconuts, sweet potatoes, and sugarcane. The women cared for the children and made clothing—loin cloths for the men and short skirts for the women. The natives were eager to exchange food and supplies for iron nails and tools, and Cook was easily able to restock his ship.

Because of a severe storm in which the *Resolution* was damaged, it was necessary to return to Hawaii. Now sure that Cook and his crew were men and not gods, the natives welcomed them less hospitably. Besides, diseases brought by the English had reached epidemic proportions. When a small boat was stolen from the *Discovery*, Cook demanded that the king be taken as a hostage until the boat was returned. In the fighting that followed, Cook and four crewmen were killed.

Now get ready to answer the questions

Narrator: 22. What is the main purpose of this lecture?

23. According to the lecturer, what were the two ships commanded by Captain Cook?

24. Why does the professor mention the name *Launo*?

25. The professor briefly explains a sequence of events in the history of Hawaii. Summarize the sequence by putting the events in order.

Narrator: Listen to part of a lecture in an engineering class. The professor will discuss alloys.

An alloy is a substance that is formed by combining a metal with other metals, or nonmetals. For example, brass is an alloy of the metals copper and zinc, and steel is an alloy of the metal iron with the nonmetal carbon.

The special characteristics of metals, such as hardness, strength, flexibility, and weight are called its properties. By the process of alloying, it is possible to create materials with the exact combinations of properties for a particular use. In the aircraft industry, there is a need for metals that are both strong and light. Steel is strong but too heavy, whereas aluminum is light but not strong. By alloying aluminum with copper and other metals, a material that is strong enough to withstand the stresses of flight, but light enough to reduce the cost of fuel to lift the craft is created. By alloying steel with nickel and chromium, the steel alloy that results is not only lighter but also stronger than solid steel.

Of course, there is an important difference between the alloys we have used in our examples and the combination of metals that occur accidentally as impure metals. Both are mixtures, but alloys are mixtures that have been deliberately combined in specific proportion for a definite purpose.

Now get ready to answer the questions

Narrator: 26. What is an alloy?

27. What does the speaker say about the properties of alloys?

28. Why does the speaker use the example of the aircraft industry?

29. What is the difference between combinations of metals in nature and alloys?

Narrator: Listen to part of a discussion in an English class.

John: British English and American English are really about the same, aren't they?
Mary: I don't think so. It seems to me that some of the spellings are different.
Baker: You're right, Mary. Words like *theater* and *center* end in *re* in England instead of in *er*, the way that we spell them. Let me write that on the board. Can you think of any more examples?
Mary: The word *color*?
Baker: Good. In fact, many words that end in *or* in American English are spelled *our* in British English, like *color* and *honor.*
John: I'm still not convinced. I mean, if someone comes here from England, we can all understand what he's saying. The spelling doesn't really matter that much.
Baker: Okay. Are we just talking about spelling? Or are there some differences in pronunciation and meaning too?
Mary: Professor Baker?
Baker: Yes?
Mary: I remember seeing an English movie where the actors kept calling their apartment a *flat*. Half of the movie was over before I realized what they were talking about.
John: So there are slight differences in spelling and some vocabulary.
Mary: And pronunciation, too. You aren't going to tell me that you sound like Richard Burton.
John: Richard Burton wasn't English. He was Welsh.
Mary: Okay. Anyway, the pronunciation is different.
Baker: I think that what we are really disagreeing about is the extent of the difference. We all agree that British English and American English are different. Right?
Mary: Yes.
John: Sure.
Baker: But not so different that it prevents us from understanding each other.
John: Well, that's what I mean.
Mary: That's what I mean, too.

Now get ready to answer the questions

Narrator: 30. What do the speakers mainly discuss?

31. How are these words referred to in the discussion?

32. What can be inferred about the word *flat* in British English?

33. On what did the class agree?

Narrator: Listen to part of a talk in an education class. A student is giving a presentation about local control of schools.

My report is on local control of schools. First, I was surprised to learn that public schools in the United States are not the same in every state or even from community to community within the state. The reason for differences in organization, curriculum, and school policies is because each school district has a governing board, called the school board, that makes the decisions about the way the schools in their district will be run. Of course, a superintendent is selected by the board to carry out policies and the superintendent is usually a professional educator, but the board, often made up of community leaders who are not professional educators, must approve the recommendations of the superintendent.

There are two ways to organize a school board. In most communities, the board is elected by the residents in their local school district. And the members usually serve without pay for three to five years. But in some districts, the school board is appointed by the mayor.

Of course, the federal government has an interest in improving education on a national level, even though schools are controlled locally. But the function of the national department is very different from a department of education in many parts of the world. This national agency is primarily involved in collecting demographics, supporting research and projects, and supervising the compliance of schools with national legislation.

Now get ready to answer the questions

Narrator: 34. What is the presentation mainly about?

35. What surprised the presenter about her research?

36. How does each of the persons identified contribute to the operation of schools in the United States?

37. According to the speaker, what is the function of the department of education in the United States?

Narrator: Listen to part of a conversation between a student and a secretary in a college dormitory.

Man: I want to buy a meal ticket.
Woman: Okay. Which plan do you want?
Man: You mean there is more than one?

Woman: Sure. You can buy one meal a day, two meals a day, or three meals a day.
Man: Oh. If I buy two meals a day, can I choose which meals?
Woman: Not really. The two-meal plan includes lunch and dinner. No breakfast.
Man: Great. That's what I would have wanted anyway. How much is that?
Woman: It's thirty-six dollars a week, which works out to about three dollars a meal.
Man: Wait a minute. Fourteen meals at three dollars would be forty-two dollars, wouldn't it?
Woman: Yes, but we don't serve meals on Sunday.
Man: Oh.
Woman: Most residents order a pizza or go out to eat on Sundays. Of course, some students live close enough to go home for the day.
Man: Okay. I'll take the two-meal plan. Do I pay by the quarter or by the week?
Woman: By the quarter.
Man: Fine. Do you take credit cards?
Woman: Yes, but you don't have to pay now. Just fill out this form, and we'll bill you.

Now get ready to answer the questions

Narrator: 38. What kind of meal plan does the man decide to buy?

39. How much does the plan cost?

40. Why do most residents order a pizza or go out to eat on Sundays?

41. How will the man pay for the meals?

42. What will the man probably do?

Narrator: Listen to part of a lecture in a botany class. The professor is talking about hydroponics.

As you will recall, hydroponics is the science of growing plants without soil, using a solution of nutrients in water. Of course, good soil has the nutrients necessary for plant growth, but when plants are grown without soil, all the nutrients must be provided in another way. This solution contains potassium nitrate, ammonium sulfate, magnesium sulfate, monocalcium phosphate, and calcium sulfate. Don't try to write down all of that now. You can refer to your lab workbook for the list of substances and the proportions needed for proper plant growth.

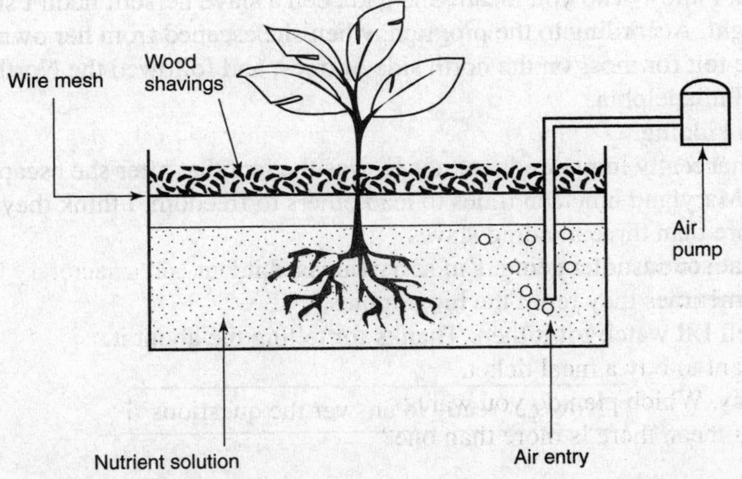

For now, let's look at the diagram that we worked on last time when we began our hydroponics experiment. Your drawing should look more or less like this one. As you know, for plants grown in soil, the roots not only absorb water and nutrients but also serve to anchor the plant. That is why the roots of our hydroponic plants are not placed directly in the water and nutrient solution. We used wood chips held in place by wire mesh to anchor the plants and allow us to suspend the roots in the tank below that contains the water and nutrient solution. Because oxygen is also taken in by the roots, we had to attach an air pump to mix oxygen into the solution. And you can see the way that the pump was attached to the tank.

During our break this morning, I'd like you to come over to the hydroponics area and examine the experiment close up. I'd also like you to take a closer look at this specimen of nutrient solution. What do you notice about this? What conclusions can you draw?

Now get ready to answer the questions

Narrator: 43. What is hydroponics?

44. Why does the professor suggest that the students refer to the lab workbooks?

45. According to the speaker, why are roots important to plants?

46. Why was the pump attached to the tank in this experiment?

47. What does the professor want the students to do with the specimen of the nutrient solution?

Narrator: Listen to part of a conversation between two students on campus.

Man: Did you watch *American Biography* last night?
Woman: No, I had class. Did you?
Man: Yes. Actually, it was an assignment for my history class, and it was excellent. It featured Harriet Tubman.
Woman: Who is Harriet Tubman?
Man: Don't feel bad. I didn't know either until I watched the show. She was a member of the underground railroad. You know, the organization that helped runaway slaves escape to free states or to Canada in the mid eighteen hundreds, just before and during the Civil War.
Woman: Oh, I know who you mean. She had been a slave herself, hadn't she?
Man: Right. According to the program, when she escaped from her owners in Maryland, she felt for moss on the north side of trees, and followed the North Star until she got to Philadelphia.
Woman: No kidding.
Man: What really impressed me though was the fact that after she escaped, she went back to Maryland nineteen times to lead others to freedom. I think they said she freed more than three hundred slaves.
Woman: That sounds interesting. I'm sorry I missed it.
Man: Sometimes they rerun the biographies.
Woman: Well I'll watch for it then. Thanks for telling me about it.

Now get ready to answer the questions

Narrator: 48. What are the speakers discussing?

49. Who was Harriet Tubman?

50. What impressed the man about Harriet Tubman's story?

Model Test 6
Computer-Assisted TOEFL

Section 1: Listening

The Listening section of the test measures the ability to understand conversations and talks in English. On the actual TOEFL exam, you will use headphones to listen to the conversations and talks. While you are listening, pictures of the speakers or other information will be presented on your computer screen. There are two parts to the Listening section, with special directions for each part.

On the day of the test, the amount of time you will have to answer all of the questions will appear on the computer screen. The time you spend listening to the test material will not be counted. The listening material and questions about it will be presented only one time. You will not be allowed to take notes or have any paper at your computer. You will both see and hear the questions before the answer choices appear. You can take as much time as you need to select an answer; however, it will be to your advantage to answer the questions as quickly as possible. You may change your answer as many times as you want before you confirm it. After you have confirmed an answer, you will not be able to return to the question.

Before you begin working on the Listening section, you will have an opportunity to adjust the volume of the sound. You will not be able to change the volume after you have started the test.

QUESTION DIRECTIONS—Part A

In Part A of the Listening section, you will hear short conversations between two people. In some of the conversations, each person speaks only once. In other conversations, one or both of the people speak more than once. Each conversation is followed by one question about it.

Each question in this part has four answer choices. You should click on the best answer to each question. Answer the questions on the basis of what is stated or implied by the speakers.

1. Man: What are you going to do this weekend? Maybe we can play some tennis.
Woman: Don't tempt me. I have to study for my qualifying examinations. I take them on Monday.
Narrator: What does the woman mean?

2. Woman: Any questions about the syllabus?
Man: Yes. Does attendance count toward the grade in this class?
Woman: No. I have an attendance requirement for undergraduates, but not for graduate students.
Narrator: What does the woman mean?

3. Man: Have you talked to Ali lately? I thought that he was studying at the American Language Institute, but yesterday I saw him going into the chemistry lab in the engineering building.
   Woman: That is not surprising. Ali is a part-time student this term. He is taking three classes at the Institute and one class at the university.
   Narrator: What does the woman say about Ali?

4. Man: Hello, Miss Evans? This is Paul Thompson. I would like to talk with Dr. Warren, please.
   Woman: Oh, Paul. You just missed her.
   Narrator: What does the woman mean?

5. Man: I am sorry. The last campus shuttle has already left.
   Woman: Oh. All right. Can you please tell me where I can find a telephone?
   Narrator: What will the woman probably do?

6. Man: Have you bought your books yet?
   Woman: I tried to, but the math and English books were sold out.
   Narrator: What does the woman mean?

7. Man: I don't have to be there until seven.
   Woman: The traffic is really bad though. You'd better leave a few minutes early.
   Narrator: What does the woman suggest the man do?

8. Man: You don't like the new graduate assistant, do you?
   Woman: No. He makes fun of his students' mistakes.
   Narrator: What does the woman mean?

9. Woman: Susan told me what you said about my accent.
   Man: I don't know what she told you, but I really didn't mean it as a put-down.
   Narrator: What does the man mean?

10. Man: I'll be right back. Can you watch my book bag for a minute?
    Woman: Sure. I'll be glad to.
    Narrator: What does the woman agree to do for the man?

11. Woman: I'm really tired of spending every weekend studying.
    Man: I hear you.
    Narrator: What does the man mean?

12. Man: Is that Mike's car? I thought you said that Mike was spending spring break in Florida.
    Woman: That's Mike's brother. He's using the car while Mike's away.
    Narrator: What does the woman imply?

13. Woman: We turned in our project today.
    Man: You did? We haven't even started.
    Woman: Well, you'd better start working. It's due in a week.
    Man: I will. I'll get it done.
    Narrator: What does the woman advise the man to do?

14. Man: Do you want to go to the International Talent Show?
Woman: Sure. Why not?
Narrator: What does the woman mean?

15. Man: Did you know that Bill and Carol are back from their honeymoon?
Woman: So they *did* get married after all.
Narrator: What had the woman assumed about Bill and Carol?

16. Man: Are you going to the review session for the test?
Woman: What's the point?
Narrator: What does the woman mean?

17. Woman: Your check isn't here.
Man: On no. What can I do?
Woman: I suggest that you call your sponsor.
Man: Okay. I'll be back.
Narrator: What will the man probably do?

QUESTION DIRECTIONS—Part B

In Part B of the Listening section, you will hear several longer conversations and talks. Each conversation or talk is followed by several questions. The conversations, talks, and questions will not be repeated.

The conversations and talks are about a variety of topics. You do not need special knowledge of the topics to answer the questions correctly. Rather, you should answer each question on the basis of what is stated or implied by the speakers in the conversations or talks.

For most of the questions, you will need to click on the best of four possible answers. Some questions will have special directions. The special directions will appear in a box on the computer screen.

Narrator: Listen to part of a conversation between two students on campus.

Woman: Where have you been? I've missed you in lab.
Man: I've been sick.
Woman: Nothing serious, I hope.
Man: Well, I stayed out of the hospital, but to tell the truth, I was in pretty bad shape. Some kind of flu.
Woman: That's too bad. Are you better now?
Man: Well enough to start thinking about school again. Now I'm worried about getting caught up.
Woman: Let's see, how many labs have you missed?
Man: Margaret, I got sick three weeks ago, so I am really behind.
Woman: Let me look at my notebook. I've got it right here.
Man: Oh, great. I was hoping you'd let me make a copy of your notes.
Woman: Sure. You can do that, Gary. And I have some good news for you. You haven't missed any quizzes. We haven't had any since you've been gone. Listen, after you have a chance to look at my notes, why don't we get together? If there's anything you don't understand, maybe I can explain it to you. It's hard trying to read someone else's notes.
Man: That would be perfect. I hate to bother you though.
Woman: No bother. I'm sure you'd do it for me.

Now get ready to answer the questions

Narrator: 18. What is Gary's problem?

19. What does Gary want Margaret to do?

20. What does Margaret offer to do?

21. What is Margaret's attitude in this conversation?

Narrator: Listen to part of a lecture in an American literature class. The professor is talking about American novelists in the twentieth century. He is focusing on F. Scott Fitzgerald.

There have been a number of important American novelists in this century, but I have chosen F. Scott Fitzgerald for our class because he is one of the more interesting ones. Born in 1896 and educated at Princeton, he wrote novels that describe the post-war American society, very much caught up in the rhythms of jazz.

In 1920, the same year that he published his first book, *This Side of Paradise*, he married Zelda Sayre, also a writer. His most famous book, *The Great Gatsby*, appeared in 1925.

Fitzgerald had a great natural talent, but unfortunately he became a compulsive drinker. A brilliant success in his youth, he never made the adjustments necessary to a maturing writer in a changing world. His later novels, *All the Sad Young Men*, *Tender Is the Night,* and *The Last Tycoon,* were less successful, so that when he died in 1940 his books were out of print and he had been almost forgotten. His reputation now is far greater than it was in his lifetime, especially since the film version of his novel *The Great Gatsby* was released.

Now, with that introduction, I am going to run the video version of *The Great Gatsby*, and then we'll divide up into groups to talk about it.

Now get ready to answer the questions

Narrator: 22. What is the main topic of this lecture?

23. Why wasn't Fitzgerald more successful in his later life?

24. According to the lecturer, what do we know about the novels written by F. Scott Fitzgerald?

25. What does the professor want the class to do after the lecture?

Narrator: The university quartet has been invited to play for a music appreciation class. Listen to a talk by the director of the quartet.

Before the concert begins, let me tell you a little bit about chamber music. From medieval times through the eighteenth century, musicians in Europe had two options for employment—

the church or the nobility. So when they were not performing at religious functions, they were playing in the chambers of stately homes. And they came to be known as chamber players.

Chamber music is written to be performed by a small group, more than one, but fewer than a dozen musicians. Pieces for more than eight players are unusual though, and it is rare to see a conductor. It may surprise you to know that any combination of instruments can be used for chamber music. The most popular are the piano, strings, and woodwinds, but chamber music has been written for other instruments as well.

Early chamber music, let's say the sixteenth and seventeenth centuries, was often written for the recorder, harpsichord, and viola. During the Elizabethan Period, there were many talented composers of chamber music, including William Byrd and Orlando Gibbons. And at that time, vocal chamber music, called madrigal singing, was very popular. Later, both Johann Sebastian Bach and George Frederick Handel wrote trio sonatas for chamber groups. This evening the University Quartet will perform two of the later pieces by Bach.

Ladies and gentlemen, the University Quartet.

Now get ready to answer the questions

Narrator: 26. What is the main purpose of the talk?

27. What is the origin of the term *chamber music?*

28. According to the speaker, which instruments are the most popular for chamber music?

29. Why does the speaker mention Johann Sebastian Bach?

30. What will the listeners hear next?

Narrator: Listen to part of a conversation between a student and a secretary in the chemical engineering department.

Woman: May I help you?
Man: Yes. My name is Bob Stephens and I have an appointment with Dr. Benjamin at three o'clock on Wednesday.
Woman: Three o'clock on Wednesday? Yes. I see it here on his calendar.
Man: Well, I was wondering whether he has an earlier appointment available on the same day.
Woman: I'm sorry, Mr. Stephens, but Dr. Benjamin is tied up in a meeting until noon, and he has two appointments scheduled before yours when he gets back from lunch.
Man: Oh.
Woman: There is a later appointment time open though, at four-thirty, if that would help you. Or you could see him Thursday morning at ten.
Man: Hmmm. No thank you. I think I'll just rearrange my own schedule so I can keep my regular appointment.

Now get ready to answer the questions

Narrator: 31. Why did the man go to the Chemical Engineering Department?

32. What does the woman say about Dr. Benjamin?

33. What did the secretary offer to do?

34. What did the man decide to do?

Narrator: Listen to part of a lecture in a health class. The professor will be talking about nutrition. She will focus on health food.

Health food is a general term applied to all kinds of foods that are considered more healthful than the types of foods widely sold in supermarkets. For example, whole grains, dried beans, and corn oil are health foods. A narrower classification of health food is natural food. This term is used to distinguish between types of the same food. Fresh fruit is a natural food, but canned fruit, with sugars and other additives, is not. The most precise term of all and the narrowest classification within health foods is organic food, used to describe food that has been grown on a particular kind of farm. Fruits and vegetables that are grown in gardens treated only with organic fertilizers, that are not sprayed with poisonous insecticides, and that are not refined after harvest are organic foods.

In choosing the type of food you eat, then, you have basically two choices: inorganic, processed foods, or organic, unprocessed foods. A wise decision should include investigation of the allegations that processed foods contain chemicals, some of which are proven to be toxic, and that vitamin content is greatly reduced in processed foods.

Now get ready to answer the questions

Narrator: 35. What is the main topic of this lecture?

36. Which term is used to identify foods that have not been processed or canned?

37. What happens to food when it is processed?

38. Which word best describes the speaker's attitude toward health foods?

Narrator: Listen to part of a class discussion in an anthropology class. The professor is talking about the Stone Age.

Professor: So, as you will recall, the Stone Age is the time, early in the development of human cultures, before the introduction of metals, when prehistoric people started to make stone tools and weapons. Can anyone remember the exact dates for the Stone Age? Chuck?

Chuck: Well, you said that the exact dates would vary for different parts of the world.

Professor: That's exactly right. I did. But in general, the use of flint for tools was widespread about two million years ago. That was the beginning of the Paleolithic Period, which is also referred to as the Old Stone Age. What can you tell me about the humanoid creatures that were alive during this period? Yes, Beverly?

Beverly: They were Neanderthals, and they were nomads. And they survived by hunting and gathering.

Professor: Very good. Beverly, can you tell us anything about the tools that they made?

Beverly: Yes, they were primarily general purpose tools such as axes, knives, and arrowheads that they used for hunting.

Professor: Correct. But we have also found some interesting tools for specific domestic purposes as well. Bone implements were being introduced in the Old Stone Age, and we have reason to believe that they were actually making sewing needles. Any ideas on why that might be so? Chuck?

Chuck: The Ice Age. They must have been cold.

Professor: That's true. The last Ice Age was about 13000 B.C. which is at the end of the Paleolithic Period. Do you remember anything else about that time that is of particular importance? Beverly?

Beverly: Neanderthal man began to decline, and *Homo sapiens* emerged.

Professor: Right. This marks the end of the Old Stone Age and the beginning of the Middle Stone Age, or the Mesolithic Period. In fact, "Meso" means "middle." Now let's think about the changing climate and the emergence of *Homo sapiens.* How would this influence the kind of tools that would be produced? Any ideas, Chuck?

Chuck: Well, with the more moderate climate, *Homo sapiens* didn't have to wander so far to hunt and gather. Wasn't it in the Middle Stone Age that agricultural villages started to develop?

Professor: Actually, it was during the Neolithic Period or the Late Stone Age, about 8000 B.C. But you are on the right track. Some of the tools previously used for hunting were adapted for rudimentary farming even during the Middle Stone Age before farming communities started to develop.

Chuck: So was it farming that marked the end of the Stone Age then?

Professor: It was influential. But the introduction of metals was usually considered the defining event that brought an end to the Stone Age. As metals started to challenge stone as the material of choice for tools, mankind entered a new era.

Now get ready to answer the questions

Narrator: 39. How did the professor define the Stone Age?

40. According to the lecturer, which two occupations describe the Neanderthals?

41. Name the three time periods associated with the Stone Age.

42. Why did tools change during the Late Stone Age?

43. What marked the end of the Stone Age?

Narrator: Listen to part of a lecture in a geology class. The professor is talking about oil deposits.

Most crude oil is found in underground formations called traps. In a trap, the oil collects in porous rocks, along with gas and water. Over time, the oil moves up toward the surface of the earth through cracks and holes in the porous rock until it reaches a nonporous rock deposit that will not allow it to continue moving. The oil becomes trapped under the nonporous rock deposit.

There are several different types of traps, but today we will talk about the three most common ones—the anticline trap, the salt dome trap, and the fault trap.

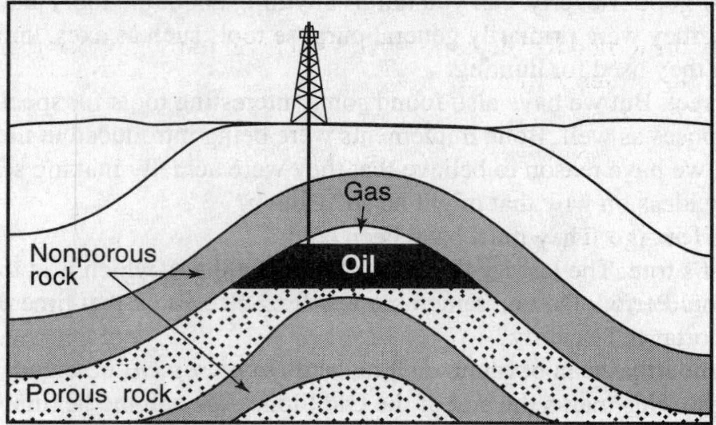

Look at this diagram. Here is an example of an anticline. As you can see, the oil is trapped under a formation of rock that resembles an arch. In this anticline, the petroleum is trapped under a formation of nonporous rock with a gas deposit directly over it. This is fairly typical of an anticline.

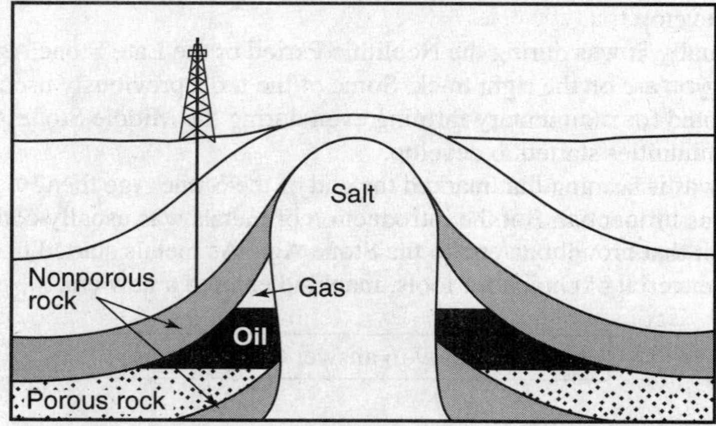

Now, let's look at a diagram of a salt dome. This salt dome shows how a cylinder-shaped salt deposit has pushed up through a layer of sedimentary rocks, causing them to arch and fracture. The oil deposits have collected along the sides of the salt dome.

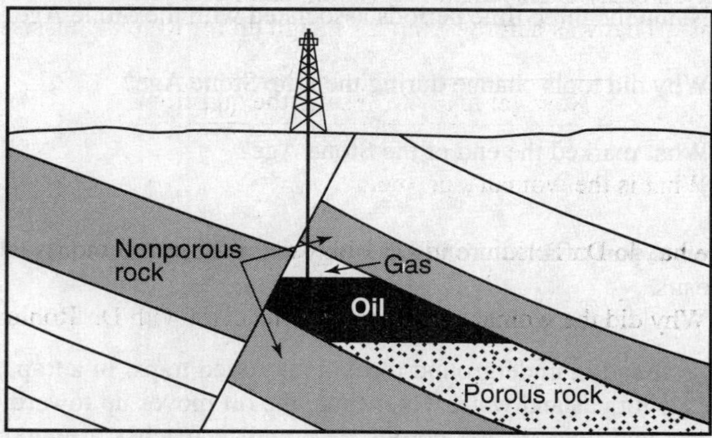

Finally, I want to show you a fault trap. This diagram represents a fracture in the Earth that has shifted a nonporous rock formation on top of a porous formation. Remember, as in all traps, the oil is collected in the porous rock and trapped underground by the nonporous rock.

Geologists study the terrain for indications of possible oil traps. For example, a bulge in a flat surface may signal the presence of a salt dome.

Now get ready to answer the questions

Narrator: 44. What is a trap?

45. Select the diagram of the anticline trap that was described in the lecture.

46. Identify the nonporous rock in the diagram.

47. According to the speaker, how can geologists locate salt domes?

Narrator: Listen to part of a conversation between two students on campus.

Man: Who is teaching the class?
Woman: Actually, I have a choice between Dr. Perkins and Dr. Robinson. Do you know anything about them?
Man: Sure. I've taken classes with both of them.
Woman: So what do you think?
Man: They are both good in their own way. But it depends on how you learn best, because they approach the class from two entirely different points of view.
Woman: I've heard that Robinson is very strict.
Man: You could say that. I'd call it traditional. He lectures every day, gives quizzes every week, leading up to a comprehensive final exam, multiple-choice as I recall.
Woman: How about Perkins?
Man: More relaxed. Uses group discussion and projects instead of quizzes. And I'm pretty sure his final is short essay.
Woman: Which one would you advise me to take?
Man: I really can't say. If you like to listen to lectures and take notes, and if you do well on objective tests, I'd say Robinson. But if you enjoy working in groups, and you do better on essay exams, then I'd recommend Perkins.
Woman: Thanks. That was helpful. I think I'll sign up for Robinson's class.

Now get ready to answer the questions

Narrator: 48. What is the woman's problem?

49. What do Dr. Perkins and Dr. Robinson have in common?

50. Why did the woman decide to take the class with Dr. Robinson?

Model Test 7
Computer-Assisted TOEFL

Section 1: Listening

The Listening section of the test measures the ability to understand conversations and talks in English. On the actual TOEFL exam, you will use headphones to listen to the conversations and talks. While you are listening, pictures of the speakers or other information will be presented on your computer screen. There are two parts to the Listening section, with special directions for each part.

On the day of the test, the amount of time you will have to answer all of the questions will appear on the computer screen. The time you spend listening to the test material will not be counted. The listening material and questions about it will be presented only one time. You will not be allowed to take notes or have any paper at your computer. You will both see and hear the questions before the answer choices appear. You can take as much time as you need to select an answer; however, it will be to your advantage to answer the questions as quickly as possible. You may change your answer as many times as you want before you confirm it. After you have confirmed an answer, you will not be able to return to the question.

Before you begin working on the Listening section, you will have an opportunity to adjust the volume of the sound. You will not be able to change the volume after you have started the test.

QUESTION DIRECTIONS—Part A

In Part A of the Listening section, you will hear short conversations between two people. In some of the conversations, each person speaks only once. In other conversations, one or both of the people speak more than once. Each conversation is followed by one question about it.

Each question in this part has four answer choices. You should click on the best answer to each question. Answer the questions on the basis of what is stated or implied by the speakers.

1. Man: It's so noisy in the dorm I can't get anything done.
   Woman: I know. I used to live in a dorm myself.
   Man: I'll have to do something different next semester.
   Woman: Why not move into an apartment?
   Narrator: What does the woman mean?

2. Man: Hi Jan.
   Woman: Hi. Are you going to school here now?
   Man 2: Yes, I transferred from community college last term. Let's have lunch sometime.
   Woman: Sounds good. Give me a call.
   Narrator: What can we assume from this conversation?

3. Woman: How many transcripts do you want me to send to San Diego State?
   Man: Just one, but I want two for myself.
   Narrator: What will the woman probably do?

4. Man: I ought to wait until Professor Bloom gets back from class.
   Woman: Not really. You can just leave a note. I'll give it to her.
   Narrator: What does the woman suggest the man do?

5. Woman: Susan told me she was really interested in social work.
   Man: Yes, but when she declared her major she chose education.
   Narrator: What can be inferred about Susan?

6. Woman: I wonder whether the grades are posted yet?
Man: I don't think so. It usually takes about three days, and we just turned in our papers yesterday.
Narrator: What are the speakers talking about?

7. Woman: Congratulations! I saw your name on the graduation list.
Man: Someone else must have the same name then. I'm not graduating until next spring.
Narrator: What had the woman assumed?

8. Man: Did you ever apply for that scholarship? You weren't sure whether you wanted to compete with all those applicants.
Woman: I decided to go for it!
Narrator: What does the woman mean?

9. Woman: We're going to the library. Want to come along?
Man: I'm waiting for the mail to come.
Narrator: What does the man imply?

10. Man: How was your break? You went to Toronto, didn't you?
Woman: I was going there, but I got a really great fare to Montreal, then I drove to Quebec and some of the little towns in the province.
Narrator: What are the speakers talking about?

11. Man: Do you want me to get anything else for our presentation while I'm at the bookstore?
Woman: I couldn't care less.
Narrator: How does the woman feel about the presentation?

12. Man: Weren't you in class Friday either?
Woman: No. I had to take my mother to the airport. She went back to New York.
Narrator: What do we learn about the two students in this conversation?

13. Woman: You must be so excited about going home after four years.
Man: Not as much as I thought I would be.
Narrator: What does the man mean?

14. Man: Do you usually bring your lunch?
Woman: I eat in the snack bar now and then.
Narrator: What does the woman mean?

15. Woman: We were just talking about you.
Man: Really? Why?
Woman: I heard you were in the hospital.
Man: I'm much better now. No need to worry.
Woman: You'd better take it easy though, or you'll get sick again.
Narrator: What does the woman mean?

16. Woman: I don't like our economics class.
Man: Neither do I.
Narrator: What does the man mean?

17. Woman: Did you find enough subjects for your research project?
Man: Not yet. I have thirty-five though, so that's a good start.
Narrator: What does the man imply?

QUESTION DIRECTIONS—Part B

In Part B of the Listening section, you will hear several longer conversations and talks. Each conversation or talk is followed by several questions. The conversations, talks, and questions will not be repeated.

The conversations and talks are about a variety of topics. You do not need special knowledge of the topics to answer the questions correctly. Rather, you should answer each question on the basis of what is stated or implied by the speakers in the conversations or talks.

For most of the questions, you will need to click on the best of four possible answers. Some questions will have special directions. The special directions will appear in a box on the computer screen.

Narrator: Listen to part of a conversation between a student and his professor.

Rick: Thank you for seeing me today, Dr. Wilson. I want to talk with you about my final grade.
Dr. Wilson: Yes?
Rick: Well, I was surprised to get a D after doing so well on the midterm.
Dr. Wilson: Let's see. I'll just check my grade book here.
Rick: I got a B, Dr. Wilson. I brought my test with me.
Dr. Wilson: Yes, you did. I have it recorded here. And you passed the final with a C.
Rick: Then I should have gotten a C+ or a B–.
Dr. Wilson: Yes, you should have, but the problem was your attendance. Twenty-five percent of your grade was calculated on the basis of class participation, and Rick, you just didn't participate.
Rick: But I passed the exams.
Dr. Wilson: Yes, I know you did. And you passed the course. D is a passing grade.
Rick: But . . .
Dr. Wilson: I'm sorry, Rick. I gave you a syllabus on the first day of class and the grading system was outlined in it. You received an F in class participation because you missed too many days, and that brought your grade down.

Now get ready to answer the questions

Narrator: 18. What prompted this conversation?

19. Where is this conversation taking place?

20. What is the grade that Rick received for the course?

21. Why did Rick receive a lower grade?

Narrator: Listen to a discussion in a linguistics class. The class has been discussing first language development in children.

Richards: Today we'll be talking about grammatical development in children. Does anyone here have any small children at home? Diane, you have young children at home, so you will be able to help us with a lot of examples. Let's start with the kind of language that we hear from twelve- to eighteen-month-old children who are just starting to use one-word sentences. What kind of words do we hear in those sentences?

Diane: "Water," "Mama," "book."

Richards: Those are very typical of one-word sentences, Diane. Your examples are all nouns. At this early stage, children are naming their world, and they need nouns to do that. But soon, by about eighteen months to two years of age, they are putting two-, three-, even four-word sentences together, and combining them in complex ways to produce a wide variety of structures. Can anyone think of any examples for this stage? Yes, Jerry.

Jerry: My son is two, and his favorite sentence right now is "Daddy up" when he wants me to carry him.

Richards: Good example. In addition to the statements that younger children use, toddlers are beginning to use commands appropriately. They also start using questions. I think one of the most interesting features of this stage is the omission of small words such as "is" and "the" as well as word endings like "I-N-G" on verbs.

Diane: Yes, I notice that my three-year-old is starting to put those endings on the verbs now, but sometimes they aren't perfect. He says things like "We runned fast" instead of "ran." All my children did that.

Richards: Good observation. What is actually happening there is that he is learning the regular verb endings and extending their use to irregular verbs. That is another very common characteristic of language acquisition in children. Perhaps the most important aspect of child grammar at age four is the active correction of previous errors. By age five, the grammar is not error-free, but there is evidence that children have learned the basic structures of their language, but, of course, recent research indicates that several grammatical constructions are still being acquired by children as old as ten or eleven. Did you have a question, Jerry?

Jerry: Yes. I was wondering if these stages are the same for children learning all languages or just English.

Richards: Excellent question, Jerry. There is evidence that the basic stages are the same for all languages.

Now get ready to answer the questions

Narrator: 22. Why does the professor call on Diane?

23. What are two charcteristics of the language of toddlers?

24. What can be concluded about the phrase "We runned"?

25. By which age have most children learned the basic structures of language?

26. What does the professor say about languages other than English?

Narrator: Listen to a professor talking with her class on the first day of the course. She will be clarifying the course syllabus.

Before we begin our discussion of today's topic, I'd like to point out a few important features on the syllabus. First, please look at the calendar. As you see, we will be meeting for fifteen weeks. The last week of November we will not meet because of the Thanksgiving holiday. But, all of the other dates are listed, along with the reading assignments in your textbook. In general, it is better to read the assigned pages before you come to class so that you will be prepared to participate in the discussion that follows the lecture.

Now, let's look at the course requirements. As you see, you have a midterm examination the last week of October, and a final examination the second week of December. The midterm is worth thirty points and the final is worth fifty points. That leaves twenty points for the project that you will be working on, and you have several choices to fulfill that requirement. You can either write a paper or make a half-hour presentation on a topic of your choice. We'll be talking a bit more about the projects in the next several weeks. Oh, yes, you will notice that I don't factor attendance into the grade, but I do expect you to be here. If you must miss class for whatever reason, please get in touch with me. My office hours are listed on the syllabus, along with my voice mail number and my e-mail address.

Now get ready to answer the questions

Narrator: 27. What suggestion does the professor make about the reading assignments?

28. How are the points distributed for the course requirements?

29. What are the choices for a project?

30. According to the professor, what should students do if they must be absent?

Narrator: Listen to part of a lecture in an astronomy course. Today the professor will talk about distant planets. He will focus on Neptune and Uranus.

Today I'm going to share a rather interesting theory with you. As you already know from your reading material, many scientists believe that the atmosphere of the seventh and eighth planets from our sun, Uranus and Neptune, have an outer film of hydrogen and helium. The atmosphere of Neptune above its methane ice clouds is about 85 percent hydrogen and 15 percent helium, and beneath the clouds, methane concentrations increase to more than 1 percent. The atmosphere of Uranus consists mostly of hydrogen with 2 percent methane and 10 to 20 percent helium, with lesser amounts of ammonia. Because of this, the surfaces of these planets are probably covered with frozen ammonia and methane.

Now Marvin Ross of the Lawrence Livermore National Laboratory in California has postulated that the methane could have separated into the carbon and hydrogen atoms that form it, and furthermore, that at the high pressure common to those planets, the carbon atoms could have been squeezed into a layer of diamonds.

Astronomers at the University of Arizona in Tucson agree that the pressures on these planets, some 200,000 to 6 million times that of Earth's atmosphere, could set up conditions whereby diamonds might form. Moreover, since the two giant planets are each nearly four times the size of the Earth, and each is nearly one-fifth carbon, the quantities of diamonds could be huge.

Now get ready to answer the questions

Narrator: 31. What is the main purpose of this lecture?

32. Which planets are being discussed?

33. The professor briefly explains a process. Summarize the process by putting the events in order.

34. How does the speaker feel about the theory?

Narrator: Listen to part of a lecture in a political science class. The professor will talk about the electoral process.

In the United States, the people do not elect the president by direct vote. This is so because the men who wrote the Constitution in 1787 believed that ordinary citizens would not be informed enough to make such an important decision, and they created a system whereby a representative group of citizens called the electoral college would be responsible for making the choice. The candidate with the most votes became president, and the candidate receiving the next highest number of votes became vice-president. But in 1800, when Aaron Burr and Thomas Jefferson received an equal number of votes, the system had to be changed to provide for separate voting for president and vice-president.

Later, when political parties had become more influential, the parties nominated candidates and then chose electors to vote for them.

Look at this diagram. Today, each political party in the state nominates a slate of electors pledged to support the party's nominees for president and vice-president. Each state has the same number of electors in the college as it has members of Congress. On election day, registered voters go to the polls to choose the electors.

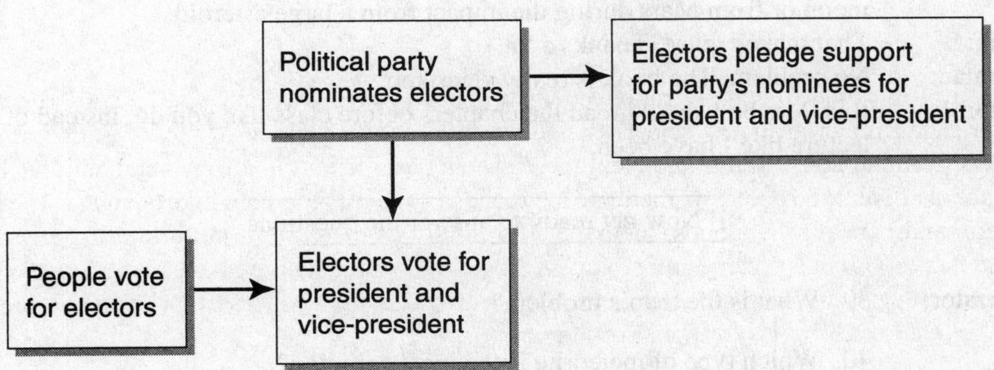

In most states, the ballots list only the names of the candidates for president and vice-president that the electors have pledged to support. This vote by the people for electors is called the popular vote, and the candidates who receive the most popular votes win all the electoral votes in a state.

Now get ready to answer the questions

Narrator: 35. What is the electoral college?

36. Why does the speaker mention Aaron Burr and Thomas Jefferson?

37. How are the people nominated for the electoral college?

38. What is the popular vote?

Narrator: Listen to a study group discussion about meteorites.

Man: Did you understand Dr. Wilson's last lecture?
Woman: The one on meteorites?
Man: Yes. I can't understand my notes.
Woman: My notes aren't great either, but I read the chapter before class so that made it a little easier to follow. Where did you get lost?
Man: Well, he said that there were three basic types of meteorites, and that they were classified according to their composition.
Woman: So far, so good.
Man: But I only have two types written down—the iron meteorite that is mostly iron, with some trace metals like nickel and cobalt, and the stone meteorite that is mostly silicates and a wide variety of minerals.
Woman: Oh, well, you are missing the stony iron meteorite that contains varying proportions of both iron and stone. He went over that one pretty fast, but he did say that the stony iron meteorite is very rare and represents only about 1 percent of the meteorites that fall to the Earth, so you might want to make a note of that.
Man: Okay. The stone meteorite is the most common.
Woman: Right. Stone meteorites account for almost 90 percent.
Man: Great. Then what did he say about asteroids and comets right at the end of the lecture?
Woman: Let's see. That was when he was talking about the formation of meteorites. And he said most meteorites are believed to be fragments of either asteroids or comets, but then he said that some stone meteorites may have dislodged themselves from the moon or from Mars during the impact from a large asteroid.
Man: That makes sense. Thanks a lot.
Woman: No problem. The book is really clear, too.
Man: It is. Maybe I should read the chapters before class like you do, instead of after the lecture like I have been.

Now get ready to answer the questions

Narrator: 39. What is the man's problem?

40. Which type of meteorite is the most common?

41. How were most meteorites formed?

42. What helped the woman follow the lecture?

Narrator: An artist from Alaska has been invited to talk about folk art to an art history class. She will be discussing scrimshaw. Listen to the beginning of the lecture.

In the period between the American Revolution and the Civil War, about 1775–1865, the hunting of whales was a major industry in America. In addition to the whale oil that was a primary item of trade, whale bones and even teeth became valuable for intricate carvings that the sailors made on them. This was called scrimshaw, although no one seems to know where it got the name.

There are two techniques for scrimshaw. One is to carve the bone into figures, in much the same way that wood or stone is carved. The other is to cut designs on the bone and then fill them with ink so that they are more visible.

This is an example of a scrimshaw from about 1800. As you can see, the results are quite beautiful, and even more impressive since the artist probably had no training at all and worked with only a pocket knife or a needle.

Like most folk artists, the sailors who practiced the art of scrimshaw tended to create practical objects such as tools, boxes, jewelry, and buttons. I have a number of examples here that I am going to pass around so that you can better appreciate the intricate details on the designs.

As you can imagine, because of the decline in whaling, there has also been a decline in the number of folk artists who produce scrimshaw. These pieces are quite rare and, as a result, quite valuable.

Now get ready to answer the questions

Narrator: 43. What is the purpose of this talk?

44. Why does the lecturer mention the American Revolution and the Civil War?

45. Identify the two techniques used to create scrimshaw.

46. Select the object that is the best example of scrimshaw.

47. Why has scrimshaw become so valuable?

Narrator: Listen to part of a conversation between two students on campus.

Man: Look. I got this in the mail, and I'm thinking about applying for a card.
Woman: Oh, right. I got one, too. And so did a lot of people on campus.
Man: So, what do you think? Are you going to do it?
Woman: No. First of all, I already have a credit card, and I think one is enough for me right now.
Man: Yeah, I have a credit card, too, but this one doesn't have an annual fee, and the interest charges are lower.
Woman: Maybe. I'm not too sure, because I didn't look into it myself, but my roommate told me that you have to carry a $200 balance to keep the card . . .
Man: So you can't pay if off every month?
Woman: No, you can't. And that means you automatically have to pay interest. It's lower, but still, you can't avoid it by keeping a zero balance.
Man: What happens if you don't carry a $200 balance?
Woman: Well, first they send you a letter warning you that the account will be closed if activity doesn't pick up. Then, after a month or two, they close your account.
Man: I see. Well, forget that. It doesn't sound like such a good deal after all.

Now get ready to answer the questions

Narrator: 48. What is the man trying to decide?

49. Why is the man interested in the credit card?

50. Why does the man decide not to get the card?

Model Test 8
Computer-Assisted TOEFL

Section 1: Listening

The Listening section of the test measures the ability to understand conversations and talks in English. On the actual TOEFL exam, you will use headphones to listen to the conversations and talks. While you are listening, pictures of the speakers or other information will be presented on your computer screen. There are two parts to the Listening section, with special directions for each part.

On the day of the test, the amount of time you will have to answer all of the questions will appear on the computer screen. The time you spend listening to the test material will not be counted. The listening material and questions about it will be presented only one time. You will not be allowed to take notes or have any paper at your computer. You will both see and hear the questions before the answer choices appear. You can take as much time as you need to select an answer; however, it will be to your advantage to answer the questions as quickly as possible. You may change your answer as many times as you want before you confirm it. After you have confirmed an answer, you will not be able to return to the question.

Before you begin working on the Listening section, you will have an opportunity to adjust the volume of the sound. You will not be able to change the volume after you have started the test.

QUESTION DIRECTIONS—Part A

In Part A of the Listening section, you will hear short conversations between two people. In some of the conversations, each person speaks only once. In other conversations, one or both of the people speak more than once. Each conversation is followed by one question about it.

Each question in this part has four answer choices. You should click on the best answer to each question. Answer the questions on the basis of what is stated or implied by the speakers.

1. Man: Could you please sign my course request form?
   Woman: I'm sorry. You have to get your advisor's signature on that.
   Narrator: What can be inferred about the woman?

2. Woman: So what are you going to do? Drop the course?
   Man: No way!
   Narrator: What does the man mean?

3. Man: Did Dr. Peterson pass back our tests today?
   Woman: No. She didn't have them all graded yet. But we can pick them up after Wednesday in her office if we don't want to wait until class next Monday.
   Narrator: What can be inferred about the man?

4. Woman: It looks like Dr. Williams is going to show some slides.
   Man: You're right. Let's sit closer to the front. I can't see very well.
   Woman: That's a good idea.
   Narrator: What will the man and woman probably do?

5. Woman: Did you like living in Montreal?
   Man: Yes. Most of the time. The weather was really cold in the winter, but the rest of the year was beautiful.
   Narrator: How did the man feel about Montreal?

6. Woman: Are you going to do the work for extra credit?
   Man: You bet!
   Narrator: What does the man mean?

7. Man: I've got to quit smoking. But how? I've tried chewing gum. I've joined a support group. My willpower only lasts about two weeks.
   Woman: It's hard. I smoked for almost ten years. Then I got one of those nicotine patches. Why don't you try it?
   Narrator: What did the woman suggest?

8. Man: You're in my American Lit class, aren't you?
   Woman: Yes, I am. How do you like the class so far?
   Man: Well, to tell the truth, I'm not too big on literature.
   Narrator: What does the man mean?

9. Woman: Can you believe it? I got an A on my final!
   Man: Way to go!
   Narrator: What does the man mean?

10. Man: Hey, I heard that you got an assistantship.
Woman: You must be thinking of my roommate. I'm not going to try to teach next year while I'm studying full time.
Narrator: What does the woman mean?

11. Man: What did you do with your notebook?
Woman: I wish I knew. I thought I had put it in my car so I wouldn't have to carry it around all day in my backpack.
Narrator: What is the woman's problem?

12. Man: You'd better hurry. They're only taking pictures for ID cards until five o'clock.
Woman: I'm on my way.
Narrator: What does the woman mean?

13. Man: What is an appropriate gift to take to some friends who have invited you to their house for dinner? I was thinking maybe some candy.
Woman: That sounds good. Or you could get a plant.
Narrator: What does the woman suggest?

14. Man: Are you lost?
Woman: I'm afraid so. I can't find Dr. Warren's office. It's number 119.
Man: Oh! The even numbers are on this side, so it must be on the other side.
Narrator: What will the woman probably do?

15. Man: But I sent my application three weeks ago.
Woman: Well that's why you haven't heard, then. It takes six weeks to process it.
Narrator: What does the woman imply?

16. Man: If you want to cash a check at the Student Union, they'll need to see your driver's license and a major credit card.
Woman: Even for a traveler's check? I have my passport.
Narrator: What does the woman mean?

17. Woman: How did the meeting go with your doctoral committee?
Man: I couldn't have been more pleased.
Narrator: What does the man mean?

QUESTION DIRECTIONS—Part B

In Part B of the Listening section, you will hear several longer conversations and talks. Each conversation or talk is followed by several questions. The conversations, talks, and questions will not be repeated.

The conversations and talks are about a variety of topics. You do not need special knowledge of the topics to answer the questions correctly. Rather, you should answer each question on the basis of what is stated or implied by the speakers in the conversations or talks.

For most of the questions, you will need to click on the best of four possible answers. Some questions will have special directions. The special directions will appear in a box on the computer screen.

Narrator: Listen to part of a conversation between a student and the dean of students on campus.

Dean: You are here because you are accused of plagiarism. That is one of the most serious kinds of misconduct at the University. It is intellectual theft.
Student: But I didn't mean to steal.
Dean: Maybe not, but copying is stealing.
Student: I didn't copy.
Dean: Yes, you did. In this case, you copied from a book instead of from a friend. It's still copying. Look, if you want to use someone else's words, you must put them in quotation marks, and you must cite the source. You know that, don't you?
Student: Yes, but . . .
Dean: Even if you don't copy word for word, but you use someone else's ideas, if those ideas are not widely published, it can still be plagiarism to use them without a citation.
Student: That is what I don't understand, Dean Conners.
Dean: Mr. Farr, your professor already gave you a failing grade for the course, and in this case I feel that is punishment enough. I'm going to give you a warning this time. But if you ever come back to my office for a similar offense, I'll have you expelled. In the meantime, if you really don't know how to write a research paper, I suggest that you go over to the Learning Resources Center for some tutoring.

Now get ready to answer the questions

Narrator: 18. Why is the student in the dean's office?

19. What is the student's excuse?

20. How does the dean punish the student?

21. What advice does the dean give the student?

Narrator: Listen to part of a conversation on campus between two students.

Man: What's bothering you? You've been really quiet tonight.
Woman: I'm sorry. I'm trying to decide whether to stay here or to transfer to a larger school.
Man: Well, there are advantages to both, I suppose.
Woman: That's the problem. I keep thinking that eventually it will be better to have the degree from a larger, more prestigious college, but I really like it here.
Man: I know what you mean. At a small place like this, we have professors teaching our classes, not graduate students.
Woman: Exactly. And, besides that, your teachers know you, and they seem to really care about you. I'm not sure it would be like that in a huge university.
Man: True. So, you are basically happy here, but you are worried about the impression that you will make with a degree from such a small college.
Woman: Yes. I'm afraid I'll be in a job interview sometime, and the interviewer will say, "And just where *is* your alma mater?"
Man: I've thought about that myself.
Woman: And?

Man: Well, as you know, I'm planning to go to graduate school, so my plan is to get really good grades here and try to get into a well-known university for my master's degree. I think that will give me the best of both worlds.

Now get ready to answer the questions

Narrator: 22. What is the woman trying to decide?

23. What does she like about the college she is attending?

24. How does the man respond to her problem?

25. What does the man plan to do?

Narrator: Listen to part of a talk in an anthropology class.

In informal conversation, the word *culture* refers to a desirable personal attribute that can be acquired by visiting museums and galleries and by attending concerts and theatrical performances. An educated person who has culture is familiar with the finer things produced in civilized society. And that's what most people think of when they hear the word culture. In anthropology, however, culture is defined in a very different way. To an anthropologist, culture refers to the complex whole of ideas and material objects produced by groups in their historical experience; that is, the learned behaviors, beliefs, attitudes, and values that are characteristic of a particular society. For a thought or activity to be included as part of a culture, it must be commonly shared by or considered appropriate for the group.

Even in a complex society like that of the United States, which comprises many diverse ethnic groups, there are practices common to all Americans, and these practices constitute American culture. In addition, the smaller groups within the larger society have shared customs that are specific to their group. These shared customs represent a subculture within the larger culture. Now, can anyone think of an example of a subculture in the United States?

Now get ready to answer the questions

Narrator: 26. What is the topic of this lecture?

27. According to the speaker, what do most people mean when they use the word *culture* in ordinary conversation?

28. According to the speaker, what do anthropologists mean when they say a thought or activity is to be included as part of culture?

29. How does the professor explain American culture?

30. According to the speaker, what is a subculture?

Narrator: A medical doctor has been invited to talk about AIDS to a biology class. Listen to the beginning of the talk.

In 1992, the World Health Organization (WHO) reported that ten to twelve million adults and one million children worldwide had contracted HIV, the virus that causes AIDS, and they estimated that by the twenty-first century, forty million people would be infected. If the current trends continue, however, that estimate will fall far short of actual numbers, which may reach one hundred ten million.

In addition, there appears to be a change in the characteristics of AIDS victims. In the 1980s, homosexual men in large urban areas accounted for approximately two thirds of all AIDS cases. Women and children seemed to be on the periphery of the AIDS epidemic. But today almost ninety percent of new adult infections result from heterosexual contact. Consequently, the rates of exposure and infection are rising for women, with an accompanying rise in the number of children born to them with HIV. In the twenty-first century, it is expected that the majority of AIDS victims will be heterosexual women and their young children.

Furthermore, research by WHO reveals that women around the world are more susceptible to the AIDS virus for a number of reasons. First, women are biologically more susceptible to all sexually transmitted diseases; second, women tend to have sexual relationships with older men who are more likely to have had multiple partners; and last, the traditional role of the man as the partner in control of the sexual activity inhibits women in many cultures from using protection.

Now get ready to answer the questions

Narrator: 31. How does the World Health Organization estimate compare with actual trends?

32. The guest speaker briefly discusses a trend. Summarize the trend by putting the events in order.

33. Why are women so susceptible to the AIDS virus?

34. Which segments of the population will probably constitute the majority of AIDS cases in the twenty-first century?

Narrator: Listen to part of a class discussion in a psychology class.

Professor: How many of you have experienced jet lag? Almost everyone? Do you know what causes it? Jennifer?

Jennifer: The difference in time that occurs when we cross time zones.

Professor: Yes. That's right. You see we all have an internal clock that determines when we should sleep, wake up, eat, or perform other bodily functions during a twenty-four-hour period. So most travelers are not able to adjust to the shorter or longer day.

David: Excuse me, Professor Roberts.

Professor: Yes, David.

David: Is it true that jet lag is worse after a flight east than it is after a flight west?

Professor: Very good question. Yes, most people can adjust a little better to a longer day than they can to a shorter day. It's also true that people over thirty who tend to have a more established routine are likely to suffer the most from jet lag.

Jennifer: Excuse me, Professor. But is there any research on how we can deal with jet lag?

Professor: Yes, Jennifer, there is. Probably the most interesting research studies on how to minimize the effects of jet lag are those that show the value of scheduling an early evening arrival. Can you imagine why that might be helpful?

Jennifer: Because you would probably just go to bed?

Professor: True enough. But there is also some evidence that light plays a role in accommodating a new sleep cycle. In addition, it seems that a full stomach increases the symptoms of restlessness and fatigue. In fact, eating a small meal on the plane should help as long as you don't find the nearest restaurant when you land. Finally, alcohol tends to dehydrate the body, which appears to make jet lag worse. So that's why it's better to drink lots of water and avoid drinking alcohol on the plane. Yes, Jennifer?

Jennifer: Does the research tell us how long it takes to adjust to a new time zone? When I visit my sister, I am waking up at three in the morning for most of my visit.

Professor: And then it's time to go home.

Jennifer: Exactly.

Professor: Well, Jennifer, some studies show that we require half a day for each time zone crossed. So if you can't include a stopover on a long flight, it is better not to schedule an important meeting for the day after your arrival.

Now get ready to answer the questions

Narrator: 35. What causes jet lag?

36. Who would suffer most from jet lag?

37. How can jet lag be minimized?

38. How long does it take to adjust to a new time zone?

Narrator: A guest speaker has been invited to talk to an education class about adult education. Listen to the beginning of the talk.

One of the most successful educational programs for adults is the Elderhostel, designed for students over the age of sixty. Initiated in 1975 by five colleges in New Hampshire, Elderhostel was originally a one-week summer program for senior citizens combining travel and college residence with enrichment courses. The concept has been so popular that it has grown rapidly to include a network of more than three hundred colleges and universities in all fifty states. Host institutions have expanded to include museums, parks, and other outdoor centers as well as traditional college campuses, and one, two, or three-week programs are now available year round. Although courses are not offered for credit, and no exams are required, the classes are taught by highly qualified faculty at the host college.

Let me write Elderhostel on the board for you. Elderhostel.

To date, hundreds of thousands of students from sixty to one hundred years old have participated in Elderhostel. Students usually live in dormitories, eat in cafeterias, and attend social, recreational, and cultural functions. All services available to students during the academic year are offered to Elderhostel students. Registration fees vary from as little as twenty dollars to as much as three hundred dollars, excluding books and transportation to the campus or community site. For many senior citizens, Elderhostel offers the opportunity for lifelong learning, companionship, and fun.

If you know someone sixty years old or older and you think they might enjoy learning, call your local college. There is probably an Elderhostel program right in your community.

Now get ready to answer the questions

Narrator: 39. What is Elderhostel?

40. Which of the statements is true of Elderhostel?

41. Which of the people in the picture would most probably be enrolled in an Elderhostel program?

42. What should you do if you are interested in finding out more about Elderhostel?

Narrator: Listen to part of a lecture in an earth science class. The professor will talk about pyrite.

I will be putting another specimen in the mineral lab for you after today's lecture. It is pyrite, also known as iron disulfide, but more commonly called fool's gold.

This is a very fine example of pyrite because this particular specimen shows the well-defined cubic or isometric crystal formations quite well. There are a lot of flat facets on the face of this pyrite. As you can see, the mineral is a brassy yellow with some green and brown streaks running through it, and it has a metallic luster. It does, in fact, look a little bit like gold, doesn't it?

But really, pyrite and gold have very different scientific properties. Pyrite is much harder than gold—about 6 on the Mohs scale. As you will recall, gold is quite soft—only about 3 on the Mohs scale. And pyrite is much more brittle than gold, too.

But what if you are on a dig, and you want to tell the difference? Well, all you have to do is heat your sample. Gold will not react at all, but pyrite will smoke and produce an unpleasant odor, a little like sulfuric acid, which is, in fact, made from pyrite. And when pyrite is struck with a hammer, it will create sparks. Actually, the term *pyrite* is derived from the Greek word for fire, and there is speculation that mankind may have used pyrite to make the first fires for cooking and heating.

Large deposits of pyrite are found throughout the world, in igneous rocks in all kinds of geological environments. It is a very common mineral. And, yes, the resemblance of pyrite to gold causes prospectors worldwide to mistake fool's gold for real gold.

Now get ready to answer the questions

Narrator: 43. What problem does the lecturer point out?

44. What will the professor do with the specimen he has brought to class?

45. Select the specimen that is most similar to the one that the professor showed in class.

46. Identify the properties of pyrite.

47. What is an easy way to identify pyrite?

Narrator: Listen to part of a conversation on campus between two students.

Man: Excuse me. Has anyone turned in a calculus book?

Woman: I don't think so. Where did you leave it?

Man: I'm not sure. I was sitting over there by the window, and I think I left it under the table. But it isn't there now.

Woman: When did you lose it? Today?

Man: Yes, just about an hour ago when I was in here for lunch. I didn't notice until I got to the library to study for my test.

Woman: That's too bad. Well, listen, sometimes people don't turn in lost items to us. There's a lost-and-found in the Student Union by the entrance to the auditorium. Maybe someone found your book and took it there.

Man: Maybe.

Woman: Do you know where the Student Union is?

Man: Yes, I do. Thanks a lot for your help.

Woman: You're welcome. Oh, wait. Another thing. If you don't find it there today, you should probably check again tomorrow. Sometimes people get busy, and don't get over there right away to turn something in.

Man: Good idea. Thanks again.

Woman: Good luck. I hope it's there.

Now get ready to answer the questions

Narrator: 48. What prompted this conversation?

49. Where does the man think he left his book?

50. What does the woman suggest that the man do?

12

FEATURED COLLEGES AND UNIVERSITIES

Many students have written to me to ask my advice about language programs and degree programs in American colleges and universities. Which college or university to attend is a very personal decision, and only you can know where you will be happy. In order to decide, you should get as much information about the school or program as you can. Use reference books like *Barron's Profiles of American Colleges* and visit web sites of language programs and schools.

The language programs featured here collaborated with me on field tests or revisions of items for the Computer-Based TOEFL Model Tests in this book and on the CD-ROM that supplements this book. All of the programs are members of the American Association of Intensive English Programs, are eligible to issue the form I-20 for you to obtain a student visa to enter the United States, and offer special TOEFL preparation courses as part of their curricula. These programs also advertise that they will provide professional ESL instructors on the faculty; multiple levels of instruction; small classes (ten to twenty students); and a safe campus area. In addition, each program has some unique features that may be important to you as you consider your options.

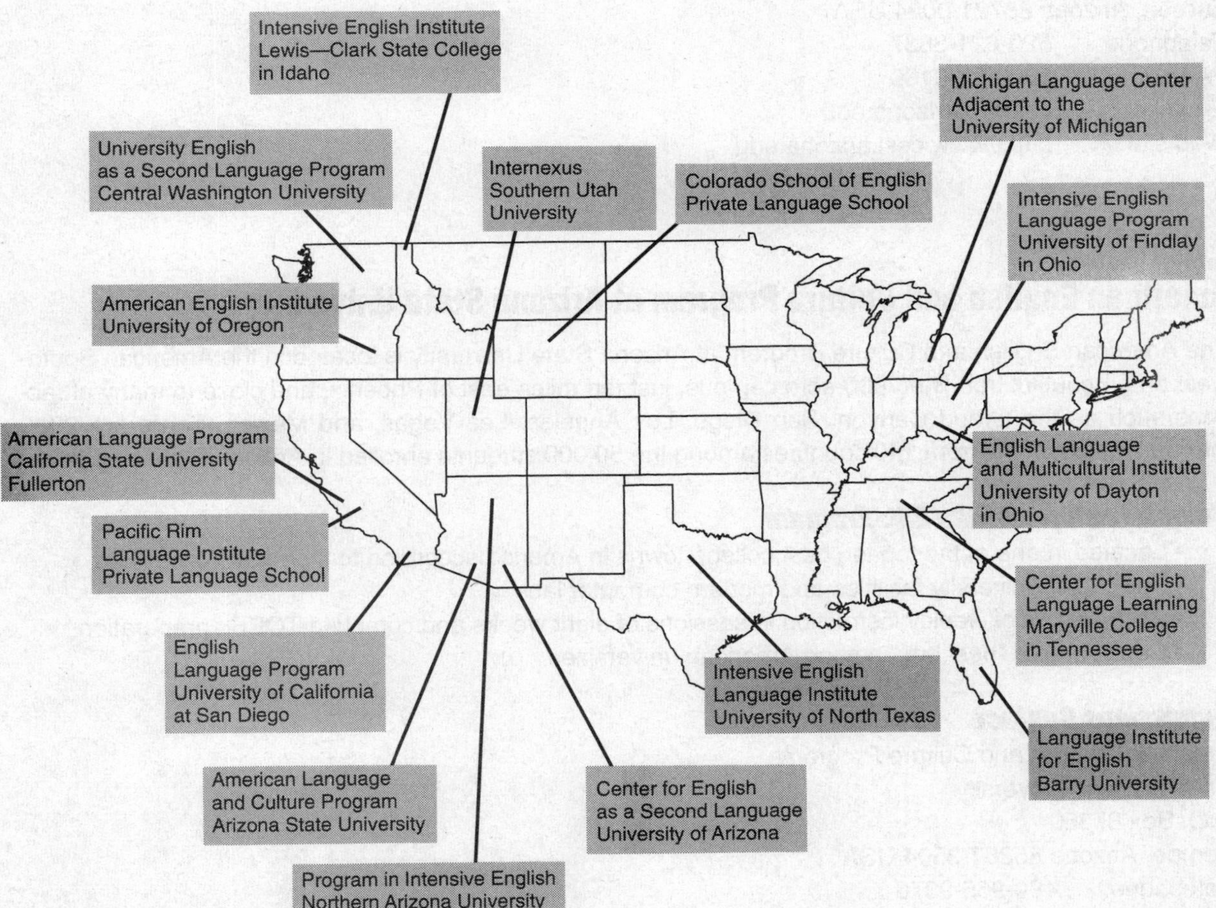

Center for English as a Second Language at the University of Arizona

The Center for English as a Second Language (CESL) at the University of Arizona in Tucson is located in the Arizona-Sonora Desert of the American Southwest, sixty miles from Mexico. There are 2150 international students among the 35,000 students enrolled in the University of Arizona.

Unique Features of the ESL Program

- Located at one of the top twenty research universities in the nation
- An international campus with students from over 115 countries
- Access to extensive facilities and services on campus
- Exceptional qualifications for faculty
- Auditing and credit courses available for qualified students

Admissions Contact

Center for English as a Second Language
The University of Arizona
P.O. Box 210024
Tucson, Arizona 85721-0024 USA
Telephone: 520-621-3637
FAX: 520-621-9180
E-mail: cesl@u.arizona.edu
Web site: http://www.cesl.arizona.edu

American English and Culture Program at Arizona State University

The American English and Culture Program at Arizona State University is located in the American Southwest on a beautiful tree-lined 800-acre campus, just ten miles east of Phoenix, and close to many attractions such as the Grand Canyon, San Diego, Los Angeles, Las Vegas, and Mexico. There are 2000 international students from 140 countries among the 50,000 students enrolled in Arizona State University.

Unique Features of the ESL Program

- Located in one of the top ten best college towns in America according to the *New York Times*
- Full use of university facilities and modern computer labs
- 21–24 hours of weekly instruction in sessions of eight weeks and complete TOEFL preparation
- Considered a "best buy" among American universities

Admissions Contact

American English and Culture Program
Arizona State University
P.O. Box 873504
Tempe, Arizona 85287-3504 USA
Telephone: 480-965-2376
FAX: 480-965-8529
E-mail: aecp@asu.edu
Web site: http://www.asu.edu/xed/aecp/esl.html

The Program in Intensive English at Northern Arizona University

The Program in Intensive English (PIE) is located in Flagstaff, Arizona, with a wonderful four-season climate. The program offers complete preparation for university course work. Northern Arizona University is a comprehensive university with degrees in many areas of study.

Unique Features of the ESL Program

- Near the Grand Canyon and many other scenic attractions
- Many extra-curricular activities available
- Curriculum designed to prepare students for success
- Automatic admission upon meeting TOEFL requirements
- English-only option available

Admissions Contact

Program in Intensive English
Box 6032
Northern Arizona University
Flagstaff, Arizona 86011-6032 USA
Telephone: 520-523-7503
FAX: 520-523-7074
E-mail: pie.nau@nau.edu
Web site: www.nau.edu/~english/tesl/pie.html

English Language Program at the University of California at San Diego

The English Language Program at the University of California at San Diego is located less than a mile from the Pacific Ocean on a 1200-acre campus in La Jolla, one of the most prestigious seaside neighborhoods on the California coast. There are 4500 international students and scholars among the 18,000 students enrolled in the University of California at San Diego.

Unique Features of the ESL Program

- Customized scheduling from a list of electives that account for 50 percent of the student's schedule
- Professional certificate programs including business management; U.S. legal systems; travel, tourism, and hospitality management
- Exceptional computer facilities and the latest computer-based instruction
- Location in an area that enjoys one of the finest climates in the United States
- Affiliation with one of the premier research universities in the United States

Admissions Contact

English Language Programs
University of California at San Diego
9500 Gilman Drive
La Jolla, California 92093-0176 USA
Telephone: 619-534-6784
FAX: 619-534-5703
E-mail: elp@ucsd.edu
Web site: http://www-esps.ucsd.edu/elp

American Language Program at California State University, Fullerton

The American Language Program is located in safe suburban Orange County 30 miles south of Los Angeles and close to beaches, cultural attractions, and entertainment. The program offers small classes with TOEFL instruction at every level and conditional admission to Cal State Fullerton, which has the second largest undergraduate business program in the United States.

Unique Features of the ESL Program

- TOEFL preparation and TOEFL examinations in all levels
- High-quality instruction and service by experienced, well-educated professionals
- Social, recreational, and cultural activities and trips included
- University courses available for advanced-level students
- Homestay and conversation partner programs

Admissions Contact

American Language Program
California State University
800 N. State College Boulevard
Fullerton, CA 92831 USA

Telephone:	714-278-2909
FAX:	714-278-7114
E-mail:	alp@fullerton.edu
Web site:	http://alp.fullerton.edu

Pacific Rim Language Institute

The Pacific Rim Language Institute is a private adult language school located in a quiet residential suburb, twenty minutes east of downtown Los Angeles. The school is approved by the Bureau for Private Postsecondary and Vocational Education and is a member of the American Association of Intensive English Programs (AAIEP).

Unique Features of the ESL Program

- Focus on conversation skills and spoken English
- Two levels of TOEFL preparation—450–500 range and 550–600 range
- Located in Asian-American community, with many stores and restaurants
- Excellent relationships with local community colleges
- Assistance with transfer to degree programs

Admissions Contact

Pacific Rim Language Institute
1719 Fullerton Road
Rowland Heights, California 91748 USA

Telephone:	626-964-0888
FAX:	626-913-9658
E-mail:	admissions@prli.com
Web site:	http://www.prli.com

American English Institute at the University of Oregon

The American English Institute at the University of Oregon is located in the beautiful Willamette Valley of the Pacific Northwest on a 250-acre campus in a suburban area. There are 1650 international students among the 17,000 students enrolled in the University of Oregon.

Unique Features of the ESL Program

- Affiliation with a highly ranked university in the Oregon system of higher education
- Orientation program before the beginning of the term
- Two hours of tutoring per week included in the tuition
- Graduation credit for ESL courses for matriculated students
- University credit courses for advanced language students

Admissions Contact

American English Institute
107 Pacific Hall
5212 University of Oregon
Eugene, Oregon 97403-5121 USA

Telephone:	541-346-3945
FAX:	541-346-3917
E-mail:	aeiadmit@oregon.uoregon.edu
Web site:	http://babel.uoregon.edu/aei/aei.html

University English as a Second Language Program at Central Washington University

The University English as a Second Language (UESL) Program at Central Washington University is located in Ellensburg, Washington, one hundred miles east of Seattle on a 380-acre campus. There are 400 international students among the 7000 students enrolled in Central Washington University.

Unique Features of the ESL Program

- Active conversation partners program
- Workshops to provide help with college applications
- Supervised visitations to regular university classes
- Conditional admission to Central Washington University through the UESL program with program recommendation accepted in place of TOEFL score
- Partnerships with other colleges and universities in the Washington state university system

Admissions Contact

University English as a Second Language Program
Central Washington University
400 East 8th Avenue
Ellensburg, Washington 98926-7562 USA

Telephone:	509-963-1375
FAX:	509-963-1380
E-mail:	horowitz@CWU.edu
Web site:	http://www.cwu.edu/~intlprog/uesl.html

Michigan Language Center, adjacent to the University of Michigan

The Michigan Language Center (MLC) is a private language school located in the Midwestern United States in Ann Arbor, Michigan, adjacent to the University of Michigan. There are 3050 international students among the 22,000 students enrolled in the neighboring academic community at the University of Michigan.

Unique Features of the ESL Program

- New sessions every six weeks
- Special seminars offered each term at no extra charge
- Conversation partner program
- Location in a small, safe, but exciting city near the University of Michigan, one of the best academic institutions in the United States
- Assistance by the MLC academic counselor in applying to American colleges and universities, as well as arrangements with some institutions for conditional admission

Admissions Contact

Michigan Language Center
309 South State Street
P.O. Box 8231
Ann Arbor, Michigan 48107 USA
Telephone: 734-663-9415
FAX: 734-663-9623
E-mail: mlc-usa@att.net
Web site: www.englishclasses.com

Intensive English Language Program at the University of Findlay

The Intensive English Language Program (IELP) at the University of Findlay is located in Findlay, Ohio, a small city in the Midwestern United States. Nearly 300 international students among the 4000 students enrolled in the University of Findlay attend classes on the 160-acre campus.

Unique Features of the ESL Program

- Long-standing tradition of educating international students from thirty countries
- Computer skills course offered as part of the advanced curriculum
- University credit awarded for intensive English students majoring in English as an International Language
- Location in an area named the best micropolitan (small city) in Ohio and one of the top places to live in the United States—near Detroit, Chicago, Cleveland, Columbus, Cincinnati
- Affiliation with a small liberal arts university that offers a large number of degree programs

Admissions Contact

Intensive English Language Institute
The University of Findlay
1000 N. Main Street
Findlay, Ohio 45840-3695 USA
Telephone: 419-424-4558
FAX: 419-424-5507
E-mail: international@findlay.edu
Web site: http://www.findlay.edu

English Language and Multicultural Institute at the University of Dayton

The English Language and Multicultural Institute (ELMI) at the University of Dayton, Ohio, is located in the heart of the Midwestern United States in a safe, suburban setting. There are 190 international students among the 9900 students enrolled in the University of Dayton, as well as 250 international students in the ESL program, preparing for study at the university of their choice.

Unique Features of the ESL Program

- Personal academic counseling by caring faculty advisors
- Highly individualized approach to language learning
- Special programs for business professionals and family members
- Supervised activities and field trips; strong host family and conversation partner programs
- Affiliation with a university recognized as a national leader in Catholic higher education and one of the top five regional universities in the Midwest

Admissions Contact

English Language and Multicultural Institute
300 College Park
Dayton, Ohio 45469-0319 USA
Telephone: 937-229-3729
FAX: 937-229-3700
E-mail: elmi@udayton.edu
Web site: http://www.udayton.edu/~elmi/

Center for English Language Learning at Maryville College

The Center for English Language Learning at Maryville College in Maryville, Tennessee, is located sixteen miles from Knoxville, near the Great Smoky Mountains National Park on a 350-acre park-like campus. There are sixty-five international students among the 900 students enrolled in Maryville College.

Unique Features of the ESL Program

- Very small classes, usually six to twelve students
- Low costs in comparison with similar colleges
- New sessions every five weeks
- Undergraduate college credit for twelve hours of ESL courses
- Affiliation with a college recognized among *U.S. News and World Report*'s top regional four-year liberal arts institutions

Admissions Contact

Center for English Language Learning
Maryville College
Maryville, Tennessee 37804-5907 USA
Telephone: 865-981-8186
FAX: 865-983-0581
E-mail: Internat@MaryvilleCollege.edu
Web site: http://www.MaryvilleCollege.edu

Language Institute for English at Barry University

The Language Institute for English at Barry University in Miami Shores, Florida, is located twelve miles north of Miami on a ninety-acre campus. There are 450 international students among the 2,000 students enrolled in Barry University.

Unique Features of the ESL Program

- Twelve levels of instruction which allow for very accurate placement
- New sessions every four weeks
- Many elective courses for advanced students
- Arrangements for conditional admission to more than 100 universities, preparatory high schools, and vocational schools
- Exceptional social, cultural, and sports activities

Admissions Contact

Language Institute for English
Barry University
11300 Northeast Second Avenue
Miami Shores, Florida 33161 USA
Telephone: 305-899-3128
FAX: 305-892-2229
E-mail: admissions@mail.barry.edu
Web site: http://www.barry.edu

Intensive English Language Institute at the University of North Texas

The Intensive English Language Institute (IELI) at the University of North Texas is located in a small university city in the Southern United States, thirty minutes from Dallas, Texas. There are 1500 international students among the 26,000 students enrolled in the University of North Texas.

Unique Features of the ESL Program

- Accredited by the Commission on English Language Program Accreditation (CELPA)
- Full-time, professional teachers and student counselors with a 12:1 student/teacher ratio, year-round classes at levels 0–6
- Graduate Preparation Course (GPC) offered by IELI, waives the GRE verbal score for admission to many UNT graduate programs
- Conditional admission for level 5 IELI/UNT students with TOEFL waiver
- Affiliation with the fourth largest university in Texas, University of North Texas (UNT), listed in "America's 100 Best College Buys," and "One of America's 100 Most Wired Colleges" according to Yahoo

Admissions Contact

Intensive English Language Institute
P.O. Box 310739
Denton, Texas 76203-0739 USA
Telephone: 940-565-2003
FAX: 940-565-4822
E-mail: intl@isp.admin.unt.edu
Web site: http://www.unt.edu/isp/

Internexus at Southern Utah University

Internexus at Southern Utah University is located in Cedar City on a 120-acre campus, within a short drive of Las Vegas as well as several national parks. There are 175 international students among the 6,000 students enrolled in Southern Utah University.

Unique Features of the ESL Program

- English Plus Program which includes activities for youth and summer travel in the national parks
- Admission for students as young as 14 years of age for short-term group programs
- Half-Half Program for students who are eligible to enroll in a part-time program of university courses
- Living language laboratory
- Affiliation with other private language schools hosted by colleges and universities in the United States and the United Kingdom

Admissions Contact

Internexus
Southern Utah University
351 West Center Street
Cedar City, Utah 84720 USA
Telephone: 435-865-8033
FAX: 435-865-8013
E-mail: sutah@internexus
Web site: http://www.suu.edu/webpages/contedu/elsc

Colorado School of English

Colorado School of English is a private language school with a campus in downtown Denver.

Unique Features of the ESL Program

- Custom programs designed for groups
- Private classes designed for the special language needs of one student
- Partnering programs for executives in the same field of work
- Sight-seeing tours combined with language study
- New courses beginning every Monday

Admissions Contact

Colorado School of English
1325 S. Colorado Boulevard, Suite 101
Denver, Colorado 80222 USA
Telephone: 303-758-3123
FAX: 303-758-3002
E-mail: cse@englishamerica.com
Web site: http://www.englishamerica.com

The Intensive English Institute at Lewis-Clark State College

The Intensive English Institute (IEI) at Lewis-Clark State College is located in a typical American town settled in a scenic river valley. There are 120 international students among the 3100 students enrolled in Lewis-Clark State College.

Unique Features of the ESL Program

- Location in an area with a mild climate
- Exceptional commitment to student services
- More home-stay opportunities than the average college program
- Courses for computer and keyboarding skills in English
- Cross-registration with three Idaho universities for students enrolled in degree programs

Admissions Contact

Intensive English Institute
Lewis-Clark State College
Lewiston, Idaho 83501 USA
Telephone: 208-799-2321
FAX: 208-799-2824
E-mail: ieiprog@lcsc.edu
Web site: http://www.iei-USA.com

udio Compact Disk

available can be used in your compact disk player to provide the audio for the . You should hear audio only. If you want to simulate the Computer-Based TOEFL, and visuals, you need a CD-ROM, not a compact disk. The CD-ROM is available from ducational Series, Inc.

phone: 800-645-3476 E-mail: customer.service@barronseduc.com
FAX: 631-434-3723 Web site: http://www.barronseduc.com

TOEFL CD-ROM Minimum Requirements

The following documentation applies if you purchased *How to Prepare for the TOEFL, 10th Edition* book with CD-ROM. Please disregard this information if your version does not contain the CD-ROM.

Documentation

MINIMUM HARDWARE REQUIREMENTS

The program will run on a PC with

1. Intel Pentium® 166MHZ or equivalent processor
2. 16 MB RAM
3. MS Windows® 95/98/NT/2000
4. SVGA (256 Colors) Monitor
5. 8X CD-ROM Drive
6. SoundBlaster or compatible sound card
7. Keyboard, Mouse

The program will run on a Macintosh® with

1. Power PC 8600
2. Operating System 8.0 (or later)
3. 32 MB RAM
4. SVGA (256 Colors) Monitor
5. 8X CD-ROM Drive
6. SoundBlaster or compatible sound card
7. Keyboard, Mouse

LAUNCHING THE APPLICATION

Barron's TOEFL CD-ROM includes an "autorun" feature that automatically launches the application when the CD is inserted into the CD drive. In the unlikely event that the autorun features are disabled, alternate launching instructions are provided below.

Launching instructions for the PC

Windows® 95/98/NT/2000:

1. Put the Barron's TOEFL CD-ROM into the CD-ROM drive.
2. Click on the Start button and choose Run.
3. Type *D:\TOEFL.EXE* (assuming the CD is in the drive D), then click OK.

Launching instructions for the MAC

1. Put the Barron's TOEFL CD-ROM into the CD-ROM drive.
2. Double-click the TOEFL Installer icon.
3. Follow the onscreen instructions.